ALSO BY ERIC BURNETT

For Children

Trapped in Tenocht̓

Held Up in

Skateboarder Steve Stops

Gymnastics Jenny Stands on ꞇwn

Baseball Bryan Steps to the Plate

For All Ages

History through Film: Volume I

History through Film: Volume II

Aztec Plays for the Classroom

Middle Ages for the Classroom

21st Century Voices

The Best American History Book in the World

The 50 Questions Every Graduate Must Answer

The Little Black Book of Skills for the Social Studies Classroom

OUR WORLD'S STORY

OUR WORLD'S STORY

The Tales, Traditions and Turning Points of the Past and the Regional Challenges of Today

ERIC BURNETT

http://ourworldzstory.com/

Contents

PART II:
The Regional Challenges of Today

This book is dedicated to
Beth, Becca and Jack

From Abiyoyo to Seletar Hill,
you've given me all I've ever dreamed of...
...and about 429 things I never thought were possible.
We've created for ourselves a pretty good gig.

Thank You

Part I

*The Tales, Traditions and
Turning Points of our Past*

I

The State of Our World

The Earth in 2013

In 2012, director Ridley Scott brought to the Silver Screen the sci-fi film *Prometheus*, a heart-warming tale of how alien scientists dabble with weaponizing viruses that can hibernate for millennia until an opportune moment arises where they can infiltrate a foreign body, hyper-gestate for a few hours and then ultimately rip themselves out of their host's abdomen. And then they take over the planet.

In this case, Earth of course was the intended target. In the film's first few scenes, archaeologists uncover cave paintings from across the globe, each indicating that an alien species of super tall, uber-buffed humans kept returning to earth to chart our progress while teasingly inviting us to their world. In 2073, our scientists accept the invitation, send our internationally-selected crew across the cosmos, and the rest of the film devolves into a race to see if the scientists can escape the face-devouring, flesh-ripping virus without bringing it back home.

But let's ignore for a minute the horror hijinks in outer space and focus more on the alien race's patient preliminary reconnaissance of our Earth. What if over the course of our existence, a band of aliens did in fact keep checking in on us to see how we were evolving? What if every ten thousand years, they landed their little spaceships, sat up on a hill and chuckled as us humans tried to survive the elements. What would they see?

Well until about 200,000 years ago, they wouldn't even see us at all, but probably some apelike, primate-human hybrid that only after about four million years turned into *Homo sapiens*. So let's start at the 200,000 years ago mark. We looked like humans, smelled like humans and made noises like humans (well, noises like fairly uneducated humans). This first version of ourselves might have physically and cognitively resembled us today, but their lives looked a heck of a lot different.

Our alien stalkers would first have trouble finding a lot of us. There were maybe five to ten thousand of us scattered across Africa and on the move, but we didn't live in large groups; instead we survived as just a few united families that walked the land looking for an animal to kill or a nut or a berry to pick. 200,000 years ago we were nomadic hunter-gatherers, and there was no guarantee we as a species were going to survive these early years.

If the aliens returned 10,000 years later, same thing. Still hunter-gatherers, living at the tip of extinction. 10,000 years more, still the same. Another 10,000 years...yep, not much changed. Yet another 10,000 years, no surprise, we're still picking non-fatal fruit and hoping some animal would walk by that we could kill with our less than impressive claws and teeth or rudimentary stone tools. In fact, for the next 150,000 years, our alien observers would be rather disappointed. We weren't changing much.

But then about 10,000 BC, we made a huge leap. We started farming. We started building towns next to rivers, we spread across five continents and we began constructing buildings that might last more than a few seasons.

2000 years ago, at the zero mark, where BC becomes AD, around the time Jesus Christ walked around the eastern Roman Empire, we were looking pretty impressive. We had empires in the Mediterranean, the Indian subcontinent and in China. Our pyramids and our great wall could be seen from just inside the atmosphere. We were making more babies and living longer. We'd grown to about 200 million people worldwide, though most of us had no idea the other guys even existed. We only traded with our immediate neighbors and if you ever led an army 1000 miles in any direction, you'd get the nickname "the Great." We were already worshipping elephant-headed gods in India, following

Confucian witticisms in China and worrying about heaven and hell in the Middle East. We fought with spears, wore fairly colorful clothes and weren't going anywhere unless an animal carried us, the wind pushed us or we walked there ourselves.

Flash-forward just a mere 2000 years this time. Let's assume the aliens realized we were progressing at a faster clip and decided to cut short their time away from us.

It's the year 2013. What would they see today? How far have we come since our hunter-gatherer days of isolation, our years as emerging empires, our worlds of daily toil and superstitious wonderings?

Let's see how far we've come? Let's see what they'd see.

They'd see there are a lot of us. Seven billion. That's a 3400% increase since year 0. At this rate, in the year 4000, we'd be up to 238 billion people.

They'd see that four billion of us live in Asia, one billion in Africa and even a few thousand live down in Antarctica. They'd see black people, brown people and white people separated by continents, but they'd also see that we were intermarrying and making mixed-race babies like never before in our history. Stigmas of interracial marriage still exist in more conservative households, but we're living in an age of unprecedented acceptance of EuroAsian, AfroAsian, AfroEuropean, and even EuroAfroAsian unions. You're more likely to have blood from many lands than you are to be 100% anything.

They'd see that we no longer live in empires, but we do live in ethnically-based tribes. We call them nations or independent sovereign states. There are about two hundred of them. The smallest is the Vatican City – about 800 people living in a walled structure less than a quarter of a square mile in size, just a few city blocks. The largest in size is Russia at 6.5 million square miles (1/8th the size of the planet), and in population, the largest is China at 1,385,000,000 and counting.

They'd see we have found different ways of keeping our people under control. Most nations have a written constitution and a democratic republic, letting their people vote and maintaining order through laws and courts. Most of these republics let multiple parties campaign for elections, saying whatever they want and letting the people (each having one equal vote) decide who will create the laws and who will execute the laws and who will judge the fairness of laws. Other countries have only one political party that wins year after year after year, or they might not let everyone vote, or they might control the news or the Internet, or they might not even count votes accurately. Some countries don't even try to fake that they're a democracy. They've held onto monarchies, basically just handing over rule from father to son to grandson, and he and his advisors get to make all the calls for the good of the nation (or their own pocketbooks). Still, others have blended the two forms, creating constitutional monarchies where their people still revere a king, but an elected body also hypothetically represents the people.

They'd see that we live longer (though maybe not healthier) lives. We pop pills when we're sick, take immunization shots when we're babies and we don't try to kill each other nearly as much as we used to. We make more food than ever before, but we also ask our scientists to find ways to better color it, shape it, flavor it, preserve it and genetically modify it. We no longer hunt, but we still gather. We head to supermarkets and fill our baskets with plastic-bagged and cardboard-boxed collections of sodium nitrate, monosodium glutamate, aspartame and corn syrup. We're fatter than we've ever been, get more cancers than ever before, yet we still wonder why the fountain of youth is beyond us.

But our alien spectators would also quickly see there is no one story of us. We are obesely rich and painfully poor. Some nations have an average annual income approaching $100,000 while other nations' citizens survive on a mere $400 a year. Some people race around the world in Gulfstream luxury jets or Japanese shinkansen bullet trains or Italian Lamborghini Superleggera sports cars. Others walk miles to find fresh water to carry back home atop their heads, use oxen to pull wooden plows through their fields and only see a motorized vehicle every few weeks. Close to a billion people each day go without food. Another billion spend their days merely moving from one digital distraction to the next. For some, entertainment revolves around sitting with some friends, chatting about the realities of life; for others, entertainment requires trip planning, gadget purchasing and appearance improving. We are a sedentary people, spending some eight to twelve hours attached to a chair, but we also have the fastest, strongest people the world has ever seen, constantly expanding our notions of what the human body can accomplish.

They'd see that we're sharing, interacting and commiserating like never before. You can eat sushi in Italy, spaghetti in India, tandoori chicken in Singapore, enchiladas in

Egypt and kangaroo hamburgers in Tokyo. You can drink a Coke in over 200 countries, buy a Toyota in 47 African nations, wander around an Ikea showroom on five continents and at every counter there's a pretty good chance the cashier will accept Visa. Companies send sales reps, project managers and resource purchasers across the globe looking for the best deal that will get their product to market cheaper and faster than their competitor. The Internet has truly leveled the world. You Skype a 1-800 number to talk to a bank rep and within seconds you're talking to an English-speaking college grad from Bangalore. You need to file your taxes, you can send your paperwork to Russia and have it back within a couple days. And if you're a kid living in Central Asia, thousands of miles from the nearest university, with a decent Wifi connection, you can download some lectures on how to make iPhone Apps from Stanford University and within a few weeks be selling your latest imaginings to the world. You can buy every product under the sun on Ebay. You can hire employees from every country in the world on Odesk. You can even go online to find a spouse, tease your friends, start a revolution or whine about the gross inequities of the teenage experience. You can upload a video to report a tragedy or you can download a virus that can wipe out your company's research. We hold the world at our fingertips, but our top searches are Bieber, Kardashian and Cruise.

They'd see that we still have trouble getting along. We created a United Nations that no one listens to, a G8 that spawns protests and a NATO that seems outdated. Billions each week go to temples on Saturdays or churches on Sundays. Each day, a billion others all stop what they're doing five times a day, lay out a rug and pray towards Mecca. We sing songs that praise our deities, pass donation plates to help out those in need, but then listen to sermons and lectures saying our faith is the only true faith and all who oppose us must perish. We are taught to turn the other cheek, follow the Eightfold Path and honor our elders, but we still exact revenge for generations-old slights, condemn those that are different and put our elders in assisted living facilities.

They'd see that we're still works in progress. They'd see that we've developed independently for thousands of years, yet we now today mingle like never before. They'd see that we've come a long way, but at different paces and with different priorities.

They'd wonder how we got to here.

And, in fact, most of us wonder how we got to here. But to answer that question we have to go back to the beginning, back to a time when our first ancestors stood up on their hind legs and peered out across a grassy plain. Back to 3.5 million years ago. Back to a little lady named Lucy.

But that is for another chapter.

2

Humans Take the Stage

Early Hominids − 3,500,000 BC > 200,000 BC

Where in the world did we humans come from? Where in the world? Well, it depends on whom in the world you ask. The Aztecs think we popped out of corn. The Egyptians think we sprung from tears. The Mongols tell a story of how a wandering lama sculpted us out of clay. Hindus tell a story about how Lord Brahma split himself in half to make a man and a woman. The Chinese believe a dog-headed man married a princess and they settled in northern China and had a lovely little family of four that went on to populate the world. And about four billion people grow up hearing about how a naked vegetarian couple frolicked carelessly around a garden until one day the bored wife decided to nibble into a naughty apple. Every civilization has a story. Every civilization has concocted some sort of explanation for where we came from, most surviving the test of time, making their way across the eras, passed down first by word of mouth and then finally written down in some holy text.

Even scientists have thrown in their two cents. They dig up artifacts and leftover animal debris, run them through carbon dating machines and come up with some estimates of how long this earth has been spinning. What did they discover? The earth is old. Really old. Freakishly old. Just how old?

No one can say for sure. The estimate keeps changing. 150 years ago, physicist William Thomson said it could be 20 million years old, or...he said it might be 400 million years old. Not really an exact calculation. In recent years we've narrowed down the number a bit. After studying meteorites, the moon and other chunks of dirt floating around the solar system, geologists now say the number is more like 4.54 billion years – that's 4,540,000,000 years for those of you who like your numbers written with commas.

This number is hard to fathom, so geologists came up with a little clock analogy to help people visualize the age of earth's creation and the key turning points in its development. If this 4.54 billion year life span was turned into a metaphoric 24-hour clock, one second into the day, the earth appeared. Four hours later, we got the first rocks. At seven hours, the first single-celled organisms popped up. Animals finally made their appearance at the 18-hour mark, and humans (after over four and a half billion years) show up at 23 hours and 59 minutes. Yep, we're about a minute old.

The first humanesque animal appeared around four *million* years ago. Anthropologists tell us hominids, or creatures that walked on two legs, emerged from a common primate (monkey) ancestor and then proceeded to evolve from Australopithecus through to our current form as *Homo sapiens*. Around the turn of the last century, scientists started using the term "evolutionary ladder" to describe this transformation from early primates to modern man, but a better choice of words would have been "evolutionary branches," because we really didn't move up in a straight direction. There were dozens of primate hominids that emerged at one time or another. Some hominid species (like Neanderthals) evolved and died out, and only one continued until we finally became the large-skulled, opposable-thumb-yielding, fire-starting, religion-creating, language-producing species we are today.

Although other archaeological finds have been made in recent years, the most famous *found* hominid remains were discovered in 1972 by American anthropologists Donald Johanson and Mary Leakey (though French geologist Maurice Taieb might like some credit seeing he was the one that invited Donald and Mary to the site). These hominid remains were named "Lucy" after "Lucy in the Sky with Diamonds," a Beatles song that kept playing over and over at the research base.

Since that time, archaeologists have made some other key discoveries, all pointing to how humans gradually evolved to survive the harsh environment of a changing planet.

And humans had to evolve because when it comes to mammals, we're pretty pathetic. We're not that hairy, our skin rips pretty easy and our teeth are pitiful (except for those two scary incisors we use to shred pizzas and vampires use to get intimate with their prey's neck). We can't jump that high. We can't run fast. And unless we forget to use our fingernail clippers, our "claws" really aren't that intimidating.

So how did we do it? How did a slow, weak, not-so-menacing species become the master of all living creatures, able to control the fate of an entire planet?

The answer – our cool thumbs, our voice box and our brains. We can craft and hold tools. We can communicate specific instructions and pass down detailed knowledge from generation to generation. And we have brains that allow us to not only plan ahead and predict, but to consider the possibilities of life beyond the tangible. We're just smarter than everyone else.

By 200,000 years ago, we had evolved into the humans you see today. All the mental and physical faculties *Homo sapiens* exhibit today were apparent 200 millennia ago; we just needed to figure out how to spread out around the world and make the most of this absurdly bountiful environment we'd inherited.

But that is for another chapter.

3

The Greatest Travelling
Expedition Ever

Hunter-gatherers – 200,000 BC > 5000 BC

About 200,000 years ago, humans were done. We'd stopped changing. Essentially the brains, the bodies and the abilities we have today, we had 200,000 years ago. Sure, we've grown a bit due to a more consistent, higher protein (possibly higher hormone-laced) diet. But, for the most part, we were done. So when you picture what humans looked like way back when, basically picture the people around you (just imagine they'd be wearing significantly different outfits and spending a heck of a lot more time outdoors).

For the bulk of human history – 200,000 years ago until about 5,000 years ago – humans had been nomads, hunter-gatherers. We started in Africa and gradually spread out first to Asia (90,000 years ago), then eventually to Australia (50,000 years ago), then Europe (40,000 years ago) and finally to North and South America (12,000 years go). We lived in small bands of family-based units, varying in size from ten to 100 people. The men hunted and the women gathered, not because there was prehistoric sexism, but because it made sense to keep women closer while they were making babies and feeding them the mammalian way. The survival of the clan depended on it. Women were also the primary food providers. They brought home the guaranteed food – the nuts, the berries, the roots, the grubs – and the men every once in awhile might track down and kill a beast, providing the clan with some much-needed protein.

We didn't live in permanent structures. We couldn't. The big food was always roaming and so were we. Predators, both human and animal, were always a danger, as we were no more than a main course in the circle of life. Our shelters might have been a skeleton-framed home made from a fallen wooly mammoth, but more than likely we lived in stick tents or stretched animal hide coverings that could be easily taken down and transported to the next location.

As for how many humans existed way back when, the numbers vary, but scientists usually settle on about only five to ten thousand – the survival of our species was by no means a sure thing. We gradually increased into the hundreds of thousands as we spread across Africa and Asia, but then for some reason our numbers drastically dropped. A recent theory being thrown around, the "population bottleneck theory," states that around 70,000 years ago, a horrific geologic event (most probably a volcanic eruption) decimated the human population, dropping us back down to only about 15,000 people. Looking at DNA across all peoples today, it appears we all come from this same source. By 10,000 BC (the eve of humans starting to move into towns), the world population had risen to about a million people, and today we're at over seven billion. So, in the first 70,000 years, our population grew about 50%. The next 70,000 years we grew a bit faster – at around a 6,600% clip. And since then, in a relatively short 12,000-year stretch, we've been rolling at about a 600,000% increase. But don't fret. After a feverish 20th century pace, it looks like our population has started to slow down, and some sociologists even predict we'll flatten out around 2050, and maybe even start going down as more and more families begin to have less and less kids.

But back to our travelling ancestors. As previously stated, our predatory desires were not exactly matched by our physical prowess, so we had to fight in groups and create useful weapons if we ever wanted a chance at a hearty meal. Although humans more often than not hunted the abundant deer, caribou, rabbits and turtles, what they really wanted were the megafauna, the super-huge beasts that could fill the clan's stomachs for weeks. Wooly mammoths were the prized meal. Yet, because of their vast size (nearly fifteen feet tall besides weighing close to 20,000 pounds) and ornery disposition, the wooly mammoth could only be taken down through a coordinated effort that combined the best projectile technology of the time with a synchronized attack. After days of tracking the mammoth's movements, the hunters would wait until the landscape was favorable – either near a canyon, a swamp or some other water source. Then, using a device known as an *atlatl,* a prehistoric slingshot that could launch a stone-tipped spear over a hundred yards at a speed of 60 miles per hour, the hunters attacked. They circled the wounded beast as it staggered away, gradually losing strength, and only when it was near death would they cautiously approach and deliver the final deathblow. Here, at the kill site, the tribe then set up camp, taking advantage of every organ available. Like the meat packing plants of the 20th century, they used everything – bones for tools, the hides for robes, the hair for pillows, the bladder as a water container, the guts for rope, the feces for fuel and even the scrotums for pouches or rattles.

We also started developing what we today might call "culture." We crafted intricate languages, with some tribes even coming up with dozens of different ways to describe their environment (like the Inuits of North America who shared 300+ words for snow). We weren't big writers (alphabets were hundreds of generations away), but we had begun, by about 30,000 years ago, to tell our stories through art – as can be seen in the famed animal cave paintings of Altamira and LaMarche. Our religions weren't monotheistic yet; we still believed in a ton of gods. We had gods for plants, for animals, for the weather, for the stars in the sky and even for a random rock that might jut out from a cliff. We believed our village elders held the keys to the supernatural and they used self-mutilation or hypnosis or herbal concoctions to communicate with the invisible world, to cure illness or to predict the future. We believed we went somewhere when we died, but we weren't sure where. We buried our fallen with tools, jewelry, and favored pets, just in case we might need them at our next stop.

We lived day-to-day, hand to mouth, and we wandered. We journeyed across continents, eventually bouncing from island to island across Polynesia, around the Mediterranean and up into Europe (after it finally defrosted) and then across the Bering Strait and down into the Americas. But eventually the food started to run out, our populations kept growing and our way of life could no longer be sustained. Something had to give. And for a few tribes, a new option emerged – farming. We could stay in one place and make the food come to us. It would be this Neolithic Revolution that forever changed the course of human history. For some, the days of humans barely surviving on the rare gifts of a harsh environment came to an abrupt end. We were becoming civilized.

But that is for another chapter.

4

We Farm

The Neolithic Revolution – 10,000 BC > 2,000 BC

Name a revolution in human history. What's the first one that comes to mind? The French? The American? The Russian Communist? The Chinese Communist? How about the Renaissance or the Reformation? The Industrial or the Scientific? Sure, they were all fairly important turning points in human history, but if you're looking for the #1, without a doubt, species-changing, grand-daddy-of-them-all revolution, you need look no further than the Neolithic Revolution.

The Neolithic Revolution? Yep, the age when food finders became food makers. In the centuries after 10,000 BC, as the ice started to melt and the rivers started to flow, across Europe, Africa and Asia, humans independently started making the one choice that would completely transform how they governed themselves, how they interacted and how they worshipped.

They started to farm.

You can't underestimate the impact of this shift from a nomadic lifestyle to an agricultural one. Once we established permanent roots and began pumping out our own food, we could turn our minds towards a host of different activities. We were no longer just surviving. For the first time, we could see what our minds could actually accomplish. We started building, inventing and philosophizing. We created governments, militaries and religions. We turned our evolution into hyperdrive. Nothing would ever be the same.

But why were humans able to make this shift? On this question, scientists and historians can't seem to agree. Some say the climate was getting drier. Others say it was getting wetter. Others claim the megafauna started to die out, so we camped out near rivers and watering holes hoping to hook a fish or spear a thirsty animal. Others even believe that as our religious rituals began demanding more and more sacrifices, we just ran out of food. Regardless of the reasons – and they might all be a little bit true – around 4500 BC humans settled down around major fresh water sources and the civilizing magic began.

For two centuries, historians all pretty much agreed that the first civilizations emerged along the Tigris and Euphrates rivers of Mesopotamia (modern day Iraq), the Indus River in India, the Nile River in Egypt and the Yellow River of northwest China. At least, that's what your sixth grade history book taught you and that's what any archaeologist worth his salt would have confirmed.

But in the 1990s, historians from Eastern Europe gathered in New York and dropped a bomb on the intellectual community. They claimed that for decades they'd been unearthing civilizations in Romania that predate those of Mesopotamia by almost a thousand years. They had known and written about these Danube River civilizations since before World War II, but no one seemed to care. Whether it was because the articles were written in Russian or because during the Cold War Era any claim made on the other side of the Iron Curtain was seen as a huge lie, these Danube River stories never made it to the mainstream press. But the facts can't be ignored. 7000 years ago, there were towns all over the Danube River valley. Artifacts prove these first European city dwellers analyzed the stars, forged metal tools in furnaces and brought water to their homes through ceramic pipes. Textbooks might say otherwise, but Iraq, Egypt, India and China aren't the roots of civilization. It's Romania.

But aside from being near rivers, what did these four (let's make it five) civilizations all have in common? It couldn't just be that they were all near rivers. There are rivers on every continent in the world. There had to be something else. In the 1997 book *Guns, Germs and Steel*, professor Jared Diamond of UCLA posed the theory that it all had to do with geography. To Diamond, a civilization's success had nothing to do with its inhabitants' brains, brawn or skin color. It was all about what was above and below the ground. Some regions were abounded with all the needed little nuggets of nature. Others were not so lucky. For Asians and Europeans, they had every geographic advantage available. They had won the ecological lottery.

Diamond first contends that Europe and Asia's animals were the easiest to domesticate. You could eat 'em, shear 'em, ride 'em, milk 'em or hook 'em up to a plow to help stir up your dirt. Diamond looked at all the animals in the world and calculated that there are only 148 that weigh over 100 pounds and eat vegetables. Of those, only 14 can actually be tamed. Eurasia has 13 of them. South America has only one – the llama. The rest of the world doesn't have any. Oh sure, Africa has a ton of huge animals, but good luck trying to get them to live peacefully on a farm. They'll either kill you, refuse to reproduce, jump over any fence you can build, or require so much darn food before they become adults that it's not even worth the effort. Africa has monkeys, apes, elephants, giraffes, antelope, zebras, rhinoceroses, wild buffalos, lions and leopards. But not a one you can ever domesticate (let alone chew up or digest). Eurasia has chickens, pigs, cows, horses, camels, goats, sheep and donkeys. You want to go on a safari, you go to Africa. You want to build a civilization, you live in Eurasia.

Our first five civilizations didn't just have a lead in the mammal-taming sweepstakes. They also had the gift of grains. Grain farmers can scatter barley and wheat seed across a field with just a few whisks of their hand, then sit back and hope Mother Nature keeps up her end of the bargain. Not so easy when it comes to potatoes, squash, rice and corn. They taste good, but they take a heck of a lot more effort to bring to maturation. The Eurasian civilizations also had the gift of latitude. From Spain in the West clear across to Japan in the Far East, Eurasia is a horizontally-spreading land mass, unlike the other major continents of the world that spread from north to south. This meant that farming and ranching knowledge could readily spread to the east and to the west. The seasons were about the same length, each day brought about the same amount of daylight and the weather was more or less comparable. A plant you could grow in Mesopotamia, you could grow in Egypt, India, Greece, Rome or Tunisia. Once the civilizations started sharing techniques and tools, they could consistently improve their crop yields, feeding more and more people with less and less effort.

So in the beginning, it was just plain easier to plant crops and raise animals in the fertile valleys of Romania, Mesopotamia, Egypt, India and China. And once man started farming, we would never go back.

We couldn't. We had started a revolution.

Crops meant more food. More food meant we needed bigger, better ways to store the food. We molded clay pots. We built huge stone granaries. At first, it was the priests who controlled these granaries, while also fulfilling their other duties as spokesmen to the gods. As more and more grain arrived, the granaries grew. They became temples, then palaces. Lured by the sedentary lives of these budding towns, nomadic hunter-gatherers threw down their spears once and for all. The population steadily grew and we started to run out of fertile land. We then had to build farms further and further away from the rivers. We needed canals to divert the river water inland, but rarely would anyone take a break from sowing his own family's seeds just to dig a ditch that might bring water to some other guy living miles away. We had to set up a system that would force people to work for the good of the whole. We set up taxes. If you wanted to stay in the town, you had to pay the priest with more grain or with your time. Few had the extra grain, so these first cities then had the laborers they needed to build the canals, and they could then also use them to pave the roads or stack the stone blocks needed to wall in our cities from invaders.

The priests had to step aside. How could they be expected to coordinate taxes, organize public projects, manage the food surplus and still find time to read the stars and speak to the gods? The civilizations were getting just too big. They reluctantly turned power over to military strongmen. These violent, born leaders enforced the taxes, protected the food reserves from foreigners and thieves and even mounted campaigns into neighboring lands to pull more territories under their domain. The age of empires had arrived.

Clan chiefs could become generals who commanded massive armies of obedient soldiers, each donning protective armor and yielding bronze or copper spears crafted by the expert metallurgists of the day. In peacetime, generals became kings. These kings built increasingly elaborate palaces, filling them with the plunder of war and surrounding themselves with hundreds of cronies, each tasked with carrying out the king's every whim. An entire network of tailors, craftsmen, artists, and scribes sprouted around the palaces to satisfy the needs of this new nobility. Our towns were up and running.

We had created civilization and with each successive generation we discovered ways to make our lives more efficient and more profitable. The Sumerians of Mesopotamia invented the first wheel, first for their wagons and then for their war chariots. The Harappan Indians designed the first plumbing system that brought water to bathrooms and took fecal matter out to the sea. The Chinese created the world's first currency, first by trading shells, then by exchanging jade and bronze coins. The Egyptians made paper to record who owed what to whom and to record the feats (some real, some imagined) of the kings.

And with each invention, with each job created, these civilizations became more and more complex. To control the chaos, we created laws. Back in Mesopotamia in 1772 BC, King Hammurabi scribed the first formal law code, an eight foot tall, black-stoned monolith that outlined the punishments for 282 behaviors, everything from what happens if you sleep with the farmer's daughter to how much money you owe if you accidentally kill your brother's ox. And the punishments were severe. Ignore your master – cut off your ear. Hit your father – cut off your hands. Curse your parents – tear out your eyes. Nurse a baby other than your boss's kid – cut off your breasts. Life wasn't easy in the ancient world, but governments realized that as populations grew out of control, the only way to maintain order was the strict, fast, uniform enforcement of laws.

Once upon a time, a nomad would never consider offending a fellow clansman. Everyone knew everyone. Offense meant ostracism and no one could afford to be kicked out of the tribe. But in expanding civilizations, where you were more likely to bump into a stranger than a family member, laws were the only way to prevent pandemonium.

One thing that was clear from the Code of Hammurabi and the other early law codes of the day was that people were valued differently. If a nobleman killed a ditch digger, he'd be fined a few sheckles. If a slave killed another – immediate death. Men could cheat on their wives. Women, definitely not. Early civilizations each created their own class systems – ruler was on top, usually followed by the nobles, then the warriors or priests, then the merchants or craftsmen and then the masses of farmers and laborers that kept the civilizations humming. Social distinctions became the accepted norm. The Indians had their Caste system, the Egyptians had their stratified pyramid and the Chinese had their five Confucian relationships. Everyone knew their place and should they forget, governments and their armies were never too far away to help send a pointed message.

Also, once the farms provided enough nourishment for the society, women became permanent fixtures in the home. For nearly all of our first 200,000 years, the labor of women was seen as equal to that of men, but with the dawn of farming, the physical prowess of men was prioritized over anything a woman could provide. They couldn't push the plow, mine the quarries or raise sword or spear in battle. They remained at home, keeping the house clean, preparing the meals and making babies. Birth rates skyrocketed. Every new kid meant another worker for the farm. Before, a woman would rarely have multiple children for these extra kids would impinge on her ability to continue to gather the necessary nourishment for the clan. Not so in these farming communities. More babies meant more labor. Once we became "civilized," the opportunities for men always outnumbered those for women. At the highest levels of society – the noblewomen and the priestesses – exceptions could always be found, but for the vast majority, the pattern had been set. Women had their very narrow sphere of influence and men had everything else. Only in the last fifty years have we seen a shift out from this woman in the kitchen norm, and with the recent demise of male-dominated manufacturing jobs, we might even be on the cusp of a new era in human history where women dominate the service field and men wander around their homes longing for the days when they were needed at the workplace.

But in these first civilizations, gender equality was on nobody's radar. We no longer had to worry about finding food, but we still had to worry. We worried about having enough water to nourish our crops, enough minerals to make our weapons and enough customers to buy our goods. We hoped our kings wouldn't turn blood- thirsty, that our lawmakers would always be just and that our neighbors would respect our belongings. Our priests became the people we embraced in times of despair, spoke to our gods for protection and watched after our immortal soul in the afterlife.

Our days were hard, our lives were still relatively short and we increasingly looked to religion to fill our spiritual voids.

But that is for another chapter.

5

What We Believe

Foundations of the World's Religions – 200,000 BC > 1000 BC

Do you believe in God or do you believe in gods? Do you have a code of conduct that rules your life? Has this code been passed down for generations? Is this code shared by millions of others?

What happens when you die? Do you go to Heaven? To Hell? To another body? To dirt?

And where do we come from? Yes, I know...our moms. But where did the first humans come from?

Man has asked these questions since the dawn of our existence. It's wired into our DNA. We're a curious bunch. Sometimes the answers to our questions might seem absurd to outsiders, but to us they feel only natural. We might believe that gods live in the clouds, or on mountaintops or in the trees. We might believe that when we die we go down a river, or to a fiery hell or into the body of a cockroach. We might believe we came from a kernel of corn, or a couple of naked people living in a garden or from stones hidden in a god's stomach.

But the one thing man has proven over our past is that we have a remarkable capacity to believe, to have faith in the unexplainable. And this is what makes life more interesting to us than it probably is for a sea cucumber. Yes, sometimes our faith is shattered, but we keep going back for more. Our capacity to have faith defines us from the other species roaming the planet eating, expelling waste and reproducing.

So over the millenniums what have humans believed?

In the beginning (no, not that "in the beginning"), for the first few hundred thousands years of our existence, man believed gods or spirits lived in nature. Usually when people think of nature gods, their minds drift to Disney's *Pocahontas*, "but I know every rock and tree and creature has a life, has a spirit, has a name." But this type of faith goes back way before Pocahontas and her Native American contemporaries, back to a time when we all hunted and gathered. These first *Homo sapiens* believed in a rudimentary form of animism, where shamans delivered rambling chants, foresaw the future and even prayed to the spirits of the clouds or the sun or the plants to help make the survival process just a little bit easier. We know these first animists believed in an afterlife because we've seen their bones buried next to amulets, jewelry and weapons, all demonstrating that the people in this world thought their stuff might be needed in the next.

The next evolution of religions took place after the Neolithic Revolution, when we started settling down next to rivers. As the first civilizations sprouted, priests took on positions of authority, and in some cases they became absolute rulers. In other cases, they ruled side by side with the tyrant, dictator or monarch. These priests were needed because not only did they know how to predict the cycle of weather (maybe a better word for them would have been "meteorologists"), but because they also were thought to have a direct connection to the pantheon of gods that decided the fate of man. In Mesopotamia, the gods were Baal, Dagon, Apsu, Tiamat and Marduk. Egypt had Ra, Anubis, Isis, Osiris and Horus. Greece had Zeus, Poseidon, Aphrodite, Athena and Apollo. India had Vishnu, Shiva, Brahma, Indra and Rudra.

Regardless of which early civilization we're talking about, their pantheons shared some similarities. First, a few of the gods were involved in the creation process. Second, some were in charge of a positive afterlife and others were in charge of the h-e-double-hockey-sticks version. Third, some gods focused on nature, specifically what it took to ensure bountiful crops. Fourth, some cared about our daily lives – when we got married, when we had kids and when we went to war. Fifth, most of these gods had human characteristics, although some might be animals and some might even be half-animal/half-man. These hybrids made it easier for us to transition from a world where we once worshipped gods of nature, to a world where we increasingly needed to believe that an omnipresent human form cared about our human reality.

The next phase of religious evolution occurred when people shifted from believing in many gods (polytheism) to believing in just one (monotheism). Sometimes this transformation lasted only a generation. Other times it became a permanent fixture of humanity. These monotheistic faiths sprung up throughout the Levant, the area we today call the Middle East. The Persian Empire had Zoroastrianism, where the god Ahura Mazda promised a joyous afterlife if you were kind to your neighbors. In Egypt, Akhenaten (King Tut's father and a rather delusional pharaoh) forced his people to believe in the one true god – Aten (a god who was not so coincidentally an incarnation of Akhenaten). But however much he tried to establish his universal monotheism in Egypt, once he died, his people quickly reverted back to their polytheistic traditions.

Yet one monotheistic religion survived, and today it has spawned the two leading faiths in the world – Christianity and Islam. This was the faith of the Hebrews, a group of nomadic shepherds who believed in one god – Yahweh (who would later become known as simply God). God constantly put these Hebrews through tests of faith, forever challenging their allegiance to Him. He promised that they alone were the chosen ones, who, because of their struggles, would one day inherit the Kingdom of Heaven. The early creation stories of the Hebrews in many ways parallel the pagan stories told across Mesopotamia, most specifically in the *Epic of Gilgamesh*. One reality true of all faiths is that to survive they must borrow from or adopt the traditions of the region. Inventing a wholly different belief system guarantees the death of your faith. Instead, in a practice known as syncretism, new faiths blend with old faiths. For example, the *Epic of Gilgamesh* speaks of a great flood that wipes out humanity, of a mysterious plant of knowledge and of a sexy temptress who brings down a clan's greatest warrior. The Hebrew Torah has Noah's flood, the tree of knowledge in the Garden of Eden and the fateful romance of Samson and Delilah. These connections could be mere coincidence or they could represent a history and a values system shared by many peoples in the region.

Another story in the Hebrew Torah was the life of Abraham. This story is not significant because of its parallels to other regional tales, but because it is critical to understanding how the eventual Christian and Islamic faiths would one day take divergent, antagonistic paths. According to the Old Testament, God promised Abraham and his wife Sarah that one day He would bless them with a family. They waited and waited and waited. As they aged into their 50s, 60s, 70s and 80s, for some odd reason, their faith in God's promise was growing thin, to the point that one day Sarah proposed to Abraham that he impregnate their servant girl, Hagar, to ensure the continuation of his blood line. This offspring, Ishmael, soon had a new baby brother when Sarah miraculously (at the age of 90) also gave birth to a child. This one was named Isaac. As the two boys grew, God wanted to test Abraham's faith, so He challenged Abraham to sacrifice his favorite son. At the moment Abraham was to slay his chosen son, God sent down an angel to stop the murder. Abraham had proved his allegiance to God, above even his love of his family.

The key question was – who was Abraham's favored son? Christians believe it was Isaac. Muslims believe it was Ishmael. This is important because the line of Isaac continues on to Jesus Christ. The line of Ishmael continues on to Muhammad. Depending on which version you believe, you could have a strong argument that Abraham's (ipso facto God's) favored son (favored religion) is either Christianity or Islam. Though many current followers might not know this story, in the early years of both faiths, it became a crucial point to support the superiority of their version.

Back to Abraham and his family drama. Ishmael and Hagar were eventually thrown out of the house, and Isaac went on to lead the Hebrews out of Mesopotamia. Eventually these nomadic shepherds were taken into captivity by the Egyptians, a state in which they remained until Moses brought them out of enslavement and took them to the Promised Land – Israel. One of the more difficult stories for non-believers to accept is that Moses parted the Red Sea to escape the pursuit of the Egyptian pharaoh. Some historians have argued that he actually crossed a little shallower strip of water called the Reed Sea. Either way, Moses and his Hebrew followers made it out of Egypt, one step closer to the Promised Land.

After walking for forty years through the deserts of the Levant, his people made it to their new home. Moses did not survive to see them arrive, but he did bring down the Ten Commandments from Mt. Sinai and these tablets outlined God's laws for his Jewish followers. Many of these laws were already fairly familiar to those in the region familiar with the Code of

Hammurabi (such as...thou shalt not steal, thou shalt not kill and thou shalt not covet thy neighbor's wife). Others mandated that thou shalt worship no other god or thou shalt worship no idol (a clear attempt to prevent the followers from reverting back to their polytheistic habits). The Hebrews embraced these laws as their ethical code, and although their story and their numbers remained relatively low over the centuries, their struggle and their beliefs became a crucial part of the holy books of both Christianity and Islam which are practiced today by over 55% of the world's population.

The world's third most practiced religion – Hinduism – also started around 1000 BC, but instead of in the Levant, this religion's roots were in the subcontinent of India. When the Aryans came down across the Indus River and shared their animistic beliefs with the native Dravidians, the resulting religion became known as Hinduism. The name Hinduism in itself is a misnomer for in actuality the religious beliefs of India were, and are, as divergent as the people in the region. There is no *one* Hinduism. The thousands of gods and thousands of methods of worship have some common themes, but unlike the firm orthodoxy of the Hebrew faith, the Hindu faith has proven itself quite open to interpretation. This grouping of faiths received the name Hinduism from Alexander the Great when he first recognized all these Indus region beliefs as those of the H(Indus) region, or "Hinduism." His relatively naïve understanding of the beliefs of the Indians has continued for some until this day. Some still have trouble defining what is Hinduism.

Some say Hindus believe in thousands of gods. Others say there's only one. Or a few. And that all of the others are merely manifestations, avatars, of the original god. In this version, when interacting with humans, the gods Vishnu, Shiva and Brahma present themselves in a variety of forms, yet each sprouts from the single, original deity.

Unlike with Hebrews who can go to the Torah, or with Christians who can look to the Bible or with Muslims who can turn to the Quran, there is no one piece of Hindu text that will give you all the key laws of the faith. However, some pieces of literature do stand out and have found their way into the belief systems of most Hindus. The *Baghavad Gita* tells the story of Lord Arjuna who is engaged in a violent battle with his family for the throne of his kingdom. He doesn't want to kill his family, but he does feel the need to take the throne for himself. He asks for guidance from the gods. Lord Vishnu descends to earth in the form of a charioteer and spends his remaining days guiding Arjuna. Their conversation provides a code for Indians to follow. Krishna warns that you should not be "attached to the fruits of activities [but] act as a matter of duty." In other words, the material world is irrelevant. We are all born for a purpose, and we must all fulfill this Kharma, this duty – no matter if your duty is to bury dead bodies, wash the streets or defeat your family in battle. The *Baghavad Gita* also provides clues on how to obtain a higher understanding of your calling. We should practice meditation (known as Yoga).

In a different story, the *Ramayana*, Princess Sita is kidnapped and her husband, an incarnation of the god Vishnu, spends his life trying to free her from her captors. This epic poem speaks of the importance of fidelity and family above all else. And the *Upanishads* speak to a host of beliefs and behaviors, one of which outlines the Hindu perspective on the afterlife. It states:

> *According as one acts, according as one behaves, so does he become. The doer of good becomes good. The doer of evil becomes evil. One becomes virtuous by virtuous action, bad by bad action... According to his deeds, the embodied self assumes successively various forms in various conditions.*

This is the belief in reincarnation. Unlike the previously mentioned faiths that promise an afterlife not of this world, Hinduism states that your soul will be reincarnated into a different body. Depending on how naughty or nice you were in your previous life, you could end up improving your position in your caste. This process could take centuries, but at some point, if successive incarnations of your soul conduct good deeds, you can break the cycle of transmigration (from body to body) and reach a state of ultimate liberation where you will know what is truly real (Moksha) and no longer live in a world where everything is an illusion (Maya). You will have escaped the misery of humanity.

By 500 BC, the roots of the major faiths of the world were firmly in place. Within a few centuries, two new challengers, in two totally different parts of the planet, would attempt to reform Hinduism and Judaism. One would be a prince, the other a carpenter. They would fail in reforming these faiths, but they would succeed in fostering two entirely new religions – Buddhism and Christianity.

But that is for another chapter.

6

From River Valleys to Golden Ages

India – Harappa to Gupta – 3000 BC > 600 AD

To know the story of the world, you must first know the story of India. For over the course of its 5,000-year history, India has seen it all. It's seen the rise and fall of the greatest early river civilization, one that dwarfed in scale the offerings of China, Mesopotamia, Egypt and Romania. It's seen barbarians from the steppe invade its lands, both redefining what it means to be civilized while also enslaving its progeny to a class system that remains to this day. It's seen golden ages of empires where leaders patronized the arts, science, education and new religions, but it's also seen centuries of regional rule where princes and kings focused more on patronizing their own pockets. It's seen its people embrace any one of 33,000 available gods, but it's also seen its people follow the more logical spiritual journey outlined by the Buddha. It's seen its people barely survive for thousands of years, trapped using the technology of the Stone Age, but it has also seen its people dedicated to the advancement of man's knowledge of the world – bringing us geometry, pi, decimal points, zero and plastic surgery. It's been the center of trade networks connecting Indonesia to Istanbul, Nepal to the Nile and Peking to Pisa. Conquerors have been awed by its majesty, missionaries have been entranced by its mysticism and ambassadors have been seduced by its riches. India is the home to the most diverse people in the world living across one of the most diverse ecosystems on the planet. It is the world in a nutshell.

To know India, we must first go back about 5,000 years to the Indus River Valley, an area of northwest India in what today is called Pakistan. Today this area is nothing but a desert. The dirt is dry, the rains rarely come and few people even attempt to survive the elements. But back around 3,000 BC, the world of the Indus River Valley painted an entirely different picture. Its forests were lush, its rivers were filled with the runoff of the Himalayan Mountains and its monsoon rains showered the valley. It was home to the largest civilization of the ancient world. Close to five million people called this valley home and it was ruled from the twin cities of Harappa and Mohenjo-Daro. Each of these cities housed more than 200,000 people, a testament to urban planning and to the complex systems of government and public assistance.

Yet before the 1920s, most of the world thought this Harappan civilization was merely the fodder of legends and that the story of India couldn't have truly begun until invaders from the north came down and organized the awaiting hordes of nomads. However, with each passing decade, archeological digs have continued to shed light on this once-flourishing society. We haven't yet figured out their writing system, but we have dug up their homes, their temples and their government buildings, and what we've found has forced archaeologists to rewrite the history books. Not only were the first Indians not uncivilized vagrants scavenging off nature's leftovers, but they were instead the founders of a rich civilization that wouldn't find its equal for a millennium. They grew wheat, cotton, rice and peas. They used wheeled wagons to transport their wares from town to town. They built ships that traded with China and Mesopotamia. They believed in fertility goddesses of nature and horned-man gods of power. Their leaders administered over a network of towns up and down the Indus River, coordinating infrastructure projects believed impossible of early man. In the main cities of Harappa and Mohenjo-Daro, they constructed walls to protect their grain storage from outside invaders, they built roads wider than today's highways and they designed plumbing systems that brought water to every home and delivered the great caca to the sea. They were ahead of their time, but like the Romanian civilizations of the Black Sea, they too would vanish from history.

But how do five million people just vanish? How was an empire of cutting-edge cities lost to history, buried beneath mountains of dirt and forgotten until the 20th century? No one knows for sure. It could have been an epidemic like malaria that wiped everyone out. Or maybe it was a cataclysmic event – a flood or an earthquake or a tsunami. More than likely it wasn't anything this fast or this dramatic. It probably just started getting hotter and drier. With each passing season, the monsoon rains probably came less and less, and as the farmers found it harder and harder to reap the crops that made it possible to survive in a city, they packed up and headed east, looking for a more consistent source of water. After generations of migrants left the Indus River Valley, the once metropolises of ancient Harappa became ghost towns. The river beds went completely dry and the last known survivors gave up on nature and joined their forefathers in the eastern lands, leaving the valley an abandoned wasteland.

At about the same time the Harappan refugees were heading eastward, another great people started arriving from the north – the Aryans. Now for many, the term "Aryan" has been eternally linked with the 20th century maniacal ramblings of Adolph Hitler, so for a moment you need to erase that image of Nazi delusions and accept that Hitler was an idiot. Aryans aren't a race of blonde-haired, blue-eyed superhumans who blessed the world with their presence, forging every last achievement of the modern world.

But they were blue-eyed and blonde-haired (and also probably bearded, dirty and pretty darn hairy). They first lived in central Asia, in countries we today call Kyrgyzstan, Kazakhstan, Turkmenistan and Uzbekistan. They were farmer nomads. They set up tents and wooden buildings, planted some crops and raised cattle, but every few seasons, they'd pack up their belongings in their wheeled wagons and head off to a new land. They were a warring people. They never fled from a fight and they had no problem kicking more settled people off their lands. They sat around fires chanting songs and telling tales of gods, goddesses and warrior-kings. And around 2000 BC, they started moving. Just as climate change forced the more civilized peoples of the ancient world to seek out new homes, so did Mother Nature force the Aryans to start their wandering expedition. This time, these Aryans didn't merely move to the next valley, to the next fertile plain. They started spreading out all across Europe and Asia. They made it all the way through northern Europe, across the English Channel and into Britain and Ireland. They moved across Turkey and down into Greece, Italy and Spain. They put pressure on the Assyrian and the Persian Empires of the Levant. And they then headed down south into India, running into the race of Dravidians who had called the subcontinent their home since they first walked over from Africa, then Arabia some ten thousand years earlier.

Everywhere the Aryans went, they left their mark. We see the Aryan thunder god stories in Norway's Thor, India's Indra and Greece's Zeus. We see the legacy of fireside chanting and epic storytelling in the Norse tales of Beowulf, the heroic poems of Homer and the poetic mythology of the Hindu Vedas. We see how the Aryans took the technology of Mesopotamia and spread it to Egypt and then into Europe. But above all, we see how the Aryan language is the root source of Sanskrit, Latin, Greek, German, English and Egyptian. So many words from Indian Sanskrit are almost exact matches with words from northern Europe and the Mediterranean. "King" is *raja* in Sanskrit and *regem* in Latin. "Snake" is *sarpa* in Sanskrit and *serpens* in Latin. The number "three" is *trayas* in Sanskrit and *tres* in Latin. And similarities between some common words like mother, father and brother can be seen all across Eurasia. The word "brother" is *frère* in French, *frater* in Latin, *phrater* in Greek, *bruder* in German, *broeder* in Dutch and *bhratar* in Sanskrit. There are thousands of similar links to be found between Indian Sanskrit and the languages of Europe, far too many to merely write off as a coincidence. There had to be one common connector, and that connector was the Aryans.

But in India, the Aryans did far more than merely introduce a language, a few gods and the tradition of storytelling. The Aryans completely transformed society. Unlike in Europe where the Aryans intermarried with the locals, in India, they chose to set up class distinctions when coming face to face with the Dravidians. In India, they established permanent laws to forever prevent the intermingling of the races, much like those laws written in the counties of the American Jim Crow South that prevented the miscegenation of blacks and whites. And like the segregated American South, the Aryans likewise divided their world based on color. They even called this system *varna*, meaning "color." The Portuguese traders had another name for it – the caste system.

According to this caste system, the invading Aryans and their warriors and priests forever stood atop the social hierarchy, while the native Dravidians were relegated to the farming and artisan positions at the bottom of the ladder. As the Aryans moved further down the Indian sub-continent, the diverse, disunited peoples shared no common story and were difficult to subjugate. They needed the caste system to maintain order. The Aryans also started writing down their epic tales, combining their stories with the array of deity stories told in the towns and villages across India. These thousands of pages of hymns, chants and fables became known as the Vedas. Through these early texts, the Aryans imprinted the new order of society, one that warned against independent thought and championed the need for unquestioned obedience to the Rajayana (warriors) and Brahmans (priests). Two worlds came together, but these worlds would learn to live apart.

For the next thousand years, during what is called the Vedic Age, these traditions became more firmly entrenched, yet the kingdoms of India developed independently without any central authority. Divided into sixteen distinct provinces and ruled like the feudal kingdoms of medieval Europe, India remained a patchwork of diverse societies, locked in a world where your caste determined every element of your humanity – from choosing your profession to choosing your spouse to determining what would come of you in the afterlife. It was a world of rules and sacrifices, of priests and kings. It was a world of inequality and suffering, of haves and have-nots.

But four events would occur in the fifth and fourth centuries BC that would forever change the course of Indian history – each inspired by a different young man who had his own unique vision of a new world order.

The first young man to change India was a prince who lived a life of luxury in a small Himalayan hill town in a place we would today call Nepal. This young prince's name was Siddhartha Gautama, and he would become...the Buddha. After a childhood of ambling between feasts and parties and horseback rides and picnics, Siddhartha started thinking his life was nothing more than one extended holiday. There had to be more to life than the gluttony that surrounded him behind the palace walls, but when he asked his father for a tour of the real world, his father was at first hesitant to reveal to his son the reality of the streets. Yet the young prince continued to hound his father until one day his father acquiesced, agreeing to have his most trusted advisors take Siddhartha on a guided tour of only the most sanitized parts of his kingdom. But all could not be hidden. Siddhartha Gautama saw the suffering of his people, saw the pitiful form of an elderly man, and saw the mourning and finality of life when he witnessed a funeral procession.

Life wasn't the carefree existence he grew up around. Life was tragic. Life was filled with misery, pain and despair. He had to find out why this was the reality of humanity. He had to find out if there was another way.

So he packed a bag, said goodbye to his family and his wealth and started on a great walkabout. He wasn't alone on the streets. In the 6th and 5th centuries BC, thousands of men took to the roads, wandering around, questioning the status quo, pondering the meaning of life. Some argued there were no gods and that we were all alone. Others, the Janes, believed we were all interconnected by a life force, somewhat like the mythical "force" that later linked Obi Won Kenobi, Luke Skywalker and Darth Vader (but without the light sabers). Still others thought maybe we were all made up of millions of tiny atoms. Hundreds of these wandering thinkers offered anti-establishment possibilities, but none of these philosophies truly spoke to the travelling prince.

He thought maybe he needed to suffer more. After living a life of wealth and grandeur, maybe the answer would come through a life of poverty. He gave away the last of his worldly possessions, stopped eating and sat for months hoping for inspiration. Nothing came to him, but a perpetual empty stomach, skin ulcers and a protruding rib cage. It had to be something else. He continued to walk across India, agreeing to live a life of moderation – not too rich, not too poor.

Eventually he made his way to the town of Bodh Gaya and sat down under a fig tree. He closed his eyes and meditated and waited. He sat and sat and sat, and 49 days later he arose and declared he had the answer. He had achieved Enlightenment. He had become the Buddha. He had discovered the path to Nirvana – freedom from all of life's problems.

He claimed there were Four Noble Truths to man's existence. First, life is full of suffering. Second, we suffer because we have unquenchable desires. We want more toys to put in our houses, we believe the grass is always greener in someone else's lawn and we hope we can be immortal and somehow escape death through an afterlife in paradise. This leads to an endless cycle of longing and disappointment. We want what we can't have and are surprisingly sad when we don't get it. But, third, he believed, you CAN in fact teach yourself to stop this cycle of want. And, fourth, once you've learned to train your mind to not want, you can escape the endless human circle of birth, life, death and rebirth. You can escape the human world of suffering once and for all.

Unlike the other religions of the age, this path required no sacrifices, no recitation of thousand-year-old hymns and no blind following of a priest who interpreted spiritual texts written in long-forgotten languages. The journey towards enlightenment required you to wage war against yourself and rid yourself of the negativity in your life that prevents you from moving forward. Buddha spoke of the Eightfold Path where you would choose the right job, the right words, the right actions and the right thoughts. You would teach yourself to be kind to others, not hurt a living creature with words or with deed. You would teach yourself to recognize when your mind or your body went astray and immediately put yourself back on course. You'd become a heck of a lot nicer.

This logical method of self-improvement was a revolution of the mind. Man for the first time could take his fate into his own hands. He didn't need to pray to a god, or listen to a priest, or sing a little medley, or perform some metaphoric ritual that required him to paint his face or kill a goat. He didn't need to hope for heaven or worry about hell. He needed to just be a better person.

Buddha continued his journey across the Indian countryside, stopping to teach his musings, hoping others would follow the path to spiritual fulfillment. Many listened, but only a few actually embraced this radical ideology. There was too much to lose. To accept the teachings of Buddha meant denying the beliefs of your ancestors, your family, your society and also giving away all worldly possessions. That is why, when Buddha died at the age of 80, after over fifty years of learning and teaching across the Ganges River Valley, his revolutionary ideas had gained little traction aside from a few devoted disciples. This Buddhism was merely just another spiritual path espoused by a discontented messenger. Its chances of survival were not good.

But then our second young visionary entered India, yet this man didn't come from the foothills of the Himalayas, and he definitely wasn't one to sit under a tree and ponder the meaning of life. He was a warrior from the far off land of Greece (well, Macedonia to be exact). He was Alexander the Great. His tales of triumph and world domination will be explored further in a couple chapters, but for now, all you need to know was that in 326 BC an army of over 10,000 Greek, Macedonian and Persian invaders stood at the shores of the Hydaspes River, on the verge of defeating the allied Indian forces, threatening to vanquish the entire subcontinent. In the previous decade, Alexander had defeated everyone who stood in his way – the Persians, the Syrians, the Egyptians – bringing each under his rule, forging an empire that united the east with the west. Nothing could stop Alexander from continuing further east.

Nothing save for his own men. They'd had enough. They were rich. They were tired. They were thousands of miles away from home. They were done. They fought the Indians this one last time on the Hydaspes River. They were victorious, and then they turned around and left. But before Alexander's reluctant return to the west, he was visited by a local lord, Chandragupta Maurya, the third young man of the ancient world to write a new chapter in India's story.

Chandragupta was inspired. He saw the power, the glory, the possibilities of Alexander's army and he dreamed of a united India. Alexander couldn't help the young prince, but Chandragupta's vision wouldn't be squashed. If he couldn't have Alexander's army, he'd make his own. He sold his dream to the regional hillside tribes, promising them riches and territory beyond their imagination. In 320 BC, he had his army and with disorder that accompanied Alexander's eventual death, the territories of western India were his for the taking. He spent the next two decades uniting the northern part of India, connecting the coastal cities of the Bay of Bengal in the east to the mountain peoples of Persia in the west. India had its first continental empire and the Mauryan Dynasty was born.

Accept for a small chunk at the southern tip, Chandragupta had consolidated much of the Indian continent, but it was his grandson, Ashoka the Great (borrowing the not-so-original title from Alexander) who decimated the last of the resisting kingdoms and truly brought all of India under one rule. Ashoka wasn't always "the great." In fact, his earliest nickname was Ashoka the Cruel. He was bloodthirsty in war and even more merciless in peace. He built a torture chamber where victims would be hacked into geometric shapes, have stakes driven into their hands and feet and have molten metal stuffed down their throats. He called this his "hell on earth" chamber and tales of his sadistic cruelty spread across the land.

But then one day he had a spiritual awakening and he realized the error of his ways. After the Battle of Kalinga in 255 BC, Ashoka walked the battlefield and was disgusted by what he saw. Hundreds of thousands lay on the battlefield, bodies shredded, limbs detached, organs oozing out of every orifice. Another 150,000 had been rounded up and would be taken away as prisoners. He didn't know what was louder – the cries of agony from the fallen or the howling wales of their loved ones.

He thought to himself, "What have I done? If this is a victory, what's a defeat then? Is this justice or injustice? Is it valor to kill innocent children and women?"

Ashoka already knew the answers. He threw down his sword and vowed to never take up arms against another. He would create not an empire of fear, but an empire of the spirit. He would throw all of his time and all of his empire's money into making India a better place. He became the final piece necessary to transform India.

Buddha had conceived the philosophy. Alexander had provided the inspiration. Chandragupta had started the empire.

Now Ashoka would put all the pieces together. He would embrace the teachings of the Buddha and passionately push for its acceptance across his realm. He commissioned thousands of miles of roads for Buddhist missionaries to share the virtue of the Eightfold Path. He spent money not on frivolous additions to his palaces, but on improving the daily lives of his people. He dug wells, planted gardens and cleaned streets. He created the first welfare state – offering money to those in need and opening hospitals to those who couldn't pay. He became the first animal activist of the ancient world, banning the killing of animals and building shelters to house the abused and ignored. He formalized the law code, inscribing the empire's edicts on pillars for all to see, and increasing the size of the police force to ensure adherence of the legal code.

In trying to bring peace to this newly united empire, Ashoka established a common currency and a common taxation system. He demanded peace on the roads. Even Buddhist monks journeying into hostile lands were taught how to merely disarm bandits they might meet along the way. Violence was the last resort. With this newfound focus on maintaining order, trade flourished and ideas made their way from one corner of the subcontinent to the other.

Some cynics argued his motives were merely a convenient public relations ploy used to preserve his power and dissuade rivals to the throne, but regardless of the purity of his reasoning, Ashoka did in fact shift the values of the land (if only for a few decades) away from the idea that might makes right, and toward a more sympathetic, generous principle of human interaction. And all of his changes came under the banner of Buddhism, and by the time of his passing, the teachings of Siddhartha Gautama were no longer merely the isolated beliefs of a disenfranchised few, but had become a dogma that in many places supplanted the firmly entrenched Hindu beliefs of the era.

Like all powerful empires, this one too would end. No leader that followed Ashoka had the credibility, the foresight or the zeal to continue this transformation of Indian society. Within two generations of his death, India regressed to its natural state. For India is not a land meant to be ruled by a central power. Its villages and people are separated by forests, deserts, oceans, rivers, mountains, plains and the steppe. Their allegiance is not to the concept of a united India, but to their local lord, their local traditions and their family's caste. A child grows up not caring about the edicts of a far-off ruler, but of the actions of her family, the expectations of her caste and the festivals of her village. A daughter is first the property of her father, then of her brother and then of the man she will marry. As she matures, she watches how her father performs his duties without hesitation – be it as a shoveler of dung, a molder of bricks or a scribe to a king. Her town's festivals signal the passage of time, bringing families together and bonding each generation to the past. Rulers might come and go, but family and faith kept the society in harmony.

With the fall of the Mauryan Empire, India didn't descend into chaos, it merely continued under the daily and seasonal rhythms defined by caste and community. For the next five hundred years, regional rule was the order of the day until 330 AD when the next great Indian empire appeared. While the Roman Empire was crumbling in Europe and as the Huns were sweeping across the steppe, a new Chandra Gupta (not the Mauryan prince from centuries earlier) married into the equally powerful Lichchhavis family, doubling his empire with one simple marriage vow. From here, the Gupta family continued to expand their holdings until they too controlled an empire stretching from the Bay of Bengal to the Hindu Kush mountain ranges. Yet, unlike the Mauryan Empire, the Guptas never tried to exert absolute authority, instead creating what was known as a "theater state." The rules were simple – pay tribute to the Guptas and you'd maintain your autonomy. Give us your money, we'll leave you alone. Deny us and we'll kill you. Because of this loose political rule, the Gupta Empire was able to survive for nearly three centuries and with the money siphoned from the countryside, the capital city at Ayodhya became the cultural and scientific center of Eurasia.

The Guptas became patrons of the arts and sciences, providing the ideal environment for men of vision and imagination to reach their intellectual potential. No cost was spared – laboratories were built, studios were furnished with the latest tools and emissaries were sent across the continent, from Luoyang to Rome to Alexandria, to draw inspiration from the greatest works of antiquity. With this unprecedented support, the Indian elite made unparalleled contributions that continue to impact our lives to this day. Although many of these developments would later erroneously be credited to others (usually Westerners), the innovations of the Gupta Indians read like a laundry list of the greatest discoveries in the history of mankind

In astronomy, Aryabhata defended the geocentric theory, asserting that the earth revolved around the sun (1100 years before the findings of Copernicus and Galileo). He also contended that the earth was round and rotated around an axis (also about a thousand years before Columbus was credited with being the first to champion this unconventional idea).

In Physics, the theory of gravity was proposed, centuries before Sir Isaac Newton analyzed why an apple falls from a tree. Newton, in thanking his European predecessors, once said, "If I should see further it is only because I sit on the shoulders of other men." Maybe he should have said, "...because I sit on the shoulders of other men from India."

In numeration, Gupta scientists created the base-ten decimal system and the numbers we know as 1,2,3,4,5,6,7,8,9 and, yes...o (these numbers were later named after the traders that shared them with Europe – thus we today call them Arabic numerals). Anyone who's ever tried to calculate their height using inches or figure out how many cups are in a quart or remember how many feet are in a mile can appreciate the brilliance of the decimal system. Thank you India.

They also created chess. Yep, chess came from Gupta India. Though instead of a horse (knight), a castle (rook) and a bishop, the early Indian version – *caturanga* – had infantry, cavalry, elephants and chariots.

They wrote the book Kama Sutra, one of the world's first birds and the bees books, which shows how two humans could best pleasure each other. You should not read this text until you are 46 years old and have been married for multiple decades.

And in medicine, Gupta doctors succeeded where others rarely dared even journey. They grafted skin, reset broken bones, practiced caesarian births and even dabbled in plastic surgery.

The mathematicians, scientists, writers and artists of the era demonstrated what a people could accomplish when a united government becomes patrons of knowledge and creates a world where humans can develop without the constant fear of violence. The Guptas were by no means pacifists. They threatened, jailed, tortured, mutilated and killed just like other rulers who want to ensure allegiance from distant regions. But they used this violence for good.

For almost three centuries, India stood out as the most innovative region in the world, rivaling the contributions of Athenian Greece in the age of Socrates, and Renaissance Italy when Michelangelo, da Vinci and Raphael stunned the western world. For three hundred years, the center of learning was Asia, but this was not the first time. For there was another nation to the east who had already made its stamp on the world's civilizations.

But that is for another chapter.

7

The Middle Kingdom Rises

China – Xia to Qin to Han Dynasties – 2200 BC > 220 AD

I f you stroll through the non-fiction section of any book store, it's pretty clear that China is making a lot of people nervous. In 2012 alone, authors spewed out books titled *Winner Take All, Is China Buying the World, China Versus the West, China Fast Forward, When China Rules the World,* and *Death by China.*

The world is worried. Well, maybe not the world - maybe just Europe and the US. And who can blame them? For the past three centuries, the world was run by European powers. They had the most deadly weapons, the most innovative scientists and the most flourishing economies. All wealth flowed through Western hands and no one could imagine a day when a beast from the east would threaten their supremacy.

Fast forward to 2013. China has close to 1.4 billion people - almost a quarter of the planet's population. They are a nuclear power, the greatest exporter of goods on earth (think *Made in China*) and they even talk of sending a man to Mars. China has jumped up the list of most productive countries in the world, currently sitting at #2 on the GDP list and quite possibly they will pass America by 2016.

And they show no signs of fading. For many this is hard to fathom. China? Where did they come from? Weren't they just a generation ago every parent's foolproof go-to country for stirring guilt around the dinner table? How many of us grew up with a mom who reminded us that "children were starving to death in China," hoping that allusion might shame us into finishing our peas and carrots?

But today's China isn't your parents' China. Gone are those 20th century decades of despair and suffering that culminated in Mao's ill-concocted Great Leap Forward that caused almost 40 million peasant deaths. Those wretched years were merely a blip in China's story, for China is a nation that over the course of human history has almost always been the most prosperous, most advanced region on the planet. Whether you checked in 2000 years ago, or 1500 years ago, or 1000 years ago or even 500 years ago, you'd almost immediately notice, like Marco Polo did in 1234, that China was "a civilization with which no other peoples could ever hope to compare."

Most of this success can be attributed to the fact that since about 1000 BC, except for just a few periods of factional rule, China has been united under one central power. No other place on the planet can claim this degree of order for so long a time. Now compare China to Europe. Sure Europe's a continent, but it's also about the same size as China. And except for a couple hundred years where the Romans spread their empire from the boot of Italy to the isles of Britain, Europe has always been divided into dozens, if not hundreds, of individual kingdoms, each involved in a seemingly life or death struggle with their neighbors to maintain supremacy. Even today there are 44 independent countries in Europe. But there is only one China.

It is this uniformity that made advancement and progress possible. China's history is told through the stories of dynasties. One potent family would rise, take over the state, unify the countryside and maintain order for generations. Inevitably, this family's fortune would fade, their leaders would prove pathetic and the peasants' lives would regress into misery and malnourishment. A new family would emerge, supplant the waning regime and launch a new age. Each family remained sovereign as long it maintained the "Mandate of Heaven," in other words, as long as heaven favored the conduct of each ruler. Should rulers become corrupt, brutal, inept, gluttonous or neglectful of their people, heaven would remove its support, paving the way for peasant revolts and rivals to the throne.

In this manner, China has been ruled by a series of families – ten to be exact. A few years back, in a classroom far, far away, a clever World History teacher devised a little trick for his students to remember the Chinese dynasties – named appropriately "The Dynasty Song." So if ever you want to impress your friends at holiday parties, just sing this little diddy to the tune of Frère Jacque (or "Where is Thumbkin?"), and you'll have the dynasties memorized in no time. If you're a bit shy about your singing chops, merely head to Youtube and type in "Chinese Dynasty Song" and you're bound to find some group of kids who threw together a little video for some much-needed extra credit. And here's the song:

> Shang, Zhou (*Joe*), Qin (*chin*), Han
> Shang, Zhou, Qin, Han
> Sui (*sway*), Tang, Song
> Sui, Tang, Song
> Yuan, Ming, Qing (*ching*), Republic
> Yuan, Ming, Qing, Republic
> Mao (*mow*) Zedong
> Mao Zedong

Not exactly the song you sang as a babykins with your mom before going sleepy, nigh-nigh, but oddly appealing lessthenone.

Let's look at the first dynasty – the Xia (pronounced "see ah") Dynasty. But wait a second, that little jingle above implied that the Shang was the first. Historians aren't so sure. For centuries, historians just thought the Xia Dynasty was nothing more than a quaint little Chinese creation myth. It told the story of a man named Yu who saved the world from a terrible flood and then united the clans. Until about 1970, most legitimate historians dismissed this story as fable, but after a few archaeological digs unearthed tombs, cities and a ton of clay pots dating back to 2200 BC, it's becoming more apparent that the Xia did actually exist. There's not enough evidence to warrant a new entry to our little dynasty song, but we're getting closer.

Another bit of evidence linking China back to an early river civilization dynasty is the intermittent discovery of scratched-up animal bones. Even into the 21st century, farmers kept plowing up oddly-shaped, randomly-marked bones. They took these trinkets to market and sold them as "dragon bones," but linguists started to realize they were something far more remarkable. They were another example of mankind's first attempts at writing. But unlike the Greeks who carved on stone tablets, the Egyptians who wrote on papyrus or the Mesopotamians who pressed down their styluses on clay, the Chinese used animal bones. They tossed the shoulder blade of an ox or the shell of a turtle onto a fire and when the bones inevitably cracked, a mystic or spiritual leader would be summoned to "read" them. He then used his bronze pen to add some of his own scratchings. These inscriptions marked the major events of the Shang Dynasty and later they evolved into the Mandarin script of today.

The Shang Dynasty lasted until about 1000 BC, when it lost the Mandate of Heaven and was replaced by the Zhou Dynasty that lasted almost 800 years. During the last two centuries of the Zhou, China steadily plunged into regional chaos. Seven kingdoms – the Qin, Qi, Chu, Yan, Han, Zhao and Wei – massacred each other without any regard for rules of combat. There was no honor. There was no safety. Just bloodshed. Warriors ransacked villages, slaughtering civilians by the tens of thousands, stacking the heads of the fallen and even cooking up cauldrons of boiled body parts they later served to the survivors. No road was safe for travel. No home was safe from plunder.

By 500 BC, a few thinkers started searching for answers. This couldn't be all that life offered. Fear. Misery. Death. There must be more?

At about the same time in India that wandering sages took to the road to ponder the meaning of life and about a century before Socrates challenged the accepted order of Greek society, in China a new age of thinkers emerged who would establish norms for human behavior that today guide over two billion souls. The most famous thinker of the eastern ancient world was Confucius. Born in 551 BC, Confucius survived a difficult childhood as his father died when he was three years old and his mother struggled to feed his eleven brothers and sisters. He married when he was 19, but a few years later he divorced his wife to further his intellectual pursuits. Domestic life was not his thing. He had theories for how to bring order to his world, but he knew he needed a bigger audience, that he needed the highest authorities in the land to embrace his ideas, or they would have little to no impact on the deteriorating state of affairs. He would make it to some of the major courts of the day, but he also would spend thirteen years wandering the seven kingdoms, sharing his ideas with all who would listen. Upon his death, his message lived on through his disciples. They continued to crisscross the countryside, meeting with officials, but also stopping to share their mentor's beliefs with the peasants and the artisans struggling to make ends meet. With each passing generation, the works of Confucius gained traction and by 200 BC, Confucianism had gained quite a following.

But what is this Confucianism? And how did it become the bond that linked an entire continent?

Confucius believed that all life comes down to relationships – how we treat others and how we are treated. He spoke of shu – the dictum that you should "not impose on others what you yourself do not desire." This should probably sound familiar because pretty much every faith - from Hinduism to Buddhism to Islam to even Scientology - speaks of the importance of treating others the way you want to be treated. Even Jesus Christ spoke of the Golden Rule, that you should "do unto others as you would wish done unto you." Confucius also spoke of chun tzu – how you should be a gracious, humble, reserved gentleman in all public settings. He spoke of li – where you should perform all rituals with the greatest attention to detail, for it is in these rituals where we make our own order and feel a fellowship with our community.

Confucius then broke all of our interactions down into five core bonds – father to son, older brother to younger brother, husband to wife, friend to friend and ruler to subject. We all have our role to play in these relationships, and if we all follow our prescribed behavior expectations, we can all live in harmony. Confucius saw the father-son relationship as the most crucial. If a son wasn't good to his father, society had no hope of ever escaping the cycle of barbarism and chaos.

"Being good" had many layers. As a child, you were expected to accept your parent's rules and punishments without question, bring honor to the house and never soil the family name. As you aged, you were expected to continue to respect your elders, earn enough money to support them when they got sick and grew tired and make enough babies to carry on the family name. This total respect and devotion to your elders was known as filial piety and it didn't end when your parents died. It just went to the next level.

Confucius taught that man must always be mindful of his ancestors, for it was these ancestors that watched over their offspring's daily lives, choosing to bring fortune, health and many children to those who properly honored the departed. For those who ignored the dead, the ancestors would have their revenge. They would rain down on their family's house any number of afflictions, from poverty to sickness to drought to infertility (both of their fields and of their wives). Every man wasn't just living his life for himself, he was living it for all who preceded him. It was his duty to follow the right path. One small mistake could bring dishonor to his entire family – both living and dead.

And for Confucius, this familial bond extended to matters of the state. Was not the emperor-subject relationship merely a symbolic extension of the father-son bond? Did not the emperor promise to protect and care for his nation's children? And didn't they in turn promise their undying loyalty, obedience and respect? Confucius believed that it was this promise that linked the Mandate of Heaven with filial piety, for as long as a ruler kept his side of the bargain, he would remain in power, but should he break the bond, he could not expect eternal submission. He could expect rebellion.

Not all Chinese thinkers, and especially not all Chinese rulers, agreed with Confucius. Not everyone thought that man was inherently good and if we just learned to play nice we could all get along. Some in fact went the opposite direction. They saw man as a deceitful, vindictive, untrustworthy, shallow beast that must have firm rules, strict punishments and the uncompromising administration of justice. They believed people weren't good because they wanted to be. People were good because they were afraid not to be. This philosophy came to be known as Legalism, and many of China's early rulers found it a heck of a lot easier to enforce than Confucius's idealistic imaginings.

The first to fully embrace this Legalism was Shi Huangdi (pronounced "she hwang dee"), the first emperor of a united China. In the centuries after Confucius's death, the Zhou Dynasty spiraled even deeper into anarchy and by the mid 3rd century BC, the Seven Great Powers again feuded endlessly for dominance. From the western province of Qin came Ying Zheng, a man who swung the pendulum of military force in his favor by first creating a cavalry unrivaled in the land and then having his engineers force tens of thousands of laborers to use their bare hands to dig through a mountain, building a canal that would bring water to their fields. Well-armed and well-fed, Ying Zheng defeated each kingdom one at a time until finally the Chu kingdom surrendered in 223 BC. Once in power, Ying renamed himself - Shi Huangdi – "the first emperor" and he renamed his conquered kingdoms – Qin-a or "China."

Shi Huangdi wouldn't last for long on the throne – just a couple decades - but his legacy would live on for the next two thousand years. He wasn't just the first emperor of China, he was the first man to rule over a truly united China. He knew he could not control the people if they continued to live under the command of their local leaders, living as if part of another country. Thus, he forced all his subjects to use the same written language, to use the same coins, to use the same measuring sticks and even use the same lucky number – six. He rewrote all the history books and banned the study of Confucian thought. When some scholars continued to follow the old way, he burned a ton of books and then threw 460 of these free thinkers into a hole in the ground and buried them alive. He took power from the lords by demanding all taxes be paid directly to him and by "inviting" all the nobles to live in his Imperial City at Xian so he could keep his friends close and his enemies closer.

He was a paranoid dude – afraid everyone wanted him dead. And they did. The barbarians to the north wanted to sweep in and ransack the fertile plains of the Yangtze River Valley and the nobles wouldn't hesitate to jump at any opportunity to squash their oppressive dictator. Shi Huangdi first took care of the barbarian threat by building a wall - a great wall. He turned the Chinese peasants into his personal slave army and commissioned the building of a fortification that would dwarf any public work ever envisioned in the ancient world. At the height of its construction, over one million peasants lived and died toiling to create this 4000-mile long (longer than the United States is wide) barricade. Over 250,000 men, women and children perished under the brutal weather conditions, sparse food rations, and back-breaking digging, carving, carrying and stacking. Those that died unwillingly offered their corpses to the project, merely becoming mixed in with the dirt and stone to become just more filler in what was then known as "the long graveyard." Once finished, the Wall really didn't pose much of a material threat – an invader needed merely go around the wall or bribe one of the guards to let him through. But symbolically, it was critical. China and civilization resided on one side of the wall. The nomadic barbarians were left on the other. And never should the two meet.

Long before his minions ever finished the wall, Shi Huangdi had already enslaved over 700,000 architects, sculptors and engineers to craft his magnum opus – a burial shrine that would rival the pharaoh tombs of Ancient Egypt. As a thirteen-year-old kid, Shi Huangdi had imagined bringing his homeland with him into the afterlife. In his tomb, he wanted nothing short of a complete recreation of his empire (though he was still some 25 years away from uniting the seven kingdoms). If you're having trouble picturing his vision, imagine one of those miniature railroad worlds where hobbyists send their trains through scaled models recreations of Main Street, USA, but instead of a small Midwestern town, Shi Huangdi wanted all of China rebuilt in one ginormous underground tomb.

In 1974, peasants drilling a well in China stumbled across a terracotta clay warrior buried deep in the dirt. Almost three decades later archaeologists have still only uncovered a mere 1% of the 4 square mile mausoleum. They've found the 8000 life-sized clay warriors, each sculpted to have unique facial features, varying hairstyles and personalized uniforms. But these clay warriors merely guard the entrance. The actual tomb of Shi Huangdi is buried deep beneath the surface, a 90-foot tall underworld palace, with a sky adorned with diamond and emerald gems and rivers of mercury weaving through the recreated countryside and cityscape. Chinese archaeologists have been slow to excavate the remaining corridors, but when they finally do, the world will most likely bare witness to the most elaborate vanity project in the history of mankind.

The irony of Shi Huangdi's burial tomb is that he actually thought he could achieve immortality. He brought in the best potion makers, herbmeisters and mystics from across his realm, and eventually settled on drinking a daily dose of mercury to extend his life. Not only did this not give him the immortality he so desperately craved, it probably killed him prematurely.

Once dead and buried, his empire crumbled almost immediately. His sons proved inept. His dynasty proved only fleeting. The people had grown disgusted by Shi Huangdi's sadistic, paranoid, oppressive implementation of the principles of Legalism, but they had grown more tired of his perpetual public works projects that drained them through abhorrent taxes and left millions of others sick, mutilated or dead (every one of the 700,000 workers who built his mausoleum were killed to prevent them from revealing the tomb's location).

Instead of plunging back into an extended warring states period like the one that befell post-Zhou China, this era of civil war lasted just short of a decade before the eastern kingdom of the Han proved worthy of the Mandate of Heaven. Yet unlike the fleeting reign of the Qin Dynasty, the Han Dynasty would live on for centuries, shepherding over what became known as the Golden Age of China. Like the Gupta Age of India, and the Golden Age of Greece (which you'll learn about right around the corner), the peace secured by the Han made possible a period of intellectual, technological and political development that would be looked back on for hundreds of generations as the peak of civilization and the foundation of all that is glorious about a people.

The Han first set out to protect its people by expanding and improving the Great Wall. Shi Huangdi's version was fairly useless, and nothing like the one we visit today. By installing hundreds of manned-towers across the expanse of the fortification, the Wall became far more than merely a symbolic barrier. China was finally protected. China then went about protecting all roads in and out of China, the most famous being the Silk Road, a network of paved paths and trade routes that extended through to India, then across the steppe of Central Asia, and finally ending at the eastern border of the Roman Empire. East was finally connected with West, and the Chinese sent their porcelain dishes (yep...china from China), jade knickknacks and silk fabric clear across Eurasia. Back home, Han engineers expanded the canal system and invented the wheelbarrow and the oh-so-useful ox-drawn plow. Farm yields doubled, then tripled and by 2 CE, China's first census recorded over 57 million people. Peacetime also brought the invention of paper making machines, a sewing loom that could spin out mountains of cloth and the iron-making furnaces that made tools and weapons stronger than anything Europe would design for centuries. Scientists created technologies such as the compass, the rudder and even the hot air balloon, the first two of which would play critical roles in future dynasties as China set out to create a naval juggernaut, the last merely a romantic way to impress your girlfriend on a third date.

But China was so much more than plows and rudders. What was truly revolutionary about the Han Dynasty was its establishment and regulation of a test, but not just any old test – the civil service exam. This was the granddaddy of them all. You think the AP exams impact your future? They ain't nothing compared to the Imperial Exam. Imagine sitting for a week in a room the size of an outhouse, writing for up to ten hours a day on facts you've been memorizing your whole life. Pass, and you join the scholar gentry, the highest honor in the land. Fail, and your entire life's study was a waste. The stakes didn't get any steeper.

But those intense stakes (and rewards) were what made this test so revolutionary. Your future was based on your merit, not your birth. There actually was a reward for studying, for learning, for dedicating yourself to personal improvement. Nowhere else in the world was this even possible. Not in India where your birth determined your class. Not in the Mediterranean civilizations of Rome and Greece where wealth and landholding determined your access to power. In China, you controlled your fate.

Well, maybe in theory you controlled your fate. Sure, *technically* anyone could pass, but you better believe the wealthy landowner kids had a huge advantage over the peasant kids. Think about it in terms of graduating from college in America. Technically, everyone can go to college, but the reality is that when you're rich, your parents can afford tutoring, test prep courses, the best private schools and they can ensure you're surrounded by equally privileged youths who will never have to worry about getting a part time job during high school to make ends meet. Pretty much the same went for Han China and for each future dynasty. Wealth had its privileges. For the rich, the civil service exam wasn't the only way to become a regional official. A rich daddy or a well-positioned uncle might pull some strings for their little er zi (son), and for the right price, prime positions could even be bought by the highest bidder.

Yet even though the game was stacked against the poor, they still had a chance. Fewer than 5% of the candidates who took the test ever actually passed, but still, that's at least a chance. In the rest of the world, meritocracy wouldn't come around for another two thousand years, but in Han China, effort meant something. Knowledge meant something.

But the civil service exam didn't merely offer hope. It kept society stable. Across the empire, everyone learned the same thing. Unlike in the US today where every state can adopt any curriculum they want, in Imperial China, there was only one way – the Confucian way. If you wanted to be a part of society, you studied Confucius. Every schoolhouse, every farmhouse and every outhouse was home to kids studying the same ideas, the same history. There came to be one shared China for everyone.

This was a brilliant plan by the Han Emperor Wu Di. He needed a way to take away power from the regional nobles, and what better way than to take away their authority. No longer would the rich lord rule his kingdom. Wu Di's civil service exam would take care of that threat with one firm stroke. He broke up the clan hierarchies, replacing them with his scholar-bureaucrats. These test-taking brainiacs leap-frogged the nobles in the social hierarchy, sitting second to only the emperor in importance. These men were totally loyal to the emperor and to the teachings of Confucius. Because Confucianism championed a society based on harmonious relationships, and because pretty much everyone spent their childhoods learning about Confucianism, with every successive generation, millions more vowed total obedience and filial piety to their ultimate father, the emperor.

In the long run, the civil service exam also probably extended the dynasties long past their expected expiration dates. Dynasties usually have one fatal flaw – they keep power within a family. That sounds like a good idea, but what if your family has some issues. What if every couple generations, your empire gets stuck with a "special" son who might not exactly prioritize the needs of his people? What if he cares more about racking up the number of concubines in his harem or finding new ways to decorate his palace with gold furnishings or devising clever methods of torturing his opponents? What if he's just off his rocker, plumb crazy? What if he's not so bright, just a few fries short of a Happy Meal? In most dynastic situations, you'd just have to bide your time, grin and hope the guy kills himself before doing too much damage. In China, sure, they still had their "special" sons, but the odds of scholar-bureaucrats stepping in to soften the damage was far greater than any safeguard instituted in the other great empires of the age (see Roman Empire for examples of "special" sons).

The Han Dynasty found a way to protect itself from itself. Nearby Korea and Vietnam soon adopted this meritocratic system and within a few centuries of Wu Di's rule, the agricultural techniques, the political structures and the economic principles of the Middle Kingdom had not only become the foundation for a nation, but for an entire continent.

This influence of one classic civilization on an entire continent only finds a parallel in one other place on earth – at the southern tip of Europe.

Over in the Mediterranean, about the time Shi Huangdi was burying his workers alive under the earthen mounds of the Great Wall of China, a bunch of competing city-states on the peninsula of Hellas molded a civilization that would become the foundation of the West.

But that is for another chapter.

8

The Middle East United

The Persian Empire – 800 BC > 300 BC

Almost two thousand years before Genghis Khan and his Mongols forged an empire linking China to Turkey, there was the Persian Empire. Five centuries before Julius Caesar crossed the Rubicon to lay the foundation for the Romans, there was the Persian Empire. Two centuries before Alexander the Great took his Macedonian warriors to the banks of the Indus River, there was the Persian Empire. The Mongols, the Romans and the Greeks often get credit for creating the largest land empires, but long before their conquering hordes subdued the known world, it was the Persians who had built the greatest land empire known to man, subjugating peoples from as far away as Greece, Egypt, Babylon and India. Born in the land we today call Iran, the Persians were the first to connect Europe, Asia and Africa, creating a paradoxical rule known as much for its unyielding violence and oppressive taxation, as for its religious toleration and progressive stance on civil liberties.

The Persian Empire started in what today would be known as the southern Iranian province of Fars – about fifty miles off the coast of the Persian Gulf and about five hundred miles away from the ancient Mesopotamian city of Babylon. In about 600 BC, the Parsi/Farsi people of this southern province were tired of being ruled by the Median people who taxed them too much, failed to safely protect the countryside and refused to recognize their own regional lords. As so often happened in the ancient world, a regional lord used a combination of military force and diplomacy to unite neighboring tribes to topple the ineffective ruler. In this case, the regional lord was Cyrus, and once Cyrus had deposed the Median ruler to the north, he united the lands under his Parsi banner. Cyrus then spread his domain through Mesopotamia to the edge of Egypt. Future kings would expand the empire even further, taking Egypt, India and many of the Greek colonies that had started popping up on the western coast of the land we today call Turkey. Cyrus established a method of government that many actually embraced. He would rule as ultimate leader from afar, but as long as every conquered region paid taxes to Cyrus, he would let local lords, known as *satraps*, control the day-to-day operations of their province. This meant that locals could keep worshipping their own gods, could keep conducting their same economic transactions and could keep practicing their local traditions. As long as the money kept rolling in, they would be left alone.

Under the rule of Cyrus then Cambyses then Darius I then Xerxes I then Xerxes II then Darius II then Araxerxes II, III and IV and then finally with Darius III, the Persian Empire flourished, amassing more riches than any land west of the Indus River and constructing temples and palaces (like the Apadana Palace in Persepolis) that dwarfed the creations of Ancient Greece. Their engineers contracted massive irrigation projects to bring water to their arid valleys and built thousands of miles of roads to connect their vast empire. Their artists polished lavish gardens and lined palace walls with intricate carvings. All of this was made possible by the elaborate and strictly enforced tax system whereby at least 10% of everyone's income (be it in crop or coin) was sent to regional lords, who then transferred a percentage to the Persian king residing in the capital of Persepolis. Some provinces, like Egypt and India, paid more, but everyone paid something. To expedite the collection of taxes, Cyrus revolutionized the monetary system, putting everyone on one standard silver and gold coin system. No longer would there be discrepancies over the value of currency. Everyone used the king's coins. Aside from founding a uniform system for transacting business, the Persian kings also enumerated a uniform set of laws, written down and enforced across the empire. Before Cyrus, laws were flexible, left to the disposition of the local lawgiver and oftentimes random or unfair. This uniform law system made life more predictable and more possible to have stable business and social contracts. Modern constitutions, bills of rights and legal contracts owe the Persians for their ingenuity in formalizing regulations.

But that was just their good side. They also had a fairly scary bad side. Sure, if you paid the Persians, life was relatively comfy. But if you chose to ignore the compulsory taxes or, Ahura Mazda (the name for their god) forbid, considered rebelling, the Parsi kings would strike down with deadly retribution. Let's just take one instance. In 521 BC, a challenger to the throne, Phraortes, led a rebellion that was quickly squashed by the forces of Darius. Darius proceeded to cut off all the rebels' noses, ears and tongues. He ripped out their eyes. He then rammed poles up the men's arses and propped them up around city squares. If that wasn't enough, he ordered their skin peeled off and then stuffed with straw. After this appetizing little punishment, not too many towns or factions considered breaking away. Persian power was absolute and unquestioned.

This is usually where history books start telling the story of Persia. By the 5th century BC, the Persian Empire had become a seemingly monolithic monster from the east, forever threatening to crush the factious city-states to the west. Cyrus and his royal progeny appeared to have an unquenchable thirst for conquest and it appeared only a matter of time before a gluttonous Persian king would set his sights on the Mediterranean peninsula of Hellas. For the West, this couldn't happen. Before Europe could have its golden ages of Greece and Rome, the Persian threat had to be suppressed. The fate of Western Civilization stood in the balance. Had Xerxes forces not first been slowed down by the Spartan 300 and then crushed by the Athenian navy in 480 BC, there never would have been the Europe we know today. Instead the continent would have merely languished as an insignificant territory under the domain of the oppressive, tyrannical forces of the Middle East.

Or that's the way European history books tell the story. Or at least that's how they've told it for the past century. Depicting the Persians as the embodiment of ancient evil reached the pinnacle of preposterousness in the 2007 film *300*, a recreation of the graphic novel that pitted the ubermacho men of Sparta against the hordes of faceless, mindless, bestial thugs from Persia. For most Westerners, this film was their first, and only, introduction to ancient Persia. Yet, it was this one-sided, demonic depiction of the Persians that so angered segments of the Iranian (modern day Persian) community that Iran's motion picture board actually lodged a formal complaint with the United Nations Educational, Scientific and Cultural Organization (UNESCO) for the film's destruction of Iran's heritage. The film presents Xerxes as a sexually deviant "oversized drag queen," a sharp contrast with the virile, buffed-out, idealized Spartan characters. His one million troops come across as monstrously disfigured barbarians, of which even the elite "Immortals" bare daggered teeth hidden behind Kabuki-esque Halloween masks.

Because of this one-dimensional representation of the entire Persian force and their leader, the final battle becomes a conflict between a dedicated, free Western army and a despotic, barbaric slave-owning regime. Director Zach Snyder simply adapted the graphic novel's classic good vs. evil conflict where the victors went on to form the foundation of the superior Western civilization, while the losers retreated to their lives of savagery, subsequently dooming the Middle East to centuries of subservience to their superior neighbors to the West.

Unfortunately for the xenophobic audience members who need this tale to be true, the reality isn't so tidy. The Persians were in fact historically tolerant and bestowed upon the world a human rights legacy unprecedented at the time. From Cyrus the Great onward, the Persian kings protected a bill of rights, even granting freedoms to women not seen elsewhere in the West until the 19th century. Cyrus, grandfather of Xerxes, proclaimed over 2500 years ago:

> *"I will respect the traditions, customs and religions of the nations of my empire and never let any of my governors and subordinates look down on or insult them while I am alive. ...I will impose my monarchy on no nation. Each is free to accept it, and if any one of them rejects it, I never resolve on war to reign. While I am the king...I will never let anyone oppress others... I will never let anyone take possession of movable and landed properties of the others by force or without compensation. While I am alive, I will prevent unpaid, forced labour. Today, I announce that everyone is free to choose a religion...No one could be penalised for his or her relatives' faults..."*

This declaration dealt with land claims, religious affiliation, women's rights, meritocracy and personal freedoms. Although many historians trace the American Bill of Rights to English tradition or even Athenian democracy, in reality, one needs look further back to Persia, where the notion of individual freedoms was first protected by a political leader. And unlike the not-soflattering Western perception of today's Iran and the Middle East, the Persia of Cyrus and Xerxes' time was highly tolerant of religions. In fact, it was Cyrus the Great who was responsible for releasing the Jews from their Babylonian Captivity. Prior to their release, for close to a century, the Jews had been exiled from their native Judah (modern day Israel), forced to live as prisoners of the Babylonians. Yet, Cyrus respected all religions and refused to hold the Jews prisoners in a foreign land. Isn't it ironic that today's Iranian president, Mahmoud Ahmadinejad, spews mountains of anti-Semitic vitriol, even threatening to blow Israel "off the map," when it was his political predecessors that re-opened Israel to the Jews. The Persian leaders of today might be less than tolerant, but the Persian founders saw the value of an inclusive society that protected personal beliefs.

The relative inclusiveness of the Persian society makes Snyder's film's depiction of Persians as slaveholders even more preposterous. No archaeological evidence exists to prove widespread acceptance of slavery, and in fact the Persian Empire became the "Promised Land" for slaves escaping captivity from Northern Africa, Southern Europe and the Middle East. This is not to say that the Persian Empire was free of violence, corruption and inhumane treatment, but to claim they were any more uncivilized than the rest of the classic world is an historical inaccuracy. As for the much-maligned Xerxes, he was actually a bearded, heterosexual emperor married to Esther (a leading advocate for Jewish freedoms) – a far cry from the effeminate, ten-foot tall, body-pierced creature that greets Leonidas in the film *300*.

Why then has recent history depicted the Persian Empire in such a negative light? Much of this portrayal can be traced back to the Greek historian Herodotus, from whom much of our knowledge of early Greece comes. Prior to the 1850s, the primary historical texts (the Bible and the work of Greek author Xenophon) championed the role of Cyrus the Great and the Persian Empires, but toward the middle of the nineteenth century, Western historians needed to devalue the importance of monarchical rule. As the United States and France emerged triumphantly from imperial control, historians sought out historical interpretations that glorified the role of democracy. Under this filter, republican governments were good. Monarchies were evil. Fortunately, the texts of Herodotus presented the Greeks in such a light - underdogs fighting insurmountable numbers, armed not only with determination and undying effort, but with firmly-ingrained democratic values. Since this time, future historians have followed this Eurocentric model established by the "Father of History," and subsequent Western texts have veered little from his analysis. Ironically, Herodotus, the champion of everything Greek, chose the Persian Empire to live, write and publish his texts, for it was there that he was granted the artistic freedom to express his views without fear of retribution.

Yet the Persians lost any chance for historical recognition for their contributions to liberal government the moment they decided to push their empire further west into the land of the Greeks. From this point further, they became the West's greatest nemesis, an enemy that would have to be dehumanized and disparaged to better demonstrate the glory and virtue of the Greek way of life. For when the two cultures finally clashed, only one could survive, and to the winner went the credit for introducing equality and freedom to the world.

But that is for another chapter.

9

It's All Greek to Us

Golden Age of Greece – 500 BC > 300 BC

Greece might have been late to the civilization-starting party, but it quickly made up for lost time. After squandering for centuries as independent city-states basically caring about nothing more than their survival, Greece emerged from its 480 BC war against the Persian Empire with a confidence, a unity and a wealth that allowed it in the next century to develop achievements that would become the hallmarks of the Western world.

However nothing about early Greek civilization would make an outsider believe the world would ever take note of these warring peoples. Spread across the peninsula of Hellas and the dozens of surrounding islands, the mountainous terrain and Mediterranean Sea prevented the Greeks from creating a united empire.

Much of what we know of these early Greeks comes from Homer's *The Iliad* and *The Odyssey*, which chronicle the greatest battle of the Mycenaean Age – the Trojan War. Though for some the name Homer conjures cartoon images of a bumbling, unhygienic nuclear power plant operator with questionable parenting skills, this Greek Homer actually lived about 3000 years ago and is seen by many as the father of Western literature. In his classic ancient tale, a prince of Troy kidnaps the beautiful Helen, only to have her jealous husband and brother-in-law, the warrior-king Agamemnon, dispatch an entire fleet across the Aegean Sea to recover the lost Greek love. Helen became the "face that launched a thousand ships" and the Trojan War became the stuff of legends. For the next three millenniums, Western warriors would attempt to match the heroic exploits of the immortality-seeking Achilles and the glory and duty championed by all that gave their lives to the siege of Troy.

After Agamemnon's forces eventually subdued the Trojans with a bit of horse-trickery, the Mycenaeans remained on the Greek peninsula until 1100 BC when their civilization vanished from the history books and Greece entered a dark age void of historical records. Whether it was a cataclysmic natural event (a la the Harappan disappearance on the Indus River) or the invasion of the barbaric Dorians from the north, the Greek city-states floundered for four hundred years until they again appeared on history's stage. And in this new and improved Greek version, the city-states were even more fiercely independent. Sparta, Athens, Corinth, Marathon, Thebes, Delphi, Argos, Olympia were just a few of the over 1500 separate societies that ranged in size from a mere few hundred residents on a secluded island weeks away from any neighbor, to the bustling city of Athens which at its peak housed over 300,000 inhabitants.

The Greek city-states chose from a few forms of government. Some were ruled by an oligarchy – a few elite men who would meet and decide the fate of the city. Most chose a monarchy, where one leader would rule until his death, and at that point his eldest male offspring would take the reigns. Still others might see a tyrant sweep in and militarily overthrow the established government and rule by whim.

Over in Athens, the city leaders decided to go in an entirely different direction, experimenting with a form of government that would lay dormant in the western world for over two thousand years until thirteen colonies on the east coast of America decided to again give it a try. And this form of government was called democracy - power by the people. Though the United States might lay claim to Athenian roots, what the Athenians practiced looked far different than the confounding show the elephants and donkeys today perform in Washington D.C. In Athens, the assembly of 6000 would be chosen by *lot* (think "lottery") from the 30,000 *eligible* citizens (women and non-citizens couldn't vote). Basically every citizen had to be ready to serve Athens. Other city-states adopted this form of government, but none was as successful as the mother of them all.

Agreeing on little more than the belief in the pantheon of gods that lived on Mount Olympus, these city-states would gather every four years to challenge each other, not on the battlefield, but in athletic competition. According to legend, Hercules built the Olympic Stadium as a present to his father Zeus, and in the year 776 BC, the first games were held. These sporting clashes brought the peoples of Greece together and the winners of the first events would be awarded an olive leaf crown and their names would be immortalized for generations. Initially the first event was the stadion – a 190-meter running race (spaced out by the footsteps of Hercules), but the games eventually tested the combat skills of boxing, wrestling, chariot racing, long jumping, javelin throwing and discus chucking. In 720 BC the Spartans suggested these events should be conducted in the nude, so, yes, these men tossed discs, sprinted around tracks and even wrestled in nothing more than their birthday suits. The Greek word for naked was *gymos*, so the next time you're in a *gymnasium*, you've returned to a true house of nudity. For the Greeks though, nudity didn't incite the adolescent boy giggles it does today, but instead the ultimate athlete was the one who showcased his talents in the buff, all slicked up in some expertly-applied olive oil.

Aside from these intermittent naked feats of fitness, the city-states would have probably existed independent indefinitely if not for the threat from the Persian Empire. In 499 BC, the Greek colony of Ionia (on the western coast of Turkey) wanted to break away from Persian control and Athens said they would support Ionia in such a move. The Persian king, Darius the Great (yep...there's that nickname again) vowed to not only punish Ionia for their plucky insubordination, but also destroy Athens, making it a lesson for all the Mediterranean world that Persia would not be challenged. Yet, the Athenians would not crumble under the might of the vastly superior Persian army. When the Persian forces landed at the plain of Marathon, the Athenian phalanx outflanked the 25,000-strong (nearly three times larger) army of the Persians. In an urban legend that has persisted through the ages, the messenger Pheidippides ran the 26.2 miles from Marathon to Athens to announce the Persian defeat, only to fall dead in his tracks within moments. In honor of this suicidal run, every year across the globe millions of aspiring runners take to the streets hoping to avoid the unfortunate climax of Pheidippides.

Persia left this battle less than pleased. But with Darius' death, his son Xerxes would have to avenge the embarrassment of Marathon. But this time Xerxes would enlist the might of all of his empire, assembling an army that Greek historian Herodotus hyperbolically numbered at 2.6 million (historians today peg it closer to 200,000). Regardless, this force was the greatest ever assembled in ancient times, and the disunited Greek city-states would have no chance against this behemoth. Attempts at unity initially failed, but after a group of 300 Spartans (and about 7000 other rarely mentioned soldiers from neighboring Greek towns) mounted a defense at the "hot gates" (Thermopylae), the rest of Greece united behind the Athenian navy (and the Delian League alliance) to repel the Persian invasion. If the martyred loss of the Spartans at the Battle of Thermopylae became the inspiration, it was the naval battle at Salamis that proved the crushing blow. Athenian general Themistocles, taking a page from the Spartans who funneled the massive forces into a narrow passageway, placed his much faster navy in the straits of Salamis and then tricked the Persian forces into entering this channel of death. The Athenian triremes, each armed with 180 rowers, continually pounded the Persian ships, leaving the waters filled with the corpses and flailing bodies of those dispatched from the sinking vessels. Within hours, the Persian navy was destroyed and no other Persian king would ever again dare enter European soil. The next time the West would tangle with Persia would be over a century later when Alexander would take the battle to Persian lands.

With the Persians defeated, the Athenians cashed in on their newfound role as saviors of Hellas and entered a period of stability which initiated an expansion of the arts and formal thought that had never before been seen on the European continent. Set up as a military alliance, the Delian League essentially became an open faucet for the Athenians. India had the Mauryan Empire. China the Han Dynasty. Greece had the Athenian Empire. Each of these empires created the stability and funding necessary for the human mind to flourish and the resulting achievements can be seen in every component of today's Western life.

In the fields of art and architecture, the Greeks set the definition for Western beauty. Their statues depicted humans in an idealized form – with chiseled muscles and flowing locks. Whether it was the three dimensional statues or the engravings on their architectural monoliths, the subjects showcased the majesty of the human form in natural poses, regularly sans clothing. To find the most buffed models for inspiration, the Ancient Greek sculptors used rock quarry workers (oftentimes slaves) to create the chiseled six-pack bod the West still admires today. In the field of architecture, the stone columns of the Greeks are today the most recognized pieces of Greek art. The Doric, Ionic and Corinthian columns, and the rectangular and symmetrical buildings they supported, have become the hallmarks of contemporary architecture. In most of the major cities across Europe, the public buildings and the facilities dedicated to the arts regularly incorporate the designs utilized in the Parthenon and other Classical Greek buildings. Take a tour around Washington D.C. and you'll bump into dozens of Greek-inspired buildings – the White House, the Jefferson Memorial, the Capitol Building and the Lincoln Memorial to name just a few.

The Greeks also put on a good show. They used open-air amphitheaters to showcase the two new forms of literature – tragedy and comedy – that continue today as staples of Western entertainment. Tales of heroes with tragic flaws and comedies mocking political leaders are just as popular today as they were in the age of Classical Greece. One needs look no further than Iron Man's hedonistic tendencies, Spiderman's inferiority complex or Harry Potter's parent issues to see how audiences love our heroes flawed. However, the tales told once upon a time in Greece would never make it past today's censors, making even Lady Gaga cringe. Whether it's the story of Sophocles' *Oedipus Rex,* which follows the plight of Oedipus as he unknowingly fulfills the prophecy that he would kill his father and marry his mother, or Aeschylus' *Agamemnon,* which describes a wife's journey to murder her husband returning from the Trojan War, or Euripides' *Medea,* which follows a wife's murder of her own children to punish her cheating husband, the plays of the Greeks were not for the squeamish and their themes of love, betrayal and violence are continually produced by Hollywood's dream factory. And as for the biting comedy that left no Athenian political, social or literary leader untouched, one needs look no further than *The Daily Show* or *The Simpsons* to see how the West still embraces biting satire.

Other popular literary genres included historical pieces, lyric poetry and philosophical essays. The lyric poetry branched off from the work of the famed poet Sappho (from the Greek island Lesbos) who years earlier wrote poetry passionately disclosing her romantic leanings. We owe today's cheesy love songs to the emotional honesty of Sappho (and you could probably argue we also owe the word "lesbian" to her as well).

But the most influential pieces of Ancient Greece have to be the work of the philosophers – primarily the work of Socrates, Plato and Aristotle (even though Socrates' work was only actually written down by his students years after his death). Philosophic inquiry didn't start with the big three of Classical Greece, but each of them took the notion of formal thought to a new level. Even before Socrates, groups known as Cynics, Sophists and Skeptics roamed the Greek countryside and the streets of Athens questioning the conventional wisdom (or ignorance).

Socrates (pronounced saw-cruh-tees, not so-crates) outlined a method of inquiry that broke down a problem into several smaller questions, believing the answer to each would eventually lead to the solution of the problem. This questioning strategy could be used to define the meaning of concepts such as right and wrong or to solve scientific quandaries (and it's still used in biology classes across America with what we call the scientific method). Socrates spent the later years of his adulthood seeking answers, believing that "I am the wisest man alive, for I know one thing, and that is that I know nothing." This incessant questioning eventually landed Socrates on trial for challenging the government and for corrupting the minds of youths. The city bosses weren't exactly pleased that Socrates was walking the streets, encouraging young men to question everything they saw. Sometimes people in power prefer when kids are seen and not heard, but Socrates disagreed. It was through the art of questioning where we truly started to learn.

But imagine if Socrates today was a high school counselor modeling how teenagers should interact with their parents. A late-night curfew discussion might look a bit like this:

Mom: Young man, why are you home so late?

Son: Mom, what do you want from me? Do you ever want me to leave home? Don't you want me to learn how to have friends? Or do you want me to just hang out with you and Dad all day? Do you want me to fear the outside world? To fear strangers and the unknown? Don't you want me to gain independence so that one day I can leave you guys and make you proud? And if you want all these things for me, don't you also agree that experience is the best teacher? Do you want me to just sit up in my bed all night long, reading stories of other kids who learned how to truly live? Are you asking me to be a mere spectator of life, to sit on the sidelines while everyone else is seizing the day? Is that what you truly want, Mom? Is it?

Broken Mom: Ummm...your Dad and I would like to extend your curfew.

You see, the world runs just a bit more smoothly when young adults just shut up and do as they're told. When they don't, we have problems. Socrates was a troublemaker, so when he was put on trial, he was found guilty and sentenced to death. The jury came down hard on Socrates, but they never thought he would actually be killed. The courts just assumed he would escape with his students to the countryside, preventing anyone from having to execute the sentence. But Socrates wasn't going for it. They said he was guilty. They said he should die. Socrates would accept their punishment. He took a sip of hemlock poison, rolled over and died. He became one of the first philosophical martyrs. He refused to apologize for his beliefs, and because he was so passionate even in death, he gained even more followers once his street strolling days were no more.

One of his students, Plato, also had a problem with government, but he didn't feel the solution lay solely in questioning. He argued in his book *The Republic* that government should be ruled by elected philosopher kings, not simply chosen randomly by lot from the general population. When you pick people randomly, you inevitably get some knucklehead that doesn't know the issues or is easily swayed by a clever speaker. Plato preferred professional politicians chosen from the upper echelon of society who would focus solely on matters of state. This recommendation falls in line with the American form of democracy. In fact, should someone ever boldly claim that the United States is the home to democracy, you could correct him and state, "Well, actually, it's a republic. I elect philosopher-kings to vote in my stead. You don't see me getting a phone call every time there is a vote in D.C on whether or not to build a new post office in Maine? You don't see me having a say on every single issue. You think the US is a democracy? I don't think so."

Aside from his political wanderings, Plato also delved into the idea of "what is truth?" In his *Allegory of the Cave*, Plato uses the metaphor of a cave to show how the world of ideas compares to the material world. Plato asks the reader to imagine a cave, and in this cave imagine a group of men chained together. And imagine this group of chained men staring at a series of images popping up on the side of the cave wall. Suppose one of these men breaks free and looks to the front of the cave. At the front of the cave sits puppet masters holding up actual objects in front of a fire. So the objects seen on the wall by the chained men are merely the shadows of the real objects. Then, imagine this same man leaves the cave and is blinded by the world outdoors. Once he eventually adjusts to the beauty and the wonder of this outside world, he returns to the cave hoping to free his enslaved brethren from their fate. Yet, when these chained men see the returned prodigal son, they see him as a crazed lunatic, and refuse to follow him outside (if you're having trouble envisioning this little scenario, go rent a copy of the 2013 animated film *The Croods*, and you can see this ignorance/knowledge, cave/outside world conflict play out in a witty little cartoon about cavemen searching for a paradise known as "Tomorrow").

At the time, many who read the Allegory (Socrates included), believed Plato's work dealt with the journey of the philosopher from seeing only the two dimensional world to finally evolving to see the world through new eyes, and never again being able to return to the mundane existence of his naïve state. But are there other connections? Why is it that so many of today's cinematic tales deal with this theme of another reality existing that dwarfs the inanity of our daily lives? Isn't it ironic that we all choose to enter a dark theater only to be taken to the worlds of the *Matrix, Avatar, Alice in Wonderland, The Wizard of Oz, The Truman Show, Inception, Pleasantville, The Chronicles of Narnia, Harry Potter*...all of which promise a world not of this world? Do we actually prefer to be controlled by the puppet masters, even when it is they who are uncovering the deception of the senses? Are we all slaves to authority figures except for the few who ignore the puppet masters and choose their own path? Does this encourage all of us to rebel against the norm? Is this why Westerners are more likely to think "outside the box" (dare I say "outside the cave")? Or does this Allegory merely symbolize the Western individual's need for self-actualization? Is this why there are so many self-help books lining the aisles of Western book stores? Is everyone trying to get outside the cave and see the light? Could the cave/outside world reference be the same as the mortal life/heaven relationship Christians embrace? Or in today's world, could the puppet masters be advertisers, the people who tell us what is correct or desired behavior? Are puppet masters companies like Listerine, who in the 1920s convinced the American people that halitosis was a disease that could only be cured with, amazingly, their product, a product once used as floor cleaner? And if advertisers are the puppet masters, then maybe the media and the TV are the greatest puppet masters of them all?

And now that a new generation of kids sit in cafeterias sucked in by their black laptops or stroll down the streets entranced by their Ishadows, maybe we're slowly becoming even more enslaved than any previous generation and, maybe, just maybe, the chance of us ever getting out of the darkness fades with every technological innovation?

Or maybe it's just a story of a cave.

Plato's student Aristotle disagreed with his teacher. He thought a cave was a cave. An apple was an apple. Fire was fire. Quite possibly the smartest man in the history of the Western world (if ever there was a way to judge such a thing), Aristotle brought to the West pretty much everything we now teach in school. The course directories of Western universities tout the disciplines once developed by Aristotle - political science, physics, logic, economics, psychology, metaphysics and meteorology. He's the creator of the literary structure of most Western fiction (rising action, climax, falling action), and he's the sorter of all things living (though his categories of "blood and bloodless," and "walking, flying and swimming" fall a bit short of our current classifications - kingdom, phylum, class, order, family, genus, species). He challenged everyone to follow his Golden Mean – never living a life in extremes. Don't be too optimistic, but don't be too negative either. Don't live in abject fear, but don't trust everyone. Basically, live a life of moderation (sounds a bit like Buddha's Middle Way). Not all of his theories proved to be correct (he proposed that the universe revolved around the earth), but they dominated as the scientific law of most Europeans until the Renaissance and Scientific Revolution took the continent in new directions.

Aside from formal thought, Greece contributed a virtual bevy of other little tidbits of trivial minutia that are a part of our daily lives. Doctors take the Hippocratic Oath promising to help and never purposefully injure their patients. Historians have the early works of Herodotus and Themistocles to guide them through the Ancient World. Astronomers have clever names for the constellations, most based on the original Greek gods. Budding high school mathematicians have Pythagoras to thank for the world famous $a^2 + b^2 = c^2$ method for figuring out the long side of a triangle. And where would we be without universities, huge marble columns and feta cheese?

But all of these accomplishments might have remained unknown to the world had it not been for a series of military campaigns that initially ended the Golden Age of Greece, but in the long run spread the era's revelations to regions that would maintain the learning long past the time this knowledge was actually lost to the Europeans.

The first of these conflicts was the Peloponnesian War that pitted jealous Sparta and its allies against the forces of Athens. Sparta refused to accept the Athenian dominance of the Delian League (and greater Greece in general), and after three decades of incessant battle, wholesale destruction and a plague that ravaged Athens, the war finally came to an end, with even the victors, the Spartans, weak beyond recognition.

Seizing this opportunity to control his southern neighbors, King Phillip II of Macedon took his army of long-speared soldiers into the heart of Greece and easily dispatched the Greek city-states. Those who didn't surrender on the battlefield, eventually succumbed voluntarily instead of wasting any more men in combat. The age of Greece was over, and it was a man from the backwards, relatively uncivilized Macedonian kingdom to the north who finally defeated the Greeks. He then absorbed the Greek armies into his massive force and dreamed of heading east, but this dream came to an abrupt end when he was assassinated by one of his bodyguards. He was replaced by his son – Alexander the Great.

Alexander, the Macedonian prince and student of Aristotle (not a bad option as a personal tutor), took the military might of his Macedonian empire and headed to the eastern edge of the known world. His quest for immortality took him through Egypt, Persia and to the edge of India. Over thirteen years, he suppressed any force that stood in his way, all the while spreading the culture of Greece (Hellenism) and integrating with the natives. He encouraged, and sometimes forced, his soldiers to marry the local women and set up Greek cities in his honor from the shores of the Nile River to the banks of the Indus Valley. Eventually he was turned back from India, more due to the desertion of his men than from his own strategic flaws.

He died months later, just shy of his 33rd birthday. His empire would eventually disintegrate as his squabbling generals could never match the idealistic, infectious fervor of Alexander or construct governments able to control the diverse peoples. But his impact had already been set in motion. Greek society spread across the Levant into India, and the cultures of Western Asia made their way back to the Mediterranean. Though only for a moment, the known world (with apologies to China), sat united under one leader, and an empire of this size, in this region would not again pop up until a small farming town in the boot of Italy gathered some steam and began spreading its way of life.

But that is for another chapter.

10

Alexander the Very Good

The Macedonian Empire – 330 BC > 250 BC

There's been a ton of "the Greats" in our history. Sumeria had Sargon the Great. China had Yu the Great. Persia had Cyrius, Darius and Xerxes...all "the Greats." India had Ashoka and Kanishka...yep...they were both "the Great." Even Korea had a "the Great" – the oh so well-known Gwanggaeto the Great who spread his empire into Russia, China and Mongolia.

These gents were all greats. They all expanded their empires, scared the living daylights out of bordering peoples and instilled pride in their own brethren who saw their influence forced across their region.

But for all their influence, they're nothing compared to the greatest empire builder of all time – Alexander the Great.

He set the bar for every future general-turned-emperor who believed power came to those who made war. Napoleon Bonaparte looked to Alexander's campaigns for guidance. Julius Caesar once wept upon seeing Alexander's likeness in a statue. Even Hitler hoped his Nazis would one day rule the world like Alexander's Macedonians.

But Alexander was the first, and like Napoleon and Hitler (not so much Caesar) he was an outsider to the people he would claim to rule, a man never truly accepted by his adopted nation as one of their own. For Alexander was from Macedonia, the illegitimate, red-headed stepchild province to the more refined Greeks to the south. Every refined culture likes to validate its own preeminence by demeaning the attributes of its lesser neighbors. For the Greeks, these lessers were the Macedonians to the north, the less-dignified, poorly-spoken, illiterate country folk who were seen as a mere nuisance to the more established city-states of the Greek peninsula.

These Macedonians might not have had the philosophers of Athens or the historians of Thebes or the poets of Lesbos, but they had King Philip II and Philip knew how to take advantage of the precarious turn of affairs after Sparta and Athens and their respective allies had beat the crap out of each other for three decades in the Peloponnesian War. By 404 BC, Greece was a war-torn, exhausted, hungry, poor, broken network of disunited city-states. Sparta might have eventually won this civil war, but no Greek emerged strong enough to repel outside invaders.

Enter King Philip II, the opportunistic Macedonian who swept in, brought the Greek city-states to their knees and established himself as King of all Greeks. At first the Greeks underestimated Philip's Macedonians, but they were far superior than the soft Athenians gave them credit. Under Philip, they had become a wealthy people, trading timber, cattle, sheep and horses. They were a resilient people, completely self-sufficient and not softened by the trappings of gluttony that had paralyzed the southern Greeks. They liked to fight, and they followed Philip into battle unquestionably.

It was at battle where Philip shined. He walked with his men, inspiring them to fight through their discomfort, willing to give their lives for their military father. And he rewarded them. He gave bonuses and promotions for those that stood out in battle and he kept them paid handsomely so their families were all well cared for. He trained his armies constantly, unlike the Greek farmer warriors who often returned to the fields after campaigns. He also had formed one of the most prolific cavalries, fed by the grasses of the rich Macedonian fields and rode by the most accomplished horsemen. He took this cavalry and this military ethos to the battlefield, where he improved the Greek phalanx by giving his men 15-foot spears, longer than any brandished in the ancient world. His men would march for days without complaint, encircle any foe with their horsed warriors and skewer any Greek hoplite before they could get within striking distance.

The Greeks were no challenge for Philip. Many allied with him as his power grew, and by 338 BC, he dispatched the Athenians and Thebians and had conquered the whole of Greece (except for pesky old Sparta which Philip realized was best to just leave alone). From here, he united the Greeks under his autocratic rule, though he still had each of the city-states send representatives to his counsel. His authority was ultimate and his words were law.

This was the world Alexander inherited. His father had already done the dirty work to subdue the only threat to absolute control of the Mediterranean, and his father had already created a military force unlike any other in the known world. Alexander spent his childhood surrounded by war and the machinations, diplomacy and politics needed to keep the peace. At thirteen, he was taught by Aristotle. At sixteen, he ruled in his father's stead while Philip was away at battle. At eighteen, he led his father's cavalry at the deciding Battle of Chaeronea that ended the autonomy of the Greek city-states.

He also had a mom that would put any contemporary helicopter parent to shame. Olympias was the fourth wife of Philip, given to the Macedonian king as a peace offering from the neighboring city-state of Epirus. To say she was a bit touched psychologically would be an understatement. This lady worshipped two things – her snakes and her son. She carried her snakes everywhere with her, and the historian Plutarch even argued she became just a bit too intimate with her snakes, using them as a replacement for her the affection of her husband. To her son, she offered the world. She believed he was the son of Zeus, that she was impregnated miraculously by a god and that her son was destined for immortality. She dispatched with anyone who stood in her (and her son's) way, even roasting alive King Philip's seventh wife, a mere teenager, and this wife's infant son. And some even believe she had a hand in the assassination of Philip, as she wanted to ensure it would be Alexander that would gain all the glory from distant victories.

He had all the tools one would need to form and rule an empire. His father gave him the army and the kingdom. His mother took care of any threats to his throne and taught him that the ends justify the means. Aristotle's classical training inspired Alexander with a love for Homer's *Illiad*, a respect for the delicacies of government, a life-long interest in the scientific method, and a moral and ethical compass for how to treat those under his rule. So rarely in history does a man with so high a political and military standing enter his adulthood so enriched by the philosophical and scientific theories of the greatest minds of the day. But Alexander was just that young man, and when at the age of twenty his father died and Alexander inherited the keys to the kingdom. He picked up where his dad left off and set Macedonia and the Greek world on a path Philip could have never imagined.

Some newbie kings at the age of twenty might rest on their father's accomplishments, content to sit back and enjoy the splendors of wealth and power.

Not Alexander.

He used his father's death as the excuse, the catalyst to invade Persia. He claimed that Philip's death by the hands of his own bodyguard, Pausanias, was actually part of a grander conspiracy hatched by Greece's age-old enemy to the east – the Persians. He would avenge his father's death by taking the Macedonian forces east, to confront and once and for all defeat the heathen hordes of King Darius.

He first had to ensure the support and allegiance of his Greek dominions. The city-state of Thebes was the first to challenge the boy-king's authority, revolting against local forces, believing the age of Macedonian rule had come to an end. They were a bit premature and Alexander made them pay. He sent in his troops to quickly put down the uprising, and to help dissuade any future dissent, he rounded up 7,000 residents, had them murdered in public, and then condemned 30,000 Thebian women and children to slavery. The other Greek cities got the message.

Once his backyard was in order, he set out to conquer the world. In 334 BC, he took his 40,000 troops to take out King Darius's forces who were stationed at the most western tip of the Persian Empire. Alexander faced off against an army of Persian mercenaries, some of whom were actually Greek, including the general Memnom. This Persian army showed how a horde of un-trained, inferiorly-armed soldiers who fought out of fear for their lives, or merely for a paycheck, were no match for Alexander's battle-hardened, inspired forces. After his victory at what became known as the Battle of Granicus, Alexander swept down through the Levant (modern day Syria, Israel and Jordan), expelling all Persian forces ruling in the region. By the time he reached Egypt, his legend had grown, and he was a man feared by all. He had defeated Memnom and forced Darius to flee from the battlefield after the Persian leader had taken control of the eastern army. Alexander then kidnapped Darius's family, holding them hostage until Darius himself would surrender. He proved a ruthless conqueror, punishing any city that did not willingly acquiesce to his demands. For Tyre, the walled-city that held out for seven months, Alexander murdered all men once he had toppled the walls, and then sold the women and children into slavery.

Egypt knew better than to resist, instead choosing to "welcome" Alexander as a liberator, eventually ordaining him as pharaoh and son of the gods. His mother Olympias had filled her baby boy's ears with stories of how he was the son of Zeus (which made her Zeus's little mortal love interest), so he took kindly to the Egyptian confirmation of his mythical heritage. For close to a year he remained in Egypt, touring the Nile, the Sahara and the Mediterranean, eventually founding a trading port at the mouth of the Nile River, the city that would become Alexandria (the first of sixteen cities named after the ever-humble Macedonian conqueror). Before leaving Egypt to resume his hunt for Darius, Alexander appointed Persians, Macedonians and Egyptians to share control of the Egyptian realm, protecting all local traditions. This establishment of joint rule and respect for indigenous cultures became the trademarks of Alexander's strategy for securing the peace in his conquered territories. He would be ruthless in battle and compassionate in peace. Don't cross him and all's good.

As he headed east toward Mesopotamia and the center of the Persian Empire, Darius made one last peace offering to the Macedonian warlord. He promised Alexander all the land west of the Euphrates, thousands of gold talents for the release of Persian prisoners, and even the hands of his daughters in marriage for Alexander or any of his closest advisors.

One of his advisors and friends, Parmenios counseled, "If I were Alexander, I'd take it" to which the ever-modest Alexander chided, "And so would I, if I were Parmenios."

No, Alexander had to defeat Darius on the battlefield. He had dreamed of meeting Darius face to face and having the god-king surrender at his feet, relinquishing all control of the East to Alexander. Only this transfer of power would suffice. Anything else would be seen as robbing Alexander of his rightful glory.

But Darius hadn't been merely sitting around after his first fleeing defeat at the Battle of Issus. He scoured the land for able bodies and assembled an army some historians calculated at over a million people. He also had his engineers construct chariots with wheels that had long knives jutting out of their axels. In theory, these chariots would cut through the Macedonian phalanx like a scythe through a field of wheat, leaving severed limbs scattered across the battlefield.

Darius hoped this little weapon's modification and his twenty to one numerical advantage might be enough to turn the tide in his favor.

Not quite. The two forces would again match wills on the battlefield, this time in Mesopotamia at the Battle of Gaugamela, but again Alexander's wit would prove too much for Darius's larger forces. All night long Alexander had a few of his men hoot and holler, feigning an attack, forcing Darius to keep his soldiers up all night. The next day, Darius's exhausted army faced off against Alexander's fresh forces and when the two sides met, there was again no contest. His cavalry merely swung around the Persian wall of soldiers and headed right for Darius's golden chariot. Again, Darius fled, this time taking with him any fleeting chance of defeating Alexander. Alexander couldn't pursue Darius as he had to return to the battle and save his own struggling forces.

And as for the Persian bladed battle chariots, they proved a failure. Alexander merely ordered his men at the last minute to step to the side, parting the sea of soldiers to let the chariots pass right by the unharmed men.

Alexander walked off the battlefield King of the East. No force would again fight for Darius – his authority was gone. Alexander sent his scouts out searching for Darius, needing the symbolic final surrender, but it was not to be. Darius's inner circle, including his cousin Bessus, rebelled against their seemingly-cowardly leader, eventually tying him up, tossing him in a wagon and then skewering him time and time again with their javelins. When Alexander eventually found the mortally wounded Darius, he flew into a rage, ordering the murder of the assassin Bessus and then a proper funeral for the man he would succeed.

Alexander had won what should have been his final battle. He had what he had come for – the Persian Empire. He controlled all the land from Greece to what we now call the Middle East. He could have stopped, merely gathered the Persian treasury, marched his men back across the Levant and returned to Greece a hero, where he would live out his days in luxury and comfort.

But this was not to be. Victory on the battlefield was only the first part of Alexander's plan. He wanted to create a lasting peace, to unify the East and the West in an empire that would last far after he parted from this world. He saw himself as the rightful heir to the earthly kingdom of Zeus and he believed it was his obligation to consolidate all the known world under one banner.

His strategy of unification would actually go far in convincing his newly conquered peoples that he was a leader to be trusted, to be revered, to be followed, but unfortunately it also sealed his fate with his own men. For Alexander wanted these Persians to be respected as equals. He wanted their customs revered and their culture adopted. He spoke with all regional priests and assured them their gods would be honored and their practices would be protected. He contracted the building of temples and ensured the people that the gods they had once been prevented from worshipping by the Persians could again be glorified without fear.

Politically, he ruled with the locals, not over them. He appointed local leaders to governorship posts and sought the recommendations of existing leaders. His men were disgusted. Persians were barbarians, not equals. They were to be ruled, not welcomed. The final straw was when Alexander began adopting some of the customs of the locals. He dined on Persian cuisine, abandoned Greek tunics for Persian pants, and most repulsively, expected all to prostate themselves when in his presence. This prostrating meant that whenever Alexander passed, every man must lay flat on the floor, nose pressed to the ground, in symbolic submission. In China this was called kowtowing, in Persia it was known as proskynesis. Whatever it was called, the Greeks didn't like it. They saw Alexander as a brother in arms, not some god needing to be worshipped, so when Alexander pressed them to submit to this custom, they were less than pleased. What was happening to their Alexander?

What was happening was that Alexander was becoming seduced by power. He wanted more. Instead of returning to Greece, he called on his men to instead head east, to where Aristotle had taught him he would see the end of the world. His men grumbled, but they still followed.

He would take his army, then 120,000 strong and made up of more Persian recruits than Macedonians, to the Kush Mountains, through Afghanistan and down into India. However, taking South Asia would not be as easy as conquering Persia.

Defeating all of Persia meant defeating Darius. Cut off the snake's head, the body dies. But with India, there was no one central ruler to be defeated, but a network of kingdoms that would need to be pacified and then independently convinced to remain under the domain of the foreign invader. Making matters worse, his army was no longer fighting in the wide-open plains of the Middle East but through tropical jungles, monsoon rains and frozen mountain passes. These elements claimed more of Alexander's men than Darius's forces ever could kill, but at each turn, Alexander proved resilient and able to employ the tactics that had made him the most innovative military leader in history.

When faced with the mountain people at Sogdian Rock who had built their fortress into a cliff, Alexander ordered 300 of his best climbers to scale the cliff in the dead of night to attack the fortification from within. When a more formidable army guarded the entry to a mountain pass, he sent thousands of his best men on a trek around the mountain to outflank the enemy. When up against never-before-seen, trained war elephants, he encircled the enemy so that they were eventually trampled under their own weaponized pacoderms. He forced his officers to marry local women to ensure alliances. He even ordered his craftsmen to build exorbitantly large chairs, tables and eating ware so that if ever his encampment was stumbled upon by the enemy, they would surmise they were fighting giants.

But he wasn't merely the king of ruse, he continued to gain his men's respect by being the first to battle, the last to eat, the last to drink, the last to take medical aid. He took little of the bounty taken through his victories, instead showering his men with the spoils of war. He sent mounds of money back to his warriors' families in Greece, set up pension plans for when the soldiers retired and established an education fund that sent tens of thousands of his army's children to the finest of schools. He had created a welfare state before there even was such a thing.

But his men still were growing tired. They wanted to go back home. They pleaded to return to their families, believing this current campaign was one more of ego than to serve and protect the glory of Greece. One officer, Cleitus, drunk with liquid courage at a post-victory party, publicly mocked Alexander, criticizing him for selling his soul to the eastern heathens and soiling his father's legacy. Alexander demanded silence, but when Cleitus continued, Alexander threw his spear, impaling his once-friend Cleitus.

Distraught over this rash act, Alexander retreated to his quarters and reconsidered his army's next step. After days of self-imposed mourning and reflection, he emerged to tell his men they would abandon his quest for the end of the world and return to Greece (granted they might need to take a bit of a detour back that might take them first just a bit deeper into India).

So his army was off again. His forces continued to swell as Alexander took in more and more Asian recruits. His battle-hardened Macedonians mocked these 30,000 Persian "ballet soldiers" as embarrassments to King Philip's once proud legion, but Alexander knew it was the best choice if he wanted to continue on into unchartered territories. Along the way he fell in love with a nobleman's daughter, Roxana, married her and eventually had a son Alexander IV. Soiling his royal blood didn't improve his reputation amongst his men, but his actions on the battlefield continued to garner their respect. At the walled city of Multa, he was the first up the siege ladder, and when the ladder broke and he was momentarily alone to fight scores of attackers, he held his own, taking down several assailants before being dropped by a spear to the his lungs.

Eventually his men broke through the city gates and carried their fallen leader, with a spear sticking out of his chest, back to his medical tent where the doctors tried to save his life. Alexander refused any rudimentary anesthesia, and his doctors then set out to extract the spear from his chest and repair his perforated lung. Alexander, of course, passed out on the table due to the pain, but he survived, and his legend grew.

After months of recovery, he returned to his lines and led his army's march back across the Persian deserts. His men died by the tens of thousands and morale sunk deeper and deeper as survival and a return to Greece appeared more and more unlikely. For Alexander, all hope was lost when his best friend and confidant Hephaestion died. Many historians argue Hephaestion was not merely a friend, but also Alexander's lifetime lover. In Oliver Stone's film biography *Alexander*, General Ptolemy claims "Alexander was never defeated, except by Hephaestion's thighs." Whether or not their love was sealed in their own special way, it is pretty clear that Alexander soon after lost his will to live. Within months, he was stricken with an illness, maybe due to poison, maybe due to malaria, maybe due to a broken heart, and on June 11, 323 BC, at the age of 32 years old, Alexander died.

On his deathbed, when asked who would rule the largest kingdom of the ancient world, Alexander responded – "the strongest."

This wasn't exactly helpful advice, and a civil war immediately broke out between his generals, each wanting a piece of Alexander's empirical pie. For forty years, his men fought each other, destroying what was left of his attempts to unite the West and the East. His wife Roxana and their son were murdered, and eventually the conquered lands were divided into three kingdoms, one of which was Egypt, ruled by Ptolemy whose family line would rule for centuries until the death of Cleopatra at the time of the Roman Empire.

So with his empire demolished and with hundreds of thousands dead due to his megalomaniacal tendencies, how can Alexander still be considered "great"? If his father's legacy was the unification of Greece and the foundation of an unbeatable army, what was Alexander's legacy and contribution to world history?

First, he did unite the East and the West. Politically it might have fallen into chaos, but Alexander established trade networks that would transfer goods, knowledge and traditions between the civilizations for hundreds of years. He spawned the Hellenistic Era, a period where the ideas of Hellas (the Greek peninsula) spread across Northern Africa, the Middle East and into India. Greek became the spoken language of the political elite, to the point where many leaders couldn't even understand the language of their own citizens. The Greek currency became the adopted norm, easing business transactions. The stoned, columned architecture of Greece spread across Asia, into the Alexander-founded cities and political centers of the burgeoning lands. Greek art, from tragedies to comedies to poetry to clothing, blended with local customs (even Buddha was sculpted wearing a Greek tunic).

Foremost among the Hellenistic contributions were the philosophical and scientific traditions of the Athenians. The Middle East became interested in scientific query, of asking questions, gathering data and logically proving hypotheses. An age of inquiry ascended across the region, replacing the antiquated, superstitious notions of how the world worked. This paved the way for the Arab enlightenment, the region's scientific revolution that would predate the European version by almost a thousand years. The penultimate symbol of the Middle East's new thirst for knowledge could be found in Alexandria, the research center of Hellenism, and home to the greatest library of antiquity – the

Museum of Alexandria. This library housed over 700,000 Greek manuscripts. Artists, scientists, poets, philosophers and historians from across the Mediterranean and from as far away as India clamored to this intellectual hub to be inspired by the many "muses" of the Greek tradition.

Of course, Alexander must also be credited for his military accomplishments. He transformed what it meant to lead an army. No longer could a leader expect to be victorious by soliciting the efforts of part time soldiers. Soldiers would be permanent, well-paid, well-trained and loyal only to the state. They wouldn't come and go as they wished, but would be dedicated to one goal – the making of war. Military commanders would likewise adopt their techniques, moving beyond merely the columned phalanx, instead utilizing the combined efforts of the cavalry, engineers, infantry, artillery and the art of misdirection. Every other western leader that would set out on their own journey of empire building would point to Alexander as their inspiration.

Even though hundreds of thousands perished and Alexander's reign only lasted about twelve years, the fruits of his dream and the efforts of his men who journeyed over 22,000 miles across the known world can not be underestimated. He set the foundation for a world where civilizations would interact and grow from each other's accomplishments instead of existing in isolation or as bitter adversaries.

He also set the precedent for western empire building, and never again would the powers of Europe be submissive to an eastern foe. In fact, the next great empire wouldn't emerge from the cradle of civilization between the Tigris and Euphrates rivers, but would spawn from a small town on a river that flowed across the Italian peninsula.

But that is for another chapter.

II

All Roads Lead to Rome

The Roman Empire – 500 BC > 500 AD

There are empires...and then there are EMPIRES. If you're talking about the biggest empire, you've got yourself either the Mongols (12.7 million miles big) or the British (23% of the planet). If you're talking about the empire that ruled over the most people, then you have the 18th century Qing Dynasty that reigned over 37% of the world's billion people. If you're talking about the richest empire, it would be hard to argue with today's American juggernaut, an "empire" that controls about $20 trillion of the world's yearly economy. Now if you're talking about longest living empires, it's a matter of semantics. The Egyptians lasted for 3000 years, but for a ton of those years they were relatively weak. The Chinese Empire has been around since about 250 BC, but depending on how you define the transfer of power due to the Mandate of Heaven, it might not make the final cut. The Mayans ruled for about a thousand years, but they don't exactly have a written history, so it's hard to trust them. And as for the Ottoman Empire, it lasted for over eight centuries, but like the Egyptians, a big chunk of that time, it wasn't exactly the most intimidating force in the region.

But if you're talking about the hands down greatest empire in human history, there's really only one that sits atop everyone's Top Ten List. There was only one empire that ruled three continents, that invented an administrative and legal system that today governs the majority of the world's nations, that spoke a language that splintered into Italian, Spanish, Portuguese and French, that combined military strategy and engineering knowhow at a level never before seen by man and that produced a religion that has today become the most practiced faith in the world.

There's only one "Greatest Empire in Human History."

The Roman Empire.

Rome's rise and eventual fall has been scrutinized by historians for centuries. How did one small, backwater village of sheep herders come to dominate Europe, the Middle East and North Africa? And how did this same empire fall into utter ruin, fragmenting off into thousands of independent fiefdoms that would never again be united? What was their formula for success, and what was their recipe for failure? For the United States, the Roman lesson is even more critical. For if the US can understand what led to the rise and fall of Rome, maybe it stands a chance of holding onto its 20th century stranglehold of world affairs for just a few more decades.

But to understand Rome, we have to go back to its beginning, back to 754 BC, back to the story of two brothers who were raised by a wolf and a woodpecker. According to the myth, Romulus and Remus were the chosen sons of a virgin priestess and Mars, the god of war (there's a more famous god/virgin birth you'll learn about later in the chapter). Their grandfather was the true heir to the throne of Alba Longa, but he was bypassed in favor of their granduncle – Amulius. Amulius wasn't too afraid of the twins' grandfather, but the sons of a god made him a bit nervous, so he sent the two babies down a river, believing they'd soon perish. But perish they did not, for they were saved by a she-wolf who let them suckle on her teats until they were mature, and by a woodpecker who brought them food five to six times a day (stop chuckling, do a Google Image search right now and you'll see tons of statues and paintings dealing with this exact subject). As they grew, they were adopted by shepherds from the neighboring hills, who raised the boys to be strong, to be wise and to be battle-hardened so they could one day restore their grandfather to his rightful throne.

So when these demi-god, wolf/woodpecker-raised twin boys finally reached manhood, they vanquished their granduncle, restored their grandfather to the throne and then decided it was time for them to go off and establish their own kingdom. They packed up their belongings and trekked about 12 miles from their family's Alba Longa to the banks of the Tiber River. It would be here where they would create a new home, but first they squared off in a fight to the death, with the winner grabbing naming rights to the new town. And guess who won? Well, when you're 23 years old and take your significant other to Italy, there's a pretty good chance you won't be visiting the wondrous city of Reme. Nope, you'll be going to Rome.

Now that his brother was dead, Romulus needed some buddies to start a town. He welcomed in the vagrants of the day – the escaped slaves, the lonely shepherds and the indebted landholders who roamed the countryside just trying to survive. Not exactly the crème de la crème of society. There was one problem. These guys might be tough, but they had a bit of trouble reproducing, because, well, they were guys. So, next on Romulus's "To Do List" was finding wives for his newfound "brothers." He asked the neighboring village of Sabine for a few of their women, but for some reason the dads, brothers and husbands weren't exactly willing to comply. So, Romulus tried option B – invite the entire village to a festival and then steal their women. They held down, beat up and killed the Sabine men-folk, and then took the ladies back to Rome.

So, let's review the Roman Creation Myth scorecard. God and virgin priestess have two boys. Two boys left to die. Two boys raised by members of the animal kingdom. Two boys kill uncle, then one boy kills brother. Surviving brother gathers gang of vagabonds to start a new village. Gang of vagabonds steal neighbors' women. Vagabonds and stolen women make babies.

And Rome was born.

For the next two centuries, a series of kings ruled over central Italy. But in 509 BC, the rich nobles wanted a bit more power for themselves, and knocked off the last ruling family, setting up the Roman Republic. This Republic became a hybrid of Roman monarchy and Athenian democracy. The rich nobles, the patricians, established a government ruled by the most respected men of society, the *senex* (the "old men"). These 300 Senators were chosen from the most prominent patrician families and they passed power down to their sons. They would discuss problems, propose laws and elect two consuls to enforce the laws. These consuls, elected to only one-year terms, would keep each other honest, but you can imagine that these two guys weren't exactly fond of each other (Imagine if Barack Obama and Mitt Romney shared the presidency. How productive do you think that little arrangement would be?)

The Romans wanted their Republic to be a civilization ruled by laws, not a civilization ruled by men. Men can be fickle. Laws, hypothetically, were stable. So again, the Romans looked to the Greeks for some advice on state building. They sent over ten ambassadors to quiz the Athenians on the best laws to implement, and these ten men came back and wrote the Twelve Tables. This assortment of laws became the precursor to the law codes that today govern the Western world. They wrote down dozens of directives and punishments, including mandates such as a) you have 30 days to pay back debts, b) children born ten months after their dad died cannot receive an inheritance (figure out why that one's a no-no), c) people can't meet at night, d) parents should immediately kill deformed children, and e) patricians can never marry plebians.

So what the heck is a *plebian*? Plebians were the "others" of the Roman world. They were the mob, the 95% of society that weren't the rich noblemen – the merchants, the landowners, the peasants. These plebians weren't too excited with this new Republic. Life was actually a bit fairer under kings. At least then they only had to listen to one stuck-up noble. Within a couple generations, they put pressure on the patricians to open the Senate to non-patricians. The patricians laughed at the idea.

But when Rome went to war with neighboring cities, the power structure of the Senate quickly changed. The plebians merely refused to fight. The patricians had a problem. They couldn't just lose 95% of their soldiers overnight, so they had to give in to the demands of the lower class. They let the plebians elect tribunes and these tribunes would then have the ability to shout "I forbid" if ever they came across a law they felt would injure the lower class. You might actually be familiar with the Latin word for "I forbid" – they would shout "Veto!"

Although neither the plebians nor the patricians were totally content with this new arrangement, this little compromise worked well for the next five hundred years. This precedent of shared power between two houses of government can still be seen in the British Houses of Lords and Commons, and the US Senate and House of Representatives. No government is perfect, but the Romans discovered a system that was about as good as it gets. They wrote fair laws, they enforced them relatively uniformly across the land, and they gave a voice to their citizens that calm the discontent and instill in the people a sense of pride in Mother Rome.

Mother Rome wasn't content to merely rule the boot of Italy. There was wealth to be had by uniting the Mediterranean world under one rule, but first, the Romans had to defeat the reigning kings of the sea – the Carthaginians. Carthage is at the northern tip of Africa, just a few dozen miles off the coast of Italian Sicily. It had amassed a navy of some 220 warships that policed the Mediterranean Sea and ensured the profits of trade always made their way into the hands of the Carthaginians. They built ships that could carry up to 100 tons of goods – everything from color dyes to silk clothing to cabinetry to jewelry to fish sauce. In 509 BC, Rome had established a peace treaty with Carthage, sharing the fruits of Mediterranean commerce. In 264 BC, the Romans wanted it all for themselves.

Carthage refused.

The Carthaginians would not go gently into that good night. They weren't ready to simply pass the baton of Mediterranean control over to the Romans. They would fight to their final man. They would fight until their civilization had been literally wiped off the map. The Carthaginians fought three wars in a century and a half, losing hundreds of thousands of soldiers, yet at one point bringing their forces down the boot of Italy, close enough to smell the wild boars and chickens roasting in the Roman capital. However, Hannibal and his forces could go no further as they had to retreat across the sea to Carthage to protect their homeland from invasion. These battles showcased every form of military strategy known to the Ancient World. They fought with elephants. They fought with horses. They fought with slingshots, javelins and catapults. The Romans sent over their legions. The Carthaginians deployed their navy. They fought with swords in closely packed phalanxes. They fought on oared trireme ships that dropped planks to enable swift, deadly boarding. They both bought Greek mercenaries. They both lost to Greek mercenaries. They fought on the sea, across the desert and through the Alps. The Romans alone lost 75,000 men at the Battle of Cannae. At the final Battle of Zama, the Carthaginians lost over 40,000.

And in 201 BC, the Carthaginians surrendered. Their men were exhausted, their land was destroyed and the Roman forces were approaching the city. They agreed to the terms of surrender – turn over all elephants and ships, pay 10,000 talents every year to the Romans and promise to never ever fight the Romans again.

This peace treaty worked for a few dozen years, but Carthage resumed its money-making ways and again became a trade behemoth in the Mediterranean. Rome was less than pleased.

They deployed 80,000 men, but this time there would be no terms of surrender. They went straight for Carthage, raped its women, murdered its sons, burned the city to the ground, destroyed the harbor and then sowed salt into all the fields so no crops could ever grow again.

Carthage was gone. Rome had won. They would spend the next six hundred years patrolling the shores of the Mediterranean, making sure profits from trade made their way back to the pockets of Roman officials.

Even though they were the undisputed rulers of the Mediterranean, Rome did not stop their war making. They couldn't. Fight – expand – tax. That was how Rome's economy thrived. To keep money flowing into Rome (and to feed the million inhabitants that swarmed to the city), the Roman Empire existed in a state of perpetual war. The more land they conquered, the more taxes they collected, the more public works projects they started and the more people they fed. Rome first spread north into Gaul (modern day France) and then up to Germania and then down through the Levant and finally across the Mediterranean Sea into Egypt. Everywhere they went, they left their mark. First they killed. Then they built roads. Then they built cities.

The generals and their loyal legions spent months, and sometimes years, away from their families, fighting for not only glory, but for something bigger. They fought for the Senate and the people of Rome. They fought because they were citizens and citizenship had its privileges. You paid few taxes, you could vote, you could never be tortured and you were protected by the rule of law. You were not a barbarian. But more than that, Roman citizenship meant admission to the most prized club in the ancient world. A Roman was respected, honored and feared. Over the course of their rule, Romans killed over five million men, women and children, and enslaved even more. But by the 2nd century AD, even with their track record of destruction, peoples actually pleaded to be brought under the Roman umbrella, as membership meant access to all the wonders of Roman society.

But Roman expansion wasn't always a sure thing. In the 1st century BC, Roman society sat on the edge of dissolution. Unable to maintain power for any extended length of time, they stood one small step from becoming yet another failed Mediterranean state.

For decades the Senate had been failing to satisfy the needs of their people. Returning soldiers found their farms stolen, their families torn apart and their loyalty quickly forgotten. The mobs of Romans were unemployed. Starving and violent gangs controlled the neighborhoods. The Senators looked powerless, as they seemed to care more about advancing their own power than helping the people (see "American Congress 2012" for more information). A revolution seemed quite possible, but General Gaius Julius Caesar, the hero of the wars of Gaul, believed he had a solution. He believed *he* was the solution. He armed his legionnaires and set them on a new target. Not another barbarian horde, but the Senate of Rome. As his troops approached the city, the Senators ordered them to put down their weapons. Julius Caesar declined. He and his troops crossed the Rubicon River (this was a big deal...troops never crossed the Rubicon) and then, to the cheers and support of the masses, he marched into Rome. He parlayed his popularity into a government position, a humble little title he liked to call "dictator for life." He wasn't going to be a consul for just a year or two. He planned on serving till death did he part. Unfortunately for Caesar, the death part came a bit sooner than expected. The Senate wasn't too fond of giving up their authority to a dictator, so on the Ides of March (March 15), they invited him to the Senate floor and then stabbed him 23 times. He died, and Rome fell into a civil war that lasted two more decades.

In 27 BC, the war came to an end and Augustus Caesar (the nephew of Julius Caesar) ascended to the throne as emperor, thus starting the age of the Roman Empire. For the next two centuries Rome lived in relative peace, an era known as the Pax Romana. The wars had ended, the people were fed, the unemployed found jobs, tradesmen walked safely from one end of the empire to the other and money started again flowing into the capital. The Pax Romana was Rome's Golden Age, and two thousand years later the world still has these Italians to thank for huge chunks of Western society.

Their biggest contribution has to be their government. Their clever little adaptation of democracy actually made it possible to govern on a large scale. Sure, Athens might have had the first democracy, but having people make decisions for a city is a bit different than asking the crowds for their opinions on how to govern an empire. Rome's system worked no matter how large or how diverse they grew. They invented representative government for the masses. Everyone didn't have a say in every decision, but every citizen could elect a local magistrate who would represent their interests to the Senators and Emperor in Rome. And Rome let their regional governors rule their provinces as they saw fit...as long as they followed a few guidelines: collect taxes, enforce Roman laws and keep the military prepared for action at a moment's notice. In this manner, Romans could rule over Greeks, Africans, Gauls, Celts, Jews, Goths, Spaniards, Turks, Egyptians and Persians. Today, for a country such as America, this type of federalism proved invaluable. The US might have a central government in Washington D.C., but it lets each individual state make the laws that best match the needs of their citizens. This lets Texans be Texans, New Yorkers be New Yorkers, and Californians be crazy. And in the ancient world, this let the Persians, Egyptians, Greeks and Gauls (and countless others) maintain a bit of their heritage while still allowing themselves to become just a bit Romanized.

And what did it mean to be Romanized? It meant your life just got a heck of a lot easier. It meant engineers would build aqueducts that could carry water to your house from far off mountain springs. It meant you would get public toilets that you could sit on when #2 just couldn't wait any longer. It meant you might get a Roman bath where you could gather with your friends and prune up in a warm Jacuzzi for hours. It meant your region's capital was going to be rebuilt, probably with a forum for shopping, an amphitheater for watching live entertainment and sewers to take your waste out of town. But most of all it meant you were getting roads. Roman military engineers built thousands of miles of roads (300,000 miles to be more precise) to first transfer soldiers and military supplies, but eventually to facilitate trade and communication. They were brilliant feats of engineering, mixing cut stones with cement to create 8-foot wide paths that could precisely hold a wagon pulled by two horses.

All roads led to Rome and it was in Rome itself that life was truly glorious. The Romans had perfected two engineering marvels – the arch and the dome. Ever wonder why 2000-year-old arches or domes don't just crumble to the ground? It's all in the keystone – the final, expertly-cut stone that locked all the other stones into place, preventing the arch from collapsing. This arch design enabled engineers to erect bridges, aqueducts and one of the most remarkable achievements of ancient architecture – the Pantheon. From the outside it's not that impressive, pretty much looks like any of the hundreds of Greek-columned buildings that line the main streets of state and national capitals. But it's the inside that was special. Its walls are twenty feet thick and it's tall enough to fit the Statue of Liberty inside with her torch just barely sticking out of the oculus that opens to the heavens. Built in 146 AD, the Pantheon remained until the 19th century, the largest domed building in the world (not too bad for a bunch of guys only working with bricks and cement).

About a hundred years before the Pantheon was finished, Emperor Vespian contracted his engineers to use their knowledge of fast drying concrete, take the design of the Greek amphitheaters and build the largest sporting complex in the world – the Flavian Amphitheater – the building you probably have heard of as the Coliseum. Today, only a shadow of its former glory, the Coliseum looks like a crumbling relic of yesteryear, with half its top knocked off and the rest just barely sticking together after dozens of earthquakes and centuries of looting.

But in its day, it could seat 50,000 people and it had some clever little engineering features you wouldn't think possible of the ancients. It had a retractable sunroof that could be closed up during heat waves. Its base had a water-tight seal and the sewer gates could be opened up to flood the bottom to create a huge pond where naval battles could be reenacted. Underneath the base were a series of hydraulic lifts so the competitors could make a dramatic appearance through the stadium floor. And these competitors, these gladiators, waged epic fights to the death. Sometimes men fought men. Sometimes men fought beasts. Sometimes the games' directors merely staged wholesale executions where thousands of slaves or criminals or any of the myriad of animals from the empire (giraffes, crocodiles, apes, hippopotami, leopards, snakes, camels) were tied up and cut to pieces. The Coliseum became the symbol of Rome's "bread and circus" campaign where emperors maintained order by promising citizens a steady supply of food and sadistic live entertainment. Nothing like some blood on the floor to distract you from your empty stomach and your boring life. Unlike the Greeks who brought us more cerebral forms of entertainment like tragedies, comedies and lyric poetry, the Romans appealed to the more base human desires for blood, carnage and spectacle. And still today we like to be entertained in stadiums. We cheer when our team scores a touchdown, shoots a basket or heads in a goal, but we also aren't too upset if we see a dislocated knee, a player knocked unconscious or a racing car burst into flames. The Romans knew what gets people's blood boiling – other people's blood. Back in the days of Roman emperors, one of the more ironic twists on these bloodsports was when the authorities ran out of criminals to feed to the beasts. Not wanting to be robbed of a chance to see his lions devour some human flesh, Emperor Caligula ordered everyone in the first five rows of the stands down into the arena where they were promptly eaten by the lions (it's doubtful that any of these spectators received a refund).

And then there's a ton of other Roman contributions that have become regulars in our daily lives. There's the Roman alphabet – that A to Z list of letters you memorized once upon a time to the tune of "Twinkle, Twinkle, Little Star." There's the Latin language that went on to become the root of Italian, French, Spanish and Portuguese (the *Roman*ce languages). There's the Julian calendar where Julius Caesar got his own month (July), his nephew Augustus got another one, some Roman gods (Mars and Janus) got a couple, and the rest just kept their old names (with the last ones simply being Latin numbers: sept=7, oct=8, nov=9, dec=10). Then there's the seemingly random contributions like the tradition of a man carrying his bride through the front door to prevent her from tripping (which would almost assuredly bring bad luck to the marriage). There's the wearing of socks with shoes to keep the footsies warm and even the cobbling of differently shaped shoes for the left and right foot. They gave us all those Roman numerals that make it so much easier to take outlining notes. They gave us some of the shorthand symbols you see at the top of your keyboard, like &, %, $ and #, and they even gave us that little thing called "et cetera" (yep...etc.).

Oh, and one more thing.

They gave us Christianity – the most practiced religion on the planet. Well, they didn't exactly give us Christianity, but they sure played a huge role in ensuring its spread across the empire. Today over 2.1 billion people follow the New Testament principles founded on the teachings of Jesus Christ, but back in 30 AD, at the time of Christ's death, there were few cues that this faith would ever be more than merely a regional cult. Now the word "cult" has a huge negative connotation in today's world, but if you head to the dictionary, cult merely means a system of religious beliefs followed by a small group of people, and when Jesus Christ taught in the towns of the Levant in the age of Augustus Caesar, his small following of devoted disciples was seen by many as just another one of the numerous cults challenging Roman authority.

Like Buddha who emerged in a time of chaos to provide a path for those in despair, or Confucius who created for China a code of behaviors to guide the masses through a world of turmoil, Jesus Christ appeared at a time when the subjects of Rome questioned if the structure, rules and systems of the Pax Romana were the only legitimate paths to follow. Was there possibly another road to take, one that didn't divide man into the haves and the have-nots, those with wealth and those without?

When discussing the founding of Christianity, you obviously have to start with Jesus Christ and what religion was Jesus Christ? Christian? Nope, he was Jewish. Christ was a Hebrew, a descendant of David, Abraham and Adam. His followers believed he was the chosen one, foreshadowed in the Torah (the Old Testament of the Bible) by Moses as the one who "shall speak unto them all that I [God] shall command him. And it shall come to pass, that whosoever will not hearken unto my words which he shall speak in my name, I will require it of him." Not everyone he encountered shared his followers' faith.

Little is known of Christ's childhood other than he grew up in the region of the Levant known as Bethlehem and spent time in Galilee and Perea (modern day Israel and Jordan). Though raised a carpenter, around his 30th birthday he began a mission to reform the Jewish faith. Travelling around the Levant, helping those less fortunate, persecuted or chastised by society, Jesus also challenged the outdated traditions of the Jewish faith where women were treated as inferior, rabbis had gained an inordinate amount of secular power and people cared more about how to properly prepare their food than they did about developing a close relationship with God. He wanted to reform the Jewish faith so that people stopped simply performing memorized rituals and learned to love God with all their heart and treat thy neighbors as they would want to be treated.

Like Socrates in Athens, this preaching of new ideas didn't go over too well with the powers that be. He challenged both the Roman authority of Pontius Pilate (the prefect of Judae), but also the sovereignty of the Jewish elders. These elders wanted Jesus silenced and Pontius Pilate ordered the torturing of Jesus Christ to convince him to recant his teachings and his claim that he was the "King of the Jews." Christ refused. The Roman authorities proceeded to torture him and then crucified him on a cross next to two petty criminals.

Hanging by cross was a common form of public punishment throughout the Roman Empire. In this form of public torture, the alleged criminal was strung to a wooden platform and hung until dehydration, starvation or the elements took his life. Centuries before Jesus Christ's crucifixion, a gladiator known as Spartacus who had united slaves across the Italian peninsula in a revolt against their Roman authorities, was captured and sentenced to death by hanging. Spartacus and thousands of his insurgents were hung on crosses that lined Roman roads for hundreds of miles, as a warning to any other person considering challenging the status quo.

But the death of Christ wasn't just another crucifixion, for his followers believed he rose from the dead three days after his death, walked with his followers and spoke of how they were to continue his message, and then on the 40th day after his resurrection, he ascended to the skies to join his father in heaven.

At the time of his death, Jesus Christ counted a few hundred adherents as his devotees, with twelve disciples chosen to walk with him closely, trusted with sharing his principles and values. It was the work of these followers and the choices made by subsequent Roman emperors (some inadvertently) that made it possible for Christianity to spread beyond the Middle East. In the decades after his death, those who knew him started writing of his life and his ministry. No one knows for sure how many "good news" writings, or "gospels," were written, but to this point historians have read not only the gospels of Matthew, Mark, Luke and John, but also the gospels of Judas, Thomas and Mary Magdalene. However, over the centuries a few of these (the first four) were officially accepted by communities or by Roman authorities, becoming part of the Bible, while others were ignored and left out of the New Testament.

Probably even more important than the gospels was the work of Saul of Tarsus. Known to Christians as Paul, Saul of Tarsus was a fervent leader of the Jewish community and even persecuted the growing Christian faith, but on the road one day, he was visited by the spirit of Jesus Christ who instructed him to change his course and embrace the one true faith. Paul used his status as a Roman citizen to spend the rest of his days working tirelessly to spread the teachings of Jesus Christ throughout the eastern Roman Empire. In the Bible, his journeys are discussed in the books *Acts* and *Epistles*, and his letters to the Roman officials and his interpretations of Christian theology became known as the New Testament books *Romans*, *First* and *Second Corinthians*, *Galatians*, *Philippians*, *Thessalonians* and *Philemon*. Eventually executed for his teachings, Paul's untiring effort firmly established Christianity throughout the Roman Empire, though it remained until the second century as only the faith of a persecuted minority.

It was the Roman emperors who played a crucial, though oftentimes unintended, role in spreading Christianity. Nero, the last surviving emperor of Julius Caesar's family, wanted to build a palace, so he burned down a chunk of his own Rome to open up some needed land. He then blamed the city's Christian converts for the inferno, sentencing them to be burned alive and ripped apart by animals in the stadium. This punishment backfired when the innocent victims stood stoically in the stadium floor, accepting their brutal torture without a whimper, believing their place in heaven would make any earthly pain insignificant. This inner strength in the face of such horrible suffering (like Jesus before them) shocked the audience and inspired many patrons to reconsider their own faith. What was it about this faith that gave men and women such inner calm, such utter confidence in the afterlife? Acceptance of Christianity steadily expanded and with each round of persecution at the orders of the emperors, Christians gained more and more acceptance in mainstream Roman circles and their nights of meeting secretly in the sewers of Rome passed into a forgotten history.

The emperors Constantine and Theodosius took Christianity to the next level, making it the official religion of the empire. Whether to maintain order throughout his realm or to simply ensure he had access to heaven, Constantine not only prevented the persecution of Christians throughout his reign, but in 337 he made a deathbed conversion to Christianity that set the precedent that Roman emperors would thereafter be linked as the leaders of the Christian church. In 391, Theodosius took Christianity to the next level, outlawing all other pagan faiths, making it a crime to visit the temples of the Roman gods or observe the holidays and traditions of their ancestors. Christianity had become the religion of the empire, and when the Roman Empire eventually fell, Christianity would survive. As the political structures collapsed, the engineering marvels fell into ruin and the military could no longer keep the roads safe, the Church still remained, uniting the continent from its spiritual center – the still capital of Christianity – Rome.

The fall of the Roman Empire would be a long process that over centuries saw the empire eventually divided into an Eastern and Western Empire. The Western Empire was overthrown by the invading barbarians in 476 when Emperor Romulus Augustus (ironic name considering his namesakes were the founders of Rome) yielded his crown to Odoacer and his motley little band of German barbarians. Why the empire fell apart has confounded historians for years. Was it because the empire had grown too large and unmanageable and the mercenaries that ruled the extremities had no more allegiance to their leaders in Rome? Was it because a string of corrupt leaders had bankrupted the empire's treasury with their opulent lifestyles and pricey bread and circus campaigns? Was it because some of these same leaders lived peculiarly repulsive lives where some emperors even resorted to raping young children, becoming prostitutes or appointing horses as head consuls (do a quick Google search for "Incitatus")? Did the people just give up on their government? Or was it because the upper class had lost its moral compass, caring more about how to fulfill their desires for sexual pleasure and sadistic violence than they did for the values that had built the Roman Republic? Was it because Rome's economic system of maintaining the empire through constant expansion, subsequent taxation and enslavement was unsustainable? Did the income disparity between rich and poor, landowner and slave, become so ridiculous that the entire empire simply stopped caring about work? Was it because their legions were no longer made up of Roman citizens, spiritually bound to Rome, but of foreigners merely doing their job for a salary? Could it have been that the barbarians sitting on the borders of the empire had become so accustomed over the centuries to Roman military techniques that they had no problem moving deep into the empire to avoid the ravaging Huns? Or was it merely because the myth of Rome was no longer an inspiration, and many thought they could better take care of themselves without the prying eyes of Rome?

Whatever the reason for its collapse, the continent would again regress into thousands of independent regions, unable to truly unite again until the European Union of the late 20th century.

But until that point in the far off future, one by one, the kingdoms of the western continent would have to decide if they would look inward and become secluded in self-sufficient fiefdoms, never needing to interact with neighboring peoples, or would they remain part of the last remnants of the Roman Empire – the eastern empire known as Byzantium – an empire that would extend the culture of the Greeks and the Romans for another thousand years.

But that is for another chapter.

12

Barbarians and Horse People

The Huns and the Goths – 300 > 600

For almost the whole of the 20th century, Western Civilization and European History courses almost without fail rehashed a narrative where Europe merely progressed from one golden age to the next. If you follow the script, first there were the Greeks, then came the Romans, and after a bit of bumbling during the Middle Ages where that pesky Church held back the European surge, the West got back on track with the Renaissance, followed by a series of revolutions that enabled it to emerge as the preeminent civilization in the world, a mantle it would boast into the 21st century.

But there's a problem with that lovely little linear tale. There was never one Europe, never one West (and if the current European Union experiment fails, there might never be). To act as if the robed wonderers of Athens merely passed the golden Western baton to the Romans who then kept it in storage until some artists in the 1500s decided to revisit the glory of the Classical Age, to merely omit all the tribes and civilizations surviving (and oftentimes flourishing) on the West's borders, leaves out some of the most dynamic characters the world has ever seen.

Let's start with the barbarians. Now the name "barbarians" is a bit difficult to get your head around. Immediately you picture a bunch of large, hairy dudes with hit and miss hygiene who run around yelling "raaaaaaaahhhhhrrr" while swinging a club and eating their food with their hands. Well, the key thing you need to realize with this depiction is that history is written by those who write, and if your people really didn't care about a written language, you pretty much had to accept that your place in history might be a bit devalued. "Barbarian" by definition is merely an uncivilized person. So, for the Han in China, the Gupta in India and the Romans in the Mediterranean, barbarians were all those people who hadn't yet embraced the joy of civilized (aka "city") life.

Yet, the term "barbarian" comes from the Greeks who whenever they listened to non-Greeks speak, all they heard was a bunch of "blah...blah...blah..." or "barh...barh...barh" sounds. At first, they used this term to cover almost everyone – Egyptians, Etruscans, Persians, Carthaginians and all those tribes to the north. Later, after more exposure to the Mediterranean civilizations, the term was rarely ever used to depict the civilizations of the south and the east, but, as for those blubbering curly haired dudes from the north, they remained barbarians for another thousand years.

But who were these first barbarians? Ironically, one man's barbarian is another man's master race. The Greeks commented that these "lesser beings" to the north couldn't reason, couldn't govern and couldn't control their animal passions. They were seen as an inferior race, one that needed to be conquered, then guided. Oddly enough, three thousand years later, the Eugenics Movement hit full speed, and countless books came out claiming that these northern Europeans were the most evolved of all of man's creatures, standing atop the racial pyramid.

For the hundreds of years after Christ's birth, these people went by tribal names like Visigoths, Ostrogoths, Lombards, Burgundians, Vandals and Franks. They were the Germanic tribes – today what we might call Germans. Hitler would later inaccurately call them his master race – the Aryans.

But from 500 BC to 500 AD, no one would have confused them as masters of anything, for they were nothing more than the outsiders who frustrated every Roman emperor from Julius Caesar to Romulus Augustus. Some emperors would push their legions further north, others would build protective walls to ensure everyone knew on which side civilization resided. Still others would actually make treaties and arrangements with these barbarians, all with the hope of maintaining the peace.

Since most of what we know about the barbarians is from the slightly prejudicial eyes of Greek and Roman historians, finding an accepted version of these people can be a bit tricky. In 98 AD, the Roman historian Tacitus described them as having "fierce blue eyes, red hair, huge frames," and living in clan-based societies where "the chief fights for victory; his vassals fight for the chief." He went on to state that all they know how to do is fight, rest and feast. They were warriors and partiers.

But they were so much more. These Germanic tribes and their traditions, their social structure and their daily lives ended up setting the groundwork for what would become life in the Middle Ages, for the millennium following the fall of the Roman Empire. As for Tacitus, he was right about one thing. They did live in small clans. Usually in small villages of seven to ten families, they set up their timbered houses in clearings amongst the dense forests. They lived with their animals (which over the centuries contributed to them having some fairly formidable immune systems) in dirt-floored, thatched-roof huts and they counted wealth based on land ownership and the number of animals (cows, chickens, pigs, horses, sheep) under their charge. They wore pants and shirts made from the wool of their sheep, oftentimes topped off with a cow-hide (leather) cap.

Like the Hindus in India, they believed not in one god, but instead in an assortment of spirits and deities that might have been specific to one clan, or be shared by many. We don't know much about their early practices, for when the Christians came into the region, they destroyed all traces of the old faiths, leaving only stories and myths to continue today. But some of the earliest Romans who entered the area noted that they were animists, believing in sun, moon and fire gods. In the far north, they worshipped the god of thunder - Thor (you might know him better as the namesake for Thor's Day...or Thursday) and the god of war – Tiwaz (Tuesday). During the month of April, they feasted in honor of the goddess of the forests – Eostre (sounds just a tad bit like the bunny holiday).

The Germanic pagans practiced witchcraft in the forests, and many of their rituals remained hidden from Christian eyes for centuries after the whole of Europe had converted. Travelling back in time 2000 years to the forests of Germania, you might have seen women concocting potions to either heal wounds or alter emotions. They might have even worshipped the most desired of all beasts – the white horse – for when these albino equines were discovered, they were almost always kept away from the commoner's gaze (these white horses then became the unicorns of western myths).

So, once again, syncretism showed up in full force. The religion of the old blended with the religion of the new to create a whole new set of practices and beliefs. But some of this old pagan stuff just couldn't be blended with Christianity. It's difficult to find some sort of connection between Christ dying for our sins and witchcraft, mythical white horses and tree gods, so a few of the unconverted just kept practicing the "old ways" at the fringes of society. But when times got tough in the Christian towns, the chosen ones almost always pointed their persecuting eyes to the "witches and warlocks" of the forest.

These clans of pagan believers gave their allegiance to one leader, a chieftain, and this chieftain in exchange promised protection and the occasional feast. Select chieftains might even rise to the status of a duke, one who would protect and demand loyalty from a collection of clans. These dukes were part military leader, part judge and part politician. They became lords, barons, counts and kings of the Medieval Era, and their absolute rule would not be replaced until the revolutions of the 18th and 19th centuries. Yet, throughout the age of the Roman Empire, it was these chieftains that continually threatened the authority of Rome.

Initially they were fought. Then they were placated. Then they were walled out (Hadrian's Wall in England and the Limes in Germania). But as time passed, they were sometimes hired out as mercenaries, pitting one barbarian tribe against another. By 400 AD, most Roman soldiers weren't really even Roman at all, but a hodgepodge of foreigners all hired to protect the dying empire.

This flimsy military structure met its eventual demise when a new barbarian horde rose from the darkness – this one more dangerous than any seen by Western eyes. It came not from the north, but from the east. It had threatened the civilization of China, forcing the Han to expand and upgrade Qin Huangdi's already fairly impressive Great Wall. It had killed everyone in its sight, sweeping in and out of villages across Asia and Europe without pause. It instigated what would become known as the Migration Period as entire races of people fled from its onslaught. It was a foe no one could stop. It was...the Huns.

The Huns pose a problem for historians. They weren't big on the whole writing thing, so all we have today to shed light on the "Hunstory" comes from the two civilizations – the Romans and the Han Chinese - who were constantly afraid these horrific horse riders from the hills would sweep down and wipe out their way of life, so they weren't the most impartial critics.

To start, scholars have trouble even agreeing on the origins of this tribe of people that would create an empire stretching from the eastern tip of the Roman Empire to the western fringe of China. Most historians point to the 200 BC group known as the Xiongnu (pronounced "shong new"), a band of herding horsemen who roamed the steppe of middle Asia. The steppe, or land between the forests of Russia and the mountains and deserts of southern Asia (present day Mongolia), is a dry, flat land with little vegetation and harsh winters that would make even the toughest nomad cringe. Only a few years after the Han brought peace to a war-torn China, the barbarians to the west, the Xiongnu, threatened to plunge the empire back into violence as they incessantly raided, robbed and enslaved the villagers of the surrounding territories. In open combat, even the numerically superior Chinese Han had no chance against the mobile, ruthless Xiongnu (who weren't exactly known for their sensitivity...one time even killing a rival king and using his skull as a drinking cup). The Chinese eventually signed to a peace treaty where the Han Emperor Gaozu reluctantly consented to deliver both his daughter as a bride gift and an annual ransom of alcohol and rice. In exchange, the Xiongnu promised to accept the Great Wall as the border between their two worlds. This tenuous peace lasted over fifty years, but eventually the Xiongnu fell apart, with some tribes blending into others, while others started moving west.

These horse people of the steppe would not be heard from again for another four hundred years, but when they did reappear on the world stage, this time they would be led by a bloodthirsty, merciless terrorist who would bring the Roman Empire to its knees. This time they would have the "scourge of God" – Attila the Hun.

Attila the Hun mastered the art of murder as spectacle. He and his bands of followers created such pandemonium that entire populations left behind their ancestral homes, fleeing the impending storm of sadism. The entire culture of the Huns was built on instilling fear and readily dispatching foes. From birth, parents created warriors. They slashed their children's faces and bandaged their skulls to create a society of grotesquely disfigured warriors who instilled horror at first sight. If their dashing good looks failed to send an opponent fleeing, the Huns had perfected a method of lightning-fast, guerilla warfare that would make any 20th century general proud. The Huns used horses on the battlefield with such stunning precision, that the phalanx warfare method of fighting that had dominated the Mediterranean for over a thousand years became obsolete. The age of the foot soldier had passed. The age of the horseman had begun.

To say the Huns lived on their horses is not hyperbole. They conducted tribal meetings on horseback, they slept on their horses and they even tenderized and cooked raw meat by packing it under their saddle (the barbarians of Hamburgh, Germany borrowed from this tasty tradition, creating a famous little dish to go with your fries). With a saddle designed with a high front and rear and stirrups unseen anywhere else in the known-world, the Huns could lock their bodies onto their smaller ponies and have a 360-degree perspective to mow down their enemies. Fifth century historian Anthemius observed, "You would think the limbs of man and horse were born together, so firmly does the rider always stick to the horse, just as if he were fastened to his place: any other folk is carried on horseback, this folk lives there." Man and horse had become one.

And when these master horsemen entered a town, their savagery became legendary. Attila, and his brother Bleda, cared nothing for running an empire. They wanted gold, nothing more. After conquering a town, they slaughtered every last woman and child and burned the buildings to the ground. They wanted their reputations to precede them, and as they continued west, more and more towns met them totally abandoned. Attila had created a war machine no one could match and those males he didn't kill, he gave a choice – join his army or die. And those that joined his force never left, for the punishment for desertion was having a long wooden pole rammed up your tushy and then having your corpse propped up in the town center so your rotting bod could stand as a subtle reminder of Attila's unquestioned power. Even his brother finally succumbed to Attila's cruelty, as he too was murdered while hunting in the forest.

Alone as the unquestioned leader of the Huns, Attila in 450 AD controlled more money than any one man could ever hope to spend in a lifetime. Under threat of annihilation, he had coaxed the protectors of Constantinople, the eastern Roman Empire, to surrender without a fight and drop 6000 pounds of gold (or $100 million in today's currency) into Attila's pocket. Everywhere he went, he left a path of destruction. He decapitated an archbishop who dared challenge his authority, he destroyed the walled fortress of Naissus with battering rams made from nearby tree trunks and he even convinced the Romans to hire him and his thugs as mercenaries to "protect" the Roman Empire (yes, the Romans hired their enemy to protect them).

Eventually he tired of his role as mercenary, and thinking himself undefeatable, squared off against Roman general Flavius Aettius in the Battle of Catalaunia, where the Roman general and his alliance of ticked-off barbarians fought back and gave Attila his first defeat. But Attila had no plan on retiring from the battlefield, and within a few years he again attempted to destroy Rome, this time by invading Italy. However, after pushing deep into the northern peninsula, he suddenly reversed course and returned to his home in the east. Pope Ley the Great claimed holy responsibility for stopping Attila, but more likely the Huns left because a plague was wiping out their forces and an army from Constantinople was mounting an attack on his rear.

Attila, however, would never make it back home. In a bizarre wedding celebration gone wrong, Attila returned with his new bride to his wedding tent, fell into a drunken stupor and ended up choking to death on his own blood. Some historians claim the cause of death was a bloody nose; others said it might have been tuberculosis. More than likely it was the sum of a lifetime of hard drinking, harder living and a weakened blood vessel that burst while he slept, leaving him to die in his own pool of blood.

Without an heir, his empire crumbled within a few decades. But the damage was done. The Huns relentless western offensives pushed the barbarian tribes deeper and deeper into Roman lands. The barbarian tribes of Germania had two choices – stay and fight the bloodthirsty Huns or cross the vague Roman borders and challenge the dying imperial forces. They chose the Roman option. With Roman defenses a mere shadow of their former glory, the Germanic barbarians lived deeper and deeper inside Roman territory. By the fifth century, the fading emperors of Rome were little more than figureheads, and in 476 AD, newly crowned emperor Romulus Augustus surrendered his throne to Odoacer, a "barbarian," thus marking the end of the Roman Empire.

Or at least what historians like to point to that date as the end of the Roman Empire. For in the east, the Roman Empire continued on for another thousand years under the reign of Byzantium, and in the west, the Pope in Rome ruled over the Church and the souls of the whole of Europe for the era known as the Middle Ages.

But that is for another chapter.

13

One Step Forward, Five Steps Back

The European Middle Ages – 400 > 1100

Wh
en Rome "fell," most of Europe paid no attention. There were no newspaper articles proclaiming the end of an empire. No heralds shouting from the highest tower, "Ding, Dong, the empire is dead." No marathon runner sprinted from coast to coast to reveal the truth. No one really cared. For the average white guy living in Europe, life looked exactly the same in 477 as it did in 476, and a heck of a lot like it looked in 376.

We're supposed to call the next thousand years in Europe "The Middle Ages," but that moniker suggests that this millennium was fairly inconsequential. We get the "Golden Age of Greece," then the "Peace of Rome," then the "Renaissance," then the "Age of Exploration," but when we talk about the years from 500 to 1500, the best historians could come up with was "Middle Ages"?

What does this imply? It implies that historians are actually the ones guilty of the number one crime of hi"story"telling - overgeneralization. Eras don't start and stop. People aren't just good or bad. And civilizations don't suddenly become stupid. The truth is, although the Middle Ages was definitely not mankind's crowning moment, the epoch that preceded this period wasn't exactly all full of brightness and joy. Wasn't it during the Roman Empire that about 30% of the people were slaves? Wasn't it during the Roman Empire that humans found it entertaining to head to the Coliseum to watch some Christians get their limbs ripped off or to watch human flesh sizzle as criminals were burned alive? And wasn't it the Roman Empire that slaughtered one million Gauls under the generalship of Julius Caesar?

Yes, Rome built some amazing aqueducts, a fairly impressive stadium and miles and miles of useful roads, but to think that the bulk of humanity living under the Roman Empire frolicked in a world of prosperity while contemplating the meaning of life definitely gives Romans far more credit than they deserve. Humans have lived in squalor for most of our run on this planet, and for those rare moments in history when for a few decades, a select few truly thrived, we cannot overlook the reality of life for the common man.

So what then can we say about the Middle Ages? Yes, for the bulk of Western Europe, the Middle Ages was an era when people struggled to survive in a dangerous world. After around 300 AD, the mass migration of Huns and Germanic tribes plunged the West into almost constant conflict. As the Roman Empire increasingly turned to mercenaries to fight their battles, the citizens of Rome and the Germanic refugees realized if they wanted to live, they had to protect themselves. Initially this meant relying on their clan's baron for whatever protection he could muster. However, by the 800s, as invaders continued to pour in from the northern and eastern frontiers, this need for protection was institutionalized. Today we call this system "feudalism." Feudalism was a relationship between a lord and his vassals. The lord promised protection. The vassals (or peasants) promised their labor. This labor might be 40 days of military service or it might be 50% of the farm's harvest. Under this system, the peasant was not exactly a slave (though a Medieval peasant might beg to differ), but was actually a landowner that "freely" engaged in this swap of protection for labor. This relationship was by no means ideal, but it did signify the end of slavery on the European continent (until the 1500s when Europeans hijacked the African slave trade from the Muslim Empire).

However, even in the centuries preceding feudalism, regions living on the fringe of the Roman Empire listened increasingly less to the mandates of the central government in far off Italy and more towards the rules of the local lord. These lords became lawgivers and law enforcers. They also controlled the means of production – the mills, the farm implements and the granaries – that made basic farming possible. Although life wasn't glitzy, these isolated villages and fiefdoms were self-sufficient. A peasant villager could live his entire life and never venture more than a few miles from his birthplace.

What else were some patterns of Medieval European life? Well, as travelling on the roads became more and more dangerous, trade came to a standstill except for the occasional peddler of goods who stopped to barter off some salt, weapons or cutlery. The silk and cotton of the East never made their way into Medieval homes, forcing the peasantry to settle for one oh-so-comfy wool outfit that had to last the entire year. If this scratchy, abrasive clothing didn't make them feel too fresh, fortunately they could count on bi-annual baths to increase their position on the hotty scale. Because of this hit and miss hygiene and the rather unbalanced diet of bread, porridge and stew, people died at a fairly rapid rate. 1/3 of babies born died before the age of two. If one lucky kid made it to adolescence, he was seen as a true gift from God. After hitting the teen years, he still needed to survive plagues, famines, measles epidemics and unpredictable violence if he hoped to make it to adulthood. The average life expectancy during the Dark Ages was about 35 years (just a hair short of the 78.6 years a Western baby born today can expect to reach). And being alive wasn't exactly entertaining. With literacy rates at an all-time low, with towns and entertainment near non-existent and with travel hindered, for the months where food production didn't dominate your every thought, life was fairly boring. For those of you imagining the Middle Ages as one long Renaissance Fair full of entertainers juggling, wearing joker costumes and dancing until just after midnight, you're confusing Disney with reality. The Middle Age was no fairy tale.

Yet, one institution held everyone together, promising a glittering future after you died, while maintaining the remnants of Classical learning – the Christian Church.

Christianity had less than humble beginnings as a cult of the lower class, meeting secretly in the sewers of Rome, but after 312 when Emperor Constantine's Edict of Milan forbade persecution of this formerly forbidden faith, the religion gradually spread across the continent. With every passing decade, missionaries pushed further into barbarian territories, converting tribe by tribe, clan by clan, until mass conversions became possible.

In one story, the missionary St. Boniface ventured into the Germanic forests and met up with a group of barbarians making a winter solstice (around December 22nd) sacrifice to the god Odin. As these pagans chanted and danced around the "Odin Tree," Boniface stepped in to stop the nonsense. He grabbed an axe, walked over to the ceremony and chopped down the tree.

And guess what the great god Odin did to this punish this madman with an axe?

Well, nothing. The Germans stood shocked. How could it be? How could a man spit in the face of their most supreme god, yet still draw life? They wondered if maybe this St. Boniface represented a more powerful god. In the coming months, these barbarians from the north started switching their allegiance, tossing aside Odin for the father of Jesus Christ. To commemorate their conversion, Boniface ordered that every year, on the anniversary of the winter solstice, each German was to take home a fir tree and place it in their home. If ever again they doubted the power of God, they needed look no further than the fir tree in their home whose shape clearly pointed to the heavens. And since the Middle Ages, every year when the winter solstice comes around, barbarians repeat this little tree in the house tradition, even sometimes claiming a white-bearded dude with a weight problem deposits boxes of goodies under its branches.

In a less touching tale of religious conversion, the king of the Franks, a warrior named Clovis, converted to Christianity to help aid him in battle. Christianity (or at least the threat of a never-ending Hell) proved to be a powerful recruiting tool. Once he himself converted, Clovis then went from town to town offering every opponent a choice – switch their allegiance to God or die. Many chose to fight with Clovis (and therefore God), and steadily his "holy army" grew in numbers, expanding the Frankish realm (aka France) to become the largest kingdom in Europe.

Whether people converted for political or military motivations or if they had an actual spiritual awakening, with each conversion, the Church grew even more powerful. A world totally separated by language and geography became a world united by the traditions of Christianity. The Church, its holidays and its sacraments became the backbone of an entire continent. The local priest was at every townsperson's baptism, marriage and death. This priest constantly balanced his flock's spiritual needs with their practical needs. A priest became the most trusted man in town. He might one day guide his followers in how to improve their crop yields and then turn around the next day to advise them on how to avoid catching a cold in the winter months. The church became the center of peasants' lives, where they would gather, where they would find comfort and where they would mourn. And Christianity had another little perk. At the end of the day, no matter how much life sucked, peasants could always look forward to a splendidly tranquil afterlife in the heavens.

Dotted across the European countryside was another religious institution that would have an equally critical role in the lives of the everyman, but also in the advancement of Western society. This institution was the monastery. Started in the eastern provinces of the Roman Empire, the first monks embraced a Buddha-esque existence by leaving society to meditate on the spiritual questions of the universe. Some (known as Stylites) went as far as to sit on the top of a tall pole in the center of town all day and all night, trying to get closer to God. All this changed with St. Benedict, who believed a true messenger of God must work to prove his faith, not merely spend his days locked in prayer or sitting on a stick.

In the 7th century, St. Benedict wrote what became known as the "Benedictine Rules," a set of behavior expectations later employed by the majority of monasteries across Europe. Monks were to remain unmarried, to surrender all their worldly possessions and to obediently listen to the mandates of the head of the monastery - the abbot. Your position in the outside world meant nothing. All were equal in God's eyes once you passed through the monastery's gates. Throughout the Middle Ages, hundreds of thousands of men chose the monastic life, either to fulfill a divine calling, to find something useful to do with their lives or even to appease their parents who believed their admission would improve their family's chances of getting into heaven. For those that chose the monastic life, each had to defer to his elder, a reality that would annoy many previously powerful men who found themselves answering to people they once passively dismissed.

Within the monastery's walls, monks divided their waking hours between prayer and labor. And there was a ton of labor to be had. Because lords realized they could fast-track their trip to heaven if they bequeathed a sizable chunk of their property to the Church upon their death, giving land became your get-out-of-hell free card. By the 12th century, the Church and its monasteries became the greatest landowners on the continent. Some monks subsequently spent their days maintaining the monastery grounds, while others basically became farmers in black robes. Still others toiled indoors, spending their days and nights holding on to the last bits of the glory days of Greece and Rome. Charged with recording the Classical learning of the great Mediterranean civilizations, monks alone preserved any connection to the rich thoughts of the ancients. As one of the few literate groups in all of Europe, these keepers-of-the-past spent hours painstakingly inscribing on parchment the documents the Church saw fit to preserve, while countless other works were either destroyed or lost to the hands of neighboring civilizations. These literate monks often then ingratiated themselves to the regional lords, assisting them with transcription of laws and correspondence with bishops and the Pope. In this manner, Church and state became informally linked, with nary a decision made without the advisement of a spiritual consultant.

For a brief moment in the early 9th century, it appeared Europe would shift into a new gear with the Church working together with regional lords to take humanity out of the darkness. One lord, Charlemagne (Latin for "Charles the Great"), took over kingdom after kingdom after kingdom until he had amassed the largest fiefdom in Europe, stretching from Scandinavia in the north to Spain in the south to the land of the Czechs in the east. In 800, the Pope invited Charlemagne, the new king of the Franks, to his hallowed home in Rome. A few weeks later, on Christmas Day in St. Peter's Basilica, Charlemagne was crowned with a new title - Holy Roman Emperor. Pope Leo II envisioned a new world where Pope and King would rule over all of Western Europe – a realm christened the Holy Roman Empire (a not so subtle attempt to recapture the glory of Rome). Once officially sanctioned by the Church, Charlemagne pushed his kingdom's borders even further. He had his holy war. He went on to fight in over 50 more military campaigns, giving every soul he encountered two choices – convert to Christianity or die. Not so surprisingly, the pagan population dropped significantly.

With all these pagans converted and the bulk of Western Europe back under the command of a central figure, Charlemagne set to improving the lives of his people and uniting Europe in more ways than merely who they worshipped. His first priority was improving education and learning. Like Alexander the Great before him, a conqueror has a unique opportunity to expand wisdom should he choose to amass the knowledge from the corners of his realm. A true patron of learning, Charlemagne enhanced the libraries of the monasteries, built schools across his empire and even tried to teach himself to read and write (not exactly a common site for rulers during this era). He then divided his empire into 350 counties, each governed by a count, who in turn answered to Charlemagne. In this manner, Charlemagne kept control of almost the whole of Europe, establishing the roots of government and creating the regional borders that still exist across France and Germany.

Charlemagne selflessly made time for himself, marrying five women, frolicking with another half dozen mistresses and eventually fathering twenty kids. This unique interpretation of marriage vows convinced the Church they might want to wait a bit before condemning polygamy and mandating the one husband-one wife policy that continued through to the 21st century. This charming piece of his personality, coupled with his proclivity to massacre any pagan leaders refusing to convert, were somewhat overlooked by the Holy Church, and in the 12th century he officially became a saint.

But Charlemagne did die (just a few centuries before he was granted sainthood). And like the 43,642 other leaders of world empires who failed to establish a clear process for determining their replacements, Charlemagne's empire slowly withered, losing influence with each successor. Not only were these leaders inconsistently competent, within a few short decades, a new stream of invaders from the north negated any advances Charlemagne accomplished, plunging the region back into chaos. These invaders came on boats that could be rowed up rivers, picked up and carried across the land. These invaders were the Vikings.

The Vikings are so much more than an American football team that sold their soul to the devil for the services of an aging quarterback named Brett Favre. They were Europe's greatest pirates (with apologies to Jack Sparrow), and their desire for quick wealth and a bit of adventure took them as far south as Africa. They then became the first Europeans to ever set foot on the Americas, when in the year 1000, Leif Eriksson came ashore on the coast of what is today called Canada (but was back then known by the ingenious name "Newfoundland"...get it "new found land").

But the American continent was only touched by the Vikings. Europe was ravaged. The Vikings learned a very useful fact about Medieval Europe – monks aren't very good fighters. Vikings rowed their knars (twenty foot long wooden war ships) up a river, hopped on out, found the closest monastery and freed the holy sanctuary of any unnecessary pieces of wealth they might find. When the monasteries ran out of loot, the villages became the next most obvious target. Taking a piece from Attila's book *How to Scare the Crapajawea Out of People In Seven Easy Steps*, they practiced a bit of depravity that definitely helped their public relations across the continent. They'd loot, they'd massacre and they'd torture. One of their more gruesome treatments of foes was the "Bloody Eagle." Vikings took a man (usually the head of the village), opened up his rib cage, tore out his lungs, dangled these little pulmonary sacks on the side of his body and then hung him in the center of town. Fair to say that neither the eagle nor his spectators enjoyed this experience. So most coastal towns simply admitted defeat and paid "protection money" (a la the mafia) so the Vikings would stop destroying their villages. These invasions lasted for over a century until Alfred the Great realized that the way to stop Vikings was to enclose towns behind walls that the invaders couldn't bypass. Viking pirates were great at sailing, pillaging and plundering. Knocking down walls? Not so much. Some Viking tribes gave up and returned to Scandinavia, others decided to settle down and live like regular, non-piratey dudes. And this was how the age of castles began.

But before jumping into the second half of the Middle Ages, let's bounce back over to eastern Europe and to a walled city that became the largest metropolis in the West, all the while avoiding ever entering its own Middle Ages, but instead clinging for another thousand years to the legacy of the Roman Empire. We head now to Constantinople, capital of the Byzantine Empire.

People tend to conveniently forget that when Rome fell, only half of the Roman Empire actually ceased to exist. The Eastern Roman Empire continued until 1453 when it was finally overthrown by the Ottoman Empire, but for the thousand years of its existence, it succeeded in preventing the European invasion of the Muslims, acted as the bridge between the eastern and western worlds and helped preserve Rome's greatest accomplishments. But to say it lasted for a thousand years is a bit dishonest. When the Turks blew up the walls of Constantinople in 1453, the Eastern Roman Empire was nothing more than a singular, walled city. The rest of the empire had steadily dissolved in the face of constant pressure from Muslim and European forces.

When Emperor Constantine first devised the idea of creating a second, eastern capital for the Roman Empire, his eyes immediately settled on the quaint little Greek town – Byzantium (known today as Istanbul). Back in the 320s, when Constantine first hatched the plan to create a masterpiece of a city from scratch, he had the greatest architects and engineers at his disposal. Humbly renamed Constantinople, this new city became the jewel of the Mediterranean. For centuries, Constantinople vacillated from being a capital that shared authority with Rome to an independent capital of the eastern half of the Roman Empire, to eventually the capital of the only part of Rome that remained. When Rome finally fell, Constantinople by default became the capital of the new Roman Empire, what historians would eventually call Byzantium, or the Byzantine Empire.

In the 530s, a few hundred years before Charlemagne got the idea, Emperor Justinian made one final push to recapture the glory of the Pax Romana. Although Justinian's forces only got as far as Italy where they crushed an assortment of barbarians, they could never hold the newly conquered territory for any extended period of time. Ironically, his only lasting legacy in Italy was his utter disregard for the architecture and art of Rome, wiping out almost all traces of the Classical Era. (So, nope, you can't blame the barbarians for knocking down all the great Roman architectural marvels. Blame that one on their own cousin to the east – Justinian).

Back in Constantinople, Justinian's legacy proved a tad more substantive. His architects built two story high aqueducts that brought in fresh water from miles away to the 500,000 citizens filling the streets. His scholars codified into one book all the spoken and written laws that had been enforced haphazardly across the empire. This Justinian Code outlined how governments, individuals and nations should behave and its principles continue to fill the notebooks of law students across the West.

Emperor Justinian was also a religious man. In fact, he believed he spoke for God. He believed he was God's messenger on earth, divinely chosen to rule in His stead. You can imagine how this "chosen one" mantle didn't go over too well with the Church. I'm not exactly sure where in the New Testament Jesus recommended his flock follow the visions of a Byzantine Emperor, but Justinian stood by his own unique interpretation. He and future Byzantine emperors encouraged this perception of a god-emperor, often depicting themselves in art as equals to Jesus and the saints. He even orchestrated elaborate ceremonies where the masses bowed in his presence after performing a series of memorized rituals. Justinian used his influence to build hundreds of churches throughout the city, even commissioning the construction of the most spectacular church in all of Christendom

– the Hagia Sophia. Translated as "Divine Wisdom," the Hagia Sophia showcased the best the empire could assemble – the most spectacular dome ever built (sorry Pantheon), the finest marble flooring ever designed and the most ornately decorated gold leaf statues ever imagined. Although the Hagia Sophia eventually boasted Muslim minarets constructed centuries later once the Turks took control in the 15th century, it remains today a testament to the opulent tastes of the ultra-pious Justinian.

However, Justinian's unique take on the Christian faith ended up severing the Church. You can probably see why Constantinople and Rome ran into a bit of conflict. In addition to the Byzantine Emperor's proclaimed status as a god-king, the two sides butted heads on a variety of issues – from the substantive to the ridiculous. They fought over thickness of bread. Romans wanted the communion bread that symbolized the body of Christ to be flat. The Byzantines wanted it fluffy. Romans didn't let their priests marry. Byzantines did. Roman priests spoke Latin. Byzantine priests spoke Greek. Byzantines saw the Pope as the leader of barbarian Europe. Rome saw Byzantium as a fossil stuck in the past. However, the greatest division stemmed from the Byzantine preference for painted icons – oil tempera paintings of saints, angels and Jesus. Byzantine churches featured these paintings prominently on their walls, enabling believers to enter the sacred halls and direct their prayers to these figures. Rome saw these artistic creations as blasphemous, condemning them as false idols, whereas Constantinople saw them as necessary windows to the stories of God for an illiterate population (odd that Western Europe had such a problem with painted stories, when more than a handful of churches boasted stained glass windows). These disagreements over yeast, priests, the Bible and idols finally led to the big split, or the Great Schism of 1054 that created two churches – the Orthodox Church in the east and the Catholic, or "Universal," Church in the west. This schism survived through the centuries, creating two Europes – a Europe that followed the Pope in Rome (France, Spain, Portugal and Germany), and a Europe that looked to Constantinople for guidance (Greece, Bulgaria, Romania and Russia). Remember this schism in a few centuries when World War I starts.

Aside from its critical role in the evolution of the Church, Constantinople also stood at the crossroads between the East and the West. As the only city in the world with one foot in Europe and one foot in Asia, Constantinople became the link between the peoples of China, India and Islam and the peoples of Western Europe. Not only did Byzantium maintain the classical learning of the Romans and Greeks, it also became the conduit for the wealth of knowledge coming across the Levant from the neighboring kingdoms. When Europe eventually decided to wake from its self-imposed Medieval slumber, the classical ideas would be theirs for the taking, but first they would have to settle the score with a new empire that threatened to not only spread into the Mediterranean, but for a few decades appeared at the doorstep of the West, ready to wipe out any hope for an independent Europe.

But that is for another chapter.

14

All Eyes Turn to Mecca

Rise of Islam – 600 > 800

Growing up in America in the late twentieth century, my generation learned little about Muslims. Sure, we heard about some conflicts over oil in the Middle East. We knew about a few athletes who had changed their names (basketball great Lou Alcindor became Kareem Abdul Jabbar and Cassius Clay is better known to the world as Muhammad Ali). And when Disney's *Aladdin* came out, we thought maybe those people "over there" once lived in palaces and had a thing for carpets and lamps. But if you'd asked the 18-year-old version of me to tell you the difference between Iraq and Iran or even which countries had the most Muslims in the world (Indonesia #1, India #2), I would have drawn a complete blank.

Then 9/11 hit and no one could ever again claim to not have an opinion about Muslims. And because for the majority of Americans, 9/11 was the first time they were introduced to Muslims, this attack became their immediate, and only, connection. The math seemed simple. Terrorists had attacked America. The terrorists were all Muslim. Muslims therefore must be terrorists. In addition to this flawed little bit of deductive reasoning, Americans also then sucked in stories of how these terrorists believed in this thing called a "jihad" where each of them automatically went to paradise if they died killing infidels. So, again, using some flawed logic, Islam must be a religion of killing.

This was what many of us believed. This was what we were being shown, and most of us never ventured to explore the topic any further.

In the decade since, some have attempted to move beyond these initial perceptions and find out more about the fastest growing religion in the world, a religion that claims more than 1.5 billion adherents, a religion that, by the end of the 21st century, will pass Christianity as the most practiced religion on the planet. We've learned that to claim all Muslims are terrorists is as asinine as claiming all Christians are members of the KKK. We've learned that to claim all Muslims share the views of Osama bin Laden is akin to claiming all Christians shared the views of Adolph Hitler.

But conflict and misunderstanding still plague Christian-Muslim relations, threatening to pull the two cultures apart. Before these severed relations can be repaired, it would help if the world knew the stories of Islam's early days as well as they know the stories of Jesus Christ as a baby in a manger, walking with his twelve disciples and dying on the cross for the world's sins.

To understand Muslims, the starting points are always one man and one place. Muhammad and Mecca. In the sixth century AD, while Europe was settling into the Dark Ages where it would remain for centuries, in the deserts of the Arabian Peninsula, a new faith sprung from the sands of one of the most desolate places on earth. Today known as Saudi Arabia, this region is one of the most inhospitable ecosystems on Earth.

Because of lack of fresh water, intense heat, minimal vegetation and unprotected deserts, the cities that popped up elsewhere in the Near East (along the Nile, in Mesopotamia and throughout the Levant) could never survive in the Arabian Peninsula. The city-states that popped up did so because of their position as bridges between the great cultures of the ancient world. But most people didn't live in the cities. They lived in the desert. These men and women of the desert became traders. They became nomads. They became Bedouins. Like the horse peoples of the steppe, the Bedouins led transient lives, constantly moving from one location to the next. Some settled in small trading towns that built up around oases in the desert, some became shepherds of cows or sheep or goats. But the majority of men in the area remained nomads, people of the land, living by a code of kinship under which all disputes were settled and all interactions were defined. A prominent saying describing these people was: "Me against my brother, my brothers and I against my cousins, then my cousins and I against strangers." This clan system defined where everyone stood. Unlike the caste system of India where priests and warriors stood at the top, or like Europe where lords demanded allegiance from vassals or even like China where the scholars commanded unquestioned reverence, in the Arabian peninsula of the 6th century, nomadic traders ruled the land and those who settled in towns were seen as soft and inferior.

This was the world Muhammad entered in 570 AD Born in Mecca into the relatively affluent Hashimite clan of the Quraysh tribe, Muhammad was orphaned at the age of six and then raised by his merchant uncle Abu Talib. Riding alongside his uncle, Muhammad travelled throughout the Near East, reaching as far north as Syria. In the 6th century, Mecca was the most prominent trading center in the region. Because of its tolerance of all religions and its forbiddance of violence within a twenty-mile perimeter, Mecca became the prime trading (and pilgrimage) destination. Its most holy site, a cube called the Kaaba (Arabic for "the cube"), housed 360 of the region's deities behind its 40-foot high stone walls. It also housed the mythical "black stone," seen by some as a gift from the heavens (seen by others as a meteorite). Aside from these worshipped relics, Mecca also permitted the practice of the two most-practiced monotheistic faiths of the time – Judaism and Christianity. Whether believing in one of the hundreds of pagan gods that watched over individual tribes or believing in Judaism or Christianity, almost all Arabs believed in the god Allah (Arabic for "The God"). Muhammad knew the teachings and the traditions of most of these faiths, both because of his experience trading throughout the region, and also because his family (the Quraysh tribe) was charged with protecting the Kaaba.

In his early twenties, with his reputation as an honest, competent merchant starting to spread amongst the clans, Muhammad was hired by Khadijah, the female owner of the most profitable caravan business in all of Mecca. At the age of 40, Khadijah had ignored the advances of many would-be suitors, instead focusing on furthering her father's business and compassionately offering assistance to the needy in her community. However, in the year 595, impressed by the character of Muhammad, Khadijah proposed marriage, and, although she was fifteen years his elder, they wed and their 25 year marriage played a critical role in the early years of the Islamic faith.

Frustrated by the continual squabbling amongst the tribes and the faltering morality of the world around him, in the year 610, during the feasting month of Ramadan, Muhammad retreated to the nearby mountains and meditated in one of the caves. Muslims believe that one night, while deep in meditation, Muhammad was startled by a voice that demanded, "Proclaim!" Not knowing what to make of this command, confused and bewildered, Muhammad returned to his wife. Although Khadijah believed the message came from the "one and only god," Muhammad spent the next three years travelling the deserts seeking truth for himself. But the messages from Gabriel, the one true god's messenger, stopped coming.

However, after three years, Gabriel reappeared and from this moment, the words of Allah flowed through Muhammad, who recorded this Message in the Quran. Muhammad shared that faith in Allah was the only path to Paradise. All other pagan gods were lies. Khadijah became the first convert to this new faith, and gradually Muhammad's family likewise began accepting this message. Many were drawn to this new faith's promise of Paradise; others embraced the strict behavioral expectations that scorned the gluttonous habits of the rising merchant classes. With these messages of hope and order, coupled with Muhammad's gifted oratorical skills he had perfected through decades of storytelling while on the caravan routes across Arabia, this new faith of Islam ("submission") increasingly became a threat to the leaders of Mecca.

In 620, the angel Gabriel again visited Muhammad, but this time he was given a winged creature that he flew to Jerusalem. There, he flew above the holy land, eventually transcending our human world, meeting the other prophets – Noah, Abraham, Moses and Jesus – and then finally speaking with God. It was at this point that Muhammad truly realized he was God's messenger.

At first, the Umayyad leaders of Mecca tolerated what they perceived as merely the ramblings of a lone man; but when Muhammad claimed he was a prophet and started degrading the pagan faiths of the vast majority of the Meccan pilgrims, the town elders realized this man and his constant criticism of other faiths were becoming bad for business. The Umayyad family had created a successful little trading hub, but if word started to spread that all faiths were no longer tolerated and protected, traders and religious wanderers might head elsewhere. These elders agreed that one night they would enter Muhammad's home and each of them would stab him, dispersing blame amongst the whole group. Yet, when they entered his home to do the deed, Muhammad had already escaped and was miles up the road, on his way to his new home – Yathrib.

This escape in the night is known as "the Flight of Muhammad," and it was this journey in 622 where the Kingdom of Islam was born.

Upon arriving in Yathrib, an oasis town fraught with its own conflicts between the rival Jewish clans and pagan merchants, dozens of villagers came to Muhammad (whose message and challenge to the Umayyad leaders had gained him a fair bit of regional notoriety), offering their homes. Muhammad declined, instead choosing his faithful camel, Qaswa, to decide where to settle. After wandering through town, the camel eventually came to rest, and this was where Muhammad decided to build his home and the first mosque to Allah. Yathrib was renamed Medina ("the home of the prophet"). Muhammad then stepped in and settled conflicts between the city's clans. From here, he gained more converts and began financing and building the army he knew he would one day need to fight his assassins back in Mecca.

Muhammad's method of gaining money wasn't exactly noble. His forces stopped all the pagan caravans trying to enter Mecca and relieved them of their wealth. This form of desert piracy was common in the day, and was essential to secure the resources needed to conquer Mecca. Within a few years, Muhammad had gone from being a successful merchant to a prophet, a politician, a trusted judge and a feared military leader. Compare these years to those of the founders of the other dominant faiths of the world, and you can see why historians recognize Muhammad as the most influential man in the history of the civilizations. Can you imagine seeing pacifists Buddha or Jesus heading an army into battle? Blasphemy! Yet for Muhammad, he was never just a religious leader. In his world of tribal conflicts and continual strife, creating a formidable military force was the only way he could ensure the spread of his faith.

This formidable force finally met the forces of Mecca at the Battle of Badr. With the religious devotion of his followers and his keen military strategy, Muhammad easily defeated the soldiers of Mecca. When his men descended to carve up those who had surrendered, Muhammad stepped in and demonstrated one reason why his faith would continue to grow in subsequent decades. He stopped their swords, claiming our enemies today will be our brothers in faith tomorrow. His practical benevolence and his persuasive message continued to attract adherents and in 630 CE, with over 10,000 armed zealots in support, Muhammad entered Mecca and destroyed the idols of Kaaba, declaring once and for all that only one god – Allah – would be allowed within the city's borders. Muhammad's reign over Mecca proved short-lived. He died less than two years later.

But the imposing allure of Islam would not cease with his passing. Within a hundred years of his death, the army of Islam had created an empire stretching further than any yet known to man, stretching from the Indian subcontinent to northern Africa to Western Europe to the borders of Byzantium. What took the Persian and Roman empires centuries to accomplish, the Muslims conquered in decades.

Why so fast? Was it because no other formidable foe stood in their way? Who could stop any organized military in the region? The Byzantines? The Persians? The barbarians of Europe secluded in their fiefdoms? No, no and no. As the Arab raids of nonbeliever caravans continued deeper into foreign lands, they had to start wondering, "Ummm...does anyone ever plan on stopping us?" But as each excursion went unpunished, the armies grew larger and bolder. Some conquered peoples converted to Islam, simply for the opportunity to partake in the plunder. Other regions actually welcomed the Arabs, as their rule promised more tolerance and cheaper taxes than their previous sovereign. Why would the Egyptians want to serve the Byzantines when they could bow to the Muslims for half the cost? Some historians argue most conversions to Islam came under threat of the sword, but this makes little sense as in the early decades, Arabs maintained a policy of actually discouraging conversion for they only taxed those outside their faith. Another economic incentive was that the Arab merchants became the only trading game in town. Similar to today's world where it behooves any would-be entrepreneur to speak English or Chinese, in the 7th and 8th century, Arabic was the link to commercial expansion. If you wanted to buy the goods coming from the East, you better speak Arabic, and it would definitely help your cause if you believed in Islam. Yet others gravitated to this new faith because of its tenets of order and personal sacrifice. These selfless ideals made so much sense in a fragmented world where violence and disorder ruled the day.

Societies in disorder need rules. People crave order. Thus Jews have the Ten Commandments. Buddhists believe in the

Eightfold Path. And Muslims follow the Five Pillars. The pillars are the non-negotiables of the Islamic faith.

First, all Muslims must praise Allah as the one and only God and trust Muhammad as his final messenger.

Second, they must pray five times a day. Originally these prayers were directed towards Jerusalem, but in 624 Muhammad declared Muslims would return to the roots of their faith, to the days of Abraham, and pray toward the building thought to have been once constructed by Abraham himself – the Kaaba. If ever you travel to a Muslim nation, you will see an arrow pointing to Mecca on the ceilings of all hotels. Most offices and buildings have also designated specific areas for their employees to recite their prayers.

Third, Muslims must make a charitable contribution (2.5% of their income). If a Muslim family doesn't have enough money, they can always pay with good deeds.

Fourth, to remind them of their reliance on Allah and make amends for past transgressions, Muslims must fast from dawn till dusk during the month of Ramadan.

And fifth, at some point in their life, Muslims must make the hajj, the holy pilgrimage to Mecca. Some might believe this final requirement isn't exactly fair in the 21st century. Requiring a trip to Arabia was one thing when the empire existed exclusively in the Middle East, but now that the religion spans six continents, it's a lot more difficult to travel across the globe to Mecca. One might think, fewer and fewer are able to make the sacred pilgrimage. But that has not been the case. Every year travel agents and tour companies arrange these pilgrimages for faithful from every corner, with over 2.5 million people annually reaching Mecca.

Aside from these pillars, Muslims also believe they should keep their bodies pure, avoiding alcohol or any other stimulants. They also believe that once you hit adolescence your every action is recorded, to be used on Judgment Day to decide how you will spend your eternity.

However, since 9/11, the two traits of Islam that have come under greatest scrutiny are the notions of jihad and burka worn by Muslim women. People wonder if jihad condones, if not encourages, the murder of non-Muslims, and people likewise wonder about the gender equality of a society that prevents women from showing their faces. The term jihad means 'struggle" and it has a ton of interpretations. It can mean the struggle to maintain your faith in a secular world, or the struggle to remain pure or the struggle against enemies. So yes, for some, a jihad could be a life or death struggle against the evil West culminating in the justification for mass murder, but for 99.34% of Muslims, they have a slightly different definition. As for the burka covering worn by women, the Quran does state that women should "extend their headcoverings...to not display their beauty except to their husbands [or other members of their family]." Yet, wearing conservative clothing was quite common to women of the Arabian peninsula long before the Quran, and, when you consider the long robes worn by Bedouin men, maybe the origin of the tradition of covering up says more about the harsh climate than it does about religious practice.

Across this harsh climate, the Arabic Muslim Empire spread relatively unstopped throughout the 7th century. By 635, just three years after Muhammad's death, Damascus fell to the Muslims, and one year later it was Jerusalem's turn. But the kingdom of Islam – Dar al Islam – would eventually be slowed, and in some cases defeated, and the first threat came from within.

One of the gaps in the Western understanding of Islam is the faulty belief that Muslims are a unified people, each condoning the actions of others. In reality, Islam is a severed faith. Like the Great Schism that separated the Church into Catholicism and Orthodoxy, and the later Protestant Reformation that threw Europe into centuries of religious conflict, the Muslims are too a divided people. Though many sects exist, the main division is between two groups – the Shiite and the Sunni – and their conflict stretches all the way back to the death of Muhammad. At that time, nobody knew who would take over his mantle as supreme caliph. It's hard to replace a prophet.

Although Muhammad married eleven women, when he died in 632, no clear successor existed. The most logical choice, Muhammad's cousin Ali was still too young. To make matters worse, the Umayyad family (remember that group of men that once tried to have Muhammad assassinated) claimed they were the most likely heirs. For two years after Muhammad's death, his trusted advisor Abu Bakr stepped in, but when Abu Bakr died, the ascension of power issue resurfaced. When Ali came of age, he ruled as caliph during a five-year civil war over the throne, but he was assassinated while prostrate in prayer. His assassination signaled that a peaceful reconciliation would never be possible, and for the next 1500 years, these two sides have competed to be the accepted spiritual leaders of Islam. On one side were the Shi'a who believed only the descendants of Muhammad could be caliph, and on the other side were the Sunni who believed the most qualified candidate should be chosen. Basically it was Ali and his followers versus the Umayyad and their followers (just remember Shi'a has an "a" for Ali, and Sunni has a "u" for Umayyad). To this day the conflict continues with 85% of the world siding with the Sunni faith and about 13% being Shi'a. In 661, the Umayyad Sunnis took power from Ali, founding the Umayyad Caliphate. In a prudent move to prevent an inevitable reciprocal assassination attempt, Umayyad leaders relocated the capital of Islam to Damascus.

The Umayyad family ruled for centuries out of Damascus until another rival to the throne emerged – the Abbasid family. Disgusted by the opulence of the Umayyad Caliphate in Damascus (and wanting a little more of the riches for themselves), the Abbasid family created a rival army. After their army defeated the Umayyad forces, the Abbasid family returned the center of Islam to the site of where civilization began, along the banks of the Tigris and Euphrates River, to Mesopotamia, to Baghdad.

Needing to assure themselves a peaceful reign, the Abbasids invited the Umayyad family to a "reconciliatory" dinner. But, instead of exchanging handshakes and singing campfire bonding songs, the royal guards wrapped the Umayyad family in carpets and then proceeded to spear the heck out of them. Only one Umayyad survived, Abdar Rahman I, the grandson of the former caliph. He fled across Africa and started a western Islamic capital in the region today called Spain, ruling what would become the most glorious city in all of Europe – Cordoba.

But it was back in Baghdad where the Islamic Empire reached its Golden Age. Yep, you read that correctly. The Golden Age of Baghdad. With the images that have come out of Baghdad due to the recent Iraqi War, many might have trouble envisioning Baghdad as a center of anything more than a violent hole of chaos. But again, you must put away your 21st century goggles and realize that for 200 years under the Abbasid Caliphate, Baghdad was the center of the world.

If you were a scholar, an inventor or a thinker living anytime between the 9th and 12th century, you wanted to be in Baghdad. Whether a Jew or a Christian, a Frank or a Mandarin, a member of the merchant class or a religious traveller, you were welcome in Baghdad. The Abbasid leaders realized quite quickly the scope of knowledge found across their commercial realm.

Their trading of goods and faith connected the world's first truly global empire. Once they saw all that their kingdom generated, they desired to bring all of this learning into one place. It was useless having the world's knowledge remaining unheard and unread in the desolate corners of their empire. Messengers brought back from the furthest corner every piece of learning ever produced. Each of these master works was then translated at the House of Wisdom into Arabic and permanently recorded. The Arab scholars perfected the great papermaking strategies of the Chinese, publishing more books than ever before. While a cultured monastery in Europe might have had three to five volumes on parchment, and the Mandarins in China might have recorded the sum of all Eastern knowledge, on the streets of Baghdad you could find dozens of bookshops selling thousands of bound books outlining everything from Aristotle's theories to the witticisms of Confucius. If not for these Muslims, the Classical learning of Greece and Rome would have been lost to the dust pile for all eternity, and the genius of the Middle Kingdom would have never made it west to Europe.

During this Islamic Golden Age, not only were ideas brought to one place and then translated for other regions to later discover, Baghdad fostered a culture of science and inquiry, advancing human knowledge to a whole new level. These Muslim scholars tossed out hundreds of advancements that are still prominent parts of our lives today.

They brought us the science of ophthalmology. Muslim doctors loved the human eye. They loved the physiology of it and they loved to dissect it. They produced theories as to how we actually see (images are actually flipped upside down and then interpreted by the optic nerve), and they even found ways to dig into the eyeball and remove cataracts.

They showed us that science and religion can work together in harmony. Yep, it was these first Muslim scholars who found no problem believing in one god while also questioning the secular and natural worlds.

They furthered our knowledge of astronomy. Muslim scientists looked to the skies and proposed theories for moon cycles, the rotation of the Earth on an axis, and also the theory that we revolve around the sun.

They established the notion of Medical Peer Review. Sometimes on the TV shows *House*, *Grey's Anatomy*, *E.R.* or even

Scrubs, the doctors all come together and have to explain why they inadvertently killed someone. The Muslims were the first to employ this type of review. They could even sue doctors for malpractice.

They dabbled in Algebra, Trigonometry, Calculus, Geometry and the Arabic number system. Though they picked up most of these ideas from the Gupta Indians, if they'd never accumulated and advanced these theorems, Europeans might be still making tally marks in the dirt or counting with that annoying MCMLXXIII method the Romans found so useful. But alas, we have the Arabic numeral system 1,2,3,4,5,6,7,8 and 9 to make counting just a bit easier.

They perfected Arabesque Art. Because Muhammad and his followers outlawed the heretical depiction of humans or animals on religious buildings, a new type of art flourished using calligraphy and intricate geometric shapes No, they didn't put together a pentagon, a triangle and a circle and call it art, but instead they manipulated the most complex patterns to decorate ceilings, walls and columns (think kaleidoscope). It's hard to explain. Just do a Google search for Arabesque art. You'll be impressed. Trust me.

And then they brought us household stuff that just makes life a lot more fun. They dabbled in chemistry, bringing us such lovely items as shampoo, bar soap, toothpaste and even that little brown cup of morning glory – coffee.

These monumental inventions (yes, I'm including soap) eventually fell into the hands of the Europeans in the twelfth century, helping inspire the region out of its Dark Ages. But before we get ahead of ourselves and start praising these Muslims as the most wonderful beings ever assembled, you must also realize they introduced the wholesale slave trade of Africans up and down the east coast of the continent, they gradually reduced the rights of women, they destroyed many local customs with their wars of conquest and they also fought in some of the most brutal military campaigns ever.

Yet, their ascent to the pantheon of world's greatest empires wasn't without roadblocks. When they attempted to conquer all of Western Europe, they were put down by Charles "the Hammer" Martel who united all the tribes of the French countryside. Their future was forever taken off course when they mounted a two hundred year campaign to capture and maintain the holy land (Jerusalem) for Muslims. These wars marked the beginning of a millennium of conflict between Christians, Jews and Muslims that continues to mark the Levant (Middle East) as the most unstable region in the world today. These wars were known as the Crusades.

But that is for another chapter.

15

Crusade for the Kingdom of Heaven

The Crusades – 1000 > 1300

What happens when the two largest religions in the world, the two religions that both preach the supremacy of their one God, the two religions that both claim dibs on the souls of all would-be converts...what happens when these two religions share the same holy land? And what then happens if the world's longest lasting religion also wants a piece of that prized property?

What happens? Perpetual conflict. Ceaseless violence. Regional instability. Worldwide concern. Justification for jihad. The fear of another Crusade.

Muslims believe Jerusalem was where Muhammad ascended into the heavens. Christians believe Jerusalem was where Jesus Christ was crucified. And Jews believe Jerusalem was promised to them by God.

Three religions. Three claims. All valid. All worth fighting for. All worth dying for.

Although the current Israeli-Palestinian conflict over the Holy Land stems more from the fallout after the post-World War II creation of Israel, the true roots of violence span back a thousand years, to 1095, to the year that started two hundred years of conflict – an era that has come to be known as "The Crusades."

In 638, the Arab Muslims took over Jerusalem and held it relatively unchallenged for three centuries. They opened the holy city to Jews and Christians, protecting all pilgrims and allowing them to worship their own personal God. Now remember, the Muslims didn't merely allow others to worship other deities because they were tolerant; they had a more pragmatic reason. As non-believers in Islam, Jews and Christians paid taxes. It behooved the first Arab conquerors to allow this freedom of religion.

By the year 1000 however, the Arab empire had started to change. Although initially united by language and faith, and continuing to accomplish artistic and scientific feats from the grand cities of Cordoba and Baghdad, the followers of Islam could never abandon their clan loyalties. The Muslim world of 1000 was anything but a united empire, more a series of independent city-states, all competing to expand their influence.

One rival Muslim clan, the Seljuk Turks, came in from the steppe (like the Huns before and the Mongols later) and overthrew the settled Muslim clans of the Levant. These new warrior Muslims took over Jerusalem and then pushed up to the gates of Byzantium. In 1095, threatened by this incursion and incensed by their own diminishing territorial claims, Emperor Alexius I of Constantinople sent out a distress call to his brother in faith – Pope Urban II in Rome. He asked for 400 of Europe's greatest knights to help fend off the Turk advance.

Pope Urban II was more than willing to oblige. He went to France, stood before tens of thousands of amped up adherents and waxed a bit hyperbolic, describing how the Turks had slaughtered innocent Christian pilgrims and unless an army of the faithful avenged this slight, these same ruthless infidels of Islam would one day challenge the very survival of the Church. Within a few months, this impassioned plea led to the mobilization of tens of thousands of Crusaders ("crux" being Latin for "cross") who headed southeast to reclaim the holy land.

But why were these Christians so willing to answer the call? Why now? The Muslims had controlled Jerusalem for over four centuries, yet Christian Europe had never been bothered enough to send down "Cross"aders before 1095. So why now? Why were they so impassioned in 1095, so willing to leave behind the only world they had ever known for a deadly land thousands of miles away? For some, it actually was the fervent belief that they fought on the side of unquestioned good versus the side of ultimate evil.

But like all other wars before and hence, the actual reasons for fighting were sometimes just a bit less altruistic.

Men left for wealth, which in the 11th century meant, men left for land. But there was less and less land to pass out. Farming techniques meant people lived longer, which meant there were more people, but the European continent wasn't getting any bigger. Plus, because of the system of primogeniture, where only the eldest son inherited his father's land, Europe had no land left for younger sons. These sons were hungry and impatient, and they would take land anywhere they could find it...and the Levant looked like as good a place as any.

Men left for power. A peasant might actually feel like man for the first time in his life and an ambitious lord might gain a few more titles. Even Pope Urban II, a man in a position one might hope was above such hedonistic desires, wanted to increase his power over the continent. As regional kings and lords were increasingly stealing loyalty from the Church, Pope Urban II saw his orchestration of a Christian victory in Jerusalem as his ticket back into the hearts, souls and minds of the faithful.

Men left for adventure. Men have always fought wars as a chance to take a break from the boredom of life. The Crusades were no different.

Some men left because they were worried about their options in the afterlife. Europe was a violent place and since the Vikings petered out in the late tenth century, there were no more bad guys to fight, so knights and lords started fighting each other. They had a lot of blood on their swords and because that pesky little Sixth Commandment stated, "Thou Shalt Not Kill" many saw the bulk of their afterlife spent in purgatory, or worse yet, the fiery fields of hell. Pope Urban II's Crusade offered yet another "Get Out of Hell Free" card (conveniently reinterpreting that inconvenient commandment). The Pope explained how God didn't mean you couldn't kill anyone; he just meant you couldn't kill *Christians*. God actually wanted you to kill infidels. Tens of thousands jumped at this opportunity to satisfy their bloodlust while saving their soul, so not only did Pope Urban assemble God's army, he also simultaneously ridded Europe of those uber-testosteroned chaps who had been laying waste to the churches and the countryside for decades.

Men left to help out their eastern brothers, the Orthodox Church, in a hope that one day the Church might reunite. A few decades earlier in 1054, the Church had split into the Catholic and Orthodox churches, and both Emperor Alexius I and Pope Urban II realized the best way to get over past differences was to find a common enemy, and the Seljuk Turks matched the job description quite impressively.

Some men left not even knowing how to fight, let alone who actually they should were supposed to kill or how they were going to survive along the way. And a ton of men left before they could even figure out these three fairly crucial questions. While the knights and lords prepared for what could be years away from home, a mob of peasants just started off to the Holy Land. Unfortunately, these "soldiers" were clueless and instead of practicing the art of patience, they confronted their ignorance by just attacking anyone who didn't speak their tongue...which turned out to be everyone. Across Eastern Europe, they slaughtered Jews, fellow Christians, innocent farmers, dark-skinned people, light-skinned people, fellow Crusaders - anyone they happened to bump into.

And when this mass of thousands finally bumbled their way to the walls of Constantinople, Emperor Alexius was less than pleased. He had asked for a few hundred super knights. He got thousands of wild, starving refugees. The Emperor kept his gates closed. He had no interest in this mob of pathetic vagrants. He ignored their pleas for food and shelter, forcing them to continue down to Jerusalem. Once past Constantinople, their fate was sealed. Their religious zeal and was quite adorable, but because these peasants really weren't trained fighters, the Turks had little trouble dispatching this mob in a few weeks.

However, this Peasant's Crusade was soon replaced by a more organized wave of soldiers – this one led by the dukes Godfrey, Bohemond and Baldwin. Over in Constantinople, Emperor Alexius looked for other solutions to his Turk problem, signing side deals with Muslims to expand his holdings and keep the peace. The three dukes were then on their own, so they pushed on down the Levant, taking over the walled cities of Nicea, Etessa and Antioch and then eventually the town of Marat al Numin.

In taking these strongholds, a few unpleasant realities slowly emerged. First, these Crusaders cared little for the Christian cause. In Nicea, Etessa and Antioch, Christians actually lived inside the walls, but they were not spared once the walls were breached. The goal was not faith. The goal was expanding power and wealth of the nobles. But ironically, even though the Crusaders started caring less and less about the faithful followers, they started caring more and more about faithful objects, or relics. Relics were any artifacts connected to Jesus Christ, his mother Mary or any one of the saints. In one case, in a town called Antioch, after priest Peter Bartholomew allegedly experienced a vision of God, he walked into a nearby church, dug into the ground and pulled out a rusty piece of metal, for which he claimed, "This is the spear that killed Christ!" He then took his incredibly fortuitous find and rallied the Christian troops. From here, tons of Crusaders made their own "finds," thousands of which returned to Europe and were worshipped for centuries to come (including such lovely little treasures as the straw from Jesus's manger and vials of milk from the Virgin Mary).

Third, the Crusaders started scaring the heck out of Muslims. They didn't just kill, they killed everything in sight. Like the most successful armies of antiquity, the Crusaders realized the power of terror. When in doubt, don't just kill men. Kill women and then kill their children. If sedentary villagers believed a horde of savages was on the rampage, they were more apt to surrender when this force comes a knocking. A group of Crusaders upped the terror quotient a few notches with their behavior at the town of Marat al Numin. After killing every one of the 25,000 men, women...and yes...children (some by burning alive, others by varying methods of swordplay), they camped out, waiting impatiently for their chance at the big daddy of booty – Jerusalem. But while there, they engaged in some behavior which would be told across the Muslim world for centuries. These crusaders started ripping apart the bodies of the dead and boiled the corpses for dinner. They put parts of children on spits and sizzled their flesh over the fire. They then devoured the bodies of the dead. This horrific story of cannibalism, though perpetuated by only a small number of Crusaders, terrified the remaining Muslim towns and only intensified the disdain for the Crusading barbarians.

Needing to avoid any further atrocities, Godfrey, Bohemond and Baldwin set out for Jerusalem. Getting into Jerusalem would be far harder than the sieges of Antioch, Etessa and Nicea. For Jerusalem stood shielded behind walls fifty feet high and ten feet thick, and the citizens of Jerusalem had cut down all the possible trees in the region to prevent the Crusaders from building siege engines. However, after days of scouring the countryside, the Christians finally found the cut tree trunks buried in a deep gully, and proceeded to build a bunch of siege engines. They then threw everything at Jerusalem and after breaching their walls, they entered the city and massacred every Jewish and Muslim man, woman (and of course, child) they encountered. One Crusader even boastingly wrote back home "there was such a slaughter that our men were up to their ankles in the enemy's blood."

Jerusalem had been sacked. After four centuries of Muslim rule, Jerusalem returned to the hands of Christians, and the Muslim world proved impotent to mount any revenge. The Muslims had been fighting amongst themselves for so many years, the idea of uniting for any purpose seemed a fool's errand. Yet with their holy city in the hands of the barbarians and with their fellow Muslims dead at the hands of the infidel, they ended up having exactly the motivation needed to exact their revenge, but it would take time.

In the decades following the attack on Jerusalem, the city flourished. While only about four hundred knights remained, Christian Europe quickly began sending down pilgrims to both visit the holy city, but also settle in the region to create a formidable Christian presence. These Christians ended up recreating feudal Europe in the region – building castles and dividing kingdoms amongst the victors. Two groups of warrior monks emerged, dedicated to protecting Christianity in the Levant - Knights Hospitallers and the Knights Templar. These Knights Templar have since popped up a ton in 20th century pop culture – they became the protectors of the cup of Christ in the *Indiana Jones* films, they became the protectors of a dirty little secret in *The DaVinci Code*, and they even inspired George Lucas when he hatched up his whole Jedi idea. But in the 12th century, they were protectors of a little pocket of Christianity amidst a region of Islam.

While the Christians furthered their colonization of the Levant, in the Muslim world a leader emerged – Saladin. Saladin started as the promising general of Nur ad Din, the newly crowned Muslim King of Damascus who had defeated Christians in the Second Crusade. Nur ad Din knew that if he could conquer Egypt, he could unite the Muslim world and surround Jerusalem from all sides. From there, he could once and for all eliminate the Christian presence in Jerusalem. Saladin had different ideas. He conquered Egypt, but he had no plans on sharing the jewel with his boss. When Nur ad Din died soon after, Saladin pushed to take the throne from the twelve-year-old heir – al Sali. Trying to protect himself, adolescent al Sali hired the regions #1 hitmen, men known as Hashashins, men who flew into fits of violence after getting high on hashish (marijuana). These elite killers, these "assassins," made two attempts on Saladin's life, neither succeeding. Saladin lived, but he soon made sure Al Sali died. Syria and Egypt finally again were under the control of one Muslim – Saladin, and the Muslim world had their own soldier of faith.

Saladin struck out for the Holy Land, luring the defenders of Jerusalem into a battle on his own terms – the Battle of Hattin in 1187. After coaxing the Crusaders into a desolate area, void of any water or sustenance, Saladin attacked, crushing the Crusader forces, and capturing the two new Christian leaders – King Guy and Renault de Chantillon. Whereas Saladin spared the king, he promptly cut off the head of Renault, a man he cursed for attacking innocent Muslim traders on caravans from Cairo. After this unmistakable defeat, taking Jerusalem became a mere afterthought. The Christians inside eventually cut a deal with Saladin for their freedom, and after nearly one hundred years of Christian rule, the Muslims again controlled Jerusalem, a role they would not again relinquish until World War I.

But the Europeans didn't know they'd never win again, so they decided to launch a Third Crusade. Who did they turn to this time? They went to the most powerful man in Europe - the Holy Roman Emperor. The ruler of what we today know as Germany, Emperor Frederick amassed an army of 100,000 Christians all bent on reclaiming Jerusalem. Frederick set off to Jerusalem with one of the greatest European forces ever assembled, hoping to once and for all defeat the Muslim invaders who had stolen Christ's home. Only one problem. He drowned crossing a river, and most of his troops simply deserted and returned home, which meant a new leader would have to take the reins of the Third Crusade.

This impossible task went to Richard I of England, known to Robin Hood fans as Richard the Lionheart. Unlike his predecessors who chose the painfully lengthy overland trail, King Richard sailed his army across the Mediterranean and joined King Guy (who Saladin had recently released from prison) in first laying siege to the coastal town of Acre. In the Middle Ages, if you stormed a city's walls, all the wealth of the town was yours for the taking. Plus, you could use this new city as a launching pad for your attacks on nearby areas, expanding your realm. Richard believed that from Acre, he could then easily attack Jerusalem. But first he had to get through Acre's walls. He tried the age-old method of building a huge siege tower and then hopping over, but the Muslims responded with their own technological secrets – a dangerous flammable cocktail known as Greek Fire. Used centuries before by the Byzantine Empire to push back the Muslims, Greek Fire was a tar-like mixture that could stick to any object and was nearly impossible to extinguish. The Muslims launched these fireballs at Richard's wooden toys and they were incinerated within minutes. Richard then tried option B. His soldiers took apart the wall, one stone at a time. He bribed each of his soldiers, promising gold coins for each rock removed. Although this plan wouldn't go down as the most ingenious military strategy of all time, it worked pretty well, eventually weakening the foundation of Acre's walls enough that they fell without needing the more typical siege tricks.

Richard then added to the not so glowing reputation of the Crusaders by promptly murdering three thousand Muslim prisoners of war when Saladin refused to pay a ransom for their liberation. Richard's forces looked prime to pierce the walls of Jerusalem.

But then he stopped. He could have made his run for Jerusalem, but he decided to stay in Acre, fortify the city and wait for reinforcements. They never came, and Richard spent another year in a back and forth power play with Saladin for control of the region. Eventually they both backed down. Saladin promised Christians safe passage on their pilgrimages to Jerusalem and the Crusaders could keep the coastal towns they'd conquered. In exchange, Richard would leave. The truce was set and the Third Crusade came to an end.

This would not be the end of the Crusades, but they would never again reach the religious fervor of the First Crusade, nor were they ever again a credible threat. There was the Fourth Crusade that got a bit sidetracked, and Italians ended up attacking and conquering Constantinople. There was the Fifth Crusade that tried and failed to capture Egypt. There was the Sixth Crusade that was more of a treaty than a war, with the Muslims temporarily surrendering Jerusalem for ten years to avoid bloodshed. Then there was the Seventh, Eighth and Ninth Crusades, one of which ended with 30,000 child soldiers being sold into the slavery. But with the Ninth Crusade, Christendom finally got the hint that Jerusalem was not going to fall, and in 1272 after nearly two centuries of warfare for the Levant, the Crusades came to an end.

However, the legacy of the Crusades impacted the region and world affairs for years to come. Europeans were shocked out of their stagnation. Their contact with the Muslims reinvigorated trade with the East, but also started the process of bringing back to Europe all the lost texts of the Classical Era of Greece and Rome. Europeans also inherited a wanderlust that eventually spawned the Age of Exploration, helping end feudalism. Feudalism also started to fade, as property started changing hands. Europe had figured out its lack of land problem. Some lords sold lands before they had left, some lords died. Serfs started buying property and the fixed land ownership patterns of the previous decade started to shift.

And for the Muslims, this marked the end of their reign as the most cosmopolitan, accepting, innovative culture on the planet. Disgusted and traumatized by the Christian barbarian incursion into the region, Muslims turned inward, dedicated to protecting their society from outsiders. Instead of welcoming the ideas of others, they rejected any contribution from neighboring peoples, and began what would be their own era of stagnation. The West was the barbaric enemy to the north. They offered nothing of value.

Although it would be the Europeans who would end up on the short end of the won-loss record in the Crusades match of civilizations, in the long run, it would be the Europeans who would progress to unimagined heights, as they would never again allow themselves to regress into the Dark Ages of their past.

But that is for another chapter.

16

The Final Strike from the Steppe

The Mongols – 1200 > 1400

By 1200, two empires stood atop the rest the world – the Muslim Empire of Eastern Persia and the Song Dynasty of China. Europe was still figuring out how to get out of the dark, Sub-Saharan Africa and Polynesia were merely the stuff of legends, and no one even knew the Americas existed (though a few hundred indigenous American tribes might disagree).

The flowering cultures of Islam and China far surpassed any other civilization of the time, and nobody appeared anywhere close to knocking them off their perches. Nobody that is, but the latest band of warriors from the steppe.

Over the previous thousand years, anytime it appeared a civilization was settling into regional dominance, the nomadic horse people from Central Asia stormed out of the wasteland and turned the civilized world into chaos. The Huns did it to the Romans, the Turks did it to the Arabs and in the 13th century, the Mongols would do it to the Persians and Chinese, but this time, these horse people would adapt and learn how to not merely conquer, but to rule. By the end of the century, they had created the largest land empire the world would ever see, stretching all the way from Korea to Germany to the edge of Egypt.

Yet in 1200, the Mongols didn't appear capable of conquering anybody. Like generations of horse people surviving the steppe, the Mongols existed in perpetual conflict with the other nomads of the region. Whether it was other Mongols or the Tatars or the Turks, these regional turf wars kept these warriors from ever being anything more than a mere border nuisance. One man changed all that and turned the warrior spirit of the steppe against the outside world, forever altering Eurasia. His name – Genghis Khan.

Genghis Khan was born Temujin – "the iron worker" – to a semi-prominent family of Mongols. His existence mirrored that of the hundreds of other clans enduring the harsh geography of the region. With temperatures sometimes hitting negative 80 degrees, with sparse water and with little to no vegetation, the Mongols were always on the move. They lived in felt tents that could be set up and taken down in less than fifteen minutes. They kept themselves warm by burning the fecal matter of their horses. They learned to ride horses and shoot arrows by the age of three. And they fought. The men were tough. The women were tough. The children were tough. If you weren't strong, you died.

In the case of Temujin's father, you died anyway. After the rival Tatars poisoned his father Yesukhei, Temujin and his mother were left alone as outcasts, fated to merely perish in isolation. But Temujin would not perish. Instead, he would make it his life's work to exact revenge on all who dared slight him or his family. By the time he was thirty years old, through his charisma and military prowess, he had reunited the clans, and he set to destroy the murderers of his father. His treatment of the rival Tatars would eventually mirror the fate of countless other peoples across Eurasia. He first beat the men in battle, he then destroyed the entire society – killing anyone taller than an axle wheel (basically anyone older than a toddler). These surviving kids were then incorporated into Mongol society, and the Tatar people vanished into history.

In 1206, the Mongols anointed Temujin their khan, their universal leader. This man, Genghis Khan, then set his sights on the Song Dynasty of China, the largest purse in Asia. For decades China had supported the Tatars, believing that as long as the barbarians to the west fought each other, China remained safe. Genghis Khan vowed to destroy China and make it his own, and by the first decade of the new century, he had created the most formidable war machine in human history.

The Mongols dominated all others through a combination of psychological warfare, non-traditional battle tactics and unquestioned loyalty to Genghis Khan. The Mongols, like the Huns centuries before, were masters of terror. If they could take a town without a fight, they would. They always gave cities a choice – surrender and become a taxed province of the Mongol kingdom, or fight and face a horrific death. Usually, the first few towns would fight. As the stories of horror spread, the next few towns rarely raised arms. The Mongols did not blink at killing every man, woman and child. They slaughtered all the animals, every kitty cat and puppy dog. They used the bodies of prisoners to help them ford streams. They piled the heads of their vanquished in a pile and smoked them. They were said to move so rapidly because they had to escape the rotting odor of the carcasses they left behind. Eventually, everybody in their right minds just raised the white flag and joined the Mongol Empire.

However, there were some not in their right mind who chose to fight. They soon died. The Mongols were extremely adaptable to the weather and to their opponents, leaving any enemy unable to predict their battle tactics. They had no problem splitting their forces into smaller groups. They attacked supply lines. They fought at night. They didn't flinch from feigning a retreat, having their mounted soldiers run away in faked distress, only to be joined by a much larger force that then enveloped the enemy force. They absorbed the locals into their ranks, both as soldiers and as critical pieces of intelligence, able to reveal weak spots in their enemy as well as teach them how to utilize regional technology. In this manner, they eventually created their own gunpowder, siege engines and a navy. Their only goal was victory, and while the other civilized people remained slaves to the military strategies of their ancestors, the Mongols constantly reinvented themselves from being merely bands of adept cavalrymen to forgers of the greatest war machine ever assembled.

And don't forget Genghis Khan. He was a brilliant strategist and ruthless leader. Death awaited anyone who retreated or ignored his orders. He wisely circumvented clan loyalties by completely reorganizing Mongol society. Instead of answering to your family's patriarch, you answered to Genghis Khan. He divided his military into groups of 10, 100 and 1000 – like the modern day platoon, company and battalion.

Because of his organization, his willingness to adapt and his utilization of siege warfare, Genghis Khan won victories that put him deep into China, but just as he was about to meet the Song forces, he was called back to Mongolia to fend off a potential coup. He would have to put off his conquest of China for another day.

After easing tensions in Mongolia, he then pushed west. After his forces pushed into Russia, he turned his forces to the Silk Road, which controlled the seemingly endless supply of trade from China through India and into Europe. He first had to deal with the eastern Persian Empire – the Khwarezmian Empire. Genghis Khan sent an ambassador requesting surrender (a strategy that was usually met with a subsequent submission to the rule of the Mongols). Yet the leader of the Khwarezmian Empire just wouldn't play by the rules and surrender. When the Mongol envoy of 1000 camels, weighted down under tons of booty, entered the border town of Otrar, the governor immediately killed the ambassador and stole the goods. Being the patient, forgiving man Genghis Khan had become, he sent another envoy, asking for an apology and a return of the pilfered goods. To this second envoy, the governor again insulted the Khan by cutting off the ambassadors' beards in public and sending back the decapitated heads to the Mongol kingdom. The governor must not have gotten the memo about who he was dealing with, because Genghis Khan didn't send a third envoy. He declared war.

He attacked from the east, from the west and even spent months marching through the previously-impenetrable mountains to attack from the north. Genghis Khan used prisoners he had captured from across Khwarezmia as human shields and once inside the walls of the capital – Samarkand – he lined up every citizen, cut off each of their heads and made a ten foot high mountain of skulls as a warning of his resolve. It's fair to say that not too many governors ignored his envoys after this display.

Now controlling the Silk Road, a large swathe of Russia and the whole of central Asia, Genghis Khan turned back east to conquer his original nemesis – the Song Dynasty in China. However, along the way, he ironically died by falling off his horse, so he never saw his dream fulfilled.

But unlike many other newly established civilizations, the Mongol Empire did not die with the passing of Genghis Khan. It was divided into three kingdoms - the Golden Horde of Russia, the Great Khanate of Northern China and the Persian Ilkhanate. In this divided state, the Mongol Empire survived, though numerous suitors continued to vie for the title of Great Khan.

Two men stood out from the rest – Timur the Lame and Kubilai Khan. Timur the Lame earned his nickname after being struck in the leg as a child while attempting to steal some livestock, leading to a limp that followed him the rest of his life. Like Genghis Khan, Timur also unleashed a lifetime of slaughter on surrounding peoples. Timur took the Mongol forces south, into India, massacring all who stood in his way. When the locals resisted him in Delhi, Timur enacted a policy that followed him through history. He chopped off the heads of all he encountered and then chucked them into a bonfire. He also got in on the skull stacking competition and made a wall of almost a hundred thousand skulls after sacking the city of Aleppo. Unlike Genghis Khan, Timur desired a magnificent capital to demonstrate his authority. Before sacking each city, he would seize all engineers and artisans and return them to his capital city of Samarkand - an oasis of gardens and engineering splendor, the pride of the Mongol kingdom. Timur the Lame, also known as "Tamerlame" to Europeans, eventually died and had himself buried in a majestic mausoleum, which he dared anyone to touch. One story has survived the ages that before his death, Timur warned that he who entered his tomb would unleash a terror on his people worse than anything Timur could imagine. Whether or not this story is true, his tomb was not opened until 1941 by Soviet soldiers. Two months later, Hitler's forces entered Russia, and in the next four years, close to 30 million Russians perished. Maybe Timur was right after all. Maybe the Soviets should have just left his remains alone.

Then came a Mongol unlike any other – Kubilai Khan. He had the warrior ethos and willingness to employ terror like his grandfather, Genghis Khan, but he also had the enlightened wisdom of a ruler instilled in him by his mother and the Chinese tutors she hired for him. Mongol moms were tough. They rode the same horses as the men, they survived the same harsh elements as the men and they also oftentimes fought alongside the men. Genghis Khan's mom taught her little baby boy to make it his life's mission to exact revenge. Kubilai Khan's mom chose to make her little tike a more well-rounded man. Like King Phillip II who brought in Aristotle to tutor his son Alexander, Sorghaghtani (Kubilai Khan's mom) brought in Confucian scholars to tutor her son. These tutors taught Kubilai Khan the importance of order in the house, order in the government and order in the empire.

He would take this enlightened mindset to China, where after a twenty-year campaign through China, he finally defeated the Southern Song Dynasty at the Battle of Yamen in 1279. In this decisive naval battle, Kubilai Khan showcased his willingness to embrace the technologies of his opponent. Years earlier he had created a navy, and at the Battle of Yamen, Kubilai Khan launched his 50 ships against the 1000 ships of the boy emperor, Huaizong. Although on water, the Mongols had not forgotten their roots and employed a bit of martial trickery. On a few of their ships, they began playing festive music, making it appear that they were about to break from the action for a bit of a dining interlude. All the while, dozens of ships moved steadily closer to the Song forces, all with soldiers hidden under huge tarps to mask their numbers. When upon the Song ships, they rained down a barrage of arrows, and within hours, the Song forced surrendered and Emperor Huaizong jumped into the water and killed himself. The age of Chinese self-rule had ended and the age of foreign rule had begun.

In an attempt to placate the Chinese traditionalists, Kubilai Khan had years ago renamed his Chinese holdings the Yuan, and now with north and south China united, he shepherded in a new era of Mongol rule, one that would last almost a century – the Yuan Dynasty. His artisans and engineers completed the construction of the new capital city – Yuandadu (present day Beijing), and he began his reign over China, a reign that forced Kubilai Khan to continually find the balance between embracing the traditions of China while expanding the empire into a new age.

Kubilai Khan's imprint on Chinese history would only mark part of the vast influence the Mongols imprinted on the world order. Their two-century romp across Eurasia not only wiped cities off the map, it also fostered wholesale political and social change across Russia, Europe and the Muslim empires. In Russia, the defenseless peasants left their lands and voluntarily entered an existence of near-slavery with any lord that could offer them protection from the invading Mongols. Like the feudal structure to the west, this landed slavery destroyed any chance for social mobility. This serfdom lasted until the communist revolutions five hundred years later. Moscow expanded its influence during the Mongol reign, as the Mongols established this previously destroyed town as the center of tax collection, unwittingly contributing to their own demise, as it would be Moscow's forces in the late 15th century that would kick out the Mongol invaders.

For Europe, although the Mongol military machine only reached as far as Germany and the outskirts of Constantinople, the reopening of the Silk Road set the wheels of European change in motion. Though the Mongols forged their empires on campaigns of terror, they then used this same threat of terror to ensure an era of peace – the Pax Mongolica. Across the Silk Road, no one dared bother a merchant or a traveller crossing the whole of Asia, leading to the common belief that "a maiden bearing a nugget of gold on her head could wander safely throughout the realm." Because of this ensured safety and promising trade network, traders on both sides of the Silk Road grew quite wealthy, especially in Europe. The merchant families of Venice and Genoa used their profits to fund an artistic revolution (the Renaissance) in Southern Europe. The stories of Silk Road traveller Marco Polo launched an age of exploration where every nation fought to find a shortcut to Eastern riches. These open trade lines also unintentionally spread the Black Plague across the whole of Eurasia. Whether on the backs of Mongol livestock brought into new regions or on the rats brought into Europe on merchant ships, the bubonic plague became the first global pandemic and signaled the first example of a devastating bi-product of interaction between civilizations. The other devastation wrought by the Mongol expansion was their legacy of combat. European nations embraced the Mongol use of gunpowder, but combined it with their plentiful iron reserves to create the next level of military might. This European rise, coupled with the Mongol destruction of so many critical areas of Muslim rule, signaled the end of the reign of Dar al Islam. Like the Babylonians, the Egyptians, the Greeks and the Romans, the Golden Age of Islam would too come to an end, and to this day the Muslim kingdoms have yet to recapture the glory of their past.

And as for the East, the Mongols under Kubilai Khan forever altered two civilizations that previously had seen themselves as impenetrable – China and Japan.

But that is for another chapter.

17

The Dragon Never Sleeps

China - Tang to Song Dynasties – 600 > 1300

C hina is *the* anomaly. Civilizations are supposed to rise and fall and then never rise again. In Europe, Rome rose, dominated a continent and then faded into history. Europe has since splintered into 47 countries.

In India, the Mauryans and Guptas created a vibrant empire, only to see its people fall victim to a series of foreign invaders over the next thousand years.

In the Middle East, the Persians, the British, the Turks and the Arabs have all taken a shot at ruling the meeting point of three continents, but each failed to maintain control over the fractious area.

Across the Asian steppe, the Huns, then the Turks, then the Mongols took turns being the master horse people of the region. But Central Asia is anything but united today.

The history of the world has been the stories of how divided people come together for a brief moment under a central empire, only to eventually fade back into sectional rule. The reality is this: humans are too different, geography is too diverse and the needs of peoples vary too much to make any kind of central rule a lasting endeavor. Even the United States of America had to compromise, creating a government that gives authority to a central power, but also to individual states and then to local cities.

At any time, citizens of America are subject to federal, state and local laws. This has become the balance most nations have had to accept.

But China's different. China has had regional lords. China has been united under one central authority. However, unlike the rest of the world, China always rises again. No matter how evil a leader, no matter how far into chaos China sunk, the Chinese always believed the Mandate of Heaven controlled their fate. Through the depths of interregional strife, one ruling family would emerge, establish a dynasty and bring an era of peace. Inevitably, this ruling family would fade once corruption, external threats from nomads and natural disasters revealed the heavens had lost favor with the ruling family. A dynasty would die, regional lords would again spend generations vying for power, and then one would emerge triumphant, forging another dynasty, and the cycle would start all over again.

So no one should be surprised that China again threatens to emerge as the world's greatest economy. They've been there before, they will be there again. If history has taught us anything it's that you don't count out China. The 18th, 19th and 20th centuries were definitely steps backwards, but China has proven that a few century blip is relatively insignificant for a 5000-year-old civilization.

When the Han fell out of power in 200 AD, the resulting Three Kingdoms period decimated society, dropping the Chinese population in one century from 50 million to 20 million. Through the 3rd, 4th and 5th centuries, China survived its own middle ages, where barbarism, violence and the utter breakdown of social order were more the norm than the exception. Yet, it was only a matter of time before the ingenuity, tradition and staggering workforce of the Chinese was again harnessed, taking China to yet another golden age.

The dynasties of Sui (581-618), Tang (618-907) and Song (960-1279) reinstituted much of what had made China great, while also expanding its culture across Asia, reaping the material and philosophical benefits that would allow the civilization to become, in the words of Venetian merchant Marco Polo, "the best that is in the world."

China never could have grown unless they overcame two rather critical conundrums – they needed to make more food and they needed to move the food faster and further.

And what was the one food China could never get enough of? Rice. But rice doesn't naturally grow in Northern China. It's too dry and too cold. In fact, prior to the Sui (pronounced "sway") Dynasty, most of China actually ate wheat or millet (looks kind of like corn), but by the close of the Song Dynasty, rice had become the dominant food for all of China. The Chinese had learned how to use a wheelbarrow, how to make the most of animal poop for fertilizer and how to build dams, dikes and canals to best irrigate the land. However, none of these developments was as important as an import from Vietnam in the 7th century that allowed the Chinese to almost overnight double their rice production – Champa rice. As a gift from the Vietnamese to the Chinese, Champa rice is a stronger rice that can grow in cold weather and actually only takes about two months to mature. This means that instead of harvesting only one batch of rice a year, the Chinese could now harvest two batches. Peasant incomes went up, the diet of the common man improved and people started living longer.

With all of this rice, China now needed a way to link its people. In the 1950s, the United States of America underwent its most weighty public works project ever – the creation of the Interstate Highway System. Although some might argue it was created to help campers explore America on weekend vacations or even to transport nuclear weapons cross country in the dead of night, the true benefit of the highway system was the ability to transport manufactured goods from the heart of the continent to the coasts in less than a few days. Like the United States of the 1950s, China of the Sui Dynasty knew the necessity of transportation for recreational, military and commercial expansion.

Like his predecessors who conscripted the labor of the masses for public works such as enhancing the Great Wall or building palaces for the royalty (both for their present and afterlife), Yang Di decided he'd kill (umm... "utilize") millions of laborers to construct the Grand Canal – a thousand mile long waterway that once and for all united the North and the South. Connecting the Yangtze River and the Yellow River, the Grand Canal was an engineering feat of remarkable proportions. The engineers connected the existing rivers by constructing intricate locks that could raise and lower the water elevation to allow a ship to traverse the changing topography. If your boat had to rise twenty feet to get to the next river, you'd park it in a lock, the water would fill the lock and you'd be miraculously raised to the next level. The doors would open and you'd be back on the canal again.

Taking close to a decade to complete and using the backbreaking labor of close to five million Chinese who moved the earth one pail at a time, the Grand Canal became the longest man made river in the world, and played the most important role in enabling China's population to grow at an unparalleled pace. Like most emperors who dream big (but kill a few too many thousands along the way), Yang Di's legacy wasn't appreciated until centuries later. Like the Qin emperor Shi Huangdi, his deadly public works projects became his undoing, causing the masses to revolt (although the peasants might have also been a bit perturbed at the fact that Yang Di took annual pleasure cruises of gluttony down the canal on hundreds of ornately decorated barges with thousands of his closest friends).

The reign of the Sui came to an end. However, like the short-lived empire of Qin, the groundwork laid in this relatively temporary dynasty made it possible for future dynasties to reach unseen heights. When the Tang and then Song rose to power, they shepherded in eras of unprecedented commercial expansion. Farmers could now start focusing on cash crops like silk, tea, oil, cotton, paper and wine, while manufacturers could mass produce ceramics, books and lacquer ware, knowing that they could send their goods to market across the empire. Instead of only policing the borderlands, the Tang and Song dynasties protected the roads of trade – both the famed Silk Road that extended across Eurasia and the internal network of commercial arteries that brought life and the potential for prosperity to the furthest reaches. The Tang and Song also actively encouraged peasants to move further away from the populated centers of the north, even taking land away from some of the wealthier landholders in the south. But don't confuse these relocation policies as the actions of an altruistic benefactor. This early take on the "rob from the rich and give to the poor" idea said almost more about the Tang and Song's desire to limit the power in the provinces, than it said about their desire to truly help out the struggling peasant.

With their empire thriving and their power relatively unchallenged, the Tang and Song took steps to remove the influence of foreigners. In the centuries following the fall of the Han Dynasty, Buddhism had spread across China. In an era of chaos and uncertainty, millions of Chinese were drawn to the Buddhist tenets of escaping the miserable cycles of life through good deeds, following a code of behavior that cared naught for class differences. Buddhism offered a solitary life of meditation for those weary of day-to-day rituals. However, the Tang and Song leaders were not too fond of the Buddhists. These monks shaved their heads, they cremated dead bodies, but most importantly, they didn't pay taxes or contribute to the economy. But they did keep asking the government to build Buddhist temples and craft grand art pieces. After peaking in the 9th century with over 50,000 monasteries and nearly a million Buddhist monks, the Chinese authorities stepped in to curtail their growing influence. Land was taken back from Buddhists, shrines were torn down and governments were encouraged to support the one true philosophy of China – Confucianism.

The philosophies of Confucius never died out, and like the Christian set of values that kept Europe together even during the darkness of its Middle Ages, Confucianism always stood in the back of people's minds, guiding their daily behavior. Adherents were challenged to be honest, to be clean, to be kind, to be humble and to be respectful. The young must show deference to their elders. Females must defer to males. Society must revere their government leaders. And in exchange, those in power must always earn their status through righteous deeds.

Unique to Chinese society, leadership was not determined by birth, by military success or by political connections. China, with its civil service exam, had created the world's first meritocracy. Any government bureaucrat could not be seated in office until he passed a week-long series of exams that tested the knowledge gained through a lifetime of study. To prevent any corruption in both the administering and marking of these exams, the Tang and Song leaders constantly revised the exam, even having students place random numbers on their exam packets to ensure anonymity. Because the exam was the key to a life of comfort and prestige, the number of students attempting the exam increased at a record pace. In 1100, 30,000 sat for the exam. Two centuries later, the number reached 400,000. By 1300, the competition for a few spots had become so intense that only one out of 333 even had a chance of passing. Compare this to the 2012 AP United States History exam that had about 360,000 students sit for the exam worldwide, with about 52% passing (or basically a one in two chance).

Although the civil service exam theoretically enabled any bright man the opportunity at government service, in reality, the wealthy disproportionately reached the highest level - jinshi. The wealthy were the only ones who could purchase any of the thousands of Confucian texts in existence, and they could provide all the tutoring needed to be successful. Over the course of three hundred years, pretty much the same few dozen families continually produced the greatest number of scholar gentry. Much like the Ivy League custom of admission by legacy, admission into the upper class of Chinese society still had a touch of nepotism, even with all of the safeguards put in place. Regardless of the social makeup of these leaders, their legacy cannot be underestimated. Monarchies and empires rely on the randomness of the ovarian lottery, but this crapshoot inevitably breeds corruption and ineptitude. Yet, in China, the ruling parties always kept the most educated advisors close to their side. In this manner, Confucian ideology remained an integral part of all decisions. Also, the existence of an educated scholar aristocracy meant that China would never face challenges for a more representative form of government from powerful nobles and military leaders from the countryside, (think of the farmers, lawyers and merchants of the colonial United States who became so annoyed with taxation without representation). Between the Tang and Song dynasties, close to 700 years passed with relative political stability, allowing Chinese culture and society to blossom.

Aided by the patronage of the royal families and the wealth flowing into the urban areas, the art and intellectual achievements of the Tang and Song eras became the envy of other civilizations. The mass production of paper and the creation of a vibrant publishing industry enabled art to flow to and from the furthest reaches of the land. The first book ever published – The Diamond Sutra – rolled off the block in 868, about six centuries before a German named Gutenberg printed the Bible. The Chinese usage of iron and their invention of steel enabled the manufacture of weapons and architecture stronger than any object man had ever crafted. The Chinese knowledge of clay and high temperature kilns enabled the crafting of the finest porcelain dishes in the world – yes, that's why your mother's fancy plates are called "china." The Chinese acceptance of Mongol stirrups led to the production of iron stirrups. The Chinese usage of a rudder and a compass enabled merchants and explorers to take goods around the world, potentially "discovering" the Americas in 1421. The Chinese aptitude for spinning silkworms led to the fashioning of the finest fabric known to man (a skill they kept from the rest of the world until a couple Byzantine monks snuck these magic worms out of China in their hollow walking sticks). And the Chinese development of gunpowder, their early experiments with rocketry and their enhancement of the crossbow enabled the formation of weapon systems that, when later adopted by the Europeans, would lead to a complete shift in global relations into the next millennium. The Chinese were way ahead of their time, and the rest of the world would take centuries to catch up.

In many ways, however, the Chinese remained as backward as any other peoples. Women were treated as inferior creatures, and children conformed to the Confucian ideal of filial piety. Young children who spoke out against their parents could be beheaded and younger brothers or sisters who struck their siblings could find themselves imprisoned for three years (imagine how much time you'd have spent in jail had this been the rule when you were a young'un?). As the wealth of China increased, the role of women deteriorated. Women were goods to be exchanged or objectified. The rate of prostitution increased as did the size of dowries. Women were something to be purchased, to be objectified. The symbol of this objectification was the inhumane practice of footbinding. Upper class mothers trapped the feet of their five or six-year-old girls in fabric, preventing them from growing naturally. As the young girl matured, her foot bones gnarled inward, compacting her feet into tiny burdens of crushed bones. Women lived in constant, debilitating pain, many unable to even stand, all so their feet would remain "feminine." When the Mongols captured China in 1279, footbinding was attacked by Mongolian women who demanded the abolishment of the inhumane practice.

Like the Shang, the Zhou, the Qin, the Han, the Sui and the Tang, the Song Dynasty would also fall out of favor, and the Mandate of Heaven again bared its fateful hand. In 1279, the invading Mongol forces of Kublai Khan swept through the southern Song Dynasty and established the Yuan Dynasty, the first era of absolute foreign rule in the history of China. Kublai Khan had to walk a fine line between remaining true to his Mongol roots, but also contending with 100 million Han Chinese bent on his overthrow. What resulted was a century long reign that saw Kublai Khan embrace the parts of Chinese society that maintained order, expand the parts that could bring in more revenue and reverse the parts that threatened Mongol values.

Kublai Khan knew his rule would only be possible if he protected the peasants. Their numerical superiority and history of overthrowing incompetent rulers meant he had to support farmers. He took land from the wealthy Chinese and distributed it to the poor. He created granaries to store surplus grain so during times of hardship the peasants could still be fed. He also realized he could not interfere with the delicate balance between spirituality and secularism. Instead of outlawing or championing any one faith, Kublai Khan welcomed all voices. Whether Confucian, Muslim, Buddhist or Taoist, all sects were welcome.

Except the scholars. More than any other group, the scholar gentry threatened to undermine Kublai Khan's rule. He initially forbade the civil service exam, instead reserving all high governmental posts for fellow Mongols. Eventually he succumbed to pressure and reinstated the exams, but only after ensuring favorable quotas for Mongol applicants. He likewise shook up the class structure, putting Mongols at the top, followed by Muslims, then Northern Chinese and then Southern Chinese.

Even more upsetting to ethnic Chinese was his treatment of merchants and performing artists. Since the age of Confucius, merchants fell to the bottom of the social hierarchy and singers, dancers and thespians of the day weren't even considered human. They were the undesirables of Chinese society.

Kublai Khan didn't exactly agree. He felt China's future rested with the merchant class. He subsequently poured even more money and labor into the expansion of the Grand Canal and focused the bulk of his military efforts on the protection of internal roads and the Silk Road. He allowed, and extensively encouraged, the usage of paper currency and even a primitive banking system. Before even his Grand Canal modifications had reached completion, he had already started designing a new capital city – Dadu (the city we today call Beijing). In Dadu where he could hide behind the walls of the Forbidden Kingdom, Kublai Khan became a rabid patron of the arts, inviting the best players from the land to perform for his court. He also welcomed the emissaries, merchants and ambassadors from distant lands. The European Marco Polo spent seventeen years in his court, while Muslim scientists arrived and improved the Chinese calendar, redirected Chinese astronomy and added to the Chinese knowledge of contemporary medical practices. Like Baghdad before, Dadu developed into a center of learning and thought, quite a far cry from the seemingly barbaric inclinations of the Mongols.

In one domain, the Mongols clearly tried to advance China's notion of "civilization." Mongol women weren't exactly what you would consider "ladylike." They rode with their husbands into battle, they spoke their minds and they walked freely down the streets of the empire. One rather impressive female member of the royal family was Khutulun. The niece of Kublai Khan, Khutulun was a tough chica, a Mongolian Fiona (a la *Shrek*), who offered her hand in marriage to any man who could defeat her in a wrestling match. Any would-be suitor had to first put up a bet of 100 horses. Win, you marry Khutulun. Lose...you're going home with a few less horses to feed. 10,000 horses later, Khutulun still had yet to be married, but her reputation only grew (as did her stable).

Needless to say, this type of woman wouldn't exactly welcome the art of footbinding and the priggish existence available to Chinese women. The Mongols pushed forth efforts to end footbinding, they increased inheritance rights for women whose husbands had died, they walked throughout the cities without concern for any rebuke and they played prominent roles in the governing of the territories and the maintenance of landholdings. Although future dynasties pushed women back into a subservient hole, for a brief moment in Chinese history, the status of women actually improved.

Yet when Kublai Khan died, none of his reforms proved enough to sustain the Mongol empire. The Mongols would one day fall to the Mandate of Heaven, but the improvements they had made to the economy and to the infrastructure continued to benefit the masses for centuries to come. Kublai Khan had also in his time created a navy unparalleled on the Asian seas. Although this navy proved unable to expand the Mongolian empire into Japan, it did prove capable of protecting commerce across the oceans and even led to maritime incursions as far as Africa and even the Americas. It also kept China aloft as the preeminent civilization on the planet – a title that was still centuries from being wrested away by the West. But they still had their own hole to dig out of.

But that is for another chapter.

18

The Land of the Rising Sun

Japan - Foundations to Feudalism – 300 > 1600

About 180 miles off the southern tip of Korea, the easternmost point of mainland Asia, lies a network of some 4000 islands, most of which are no more than mere chunks of volcanic rock poking out from the Pacific Ocean "Ring of Fire." Their surface would remind a visitor more of a lifeless moonscape than of a beachy paradise. But on four of these islands – Hokkaido, Shikoku, Kyushu and Honshu – a civilization sprung up that rivaled any groupings of man in world history. Uniquely located to develop independently from neighboring threats, but situated close enough to benefit from the cultural advancements of nearby China, this relatively insignificant archipelago would in the 20th century emerge as one of the most powerful military and economic forces the world has ever seen. But how could a nation of disconnected islands and jagged mountains, where only 18% of their land is actually inhabitable, evolve into one of the (if not the number one) most advanced civilizations on the planet?

Japan definitely didn't start off looking too impressive.

You didn't always need a boat or a plane to get to Japan. Once upon a time, Japan was actually connected to Asia. Until about 15,000 years ago, Japan was linked to the mainland by an ice bridge, somewhat like the Bering Land Bridge that connected Alaska to the Asian continent, allowing fleeing and foraging nomads to wander down and populate the Americas. The first to walk across this icy land link were the Ainu people, the Japanese people's earliest ancestors. If you were to look at them today, they wouldn't resemble the Japanese stereotype. They have lighter skin, a lot more body hair and look more Polynesian or white Russian than Japanese. The men love to grow their beards down to their belly buttons, and sometimes their envious wives permanently tattoo their chins with faux facial hair to keep up with their hubbies. Tragically, these first peoples met a fate much like other indigenous peoples from around the globe, seeing their numbers dwindle due to disease, murder, intermarriage or marginalization. Today, only about 200,000 of these fair-skinned "former Aborigines" actually still survive, and although they have been officially acknowledged by the Japanese government, they still exist as the outcasts of mainstream Japanese society.

But this wasn't always the case. Until about 10,000 BC, about the time planters out in Mesopotamia decided to set up homes and give farming a try, the Ainu clans spread out across the northern island of Honshu. They were the sole residents of these volcanic isles. In the last couple decades, historians have found a series of intricately patterned clay pots from the Ainu, and if carbon dating machines are accurate, these pots stand out as the oldest pieces of pottery in human history. Like in the river civilizations of Mesopotamia, Egypt, China and the Indus valley, these pots were also used for storing food. Unlike their mainland counterparts, these pots had rope-like patterns adorning their outside surface (potters would take a stick rapped with rope and press it against the outside for a fine finish that surely impressed). These pots defined the people of these early Japanese days so well that the time period between 10,000 BC and 300 BC was known as the Jomon ("cord patterned") Period. Egypt had its Age of Dynasties, India had its Bronze Age, Babylon had its Iron Age...and Japan? Japan had its age of pots.

Although the topic of pottery demands more attention, please, oh please, let this be the last I speak of the glory of clay crockery. For Japan in its early years was so much more than heated clay. Over these ten thousand years, it saw a steady stream of immigrants from mainland China and Korea, though these fresh settlers would have to make their way across the East Sea on boats before reaching one of the more hospitable islands. Over the millennium, these East Asian immigrants supplanted the Ainu people, yet remained hunters, gatherers and fishermen. It wasn't until about 500 BC that these Korean/Chinese/Ainu hybrids tried out the whole farming thing, and it was then that they began building more permanent wooden houses, leaving behind some of their nomadic traditions.

But they still didn't write anything down. Long after Plato was philosophizing about a republic, Buddha was scribing the Eightfold Path and the Chinese were copying the Confucian dialects, Japan had yet to write down a word. Literate Koreans were in high demand and each powerful clan lobbied heavily for the pen of one of these migrant Korean scribes. It wasn't until the 6th century AD, about the time the Roman Empire had fallen into ruin, that any Japanese scholar attempted to enumerate the Japanese spoken language.

It was here that Japan made its first big cultural leap, and this leap can be attributed almost entirely to the efforts of a power hungry clan who eventually enrolled Japan in a crash course of Chinese Civilization 101. Before the 3rd century AD, when Korean and Chinese ambassadors walked the roads of Japan, they saw a land with no central government and simply a ton of independent clans ruled by tribal chieftains who worshipped animal gods or clan elders who claimed they were descendants of deities. Like the Germans to the Romans, these were the backwards barbarians. Their architecture was anything but impressive. One might see large mounds of dirt meant for a dead leader or an egotistical noble, but there were really only a few cleverly-crafted wooden huts that might last a season or two. This wasn't to say that it was a land in chaos. Actually, everyone who visited noted how peacefully the people lived. Theft and murder were practically unheard of.

The Yamato clan was the first to take advantage of this relative passivity and calm to unite the clans. Every civilization goes through a period where society devolves into regional kingdoms, simultaneously causing every society to endure a subsequent period when one clan leader gets the bright idea to use his authority and muscle to expand his holdings. Because the Yamato family controlled the fertile rice plains, they had a huge advantage when it came to trading influence, wealth and the feeding of their people. In the 3rd and 4th centuries AD, with each successive generation, the Yamato family used warfare, coercion and treaties to expand their territory, and by the mid 300s, their holdings expanded into southern Korea. This was the first hint of a nation we would later call Japan.

The Yamato ruling family legitimized their rule through faith. They claimed to have descended directly from the sun goddess Amaterasu who lives in the heavens, each day blessing Japan with a new dawn. According to legend, Amaterasu sent down her grandson to unite the kingdoms under one rule, and it is this grandson, Jimmu, who rose as Japan's first emperor and became the founding father of the Yamato family line. Today, the emperor of Japan, Akihito, resides as the latest in an empirical line that dates back over 2600 years, the oldest claim held by any current monarch. Though at times (including today), the role of the emperor was solely symbolic, during other eras, his seat stood as the sole uniting force of a people reticent to dissolve the clan system.

Once they had an empire, the Yamato clan looked to the west for inspiration, to a fairly accomplished civilization, to the Chinese. Over the next two centuries, they sent hundreds of officials to Chinese courts to learn of their scientific advancements, their engineering achievements and the most important skill of all – their governing tricks. They employed Chinese irrigation systems, adopted innovative agricultural techniques and underwent a wholesale adjustment of their regimes, creating generations of scholar-bureaucrats best prepared to govern outlying provinces. The Confucian ideals of filial piety, respect for your elders, proper etiquette in all human interaction and loyalty to rulers became hallmarks of Japanese society.

Even when the Yamato clan was usurped by a rival clan, the Soga family, the Confucian ideals and Chinese bureaucratic state remained entrenched in everyday life. The Soga clan took the love of all things Chinese to the next level. More court ambassadors and scholars journeyed to China to learn the proper way of behaving, and returned to build cities modeled after the Chinese grid structure. They instituted a census to better collect taxes from all residents and determine how to distribute land more equitably. Japanese scholar-bureaucrats began to speak and write in Chinese, a difficult feat considering you have to learn over 80,000 characters (compared with the only 26 consonants and vowels needed by English speakers). Once they learned Chinese, wrote poetry in Chinese, transcribed the Buddhist scripture in Chinese and dabbled in the art of Chinese calligraphy, the scholars attempted to use the Chinese characters to represent Japanese speech. It didn't work so well. Japanese scholars spent the next four centuries, until the 9th century, creating a new written language, some using Chinese symbols, and some using new symbols that represented sounds.

Once the Japanese had a stable government, a productive labor force, a functioning language and a connected kingdom, it was time to go the path of all great empires – get complacent, get gluttonous and watch your kingdom fall into chaos.

By the 8th century, the government kept demanding more and more from its people, but delivered less and less. Peasant fathers no longer wanted to lose their sons to compulsory military service for the emperor. Farmers no longer were willing to see their rice harvests sucked up by some faraway leader. And in the far off court of Kyoto, the royal family spent more and more of their wealth on elaborate ceremonies, fancy summer palaces and the mounting cost of purchasing all the sensual delights available to the wealthy. While the royal families were away satisfying their desires, the countryside devolved into a culture of violence and thievery. Goods could no longer be safely transported. The central government was unable to hold up their end of the deal. Enough was enough.

Local lords started hiring their own private militaries. Landowners took up arms. Even Buddhist monasteries hired their own oxymoronically-titled "warrior monks" to expand and protect Buddhism. All hell was breaking loose.

So Japan entered into its Middle Ages, an era comparable to the European Middle Ages, where local lords demanded allegiance from mounted warriors, where peasants gave their loyalty (and a share of their harvest) to these lords in exchange for protection. Like Europe, this entire civilization shut itself off from the outside world and became hundreds of self-sufficient little fiefdoms scattered patchwork across the islands. This was the age of lords, the Japanese daimyos and of their warrior servants - the samurai.

During the Japanese Middle Ages, you were either a daimyo, a samurai or a farmer. Not a lot of other options. Rice was currency, so the farmers cultivated the money that kept the system going. They promised big chunks of their rice harvest to their daimyos, who then took this rice and used it to compensate their samurai for protecting the fiefdom. Daimyos built huge fortifications, or castles, that sat at the center of towns, acting as marketplaces and mills during peacetime, and sanctuaries from enemies during times of war. Like in Europe, lords were never happy with the status quo, always intent on forming alliances or staging military campaigns that might increase their landholdings. More land meant more rice, and more rice meant more wealth and power. This form of feudalism came about five hundred years after the European version and lasted far later, until almost the 18th century. It wasn't the Golden Age of Japan, but it has become the most romanticized age of Japan. Like the stories of Snow White, King Arthur and Robin Hood that continue to be passed down from generation to generation, these stories of ruthless daimyos and their selfless samurai are likewise passed on in Japan from father to son, but are also rehashed again and again today in Japanese cinema, anime, video games and television.

The Japanese just can't get enough of these sword-yielding heroes of yesteryear.

And who can blame them? Samurai are fearless, deadly and willing to give their life without a second thought. They never surrender, never show emotion in battle and can never be found without their katana, the badassedest weapon on the planet. This 2 ½ foot long curved blade was fabled to be so sharp that it could slice a man in half from skull to groin, and the man would still keep walking for a few steps (undoubtedly the inspiration for more than a few of George Lucas's far, far away light saber duels).

But that was just one type of samurai.

They were so much more than elite swordsmen.

In fact, initially, their weapon of choice was the bow and arrow, and they practiced for years to master the skill of hitting moving targets from horseback. Even today, mounted archers tour Japan showcasing their talents at national parades or when foreign ambassadors are shown around. Fortunately, in this ritual demonstration known as yabusame, archers no longer use dogs as targets, but a less vulgar, and a definitely quieter, circular wooden board.

Samurai were not all noble men. In times of war, a daimyo might call for a mass roundup of peasants and give them temporary samurai status. These armed farmers would bring their pitchforks, axes, hammers or hoes (or just hope to find some dropped weapon of a fallen enemy), and then they'd try to stir up as much mayhem as possible before returning to their rice-harvesting lives.

And samurai weren't all men. Over in the European Middle Ages, the ideal woman was demure, delicate and defenseless. Her value in society was minimal – make the babies, take care of the babies, keep her mouth shut. The classic tale of western medieval female passivity is Snow White – the girl is hated because she's cute, eventually put into a coma by an ugly step mom and then only saved when a strange man kisses her. Why does he kiss her? Because she was silent, pretty and passive. Personality really wasn't a priority in Europe.

In Japan, the role of women was also domestic to a large degree, but samurai wives were expected to learn the tools of warfare and defend the daimyo's holdings to the death. Some women even fought alongside their husbands – the most famous being Tomoe Gozen who sought out her husband's killer, cut off his head and then retreated to a convent where she spent the rest of her life in prayer. A couple sisters also mastered the art of revenge after they witnessed the murder of their father. For the rest of their childhood and into adulthood, they mastered the weapons of the samurai, and when the opportunity finally arrived they avenged their father – one daughter trapped the samurai's sword with a long chain, the other cut him to pieces with her naginata. These early female martial artists eventually faded from society, and women were again expected to master the art of homemaking.

The one trait all samurai shared was the strict adherence to bushido – the way of the warrior. Like chivalry to a medieval knight, this code of ethics marked the path of all samurai. They were to be honest, to be frugal, to be loyal and to fight to the death. They could never surrender. These expectations resembled those of European knights (except for maybe the being frugal part), but for the samurai, bushido went even further. The "to the death" part was taken literally. Should a samurai fail to live up to his duty – should he lose in battle, prove disloyal or embarrass his daimyo – the only acceptable option was seppuku – suicide. The European Church forbade suicide (it assured a one way ticket to Hell), but in feudal Japan it was the only acceptable way to wash away one's sins and restore honor to the samurai's family.

This ritual suicide usually was performed in front of an audience. A samurai could restore his honor with a clean, stoic taking of his life. Easier said than done. The disgraced samurai took to his knees, opened his robe and then used a small knife to cut through his stomach and intestines. Self-disembowelment can cause a bit of discomfort, so oftentimes a samurai would have a respected friend or family member act as his second should he pass out from the pain or fail to finish off the job, agreeing to decapitate his buddy should he not be up to the task.

The other part of bushido not seen in western chivalry was the expectation that the samurai embrace the arts. A true samurai was refined, cultured, literate and at one with nature. To replicate the serenity and beauty of Japanese forests and mountains, he might manicure his garden of flowers and bonsai shrubs or engineer fountains that fed into ponds filled with golden fish. He might recite poetry or play a musical instrument or spend hours raking a sand garden while meditating on the meaning of life. He might even paint landscapes or refine his intricate calligraphy. Whatever the artistic pursuit, the goal was being at one with nature – a part of this world, not one trying to control this world. The killer instinct they had refined on the battlefield had to be left at the doorstep of their homes, for once inside, a samurai was a man of introspection and inspiration.

But it was on the battlefield where they made their reputations and where legends were born. For most of the Japanese feudal era – the Heian, Kamakura, Muromachi and Sengoku periods – battles were waged against rival clans. This perennial power play was briefly interrupted in 1274 when Kublai Khan and the Mongols constructed hundreds of boats and set sail from China to conquer Japan. The daimyo clans and their samurai warriors briefly united to defend their homeland against the Mongols, a fierce tribe of conquerors who had created the largest land empire in human history – stretching from Eastern Europe to Korea. Initially, they didn't have a chance. Samurais kept expecting Mongol warriors to break away from the pack and fight in mano-y-mano duels that would determine honor and combat superiority. But the Mongols had other plans. They fought as a unit and blasted the Japanese coast with their never-before-seen exploding iron bombs. Japan might have lost the islands had not a storm crashed down on the Mongol ships, forcing them to return to China to regroup. Seven years later, Khan returned with an even greater armada of over 120,000 troops, but again, they would be pushed back, not by the samurais, but by a violent typhoon that utterly demolished the Mongol fleet. The samurai took this intervention as a sign that the gods favored them over all would-be invaders, and they thanked the gods for answering their prayers by sending kamikazes - the divine winds.

With the Mongols gone, Japan again withdrew, regressing into a continued cycle of peace and civil war between rival daimyos.

Smaller clans were eventually swallowed by more powerful lords and peasants continued to slave away on their rice fields. Some peasants eventually gained enough wealth to say goodbye to the farm, becoming merchants at one of the burgeoning towns that catered to the expanding tastes of the daimyo nobility.

But all feudal eras must come to an end, and in the final decades of the 16th century, three men emerged to unite the whole of Japan under one banner. The samurai would again be called on to test their loyalty on the battlefield, but this time the winners wouldn't merely absorb a few more chunks of neighboring land.

This time, the victor would be handed the keys to the entire kingdom of Japan.

But that is for another chapter.

19

A Light at the End of the Tunnel

Europe - The High Middle Ages – 1200 > 1500

In 1914, the countries of Western Europe controlled 80% of the world's population. In 1969, this same West put a man on the moon. In 2000, they then put a portable telephone in everybody's pocket.

In 1000, the West lived in dirt-filled hovels. In 1000, the West was afraid to venture outside itself. In 1000, the West was probably the most backwardly primitive piece of real estate on the planet.

So what happened? How did the West break out of it's self-imposed slump to rejoin the pantheon of the world's greatest civilizations?

First, Europeans started eating better. You'd be surprised how little your society can progress when it's hungry. Try it sometime. Don't eat for a week and then try to write poetry, harness electricity or create your own original algorithm for calculating the circumference of a circle.

The West was late to the agricultural party, and when they arrived, their available tools were ill-suited to the environment. The plows of the Mediterranean, Mesopotamia and the Nile River Valley were great when your lands flooded and the nutrient-rich soil sat a mere inches below the surface. Northern Europe has different dirt. Now, without exploring the stimulating perplexities of the composition of soil, you need to just trust that Northern Europe's good dirt is far deeper beneath the topsoil than the good dirt in other places. Subsequently, for millennia, Europeans did the best they could with an ox and a puny plow, but then, one day (it was a Thursday I believe), the Europeans found a better way of making crops, and the rest is agricultural history. They invented a heavy plow that could pull the prime soil to the surface, they created a collar for horses that wouldn't rip apart their necks and they rotated their crops using the oh-so-efficient three-field system. The three-field system enabled farmers to plant wheat on 1/3 of their land, peas or beans on another 1/3 and nothing on the final 1/3 (letting it lay "fallow"). By leaving the field fallow, and maybe even allowing your animal fertilizing machines to plop down their little nuggets of nourishment, the soil's fertility rejuvenated, making the land far more productive.

Once their bellies were full, Europeans could start looking for other ways of making money. As the threat of bandits gradually decreased and the lure of foreign goods steadily increased, men started hitting the road to try to quench the region's growing thirst for luxury goods. These "dusty feet" might bring back spices, silks or ceramics from the East (china from China?). The lords quickly jumped on this get-rich-quick idea and allowed these merchants to set up shop in towns. At these markets, the townspeople (known as "burghers") might lend money, they might sell recently acquired specialties or they might provide one of the many services offered by the butcher, the baker and the candlestick maker. Not surprisingly, millions left the farms for town-life, hoping to make a buck as one of the many smiths – arrowsmiths, blacksmiths, silversmiths, locksmiths, goldsmiths or bladesmiths. No wonder the leading surname in the West is "Smith" (followed closely by those famous people who liked to turn grain into flour – the Millers). As these burghs, or boroughs, grew, their inhabitants increasingly demanded more rights and because a growing number of these merchants were rolling in the dough, the regional lords had to start listening to the merchant commoners. Families like the Medicis of Italy or the Fuggers (not kidding about the name) of Germany even started loaning money to governments, making these medieval businessmen serious rivals to the thrones.

And these thrones had a seemingly endless thirst for money. Here was the problem for kings. They had to share their money. Their number one revenue stream – taxing the peasants – was being currently drained by those pesky lords who insisted on maintaining feudalism. The kings had a few ways of getting rid of the lords. If you followed the lead of King Louis the Fat (actual title), you could ride around your countryside imprisoning anyone who opposed you, or you could tie the private areas of your enemies to a rope and then hang them in the city square. But for the majority who disagreed with genitalian public torture, they chose a fairly successful method for increasing their holdings. Step One - Tax the people under your control. Step Two - Use the money to buy an army. Step Three - Use the army to defeat the lords. Step Four – Repeat steps one thru three.

By the 14th century, any king worth his salt had a standing army of tens of thousands of paid soldiers willing to do their lord's bidding. The knights were no match for these armies, as the new weapons of the era doomed chivalry and knighthood to the dustbin of history. The crossbow and gunpowder could not only knock the mightiest knight off his horse, but these new tools of war could be mastered with a minimum amount of training. Unlike the path to knighthood that took a couple decades and cost a ton of money to sustain, standing armies could pulled together from any old hodgepodge of ruffians. And once they were under a king's service, they would have access to the most deadly weapons of the era. The Welsh longbow was the superweapon of the Middle Ages. Sometimes taller than its archer, because of the longbow's accuracy and force, it could pierce a mounted knight's armor from hundreds of meters away. It was used with great efficiency in the Battle of Hastings where William the Bastard's expert marksmen pretty much negated any advantage of the English cavalry. This victory allowed William (who from thereafter chose to be called "the Conqueror") to divide up all of England amongst his faithful followers, making him the most revered king in all of Europe. Eventually the descendants of these lords became a bit less faithful to their king, and this change in heart contributed to the next evolution in government. But I'm getting ahead of myself.

Between the town burghers who wanted more say in how their taxes were used and the lords who felt their voices should be heard, the kings of Europe had to decide to what extent they would accept advice from the common folk. To avoid revolutions, rational kings placated wealthy merchants and influential lords by creating parliaments. England went the furthest by allowing representatives of the royalty (the House of Lords) to meet with reps from the boroughs (the House of Commons), and over the rest of the millennium, English monarchs varied to what extent they wanted the "advice" of the Parliament. Some chose the absolute monarch approach. Others chose to reluctantly relinquish just a bit of power. And by the time the European monarchies made it to the 21st century, the remaining princes and princesses, dukes and duchesses sadly resigned themselves to becoming mere figureheads whose primary role was to intermittently appear topless in tabloid magazines or stage rather gaudy public weddings.

Nevertheless, the bulk of Europeans never really noticed this transfer of power from the nobles to the commoners. But they did start to notice the expansion of learning, which, instead of being controlled by monks surviving in the isolated confines of their monasteries, started to spread through the towns and even into the countryside. There wasn't one event that opened European's eyes to the beauty of knowledge, but a combination of factors that ended up putting books in the hands of the masses. First, when the Crusaders made contact with Muslims in the Levant and in Spain, they ended up wading through the mountains of literature the Muslim scholars had accumulated in the previous three hundred years. Not only did this knowledge include the classical learning of Greece and Rome, but it also showcased the vast knowledge gathered from India and China. European scholars took these Arabic texts and began transcribing them into the vernacular (local languages) of their region.

Disseminating this information to the public became the next step. They needed to learn how to make paper, then how to quickly print books and finally how to build universities so people would have a place to actually learn what was in the books. Before paper and the printing press, copying books was an extremely laborious process. Basically, someone wealthy would first have to find an original copy, then they'd hire a scribe to rewrite the book one word at a time, and then, after one to two years you'd have your book finished and you could return the original book to its owner. Not exactly efficient. This process was so time consuming and expensive that most churches didn't even have a Bible, just a few pages of some critical prayers – basically a Wikipedia summary of the Holy text.

But in 1450, in a little town in Germany, Johan Guttenberg created a press where a master smith would mold thousands of little lettered tiles (in 52 different designs...why 52 if there are only 26 letters in the alphabet?) and then place them on a metal plate to match the text of the author. This metal plate could then be doused with ink and used as a stamp to print hundreds of the same page. This process was then repeated for each new page of text, and then a bookbinder would connect all the pages together. Instead of one book being made in a year, thousands could be published in a few months. Books started circulating through towns and, even though few could afford an original copy, the books were passed from person to person and the knowledge likewise began to circulate. A continent began emerging from the Dark Ages.

Not all of this printed material focused on the classics of antiquity. In fact, the first printed material published in mass weren't even books at all, but playing cards. The Muslim Empire shared this little pastime with the Europeans and the 52-card deck we still use today, including the images of the king, queen and jester, look almost identical to their appearance nearly 700 years ago. So, the next time you're playing Blackjack or watching the World Series of Poker, thank the Arabs for the idea. After their foray into playing cards, the publishing world expanded to include documents criticizing the church and the government, medical and scientific treatises, and even travel books.

The most famous travel guide (it was the Lonely Planet of Medieval Europe) belonged to an imprisoned Italian named Marco Polo. Back then, Mr. Polo was so much more than a grating pool game of hide and seek. In the 13th century, Marco Polo joined his father and uncle on a trip across Asia, and wound up living in China for almost 20 years. Under the permission of Mongol leader Kublai Khan, who had recently conquered China, Marco Polo freely wandered the Chinese countryside, absorbing the technology, the systems of rule and even the fashion of his accommodating hosts. He finally returned across the Silk Road to Europe, only to be robbed and thrown in jail (for appearing to be on the wrong side of a civil war with Venice) once he reached the doorstep of Europe. While in jail, one of his jail mates, a romance novelist named Rusticiano, started scribing his story, and within a few years *The Travels of Marco Polo* sat on the bookshelves of traders and scholars across Europe. The age of exploration had its inspiration.

To make sense of all this new information coming from all corners of the globe, formal institutes of research and learning sprung up, granting degrees once varying levels of knowledge were attained. Formal education had existed prior to the Middle Ages, but these monastic schools were controlled by the Church and were oftentimes outside the city centers. With the growing urban population and the rising need for an educated clergy, in the 11th century, the first formal universities appeared. First was the University of Bologna in 1088, followed within a few decades by the Sorbonne, Oxford and Cambridge. Although started with a direct connection to the Church, within a few generations, the universities broke free, and, like the guilds that controlled commerce in the cities, the universities became self-sufficient bodies, able to conduct research and instruction without the prying eyes of the Church or the tax-collecting hands of the royalty. This tradition of self-sufficient institutions of higher learning, granting bachelors, masters and doctorate degrees continued to expand, and have today become the final academic hoop needed to jump through for anyone hoping to attain wealth or success. Western institutions continue to dominate the world's higher learning destinations. In 2010, they accounted for all of the top-10 ranked universities in the world (Harvard, Yale, University of London, MIT, Oxford, Imperial College of London, University of Chicago, Caltech and Princeton).

From one of Europe's greatest accomplishments, we now head to possibly its darkest hour, but also to the event probably even more critical to its emergence from the Middle Ages – the Black Plague. One of the unfortunate bi-products of global trade networks is that in addition to sharing knowledge, goods and people, these trade networks also link people who like to share their germs. Before there was bird flu, H1N1 or SARS, there was the bubonic plague. Carried by fleas who lived on rats that travelled on ships, the bubonic plague started with some swollen sores that oozed gunk, which then turned into high fevers and frequent vomiting of blood, followed by death. No one knew what to do to stop this massive epidemic that eventually claimed close to 1/3 of Europe's population. Some people drank copious amounts of alcohol, some wore perfume, some walked in sewage, some even drained the blood of the ill thinking that might eradicate the disease. Nothing worked.

Within a few years, society fell into chaos. Farms and homes sat vacant. Nobody worked the lands of lords, and fields fell into disrepair. According to urban legend, children then created adorable little nursery rhymes about puss-filled sores

Ring around the rosey (puss-filled sored)

Pocket full of poseys (worn to fend off the disease)

Ashes, ashes, we all fall down (darnit...we keep dying)

This little nursery myth is about as accurate as the one that links America's naughtiest word to a supposed law forcing couples to put up a sign outside their home saying they were Fornicating Under Consent of the King. But, alas, the truth isn't as titillating as the fiction. The "Rosie" song first popped up in a Mother Goose book in the 1880s and the naughty word's origins have never been proven.

But I digress...back to the plague.

Those Europeans who did survive struggled to live on the meager food available. When the lords attempted to force the surviving peasants back into their little feudal land/protection agreement, the peasants realized their newfound bargaining power. Peasant revolts became the norm, and lords eventually realized they had to throw in the towel and start paying wages. That new relationship, and the fact that many lords perished along with the common rabble, meant that more lands could be purchased by those with the white blood cells needed to fight off this deadly scourge.

The Church also lost face as it proved powerless to stop the rampage, striking a huge dent in the credibility of Christianity as the savior of mankind. When prayers kept going unanswered, people started looking elsewhere for relief. But this time the Church would be unable to stop the quest for truth. No matter how much the priests threatened eternal damnation, heretics continued to look to nature, to science, to their own imaginations for solutions to man's problems. The Church was no longer above reproach. A crack in the Church's control of thought had been exposed, and Europe could never go back. They could only go forward.

But that is for another chapter.

20

Checking in From All Corners

Polynesia, Africa and the Americas – 400 > 1500

By the year 1500, all the continents of the world were populated by humans. But by that year all the continents were definitely not connected. Sure, there was the Silk Road criss-crossing Asia. There was the Indian Ocean trade network linking East Africa to East Asia. There was even a Trans-Saharan caravan trail connecting the gold-producing regions of West Africa to the Middle East. But still, about 75% of the planet sat isolated from the other continents. The indigenous peoples of the Americas, Sub-Saharan Africa and Australoasia might have interacted with their neighboring tribes, but they definitely didn't meet up with travelers from across the oceans. They might not have seen themselves as isolated (living sometimes in cities far larger than the towns of Medieval Europe), but by today's standards, they were on their own.

We don't know a ton about these early inhabitants of the "new worlds," not because they didn't have vibrant, complex, advanced civilizations, but because they failed to do one thing that makes history possible. They didn't write. Yes, they drew pictures on their monuments and carved monoliths to illustrate their daily lives or to honor their gods, but that just doesn't count. So unfortunately, our knowledge of their early years is fairly negligible compared to the mountains of records we have of the Mediterranean and Asian civilizations of the ancient world.

Archaeologists have uncovered a ton of evidence (especially of the major civilizations of Mesoamerica – today's Latin America), but still most of our accounts of their worlds come not from actual members of the civilization, but from the explorers that would run into them over the course of the 16th and 17th centuries.

But let's try to go back a few hundred years and try to make sense of what was going on in their worlds prior to the Age of Exploration that once and for all linked the world together.

Over in the Americas, there was no one civilization that dominated the entire continent. There was no singular group of Indians all following the same leader and glorifying the same gods. By the time Columbus arrived in 1492, thousands of groups of Native Americans had already set up shop around the Western Hemisphere. Some were small groups that stayed hunter-gatherers. Others created efficient empires that boasted highly "civilized" methods of agriculture, government and human interaction.

How many tribes do you think existed on the North American continent? Take a guess. Four? Twenty? 260 million? Well, not quite 260 million, but here are just a few:

Abnaki Alabama Aleuts Algonquin Anasazi Apache Arapaho Arawak Arikara Assiniboin Aztec Beothuk Cabazon Caddo Catawba Cherokee Cheyenne Chickasaw Chinook Chippewa Choctaw Chumash Comanche Cree Creek Crow Delaware Erie Eskimo Flathead Haida Hidatsa Hohokam Hopi Hupa Huron Ioway Innu Inuit Iroquois Kaw Kickapoo Kiowa Klamath Kootenai Kwakiutl Mahican Makah Maliseet Mandan Mayan Melungeon Menominee Metis Mississauga Modoc Mohave Mohawk Mohegan Montagnais Mound Builders Narragansett Navajo Nez Perce Nootka Olmec Osage Ottawa Oto Papago Passamaquoddy Pawnee Pennacook Penobscot Peoria Pequot Pima Ponca Potawatomi Pueblo Quanah Parker Quapaw Sauk Seminole Seneca Shawnee Shoshone Shuswap Sioux Squanto Tlingit Toltec Tonkawa Ute Washo Wampanoag Wichita Winnebago Wovoka Wyandotte Yakima Yuchi Yurok Zapotec Zuni

As you can see, there was no one Native American nation, religion, language or government. Not only were they not unified, but many of these tribes had conflicts with each other that the Europeans would later exploit to their advantage.

But I'm getting ahead of myself.

To the south it was a bit different. In the southern area of what we today call Mexico and along the western coast of South America, two civilizations flourished at a scale only matched by the Romans, the Mongols, the Muslims, the Indians and the Chinese. These two civilizations were the Aztecs (the Mexicas) of Mexico and the Incas of modern day Chile. Together these two regions made up what was later called Mesoamerica – or "middle America."

The Aztec civilization had built on the foundations established by first the Mayans and then the Toltecs. Most people hadn't heard of the Mayans until 2012 when some of the cognitively-challenged members of our species started pointing to this civilization's calendar as a clue that the end of the world was coming at the end of the year. Even though Hollywood made a film that proved otherwise (cleverly-named *2012*), the year came and went, and yet another doomsday prophecy fell into the ignored graveyard of man's end time's predictions. But before the Mayans were inspiration for Hollywood fodder, they were a dynamic society that built stone temples and an acropolis, invented floating gardens that resisted frost and could be farmed year round, developed a system of math that included place value and the number zero and organized a capital city at Teotihuacan that by 700 AD was the most-populated city on the planet. It was first established around 2000 BC, at the time of the great Egyptian empires, and continued uninterrupted until the arrival of the Spanish in the 16th century.

However, before the Spanish arrived, the Mayans were challenged and eventually overpowered by first the Toltecs around the year 1000, but ultimately by the Aztecs in the 14th century. Like the Mediterranean powers of Persia then Greece then Rome, all the three major powers – Mayan, Toltec, Aztec – continued to exist even when one of the other tribes proved superior.

The reign of the Aztecs was brutal and complex, but on a scale far surpassing their predecessors. The Mayans might have built the Great Plaza at Tikal and their capital city of Teotihuacan might have housed 200,000 people, but the Aztecs did them one better. They built a capital city in the middle of a lake, Lake Texcoco, and then surrounded this island city with floating gardens and two causeway land bridges that connected the capital to the 500,000 surrounding villagers lining the lake's shores. This capital city, Tenochtitlan, was one of the most advanced and disturbing cities of human existence.

It housed astronomers and mathematicians that plotted the stars more accurately than many of the famed skygazers of Europe's Scientific Revolution. The Aztecs required every one of their kids to go to school, regardless of gender (the Western world wouldn't require universal compulsory education until the 19th century). They developed law codes covering every offense from theft to adultery to public drunkenness, with punishments ranging from a public head shaving to having your heart ripped out in public. They had divorce courts that awarded half of all a husband's assets to his wife. Aztec markets offered everything from human slaves, to falcons and partridges (with or without the pear tree), to medicines made of crushed black beetles, to obsidian and jade necklaces, to jaguar hides to be worn by elite warriors. The Aztecs invented a ball game that was a little bit soccer and a little bit basketball, where players used only their hips to bump a ten-pound solid rubber ball into a cement hoop ten feet off the ground (imagine what those hip welts looked like). They mastered the art of agriculture, assigning men each day to collect human feces to fertilize their thousands of individual chinampas (floating farmlands) that grew corn and squash.

Stars and schools and divorce and birds and ball games and farming are all truly fascinating, but let's be serious. When people think of the Aztecs, they think of one thing. These guys liked to kill people. They believed their gods must be ceaselessly appeased with blood sacrifices, so they obliged by running a constant stream of victims to the roof of their temples, where the high priests would thrust obsidian daggers into their chests, and then rip out their still beating hearts to show to the onlookers below. The bodies were then heaped down the side of the temple, creating a mound of corpses fifty feet high. In one four-day festival, 80,000 lives were taken to hopefully ensure a bountiful harvest.

And where did all these victims come from? Some actually volunteered for the honor, but most were captured from villages across Mesoamerica. An entire industry of hunting humans for sacrifice emerged, making the Aztecs none too popular in the region. If ever a high-level village elder or warrior was taken, his captor would earn the distinction of getting to wear his captive's peeled-off skin around town for a month, after his family chopped up his carcass and dined on his flesh. The Aztecs were annoying because they kept eating people, so by the time the Spanish arrived in the 16th century, the neighboring tribes needed little convincing to align with the European invaders to topple their carniverous

Aztec oppressors. But for two centuries, it reigned over a golden age that rivaled anything the Eurasians had produced to that point.

To the south of Mexico and the Aztec kingdom sat the equally impressive Inca Empire that stretched down the western coast of South America, covering the countries today called Bolivia, Chile and Peru. Unlike the Aztecs who lived around the lakes of central Mexico, the Incas survived in the high mountains of the Andes. They created an empire in the heavens, building 25,000 miles of trails, carving out terraced mountain farms for their corn, potatoes and tomatoes and erecting a summer estate for their king 8000 feet above sea level (one of today's new Seven Wonders of the World – Machu Pichu). Like the Aztecs to the north, the Incas controlled their empire without iron tools, without horses and without wheels. Their largest pack animal was the llama and their largest protein source was the guinea pig. They survived and thrived through man's labor. Their messengers ran the Inca trails, their farmers used their bare hands to plow the fields and their soldiers fought threats to the throne with clubs and slingshots.

In the rest of the Americas, no other empire challenged those of the Aztecs and the Incas. Most of the 90 million inhabitants from the Arctic to the tip of South America survived independently, as hunter-gatherers, as farmers and as traders of natural resources. They recorded little of their successes in writing, but their tombs, their stone temples and the stories told by the later European invaders speak to the cohesion, the triumphs and the trials of the American tribes.

Across the Atlantic, an entire continent was likewise evolving sporadically, with some clans continuing to wander the plains using the tools of hunter-gatherers 100,000 years ago, while others developed into kingdoms wealthier than any realm in Europe or the Far East.

Africa's a hard region to introduce. No singular empire dominated the continent. No singular religion unified all its people. No writing, economic or social system emerged to unify vast stretches of the continent. It was just not possible. Africa is just too huge to ever unite. When you picture Africa, you have to ignore the Mercator map projection you grew up with. In that world map (the one with Europe dead set in the middle), Africa is big, but it really only looks about twice the size of Europe, just a bit bigger than South America. But this map is a joke, skewed both to fit all the continents on one page, but also to reinforce the

Eurocentric perception of the world in the 16th century. The real Africa is larger than the United States, India, China, Mexico, Japan and Western Europe COMBINED (check out the Peters Projection Map). There was no way any one civilization could ever have dominated this entire continent. Rome couldn't have done it. The Mongols couldn't have done it. The Muslims tried, but they couldn't have done it. No central empire could have ever connected the impassable deserts, the deadly swamps, the impenetrable forests and the vast plains filled with an ark full of hungry carnivores.

Organizing the continent was made even more difficult because the Africans weren't exactly prolific writers. Except for a few kingdoms on the coasts or the Muslim-controlled lands up north, Africans weren't the most impressive historians. They preferred to entrust their tribe's stories to a village elder, walking libraries who passed down all their people's knowledge from one generation to the next. They also really didn't need writing. First, much of their land was shared by the whole clan, and you'd be surprised how little you need laws when there aren't property issues. But also, remember that written language first developed as a way of recording business transactions or cataloguing detailed laws when societies grew so large that you couldn't trust your neighbor anymore. This population tipping point was rarely reached in Africa, so local clans just stuck to the decisions of their village chieftains or trusted the words and deeds of each other because you knew if you screwed over someone in the tribe, there was a pretty good chance you'd be expelled, forced to survive out on your own in an unfriendly wasteland or just killed.

Civilizations also didn't develop on a large scale because they lacked massive agricultural projects. It was hard to farm tons of acres because the continent lacked huge domesticable animals (it's a bit tough to hook up a rhino or a hippo to a plow and ask it to politely till the soil), so they could only farm as much as their human labor would allow. This meant farming remained relatively small-scale and rarely allowed for the food surplus needed to launch an evolution of civilization.

This didn't mean that Africa didn't have its great civilizations. It just meant that their golden civilizations remained restricted to one region and their reign was relatively short-lived. The great civilizations had one thing in common – they were traders. They would tap into a resource demanded by their neighbors or the Eurasians, they would mine that resource until it ran out and they would set up markets and trade routes inviting would-be travellers to take their commodities to far away lands. The most-coveted resource varied from generation to generation. It might be gold or slaves or salt or timber or rubber or sugar or coffee. Today it's oil. Regardless the type of good, these resources almost always were more of a curse than a blessing, for they brought only temporary wealth to a region and unfailingly crippled the economic development of the African peoples. What incentive was there to learn how to manufacture goods when you could just dig a hole in the ground and find instant wealth?

And it was this instant wealth that brought a few African empires to the attention of the world's markets. Foremost among the great African empires was the Kingdom of Mali in northwestern Africa, home to two-thirds of the gold reserves on the planet. In most parts of the world, you can only get gold by digging deep into the earth's crust, but in Mali the gold lined the beds of the Niger River. The kings of Mali used this wealth to enrich their own pockets, but also to build universities and huge trading centers in towns like the famous Timbuktu. Salt trading nomads from central Africa brought in hundred-pound blocks of salt to Timbuktu, bringing the gold they picked up back across the Sahara to the trading ports of the Mediterranean Sea. In the 14th century, one man, King Mansa Musa decided to take his pilgrimage to Mecca, a fairly common practice for ordinary Muslims, but this man was no ordinary Muslim. He was the richest man in the history of the world (he was seven times richer than Bill Gates is today), acquiring over $400 billion in profits made off his gold and salt empire. Along his way to Mecca, Mansa Musa stopped off in Cairo with his caravan of one wife, five hundred concubines, five hundred slaves and sixty thousand porters. As he walked through the streets of Cairo, the locals were blown away by his entourage – even the slaves all carried golden staffs. Mansa Musa had no problem rubbing these foreigners' noses in his wealth, tossing bags of gold around town, totally destroying the Egyptian economy. From this moment on, Timbuktu was labeled the Golden City of Africa and, over the centuries, the myths of a city lined with gold kept enticing Europeans to make their way into the heart of the continent, looking for Africa's own El Dorado.

But lost in the myths of Timbuktu's astounding (yet temporary) golden wealth was the fact that the Mali kings had established the most advanced libraries of the 14th century. 25,000 students attended the universities of Timbuktu, ingesting the knowledge from the 300,000 scrolls lining the walls of the academies. Everything the Greeks, the Muslims, the Indians and the Chinese had ever conceived could be found in Timbuktu.

But alas, this part of Africa faded into history like every other city of the world that survived solely on its prestige as a market on a major trading route. For once the gold dried up and the salt stopped coming in from the desert, men stopped making their way across the Sahara. Timbuktu died a slow death and when the Europeans finally found the famed city in the 19th century, it was a mere shadow of its former grandeur.

This precarious position as a regional trading giant was also shared by the kingdoms of Africa's east – the Swahili Coast. Connected to the Indian Ocean trade network for over a thousand years, dozens of east African port towns gained wealth and prestige by processing the goods from the interior of Africa and loading them onto the Arab trading vessels for their passage to India and the Orient. Because the Muslims dominated this trade from the 10th century forward, many of these kingdoms developed a multicultural flair – creating faiths, art and economic and political systems that were a hybrid of African customs and Arab tradition. Locals adopted Islam, and the area's architecture (with aqueducts, arches and intricate geometric carvings) looked more like a city in the Middle East than one from the African interior. Rulers grew rich off import and export taxes and most were content simply watching their city-state prosper. They rarely competed with each other, instead focusing on being trusted hosts, guaranteeing the safety of traveller's goods and the comfort of their guests. The greatest of the Swahili city-states was Kilwa, that by the 15th century controlled dozens of coastal and mainland cities, like Zanzibar, Mozambique and Madagascar.

However, when the Portuguese arrived in the 15th century, the city-states of the Swahili Coast crumbled before the supremacy of European gunpowder, immediately handing over their wealth and their trading empires to the sea invaders.

Another of the great African empires to rise and fall with the riches of resource extraction was the Kingdom of Zimbabwe, a landlocked region in southern Africa that prospered by sending gold and copper to the Swahili Coast. Unlike the other empires of Africa, the Zimbabwe people erected huge stone cities, similar to the ones found in the great civilizations of the Americas and Eurasia. Zimbabwe actually means "house built of stone" and every one of the 18,000 residents had their own stone home. Though most of these smaller stone abodes have vanished over the last five hundred years, a giant walled King's Court with its five-meter thick walls (looking remarkably like the castle walls of Europe) can still be visited should you ever find yourself walking around southern Africa. But like its trading partners to the east, once the Portuguese arrived in the 15th century, the age of Great Zimbabwe came to an immediate end, as the Europeans would establish themselves as the sole benefactors of the African resource trade. And since that day, Africa has struggled to escape the grasp of outsiders entering its land to siphon off the gifts of nature their continent holds beneath the soil's surface.

One region that remained relatively free of European touch was the network of Polynesian islands dotting the Pacific Ocean. Few historians ever discuss the impact of the Polynesians, but their reach was nothing less than remarkable. Using nothing more than wooden canoes and their knowledge of the stars, the Polynesian peoples spent three thousand years colonizing the islands of the great Pacific Ocean, a body of water that covers nearly 1/3 the earth's surface. Historians trace these first ocean sailors to the island of Taiwan off the coast of China. Today, Taiwan is peopled 98% by Chinese from the mainland, but that remaining 2% are the descendants of the first Polynesian explorers. Sometime around 1000 BC, about the time of the Trojan War over in Greece, a Polynesian clan set off in canoes, looking for independence from their fatherland. They then settled nearby islands, showing that colonization was possible. Generation after generation set off further south and further east, looking for new lands to settle. The Polynesians never really developed agriculture, instead choosing to hunt, gather and fish. When a new island's resources couldn't keep up with their needs, an adventurous clan would hop back in one of their wooden canoes and head out again on the high seas. They replicated this process of exploring, colonizing, exploring, colonizing over the next 1500 years, ultimately making it all the way to Easter Island, nearly ten thousand miles away from Taiwan. Through the course of these voyages of discovery, the Polynesians settled over one thousand islands, spreading their culture all the way to the tip of New Zealand (and some even believe to the shores of South America).

Each settlement demonstrated the recognizable traits of the Polynesians. Whether in Hawaii or New Zealand or Samoa or Fiji or Micronesia or the Auckland Islands, the settlers all mastered the science of navigation and engineered out-rigger canoes that could criss-cross the ocean, trading with nearby island communities or fishing in the open seas. They usually lived in small family units, with four or five communal houses clustered around a garden. Because resources on these islands (often volcanic atolls) were scarce, to survive they had to share. If you didn't share, you'd die. Because of this environmental reality, private property was rare, so similar to many African clan-based societies, formal laws and a written language were a waste of time.

But that isn't to say the Polynesians didn't like to write, they just so happened to like to write on themselves. The last couple decades have seen the whole tattoo craze spread beyond the biker gangs of the west coast, to becoming so mainstream that everyone from frat boys to teenage girls with individuality issues are getting "inked." You can blame the Polynesians for starting this trend thousands of years ago. They'd use a carved bone needle to jab ink from a candlenut under the skin. But unlike today where people choose to scar themselves with stars or crosses or angels or dragons or some clever little saying from Buddha, back on the Polynesian islands, tattoos represented your class in society or how many sexual partners you'd had.

Before you lost your virginity and got one more tattoo mark, your village had to plump up. In a practice known as fattening, Polynesian adolescents were removed from the village and force-fed for months, if not years, to hopefully add on a few more pounds of flesh to make them more sexually attractive. There's also a bit of Darwin at play as the chunkier Polynesians had a better chance of surviving the long voyages from island to island. So, if you've ever wondered why wrestling's "The Rock" or the New Zealand's rugby "All Blacks" are so huge, you can look back to the realities of their ancestor's dating practices (or maybe it's because they work out a ton and eat some very effective protein shakes).

Polynesian culture isn't best known for its tattooing and fattening. Today when most people think of the island peoples, they think of surfing or hula dancing or people who just seem to smile incessantly. And of course there are those stone-headed statues on Easter Island – the moai. With their distinctive design where their heads are about the same size as their bodies, the moais could weigh up to eighty tons and be as tall as a three story building. Carved out of stone blocks, and then dragged on log rollers to the coastal perches, nearly 900 were crafted in the 13th and 14th centuries. Tragically, the Easter Island settlers cut down every single tree on their island to construct and move the statues, causing their ultimate extinction.

By the 15th century, across the globe, man had stretched out to every habitable chunk of land, living in clans or cities or even in complex empires. Today, the cultures and the contributions of the Americas, Africa and Polynesia continue to pop up in our daily lives, but for their stories to be told, they would first have to be found and linked by a people unwilling to let others live in isolation. These people, these Europeans, would in the 1400s begin the two century long challenge of uniting the entire globe, partly for selfish reasons, but also simply for the sake of satisfying man's passion for discovery – a passion that still exists to this day.

But before the Europeans could even consider exploring the world, they first had to get their act together and escape their Dark Ages. They'd need a few revolutions to get that ball rolling.

But that is for another chapter.

21

Europe Reopens Its Eyes

Europe - Renaissance, Exploration and Reformation – 1400 > 1700

In less than one hundred years, the face of the globe changed, and the countenance of Western Europe would never be the same again. Though the world of 1550 might have looked pretty similar to the world of 1450, the choices made and the feats accomplished set the wheels of progress turning in directions that would totally alter how humans interacted.

Feudalism took its last breaths, making way for the formation of the nations of Spain, France and England. The two continents previously unbeknownst to the civilized world appeared from out of nowhere when an Italian sailor accidentally bumped into some islands off the coast of Florida. European art and culture blossomed into an era of creativity and expression not seen since the days of Pericles' Athens. And the Catholic Church faced a violent and unrelenting challenge from Protestants that would leave a fractured Christendom unable to ever again unite.

It all started in 1492, the year Columbus sailed the ocean blue. That was the year the Spanish monarchs Isabella and Ferdinand once and for all kicked the Muslims out of the Iberian Peninsula (that little square chunk of land that juts out from the bottom of Europe). Ten years later, Leonardo da Vinci painted the most famous face in the world – the Mona Lisa. In 1507, Michelangelo laid on his back and finished the ceiling of the

Sistine Chapel. In 1517, a priest named Martin Luther nailed an essay on the door of a church in Germany, condemning Christianity for being home to a bunch of hypocrites. And in 1522, Ferdinand Magellan's crew returned from man's first circumnavigation of the planet. In just thirty years, European persistence had inspired its first nation, its greatest works of art, the custody of two landmasses that would feed Europe's wealth for centuries to come and a religious revolution that forever altered the power structure of the continent. These three decades were just the crowning triumphs of the eras historians later dubbed the Dawn of Absolutism, the Age of Exploration, the Renaissance and the Reformation.

Yet to deal with each separately almost misses the point. These five movements - one dealing with political reform, one with exploration, one with artistic inspiration, one with feats of navigation and one with religious reform – though seemingly disconnected, all erupted from the same umbrella of thought percolating through the greatest intellectual, artistic and political minds of Western Europe. This fresh philosophy, this "humanism," directly challenged the Catholic Church – a secular response to the superstitions that kept Europe under a veil of ignorance for the thousand years of the Middle Ages. Even without a degree in etymology, you could probably figure out that humanism is the belief in...well...humans. In the 15th and 16th centuries, humanism was the feeling that humans had so much more to offer than the blind acceptance of religious rituals. Man's imagination had been ignored. His mind had been wasted. But no longer. No longer would the Church be the sole source of wisdom. No longer would people merely survive this mortal world, clinging to the hope that their immortal existence might make up for a squandered life. Humanism offered an alternative to faith in an invisible god. It offered another source of inspiration. Man himself. Over the next hundred years man would experiment in ways he never would have before considered. And he had no one to thank but himself.

But these revolutions took time. In fact, like in most artistic and philosophical golden ages, the masses probably never got the memo that their lives were supposed to be golden. Initially, these breakthroughs were only felt in the bustling ports, thriving merchant city-states and sheltered palaces of the elite, but for the next few centuries, the world would look back at this era as when the rise of Europe (and the relative enslavement of Africa and the Americas) truly began. Not since Greek antiquity, when the ideas of a relatively small faction of learned men had been shared by Alexander across the known world, had so many peoples been forever altered by so few inspired visionaries.

None of these movements would have been possible had feudalism continued to keep a continent locked in seclusion. So what happened in Western and Southern Europe in the 14th and 15th centuries that made such a huge change possible? First, the rise of merchants and the growing prosperity in towns threatened to undermine the unquestioned power of regional lords. No longer did people have to live near the protection and the resources of a baron, a duke, a count or an earl. Instead of meeting at fairs once or twice a year, merchants set up permanent markets, and towns became centers of power. Next, traders needed money to take their goods afar, and early banks appeared, granting loans and extending credit. At first, it was only the Jews who could lend money (since the Bible forbade usury – the loaning of money with interest), giving this persecuted group a head start in an industry that would become a necessity when European economies commercialized. As the Church reduced its restrictions on money lending, more Christians entered the field and money started flowing through the hands of new classes of people, not merely through the palms of the provincial lords.

With all of this newfound wealth to be made from trade and banking, it wasn't long before monarchs wanted more for themselves. Throughout the Middle Ages, kings might have been seen as the chief monarchs of emerging nations, but the nobles all stood between them and absolute, unquestioned power. The nobles had first dibs on peasant taxes, they controlled the warrior knights and their landholdings and prominent voices meant they had to be consulted should a monarch want to extend the nation's boundaries.

Kings weren't exactly fond of this arrangement. They wanted absolute power and the idea of having to consult with lords was more than a bit annoying. So when gunpowder finally entered Europe, they had their chance to tilt the power even more in their favor. Before, in the Middle Ages, nobles could barricade themselves inside their impenetrable castle walls or send out their trained knights to foil any royal power play. A king could try all he wanted, but a fortified lord behind stone walls was a tough nut to crack. But within one generation, gunpowder made castles and knights obsolete. What match could a stone wall be for a well-placed cannonball? Could a mounted knight with a lifetime of training survive a well-aimed musket? And when you combined the two – a gunpowder-fed artillery with a musket-yielding army – medieval warfare had no chance of survival. The age of knights had ended. One by one the nobles lost their kingdoms, with each loss only increasing the power of the monarchs.

But kings still needed money. Money made the whole system work. More money meant more weapons. More money meant more armies. More money meant more ships. They needed money, so they taxed. They borrowed. They encouraged trade. They promoted local manufacturing. They even gave money to crazy seamen who believed they could find shortcuts to Asia (we'll talk about Chris and Ferdinand in a minute). And the investments paid off. The risks proved worth it. Money started rolling in from all corners of the planet, and with each new revenue stream, more land could be taken over and more profit-producing enterprises could be financed.

By 1600, four new nations appeared, each demanding unquestioned loyalty from their countrymen. Portugal, Spain, France and England shared the traits of this new era of absolutism, this age of national dynasties. They forced everyone to speak the same language. They made everyone use the same money and made everyone use the same units to measure goods. They created one set of laws enforced by a network of bureaucracies. They constructed absurdly lavish palaces and established elaborate ceremonies, each maintained to showcase their godlike supremacy. And as for the nobles, their voices were relegated to the newly formed parliaments and national assemblies, governing bodies whose power varied based on the whims of each subsequent monarch.

But above all else, they expanded. The more land they gobbled, the more power they yielded. Expansion triggered their ascendancy, and only with expansion could they maintain their power. And as the resources of the European continent increasingly fell into the hands of fewer and fewer monarchs, the kings of western and southern Europe looked to distant shores for new sources of wealth.

Although the days of England, France and the Netherlands ruling the seas would one day come, in the 15th century, the only countries with a true sea presence were Portugal and Spain. If the world was going to be mapped, it would be by a navigator sailing under the flag of one of these two nations on the tip of the Iberian

Peninsula. Long excluded by the Italians from the Mediterranean trading networks, the Portuguese and Spanish rulers realized if they wanted to secure a share of the mountains of wealth promised by the Asian manufacturers, they would need to find a new course to the Indies. At the end of the 15th century, the Indies had become the general term for any of the desired trading posts in Asia, be it India, China, Japan, Malaya or Java (Indonesia today). Any semi-intelligent merchant knew that the key to wealth was the Indies, with its spices, its silks, its unrivaled pottery and its luxury goods. A successful expedition guaranteed a 1000% return on their investment, and every emerging nation knew what greatness could be purchased with this money, but more important, what risks existed should their neighboring country find the unknown path first. The race was on.

By the end of the 15th century, a convergence of factors materialized that set in motion an unprecedented Age of Discovery by Portugal and Spain. In 1453, when the Ottoman Turks conquered Constantinople, destroying the Byzantine Empire once and for all, the trans-Eurasian Silk Road, that had for centuries brought goods from Asia, was now cut off. For a couple hundred years, the Mongols had protected the salesmen of the Silk Road. But no longer. With an unpredictable Muslim power replacing the Mongol-enforced peace, European merchants were at the mercy of these Muslims. Yet with so many goods just waiting to be imported, traders realized if they couldn't go through the Islamic world, they'd just have to find a way of going around it.

Ironically, it was the Muslims who made Europe's Age of Exploration possible. It was the Muslims that brought the nautical technology from the East that allowed Europeans to sail out of sight of land and start heading into open waters. They passed on the compass, a triangular sail that could catch the wind and the astrolabe for reading the stars. Navigators could finally use the sun, the stars and the earth's own magnetism to guide their ships across the open seas. Ships were then built stronger, faster, with three masts and a bigger, more accurate rudder. Sailors could catch the prevailing winds and sail away to far-off lands. And with their newfound gunpowder-fed cannons, no pirate dared threaten these imposing beasts.

And why were Portugal and Spain the first out of the gate? With their geographic proximity to northwestern Africa and the Atlantic Ocean, their independently powerful and moneyed monarchs and their direct link to the navigational knowledge of the Muslim world, Portugal and Spain were the most likely contenders to find a water route to Asia. For decades, Portugal had flirted with the western coast of Africa, hearing stories of endless supplies of gold and even of a mythical Christian leader named Prestor John (a long lost monk who many Europeans believed had established a Christian empire in Africa). If Prestor John could be found (or so the story went), his empire could be united with the European forces of God to encircle the Muslim forces. This mythical reunion was nothing more than a wild fantasy. But the gold was real.

The first to actively explore Africa was Prince Henry of Portugal. The world has had Alexander the Great, Richard the Lionhearted, Attila the Hun and even Vlad the Impaler. But when it comes to a really cool nickname that will impress the ladies at the local pub, look no further than Prince Henry the *Navigator*. Prince Henry rose to power on the heels of his military victories that pushed the last Muslims out of Portugal. In one of the last Muslim strongholds, the city of Ceuta, Henry not only found the indispensable libraries representing the sum total of Muslim learning, but he also came across a vast storehouse of spices, including most notably pepper and cinnamon. Henry could have merely sold these luxuries on the open market, fetched a handsome profit and our story would have ended there, but Henry had a bit more foresight. He knew that the man who could monopolize this spice trade would be the man who could enrich his kingdom. Prince Henry then, in the southern city of Sagres, established a school of navigation to improve the maritime technology available to Europeans, but also answer questions such as "Why does the North Star, a navigator's most reliable landmark in the sky, disappear when sailors venture further south?" These astronomers, navigators, biologists and chemists began dispelling the major myths of the day – that the ocean boils when you head south, that the sun touches the ocean, that the earth was flat. Many learned Europeans had already deduced these realities, but at Henry's school, his scientists fueled the captains with the confidence to head further and further south along the west coast of Africa. With each expedition, the Portuguese explorers leapfrogged each other, heading a few more miles south, mapping the terrain, making contact with locals and potentially heading inland to look for gold and Prestor John. But to actually make it to the southern tip (a distance of about 5000 miles), someone would have to be willing to leave Europe for what could be years and refuse to return until the destination was reached. That man would be Bartolomeu Dias.

Dias set sail in August 1487, and seven months later, he had finally reached the southern tip. Going around Africa scared the bejeepers out of Dias's crew, as the waters beneath the tips of continents aren't known for being especially friendly. When you have two great oceans colliding, the storm patterns make for deadly waves with violently unpredictable winds.

But he made it around the tip. Once on the eastern side of Africa, Dias wanted to continue toward Asia, but his crew felt they shouldn't push their luck any further and should instead get back to Europe while they still had their lives. Dias agreed and returned to Portugal in December of 1488, and his Christmas present to the king was the knowledge that the Portuguese had been further south than any other European. As he recounted his treacherous trip around what Dias named the Cape of Storms, the Portuguese monarch King John II thought it might be prudent to rename the route something a bit more positive to encourage future navigators, thus the southernmost point of Africa became known to the world as the "Cape of Good Hope."

Now that the southern route around Africa was proven passable, Portugal's Vasco de Gama set out in 1497 to finish what Dias never could – reaching Asia by sea. Instead of hugging the coastline for the entire route, when de Gama reached the southern tip of North Africa (where the continent shoots eastward for a thousand miles), he chose the shortest direction between two points and headed diagonally down to the cape. Although Columbus would receive a ton of praise for his fearlessness in heading across unchartered oceans, it was de Gama who spent the longest time on the open ocean without site of land. Columbus was gone for five weeks, de Gama for thirteen. When he finally hit the Cape of Good Hope, he headed up the east coast and met some Indian traders who showed him how to catch the monsoon winds of the Indian Ocean. On May 20, 1498, about a month shy of one year, de Gama reached Calicut, India, becoming the first European to reach Asia by sea. No European would ever have to trade across the treacherous, costly Levant and Silk Road again. Within a decade the Portuguese had set up ports all around Africa and South Asia, even reaching as far as modern day Malaysia at a trading town called Malacca. The Portuguese had succeeded in opening up the Indies, and over the next century, spices, tea, ceramics, textiles and even slaves flowed freely from East to West, while European gold ended in the hands of the East.

With the southern route securely in the hands of the Portuguese, the Spanish could only go one other direction - west. However, nobody really wanted to head west. Nobody except for a persistent Italian sailor from Genoa, Italy. Christopher Columbus (or Cristoforo Colombo to his mom and dad) spent his adulthood on the seas. He made up for his lack of schooling by learning from everyone he encountered. He learned the latest navigation techniques from the Portuguese. He listened to of tales of a "new found land" from the Viking descendants he met in England. He read of Marco Polo's adventures and Ptolemy's theories of the earth's spherical shape. He took all of this knowledge and came up with the theory that right on the other side of the Atlantic Ocean rested the Indies, ripe for the taking. He took his theories and his calculations to the thrones of Europe. Somebody had to be willing to finance his dream. But the Italians, the French, the Portuguese and even the Spanish refused to accept his proposal.

But he persisted. After seven years of patiently pleading his case, he finally convinced Queen Isabella of Spain that the potential rewards far outweighed the negligible risks. With a few ships – the Nina, the Pinta and the Santa Maria – he promised he could radically cut the distance to the Indies, allowing Spain to monopolize sea trade.

Columbus set sail in 1492 on a trip to Japan that he thought would be about 2,500 miles. He was just a bit off. Japan is actually about 10,000 miles away from Spain, and had Columbus and his crew not bumped into these little chunks of land known today as the Americas, his crew would have starved to death and his ships would have ended up at the bottom of the sea.

But Columbus did hit land, a small island called Guanahani inhabited by the Tainos. Columbus insisted these people were from the Indies, and erroneously named them Indians. His first account of these people didn't bode well for how they'd be treated in the coming century:

> They do not bear arms, and do not know them, for I showed them a sword, they took it by the edge and cut themselves out of ignorance. They have no iron. Their spears are made of cane...They would make fine servants...With fifty men we could subjugate them all and make them do whatever we want.

Ahhh, what a lovely sentiment? Columbus wasn't exactly the poster child for humanitarianism. But racial equality was the least of his concerns. He wanted Asia.

And Columbus truly believed he had, in fact, found an island off the coast of Japan. Until his dying day, he insisted this land was Asia. He took several more trips back and forth across the ocean, each time finding more islands in the Caribbean. Though he proved a capable navigator (if maybe off course by a continent or two), he was less impressive as a governor, and his legacy of rule was seen as nothing more than a period of chaos, murder and plunder for gold. After initially being seen as a hero, he spent some time in jail for his bungling of these newfound lands and died not knowing the true import of his discovery. Portuguese explorer Amerigo Vespucci eventually set foot in Uruguay, and when in 1502 German cartographer Martin Waldseemuller created a map with Amerigo's name next to the Nuevo Mundo (new world), the Americas had their namesake.

Although Columbus received little initial credit for his discoveries, even losing out to Amerigo for the naming rights to these new lands, his efforts set in motion centuries of exploration and discovery that would wipe out civilizations that had prospered for millennia, transport civilizations to unknown lands and unite the globe in trade networks that moved not only peoples, but goods and ideas. Some of these exchanges were conducted peacefully, but for the most part violence and death followed each new discovery. Historians have since debated whether Columbus was a hero or a villain, but regardless of the ethical judgments surrounding his discoveries, his findings allowed humans to expand further than ever thought possible.

While the Spanish and Portuguese were expanding their boundaries, back home in Europe, a group of artists and thinkers began expanding the possibilities of human creativity. In the flourishing city-states of Italy, the humanistic trend toward self-discovery meant that artists could again begin testing the limits of imagination. Whereas throughout the Middle Ages, art remained two-dimensional and centered on the depictions of saints and Biblical stories, during this artistic revolution known as the Renaissance, man again became the muse and those possessing the skills of perspective and realism became the most prized craftsmen (sort of like in the Golden Age of Athens). Although the Renaissance would eventually spread across Western Europe to include a literary transformation, the first (and most famous) pieces came from Florence and Rome and revolved around achievements in painting, sculpture and architecture.

Before looking at the works of da Vinci, Michelangelo, Raphael and Donatello, we must first ask the questions: Why 1500? Why Italy?

Was it because the Italian peninsula was home to thousands of Roman sculptures and monolithic ruins left over from the Pax Romana, constantly reminding the locals of a past far more glorious than their current state? Was it because so many Muslim recordings of antiquity began flowing into Italy, spawning a revived interest in Greece and Rome? Or was it because immeasurable wealth rested in the hands of opulent patrons, more than willing to throw a few coins at the artistic community?

Yes.

Whether it was the merchant Medicis of Florence or the pampered Popes of Rome, there was money to be spent, and what better way to distribute wealth than to hire artists to decorate their homes, palaces, churches and tombs?

Regardless of the reason, from 1475 to 1525, the greatest works of the last thousand years streamed from Italian hands. Venetian Leonardo da Vinci used his knowledge of the human body gained through his examination of cadavers to sketch hundreds of images of the lifecycle of man, from the womb to the grave (most notably the Vitruvian Man...that sketch with circles and a standing man with arms outstretched). He masterfully painted The Last Supper and the Mona Lisa, the most recognizable piece of art in the world (yet don't be surprised if you're a bit underwhelmed by its size when you visit it in the Louvre). And in his spare time, he invented the helicopter, the parachute and the submarine (though worried his ideas might be used for war, he encoded all of his ideas in backwards text). Da Vinci became the world's first Renaissance Man, a man at the top of his game in so many fields.

If da Vinci was the number one symbol of the Renaissance, Michelangelo was a close second. Commissioned almost exclusively by religious leaders to bring the Bible to life, Michelangelo still found a way to throw in his humanistic touch. He was asked to sculpt the boy underdog from the Biblical battle of David versus Goliath. He returned with a fifteen-foot tall naked man whose private parts have shocked citizens and visitors to Florence for generations. When asked to recreate the stories of the New Testament on the ceiling of the Sistine Chapel, Michelangelo returned to Pope Julius II a fresco with women that look like bodybuilders with breasts and a central image of God giving life to Adam, a reclining figure depicted as more dominant than even the likeness of God. The ceiling was not exactly what Julius had ordered.

Although da Vinci and Michelangelo are the most renowned, the patronage of the merchant families and the Catholic Church created a network of artists who filled Italian homes, city squares and places of worship with frescoes, statues, fountains, paintings, ceilings and entryways. Donatello mastered the art of bronze statuary. Raphael created the School of Athens and the Sistine Madonna (that painting with the two adorable little cherubs gazing into the sky).

Once the artistic revolution was underway in Italy, it wasn't long before the rest of Europe joined the movement. With the printing press able to spread the works and the philosophies of the Renaissance into the libraries of the wealthy and the pious, with the rising frequency of travellers and with the myriad of wars that brought peoples into contact with these new forms of creativity, the Renaissance spread into France, the Netherlands and then England. These 16th century pieces continued to have a religious undertone, but the focus on the beauty, and sometimes the ugliness, of the human form increasingly dominated. When the imagination and creativity of the visual arts spread to the written arts, a new age emerged where with a pen and a wicked wit, artists could bring down even the most prominent member of society.

In England, by the end of the 16th century, William Shakespeare was spinning out dozens of plays and poems that explored the greatest moments in European history, while also dealing with themes of the fallibility of the human spirit. His cutting comedies and bitter tragedies gained an audience with the lowest classes, and his plays performed at the Globe Theater gained a cult following. Ironically, today the original works of the barb are seen almost as too highbrow for us mortals, but his themes and characters continue to be seen in films such as *Ten Things I Hate About You, O, She's the Man* and the inevitable *Romeo and Juliet* or *Hamlet* recreation that surfaces once every generation (think *West Side Story* and *The Lion King*). And who couldn't recognize a good Shakespeare quote – "to be or not to be," "it's all Greek to me," "all the world's a stage," "eaten me out of house and home" or "to thine own self be true?" Shakespeare might not have created the English language, but he could be seen as the one who advanced it the furthest, himself adding what some etymologists believe to be some 3000 new words to the English lexicon.

By 1600, the Renaissance had transformed the world of creativity, and Europe would never again return to the days of artistic stagnancy. Though initially funded by the Catholic Church, with each piece chronicling the mind, body and soul of man, the Renaissance and its shift away from spirituality steadily tore cracks in the unquestioned foundation of the Church. These cracks would eventually become irreparable fissures when one man chose to publicly challenge Christendom, unintentionally spawning the creation of dozens of new faiths, all rivaling the supremacy of Europe's first Church.

As the Middle Ages trudged along, the Church steadily lost its monopoly on the minds of Europeans. After Europe's less-than-impressive oh-for-nine won/loss record against the Muslims in the Crusades, it was a bit tough to swallow that God only had one chosen people. When the Church failed to quell the suffering of the Black Plague, some questioned the value of a faith that couldn't even keep people alive. But even with these challenges, few dared publicly confront their religious superiors for fear of torture, both in this life and the hereafter.

Yet by the 1500s, the centuries of clerical abuses had started to become too much for even the most pious followers. Priests weren't exactly the immaculate models of godliness. Some married. Some had mistresses. Some even had children. Some cared more about securing their garish lifestyles than protecting the souls of their parishioners. Some fought in wars. Some didn't even show up to their parish, and when they did, their illiteracy prevented them from accurately reading the Bible. And for some reason, the priests' interpretation of the Bible always ended up in an appeal for more coins in the offering plate. Some priests started money lending and others even sold vacated religious positions to the highest bidder. Even merchant families (like the Medicis) could become Popes. Of course, not all the clerics were wicked or incompetent, but like the Catholic Church of today, a few guilty clergy can spoil the reputation of the entire faith.

The above transgressions were annoyances, but not enough to bring down the Church. In 1517, caught up in the artistry of the Renaissance, Pope Leo X commissioned the restoration of St. Peter's Cathedral, and to raise the money, he conveniently redefined the centuries old tradition of "indulgences." Pope Leo X promised that for a few coins, you could free your ancestors from purgatory and put them on the fast track to heaven. These "Get Out of Hell Free" cards followed a price index based on your status in life. A king might pay twenty gulden, whereas a farmer might pay only one. With this payment, no matter your uncle's, your father's or your brother's crime, any one of their souls could be freed.

This little scheme posed a few problems. If you could merely buy yourself out of Hell, why follow the commandments when on earth? If the Pope really had the power to free your soul from Hell, why didn't he just do it out of the kindness of his heart? And what of faith? Did you even need to believe in God? Wasn't that little, fairly significant nugget a criterion for Christian salvation?

In Germany, the indulgences had become quite common, and with salesman such as John Tetzel peddling salvation through his carnival-like performances, more than a few eyes started to turn. One man saw these indulgences for what they really were – a blatant scheme to rob the people. And this man had had enough. At the university at Wittenberg, this man, a professor of theology named Martin Luther (not that Martin Luther...this one's last name isn't King) couldn't stand the corruption and hypocrisy any longer. So what did he do? How did this Martin Luther fight the power?

He wrote an essay.

Not just any essay, but an essay with 95 subcategories - his 95 Theses. He took this outlined list of the Church's indiscretions and nailed them to the door of the Wittenberg Church. At this point, he had no intention of bringing down the Church; he just wanted to start a conversation with his fellow theological brothers. However, his message went far beyond the inner circle of clerics in Germany. The printing press stepped onto the European stage and took what could have been a mere footnote to Church history, and created a movement. If you lived in a town in 1522, you'd have heard of the 95 Theses. Not everyone could read, but everyone could listen, and there was always someone in town willing to report Luther's finding to an attentive audience. Luther wasn't done. He followed up his formal complaints with a series of pamphlets and sermons, each challenging the legitimacy of Church doctrine.

Should priests marry? Should priests be literate? Were priests even needed? Or could a man simply believe in God and that be enough? Did he have to go to a building on Sunday to go to heaven? Or merely trust that Jesus died for our sins? Should the Church advertise relics (the bones or sacred belongings of the saints) to expand their audience, or should the words of the Bible be the sole spiritual commercial?

The Pope was less than pleased. He ordered Martin Luther to renounce his teachings, but Luther continued. The Church faced a tough decision. Punish Luther, he becomes a martyr. Ignore Luther, his message continues to spread. The solution – put Luther on trial. Luther was brought before the Diet of Worms (not an uncouth menu selection, but a meeting of the princes of the Holy Roman Empire at a city called Worms). The Holy Roman Emperor gave Luther a choice – recant or die. But Luther could not recant. He could not deny his beliefs when he knew he was right. Nothing in the Bible contradicted his teachings. He knew he was on the right side of the truth.

The Church was stuck. They couldn't kill him, but they couldn't just let him directly challenge the Church and go free. His punishment was ostracism. They let him go free and vowed to punish any man who gave him aid. And should a defender of the Church kill the rebel, oh well, it was out of their hands. The assailant would not be punished. They essentially dared a Christian follower to assassinate Martin Luther. Luther was released.

But Luther was never killed. He was never again arrested. Instead, Prince Frederick III of Germany outwitted the Church, by "kidnapping" Luther and hiding him in Wartburg Castle for a few months. Luther spent his days of banishment rewriting the Bible in a language his German brethren could actually understand. But in 1522, there was no singular German language, simply dozens of provincial languages like Bavarian, Saxon, Low German and High German. If Luther was to translate the Bible from Latin to German, he would have to invent the German language. In 1534, he finally finished his magnum opus, writing the first of what would become dozens of Bibles written in dozens of languages. These new versions completely flipped the power structure of the Christian faith. No longer would the writings of the followers of Christ reside solely in the hands of those that spoke Latin. Now, anyone could read the Bible. Now, anyone could *interpret* the Bible. Dozens of new faiths emerged, and each of these "protesting" faiths offered an alternative to the Church. Each of these new sects became part of what is today known as the *Protestant Reform*ation.

But the Church wasn't going to take these challenges sitting down. The Church responded by declaring they were the one, true, "universal" faith. And the Latin word for "universal" was "catholic," – thus the Church was renamed the Catholic Church. But a simple renaming wasn't the only alteration the Pope made from Rome. The church leaders then mounted their own Counter-Reformation, becoming even more strict, more dogmatic. They had no intention of giving in to the Protestant challenge. You were either with the Church or you were against it. And if that meant war, the Catholic Church was more than willing to take up arms. Princes, lords and kings took to the sword, killing each other to prove what was the one true faith. The continent fell into an age of chaos, as soldiers of God waged war for the hearts and minds of Europe. Hundreds of thousands of men, women and children, from England to Germany to Norway to Spain, would perish.

Martin Luther's publishing of his Bible, and this ensuing century of warfare, nailed the final stake in the coffin of the Middle Ages. Europe's epoch of mediocrity began to fade, and a new Europe emerged. This new Europe would be stronger, mobile and empowered by both a revolutionary zeal and a newfound faith in humanity that would take them across the globe. For the select few merchants, artists, explorers, patrons, patriarchs and politicos who ushered in this rebirth, Western Europe felt like it was living through a new golden age.

Yet like all golden ages, this one too came to a premature end, but what emerged from this prosperity of the human spirit surprised even the most disheartened cynic. What did Europeans think would happen when the institutions that stabilized the continent for a thousand years were completely uprooted? What did Europeans think would happen when previously isolated civilizations came face to face with a people bent on stealing their wealth at any cost?

What happened? Europe and the lands its explorers and settlers touched entered into a century of violence and upheaval that forever restructured the power of peoples and regions.

But that is for another chapter.

22

The Century of Death

Europe - Revolutionary Impact - 1500-1650

In a perfect world, revolutions would make life better for people. In our world, this never happens. At least not initially. The French Revolution flirted with equality before putting its citizens through the guillotine and a bitterly fruitless series of continental wars. The Industrial Revolution forced its participants to survive decades of urban squalor before reaping the benefits of an advanced economy. And the Russian Revolution...well...let's just say the twenty million people that perished probably would have preferred life just the way it was.

But what about Europe's little 16th century foray into the world of change? What could possibly go wrong when people started meeting new neighbors and asking questions about their God?

What could go wrong?

Well, where would you like me to begin?

When Prince Henry and his Portuguese fleets first set out down the African coast, ushering in an era of exploration, the goal was spices. Cheap, plentiful, little savory morsels of Eastern pleasure. But when an eastern sea route was finally established and a couple continents were inadvertently discovered, what the world got was so much more cataclysmic than merely the exchange of some items that would end up in the spice cabinets of European nobility.

In the Americas, life as the natives knew it ceased to exist. Depending on which historian you ask, in 1500, when Columbus first arrived, the Americas were home to anywhere between 40 million and 100 million people. Two centuries later, they were at five million. Though the Black Plague was truly devastating and the Holocaust marked an era of unrestrained horror, the plight of the American indigenous populations has no equal. Some call this loss of life a genocide, but that moniker seems to fit better when premeditated slaughter accompanies the carnage. With the Americas, almost all of the death came from the silent killers of disease.

The American continents, insulated from the germs that had bounced around Eurasia for millennia, were no match for the invasion of smallpox, measles and the flu. Within a few decades of the first Spanish arrival, entire Caribbean island populations disappeared. Those that survived were too weak to even put up resistance to the technologically superior Europeans who then stepped ashore. Going back the other direction, syphilis infected the continent of Europe. Although this disease took decades, not weeks, to destroy the bodies and minds of the infected, it did kill millions and eventually forced Europe to adopt strictly conservative (aka "monogamous") sexual practices to limit its spread.

The exchange between the Old and the New World of not only these diseases, but of goods, ideas and people, has become known as the Columbian Exchange or the Transatlantic Trade Route, and this route forever altered the civilizations on three continents. Each region was the recipient and the donor of a host of gifts, oftentimes swapped without unanimous consent.

Whereas the disease-swap led to nothing but calamity, the introduction of varying crops across the Atlantic unmistakably improved the overall diets of everyone touched. For the Americans, the arrival of cows, sheep, goats and pigs meant the addition of entirely new protein sources. The Europeans brought back tomatoes, potatoes, corn, avocadoes, chilies, chocolate and vanilla from the Americas. These items provided the color, the flavor and the vitamins sadly lacking on the European menu (most Medieval Europeans had for centuries survived on beef, bacon and bread). These American imports put the sauce on Italian pasta, the chocolate in French pastries and the chilies in Spanish tapas.

Though not exactly edible, and with rather dubious effects, tobacco also made its way to Europe, becoming for many regions the number one cash crop for all would-be settlers. These items made their way throughout the Mediterranean and across continents, even altering the eating habits of Sub-Saharan Africa. With diets more balanced and stomachs more full, all recipients began living longer, better able to survive the inevitable periods of famine and illness.

But people became the most recognizable import and export. Some left by choice. Some left by coercion. Some were kidnapped and sent across the Atlantic. When the Portuguese first arrived in West Africa, they were quick to involve themselves in the slave trade already made profitable by African and Muslim merchants. When the indigenous American populations proved unable to meet the labor demands of the European settlers, Africa became the most obvious source of cheap labor. More than twenty million people were taken from West Africa, with only ten to twelve million actually ever surviving the trip. The majority of these slaves went to the Caribbean and South America (most notably Brazil), but because in the early years of the slave trade little thought was given to the lifespan or viability of forced servitude, more and more slaves were brought over to replace those that died under the brutal conditions. Why create conditions for slaves to live longer when it was easier to just replace the dead with a new batch fresh off the boat? And the bulk of these slaves sent to the South were men who rarely lived more than a few years before perishing under the misery of bondage. In North America, males and females were imported in relatively equal numbers, allowing for marriage and reproduction. Although the Southern United States imported relatively few slaves, its policies of directed slave marriages and legal enslavement of all slave offspring meant that the populations would not only increase, but would remain intensely segregated from the privileges of the white community. In South America, blacks and whites weren't as segregated and the resulting intermarriage between the races led to a more vibrant cultural exchange than what was found up north.

The types of Europeans who emigrated west also differed across the New World. Along the eastern coast of North America, the British sent over entire families and towns to become permanent colonists. These colonists (think Pilgrims) oftentimes came from newly Protestant backgrounds, intensely independent with a work ethic that scorned the shirking of labor. These pious immigrants, believing they were God's newly chosen people, wanted to create a "city on a hill" for all others to emulate. This independence, bordering on arrogance, became the foundation for what would be a people unwilling to remain under the rule of their English mother country.

In the Spanish and Portuguese colonies to the south, a different dynamic emerged as the young male victims of primogeniture left their European homes in search of land and prosperity. Upon arrival, the encomienda system granted each white man the services of all natives living on any land taken or bequeathed. These products of old nobility hated the idea of getting their fingers dirty, instead forcing the indigenous populations to take up all menial tasks. For those Native Americans hardened by living under the rule of the Aztecs or the Incas, this was merely the exchange of one oppressive ruler for another, but for the hundreds of independent tribes unaccustomed to forced servitude, this condition proved unbearable, leading many to choose suicide or, at the very least, infanticide. Although clearly a hierarchical relationship, the European-Indian interaction in the south provided for far more intermarriage than in the north where European-Indian unions were almost nonexistent (at least after the early years when Pocahontas-John Rolfe unions were more common). Because Southern European men often arrived without a woman in tow, they were more willing to hook up with the locals. The resulting mestizo population of mixed heritage parents also contributed to the cultural exchange throughout what would become Latin America. Because of this vast mestizo population, although European descendants would hold governmental and religious positions of power for centuries to come, Latin American society wasn't simply a recreation of Old Europe, but instead a world where indigenous values and traditions blended with those of the West.

The impact of the Europeans on the Americas has no parallel. Where else, on such a grand scale, were a people able to completely destroy one civilization, replacing it with another? Although in North America this process took far longer, the results were the same. Within three centuries, the two continents once inhabited by hundreds of unique, independent peoples became regions almost exclusively inhabited and controlled by Europeans. These Europeans imported and mandated their Christian faith, their governmental systems and their technologies, all of which kept the indigenous populations subservient, or at the least, irrelevant.

This ability to completely subjugate populations was not possible in the Asian areas discovered by European explorers. Though by the 19th century the story would be different, in the 1600s the Europeans were no match for the advanced civilizations of India and China. India initially laughed at the European attempts to trade, and the Chinese likewise saw no value in the European goods brought to market. Because time and again Europeans met Asian peoples relatively immune to European illnesses while also able to assemble formidable military forces, the Portuguese, the Spanish and the Dutch contented themselves with merely securing trading rights in critically-located ports. Ironically, the Chinese would eventually find one product of value the Europeans could offer – silver.

The one item the Americas had in bulk, which the Chinese ceaselessly demanded, was bullion – gold and silver metal. The gold and silver deposits in the soil of the Americas became an unexpected boon to the Portuguese and Spanish. When the Spanish conquistador Pizarro first encountered the Incas in 1534, he kidnapped their king Atahualpa, demanding a gold ransom that would fill a room vault bigger than a McMansion family room (22 feet by 17 feet by 8 feet high). They got the ransom, but they killed Atahualpa anyway. Pizarro and his men then amassed eleven tons of gold and twenty-five tons of silver. Pizarro alone walked away with a fairly impressive stash that today would be valued at over $400 million. Pizarro's haul led to the first of what would be many American mineral rushes with Spanish silver mines popping up all over Mexico and South America. By 1600, South America provided 80% of the world's silver, with almost all of it going to China. Spain purchased the luxury goods from China, while China used the silver to turn their economy from one of paper currency to one of a more durable material. Unfortunately for the Spanish, they failed to use this gold and silver rush to develop a permanent, diversified economy, instead just sending it to Northern Europe to buy the luxury goods coming out of England, France and the Netherlands. This fatal decision to bypass economic improvement meant that when the mines inevitably dried up (pay attention oil-rich Saudi Arabia), the Spanish economy fell into disarray, and in 1588, when the Spanish fleet (its Armada) was defeated by the British, the age of Spanish maritime dominance came to a crushing end.

This clash on the seas was not the only military conflict facing Europe in the century following the humanistic revolutions of the 16th century. While the Americas and Asia adjusted to the new European explorers, traders and settlers, Europe plunged into a series of "wars of religion," each making it all too clear that Europe would never be a united land again.

When Martin Luther nailed his 95 Theses to the door of the Wittenberg Church, he had no intention of starting a revolution, but a revolution was what he would get. Within a few years of publishing the 95 Theses, peasants across the land seized this moment to demand more rights. They destroyed monasteries, plundered castles and left towns utterly devastated. Luther made his opinion on this peasant revolt relatively clear when he wrote the oh-so-subtle pamphlet titled "Against the Murdering, Thieving Hordes of the Peasants." Eventually Luther threw his full support behind the princes who employed all their military capabilities to put down these insurrections.

But the wars were nowhere near being resolved. The princes of Western Europe realized this was the perfect time to expand their influence by snatching Catholic lands. In 1500, the wealthiest landholder in all of Europe was not a prince, not a merchant, not a banking family, but the Catholic Church. Over the course of the Middle Ages, millions and millions of acres were bequeathed to the Church, sometimes because the haves wanted to help the have-nots, but more often, it was the soon-to-be-dead that wanted to increase their chances of spending an eternity north of Hell. So when Luther made it acceptable to formally challenge the Church, the priests took this opportunity and ran with it. Newly-Protestant princes began attacking neighboring Catholic parishes, and with the religious zeal of pent-up peasant armies at their disposal, they readily dispatched their weaker foe, taking control of all lands and taxations. In this manner, realms expanded and the Catholic Church mounted a formidable defense. After this back and forth maneuvering for power, in 1555, German princes agreed to the Peace of Augsburg where individual princes decided the one accepted faith for their kingdom. Because princes could change their mind to suit their economic and political agendas, some regions found themselves switching their allegiance between the Protestant and Catholic faiths with every subsequent transfer of power. A noble father might be Protestant, yet his son might choose to be Catholic. And whatever their lord of the moment chose, the people had to follow. Europe became a forever changing patchwork of Christian denominations. The one institution that had united Europe had fallen and instead of one unrivaled Christianity, the continent was forever replaced with competing Christiani*ties*.

In addition to meeting violence with violence, the Catholic Church responded to the calls for reform by instituting the Counter Reformation. At the 1545 Council of Trent discussions, the Church reversed its policies on indulgences and agreed to strictly monitor the behavior of all clerics, but instead of moving forward and evolving to meet the perceived changing needs of Europeans, the Church actually became more conservative, explicitly establishing the rules, behaviors and teachings followed by the priests, defining once and for all the one, and only, way that the Bible could be interpreted. Any other perspectives would be deemed heresy, subject to punishments that could include a painful death. The decades of European humanism where individuals had started believing they could challenge the Church were over. In one of the most comical interpretations of the Council of Trent, Pope Paul IV mandated fig leaves be sculpted, painted, sketched or planted on the genitalia of all Renaissance pieces depicting nude subjects. And the Renaissance was over.

Though the covering of men's private parts with vegetation might appear odd by today's standards, the edict that had more drastic consequences was Pope Paul IV's absurdly-titled "Cum nimis absurdum" that established ghettos for Jews, preventing them from living amongst the Christians. This precedent of religious intolerance gained speed as the century passed, leading to the expulsion of Jews, Muslims and non-believers from all Christian towns. One group drawing far too much unwanted attention were unmarried older women who were a burden on a town's resources and a blight on society. These spinster women (who God forbid made it to thirty without finding a husband) oftentimes lived on the outskirts of towns or in broken down shacks deep in the forest, and drew the ire of mainstream Europe. These "witches" were then blamed for every possible calamity that could befall a community – miscarriages, famines, accidents or freaks of nature – and the punishments imagined by their accusers frequently surpassed the sadistic. Instead of merely killing the accused, Europeans experimented with ovens, thumbscrews and a myriad of other devices that caused excruciating pain, like the Pear, the Judas Cradle and the Iron Maiden, but I shall entrust you with a Google search should you require the R-rated details.

As witches were being persecuted, groups were being banished and individuals were being burned alive for heresy, wars started up again across the continent, these being even more brutal than the earlier princely rivals. Armies that fought for a Catholic prince, might end up fighting for a Protestant prince and then surrendering to a Calvinist prince. Save for personal advancement, few could predict what would motivate a prince to take his people to war. For 30 years between 1618 and 1648 (a conflict known cleverly as the Thirty Years War), all of Europe fell into a continental bloodbath, not the last time independent European nations would test their arms against neighbors. Victors were unclear, motives were vague, but the one thing that was consistent was the carnage inflicted on the peasants. Towns vanished, crops were destroyed and famines and plagues wiped out populations. Within one generation nearly one third of Germany's population perished, with the only one result being that Europe proved it could never unite again.

What started out as a century of promise for the possibility of human achievement ended with the fracturing and destruction of civilizations. For the first time, the world truly had a global trade network. With European ships connecting the Americas to Europe to Africa and to Asia, the supremacy of the Muslim empires and the nomads from the steppe came to an end. Europeans could merely bypass these land empires, leaving central Asia to fall into an era of stagnancy. For the first time, the civilizations of the American continents completely fell to foreign invaders from across the ocean. For the first time, Europe failed to handle a challenge to its religious superiority, and instead fragmented into dozens of nations all warring for supremacy.

But again, man, unwilling to see the march of progress stopped too soon, would demonstrate his resiliency and challenge the backwards steps taken during the 16th and 17th centuries.

But that is for another chapter.

23

The Cannon and the Crescent

Muslim Empires of the Near East – 1400 > 1700

Remember how the Europeans all of a sudden decided they might want to try out their new boats and see if they could find a shortcut to the East?

Refresh my memory – why did they do that again? It wasn't that Europeans finally learned how to sail or that they discovered some magical floating wood in a forest far, far away. No. The main reason the Atlantic countries of Portugal, Spain, France, England and Holland went exploring was because their access to all the fineries of Asia had been cut off. They wanted the spices, the jewels, the fancy plates, the carpets, the silks and cottons of the East, and just when their thirst was being whetted, the Muslims started getting other ideas.

You see, the West was late to the world of trade. Sure, the Romans and Greeks had controlled the Mediterranean Sea for great portions of the world's history, but when it comes to truly global trade, Europeans were the new kid on the block, and starting to be a bit annoying. By 1492, the Muslims, the Mongols, the Indians and the Chinese had already been sailing across the oceans for centuries and had established relationships so that goods flowed freely from empire to empire with little interference from outside powers. But then the Europeans decided they might want to wake up from their self-induced technological slumber and start seeing what the world had to offer, and what they saw didn't exactly assuage their inferiority complex.

Between China and Europe sat three empires – the Ottoman, the Safavid and the Mughal – who each alone possessed a technological advancement, a cultural refinement and a military dominance that made the Europeans reconsider their place in the world's hierarchy. These three Muslim empires, these Gunpowder Empires, controlled the lands from Austria in the west, to Mecca in the south, to the far reaches of India in the east. They worshipped at the most magnificent house of God in the world (the Hagia Sophia), they constructed the most beautiful building on the planet (the Taj Mahal) and they amassed a larger percentage of the world's economy than even the Americans today. The Ottomans controlled what we today call the Middle East, the Safavid Dynasties ruled over modern day Iran and the Mughals united the land today known as India.

Each of these empires took advantage of the power vacuum left behind when the Mongols receded into the steppe, and for over three centuries they held on to vast land empires that ensured global power politics would still have to go through the heart of Asia. However, even though their weapons and their religious zeal created three of the most formidable empires of the last millennium, their decadence and their obsessive resistance to Western innovations meant that when they did meet face to face with European might in the 18th and 19th centuries, they were lagging far behind in most areas of economic, social and military achievement.

But in 1400, you'd be hard-pressed to find any intellectual who would claim the Europeans were anything more than merely the annoying younger sibling to the much more mature eastern empires of the Ottomans, the Safavids and the Mughals.

First, the Ottomans. Directly to the east of Europe, these were the people who most immediately threatened Christian Europe. The Church's track record against the Muslim warriors wasn't exactly impressive. After their first victory in the Crusades, the West suffered loss after loss after loss to the Muslims and by 1300, it appeared Europe's claim to the Holy Land would never again be anything more than just a hollow threat. And when bands of nomadic Turks came out of the steppe in the 14th century, the delicate balance that had existed since the Crusades was shattered. This new antagonist sought nothing less than the conquest of all of Europe.

Like the Seljuk Turks centuries before, this new group of Turks were master horse people like their steppe brothers, and they also fought with the religious passion shared by their nomadic Muslim forefathers. Known as ghazis, or warriors of faith, each of these small tribes survived by raiding the agricultural enclaves across the Levant and then retreating back into the security of their homeland. But one of these groups of Turks chose to not retreat to the steppe. Instead they decided once and for all that they would conquer the sedentary peoples of the eastern Mediterranean, destroy their walled cities and then unite an empire under their rule. The leader of these horsemen was Osman, but to the Europeans suffering from perhaps a subtle speech impediment he was Othman, and his followers – Ottomans.

Osman led his ghazis on a series of raids and military skirmishes on the eastern fringe of the Byzantine Empire, and in 1302 his horse forces captured parts of Anatolia (the region we today call Turkey). Some of these raids were fought for the will of Allah, others for power and prestige, still others for booty. But unlike his predecessors, Osman's Turks didn't retreat. They settled in previously Byzantine towns like Nicaea (where the Church decided in 381 they'd worship the Father, the Son and the Holy Spirit) and then in Bursa (a useful little town right across the water from Constantinople).

Osman would die before stretching deeper into Byzantine lands, but he put the Ottoman foot in the door, allowing successors to push the crack open a bit further over the next hundred years. And with Muhammad II's ascension to the throne in 1444, the European gates were thoroughly blown wide open. Muhammad II (aka Mehmed II) made his number one priority the seizure of Constantinople, the last symbol of the Roman Empire, and the final piece of the Ottoman Middle Eastern puzzle.

By 1453, the Byzantine Empire was a sad little shadow of its former glory. Its population had peaked centuries earlier at over a million people, but when Mehmed II came pounding on its walls, it was at a mere 50,000. Its control over the Mediterranean region that once stretched across three continents and even down into Italy, had been reduced to a sliver of Christendom, entirely surrounded by the empire of the Ottomans. Like the Roman Empire that saw its 1000-year reign end when the inauspiciously-named Romulus Augustus relinquished authority to the barbarian nomadic hordes, the Eastern Roman Empire likewise saw their

1000-year reign end with the empire's namesake at the throne – Constantine XI.

In one of the most important turning points in world history, the choices made by Constantine XI and Mehmed II flipped the directions of two civilizations – the West and the Kingdom of Islam. Secure in his castle, Constantine XI had no reason to fear this latest challenge to his empire. Sure, Mehmed had over a hundred thousand troops, and Constantine had just seven thousand. Sure, Mehmed had set up a fort on the other side of the Bosphorous Sea where he could launch his final attack. And sure, Mehmed had 125 ships stationed at the ready, while Constantine only had 26. But what did Constantine have to fear? Constantinople had survived for a thousand years, and the walled behemoth hadn't been conquered yet, so why would these former horse people from the east pose any more of a threat?

Well, this time it would be different because Mehmed had gunpowder, and the hundred-foot-tall, thirty-foot-wide protective walls that surrounded the city would be no match for the iron balls of destruction under Mehmed's employ. Ironically, the cannons and their requisite technology had been offered to Constantine months before the battle by the most decorated metallurgist in all of Europe – Orban of Hungary. Orban's offer of assistance fell on Constantine's deaf ears, so like the free agent weapons manufacturer he was, Orban went across the Bosphorous and entertained a meeting with Mehmed. Mehmed wouldn't refuse, and at his disposal came 50 cannons and one super cannon named Basilica – a 27-foot-long beast, the largest in the world. Had Constantine initially agreed to this offer, history might have played out a bit differently, but the moment he declined this gift of military hardware, his fate was sealed.

Constantine tried one last defense. He extended a massive chained fence across the water so that no boats could enter the sea to attack Constantinople from the north. Mehmed scoffed at this feeble obstacle, simply ordering his men to cut down a bunch of trees, slaughter hundreds of sheep and oxen and then use their boiled fat to grease up the logs so his men could drag 70 of his ships over land. Imagine the faces of the defenders of Constantinople as they gazed across the straits only to see a parade of boats being yanked across the hillside on greased planks. When Mehmed's men dropped their ships back in the sea, the siege began, and after one month of firing everything he had at the last bastion of Christendom in the Middle East, the walls were breached, Constantine was slain and the city finally fell.

For Europe, this meant that the Muslims were now in full control of the eastern European passage to Asia. They could tax any goods entering or exiting, and they showed no signs of stopping at Constantinople. The European nations knew at this point that if they were to fully pull themselves out of the Middle Ages and continue to benefit from their trade with the East, they'd need to find some other routes, thus launching the European Age of Exploration.

But for the Ottomans, exploration was last on their "To Do" list. First they would need to secure their winnings, then they would commission glorious public works projects to symbolize their unmatched superiority and their spiritual pre-eminence, and then they would see how tough it would be to conquer the rest of Europe.

This task first fell to the hands of Mehmed II and his successors, but it was with Suleiman the Magnificent that the Ottoman Empire reached its true golden age. Suleiman inherited an empire already rich in power and in artistic inspiration. When Mehmed II conquered Constantinople, he transformed the largest church in all of Christendom into a mosque. Take down a few icons of some saints, destroy a bunch of mosaics, throw up some minarets, remove the crosses decorating the halls and...presto – you've got yourself the biggest mosque in the world – the Hagia Sophia.

Suleiman would not merely rest on the achievements of others. He embarked on a series of public works that perched the Ottoman Empire above all rivals. From his childhood, Suleiman was destined for greatness. He was born almost exactly a thousand years after the prophet Muhammad and he was the tenth sultan of the Osman family. He was named after Solomon, the Biblical creator of the first temple of Jerusalem and possibly the greatest political leader in Jewish history. With a pedigree of such import, the expectations for this boy leader were immense.

Yet by the time of his death, Suleiman had surpassed every one of these boyhood expectations, leaving a legacy few could have ever imagined. While in the 16th century, the West was still admiring the works of Michelangelo and da Vinci, the Ottoman Empire claimed a man whose brilliance quite possibly trumped anything the European Renaissance offered.

Suleiman was a philosopher, a warrior, a poet, a patron of the arts, an engineer, a goldsmith and a leader without equal. To his people, he was Suleiman the Lawgiver, but his achievements spread far beyond merely bringing peace to a region known for its instability. His own people praised Suleiman for his ability to be both a ferocious warrior and a restrained politician. Suleiman let his regional ministers rule as they saw fit, as long as criminal laws were stringently enforced, merchants conducted all transactions ethically and the taxes continued to stream into the capital without indiscriminate corruption or exploitation. To the diplomats who made their way to the streets of Constantinople, or by chance found themselves at the foot of the great Suleiman, the Ottoman Empire stood unrivaled. His aqueducts surpassed the engineering of the Romans, his humbly named Mosque of Suleiman almost surpasses the Hagia Sophia in design and opulence (while simultaneously housing the Muhammad-mandated libraries, schools and hospitals) and as he walked amongst his people he demanded total silence. For a religion and a people who preached there is no god but Allah, Suleiman came closer than any other Muslim leader to attaining a status as a god on earth.

And he also had a fairly impressive collection of lady friends, in what became a staple of the Muslim Gunpowder Empires – the harem. A harem is a collection of women – girlfriends, entertainers and servants – who must attend to the sultan's every wish. The Ottoman version of the harem might not have been as naughty as the European stereotypical depiction that has played out time and again in Hollywood flicks dealing with what happened on those lonely Arabian Nights. Nor was it as well-staffed as the harems of their Mughul neighbors (Akbar the Great settled down with 5000 concubines and 26 wives). Yet Suleiman's private residence was still stocked with numerous options for his personal amusement. Most of these female companions were chosen for political reasons by either his advisors or his mother (a Gunpowder sultan wasn't exactly able to tell his mother that the latest offering wasn't his type). Because Muslim law allowed four wives and as many concubines as could be properly supported, there were more than a few male offspring vying for the throne when dear old dad finally kicked the bucket. This led to countless behind-the-scene dramas (oftentimes orchestrated by power-hungry moms) and even the occasional assassination attempt on elder brothers or even dad (Suleiman had his own son executed after a foiled assassination attempt). These hereditary fights would make any dad paranoid. But daddy-mommy-concubine tiffs were the least of the Ottomans' worries. For just outside the empire's boundaries, any number of nomadic Muslim tribes sat waiting for the opportunity to jump in and wrest the crown of the Muslim world away from the House of Osman.

These incessant internal and external risks meant that the Ottoman emperors had to establish a secret military force whose honor and allegiance would never come into question.

Enter the janissaries. Since no Muslim could be trusted to protect the sultan, the Ottoman armies crafted the perfect plan – kidnap Christian boys at a young age, bring them back to the palace and then use the rest of their adolescence to teach them to not only be elite fighters, but be the most educated, reliable men of society. This wasn't the first, and wouldn't be the last, time autocrats appreciated the advantages of having an elite corps of devotees ready to obey any command without complaint. Adolph Hitler tried this out with his Boy Scout-esque Hitler Youth program in the 1930s and Pol Pot perverted the idea even more in Cambodia in the 1970s (no, I'm not saying Boy Scouts follow Hitler...read the sentence again). Both men took the minds and the bodies of the nation's youth and molded them into fanatical protectors of the throne, praising the leader above all. For Mehmed II, Suleiman and every subsequent Ottoman sultan, these janissaries were the empire's elite corps – the best-trained military force, the most trusted political advisors and oftentimes even the highest ranked government leaders. They maintained order throughout the kingdoms and spread the Ottoman reach deep into Europe and far into the fertile crescent of Mesopotamia.

But past Mesopotamia, the Ottomans could go no further. They would have to share the Muslim realm with their adversaries to the East – the Safavid Empire. Although also a member of the Gunpowder Empire club, the Safavids were no friend of the Ottomans. Yes, to an outsider, they might look like interchangeable parts, but these same people might erroneously think Iranians and Iraqis see each other today as inseparable brothers-for-life. Admittedly, both fought for Allah, both used their unique fusion of cannons and nomadic confidence to blow their enemies off the battlefield, and both, once settled, created worlds where some of the most stunning works of art could be produced. Both even lacked trust in their fellow Muslims and looked outside their realm (mostly in Russia) to find young boys to kidnap and then convert to obedient defenders of the empire.

But to be honest, they hated each other. Some art historians might claim it was because the Safavids chose architecture that was far less bold, ostentatious and massive as their neighbors to the west. Nowhere in the Safavid kingdom was there a piece of architecture that came close to rivaling the Mosque of Suleiman. Instead these successors to the Persian realm chose to create what could be the most beautiful city in the world, a city I'll bet you $47.32 you've never heard of before – Isfahan. Recently deemed a World Heritage Site, this stunning city boasts bridges you could never imagine, mosques more colorful than any in the Muslim world, and because it was the heart of rug manufacturing, a collection of the most intricately crafted Persian carpets you will ever see. Today, it is these carpets that are the most enduring international legacy of the Safavid Dynasty. Today, few will ever get their passports stamped in Iran on their way to visiting Isfahan, but 30% of the world's carpets come from Persia (today known as Iran), and over one million Iranians continue to hand weave these masteries of detail and color. The Safavids had built an oasis in the desert to showcase their creative passion.

But let's be honest. They didn't hate each other because one's art was a bit fancier than the others. They hated each other because a religious rift dating back to Muhammad could never be reconciled. The Ottomans were Sunni. The Safavids were Shi'a. At the heart of this conflict was who had the right to succeed Muhammad as heir to the kingdom of Islam. Should it be the one who claimed blood relation to Muhammad? Or the one seen as the most fit for the title? The Shi'a believed you must be a descendant of Muhammad. The Sunni didn't. But like the Protestant-Catholic division that evolved over the centuries into so much more than mere ideological quirks, the Sunnis and the Shi'as saw themselves as diametrically opposed sects. In 680, the Shi'a believed only Hussein, the son of Ali (who was the son-in-law of Muhammad...the closest Islam could find to a true relative to the Prophet), should have first dibs on the caliphate and so they met the Sunni on the battlefield. When Hussein was eventually defeated and beheaded, the Shi'a had their martyr, and ever since, the Shi'a faithful have seen themselves as oppressed and the Sunnis as the oppressors. Today, 90% of the world is Sunni, and because it is the Sunni who control most of the leadership roles politically and economically, many Shiites today still see themselves as historical victims.

Another difference between the two Muslim empires was how they dealt with nonbelievers – the jizya. Unlike the Ottomans who practiced religious tolerance, allowing all Christians, Jews and Zoroastrians to continue their practices as long as they continued to pay taxes, the Safavids mandated everyone convert to the Shi'a faith or face exile, or even death.

So when the Safavids stopped the Ottoman eastern advance at the Battle of Caldiran in 1514, the Ottomans' desire for an empire stretching through to India was squashed. But the Ottomans refused to retreat and after 150 years of war, the Ottomans took over Mesopotamia (today's Iraq), while their hated enemy resided next door in what today we call Iran. And the Iranians (the Persians of the day) never forgave the Sunnis for stealing their land. In fact, one reason America was so hesitant to pull their troops out of Iraq after the 2002 war was their fear of what Iran would do next. Would they immediately throw their full support behind the Shiite minority, and try to wrestle away the portion of the Middle East the Safavids believed they earned 500 years ago? We're still waiting to see the answer to that question.

But the Safavids and the Ottomans weren't the only Muslim empires laying claim to the Near East. The Mughal Empire ruled the Indian peninsula for three centuries until the British arrived and pushed them out so they could take their turn controlling one of the wealthiest regions in the world.

In 1500, India held close to 150 million people, and its economy made up one-fourth of the world's wealth (by comparison America's GDP today is about 22%). They had the only diamond mines in the world, and their spices, jewels and textiles were such the envy of the world, that Europe sent men in boats in every direction just to be the first to control access to the subcontinent. All roads might have led to Rome, but all wallets led to India.

So when the nomadic Muslim prince Babur realized he was never going to recapture his native homeland of Afghanistan, he decided to instead try his hand at the little jungle paradise to the east. Claiming relation to Genghis Khan himself, Babur came from a warrior pedigree and by the time he was in his twenties, he'd already fought in a couple dozen wars and knew how to employ some of the most intimidating military strategies of the era. He taught his 1000 war elephants to use their trunks and feet to rip apart soldiers on the battlefield, he built hundreds of cannons that could launch projectiles over a thousand feet and he ruled over an army of archers who employed a composite bow more powerful than the English longbow that ended the reign of knights in Europe.

At his death in 1530, Babur had expanded his empire across the regions we today call Pakistan and northern India. His successors built upon his military legacy, but then focused on constructing a series of dynamic structures, each coming to define the Indo-Muslim style. Like the Ottomans and the Safavids, the Mughal shahs first wanted to create paradises on earth. The steppe was a harsh, dry, unforgiving ecosystem, and water was always a commodity in short supply. The Quran spoke of heaven being a paradise with rivers flowing from four directions, so because of the geographic realities of the region and the glorious stories of paradise established by their holiest scriptures, the Mughals set out to redefine architecture and synthesize nature and art like no one before.

When the grandson of Babur, Akbar the Great, rose to power, he first set out to create a palace where he could keep his enemies close. This palace was Fatehpur Sikri. Like France's King Louis XVI who later secluded and pampered all the regional lords in the gloriously gluttonous palace at Versailles, Babur built a complex where he could display his supremacy, while keeping close any would-be challengers to the throne. Fatehpur Sikri had all the engineering wonders of a Roman bath, while keeping the cultural intricacies of his Mongol heritage. Because Fatehpur Sikri was in the middle of a desolate, arid region miles from any reliable water source, Akbar's engineers and army of laborers had to first dam water to create a man-made lake, and then construct waterwheels that continuously raised the water to the elevated hillside structures. This water then circulated through a series of baths, fountains and aqueducts to keep the buildings essentially air-conditioned in a climate where the sizzling summer temperatures could frequently surpass 110 degrees. With an eye to his past, Akbar laid out the structures in a configuration that mimicked the nomadic tent patterns of his forefathers, actually encasing the very wood from nomadic tents inside the stone pillars. However, despite its engineering innovations and its reverence to the past, Fatehpur Sikri could not survive the elements, and the harsh climate forced it to be abandoned less than 50 years after its founding (though it still exists today as it did four hundred years ago, just a short drive away from the Taj Mahal).

Fatehpur Sikri's place on the world's stage might have only been a blip, but for those few decades, it was a place to behold.

Like Suleiman to the west, Akbar was a man of the ages, and he treasured the art and the philosophy of those in his presence. His unquenchable desire for knowledge brought thousands of spiritual, philosophical and cultural leaders to his doorstep. Weekly he met with Christian, Muslim and Hindu envoys, debating the intricacies of each sect's dogma. Though illiterate himself, he was an astute listener and even attempted to design a new religion which fused the major tenets of Islam and Hinduism - Din-e-Ilahi. This religion wasn't exactly popular – only a couple dozen ever converted and even his kids ignored him and his attempt at spiritual harmony. When it comes to religion, Akbar also uniquely interpreted the Quran's edict that no man shall have more than four wives. In his harem of over 6000 women, each protected by her own personal eunuch, he maintained relations with a couple hundred wives and countless other lady friends.

As Akbar continued to expand his realm through war, his wealth continued to surpass even the gaudiest of heights. By the time Shah Jahan took the throne, the Mughal Emperors had made the Indian population their ticket to opulence. And speaking of thrones, Shah Jahan set his artisans to making a royal chair like nothing the world had ever seen – the Peacock Throne. The Ottomans might have started the idea of making a fancy throne adorned with every gem they could get their hands on, but Shah Jahan went just a bit over the top. At over six feet long and four feet wide, it used over 2500 pounds of gold, over 500 pounds of emeralds and rubies and a 186-carat diamond. Considering the average wedding ring has a diamond that is less than a carat in size, this Koh-i-Noor diamond was fairly impressive. If the throne was around today, it'd fetch over a billion dollars on the open market (and who knows how much the folks at Ebay would splurge). But alas, the Persians claimed it as booty from the Mughals in the 1700s, and since it's been stripped and sold off across who knows where.

But Shah Jahan didn't stop there. Considering his name actually means "king of the world," it's fair to say this man didn't do anything on a small scale. The Peacock Throne was an impressive piece of furniture, but Shah Jahan truly outdid himself when it came to architecture. For it was Shah Jahan who designed and orchestrated the construction of what many believe is the most striking, most recognizable (sorry Eiffel Tower) building in the world – the Taj Mahal. Taking 22 years and 20,000 expert artisans from across Europe and Asia, his masterpiece cost over 32 million rupees (about $1.1 billion dollars in today's US money). Its minarets, domed ceiling and marble walls were adorned with countless precious stones, mosaics and careful brushwork. Unlike the European works of the Renaissance that showcased the splendor of the human form, Muslims weren't allowed to paint or sculpt any type of mammal – be it human or otherwise. It would have been an affront to Allah.

So the Taj Mahal, like other Muslim works, showcased the skill of its artisans through ornate lettering of sacred texts, elaborate geometric patterns and meticulous carvings. According to legend, Shah Jahan didn't ever want another ruler to build a temple better than the Taj, so he cut off the hands of every artist and architect who worked on the memorial (not exactly the severance package they were expecting).

Unfortunately for the average Indian, these grandiose projects meant a continual tax burden and perpetual need for expansion through military conflict, leaving the masses forced to live in a state of permanent starvation at the mercy of the whims of regional lords. These pricey pet projects also meant that the Mughal shahs were ill-prepared for the growing power of the Europeans. And when the British finally arrived in the 1700s, they were met with a civilization facing collapse. Famine, constant civil wars, natural disasters and disease all weakened the subcontinent's ability to fend off the advances of a persistent and well-armed foe. The age of India being ruled by foreigners had only just begun, but this time, instead of the invading forces coming from the steppe, they arrived by boat from the far off British isles.

But that is for another chapter.

24

Chinese Expansion and Withdrawal

China - The Ming Dynasty – 1400 > 1600

While the Near East and India were adjusting to the rule of the Muslim nomads, Europe was pulling itself into a new age of exploration and self-discovery, and the Americas were surviving the onslaught of the trans-Atlantic forces, over in the East, the civilizations of Japan and China were trying to maintain their traditional roots while surviving internal disorder and threats from beyond the horizon.

Like the rest of Eurasia, the prospect of Chinese autonomy ended when the Mongol hordes took control, spreading their empire from the Pacific Ocean to the borders of central Europe. During their nearly century-long reign, the Mongols upended society by devaluing the age-old superiority of the Mandarin bureaucrats, replacing Confucian order with arbitrary violence and inconsistent law enforcement. The Mongol lords then connected China to a transcontinental trade network that left the previously isolated peoples open to the wandering eyes of traders and missionaries from the West.

As the Mongol control over their vast empire dissipated, chaos and famine ruled in the countryside. For one young boy, Hongwu, the despair of the later Mongol years hit just a little too close to home. His parents were homeless, they sold his siblings just to survive and just when Hongwu reached adolescence and thought life couldn't get any worse, his parents died, leaving him to roam the countryside looking for scraps. And where did a young boy with no hope turn in times of misery? The monastery. He joined a Buddhist monastery, but even they lacked the resources to feed and shelter him, so he again went on the road, living off the hit and miss kindness of strangers. Exhausted by the futility of this existence, Hongwu finally joined the army. Here he showed a knack for killing people and leading others in battle. Hongwu turned his little band of brothers against the Mongol invaders, conquering village after village, eventually gaining enough strength to kick out the last of the Mongol rulers. It wasn't that hard to gain support for his little venture, as year after year the mounting droughts, famines and floods intimated the Mandate of Heaven was lost and another dynasty needed to fall.

With the barbarian invaders finally expelled, Hongwu established the Ming Dynasty and vowed to fix every ill that vexed his childhood, bringing back the romanticized order from dynasties past.

Task #1 – Help out the poor. China had millions of acres of unfarmed land, so Hongwu declared that whoever cultivated these new fields wouldn't have to pay taxes. He helped bring water to these vast, arid regions by ordering the construction of dams, dikes and levees. These choices seemed noble at the time, but with a few decades, most of these lands were merely snatched up by rich landlords, not the poor for which they were intended. Hongwu believed he could reduce taxes if he cut off a chunk of money normally used to house, feed and arm the military. Instead, he would give every soldier a parcel of land. These soldiers would hypothetically use this land to feed their families, purchase their needed weapons and pay for the training necessary to perform in combat. This idea worked in theory, but few soldiers could ever earn enough profit from their harvests to make ends meet. So did Hongwu succeed at his first task? Not really. Yes, more food was produced every year and the government's balance sheet wasn't in such dire straits, but for the most part, the poor stayed poor and the rich kept getting richer. So Hongwu went back to the drawing board.

Task #2 – Bring back the scholars. Hongwu wasn't exactly a fan of the scholar-gentry, the masters of the civil service exam. In his childhood, these were the smug elites who scoffed at his illiteracy. The Mongols, under their rule, had rid themselves of the scholar class and Hongwu was inclined to keep them out of government. But tradition and their track record forced him to reconsider. In 1383, he decided he would bring back the civil service exam to determine which men truly were the most qualified in the land. But this time, the test would be even more demanding than the previous editions. Each year, tens of thousands of would-be government bureaucrats locked themselves in rows of testing chambers (think outhouses) and spent days filling out the exam booklets. Questions like "Unscramble the following words and analyze their relevance: Beginning, good, mutually, nature, basically, practice, far, near, men's" or "Write an eight-legged essay (kind of like the five paragraph ones we all grew up on) on the following: Scrupulous in his own conduct and lenient only in his dealings with the people." The Ming leaders expanded the passage rates by creating tiers based on scores, assigning subordinate degrees for those who didn't shine the brightest. Even with this extended opportunity, the tests were still killers. Many a potential scholar killed himself once he realized his chances of passing the dreaded test were slim to none. Some even resorted to trying to bribe test moderators or creating "cheat shirts," elaborate cheat sheets with thousands of miniscule characters scribbled on their underwear. Even with the crushing pressure and potential for immorality, under the Ming emperors, thousands more Confucian scholars earned the elite status that was their ticket to lifelong employment and immediate respect. If only they would fulfil their job requirements honestly.

Which leads us to his Task #3 – Ensure loyalty and eradicate corruption. Like many men who come from humble beginnings and then achieved absolute power (think Hitler and Stalin), Hongwu became a bit paranoid once he sat in the emperor's chair. He killed or expelled anyone who dared disagree with him, and those who used the public coffers also found their lives shortened. A fairly grotesque man, with pot-marked scars covering his face and a jawline resembling a warthog, Hongwu wasn't exactly respected for his rugged good looks. He was feared for his violent temper and ruthless retribution. He had no problem beheading foes, but he much preferred public humiliation. He'd drag any man caught in a scandal into the public square, spread the offender's legs and then whip his bare butt until the flesh drained blood onto the street below. This punishment is still sometimes used in Chinese-influenced societies today. One such incident in Singapore in the 1990s involved an American high school kid named Michael Fay who stole a few road signs and scratched up some cars. When he was finally arrested, President Bill Clinton pleaded for leniency, but the boy was taken out and whipped with a four foot long rattan cane. Students in the Ming Dynasty were likewise kept in order, but their punishments were just a tad bit more severe. One student who vocally criticized his teacher was beheaded and his head was put on a pole in front of the school. Remarkably, student attention levels improved significantly.

Not exactly a trusting boss, Hongwu did find one group he could depend on, a group of men whose loyalty was unparalleled. Men who would never lead a violent revolution, who would never be caught bedding one of the royal concubines and who would answer his every call. These men were eunuchs. Kidnapped at an early age, these young boys had their testicles cut off, thus weakening some of the mammalian desires that tend to get men into trouble in imperial courts. Hongwu and later Ming emperors could trusted their corps of 70,000 eunuchs to not only protect the throne, but to faithfully execute court wishes.

The most famous eunuch of the Ming Dynasty was a Chinese Muslim boy, stolen at the age of eleven and brought to the imperial court to serve the emperor. This boy would become known to history as Zheng He, and his sovereign master was not the violent, obsessive, hyper-protective Hongwu, but the third Ming monarch, a man far more open to the splendors of the outside world. His name – Yongle. Yongle wasn't a slave to the past, but an innovator and a visionary. He had his scribes acquire all the knowledge of the land, creating an 11,000-volume encyclopedia. He moved the capital to Beijing in the north where his army of engineers constructed what would become known as the Forbidden City. He expanded and repaired the Great Wall so his forces could ignore the northern border and focus on the wealth waiting for them across the seas.

Yongle and his most trusted aide Zheng He then created an armada greater than anything the world had ever known. In the early 1400s, when Europe was still a century away from their famed Age of Exploration, the Chinese were already embarking on their own tour of the continents. Near the Yangzi River, Zheng He erected dozens of dry docks, some three times the size of football fields, to build some of the largest ships ever imagined. After tens of thousands of craftsmen worked night and day for years to finish the fleet, the river was flooded and the ships headed out to sea. And these ships were not your fairly standard European variety. No, these beasts of the sea were something to behold. Let's put it into context. Columbus's adorable little Niña, Pinta and Santa Maria that "discovered" America were about 60 feet long. Zheng He's were close to 400 feet long. Basically, you could put five of Columbus's ships in the hull of one of Zheng He's and still have room for an army of elephants to roam the deck.

Once completed, Yongle sent his fleet across Asia, to Africa (and some even believe to the New World) to gain trading partners, secure alliances, but also to just flaunt the majesty of the Ming Dynasty. This navy of 300 ships, manned by 28,000 sailors, dwarfed the combined forces of all the European nations during the Age of Exploration. When this army of ships entered any harbor, the foreign leaders could do nothing more than to bow down to the superiority of the Chinese. Zheng He's Muslim background and his father's own experience on his pilgrimages to Mecca, meant that Zheng He was welcomed in ports throughout the Muslim world. By the end of his seven voyages and his nearly two decades on the seas, Zheng He added over 50 tributary states to the Chinese empire. Although many of these states only paid lip service to the firepower of Zheng He's navy, immediately reverting back to the status quo once the ships were out of sight, no one could argue that China didn't spread its influence from Southeast Asia to the coastal kingdoms of India and even to the southern coast of Africa. In his book *1421: The Year China Discovered America*, author Gavin Menzies even claimed Zheng He made it to the Americas, stating that the discovery of Chinese anchors, traditions and even DNA in indigenous peoples prove the Chinese made it to the shores of California a century before the Atlantic explorers.

Regardless of whether he made it across the Pacific, Zheng He's voyages cannot be overstated. By 1430, China could have become a global superpower, firmly positioning its forces in the dozens of tributary states dotting Asia and Africa, possibly even colonizing the Americas before Europe even thought to head out across the Atlantic. But alas, in one of the most critical turning points in world history, the Chinese totally and abruptly abandoned their navy. When Yongle and Zheng He died, so did China's forays on the seas. All ships were burned. All records destroyed. All maps thrown into the dustbin of history. China stood at the edge of establishing a global influence which would have surpassed even the Mongols, but they inexplicably pulled back. Whether it was for fear of the influence of outsiders, or the need to spend government funds on protecting the northern border, or the frustration that merchants were gaining too much power in society or because the trips were too expensive, China ceased its overseas expeditions, opening the door for the Europeans to begin their assault on the world's resources.

Who knows what would have happened had China followed Zheng He's exploration with European-style colonization and trade. Would Portugal have ever been able to reach India, or would the Chinese have stopped them before they even made it around the Cape of Good Hope? Would the Dutch, the Spanish, the British, the French and the Portuguese have landed merchants and missionaries across Asia, or would the Chinese have been so firmly entrenched that no European power would ever dare attempt come ashore on one of their skimpy ships? Regardless of what could have happened, it never did. The Ming emperors withdrew to their Forbidden City and focused on the internal happenings of their people. It wouldn't be the last time China would enter prominently into world affairs, but it would take another 500 years before it could again call itself a world superpower.

When the Europeans arrived in the 1500s, Chinese civilization by most definitions still surpassed that of the Europeans – but the gap was closing. The first Portuguese and Dutch merchants knew there was still an unquenchable thirst back home for Chinese silks and porcelain. The Chinese kilns at Jingdezhen produced enough porcelain to fill the demand of all the world's markets. They had created a Henry Ford-esque assembly line process where the superheated kilns spewed out thousands of pieces of pottery a day. During this era, traditional designs of nature and harmony continued, but the Chinese began taking special orders, reproducing the worlds of their European and Asian customers.

At first, the Chinese wanted little do with the Europeans. For the previous few centuries, trade was almost always one-sided. The Chinese just didn't want anything the Europeans offered. In fact, the first Europeans were expected to kowtow (lay their bodies to the ground in symbolic submission and then crawl forward) to the imperial leaders, not exactly a demand the Europeans were accustomed to fulfilling. However, unlike in previous dynasties, these new Europeans offered a good China desperately wanted – silver.

The Yuan Dynasty under the Mongols had issued paper currency as the primary method of trade, but the Ming refused to continue that tradition, instead wanting the more durable silver. Yet as the Chinese economy expanded, requiring more silver pieces, Chinese authorities couldn't keep up with the demand. Enter the Europeans. The Spanish and Portuguese silver mines in the Americas were yielding a seemingly inexhaustible supply of silver (and gold), and most of this silver ended up filling the coffers of the Chinese government. Because of this need for Western silver, the imperial guard reluctantly opened their ports to trade, under the condition that the government controlled all transactions and the only ports open to international trade would be at Macao, Canton and Peking. As China became increasingly involved in these newly created global trade networks, their society gradually began to change in ways repellent to Chinese traditionalists. The lowly merchant classes were becoming wealthy off this new exchange (though much of their income was taxed and ended up in the throne's coffers), and the missionaries that arrived with the traders were becoming more of a nuisance. If the Jesuit and Franciscan missionaries gained momentum converting locals to a religion valuing an invisible god, might they totally sabotage a society rooted on strict secular gender and age relationships? Fortunately for the Chinese bureaucrats, because the Chinese lacked a tradition of monotheism, few converted to this Christianity. These missionaries continued to impress the imperial court with the accuracy of their clocks, calendars and weapons, but they never converted any large number of people to this foreign faith.

Although the Church would never crack the Confucian grip on the masses, the influx of silver did thoroughly embed itself in daily life. Subsequently, when the flow of silver dried up in the mid-1600s, the Ming were doomed. The Ming could no longer deal with the natural disasters that once again decimated the countryside. The age of the Ming ended, replaced this time with barbarians not from the steppe but from northeastern Manchuria. These Manchus would establish the Qing Dynasty, and from their perch in the Forbidden City of Beijing, they too would begin the challenge of finding the balance between territorial expansion, infrastructure improvement and peasant appeasement. However, as the Europeans continued to push their trade deeper into the interior, the Qing Dynasty progressively found themselves ruling over an empire no longer holding the a position of global supremacy. The era of China's dominance was over.

But that is for another chapter.

25

Leave Us Alone

Japan – Tokugawa Shogunate and Isolationism – 1500>1700

O ver the course of its existence, its unique geography right off the tip of eastern Asia allowed it to always determine the extent to which it wanted to be touched by the civilizations of others. In the book *The Clash of Civilizations,* Samuel Huntington speaks of eight civilizations – Sinic, Hindi, Islamic, Western, Orthodox, Latin American, African and Japanese. Seven of these civilizations span multiple continents. Only one is a country in and of itself. Only one has been able to remain separate from the world, choosing on its own terms when it wanted to open its doors to outsiders, and to what extent they wanted to keep their doors open. Only one has been able to choose its path.

Japan.

Japan had run-ins with the Koreans, the Chinese and the Mongols. Each was repelled. In the 16th century, when European powers spanned the globe looking for willing (oftentimes reluctant) trading partners, Japan at first warily welcomed the hygienically-challenged, red-haired devils. Yet within a century, these strangers were banished, and the island nation returned to isolation, taking what it wanted from European culture and forbidding all that might contaminate Japanese society. In the next three hundred years, as Europe gradually put one country after another under its sphere of influence, Japan remained inaccessible, immune to the progress of the known world.

But it still was progressing. Just on its own timetable.

First, Japan had to escape its own Middle Ages. In Europe for a thousand years, the Middle Ages meant thousands of independent lords ruled over their fiefdoms, demanding allegiance and wheat from their peasants in exchange for protection secured by well-trained knights. Japan's feudal world looked fairly similar. In Japan, the lords weren't barons or dukes or counts, but daimyos, and the peasants' grain of exchange was rice. These daimyos employed sword-yielding samurai to protect the peasants and to ensure the timely payment of rice tributes. Both of these feudal worlds would come to an end. For Europe, the continent would need a plague, a Renaissance, an Age of Exploration and gunpowder to exit the Middle Ages.

For Japan, the 6,852 islands would need three men. The Three Unifiers.

Oda Nobunaga. Toyotomi Hideyoshi. Tokugawa Ieyasu.

These three men all came from relatively humble origins. They weren't the wealthiest or the most powerful daimyos. In fact one, Hideyoshi, was simply a lowly peasant. But the three together ended the centuries of chaos, violence and regional warfare, uniting Japan in a 250-year period of peace. Though at times allies and at other times foes, these three men each played a vital role in creating modern Japan. Even today, Japanese schoolchildren memorize the poem of the great unifiers, a tale that shows how each man distinctively approached the challenge of unification. In this poetic allegory, the three men sit in a room watching a cuckoo bird that refuses to sing. They responded:

> *If the cuckoo doesn't sing, kill it!* – Oda Nobunaga
>
> *If the cuckoo doesn't sing, let's make it to* – Toyotomi Hideyoshi
>
> *If the cuckoo doesn't sing, let's wait until it sings* – Tokugawa Ieyasu

Nobunaga was the warrior, Hideyoshi the immovable force and Ieyasu the patient planner. Although at one time or another each man could be violent, forceful or patient, these three approaches also represented the different periods of Japan's evolution.

In the 1540s, Oda Nobunaga, although only the heir to a small domain, used his military prowess to defeat rival daimyos and set up base in Kyoto. Willing to use guerilla warfare and

Portuguese gunpowder, but also free of rival daimyo in his region, Nobunaga was able to gradually strengthen his forces, adding province by province to his holdings. By 1580, he had either annihilated or forced 1/3 of the country to submit to his authority. He was the most powerful ruler in the land. He improved the economy by creating castle towns, and he linked them all by constructing a network of roads to aid in both commerce and the movement of troops. But along the way he made enemies. Known for treating his subordinates like trash, teasing them for their weight or their hairline or their feminine behaviors, Nobunaga wasn't exactly well-liked. In 1582, one of his generals, Akechi Mitsuhide surrounded Nobunaga's unarmed castle and burnt it to the ground. Whether Nobunaga died in the fire, at the sword of an assailant, or by committing suicide, no one knew for sure. But regardless, Mitsuhide was to blame.

Enter Toyotomi Hideyoshi. Hideyoshi's story was a rags-to-riches tale. He was noticed by Nobunaga, both for his skill in castle-building, but also for his less than intimidating presence (Nobunaga liked to call him "the bald rat"). He was taken under the general's wing and made a foot soldier. Hideyoshi rose through the military ranks, becoming first and officer and then one of Nobunaga's most trusted generals. When Nobunaga was struck down, the first of his generals to seize the opportunity and avenge his death would earn honor, wealth and the keys to Nobunaga's kingdom. Hideyoshi outmaneuvered the other heirs to the throne, hunting down and killing Mitsuhide eleven days after the initial castle burning and then presenting his head to the grave of Nobunaga as a symbol of retribution.

Hideyoshi then became the supreme ruler of central Japan.

But he knew this was a precarious position. Dozens of daimyos wanted him dead, so Hideyoshi gathered allies who would help him sweep across the countryside, putting down any would-be competitors for the throne. By the 1590s, all of Japan had surrendered, so Hideyoshi then made sure the allegiances he had won on the battlefield would remain for generations. He sent out his surveyors across the land to register all rice crops and measure all domains. He then repositioned all the daimyos, uprooting them from their familial fiefdoms and depositing them in new locales, ensuring they would keep their wealth but lose their regional support. Hideyoshi then mandated all peasants stay on their land, never taking up arms. He forbade samurai from ever returning to farming. He formally split society in two, ensuring the path from poverty he had taken to the throne could never be replicated. He created a warrior class all swearing allegiance to one man – himself.

As with most warriors, Hideyoshi was not content to merely enjoy the fruits of his years of conflict. Once a warrior, always a warrior. Hideyoshi next turned to conquering Korea. For a people so used to remaining isolated from the barbarians to the west, this military expedition marked a turning point in Japan's history. Not only had it recently accepted Christian missionaries and merchants into its boundaries, Japan was now actively seeking out contacts and territory outside its protected sphere. Hideyoshi eventually paid the ultimate price for this foray into international domination, losing both the battle for Korea and his life...which opened the door for...

Tokugawa Ieyasu. When Hideyoshi started passing out new lands to his daimyo, he granted one of his most trusted allies – Ieyasu – a chunk of land near a meaningless filling village called Edo (a fishing village that today goes by the more familiar name – Tokyo). While his mentor Hideyoshi was centralizing his authority and taking the war to Korea, Ieyasu was back in Edo increasing his wealth and strengthening his military for the moment when he would step onto Japan's stage. In 1598, Hideyoshi's own son was merely an infant and Ieyasu's decades of allegiance to first Nobunaga and then Hideyoshi proved to the rival daimyos that he was a rightful heir. But rival clans still resisted his ascension, and at the Battle of Sekigahara, Ieyasu and his alliance of 90,000 troops faced off for one final battle for Japan. With a superior strategy on the battlefield (and also a few well-placed bribes to get his foes to change sides mid-battle), Ieyasu obliterated the last of the resistance, leaving himself as the sole ruler of all domains. Standing on the shoulders of the men who came before him, Ieyasu then returned to his home in Edo, launching the Tokugawa Dynasty that flourished uninterrupted for the next 250 years.

Each of the three unifiers had played a critical role, but it was Tokugawa Ieyasu who survived to the dynastic finish line. To this day, Japan still recognizes the work of each man, proclaiming, "Nobunaga pounds the national rice cake, Hideyoshi kneads it, and in the end Ieyasu sits down and eats it."

However, in order to eat the metaphoric cake, Ieyasu first guaranteed no other could ever steal it from his shelf. Sekigahara was a decisive battle, but any wise leader knows that defeated men produce vengeful sons, and the Tokugawa reign was anything but assured when he declared himself shogun (supreme leader of Japan) in 1603, inventing a family tree that linked him back to the emperor's family.

Ieyasu then tried his own spin on the age-old advice, "Keep your friends close and your enemies closer." Taking a page from his predecessor, he again uprooted the daimyos, this time depositing them in a protective circle around Edo. Friends and family held the lands closest to Edo. Those who proved their allegiance in battle made up the next ring. And for the daimyos he couldn't trust, these men were banished to the outskirts of Japan, still in a position of power, but hardly able to ever again mount a credible threat to the throne. Ieyasu then "invited" daimyos to make biannual trips to Edo where they would reside under the watchful eye of his court. This requirement not only prevented the daimyos from ever being home long enough to organize a credible military force, but also completely sacked the daimyos of their wealth. No self-respecting daimyo would parade to Edo without decking out his travelling entourage in the most elaborate clothing, jewels and transportation, so the trip alone could completely drain a daimyo's treasury (especially those outcast daimyos that had to journey from the northern and southern extremities).

Ieyasu also looked to his own past for additional ways to ensure allegiance. As a boy, Ieyasu was ceremonially kidnapped from his home (like the other sons of powerful lords) and forced to live with his father's rival daimyo. No respected daimyo would risk his honor or the life of his heir in a staged rescue, so these little abductions proved quite effective. Under the Tokugawa Shogunate, Ieyasu modified this program so that each daimyo could either bring his entire entourage to Edo (which could number as many as 300 advisors, porters and support staff), or he could merely leave his eldest son as a special guest (aka "hostage") of the shogun. Either way, the daimyos were stuck. The Tokugawa shoguns made it clear who were the powerful and who were the powerless. The daimyos' wings had been clipped.

Once Ieyasu had geographically carved up society, he then looked to China for strategies for organizing the rest of the masses. China had maintained order in the largest civilization on the planet through the defined classes and relationships outlined under Confucianism. At the top of Chinese society were the scholar-bureaucrats, next were the farmers, next the artisans and at the bottom were the merchants. Scholars earned their place as the ruling hierarchy through a lifetime of study, farmers provided the food needed for survival, artisans created the goods fundamental to everyday life and merchants (who created nothing) lived like parasites off the labor of others.

In the Confucian world, the businessman was the lowest of the low. Compare this system to modern day America where if the younger generation asked what they'd want to be when they grow up, few would want to be lifetime scholars and even fewer would tick off farming as their career of choice. Yet from the Zhou Dynasty nearly 3000 years ago, China has valued education of the elite and labor of the peasantry above all else. Conversely, America, since its founding at Plymoth Rock and its early settlements at Jamestown, was a nation of merchants and religious zealonts, who each hoped to prosper in this new world. But in China, the merchant was a cancer and the religious fundamentalist the outcast.

Japan chose the Chinese model.

Japan had merchants, it had artisans and of course it had farmers, but they lacked the scholars. Where would Ieyasu turn for this class? Who would be the most obvious candidates for an educated ruling elite? Of course, there was only one option - the samurai. Only the samurai would receive access to the finest education, only they would sit for the civil service exam and only they would administer the mundane day-to-day necessities of a centralized government. They could keep their honor and their connection to their past by being the only ones who could carry a sword, but with the peace of Tokugawa, the need for a warrior elite vanished. Over the course of the Tokugawa Shogunate, the once feared, battle-hardened military elite slowly evolved (or devolved depending on your point of view) into paper-pushing bureaucrats more likely to be seen behind a desk than on a battlefield.

The mounting prominence of the merchant class was another challenge to the prestige fo the samurai. As more and more daimyo moved to the city centers and as increasing crop yields enabled more farmers to move to urban areas, the populations of Japan's largest cities exploded (the adorable little fishing town of Edo housed over a million people) leaving Japan primed for a commercial revolution. Merchants always benefit when their clients are rich, and with the state-mandated requirement of biannual court attendance for all daimyos, entirely new services and goods were crafted to cater to this endless cycle of visiting nobility. Appearance and reputation meant everything to the Japanese aristocracy. Make something fancy, they'd buy it.

The daimyo estates were losing up to 25% of their income on the trips to Edo, and even more than that keeping up with the latest Edo fashion trends. The wealthy found themselves surprisingly penniless, and this was where the merchants lent a helping hand. The merchants offered the daimyo, and their samurai, loans to keep them living the good life. But through this relationship, power slowly flipped, and it was the samurai who ended up serving the merchants. By the mid-19th century, of the 1.7 million samurai, nearly all had either settled into lives of sedentary labor or had grown indebted to the merchant class. The Confucian hierarchy that valued the samurai bureaucrats had become a mere shadow of its earlier intent. Merchants might have technically sat below the samurai, but for anyone who walked the streets of Edo, there was no doubt where power truly resided.

And anyone who walked the streets of Edo also started seeing some forms of entertainment that were a paradise to the senses. Edo, Kyoto and Osaka each had their own special districts where the night arts entranced the wealthiest of clients. These "floating worlds" provided art, theater, sport and even a few probably-shouldn't-be-mentioned amusements. One of the first crafts that awed the eyes of the Europeans arriving in the 17th and 18th centuries was the vibrant woodblock printing that produced Japan's own cultural postcards. Initially merely black and white prints created centuries earlier to illustrate Buddhist teachings, by the Edo period, these wood-carved, multi-colored recreations provided an insider's view of the nightlife of these urban Tokugawa socialites. These stamped prints revealed glimpses of the flamboyant kabuki performances, the masterful sumo wrestlers and the forbidden arts of the geishas and courtesans.

In the area of live entertainment, the kabuki theater became the answer to the classical noh theater that failed to appeal to the increasingly hard-to-please urban customer. Noh productions were eight hour long bore fests of screeching instruments and recycled stories of historical figures from time long ago. Going to one of these performances felt more like work than relaxation. The kabuki theater was different. It was colorful, emotional and built on the element of surprise. Men played all the on-stage roles - both male and female. Their decorative, excessive makeup is the most recognizable component of kabuki theater, with exaggerated colored expressions juxtaposed against a white powder foundation, making it seem as if the actors were wearing masks. Unlike their noh compatriots who only rehashed historical tales, the kabuki performances oftentimes focused on doomed romances (where both lovers end up committing suicide) or clever critiques of the nobility and government authorities. The kabuki shows also promised climatic twists, using both a rotating stage and hyper-dramatized behavior of the actors. But still, these endurance fests were not for the faint of heart, clocking in at a hefty five hours in length. Clearly shorter than the noh performances, but not exactly the 22 minute sit-coms that nowadays service attention-span-challenged Westerners.

For those Japanese customers without five hours to kill, there emerged a bit more violent option – sumo wrestling. Like block printing and theater, sumo had been around for centuries, but the stability of the Tokugawa Era turned the sport mainstream. In its early years, two fairly chunky men would gather in an open field, surrounded by an audience and try to knock the person down or toss him into the spectators. For those standing in the audience, this second outcome oftentimes caused a fair bit of discomfort. The sport changed forever when Oda Nobunaga (yes...the man who wanted to kill the shy cuckoo bird) staged a tournament at his castle, inviting the top sumitori from across the island. 1500 men answered the call, but in order to speed up the matches (and save a few spectator lives), Nobunaga put in a circular boundary that became a permanent fixture of the sport. Years later, these sumitori came from the growing rank of ronin, master-less samurai, who looked for some means of subsistence in a world where the daimyo hostage system and the transformation of samurai into scholar-bureaucrats left few job options for the warrior samurai needing a venue to showcase their burliness.

Still this wasn't enough. What did the floating market offer to those wanting just a bit more from their evenings out on the town? For those not wanting to test their viewing endurance at a kabuki performance or watch portly dudes with awkwardly-positioned undergarments locked in a waddle to the death, there was a network of female companions available for their pleasure. In the urban worlds of Edo, Osaka and Nagasaki, government officials set up districts where men could employ the services of geisha, courtesans or even prostitutes. Set up in part to prevent the political dramas that almost always surface under dynastic rule (where women spar behind the scenes for power and influence), these carefully-regulated districts clearly defined the differences between each of the pleasure women. Geishas were the sophisticated, accomplished entertainers, skilled in the arts of the tea ceremony, classical dance, musical performance and poetry. Taken from their families at an early age and sold to geisha houses, these girls became the property of their house mother, hoping if they perfected the talents of satisfying male companions, they might one day catch the eye of a wealthy male patron, becoming his sole mistress. Courtesans and prostitutes were the last of the "women of pleasure," with courtesans also offering entertainment, whereas prostitutes...well...prostitutes had basically one purpose. Because these women all operated out of the same general geographic region, and because some geisha and courtesans achieved a revered status, an entire sex trade emerged where families might unwittingly sell their daughters into prostitution, thinking they had set their daughters up for a life of luxury and safety in one of the prestigious geisha houses. Although geishas lost prominence during World War II when American soldiers referred to any pleasure worker as a "geisha," these talented women still survive today. Segments of Japanese society (like they did centuries ago) continue to demand their wives remain demure, reserved and modest, but aren't timid about going out and looking for something less wholesome on the side.

While the urban performing and visual arts expanded and the merchant class prospered to the detriment of the samurai, the central government also had to deal with the ever-present threat of European expansion. In the 16th century, when some rough winds knocked a Portuguese ship off course, washing it up on the beaches of Japan, the land of the rising sun could no longer ignore the bearded barbarians. Initially the Portuguese weapons and Christian missionaries were welcomed by the daimyos and merchants. Oda Nobunaga's military victories stemmed in large part from his willingness to employ the European firepower, and unlike the Chinese masses whose Confucian values deemed Christianity an absurd practice, the Buddhist adherents were far more accepting of the premises of Christianity. For a people who followed an Eightfold Path promoting right speech, right action and right intention, Jesus Christ's Sermon on the Mount teachings of "turn the other cheek," "judge not, lest ye be judged," and "whatever you want men to do, do also to them" blended fairly easily with their previous moral standards. By the early 1600s, missionaries had converted over 300,000 souls. This started to cause the Tokugawa shoguns a bit of concern. Was the ultimate authority for the converts the shogun? Or was it the Pope in Rome? And when would the missionaries stop? Were they happy with 300,000 converts, or would they persist until everyone turned from the traditional Japanese belief systems?

And then they heard from across the sea that in the Philippines, the Christians had revolted, taking over the country, leaving the Filipinos merely the servants of their European lords. The Japanese had seen enough, and forced all Christian Japanese to revert to the old beliefs. Some Christian converts remained resolute. In 1638, the forces of Christianity rebelled against the forces of the Tokugawa regime. Granted, most of these peasants fought not because they cared so much about losing Christianity, but because they were starving to death due to high taxes. But the shogun's 135,000 troops needed little incentive to cut down these so-called, God-fearing farmers. 38,000 Christians died in this Shimabara Rebellion, representing the end of the Christian influence over Japan's peasantry. Within a few decades, no one dared admit to believing in God. Christianity had been wiped out.

At the same time Christianity was being extinguished and the missionaries were being expelled, the western merchants were also being denied entry to Japan's shores. Though initially Japanese daimyos welcomed the goods these merchants brought from both Europe and from their trading posts across Asia, the shoguns knew that to maintain absolute power, no outside influences could be tolerated. All ocean-going Japanese vessels were burnt, no Japanese could leave the islands, any that had already left could never return and trading with Europeans was outlawed - except for at one place.

The shogunate didn't want to completely cut themselves off from European trinkets and expertise (who knew what little inventions the Europeans might discover next), so at a tiny island in the harbor of Nagasaki, only Dutch traders could bring their wares to market. Why the Dutch? Well, the Protestant Dutch had made special friends with the central powers when they lent them weapons and gunpowder during the Shimabara Rebellion to wipe out their Catholic enemies. In this way, the Protestant/Catholic tensions that had plagued Europe ever since Luther's Protestant Reformation now made their appearance on the other side of the world. And because the Dutch had proved their allegiance (and they didn't have that pesky little figure known as the Pope commanding obedience from Rome), they were granted limited trading rights at the man-made island of Deshima. Although tolerated, the Dutch were never welcomed. If they ever doubted Japan's true feelings, they need only look at the shoreline, adorned with the hanging skulls of Europeans who tried to go ashore, a morbid warning to not sway from the shogun's authority. When they arrived at port, they were essentially quarantined, unable to interact with any but the crown's chosen intermediaries. Even on occasions when they lost men at sea, they could not bring the deceased ashore for a proper burial. It was a tenuous relationship, but it enabled the shogun to keep a cautious eye on the happenings of the West.

So when the Europeans finally returned in force (this time in 1853 when it would be an American armada that would enter Japanese waters), the nation was alarmed by this Western display of power, but not wholly unprepared. Their economic system had evolved to where the merchant class had amassed a high degree of wealth, the credit and banking system had subsequently matured and the city dwellers had grown accustomed to obediently following the mandates of their now urbanized samurai. The necessary factors were in place for Japan to accomplish their own industrial revolution in just a few short decades, a task that took their Western counterparts almost a century to direct.

Japan might have taken a different approach than the rest of the civilized world, but when the Tokugawa Shogunate finally ran its course, the resilient, insular, obedient populace would have no problem catching up and even surpassing its international rivals.

But that is for another chapter.

26

Goodbye to the Old World

Europe – Scientific Revolution and Enlightenment – 1600 > 1800

L ooking through our hindsight glasses, it would appear that
by 1600, Europe had everything it needed to rise to the top
of the sociological food chain, finally competing with the
superior civilizations of the East. After the waning days of the
Romans, the Europeans slipped into a deep sleep of ineptitude,
seemingly oblivious to the intellectual evolutions of the Muslim,
Indian and Chinese empires. But by 1600, wasn't Europe ready to
eclipse the rest of the world, and for the first time since the
Greeks, establish that they were the center of all learning and
innovation?

Not yet.

Had they started to learn how to farm efficiently? Check.
Had people started moving to cities where the process of change
could occur more quickly? Check. Had universities begun
springing up throughout these budding towns so learning could be
freely dispensed? Check. Had the legitimacy of the Church been
challenged by the Crusade failures, its impotency to stop the Black
Plague and the Protestant Reformation? Check. Had the printing
press been invented so knowledge could be shared efficiently
across the continent? Check. Had the Europeans explored beyond
their borders, bringing back not only the wisdom of other peoples,
but the wisdom of their own ancestors? Check. And had the

artists and great thinkers of the time started looking more to themselves and humanity for inspiration? Check.

But still, Europeans were a bunch of knuckleheads. It's not that these pale-faced humans weren't smart (intelligence doesn't just get lost for a thousand years), but they were illogical. And they were scared. Brilliant men did exist, but in a sea of absurdity and persecution, who would have the courage to actually stand up to reveal that the emperor's new clothes weren't exactly attractive? All around Europe, it appeared the intellectual gains of the Renaissance, the Age of Exploration and the Reformation were only mere blips in the development of the European noggin, because the irrationality of society kept returning. In 1600, people still hunted down and tortured witches, blaming them for unexplainable acts of nature. Women were still treated as inferior members of the species, to be protected and confined to the domestic sphere. Children were to be seen and not heard, to be beaten not praised. The ill were still vulnerable to the wacked out theories of pseudo-doctors, where even the most important individual in society might die from being bled to relieve a headache.

The world was still a scary, unexplainable place where humans' only chance at survival was appealing to God to help protect them from the danger and the devil that lurked around every corner. The masses passively accepted their authority figures, merely wandering through the darkness, unable to get out of the cave of misunderstanding to finally see the light. To paraphrase the prophetic words of famed *Matrix* mentor Morpheus, the "world had been pulled over their eyes to blind them from the truth."

What would it take to finally push Europeans over the edge, pulling them for the last time out of the abyss, opening their eyes to the light of understanding? What would it take? Well...two more revolutions of the mind – first the Scientific Revolution and then the Age of Enlightenment.

It's hard to pinpoint exactly when the Renaissance, the Age of Exploration and the Reformation ended and when the Scientific Revolution began. The scientists, engineers, doctors and mathematicians who cultivated the discoveries that defined this era inherited the knowledge of those that came before. Navigators had already begun tinkering with devices to aid navigation and Renaissance artists (Leonardo da Vinci included) were already dissecting cadavers and considering focal points and perspective to better capture the natural world on canvas.

Yet when Nicolaus Copernicus, a Polish monk, finally got up the nerve to send his theories on the universe to the Pope, a new age had begun. Copernicus argued that the planets, the stars and the heavens didn't go around Earth, but instead, that the sun was the center of our solar system and Earth was nothing but an insignificant third rock from that star. This heliocentric theory directly contradicted the Church's geocentric theory where God positioned mankind at the center of the universe. The Church was in no mood for another challenge from a mere mortal. Already defending itself against Martin Luther and his theological adherents who had plunged the continent into a century of skepticism and chaos, the Catholic Church was none to pleased to have yet another critic defy their sovereignty. In the decades after the Reformation, the Church had executed its own Counter-Reformation, reforming some of its less favorable behaviors, but amping up its persecution of non-believers. Just when they thought they were making headway in restoring faith in the Catholic Church, Copernicus had to go and knock a few more dents in the Church's ecclesiastical armor. Ironically, the Church only had itself to blame for Copernicus's research into the structure of the universe, as it was the Church that hired Copernicus to precisely date all the major religious holidays. While on this task, he noticed that the Church's calendar didn't work because the Earth's actual orbit looked nothing like what had been accepted by the Church's great minds for fifteen centuries. Copernicus died without ever seeing the fruits of his theories, but within a century, the Copernican Revolution was fully underway.

When the 17th century arrived and a new generation of tinkerers, hobbyists and part-time scientists started looking further into the heavens and through the natural world, they had in their toolbox all the instruments needed to catapult Europe into modernity. They had microscopes and telescopes forged from the lenses of the master glassmakers of Venice. They had the most accurate scales and clocks in existence. And they had Gutenberg's printing press so all the findings of the great thinkers could be shared and scrutinized by the scientific community for centuries.

Around this same time, Lord Francis Bacon hogged the spotlight by finalizing a methodology for how all scientific inquiry should be conducted. Bacon believed all true experimentation required a hypothesis, meticulously recorded data, analysis of these results and then the publication of conclusions for others to repeat, test, refute or validate. Even today, Bacon's scientific method determines how our nation's high school students dissect their frogs, sort their Mendel's peas and mix baking soda and vinegar for a fun little explosion. Bacon lived and died a scientist, actually perishing from the flu he caught while standing outside in the freezing cold, jamming snow up a chicken's rear end trying to ascertain the effects of refrigeration on flesh.

Across the West, scientists experimented, recorded and published, and because they documented their findings in their native tongue and not the antiquated Latin of their predecessors, any literate individual with a sense of inquisitiveness could become a member of the unofficial fraternity of European scientists.

By the mid-17th century, discoveries were popping out from all corners of the scientific community. In astronomy, Brahe, Kepler, Galileo and then Newton, each building on the work of the other, used the devices at their disposal to prove the nature of our solar system and the role of gravity in keeping all the celestial bodies in orbit. Tycho Brahe set up formal observatories to collect more information on the planets than any man before; Johanes Kepler took his mentor's notes and used his math skills to publish his theories on the motion of planets; Galileo Galilei improved upon the design of the telescope so it brought images 32 times closer to the human eye, eventually making it possible to prove that moons orbit Jupiter, that spots exist on the sun, and that the moon is made up of craters, mountains and dirt just like earth; and Sir Isaac Newton, standing firmly on the shoulders of these giants of astronomy, proved that the movement of these celestial bodies, and all of nature, is defined not only by the law of gravity, but also by laws of motion which govern how all objects interact. With Newton, the Copernican Revolution was complete. Though only a half dozen of the most learned men could even comprehend Newton's *Principia Mathematica*, the world of mysticism and faith would never be the same. Laws governed the behavior of objects, not laws by an unseen god. Even to the average Joe who knew nothing of Newton's laws, he could still look to the skies and the infinite planets and stars and wonder - Where then is heaven? Are we not God's special creatures? Where even is God?

A century before, neither scientist or learned man would dare publicly admit to not believing in God. But by 1700, atheism was increasingly accepted, no longer a guaranteed death sentence.

Yet the discoveries were not reserved merely for the astronomers. In math, Pascal invented a mechanical calculator that could add, subtract, multiply and divide. In the physical sciences, Otto von Guericke created a machine that could generate electricity, and then Benjamin Franklin discovered with a key and a kite that electricity came from lightning. In the medical world, Ambroise Pare revolutionized surgery, Andreas Vesalius proved that hearts pump blood and Pierre Fauchard figured how to properly care for teeth and extract them when necessary. In the world of biology, Carl von Linne sorted all living creatures into the much-memorized categories of kingdom, phylum, class, order, family, genus and species.

The list goes on and on and on...and then on some more. Between 1600 and 1800, the world as they knew it became the world as we know it. This is where all the fathers came from – the father of dentistry, the father of surgery, the father of chemistry, the father of physiology, the father of anatomy, the father of mineralogy and the great grandfather of them all - Sir Isaac Newton. Each of these men adhered to the precepts of Bacon's scientific method, turning the West for the first time into the center of all learning. Now, when the Europeans went to the shores of China, Japan, India or the Muslim empires, they wouldn't be merely discounted, but their books, their gadgets and their methods would be first respected and then coveted. Yet unlike the engineers and scientists of the East, the West operated under a model of pure science – where knowledge was the only goal and curiosity the leading motivator. In the classical ages of China, India and Islam, the discoveries were usually made with a purpose in mind – have a problem, solve a problem. This fixation on applied science restricted Eastern scientists to the world they needed to fix, whereas in the West, so much more was learned about the natural world as scientists were free to explore where no man had gone, purely for the sake of knowledge. Nothing more. Granted, if a fortune could be made from the discoveries, later Western entrepreneurs would prove more than willing to reap the benefits, but for this two-century period, science was pure and discoveries came in rapid succession.

With each discovery, the world became more and more under man's control, not the other way around. We no longer moved at the whims of nature, but it was we who could make nature bend to our will. In later generations, Western man would begin harnessing the gifts of nature like no civilization before, turning the environment into the materials that would propel the West to global dominance.

But this is not to say that all of Europe on the scientific bandwagon. The Church continued to fight the battle for universal truth, scientists were still persecuted and jailed for their findings (Galileo spent the rest of his life under house arrest after refusing to deny his research), and the mass of Europeans still believed witches lived among them and little store-bought talismans or passed-down rituals could be turned to for guidance and protection. But before we lambast the ignorance of these mental midgets, should we not also admit that many of the most learned of the West today continue to knock on wood, stay clear of black cats, walk around opened ladders, save their mother's backs by avoiding cracks or believe that God created man, that Darwin's evolution theories are preposterous, that Noah fit every species of every animal into a boat and that the Biblical Jonah lived in a whale for three days? The more and more our world seems governed by the laws of science, the more and more man continues to cling to the safety and faith of our past.

The true import of the Scientific Revolution was not what it did for the natural world, but what it did for how humans interact with their environment. We no longer had to wait for nature to have its way with us. Man could define, predict and even alter his existence. From here, man would not try to simply define the laws that governed the natural world, but find the truths that govern how man should interact with his fellow man. This was the last of the revolutions of the mind – the Age of Enlightenment.

Thomas Hobbes and John Locke were two of the first to delve into creating irrefutable laws of the invisible universe – where governments and nobles ruled, where everymen submitted and women and children suffered in a world of irrelevancy. Hobbes, a contemporary of Galileo, believed that like the planets that revolve around the sun in a predetermined manner, so did humans follow a predestined course. Men abide by one natural law – they are selfish to the core. When all the societal niceties and traditions are stripped away, man is revealed as a being in constant battle with others – for power, for wealth, for survival, leading to a life that is "nasty, brutish and short." According to Hobbes, man then needs government to implement and enforce laws to control his naughty tendencies. Governments need men to abide by said laws. This give and take amounts to a "social contract" where each side plays a role to ensure society doesn't revert to its natural state of anarchy.

Not exactly the most positive take on humanity. Enter John Locke, the Brit with a bit happier spin on the human species. To Locke, man is born with a clean slate with no predetermined path. Then, from his first breath, he begins to sense the world around him, and it is the product of these sights, sounds, touches, tastes and smells that mold man. No one has an advantage at birth and we are all by nature merely observers, taking in the evidence of our lives to determine our course. In the whole nurture vs. nature debate, let's just say Locke is at the far end of the spectrum defending the nurture point of view. Locke then states that the role of government is not to ensure we fall back into a state of selfishness, but to instead protect the natural gifts we all inherit upon birth – life, liberty and property. To Locke, this is the social contract, and should ever government fail to protect this holy triad of personal freedoms, society had the right, no, the *obligation* to overthrow the government and demand protection.

In the century that followed, inspired by the findings of Hobbes and Locke, and benefitting from the structure of the scientific method, a series of thinkers, satirists, writers, poets, musicians, philosophers and historians emerged, each using logic and reason to help better understand the human condition. Although the famed works of these thinkers popped up in urban areas across Western Europe, it was in Paris that a new demographic stepped to the forefront of intellectual change. This group was made up of wealthy, literate, connected women who tried to outdo each other in their weekly get-togethers where the brightest minds of the days assembled to hash out answers to the questions – why do we behave the way we do and how should we behave? At these *salons* (think 18th century version of today's "book clubs"...albeit with a bit more impressive guest list than Cindy Housewife could assemble to discuss the merits of *Fifty Shades of Grey*), men such as Voltaire, Montesquieu, Rousseau and Diderot gathered to finish conversations they couldn't hold at the universities or the other accepted venues of the day. The women were not merely passive hosts, but actively engaged in the discussions, oftentimes pushing the discourse to subjects previously considered untouchable.

For Voltaire, organized religion had to go. Raised a Catholic, he saw the Church as the great corrupter and suppressor of the human spirit. To him, God was merely a clockmaker, a being that created the world, all the plants, the animals, the intricacies of human behavior and then started the wheels of time turning, leaving us all to do with His world as we wish. This new faith, this Deism, dismissed the notion that God actually cared about our daily lives. He was merely the great Creator. He started the ball of life rolling and then just let it all play out without his interference.

Voltaire saw no logical place for the Catholic Church in man's daily life. He encouraged religious tolerance, believing that the acceptance of all faiths would free the world from war and allow man to truly reach his potential.

Montesquieu and Rousseau concerned themselves more with how to govern. Montesquieu saw that whenever all power to govern rested in the hands of one man, the fate of the state depended solely on the mental and ethical capabilities of this man. This totally centralized power was great if your king was an enlightened dictator, but more often than not, he was a gluttonous, egocentric, paranoid pig of a man. From generation to generation, a people's standard of living could vary, not by any decision they made, but because of the unchecked whims of their leader. Montesquieu offered a solution. Check power. Balance power. Create three branches – a lawmaking branch (legislative), an enforcing branch (executive) and the branch of final judgment (judicial) – and the success of a nation would be determined more by the strength of their laws than by the minds of their leaders. Rousseau piggy-backed Locke, believing "all men are born free," but then also adding that they are "everywhere in chains" - chained to their Church, to their lord, to their land. But to Rousseau, this was not always the way. Before humans walked down the paths of civilization, they were closer to their natural state. As noble savages, we lived in a world of equality and relative peace, and it wasn't until we settled into societies that we went off course, creating a world of haves and have-nots - those few who enjoy the fruits of humanity's labor and the masses who suffer at their exploitation. The only solution is to give every citizen a say in government by granting him the right to vote. He could then choose with the ballot who he desires in power, kicking out those who break the social contract.

Outside the sphere of government, two other men contributed significantly to the era – one dealt with how we punish our rulebreakers and the other with how we run our economies. Cesare Beccaria believed the criminal justice system was inherently flawed. We beat our children, torture our suspects and publicly humiliate and murder our guilty. A true civilization should not destroy those who've sinned, but should rehabilitate them so they can re-enter society and contribute to their fullest. Should little Barack smoke some pot in high school, we shouldn't cut off his hands and display them on a fence for all to see. No...we should have a talk with little Barack, show him the error of his ways so that he can one day be president. Beccaria's ideas had a significant impact on how children and prisoners (odd putting those two together) were treated, contributing centuries later to a situation where Western youth today feel entitled and free to question authority without any real fear of cruel or unusual punishment. Some teachers and parents long for the good ol' days.

Adam Smith cared little for prisoners. He concerned himself with man's pocket book, with obtaining wealth and with how economies should be run. To Smith, only one entity truly knew what products and what services should be provided, and it wasn't the government. It was the market. Entrepreneurs decide what to make and consumers decide what to buy, and if Thomas Hobbes was correct, since both parties are selfish at heart, they will eventually arrive at an equilibrium point where goods can be shared. If a man wants to invent some animal-shaped pottery that when watered grows into a plant (a la the famed "Chia Pet") then all the more power to him. If there are consumers to buy the product at his established price then the product should exist. If no one buys the product, the entrepreneur then needs to either lower the price, improve the product or get out of the animal pottery growing business. In this manner, the invisible hand of the market pushes all parties to improve the quality and quantity of the goods and services provided. And we all benefit. This idea didn't go over so well with the governments of Europe who preferred telling their colonists and their merchants where, how and what to buy and sell.

One of the crowning achievements of the Age of Enlightenment was Diderot's creation of Europe's first encyclopedia, not so ironically named *The Encyclopedia*. Diderot took the sum total of all man's knowledge and started writing it all in one convenient location. He called on the greatest Enlightened philosophes of the age to contribute to the master work, and when it was all done, it numbered over 18,000 pages, with 72,000 articles, 3200 illustrations, all bound in 35 handy dandy, convenient volumes. However, not everyone had access to Diderot's encyclopedia. Not only was its cost a bit prohibitive (only 4,000 were ever published), but its mere size wasn't exactly something your everyday merchant could store on his bookshelf.

But the knowledge was out there, open to the world. As literacy rates increased and as universities began freely sharing the views of these Enlightened thinkers, ensuing generations grew up envisioning a world where the theories of their predecessors actually came to fruition.

Oddly enough, it wouldn't be in Europe where these ideas would finally get their chance to prove their merit, but in one of England's coastal colonies – a region on the east coast of the Americas, where the leaders of a collection of port towns and plantations saw to it to question the authority of Mother England, wondering if power need truly reside across the Atlantic Ocean. But could this upstart society of religious exiles and forgotten European sons ever truly break from a millennium-old civilization with one of the most powerful militaries on the planet, and then actually live by the mandates of Locke, Montesquieu, Beccaria, Smith and Rousseau?

Yes...I think they just might have a chance.

But that is for another chapter.

27

The Beast from the East

Russia – Kiev Rus to Catherine the Great – 1400 > 1800

I just know I'm forgetting someone. Who could it be? Let me think. Did I mention the first river civilizations? Check. First great empires in China, India and the Mediterranean? Check. Empires from the steppe? Check. Rise and fall and rise again of Western Europe? Check. Gunpowder Empires? Check. Feudal ages of East Asia? Check. I think I even covered peoples in the Americas, Africa and Polynesia, peoples who never even bothered to write their history down.

So who am I missing? Let me take a look at a world map and see who was left out.

Ahhh...there it is. Of course. How could I have missed it?

Mother Russia. The biggest country in the world by a long shot. How big is it? It stretches across two continents - making up 51% of Asia and 49% of Europe. It's twice as wide as the United States. It spans nine different time zones. You could fit 160 of today's nations within its borders and still have some room left over for some fields of corn.

Russia is huge. And unlike the vast empires of the Romans, the Mongols and the Ottomans, Russia is still around. The rest have all faded with the times and their holdings have long since become independent.

But not Russia. Russia's still going strong, and after surviving more than a few hiccups after the fall of the Soviet Union in the 1990s, it's back up to being among the world leaders. Number eleven in GDP. Number nine in population. Number three in military expenditures. And number one in nuclear warheads.

Throughout the 20th century, Russia stood as the West's arch nemesis. Even though the Western nations formed tentative alliances with Russia during World War I and then World War II, the Russians were never really seen as "one of us" and as their population, their industry, their military might and their influence on the developing nations of the world peaked in the decades of the Cold War (1945-1989), many wondered if our world would come to an apocalyptic end at the hands of the Russians (with more than a little goading from the good ol' United States of America).

But here we are. The planet survived.

The Cold War might be behind us, but Russia still remains one of the most powerful, if least understood, nations on the planet.

But they weren't always the beast from the east.

The beginnings of Russia date back to the late 9th century when bands of Vikings (called Rus) ventured up and down the dozens of waterways branching off of the Black, Baltic and Caspian Seas, eventually establishing "the land of the Rus" – Kiev Rus. Each successive Grand Prince of Kiev (from Sviatopolk the Acccursed, to Yuri the Long Arms, to Vsevelod the Big Nest, to Dmitry the Terrible Eyes) added to the feudal wealth of the Rus, making this region one of the wealthiest kingdoms of feudal Europe. The kingdoms of Kiev Rus expanded a lucrative trading relationship with the Byzantine Empire down south, but like every other civilization of Eurasia in the 12th century, they surrendered to the Mongol hordes of Genghis Khan and his progeny.

For the next three centuries, the Mongol Khanate of the Golden Horde controlled the economy of Kiev Russia, but instead of living amongst the Russian people, the Mongols remained in the steppe, letting the Russians rule themselves and collect their own taxes. And as long as the taxes kept flowing from Russian to Mongol hands, they were more or less left alone. In this way, the Mongols and the Russians maintained a relatively uneasy truce – Mongols promised to stop massacring villagers if the villagers promised to pay their taxes on time. This little arrangement seemed to work, but it still didn't stop the Mongols invading the southern borderlands every couple generations to remind the Russians who was really in charge.

Around the late 15th century, the tide started to change. The Mongols were still interested in Russian taxes, but less willing to be bothered by costly and brutal military campaigns. They'd gotten lazy. The noble princes around Moscow, who had been the Mongol's tax collectors for centuries, started to talk of a rebellion, and in 1462, under the leadership of Ivan the Great, they united the countryside and waged an all-out war on the Mongols. Seeing the power of religious fervor, Ivan sold this war to the people as a war for God, his people's one final chance at driving the infidel from their holy land. And it worked. In 1480, the final Mongol force surrendered and Russia was again free.

Russia then knew it needed to expand. Russia is one of the most vulnerable regions in all the world. To the south it has the indefensible steppe where for a thousand years horsemen had plagued agricultural communities trying to survive. To the west were the European dynasties that perennially wanted to expand their holdings for both narcissistic and economic ends. To the east were the vast Siberian plains, an inhospitable climate where only the strongest could survive. And to the north was...well...the North Pole (so at least they didn't have to worry about that frontier).

To make matters worse, Russia only had one water port, Arkhangelsk, and it was frozen for most of the year. Russia was landlocked and surrounded on all sides. Their leaders determined the best defense was a fierce offense. They needed to enlarge their empire, but instead of fighting the superiorly-armed Europeans, they pushed to the south and to the east, kicking out the last vestiges of Mongol control, each time settling Russians in the freshly-conquered lands.

In this way, the Russians looked a lot like the Western Europeans who settled the Americas after Columbus's voyages at the end of the 15th century. The Russians would send explorers, then soldiers, then settlers. It turned out they could find an explorer, a soldier and a settler all in the same person – a Cossack. Cossacks were the baddest men on the plain. Imagine a cross between an American cowboy, a European knight and a Hun. They could live on their horses, survive the harshest environments, destroy any army they faced and when all opponents were finally vanquished, they could rest a bit, build a few communities and raise their families. They were independent warriors for hire to the highest bidder. They were feared by villagers and nobles alike, and they established settlements all across Russia. The merchant Strogonov family hired Cossacks to settle and build forts in Siberia so that they could open up trade routes to the Pacific Ocean. Eventually these warring, settling Cossacks made it across the Bering Strait to Alaska. From there, they set up forts and colonies all the way down the American west coast, with thousands creating settlements in the regions we today call Washington, Oregon and California. By 1800, Russia had established an empire that spanned three continents – only Spain could say it came anywhere close to controlling as much land.

As the territorial claims started piling up, Russian leaders had a choice – force all of their inhabitants to conform to one Russian culture, one Russian economy, one Russian political system, or learn from their Mongol conquerors who discovered the benefits of relinquishing just a bit of autonomy to your dependents. You could waste all of your money and resources trying to pound people into submission or you could just let them be. Russia compromised. Russian inhabitants of the far Siberia, Eastern Europe, Americas and the far off steppe could wear what they wanted, believe what they wanted and practice all their old cultural traditions, but they had to submit to the total authority of Russian rule (which mostly meant ensure taxes go back to Moscow or St. Petersburg). And for the most part, the newly-conquered were OK with this arrangement, for it really wasn't a new arrangement at all. Most kingdoms and villages across Eurasia had been paying taxes and following laws of distant conquerors for centuries. How much different would Russian rule really be?

They would soon find out. A succession of Russian rulers was growingly attracted to the ideas coming out of France, England and the Netherlands. These nobles tried to play the delicate game of embracing some of the innovations of Western Europe while simultaneously ensuring power continued to rest in the hands of one ruling family. After Ivan the Great (Ivan III) gave way to his son Ivan the Terrible (Ivan IV), Russia became the monolith it has remained until today. Ivan the Terrible saw himself as the creator of a new Roman Empire to the East, replacing the Byzantine Empire that had fallen to the Ottomans a century earlier. He created a new title of Czar (Caesar) and killed any noble that stood in his way. He made it clear from the beginning of his rule that he would not be sharing authority with any parliament or band of nobility. He would stand at the unquestioned top of the political pyramid, with all answering to his every whim. He alone appointed regional officials to execute his business and he also created a secret police that kept all Russians on their toes at all times. No one ever knew who was watching, who was listening. Dissension was not tolerated under any circumstance. Freedom of speech was not even considered. The threat was clear – speak out against the Czar and die. Disobedient individuals could be stolen in the dead of night or hung up in the city square. Entire villages were wiped out with one order from the lips of Ivan.

Towards the end of Ivan's life, after the death of his wife, he clearly lost his mind, thinking everyone was out to assassinate him. In one mad fit of rage he even beat up his daughter-in-law and killed his son, the heir to the throne. Years later, Ivan died, passing his throne to his feeble, cognitively-challenged, older son Feodor. At this point, Russia could have fallen back into an age of factionalism, but the nobles of Russia, the boyars, chose to look to Ivan's wife's family for leadership. Her family was the Romanovs, and they would rule for the next three hundred years until 1917 when they were overthrown during the Communist Revolution.

But in that time, the Romanovs built on the autocratic traditions of Ivan IV, while expanding the cultural refinements of the Russian people. The two most influential Romanov leaders of Russia's history were Peter the Great and Catherine the Great who transformed Russia in the 18th century to make it an empire on par with the European dynasties to the west.

First let's look at Peter the Great. Peter took over the throne in 1682 he quickly measured up his empire and recognized he had a huge problem – his Russia had fallen centuries behind its European peers and if he didn't catch up quickly, it would only be a matter of time before the Western powers turned their imperialist tendencies east. So, he devised a pretty ingenious plan – he would dress up in disguise, travel all around Europe and learn everything he possibly could from European scientists, philosophers, artists, manufacturers and military officers. There was one problem – he was 6'8" – which is fairly huge by today's standards, but back in the 17th century where the average male was just a bit over 5'2" tall, he was a freak of nature. But that didn't stop him. He dressed in rags, got jobs building ships in Holland and even tried meeting with the French monarchs to see if they'd support him in his bid to defeat the Ottomans.

He wasn't successful gaining any military allies, but his 18-month fact-finding mission proved a success. He returned to Russia full of ideas, and he spent the rest of his reign making sure they came to fruition. First, he needed a warm water port. Arkhangelsk was useful for a few months out of the year, but Peter knew that if he wanted to be a full partner in the trade game, he had to be able to get his ships out to sea. He used his knowledge of shipbuilding to design a navy that was then set to the task of capturing any port that would not freeze over during the fall, winter and spring. He sent his navy on campaign after campaign after campaign, but time and again, the Swedes, the Ottomans and even the Poles pushed him back. It would take him 22 years, but he eventually grabbed a port on the Baltic Sea and one on the Caspian Sea.

But that was only the start. There was more to Westernization than merely joining the world of sea trade. He also set to pull Russia out of its Middle Ages. Problem #1 were the nobles. They were trapped in the past, making money off of agriculture like they had for over five hundred years. They had become gluttonous and lazy and were a drain on the economy. They were useless to him. He started to surround himself not with noble advisors but with trained bureaucrats appointed based on merit, not on birthright. He established a universal law code and a uniform tax collecting system so that the entire empire followed one set of rules, not merely the whims of local lords. He replaced nobles who served no purpose with local magistrates that would answer only to Peter. And to symbolically demonstrate that the past was behind them, Peter forced all nobles to cut off their beards to better resemble the clean-shaven faces of Western European nobility.

If the nobles were annoyed with Peter's attack on their facial hair, they were even less pleased with the rights he began extending to the female nobility. He forced upper class women to start wearing the latest fashions, to begin attending higher level schools and to leave the home and actually attend social events with their husbands (especially the soon-to-be world renowned ballet).

But these social changes impacted only a select few from the upper class. Peter's most lasting changes involved his treatment of the remaining 99% of society. Seeing that the growing Middle Class in Europe posed a huge threat to the monarchies, Peter knew he had to control economic growth to prevent what could become class warfare. Instead of creating an economy ripe for entrepreneurialism, Peter created a system where any manufacturing or commercial industry was totally controlled by the government. In countries like France, Holland and England, merchants were getting rich off the commercial opportunities from the global trade networks. In Western Europe, if you had an idea of how to make a buck, you could get a loan from the bank, start a firm and start spinning out wares. Western Europe was home to the new rich, a group of business builders known as entrepreneurs. But this private industry would never be tolerated in Russia. Peter controlled all enterprises, and he also controlled the workforce. Instead of advancing the rights of the lower class, providing an opportunity for their upward mobility, he actually reversed their freedoms, making them fundamentally slaves for life.

Peasants in Russia were called serfs, but they were treated less like the peasants of Medieval Europe and more like the African slaves of the plantation American South. They were born into serfdom and could not escape. They were slaves to the land and prevented from taking any other job. They lived by a different set of laws than their landholders and lived in a constant state of starvation. Over 50% of the population was made up of serfs, and this percentage would remain the same until the 20th century. Peter used this serf labor army to fill his newly created mining and iron-making industries, and he even used them to build his new capital – St. Petersburg (a task that killed over 100,000 serfs before it was completed). Every industry created was built not for the sole sake of profit, like in the West, but to benefit the empire and its ability to wage war. No superfluous industries were pursued. Few luxury goods were produced. Peter was content to merely import the finest luxuries from Western Europe, while trading away his nation's iron, grain, timber and animal furs.

But that's not what made Peter truly great. What made him great was that he was one of the more interesting political figures in history. This man had some unique hobbies. He had his conservative side that liked to build chairs and design pots. He had his physical side he used to impress his guests. He could sleep standing up, roll up a silver platter into a scroll with his bare hands and drink a shot of vodka every 15 minutes for an entire day and wake up the next morning and go hunting while his drinking buddies were passed out in the palace. He was also a collector. He liked to collect teeth (tens of thousands of teeth to be exact...many from his enemies who made for unwilling dental patients). But his greatest collections were housed in his "art chamber" – the Kunstkamera – the world's finest freak show.

Peter was annoyed by the superstitious and irrational minds of his Russian people. He still heard stories of villagers believing in monsters and devils and all sorts of mythical beasts. He wanted to prove that there was a reason for all things strange, so he set his museum curators on a continent-wide search for any physical human abnormality. He wanted to collect and then display his own "freak show." He wanted to show that deformities were just nature's accidents, not the supernatural practices of sorcerers.

He ordered all deformed, still-born babies to be sent to St. Petersburg. He wanted the skulls and the bodies of any dwarf, giant or human anomaly added to his collection. Three hundred years later his collection is still intact, so if you ever want to see two-faced babies, Siamese twins, human mermaids or any other genetic mutation known to man, feel free to stop by the Kunstkamera for a glimpse into the surreal.

When Peter II died, Russia lost one of the most charismatic, passionate and resolute leaders in its history, but within a decade Catherine II, Catherine the Great, would take over the Romanov crown and take Russia even higher, to its true golden age.

Catherine the Great assumed the throne of Russia after her husband, Peter III, mysteriously died after being emperor for a mere six months. Catherine was never proven guilty of plotting the assassination, but she wasn't exactly disappointed that she no longer had to deal with a man she often described as the most boring, dull man in any room. Once in power, Catherine had a bit of a problem acting like a lady. She had no desire to play the role of a submissive female noble. Instead she ruled over Russia with an iron fist, striking down all enemies and never swaying from a battle. She extended Russia's borders even further, to the Black Sea in the south, clear to California across the Pacific Ocean to the west. Nobody in Europe knew what to do with her. She worked harder, longer hours than any monarch from the West, she toured her country trying to talk to as many of her people as her energy would allow, she wrote countless letters to the Enlightened thinkers of France, England and the United States, and she even had no problem parading a slew of "favored" men into her bedroom, one after the other.

She tried to finish the Westernization her great-uncle-in-law, Peter the Great, had started a generation earlier. She gobbled up the greatest art pieces of Europe, depositing them in the Hermitage Museum. She forced her nobility to educate themselves in the writings of the Enlightenment. She built orphanages, schools and hospitals. She was even willing to risk her own life to prove her faith in Enlightened theories. She was a true believer in the power of science and she proved her convictions by being the first prominent Russian to inoculate her family against the smallpox vaccination. Smallpox was the scourge of Europe, killing millions and marking millions more with pox scars. The cure for smallpox existed, but no one was willing to take the inoculation, for fear that it might be the devil's potion. Catherine scoffed at this nonsense. She took the needle and the vaccination, and her courage inspired countless millions of others to follow in her footsteps.

But oddly, she found nothing hypocritical about embracing the Enlightenment while keeping more than half of her population enslaved. She gave more power to regional lords, taking away any remaining freedoms from the serfs. Russia was one of the few places where as the state evolved, its people actually regressed. Her subjects might have held her in awe, but they also were sick and tired of barely clinging to life while royals sat hidden away in their palaces playing card games, using diamonds as gambling chips.

Towards the end of her rule, Catherine stared down several threats to her throne. In one instance, the Pugachev Rebellion of 1775, tens of thousands of serfs banned together demanding an end to serfdom, taxation, the military draft and landed nobles. This band of rebels fought a guerrilla war across the countryside, but Pugachev was finally captured and brought to Moscow in an iron cage. Catherine chopped off his head and had his body cut into four chunks to be hung in the four corners of the capital city as a warning of how rebels would be treated. A few years later, after seeing the deadly fruits of the French Revolution, she started censoring the same Enlightened writings she championed earlier in her rule, realizing maybe it wasn't the best idea to Westernize too much. By the time she died in 1796 (after suffering a stroke while sitting on the toilet), her empire was no longer seen as the inferior step-brother of the European monarchies.

Nope, by 1800, Russia was a force to be reckoned with. Its empire would last another century, even when one by one, the European nations succumbed to revolution. And when a tiny general from France tried to invade Russia in his quest to conquer the world, it would be Russia that would swallow his ambitions, sending him home defeated with nary an army under his charge.

But that is for another chapter.

28

The Documents Heard
'Round the World

The United States of America - Founding – 1700 > 1800

And now we get to a country you might have heard of before. I'll give you some clues. It has the third most people and the fourth most land. It has the largest economy in the world. It has the largest military in the world. It's home to the most desired universities, the greatest technological innovations of the 20th century and MTV. Its breakfast cereal aisles are legendary. Its fast food restaurants are global icons. It makes the movies everyone wants to see and the music everyone plugs into their ears. Its embassies around the world have the longest lines of any foreign country – those lining up to protest its foreign policy and those lining up just hoping for a chance to win the immigration lottery and possibly set foot in the nation where the streets are lined with gold and anyone can make it to the top.

It's everywhere and its global reach touches everyone. You can go hiking in the most remote hills of the Himalayas, stop off in the islands of Papua New Guinea or get stranded on the coast of Antarctica, and you will see its footsteps. Love it or hate it, everyone has an opinion of it.

It is the United States of America.

Although its reach is incomparable today, its beginnings were less than intimidating. After Columbus touched ground in the Caribbean, the European powers of Spain, Portugal, France, England and Holland set off exploring and colonizing all across the two Americas. By the mid-1600s, the Americas were a patchwork of land claims, sparsely populated by the outcasts and the fortune seekers of Europe. Spain by far had the most territory, controlling almost all of South America, the entirety of Central America and all lands west of the Mississippi River. Portugal held the eastern portion of South America, what would one day become Brazil; France laid claim to the areas around the Mississippi; Holland briefly held some ports on the eastern coast (New Amsterdam - aka "New York" - was their most prominent); and England ruled over a series of thirteen colonies huddled closely against the Atlantic Ocean.

Throughout the 17th century, these northern English colonies weren't even the most desired holdings in the Americas. The Caribbean islands produced the sugar that fetched a hefty sum on the world markets and the silver and gold mines of South America dug out the bullion that made the world exchange possible. The British thirteen colonies were a mere afterthought.

Yet as the mines dried up and the market for sugar became saturated, the more diverse economies of North America forced Europe to take notice. For the first half of the 17th century, although technically ruled by Britain, the colonists survived relatively autonomously. England was embroiled in one of its seemingly endless string of wars with continental Europe, leaving the port cities of the Americas to trade their wares relatively unencumbered and leaving the southern plantations to grow wealthy off of rice, indigo and the conveniently addictive crop known as tobacco.

By 1750, the inhabitants of these British colonies had arguably the highest standard of living on the planet. Their Protestant work ethic had them working hard all day to secure their place in heaven, their natural resources on the vast continent seemed inexhaustible and their location made them able to readily enter the world markets with minimal transportation difficulties.

But in 1756, everything changed. Britain and France started dueling in yet another war. This one would last for seven years (named oddly "The Seven Years War") and would involve British and French holdings across the globe. The British colonists became mere pawns in this global game, but as they combined their forces with those of the feared British redcoats, the French forces were subdued, opening up British territory all the way from the Atlantic to the Mississippi. After this French and Indian War (as it was called in the colonies), life started to change for the citizens of Massachusetts, Connecticut, Rhode Island, Delaware, Pennsylvania, New York, New Jersey, Maryland, Virginia, North Carolina, South Carolina and Georgia.

Out of fear the crown would have to protect the colonists against the unpredictable Indians, Britain forbade the colonists from settling on the freshly-acquired territory to the west. This constraint frustrated the colonists. Why the heck did they just finish fighting the French? Weren't they owed all this new land they secured? Plus, the British troops didn't leave, and since there weren't a lot of British bases set up for the soldiers to catch some sleep, they were often housed in the homes of the locals (not exactly a desirable situation for a farmer father with impressionable munchkins living under the same roof). And because England fell heavily into debt funding the little French and Indian War, they decided to start actually collecting the taxes they had been a little lax collecting over the previous century. This was where the colonists had enough. Unwanted houseguests were one thing. Cutting into their pocketbooks could not be tolerated.

Imagine a young adult who graduates from high school, heads to college and has the best four years of his life. He has total freedom to make his own choices, he has more free time than he could ever imagine, his food supply is pretty consistent and there's no one to tell him he needs to be home by 12:00. But then, due to unforeseen circumstances, he reluctantly returns home to his parents' house at the ripe age of 22. Back under his parents' roof, his mom nags him about the cleanliness of his room, his dad wonders why he gets home in the wee hours of the night and no matter where he walks, there's always someone's meddling eyes following his every move. This scenario rarely ends well. Once you get a taste of freedom, returning to the world of living under the thumb of another is just a bit disconcerting.

The colonists felt this discomfort. Well maybe not all the colonists. Mostly just the wealthiest merchants, traders, shipbuilders and landowners felt the sting of British meddling. Their profits dwindled as the British again wanted to determine what was produced, how it was produced, how it was shipped, where the goods ended up and how much off the top ended up in the hands of the British government. The decades of self-governing were gone. The new age of taxation without representation had begun.

The wealthy 10% knew something had to change. What happened next appears in hindsight as a carefully orchestrated attempt by the wealthy and learned elite to manufacture conflict, to inspire the masses to rise up and to throw off the shackles of colonial servitude. In reality, the events that unfolded over the second half of the 18th century were probably more sporadic reactions to increasingly oppressive British policies, but because all of these revolts, protests and boycotts happened at the tail end of the Age of Enlightenment, what could have merely been a brief blip of dissension became a revolution that would change the world.

Two factions spurred the American revolutionary movement - the militant, prone to violence rabble-rousers led by Samuel Adams (yes, that guy on the beer bottle) and then the educated, classically trained thinkers who saw Western Civilization at a great crossroads. These thinkers were not merely passive readers of the European Enlightenment. They were active participants. Benjamin Franklin was well known in the salons of France, and the writings of Thomas Jefferson and Patrick Henry were followed with as much interest as were once Rousseau, Montesquieu and Voltaire. But it was the job of the Sons of Liberty, a loosely-organized group of young men willing to step a bit outside the law, to bring the issues facing the men of the port cities (primarily those living in Boston) to every colonist on the Eastern seaboard. Tax collectors were stripped naked, tarred, feathered and mocked as they staggered through the streets with flesh on fire. British goods not subjected to the same strict tariffs as American goods were destroyed (a la the Boston Tea Party). Signs were made. Slogans repeated. Misunderstood acts of violence where errant snowballs led to accidental deaths were blown into catastrophic events (see "Boston Massacre"). Steadily, more and more started to entertain the thought of independence, but still, by the mid-1770s, John Adams admitted that 1/3 of the population were patriots wanting independence, 1/3 remained loyal to King George and 1/3 were apathetic and worried more about whether or not their corn was going to grow than if they had to pay taxes to some fancy-pants-wearing dudes across the Atlantic. These numbers shifted more toward the patriotic camp after the publishing of Thomas Paine's *Common Sense*, a piece of American Enlightenment, written in the language of the common man, succinctly outlining the economic, social and political reasons for breaking from British rule.

In 1776, representatives from the thirteen colonies gathered in Philadelphia to discuss how to best deal with the mounting tension. Like the population as a whole, these delegates struggled to come to grips with how to proceed. Eventually, after months of debate and after actual shots were fired by George Washington and his newly-formed Continental Army, the delegation entrusted lawyer John Adams, philosopher and tinkerer Benjamin Franklin and plantation aristocrat Thomas Jefferson with the responsibility of writing a Declaration of Independence. Thomas Jefferson took the lead and what resulted was a masterful blend of Enlightened thought and scientific reasoning. The document begins with Locke's take on natural rights, alludes to Voltaire's depiction of a Creator God and then rounds off with Rousseau's directive that a persecuted people have the right to rebel. It reads:

> *We hold these Truths to be self-evident, that all Men are created equal, that they are endowed by their Creator with certain unalienable Rights, that among these are Life, Liberty, and the pursuit of Happiness—That to secure these Rights, Governments are instituted among Men, deriving their just Powers from the Consent of the Governed, that whenever any Form of Government becomes destructive of these Ends, it is the Right of the People to alter or abolish it, and to institute a new Government, laying its Foundation on such Principles, and organizing its Powers in such Form, as to them shall seem most likely to effect their Safety and Happiness. Prudence, indeed, will dictate that Governments long established should not be changed for light and transient Causes; and accordingly all Experience hath shewn, that Mankind are more disposed to suffer, while Evils are sufferable, than to right themselves by abolishing the Forms to which they are accustomed. But when a long Train of Abuses and Usurpations, pursuing invariably the same Object, evinces a Design to reduce them under absolute Despotism, it is their Right, it is their Duty, to throw off such Government, and to provide new Guards for their future Security. Such has been the patient Sufferance of these Colonies; and such is now the Necessity which constrains them to alter their former Systems of Government.*

At this point, Jefferson had his audience's attention. He was writing to the leaders of not just Britain, but the leaders of all Western nations. He was writing to an intelligentsia nourished on a steady diet of British and French philosophes. He was writing to prove the perilous path America was embarking on was, although without precedence, not without merit. The thinkers of Europe had spent the last century talking about an ideal civilization. The American colonists were going to create it.

The Declaration was of course met by England as an act of war and over the next seven years, the colonies erupted in a war that stretched from Canada down to the southernmost colonies. Eventually, under the leadership of George Washington, who precariously maintained his band of farmer-soldiers and with the financial, military and naval assistance of the French, the British were defeated, leaving the colonists faced with the hardest part of a revolution...actually creating a new government.

Their first attempt was a fiasco, so much so that America doesn't even recognize its first eight presidents (John Hanson was the first, George Washington actually the ninth). Wanting to prevent a return to monarchy, the 1776 Articles of Confederation loosely bound together the thirteen colonies under a series of laws doomed to fail. Each state, regardless of size, received one vote. Tiny little Rhode Island held as much power as mighty Virginia. The legislature needed 9 out of 13 votes to pass any new law, which was nearly impossible for a people who rightfully only cared about the prosperity of their colony. Taxes were optional, no navy existed to enforce the seas and every colony produced their own currency. America was a region in competition, not a region in cohesion.

Then, in 1787, America looked like it might be in for a civil war, but this time it would be the poor fighting the rich, not the Americans fighting the Brits. Unable to pay his taxes and feeling dooped by a nation that promised him freedom if he fought, Daniel Shays led a band of Revolutionar War veterans across the farmlands of Massachusetts. With pitchforks and muskets in hand, they threw the countryside into chaos.

Enough was enough.

Again the Founding Fathers gathered in Philadelphia, but this time not to declare independence, but to create a Constitution that would keep their fledgling nation from falling into the abyss.

Facilitated by Constitutional Convention President George Washington, the convention delegates crafted a masterpiece of compromise that has stood the test of time, able to adjust to the changing needs of society and equally able to maintain order when the inevitable foibles of man could have easily brought the nation to its knees. Like the Declaration of Independence that preceded it, the Constitution was imbued with Enlightened thought.

Montesquieu's separation of powers became America's Congress, President and Supreme Court. Voltaire's freedom of speech and religion became America's First Amendment. Beccaria's opinions on the fair treatment of prisoners became the Eighth Amendment. Smith's notions of capitalism became the Congress's charge to protect trade and intellectual property (copyrights and patents). Rousseau's belief in direct democracy became America's elections. But Hobbe's lack of faith in humanity led to the electoral system where Americans semi-vote for the president, but a third party actually makes the final call. By 1788, the United States of America had a functioning government, a truly revolutionary way of running a country.

It has become fashionable of late to criticize the American Revolution as being nothing more than a transfer of power from one group of wealthy white men to another group of wealthy white men. In his book *A People's History of the United States*, author Howard Zinn speaks of "A Sort of Revolution" where the entire movement was crafted by an American elite intent on insuring their own prosperity by removing any external threats to their total control of society. To Zinn, how could historians call this a revolution when only 10% actually could participate in the democratic process (women, the property-less and slaves were excluded)? Or how revolutionary was it when the monarchical structure of Britain with its parliament and chief executive named King George was replaced with a Congress and a chief executive named...George (Washington)? Wasn't this just the same old, same old?

No. This George voluntarily stepped down after eight years, allowing free elections to take place. This George allowed the Congress to create legislation without interference, vetoing only two pieces of legislation in his eight years of office. And this George established a court system that ensured the rights of the Constitution were enforced at all phases of governance, so that every man was equally able to pursue happiness.

But yes, America fell short in a number of areas. Slavery still existed. Women played a very insignificant role in the government for another century and property-less males wouldn't have a full stake in government until the 1830s. However, it was a start, and from this revolution, over the next two centuries, one by one the nations of the world followed suit (139 and counting), creating their own constitutions that look remarkably similar to the one created by the Founding Fathers long ago in the secluded meeting halls of Philadelphia.

Though America started the democracy ball rolling, the revolutionary momentum didn't truly start moving until the European nation with the most obscene absolute monarchy faced its own challenge to the throne. For when this nation fell to the empowered masses, the rest of Europe couldn't merely discount the shift as a bizarre anomaly from the uncivilized frontiers of the Americas. When revolution came to Europe, monarchy entered its dying days. Representative government was here to stay.

But that is for another chapter.

29

You Say You Want a Revolution?

France – Revolution to Napoleon – 1700 > 1850

When the American colonies ripped themselves away from the grasp of the British Empire, it registered as merely a blip on the world's radar. These newly created United States were no more than a baker's dozen of frontier settlements clustered between the Atlantic Ocean and the vast unknown of the western territories. Sure, it was fairly impressive that this plucky little band of upstarts dared challenge the might of the British army, but at the time, few in Europe actually worried that this American model might in any way upset the social and political status quo of the continent. The American Revolution caused little concern.

But the French Revolution? That definitely made the monarchs of Europe sleep a little less soundly.

By the mid-18th century, France was the preeminent nation in Europe. It was the big boy on the block. It housed 28 million people, making it the third most populated country in the world behind China and India. Its colonial holdings spread across five continents, from the Mississippi basin in the Americas to the southeast coast of India. More important than territorial holdings was its cultural influence.

All eyes looked to France to see how to dance, how to dress, what to eat, what to watch, what to think. French was the language of diplomacy. Any educated man spoke French. The greatest literature and enlightened thought was written in French. Their monarchy was the crown jewel of the Western kingdoms. King Louis XVI's palace at Versailles was the model all others tried to imitate. France was the greatest nation of Europe. In 1785, revolution wasn't on even the most subversive tongue. No way. It could never happen. France was too big to fail.

But it did. In less than 25 years, the monarchy that had ruled for close to a thousand years was overthrown and a new social and political order completely reversed centuries of unchallenged order. Like with the Industrial Revolution in England, looking back, it seems the writing was on the wall; all the causes were right there if someone would have just taken the time to look. But in reality, the revolution never started with any radical changes in mind, but gradually transformed into something out of anyone's control. Some might even argue that it wasn't so much the demands of the revolutionaries that plunged France into the abyss, as it was more the exaggerated reactions of the counter-revolutionaries that turned what could have merely been a modification of a system of government and class control into a wholesale bloodbath.

Although France appeared the model to every realm from Belgium to Russia, beneath the glittering façade of Versailles and the majesty of the nobility rested serious problems that needed to be solved. The French class structure, the *ancien regime*, had defined everyone's role in society for over three hundred years. Under the ancient regime, the nation was divided into three classes, or estates – the First Estate (the clergy), the Second Estate (the nobility), and the Third Estate (everybody else). The First Estate numbered to about 130,000, consisting of priests, bishops, monks and nuns. Although the smallest in size, they were the nation's greatest landholders (over the years inheriting the vast tracts of lands bequeathed to them by the soon-to-be dead hoping for some preferential treatment in the afterlife). The Second Estate numbered around 600,000 and was made up of both the Nobles of the Sword (who could date their pedigree back hundreds of years to the wars of the cross) and the Nobles of the Robe (who had recently bought their way into nobility and who filled all major government positions). The Third Estate was the rest (about 27 million) of the nation – the bakers, the farmers, the doctors, the lawyers, the bankers, the merchants, the man in the factory and the man walking the street. They were separated by wealth, region, education and behavior. Some of the lowest members of the Third Estate lived in horrific squalor, barefoot in the countryside, using the medieval tools of their distant ancestors. Others resided in the glorious urban mansions of Paris, products of a fledgling Industrial Age (more to come in a couple chapters) that made millionaires out of entrepreneurs willing to risk their wealth. Yet, they were all united by one trait – the bitter reality that they were not members of the First or Second Estate. This distinction meant that they alone had to pay taxes and they alone were not privy to the privileges of the higher class – they couldn't be officers in the military, they couldn't hunt, they couldn't wear a sword, and in a court of law, if they were arrested, they were tried and punished by a different set of standards. The Third Estate was below the Nobles and the Clergy, and no matter how much wealth they ever attained (and some even got richer than the members of the other two estates), they remained inferior.

Although this state of inequality caused frustration, it didn't cause revolution. This was brought on by a financial crisis. France was in debt. France was on the verge of bankruptcy. After decades of war against England, including the most recent financing of the American Revolution, the federal coffers were nearly empty. This situation wasn't aided by the existence of Versailles, the king's palace. Built initially as a summer hunting retreat for the royal family, King Louis XIV eventually transformed it into a palatial residence of over 700 rooms, able to house close to 20,000 people at a time. King Louis liked to keep his enemies close, so from time to time, he would invite the nobles of the realm to stay as guests in his home – both to keep an eye on them, but also to make sure they realized who really had the power (the man who owned the 87 million square foot palace). The keepers of Versailles then not only had to pay to keep the bushes trimmed, the fountains flowing and the floors clean, but they also had to see to the every whim of the pampered royalty. This cost a fortune. In today's dollars, you couldn't even put a price tag on its construction and maintenance fees (probably somewhere around $2 billion), but in looking at the state budgets of the 18th century, the feeding, housing, caring for and pleasuring of all the residents could take anywhere from 5 to 15% of the nation's annual expenditures.

The economic straits weren't alone caused by the financing of some ill-advised wars (though the United States was pretty thankful for the help) and the bankrolling of the king's swanky palace, the biggest issue was that the groups most able to pay, the groups with the largest landholdings, these were the groups actually exempted from paying taxes. It's not that they paid less tax. They paid no tax. France could never hope to escape their financial dilemma if they didn't increase their revenue stream, and the Third Estate was all tapped out. You just can't get blood out of a turnip (with the Third Estate playing the role of the turnip in this extended metaphor). Every finance minister Louis XVI appointed came up with the same recommendation – tax the nobility and the clergy. These recommendations posed a couple problems. Not only did the upper estates vehemently resist any attempts to alter their status, but even more important was that the more the finance ministers publicized the predicament, the more the masses hyper-scrutinized the affairs of the state. In an age where scores of newspapers were launched every year, the spindrift ways of the royal family became fodder for the urban dailies. Whereas for a century, a rare few might have whispered about the happenings at the Chateaux de Versailles, now hundreds of thousands openly questioned the expenditures of the royal family.

When in 1788 the First and Second Estate were once again strongly advised that they would need to reluctantly embrace the need for universal taxation, the nobles and clergy made a choice they thought would settle the issue once and for all, but instead opened a Pandora's Box that could never be closed. They dug deep into their bag of tricks and suggested a reconvening of the Estates General, an archaic, seldomly-used assembly of the three estates that hadn't been called since 1614. The king acquiesced, setting the date for assembly for 1789. Both sides thought this meeting could only benefit their cause. Even though the Clergy brought 300 delegates and the Nobles brought 300 delegates and the Third Estate brought 600 delegates, because each estate only counted for one vote, the upper estates believed they would win any vote 2-1. And the king was equally cocky, thinking his presence alone would awe everyone into supporting any royal mandate. They all didn't account for one group – the Third Estate.

In the summer leading up to the Estates General, each region selected a representative to send to Versailles. As important as the delegates chosen (which were almost always lawyers or the most competent speakers in the towns) was the creation of a list of complaints. Any leader knows you rarely want to ask your minions if they see any problems. Chances are they do, but once you get the ball of complaints rolling, it's hard to stop the momentum. The delegates started recording all of these grievances in what became known as the *cahiers de doleances*, and as each new topic was introduced and circulated, hope rose amongst the voiceless that change may be possible. When the doors to the Estates General opened on May 5, 1789, what entered wasn't merely a group of awed members of the lower class excited to just be invited. What entered was a body of the oppressed, impatient to be heard.

Everyone entered, the King arrived and the minister of the proceedings jumped right to the topic of taxation. But the Third Estate didn't flinch. They wanted to discuss the issue of representation, but more specifically, the issue of voting power. They didn't want to meet separately (by "order") with each group casting one vote. They wanted to meet together, each casting a vote by delegate (by number of "heads"). This suggestion posed a bit of a problem as the Third Estate alone had 600 heads, equal to the combined total of the Nobility and Clergy. As tensions rose and no resolution to this voting issue appeared possible, King Louis XVI terminated the meetings. Or so he thought. From a distant corner of the room, one man (the scandal-prone journalist Mirabeau) stood up and proclaimed he would "not leave except at the point of a bayonet." The crowd was shocked. Didn't this mere mortal get the memo? You're not supposed to disagree with the King. He was God's chosen one. But Mirabeau had spoken, and the gauntlet had been set. The King could cower and acquiesce yet again, or he could respond with force. He chose the latter.

In the next five months, France would implode. First, the Third Estate called itself the National Assembly and invited anyone from the First and Second Estate to join them. Seeing the writing on the wall, a few liberal clergy and enlightened nobles crossed party lines and joined this newly created governing body. Seeing the sides starting to unite, Louis panicked, locking them out of their meeting hall, to which the arriving delegates merely found the largest nearby meeting place (an indoor tennis court) and resolved they would not disband until they wrote a new constitution. Louis, seeing that this could turn violent quickly, ordered his army to protect Versailles from seemingly inevitable chaos. Meanwhile, 20 miles away in Paris, hearing of the rebellion of wills in the king's palace, Parisians drew more frustrated over a condition closer to their hearts (well, actually, close to their stomachs). The recent bread harvest had been less than impressive, and the price of bread had skyrocketed to nearly 80% of a worker's daily income. Just for bread. As the city rumblings increased, so did Louis' military force. Parisian mobs of mothers and laborers started fearing the worst, that Louis' troops would descend on them, adding further oppression to their already miserable state. If a showdown was what the king wanted, they would need to arm themselves.

On July 14, 1789, a mob of close to a thousand Parisians stormed the Hotel des Invalides (once a military hospital, but also a storeroom of weapons), stealing cannons and muskets. They then headed to the Bastille, a medieval fortress that had over the centuries become a prison for anyone who dared oppose the king. After hours of back and forth cannon volleys, the governor of the Bastille agreed to discuss terms with the mob. Possibly not understanding what a truce meant, the mob promptly stormed through the gates, stole whatever gunpowder they could find, cut off the governor's head with a pocketknife and paraded it around Paris. So what was the fruit of the mob's little outburst? They freed seven prisoners (two of which would later be sent to an insane asylum, four of whom were in for petty crimes and the last who was sent to prison by his parents), they added a bit of ammunition to their stockpile and they killed a few of the king's soldiers. But like the Boston Massacre that killed a grand total of five men, the Bastille's magnitude couldn't be truly judged until the papers spun the tale. Within a week, the stories circulated that the people had spoken and that the symbol of tyranny had been destroyed. The line had been crossed. The king's faithful children no longer unconditionally loved their father. Shots had been fired. The revolution had started.

All across France, the story of the Bastille fed people's imaginations. Everyone then wondered – what would the King do next? He must have his revenge. Mustn't he? New rumors popped up that the King was assembling all the lords and clergy to put down the Third Estate. July and August became the months of the Great Fear, where peasants across the countryside wondered if they would soon pay the price for the actions of the Parisian mob. Deciding to not wait to be attacked first, many of these peasants seized the moment to ransack the property of the landed and the religious. The Great Fear became the great opportunity to randomly murder people who once slighted them and possibly burn down their houses along the way. Churches were destroyed, lords were pulled out of their homes in the middle of the night and mutilated, courthouses were raided and property claims were destroyed. All across France, the nobles and the clergy feared for their lives. Some stayed, hoping to survive the chaos. Others got out as soon as possible. These émigrés fled to the safety of neighboring kingdoms, hoping to return once their world came to its senses. Many never returned.

Spurred on by the actions of the Parisian mob, the National Assembly sped into overdrive. Within two months, they passed laws that wholly transformed French society. Well, maybe not yet. In 1789, they were merely a series of well-intentioned ideas brainstormed by an assembly reared on Enlightenment ideals and infused with a self-assurance that they should take this extraordinary moment and see what they could pull off. In August, they penned the aptly named August Decrees that outlined 19 principles including the abolition of 1) feudalism, 2) a lord's right to administer trials, 3) the forced payment of tithes (10% taxes) to the church and 4) legal exemptions granted to nobility and clergy. They even dealt with some less momentous issues like the caging of pigeons during off-hunting season and the singing of patriotic songs while in church. A few weeks later they signed the Jefferson-inspired Declaration of the Rights of Man. The Declaration of Rights was more like the American Bill of Rights. It said you could say whatever you want, write whatever you want and practice whatever religion you want. No matter your birth or your status, your property would be protected and in the eyes of the courts you would be treated the same as others. And lastly, it said the power to rule didn't come from God and it didn't come from the royal family. The power to rule came from the people. Anyone who might climb to the top of the ruling hierarchy did so by the pleasure of the people. Should you anger these people, should you not protect their rights, you would no longer be needed. Louis' grandfather King Louis XIV once allegedly (and arrogantly) said, "I am the state" - but a century later the people could finally proclaim, "No...actually, WE are the state."

But still Louis XVI would have none of this. All the National Assembly's posturing and proclamations were nothing but mere annoyances to him. Who was this National Assembly anyway? A bunch of people from the Third Estate coupled with a few noble and cleric traitors who decided to switch to the dark side? All this so-called National Assembly was doing was writing down a bunch of pie-in-the-sky ideas that no one would ever enforce. It's one thing to write down a bunch of so-called laws or rules. It's another thing to actually execute them, and as far as King Louis XVI was concerned, he was the only one with the authority to enforce anything. And he had no intention of implementing any of these notions.

Until the women got angry. On the streets of Paris, women were getting ticked off. A series of poor harvests meant the price of bread reached ridiculous levels. Unlike the British across the channel, the French never embraced the New World foods like the potato. Their diet relied on bread, so when the price of bread almost doubled in just one year, the women found it impossible to feed their families. This was where the revolution went from merely being a set of ideas to being a movement with force and the backing of the masses. The Estates General was a meeting of the brightest minds of the Third Estate. The Storming of the Bastille was a mob that got caught up with the emotion of the moment. The bread shortage was truly the catalyst that pushed people out of their homes and onto the streets. Enough was enough.

A rumor started circulating that the royal family was hoarding all the grain in Versailles. Many found this rumor fairly believable as the reputation of the queen, the Austrian Marie Antoinette, wasn't exactly glowing. The tabloids clamoring for the public's attention filled the streets with stories of her naughty behavior. As a foreign princess, she was never totally accepted. Depending on who you asked, she was either a reckless gambler, a philanderer, a plump princess, an opera connoisseur with her own delusions of becoming an actress or merely an air-headed bimbo who cared for little more than putting on fancy clothes and wearing puffy head pieces. She was often referred to as the Austrichienne ("chienne" is a dog...try to figure out what they were calling her).

The media didn't help her reputation. In his book *Confessions*, Enlightenment author Jean Jacques Rousseau mentioned a princess who was so indifferent to her people's hunger that she said, "Let them eat cake!" (he actually wrote, "let them eat brioche," but you get the idea). The people thought Rousseau was talking about the Austrian queen. But the truth was irrelevant. As anyone who has ever survived adolescence can attest, the origin of a rumor isn't nearly as important as what it eventually becomes once the masses manipulate it to fit their needs. By October 1789, a Parisian mob of 7000 women believed that the arrogant chienne *did* have a ton of food stored in Versailles, that she *was* wasting the people's money on her own pampering, and that she must be so clueless to the realities of life that she had the gall to suggest they should just find some cake to fill their tummies.

So they marched. For 20 miles they marched. Their ranks gradually swelled to include a few dozen men, and even the king's own guards who followed close by, not knowing what exactly to do with a parade of women carrying garden and kitchen tools. The guards hadn't really been trained to deal with such a sight. When they reached Versailles, ripe with venomous anger and howling stomachs, the women easily overthrew the king's guards, cut off their heads and stuck them on a couple poles (this head-pole thing was starting to become routine) and then ransacked the palace searching for the little chienne. She eventually walked out onto the balcony and stared down the crowd, even though they had cannons and muskets sighted in on her painted muzzle. Their desire for blood turned into a desire to "protect the royal family." The mob forced the king, the queen and their son to pack their things and head back to Paris, "escorted" by the female mob. The hungry women had left Paris wanting bread. They had returned with the royal family.

Not surprisingly, soon after, King Louis XVI recognized the National Assembly as the legitimate government body. It was kind of difficult to argue when you had a mob threatening to kill your spouse and run your own head on a pole. But though Louis might have sided publicly with this newly-founded assembly, he privately conspired to return life to the good ol' days. His new home/prison was in the heart of Paris, at the Tuileries Palace (which has since been destroyed and today is basically the front yard to the Louvre Museum). The king wasn't content to ride out the storm, granting a few concessions to the stirred up mobs. He entered into a series of private correspondences with the French émigrés and the nobility across Europe. They promised to help him regain the throne. Louis believed if he could just make it out of France, he could drum up enough support from the neighboring monarchies that he could put down this insurrection and resume his life of self-indulgence.

So, on the night of June 21, 1791, Louis, his family, some nannies, some servants and some friends hopped on a bright yellow carriage and tried to escape to a protected fortress in the border town of Montmedy. Pathetically, not understanding the gravity of the situation, the king kept ordering his escape party to stop and take breaks. He even had the audacity (let's call it "stupidity") to walk alongside the carriage enjoying the views. Eventually he was recognized by a postmaster named Drouet (who allegedly recognized the king after comparing his profile to a noggin on a coin) when Louis asked to stay the night in Varennes. The next morning he woke up and was met by a mob of revolutionaries who volunteered to accompany the king back to Paris.

This was the tipping point. Any chance for reconciliation was gone. Though some wanted to maintain the position of the king (even actually giving him authority in the newly-created Constitution), others saw this latest episode as another example of how little the royal family could be trusted. On his road back to Paris, his carriage was spat on, and mobs of angry belligerents all wanted a piece of the traitor. The line had been drawn – you were either for the traitor and maintaining the royalty of old or you were for liberty and equality, for a new day, for revolution. In that National Assembly, everyone's allegiance was clear – if you believe in conserving the royal family, you sat to the right, if you believed in transforming the power structure, you sat to the left. This designation eventually became the left wing/right wing, liberal/conservative political schism that has lasted till this day, but in the months following the royal family's return, it became the divide that upped the level of violence. You were either with the revolution or against it.

When the revolution moved to Paris, the major playmakers no longer saw themselves as members of the First, Second or Third Estate. That ancient divide had been replaced by a new form of organization – the political club. Dozens of clubs popped up across Paris (and eventually across the country), each having their own idea for what life should look like in a new France. There were Jacobins and Girondins and Feuillants and Carabots. Robespierrists and Enrages and Dantonists and Republican Women. Before, the Third Estate was united in their frustration with the current regime, but once they saw change was actually possible, they began splintering across ideological lines. Some focused on enforcing the constitution of 1791; others said it didn't go far enough. Some wanted to declare war against Austria; others wanted to maintain neutrality. Others focused on economic issues like controlling the price of goods. Some cared more about social issues like expanding the role of women or allowing gay marriage. These clubs fought with each other for power, and yet power was fleeting. Another rival always stood at the ready, eager to jump in and seize control of the government should any party fall out of favor.

And then France went to war. Partly wanting to return their nation's daughter to the throne, but mostly needing to ensure this anti-monarchy absurdity spread no further, Austria declared war on France in April of 1792. Now the French could unite against a common enemy outside their borders. The political clubs started to raise the level of vitriol. Anyone not siding with the revolution could then be seen as not only a traitor to the cause, but as an enemy sympathizer. Who then became public enemies #1 and #2? The émigrés and the royal family. Why else would anyone willfully leave France other than a hidden desire to sabotage the revolution? This became the excuse needed to seize all the lands of the émigrés and pass them out to the masses in one of the greatest land re-distribution schemes in European history. But what about the king? He couldn't be trusted. With his loyalist supporters and his familial connections to the enemy, he had to be killed. In June 1793, he was stripped of his title, stripped of his honor and then stripped of his head. The guillotine had taken yet another life, but not just any life, the life of a king, a person once seen as God's representative on earth. The European nations sat shocked at this turn of events, and even many Frenchmen thought the revolution had gone too far.

Enter the Reign of Terror.

Maximilian Robespierre and his Parisian faction known as the Jacobins took over the National Assembly, promising to ensure the spirit of the revolution of 1789 continued and that no one's personal desires or greed stood in the way of the realization of both the August Decrees and the Declaration of the Rights of Man. The counterrevolutionaries who popped up after the death of the king had to be silenced. What better method than the guillotine? Initially implemented because it was seen as the most humane, efficient way of off-ing someone's head, it later became the symbol of this most violent period of the French Revolution. So many thousands lost their lives to the guillotine that some began to openly question the humaneness of the practice. Onlookers spoke of decapitated heads biting at each other as they sat in a bag or the recently chopped blinking several times before finally expiring. Eventually observing scientists concluded that after the guillotine did its dirty work, the brain actually did remain alive for a bit – thirteen seconds on average to be exact – undoubtedly the longest thirteen seconds of the victim's life.

As soldiers died on the battlefields throughout Western Europe, within France, neighbor turned against neighbor and brother against brother. These civil wars for control of the throne cost close to 40,000 lives, with both enemies and supporters of the revolution meeting a violent end. In Paris, Robespierre established the Committee of Public Safety (always be afraid when countries create groups to ensure safety...pretty good chance your safety will feel anything but protected), who presented weekly reports on how the war against Austria was progressing and who might be an enemy of the state. Trials were held, sentences were passed and executions were performed. At first, the Committee actually put on an air of legality to the proceedings, but within a year, the farce had become a witch hunt and anyone could send an enemy, political or otherwise, to the gallows. Some trials even involved entire groups of people tried simultaneously with no evidence presented, except for the knowledge that the defendants disagreed with how the government was run. Blood continued to flow and heads kept rolling, until the Convention had had enough. On July 27th, 1794, Robespierre rose to the podium yet again, spewed out another of his never-ending lists of enemies of the revolution, but this time the crowd didn't buy his argument. The crowd shouted, "Down with the tyrant!" This time it would be Robespierre that would be arrested. And the next day he was guillotined, which officially ended the revolution.

Now the pendulum swung the other direction. The French wanted a return to order. This period, known as the Thermidorian Reaction, saw an attempt by the conservatives to calm the entire pulse of the nation, bringing back a semblance of order. Instead of a king or an assembly, this phase of the revolution saw the rise of the Directory – five men who would jointly decide on how best to enforce the laws of the nation. This was a total failure. There's a reason why countries don't have five presidents, five kings or five dictators. It's not exactly efficient. Inflation rates skyrocketed, the economy was in disarray and bread prices shot to levels even worse than those before Louis XVI's ouster. The people had had enough. But where do you turn when you need true order imposed? Where do you turn when you need a man strong enough to battle the forces of the right and the left? Where do you turn in your time of need?

You turn to the man nicknamed "the little corporal" - Napoleon Bonaparte.

In 1799, the man seen centuries later as "short," made one of the biggest power plays history had ever witnessed. This 5'6" hero from the former Italian island of Corsica, entered the government building of the Directory in 1799 with his army of followers, formally ended the proceedings and announced he would assume power over the government until he could guarantee stability.

And it worked. After almost a decade of chaos, the French people were more than happy for a little coup d'etat. After all the starvation, terror and death of the revolutionary years, all the people really wanted was a little bit of peace - even if that meant handing over power to an enlightened dictator. Napoleon sensed the mood of the Parisians, and of France as a whole, so when word got out that he had held the legislature at gunpoint until they agreed to crown him "First Consul," few batted an eye. The entire French Revolution had been fought to close the era of absolute rulers, to give power to the people. But when it turned out the people were crazy or power-hungry or short-sighted, the ideals of the revolution could be temporarily ignored if it meant a taste of stability.

Napoleon believed only he knew exactly what his people wanted. He also knew he would have to dance precariously between employing the dictatorial powers necessary to exact change, while continuing to appear as a son of the revolution. Napoleon had mastered the art of public relations during his military campaigns across southern Europe and into Egypt. He knew wars couldn't be won without the seven P's (Proper Prior Planning Prevents Piss Poor Performance), but he also knew morale and public perception kept his men inspired and kept the families back home loyal to the cause. As a battlefield commander, Napoleon made sure his every victory circulated through news pamphlets and socialite circles, and he ensured his every defeat never hit the public's eyes. He was so successful at controlling his own public perception, that even after he was soundly defeated in Egypt and had to abandon his men on the battlefield, he still received a conquering hero's welcome when he returned to the streets of Paris.

As first consul (aka "president"), he again pandered to the crowds. He rewrote the law books. The dreams of the early revolution were formalized by law. Feudal bonds were forever broken. All private property was protected. He created an official legislative branch to write laws and separate government departments (think Treasury Department, State Department and Agricultural Department) to execute the will of the state. He separated the church and the state, but also made sure the Catholic

Church was again protected. The French could worship freely and the clergy could apply for government jobs. Segregating Jews was forbidden. But above all else, classes were equal under the eyes of the law. You netted no special favors simply because of your parents' status. All government jobs were open to all classes – merit trumped birth. He created a unified nation. He gave France a national bank, a national anthem, a standardized currency and a uniform decimal measuring system to expedite trade across the nation. These reforms all became part of what was called the Napoleonic Code, and as Europe watched France prosper, they too then realized the value of these modifications, many (like Belgium, Italy, the Netherlands, Poland, Portugal and Spain) even choosing to likewise enforce national codes and institutions.

But Napoleon also knew when nationalism, liberty and equality had to be disregarded. He cracked down on freedom of speech. He closed down newspapers critical of his throne. He sent his spies out looking for rivals. He imprisoned thousands, held them without trial and sentences many to death. The days of taking your voice to the streets were gone. The people demanded order and Napoleon fulfilled their wishes, even if that meant forsaking the rights of man.

He also knew that the role of consul was beneath him. He wanted to recreate the Roman Empire. And he needed a title that fit. So on December 2, 1804, at the Notre Dame Cathedral, Pope Pius VII arrived from Rome and officially anointed Napoleon, Emperor of France. From that moment, nothing could stop his ascension.

He then took another page out of the Roman Empire's *Strategies for Keeping the Masses Happy* handbook. Feed them and make them feel proud. And he could kill two birds with one stone. How do you feed millions of people and simultaneously make them love their country so much they forget about economic despair? War.

They'll satisfy their anger with the blood of the enemy, and they'll satisfy their stomachs with the spoils of battle.

Napoleon raised armies and took France's revolution across Western Europe. It wasn't hard to find a country to fight. The monarchies of the West all feared that one day the revolutionary ideals of France might spread across their borders. Napoleon knew he was surrounded, so instead of waiting for his foes to align, he took the war to them. From 1803 to 1815, France fought a series of endless wars against everyone from the Russians, the Prussians, the Spanish and the British to the Persians, the Ottomans, the Swedes and the Swiss. In the first few years of his campaign, it looked like no one could stop Napoleon. He took his million troops, his application of every bit of military technology and strategy known to the West, and his promise to give his soldiers honor, a daily meal and an enemy to focus their anger, and created an empire that by 1810 covered Span, Naples and parts of Germany. Even at the Battle of Austerlitz where Napoleon was outnumbered by Russian and Austrian forces, Napoleon proved adept at pumping up his forces and splitting up the overconfident alliance from the east. A wise man would have been content with his victories, secured his borders and sat back and ruled over the largest European empire since the Romans.

Napoleon wasn't this wise man. He was bombastic, egotistical and he had surrounded himself with "Yes Men" who were more apt to support his misguided schemes than call him on the error of his ways. So what did Napoleon do after he won his greatest battle against Russian and Austrian forces? He invaded Russia. He took 600,000 men and marched on Moscow. This was a mistake. There was no way he could keep that size of a force fed and healthy, so in the summer of 1812, across Eastern Europe, tens of thousands fell to starvation and disease. The only thing keeping his troops alive and Napoleon's faith unchallenged was Moscow. If he could just get his army to Moscow, they could live off the land and the riches of the city. They could sleep in the beds of the Muscovites, drink from their water and recover from the thousand-mile journey.

Brilliant idea except for one problem.

Moscow burned itself to the ground. The French entered an abandoned city with no food, few homes and a destroyed infrastructure. Napoleon had a choice to make. Keep his men in Moscow and rebuild the city or head back to France. He returned back to France – in the winter. This choice signed his soldiers' death warrants. There was no way they could survive the Russian winter. As they marched back home, they froze, they starved and one by one, they were picked off by Russian guerilla fighters who never gave the soldiers a moment's rest, attacking unexpectedly and then fleeing to the safety of the forests. By the time Napoleon re-entered Paris, only 30,000 men had survived – 5% of his original force. He had failed and the luster of his initial glory had darkened.

Napoleon could no longer hold onto power. His military campaigns had bankrupted his treasury. He even resorted to funding French pirates across the Atlantic and selling his French holdings in the Americas (the Louisiana Purchase) for some quick money. But it was not enough. His little trip to Russia weakened his control of his other territorial holdings. His states in Spain and Italy began to rise up, and even in Haiti, a band of slaves proved too much for Napoleon's diluted forces. His own men were tired of fighting, and after a couple years of relative peace, the Russian, British and Austrian forces mustered an army of a few hundred thousand soldiers and surrounded Napoleon. This time he could not escape and he could not win. He surrendered and was forced into exile on a small little island called Elba off the coast of Italy. This exile was only temporary, as he escaped in 1814 and returned to Paris. He again tried to muster a force able to defeat the allied forces of Western Europe, but at the Battle of Waterloo on June 18, 1815, he was routed for the final time. This time the allies exiled him to St. Helena, a tiny little island in the middle of the Atlantic. There was no way he could escape from this desolate island prison. He lived out the rest of his days, dying six years later in 1821.

Yet Napoleon had left an imprint on Western Europe that would last until the 20th century. Seven million men lost their lives in the Napoleonic Wars, monarchs almost lost their thrones and an entire continent was confronted with France's little experiment with liberty, equality and brotherhood. The European powers knew they had to make sure a Napoleon could never rise to power, and that the madness and turmoil of the French Revolution could never terrorize the region again. In France, the revolution continued on for another few decades. The nobles and the royal family would return and try to reverse many of the reforms of the revolutionary era. In 1848, it looked like France hadn't learned a thing. The people were starving, the nobility looked to be living the good life and a new generation of the poor thought they could change their world again. There were marches, declarations, protests and bloodshed. One king stepped down. Another despot took his place. The rest of Europe was getting tired of this seesaw of French politics, knowing that "whenever Paris sneezed, the rest of Europe caught a cold."

The European powers decided they would be wise to reform their governments voluntarily before their citizens forced the issue. One by one, the West abolished slavery, gave all men the right to vote, abolished the death penalty and improved the workday by exacting a ten-hour day maximum and mandating safe working conditions. The European powers also met at the Congress of Vienna to redefine their borders so that no singular nation would dominate the rest. The boundaries of Germany expanded, but its 360 states merged into a 38-state German confederation. Some nations absorbed their neighbors. Others ceased to exist. Boundaries that had been fought over since the Middle Ages were established and ratified by all the signatories. Europe had caught a glimpse of what industrialized war could do to their continent. They wanted to make sure the Napoleonic Wars were never replicated.

And they did keep the peace for the rest of the 19th century.

But then the 20th century started, the horror stories of Napoleon had long since been forgotten and each European power falsely believed that if a war was to be fought again, it would be quick, effortless and relatively bloodless.

They couldn't have been more wrong.

But that is for another chapter.

30

Latin America Stands Alone

South American Revolutions – 1800 > 1900

When looking at the major movements across history, we often try to see patterns or blueprints that essentially show us that life moves forward in some sort of a predictable manner. Karl Marx believed, "History repeats itself, first as tragedy, second as farce," meaning if you think it was pretty pathetic having to watch humans destroy themselves the first time around, it's pretty darn ridiculous when they don't learn from their mistakes and go through the same motions again and again. In the 20th century, philosopher George Santayana penned a similar thought with "Those who cannot remember the past are condemned to repeat it." These philosophies, coupled with our human partiality to making over-simplified comparisons, have led a generation of wannabe historians (present company included) and media pundits down the path of hyper-generalization.

It's gotten to such an extreme that in the weeks following the 2011 Middle East revolutions, when teachers unions in the American Midwest went to the streets to protest their salary cutbacks, commentators took to the airwaves crying, "America has become the new Tunisia" or "This is Egypt all over again." No. It really wasn't. But it doesn't just stop there. In recent years, it has become almost a competition between political pundits to see who can out-analogize their enemy. Take the portrayal of Barack Obama. One minute, he's Martin Luther King Jr. and the next, he's Lyndon B. Johnson. A couple months later he's being compared to Josef Stalin, only to be followed by the obligatory comparison to this century's poster boy for villainy - Adolf Hitler. But is Barack Obama "just like" any of these men?

The truth is – no. As unentertaining as this might sound - nobody is just like anybody else, and history doesn't repeat itself.

But there are patterns.

So when we take a look at Latin America and their political revolutions of the 19th century that freed two continents from the grasp of European empires, we must be careful not to draw too many parallels to those experiments in the United States and France. It would be easy to merely assume the dominos of popular sovereignty merely fell down across the United States and France and then hopped back across the pond to South America. But be careful. The Latin America of 1800 had little in common with the United States of 1776 or the France of 1789, so although we might be able to find some parallels, it was their differences that pushed them down far rockier roads to independence, leaving the nations a jumbled mess and subservient to the Western world through to the 20th century.

In 1800, the Latin American colonies were ruled almost exclusively by Spain and Portugal. In the year following Columbus' discovery of the Americas, the Pope facilitated an agreement (the Treaty of Tordesillas) wherein the New World, Portugal could claim all lands east of Columbus' discovery (Brazil), leaving Spain all lands to the west (pretty much everything else). This meant that by 1800, Spain ruled an empire that stretched from northern California, down through the west coast of Mexico and South America, all the way to the most southern tip of the Americas – Cape Horn. And Portugal got Brazil (this is why today the Brazilians speak Portuguese and everyone else south of the United States speaks Spanish).

Though separated by language and mother country, these regions shared a few similarities. They were Catholic, they were ruled by monarchies, they respected the power of the fist over the power of the pen and they were diverse. Their societies were intensely divided by race. At the top of the power pyramid were the peninsulares, composing 1% of the population. These were the Europeans born in Spain or Portugal who controlled the highest positions in government and owned the most profitable land and businesses. Below these European-born elite stood the creoles.

Making up 10-20% of the population, these sons and daughters of the peninsulares were born in Latin America and were also quite wealthy, but they still remained one rung below the peninsulares. The remaining populations were the mestizos, the Amerindians and the slaves. In the eyes of the law, slaves had about the same rights as a cow or a horse, the Amerindians existed outside of society and the mestizos were those of mixed ancestry who lived for decades in the awkward purgatory of not being fully Amerindians, but also not being wholly creole. Their class structure went like this: peninsulares (European born Europeans), creoles (American born Europeans), mestizos (half-European, half-Amerindians), Amerindians (the locals) and slaves (Africans kidnapped and brought to the new world). Basically, the handful of white people dominated the political and economic spheres, leaving the darker-skinned peoples void of any observed rights.

This clear inequity was increasingly challenged as the works of the Enlightenment were shared, and the feats of the French and American revolutions spread. But in Latin America, who would be the revolutionaries? Who would ruffle the feathers of the empowered while enraging the masses? Who would be their Thomas Jefferson? Their Robespierre? Their George Washington? Their Napoleon?

If revolution was to come, it would have to come from the creoles. But in 1800, very few of these educated creoles were willing to risk their privileged statuses and challenge the status quo. Though they only needed to overthrow a mere 1% of the population, they also realized that to do so would mean riling up the lower classes, and once this pot or rebellion was heated up, who could predict if it could ever be cooled down again.

But the true catalyst to revolution was not the stories of the American and French revolutions, nor of the ambitious enlightened theories of the European philosophes. The Latin American revolutions sprung from the power vacuum created by Napoleon's little forays across Europe. At the turn of the 19th century, the nations of the Iberian Peninsula (like the rest of continental Europe) focused all their attention on getting rid of the little corporal from France. In 1807, Napoleon invaded Portugal. In 1808, he invaded Spain. King John VI of Portugal saw the writing on the wall and fled the Old World for the safety of his Brazil where he could enact his own unique interpretation of liberty, equality and fraternity. Next door in Spain, King Ferdinand II wasn't so lucky. He was forced to give up his throne that was then filled by Napoleon's habitually-inept brother, Joseph Bonaparte. With Ferdinand II out of the picture, the Spanish chain of command out in the Americas was a bit up for interpretation. Should the peninsulares follow the mandates of the ousted king or the new regime of Napoleon? In Brazil, this question would be postponed for a few decades as the mother country's king now housed himself in the New World.

But in Mexico, the Europe's Napoleon-caused chaos signaled a chance for change, and unlike in the United States and France, the first spark came not from the propertied elite vying for unchallenged power, but from the voice of a priest from the small town of Dolores. In 1810, instead of delivering his standard Sunday sermon, Father Miguel Hidalgo issued what became known as the "Cry of Dolores," inciting the 300 men sitting in attendance to rally behind their holy father and pull their country away from European oppression. From this moment, Father Miguel Hidalgo would no longer merely be the religious leader of his parish's flock. He would become the father of the Mexican revolution.

At first, the creoles and land-owning mestizos favored this idea of revolution from below. In their eyes, once the peninsulares were gone, they'd be able to slip comfortably into their former leaders' shoes. But unfortunately, the riotous thousands who first only targeted the offices and homes of the peninsulares, eventually pointed their shovels, knives and pistols at any member of the propertied elite. At this point, Hidalgo's little revolution had to be put down. He was quickly arrested, sent to trial and less than eleven months after his first speech, his body was introduced to an array of bullets from a firing squad. Revolutionary hero #1 – dead.

But the revolutionary dam had been breached.

Next up, Jose Maria Morelos, also a preacher and a student of Miguel Hidalgo. He picked up where Hidalgo left off, proving himself a far more impressive military commander than his mentor. Morelos beat the Spanish in a few dozen battles before eventually taking the coastal Spanish stronghold (and modern day Spring Break destination) Acapulco. Not content with mere military victories, Morelos took a page from the US guide to revolutions, forming a national congress, writing a Constitution and even formally declaring independence. He too was quickly captured, tried and executed by firing squad. Revolutionary hero #2 - dead.

If Mexico was ever to break free from Spain, they'd have to enlist the support of the creoles. Enter General Agustin de

Iturbide. In the early years of the Mexican independence movements, Iturbide actually fought *against* the revolutionaries, but events in Spain made Iturbide and his reps from the creole class reconsider their loyalties. When it appeared King Ferdinand was losing power back in Spain, it wasn't clear if he would take the path of Portuguese King John VI and retreat to Mexico to claim his American throne. And even if he didn't flee the chaos of Europe, how long was it really going to be before the masses rose up in unison, flipped society and established a republic? Either way, the creoles stood to lose, so instead of waiting to see how this drama played out, they took the initiative, forged a tenuous alliance with the Church, the landed elite and the revolutionaries, and secured independence for Mexico in 1821. General Iturbide then promptly crowned himself emperor, trashing any liberal hopes of a more democratic republic. Many were none too pleased with this turn of events, and eventually a new military force under the leadership of Antonio Lopez de Santa Anna moved into the capital city, toppling Iturbide, the recently crowned emperor. He was then arrested, tried and executed by...you guessed it...firing squad. Revolutionary hero #3 - dead.

When Santa Anna assumed power, a few Latin American revolutionary precedents had already been set. First, Mexicans don't like their traitors. Go against the government, you will die. Second, you can be a hero one moment and dead the next. Third, constitutions are adorable ideas, but they don't actually have to be followed. Fourth, and most importantly, military leaders, or *caudillos*, controlled Latin American politics. The key to gaining and maintaining power rested in the hands of the army leaders. Violence consistently trumped diplomacy.

Santa Anna, the great hero who overthrew the evil emperor, increased his popularity through the 1820s as Mexico survived constant coups. He watched from his estates as, one after another, "elected" presidents found themselves confronting a rival army at capital's footsteps. This rapid succession of deposed leaders ceased for a bit when Santa Anna, the protector of Mexico, the conqueror of Spain, the "Napoleon of the West," rose to the presidency in 1833, a title he maintained off and on for the next two decades. But in 1857, again the disenfranchised, suffering horde grew tired of a president who cared nothing for the little guy, instead simply making sure the rich could keep getting richer. The Amerindians sought a leader from their own ranks. Benito Juarez, a non-military "Indian of the original race of the country," rose from his peasant background to become an accomplished lawyer and a respected champion of equality. With the backing of the United States, Juarez financed a coup of his own, replacing Santa Anna and promising to finally bring true representative government to the struggling nation.

This promise would have to be put on hold as the Mexican nobility had different plans. The peninsulares and the creoles had no intention of handing over power to a commoner. Unable to defeat Juarez on their own soil, but also not willing to accept an inferior stake in society, members of the Mexican nobility sent out a plea to Europe for help. Napoleon III of France answered the call. This Napoleon saw Mexico as his chance to again hold a French empire in the New World, while also draining the profits of the Mexican silver mines. He dropped his French troops in Mexico, defeated Juarez and then looked back to Europe for a candidate to install in the throne. France had recently reconciled with their bitter enemy Austria, so Napoleon III agreed to send Austrian emperor Franz Joseph's brother to rule Mexico. This actually worked for a few years in the 1860s, as Austrian Maximilian became the Emperor of Mexico (until of course Juarez formed a new army, overthrew Maximilian, and had him killed by...wait for it...firing squad).

France was out of the American empire business once and for all, and this turned out to be a victory much-needed by the Mexican people. A few years earlier, they had suffered a humiliating defeat at the hands of the USA when a border skirmish in Texas devolved into US troops marching on Mexico City. Surrounded and outgunned, the Mexicans surrendered and accepted the United States' fifteen million dollar offer to buy all northern territories from Mexico. This little land heist left a bitter taste in Mexico's mouth, especially since one of the newly-acquired regions (a place called California) ended up being home to one of the greatest gold discoveries of the last five hundred years. Mexico had already lost their prestige to the Americans; they regained a bit of their self-respect by repelling the French so they could try their hand at democracy.

Down in South America, the Spanish and Portuguese holdings were having an equally messy time securing self-government. Instead of looking at how every one of the remaining nineteen nations gained independence, let's just focus on the three biggies – Brazil, Gran Colombia and the United Provinces of the Rio de la Plata. Now the first one you might recognize, especially if you've kicked a soccer ball, but there's a pretty good chance you'd be out of luck if you tried to book some airline tickets to one of the last two. That's because they no longer exist. But they did for a brief moment in the early 19th century. It actually looked like the world was headed towards creating a United States of Latin America.

At the northern tip of South America, right where the continent turns into the Isthmus of Panama, a wealthy, educated planter named Simon Bolivar had a vision for a united nation he called Gran Colombia. Bolivar was something of a hybrid hero. He had the international diplomacy skills of a John Adams, the enlightened knowledge of a Thomas Jefferson, the military acumen of a George Washington and the toughness of a street fighter. Foreign dignitaries treated him as an equal. His troops trusted him as a man who would fight side by side with them to the end. He couldn't throw off imperial rule without a coalition of the not-so-willing. He criss-crossed the countryside, finally convincing the slave-owning plantation gentry, the cowboys of the interior valleys (the llaneros), the Amerindians living in the mountains and even the freed (and soon-to-be freed) slaves that they all could benefit from independence.

The Amerindians, the largest portion of Spain's American empire, were the hardest to convince. They rightfully had trust issues as they had survived centuries of brutal slaughter. Most recently, the European leaders viciously repressed Tupac Amaru's revolt in 1780. Tired of the rampant persecution that left his people penniless, exploited and demoralized, Tupac Amaru II (a mestizo with a familial claim to Incan royalty) staged a rebellion against Spain. It lasted a few months before he was captured and forced to watch the brutal murder of his family before he was tied to four horses. These horses tore his limbs from sockets, leaving his ripped appendages to be staked across the region as a reminder of Spanish superiority. This event didn't exactly improve Amerindian-Spanish relations.

So even after Simon Bolivar convinced many of the Amerindian tribes to join his cause, they were rightfully cautious. Bolivar's precarious alliance gained one more critical supporter after he travelled to Jamaica. There, he secured the services of British mercenaries fresh off the Napoleonic battlefields and more than willing to lease their military gifts to the highest bidder. The Spanish proved no match for Bolivar's hodgepodge of mercenaries, slaves, Amerindians and nobles, all financed by England's war chest. In 1824, Bolivar's forces overpowered the Spanish army, securing independence for his Gran Colombia.

At the same time as Bolivar was weaving together a political and military alliance, Jose de San Martin was persuading cowboys, former slaves and some ranchers to fight for his noble cause. He too was able to defeat the Spanish, and in 1824, he established the Provinces of the Rio de la Plata. But both Martin's and Bolivar's experiments with a federation of united states ultimately failed. Whereas the thirteen US colonies all shared a common British background and were all nestled along the East Coast, the Latin American nations proved too divergent to forge into any lasting union. The topography was insurmountable, no real network of roads existed, the diverse populations proved unwilling to compromise for a distant people they never met and the entire idea of democracy proved absurd to a people who only knew hereditary monarchies. By 1831, Gran Colombia had splintered into Colombia, Ecuador and Venezuela. The Provinces became Argentina, Bolivia and Chile. The dream of a United States of Latin America died.

To the east, in Portuguese Brazil, the path to sovereignty took a bizarre route that, although unorthodox, provided the new nation with the stability it would need to survive and prosper after independence. Unlike the Spanish colonies that saw a power vacuum when Napoleon toppled the crowns of the European powers, Brazil actually saw their monarch, King John VI, flee the peninsula, taking refuge in Rio de Janeiro. He continued to rule Portugal while in exile, but when Napoleon was eventually defeated, he rushed back to the comfort of his palaces in Portugal to rule his people in person. The timing of his repatriation couldn't have come at a more dangerous era in Latin American politics. If King John didn't make some concessions to the people, he would soon find his American holdings going the way of the rest of South America. So he turned Brazil over to his son Pedro. Unlike his father, Pedro knew only Brazil (he had arrived when he was nine), and saw himself more as a son of the Americas than a son of royal Europe. He understood the frustration of the Brazilians, believing their plight a just and noble cause.

And this was where the Brazilian independence movement swayed from the creole-led military insurrection blueprint that had freed one nation after another. This revolution was led by one man – Emperor Pedro. In 1822, he declared independence, and his father did nothing (some might argue it was because a father didn't want to fight his son; others might say it was actually the father who came up with the whole idea to ensure Portugal would keep at least a little bit of influence). Pedro then set up a constitutional monarchy that pulled the creoles into an assembly while coincidentally keeping him as emperor.

This little arrangement kept the peace for a few more years, but Pedro increasingly made enemies with the wealthy landowners. First he condemned slavery as the cancer of their society, but more importantly he ruled over a failing economy. Inflation was out of control and trade with Europe sunk to new lows. As tension mounted, Pedro felt he too would soon be overthrown, so he did what any other man would do in his position. He hopped on a boat for Portugal, leaving his son to run the country.

The problem was...his son, Pedro II, was only five years old. Now, even taking into account that kids might have matured faster in the 19th century, odds are this mini-man wasn't able to fully administrate the economic and political needs of this vast nation. For the next ten years, a regency made choices for him until he reached the ripe old age of fifteen when he could officially be crowned Emperor of Brazil. He held this position for another 40 years, only being overthrown in 1889 by a military coup. In these forty years, he brought peace, stability, expanded personal freedoms and rapid economic growth to Brazil, making it the dominant nation in a region which struggled to gain its footing.

In the decades that followed these revolutions, Latin America labored to create governments and economic systems that would prove lasting and inclusive. One of the primary debilitating factors was the existence of caudillos, local warlords who always sat in the background threatening to rise up and overthrow whoever sat in the president's seat. The elected officials could totally trust that their reign wasn't in jeopardy, so they subsequently drained the government coffers creating personal militaries that could combat the inevitable coup. Another impediment to an enduring government was the complete lack of a political tradition. Unlike in the thirteen American colonies to the north where England allowed the individual counties and towns to run their own elections and create their own assemblies, no such pattern of representative government existed in the hierarchical Latin American nations. As products of the Iberian monarchical governments that limited personal freedoms and granted rights based on birth, the creoles, mestizos and Amerindians knew little of how a Bill of Rights could actually function. Likewise, the Church stood in the way of a reorganization of society. The Founding Fathers of the United States of America were Protestants or Deists who wanted to ensure a separation of church and state. In Latin America, the Catholic Church had too much to lose. They were huge landowners in their own right, but they also controlled intellectual thought, maintaining a monopoly on the education system. Any constitution that might encroach on these rights would not be tolerated.

Lastly, the Latin American nations, all twenty of them, housed populations that proved too diverse to rule. On one end of the spectrum they had the remnants of European nobility, expecting to be treated with deference and obedience. At the other extreme, they had the vast Amerindian population who either existed in abject poverty or remained completely outside the sight of "civilized" society. They had a clergy who wanted to maintain order and control the minds and souls of the people through God's will. They also had a growing liberal elite who wanted to see rights awarded to individuals in the model of the western European nations. There were city dwellers who toiled their days away in the factories, miners who survived a life in the darkness of the mountain tunnels and ranchers who lived in the open plains. How could any one leader appease the needs of these groups? Every time a constitution was created to set the country on course, one of the disenfranchised groups would cry foul, claiming they were being ignored. An opportunistic leader would inevitably jump into the fray, promising to better equalize society. If this populist hero ever did take power, he would almost assuredly underwhelm his constituents, and the cycle of discouragement would start all over again.

Even when political rights eventually trickled down, for many, it was their economic despair that posed the larger problem. For three centuries, the Latin American economy was crippled by an economic system where Europeans stripped the region of its raw materials and kept its indigenous population illiterate and consigned to agricultural and mining labor. When the Latin American nations finally emerged and tried to enter the global marketplace, they were at an extreme disadvantage. A century behind England's Industrial Revolution, the Latin American emerging manufacturing sector couldn't compete with the cheap goods that continued to pour into their ports from across the pond. Not only did they have to make up for lost ground, but their urban populations swelled at such rates that no amount of municipal planning could keep pace with the massive infrastructure nightmares. As more and more Church lands and small farms were picked up by corporate landholders, millions more displaced peasants migrated to their final option – the cities. That pattern of displacement and urbanization has continued into the 21st century, with Latin America today laying claim to three of the top ten most populated cities in the world (Mexico City – 21 million, Sao Paolo – 18 million and Buenos Aires – 13 million).

As the Latin American nations strained to cope with the array of obstacles that emerged once they freed themselves from European rule, across the globe, nations had to deal with the new threat from the West. For in the late 19th century, European nations possessed a newfound voracious appetite for resources and markets to appease their industrial gods. They roamed the seas, equipped with naval forces armed like no other in the history of the world. Anyone in their paths faced one decision – trade or be conquered. How each nation answered that question would determine their fate into the next century.

But that is for another chapter.

31

Man and His Machines

Europe – Industrial Revolution – 1750 > 1900

And yes, once again we're back to the land of revolutions. But this time the stakes are a bit higher. Sure, each of the preceding revolutions altered how we look at the world, but how much did they really change the lives of the average Joe? In 1500, the average European spent his days stuck on a farm, plowing the same land his family probably farmed for generations, hoping that, through God's grace, the forces of nature would be kind enough to allow his family to survive just one more year. Three hundred years later, after all the so-called revolutions, how much had really changed?

Was this peasant suddenly a famed artiste peddling his wares to eager patrons across the continent? No. Did this peasant become a swashbuckling sailor braving the high seas to discover new lands? No again. How about when it came to his relationship with God? Did he now believe in Olaf, the great god of tree bark? Nope. His God was still the god of Noah, Abraham, Moses and Jesus. OK, he must have changed his perception of the world, constantly employing the scientific method to grasp unexplainable phenomena? Not exactly. Do you really think the average peasant cared that there were craters on the moon or that gravity makes fresh fruit fall to the ground? Pretty sure, neither of these thoughts kept him awake at night as he slept cuddled up to his portly pig (not his wife...an actual pig) in his one-room shack.

Well, he must have felt more enlightened, like he could stand up to the lords and ladies of the shire and change the world solely through the power of his convictions? Nope, he still fell prostrate to the man. So the political revolutions of the United States and France must have made his life better? Didn't he now have a Constitution, enumerated rights and even an all-powerful legislative branch that constantly tried to devise ways to allow him to pursue his happiness? No, in fact, he probably felt like the rich people who used to rule him were merely replaced with new rich people sporting slightly different accents.

The truth is that every one of the European revolutions of the sixteenth, seventeenth and eighteenth centuries affected only a small portion of the population. Looking back with our 21st century goggles, we can see that these little revolutionary turning points all put us on the path to where we stand today, that each transformation took us one step further away from our Dark Age past and toward our modern lives filled with joy, peace and online shopping opportunities. But for the everyman, for that lowly peasant who didn't have access to the art, the ideas, the experiences and the literature of the more affluent members of society, for that man, the changes were anything but revolutionary.

Then came the Industrial Revolution. This one was the biggie. In the history of mankind, this revolution ranks up there with the discovery of fire, the wheel and his and her clothing ensembles. Only one other revolution in human history comes close to altering the lives of regular people to such a vast extent as the Industrial Revolution – the Neolithic Revolution.

For the first 150,000-year reign of *Homo sapiens*, we spent our lives roaming the countryside in constant pursuit of new sources of food. Then came the Neolithic Revolution when we settled into a more stable existence next to water sources where we started growing crops, allowing a small percentage of our civilization to use whatever free time was available to organize governments, fashion an assortment of newly-needed goods and define who and how we were to worship. Though it took on a variety of forms from region to region, this agricultural existence worked for the next 10,000 years.

Until 1750, when a series of tinkerers, entrepreneurs and visionaries took the world in a direction that changed everything about how we live our daily lives. Within a mere century, the European peasant, who like his forefathers before who had lived as slaves to the inescapable cycle of farming, finally found himself living in a city, within walking distance of markets that sold every stuff and thing the human mind could concoct. And since these decades, one by one, the rest of the world has industrialized, continuing to take the global community further and further from our agricultural roots that were founded millennia ago on the banks of the Tigris and Euphrates rivers.

To "industrialize" means to change how goods are made. Before 1750, there were two ways to produce a good, market the good and move the good. You could either use manpower or animal power. Subsequently, there was always a limit to how much could be made. You could only go as fast as your two-legged or four-legged workers could take you, and because the speed of a human, a horse, a mule, an elephant or a camel hasn't changed that much in a few thousand years, our production efficiency really didn't improve that much either. Industrialization meant, however, that goods would no longer be made by man and his pets. They would be made by machines. And this was what changed the world.

In retrospect, it looks obvious that by 1750, England had all ingredients needed to head down the path of industrialization. Their land was blessed with a seemingly inexhaustible supply of coal and iron ore. Because it's an island, there was no point in England further than 100 miles from the sea – any good made could get out to the open seas with relative ease. It had a massive population of would-be workers. With the diet additions of the Transatlantic trade and the improved health due to sanitation and medical breakthroughs, more and more Englishmen were born and lived longer.

These workers were also "freed" from their land due to a series of recently passed laws that made it impossible to survive in the countryside if you weren't a landowner. Prior to the 1750s, English towns almost always had an area known as "the commons," where anyone was free to use the land as they pleased. These common areas (think National Park without the park ranger, the fragrant outhouses and Smokey the Bear) could be ten acres; they could be thousands of acres. Townspeople shared these lands for hunting, cutting down trees or even farming. A man who didn't own land could survive for years on the commons (in fact Robin Hood made himself a hero hanging out in the Sherwood commons). However, as England's population increased, would-be landowners pressured the English Parliament to make more land available for private ownership. Where did they look? The commons. The Parliament eventually passed a series of Enclosure Acts that essentially partitioned the commons into individual tracts of land. They then lined the lands with hedged fences and sold it to the people. Those with money now had their property. Those without were homeless, and these vagrants became the workforce England's cities would soon crave.

England also had three other fairly critical characteristics. They had the right amount of cash, the right government and the right mindset. By 1750, they had grown wealthy off their colonization, exploiting the natural resources and a percentage of the profits from their overseas kingdoms. During these ages of exploration and colonization, England had developed a banking system that not only extended credit to entrepreneurs, but also facilitated individual investment in shares of a corporation. People bought stocks. And unlike the other European nations, England enacted property laws that firmly protected this newly-minted wealth, providing the assurance needed for continued entrepreneurship. These property laws extended beyond owning chunks of dirt or a building. They included intellectual property. You owned what you envisioned. In England, if you invented a gadget, you'd be the one getting rich off that gadget. Lastly, England benefited from their knowledge of the ideals espoused during the Scientific Revolution and the Enlightenment. A nation of men schooled on the scientific method and the belief that man had the power to manipulate nature saw the world differently than those who came before. These men saw the problems of production, energy, transportation and communication as merely obstacles to overcome, obstacles that with the right planning and investigation could be readily surmounted.

This was where the inventors entered the scene. England already had a successful textile industry. For two centuries, it had relied on the putting-out system (not the 21st century high school version of "putting out"), a system where a man with a wagon full of thread dropped off his materials at a woman's cottage and she then spent her nights and the cold winter days weaving the fabric into some sort of wearable piece of clothing. This system worked, just not fast enough. In 1764, a weaver named James Hargreaves invented the "Spinning Jenny" which could produce fabric eight times faster than before.

A few years later in 1768, Richard Arkwright created the water frame, a device that used the energy of running water to weave thread. Though some claim Arkwright stole the idea from another man, it was Arkwright who took the idea and put it to work on a massive scale. Today known as the father of industrialization, Arkwright eventually built a series of factories adjacent to the rivers of Derbyshire County, and then watched as his businesses exploded. Soon others wanted in on the Arkwright magic, and water-run factories started popping up across England. This was the beginning of the Industrial Revolution. Textiles were the goods, and the machines were the producers. Arkwright had revolutionized manufacturing and for his effort he received a knighthood from the king and millions of dollars from those wanting to use his patents to the water frame. He became the world's first industrial capitalist. Before there was Gates, Jobs and Zuckerberg, there was Arkwright.

But he was only the beginning.

The next problem that needed to be solved was the placement of factories. Factories had relied on waterpower, which meant for your business to flourish, you had to stick your factory next to a river. But there was only so much river real estate available. To grow your industry, more energy was needed from a more mobile source. James Watt looked to the coalmines for inspiration. One of the difficulties in mining coal was the deeper the miners dug, the more their tunnels filled with water. Pumps were set up to extract the water in a never-ending series of bucket-liftings. This method was unfortunately inefficient as horses (and their horsepower) were the only energy sources available, so mine operators experimented with steam engine pumps. Using steam as a power source dates back to the Pax Romana, to a mathematician named Hero, but it could never be used at a sizeable scale, because so much time, energy and money was wasted in trying to cool the engine down so it wouldn't overheat or explode. Watt figured out a way to cool the steam engine down (which I won't even try to explain because it has to do with cylinders and indicators and other mechanical doodads and I frankly don't get it myself), and he also figured out how to make the steam engine turn a rod in a circular motion, meaning it could now power any number of motors or wheels. And in honor of his contributions to power, we forever after have measured energy using a unit called Watts.

Within a decade, English tinkerers came up with another innovation that helped take the Industrial Revolution to the next level – puddling. Not exactly an intimidating word, "puddling" is the process of turning iron ore dug from the ground into actually usable iron or steel. For centuries, metallurgists had already figured out how to heat charcoal, melt iron and shape it as they saw fit. But this took a long time. A master metallurgist might spend hours in front of a furnace and only pull out a cubic foot chunk of usable iron. Wood subsequently remained the most commonly used material for construction, and iron was only used sparingly (and usually for weapons). Puddling however ended the age of wood, and brought the West into the age of heavy industry, the age of iron. Puddling uses coal, a brilliant little gift of nature that has 300 million years of stored energy. Once upon a time, the rainforests covering the earth were slowly buried deep beneath the earth's layers, but before they fell to the powers of the plates, they had stored up thousands of years of the sun's energy. By the time the British dug up this precious little energy gem, it had become the world's perfect alternative energy (until oil came around in the 20th century).

The puddling process could produce much higher temperatures than mere wood fires, and this heat, coupled with frequent stirring, made the iron more moldable. With this evolution in material production, England could produce iron eight times faster than before. England skies were filled night and day with the coal burning furnaces that churned out iron bars, rails and sheets at a record pace. This nation that produced 17,000 tons of steel in 1740 was producing over 3,000,000 tons of steel in 1840. England became the "workshop of the world" and one after another, investors and inventors jumped at the opportunity to make a financial killing.

The entrepreneurs were off and running. The steam engine could be hooked up to any factory machine and could power it almost indefinitely. All that was needed was a ready supply of coal to heat the machines. Canals were built to carry the coal from the mines, but still, a cheaper, more efficient transportation method needed to be created to move the coal from the distant mines to the heart of the factory district. Why not hook up a steam engine to one of those horse drawn carriages? The first steam engine car was attempted in 1769, but it wasn't exactly efficient. It had three wheels, travelled at a staggering 2.5 miles an hour (just a pinch slower than how fast humans walk), and was linked precariously to a steam engine that jutted out from the vehicle (picture a freakishly huge tricycle attached to a huge barrel of boiling water). This awkward design, coupled with the fact that there were maybe only a few dozen paved roads in all of Europe, meant the mechanical car would have to wait a century until Daimler Benz came up with a better-looking four-wheeled version.

But was there another option? What about if someone combined the power of the steam engine with the durability of iron rails? Couldn't someone just attach a steam engine to a carriage, link it to a bunch of other carriages and then slide it along miles of elevated, parallel rail tracks? Someone did. In 1804, engineer Richard Trevithick's steam locomotive made the first trip in Wales, launching the start of the rail age. England, soon joined by the United States, would spend the rest of the 19th century producing more iron than anyone in human history, criss-crossing their nations with steel rails, making trans-continental travel seamless and putting every citizen within days of sending their goods to the global market. By 1900, America had put down nearly 200,000 miles of railroad track, and, coupled with England, they accounted for 90% of the world's railways. The goods made in record time could then be brought to market almost instantly. Over the course of human history, man had never been able to transport goods over long distances at an average rate faster than five miles per hour. Trains could guarantee speeds of up to 40-50 miles per hour.

The steam engine didn't only transform travel by land. No longer would transoceanic journeys sit vulnerable to the randomness of nature. Seasonal currents, unpredictable storms and fickle winds constantly threatened the success of the sailing ships that took to sea. Once the steam engine met the screw propeller, trips across the Atlantic could be made in half the time at 1/7 the cost. In 1607, the Mayflower travelled from England to the United States in 67 days. By 1800, sailing ships peaked at making the journey in about a month. Steam ships left these vessels in their wake. By 1850 the trip was made in eleven days, and by the end of the century a German vessel could cross the Atlantic in just over four days (today a United Airlines flight takes just about six hours).

As coal and iron continued to pour into the factories, and finished goods rapidly streamed out to the international market, factory managers had to increasingly modify how they organized their workforce and their physical resources. The most basic change was figuring out where goods should be produced. Under the domestic putting out system, raw materials were brought to the laborer. Now the laborer was brought to the raw materials. Factories proved to be the only buildings large enough to house the massive steam engine machines, as well as the huge labor pool needed to make the purchase of said machine worthwhile. Often, the factory owners even built nearby tenements (the mother of today's apartment slums) so their workers could roll out of bed, stagger to the factory and work from 6:00 in the morning until 9:00 at night. Slaves to a clock and rarely ever seeing the sun, these workers were then taught to follow a Monday through Saturday workweek. The inclusion of Monday as a work day was a tough adjustment for many, as Monday had almost become a hangover day, where those who partook in a bit too much fermented ale the previous Sunday eve stayed at home to sleep off their drunken revelry. To take even more of the fun out of work, the factory managers divided labor so that each hand specialized in a task he would repeat thousands of times, day in and day out. This specialization of labor turned work into a mind-numbing, repetitive process, sucking the spirit out of their workforce. But worker happiness was the least of the new entrepreneurs' concerns, for coupled with the new machines, these cogs could spew out products hundreds of times faster at one-hundredth the cost.

Just as all the features of the Industrial Revolution coming together – improved energy sources, transportation networks and methods of organization - an agricultural tragedy created a need for even more workers to feed the insatiable hunger of the factory beasts. A few of the creations of the industrial age were the mammoth farm tractors, seed drills and threshing machines that plowed the land, planted the seeds, watered and fertilized the fields and harvested the crops faster than any group of men ever could. Since the dawn of farming in Mesopotamia, the Indus River valley and the Yellow River in China, man had unfailingly tried to improve his tools, but inevitably he always remained handcuffed by the speed of animal or human power. The coming of the agricultural machines meant the death of the independent farmer. He couldn't afford to buy the machines, and he couldn't grow the crops at a rate that could ever compete with his more capital-rich neighbor. Hundreds of thousands of farmers found themselves unable to make ends meet on the farmlands their families had held for centuries, they too being forced to hopelessly relocate to the cities. In the 1840s, these displaced farmers were joined by the millions of Scottish and Irish who were fleeing the potato famine that had killed over 1.5 million of their brethren.

Unfortunately, the cities that met these millions of migrants were in no way ready for the pace and scope of the urban migration. Hundreds of families lived side by side in the squalor of a tenement, buildings that might only have a couple windows per floor, one bathroom to be shared by a dozen families and no running water. Chamber pots of feces and urine were merely dumped out onto the street and hygiene hit all-time lows as many would not bathe for months, if not years. With thousands of strangers hacking phlegm on each other, living in each other's filth and excrement and eating in the same bacteria-infested living quarters, diseases like cholera, typhoid and tuberculosis found the optimal environment to be fruitful and prosper. In the 1840s and 1850s, these three diseases accounted for over a third of all deaths in major cities, and until the governments could find a way to separate the drinking water from human waste, these numbers continued to climb.

Escaping the tenement brought little relief. The canals and rivers were filled with human sewage and the toxic run-off of factory waste. The air was filled with the smoke of the ceaseless coal fires that coated every wall, window and vehicle with black dust. This black dust and the other toxins introduced to man's daily life meant a surge in the number of cancers and other maladies that first debilitated and then took the lives of their urban victims. Entering the factory or the mines presented yet another series of hazards that threatened to handicap, maim or even kill the insignificant human cogs in the machine. With no safety regulations, the exhausted men and women could readily lose a limb or even their lives.

For children, life was unbearable. At the age of eight, city kids were expected to bring home a wage, having to accept a mere ¼ of the pay of their adult counterparts. These diminutive workers became the ideal candidates for the plunging into the darkness of the coalmines or cleaning and repairing the factory machines. In the mines, the 16-hour days bent over in the darkness of the tunnels led to stunted growth, malnourishment and all the lung diseases afflicting their elders. In the factories, their fatigue and inconsistent attention spans led to a slew of industrial accidents that took their lives or forever cast them among the rising number of invalids roaming the streets. The factory owners had no incentive to improve the working standards or provide health insurance. An army of the destitute waited outside their factory gates more than willing to step in to replace any fallen worker. A woman whose misplaced hair pulled her into the machine, ripping her skin from her skull, could expect to be replaced on the line within the hour. Mortality rates skyrocketed and life expectancy for these urban poor plunged to a mere 30 years of age.

It would be too easy to focus on the urban filth and despair facing these first generations of industrial laborers, but this requisite phase of misery was short-lived and the long-term benefits more than made up for these few decades of hopelessness. Remember, the Industrial Revolution marked the most radical shift in human history, and not merely because it made life pretty uncomfortable for the first few generations of workers. For the growing middle class of factory managers and entrepreneurs, an entire world of consumption became available. Before, only the landed aristocrats and nobles had access to the finer things in life, but now the man who started a company and made it profitable could expect to employ servants, adorn his house with prized art and furniture, clothe his family in the freshest fashions, enroll his children in the finest schools and find entertainment in one of the many growing entertainment venues that included theaters, museums and restaurants.

The existence of this growing managerial class, a group later labeled the bourgeoisie, always stood in stark contrast to the vast working class, the proletariat. Unlike the Western birthright class distinctions that appeared almost divinely chosen, these industrial distinctions were based solely on money. One group earned the money from the labor of another. But because this newly-wealthy class was always within sight of the laborers, their status always appeared just within grasp. If the father couldn't reach a life of comfort, maybe then could his son, or more probably, his grandson. Wealth determined class, not birth (though being born to an already established family still had its advantages).

But still, why was this revolution unlike the rest? To what extent was it truly transformative? First, it transformed family life. Before, moms and dads worked all day with daughters and sons. They worked together, they ate together, they worshipped together. Dad was the boss, mom stayed in the house and children only spoke when spoken to. Not after industrialization. As children entered the workforce and moms left the home to make a wage at a factory, family dynamics changed forever. Instead of going through life together, families merely caught up with each other at night with a "What did you do today?" The labor of fathers was "outsourced" to the much cheaper females and children. Role models stopped being family elders and started being the titans of industry. Wealth became the end-all, be-all...and it still is today. Ask any soon-to-be high school graduate what they want to be when they grow up, and the answer they'll most likely come back with will be – RICH. Few will respond with "I just hope I have a strong balance between spirituality and community service, while maintaining a strong rapport with my parents through to their golden years." Eventually though, these empowered women and children survived the despair of urban filth and horrific working conditions and gradually found their voice. By the 20th century, they were speaking out and demanding rights never thought possible in earlier eras. The lines of gender and age appropriateness had been severed.

Second, the West could unofficially start taking over the world. Save for a few golden centuries of the Greeks and Romans, for the whole of human history, by any yardstick, the West fell far behind the worlds of the Muslims, the Indians and the Chinese. Not anymore. With their mass-produced munitions that could put a gun in the hand of any able-bodied youngster, their steam-powered ships that could journey up rivers deep into the heart of an inland empire and their colossal supply of cheaply produced goods, no society was safe from the voracious touch of the Western industrialized powers. England took the early lead over Germany, the United States, France, Belgium and the Netherlands, but the rest of the West soon caught up. England's arsenal of steel weapons dwarfed the rest of the world, their ships accounted for ½ of the world's entire maritime supply and their population skyrocketed (London housed three million inhabitants in 1860, making it the largest city in the world). Over the course of the second half of the 19th century, the Western European powers subjugated almost the entire planet, placing close to 80% of the world's population under its economic or political sphere. This geopolitical shift completely flipped the power balance that had existed since the age of the Guptas, the Zhou Dynasty and the age of Muhammad. We have all inherited this world where the West dominates and only in the last decade have the perennial power players from the East returned to their perch as the dominators and not the dominated.

Third, people started being naughty. For centuries in the West, human behavior was under the constant watchful eye of village elders, the church hierarchy and their parents. Now they were on their own. The Ten Commandments became more recommendations than absolute laws. The symbolic shift in cities where factories stretched further to the heavens than church steeples meant city dwellers now worshipped the almighty dollar over the teachings of Jesus and the mandates of God. After a fifteen-hour day at the factory, workers were more inclined to hit the pub than the pew. Alcoholism rates swelled and as more and more men found themselves unemployed, robbery, gambling, prostitution, assault and even murder became commonplace. The city governments fell far behind in their ability to regulate these mounting indiscretions. Regional and ethnic gangs filled the power void, offering "protection" to those trying to survive in a world of chaos and random acts of violence. Until the municipalities found a way to police the streets and provide jobs and social services to the disenfranchised vagrants, the values once dictating individuals' daily choices were replaced with the most base survival instincts.

Fourth, the meaning of work forever changed. Man used to be self-sufficient. On the secluded farms of Europe, a farmer built his home, crafted his furniture, milked his cows, harvested his crops and taught his children. But the age of the family farm ended. By 1860, nearly 70% of Englanders lived in cities. Once farming went the way of the industrialized factory, a few men with some machines could produce far more than when the entire population worked the fields. For those who once spent a lifetime mastering a skill - the blacksmiths, weavers, metallurgists and craftsmen – the age of machines meant the end of their value. In a stroke of one generation, the skills that had for centuries been passed down from master to apprentice, became obsolete. A twelve-year-old in front of a spinning loom in Liverpool could produce more clothes than a skilled weaver in Delhi could ever imagine. The farmers and the artisans who built their world with their hands became interchangeable parts in the nation's economy. Now, we can't over-romanticize life on the farms (it was pretty darn boring hoeing a field or picking ripened fruit), but the sense of completion, the feeling that you were working toward a higher goal, vanished as man became slaves to the weekly pay stub. Some raged against the machine, forming a posse of the ticked off to enter the factories and destroy the challengers to their livelihood. The most famous group, the Luddites, demolished the automated looms and riled up the working class, scaring the bejeepers out of factory owners. Eventually, the British legislature made destroying a machine a capital offense, punishable by public execution. Even today, the term Luddite has come to represent anyone unwilling to embrace the latest technology – "Hey Tiffany, I can't believe you haven't bought the iPhone 27 yet. You're such a Luddite."

And lastly the relationship between employer and employee created tensions that would eventually explode into cries for change, or, in some cases, revolution. The workers of the world got tired of taking orders from the man, and once the powerless masses realized their strength in numbers, they began pressuring the legislative branches and their bosses for the big three – fewer working hours, better working conditions and improved wages. Sometimes this pressure manifested in the creation of labor unions that collectively pushed for more rights, but other times more drastic measures were needed. By the end of the 19th century, men began considering the words of Karl Marx and his theories that the factory owners could be overthrown, launching humanity into its next and last stage of economic development – a world where all goods were shared equally amongst the community, a world not unlike life before the Neolithic Revolution.

But that is for another chapter.

32

Europe Takes Over the World

Europe - Imperialism – *1750 > 1910*

By 1850, all of Western Europe was well on its way to full industrialization. The rewards were just too great, and the costs were reasonably easy to overlook. The innovative machines and techniques that launched England to the head of this production revolution were soon copied by France, Belgium, Germany and the Netherlands. An island revolution became a continental revolution. Then it hopped over the pond and hit the United States.

It could have ended right there. The West could have maintained its monopoly on industrialization for probably a few more centuries, and the world would be none the wiser. The great civilizations of the world – India, China and Dar al Islam – weren't exactly clamoring for all things Western (their previous experiences had proven the futility of trading with these backwards people), and the rest of the world was content to live regionally-isolated, independent lives of farming, herding, hunting and gathering.

But Europe wouldn't have it. Partly out of the desire to help out the unenlightened of the world, but mostly to feed the unquenchable thirst of the factory beasts, the Western European nations spent the second half of the 19th century taking their tools and their knowledge to the furthest corners of the planet. By

1914, at the onset of World War I, close to 80% of the planet's population was under the economic or political domination of a Western power. From the rainforests of Malaya to the harbors of China, from the coast of Australia to the plains of inner Africa, and from the fields of Argentina to the mountains of India, the non-Western world had become the producers of the raw materials needed to feed Western machines and they also had become the needed consumers of the vast goods spat out by these machines. The factories might reside in the sprawling cities of London, New York, Paris, Berlin, Chicago and Vienna, but the raw materials came from the hands of villagers sometimes more than 10,000 miles away. In this era that would become known as the Age of New Imperialism, Europe had created a truly global economy, and we could never go back to being isolated again.

But why in 1850? How was this possible? Through the revolutions of the 16th to 18th centuries – the Renaissance, the Scientific Revolution, the Reformation, the Enlightenment and the political revolutions – the West learned that they were not merely inhabitants of the earth, they were the masters of it. They no longer were subject to the superstitions and randomness that kept man trapped in ignorance. Man was the one who controlled his fate, and he could use the resources of the planet to make machines to make his life more productive and more efficient. Once man had the mindset, a confluence of events and ideologies made the second half of the 19th century the starting point for Western Europe's march across the world.

Perhaps the greatest motivation for expansion was money. Money makes men move, and in the case of the Industrial Revolution, profit was king. But by the 1850s, profits were slowing down. The unprecedented growth rates achieved in the first phases of the manufacturing revolutions were unsustainable, and as more and more European nations borrowed the techniques of the industrialized, it appeared growth would soon flatline. Unemployment rates started climbing, the raw materials needed to make the goods started running out and the continental buyers able to gobble up the goods had already purchased everything they could afford. If the entrepreneurs were to survive, they'd have to look outside Europe and the United States to get past the invisible productivity barrier that threatened to undo the entire system. So they started looking elsewhere for the tin needed for their canning; the cotton needed for their textiles; the coal needed to fuel the machines; the rubber needed to finish their goods; the iron needed to build the infrastructure; the copper needed to connect the telegraph lines; the corn and wheat needed to feed their workers; and the tobacco and coffee needed to keep the city dwellers drugged up and ready to work another day. Once they found which nations could best supply these raw materials, they could then call on these same peoples to buy the goods once they rolled off the factory floor.

Yet the Europeans weren't solely motivated by the promise of economic gain. They also thought it was their obligation to help out the "little, unfortunate colored people" of the world. Today, to make such a statement generates cries of racism, but in the 19th century this arrogance had become the common perception amongst Western elite. Basically, Europe was the first to industrialize, create representative governments and see the planet as something to be controlled, so it was obviously the home to the most advanced peoples. Wasn't it?

Literature was used to justify this belief. Charles Darwin's *The Origin of Species* was intended to show how species in the natural world survived or perished based on their ability to adapt to their environment. The species that had developed the most useful adaptations had survived as the fittest, the rest suffered the path of extinction. To some, this theory of evolution could be likewise applied to the human race. In an odd bit of creative analogy-making, the white man must then be the most dominant of the human species because they had risen to the top of the industrialized ladder. This belief in biological determinism, that some races are just better than others, became en vogue amongst the more educated classes, even leading to so-called scientific experiments that attempted to quantitatively rank each race from smartest to most dense. In one ridiculous experiment, scientists actually gathered thousands of skulls, filled them with little silver balls and then measured which skulls could actually hold the most balls. More balls=bigger head=smarter person. And guess what they found? Yep, in a stunning turn of events, these European scientists found that Europeans were the wisest on the planet, followed far behind by the peoples of the Americas, Asia and Africa. For those of you who have friends with big noggins, you probably already know that big heads quite regularly have nothing to do with IQ, but you're just not interpreting the data through 19th century Western eyes.

In 1899, Rudyard Kipling actually mocked this justification for Western imperialism (though many of the time thought he was actually championing the need for Western help) in his poem *White Man's Burden*. It mocked the pervading conviction that the less civilized of the world were waiting for the West to take over their nations, showing them how to properly live. Kipling sarcastically speaks of "sullen peoples" who were "half-devil and half-child." He recounts the need to wage "savage wars of peace" to "fill full the mouth of Famine And bid the sickness cease." The world was waiting for a hero to save them from themselves.

Answering this call to help out the poor and uncivilized were an army of missionaries and philanthropists, a 19th century version of today's Peace Corps, who accompanied the captains of industry to every country that felt the touch of industrialization. In the late 19th century, this chance to proselytize to peoples who had never heard of God was an opportunity that they felt had to be embraced. In bringing God's message to the people, they could also bring them education and better health. One additional motivation was to hopefully end the seemingly vulgar, uncultured behaviors of the heathens. Westerners looked in disgust at the barbaric practices they encountered. They felt they had to act once they heard the stories of continued slavery, girls who had to marry at eight years old, men who married more than one wife, families who killed newborn daughters and communities that forced widows to commit suicide by fire upon the death of their husbands. These missionaries, nurses, teachers and humanitarians would help bring these people out of the darkness and into the light of proper behavior. They weren't always welcomed with open arms.

Aside from the profit hunger and cultural arrogance, many of the reasons for colonizing the world concerned geopolitical issues that meant nothing to the people of distant lands. As each of the European nations evolved, they started to take deeper pride in their country's history and their country's place in the world. At about this same time, compulsory education was popping up all over Western Europe, meaning generations of children were raised hearing of their country's heroes, their victories in battle, their famed artists and their unsurpassed customs and traditions. This growing sense of nationalism meant that citizens were more than willing to support their governments as they amped up their militaries and journeyed outwards to prove their superiority. Just as the high school boy pumps iron for hundreds of hours to hopefully look tough and intimidate some of the other wanna be alpha males, Western Europe also started finding ways to puff up their holdings, as any territorial addition to one's domain was one less for its Western neighbor. Another way to prove your status was to build huge armies. Napoleonic ideas of conscription, where able-bodied men were drafted into military service, meant Europe had massive standing armies that could be deployed at a moment's notice. By 1914, Russia had an army of over 1.3 million, Germany and France had close to a million and even Austria had about 500,000 soldiers.

Even more impressive than the sure volume of the forces was the awesome firepower each man wielded. Two of the more noteworthy goods produced by the Industrial Revolution were the breechloading, repeating rifles and machine guns. In 1800, an expert rifleman might be able to load, reload and fire off maybe three rounds a minute. The repeating rifles could shoot fifteen rounds in fifteen seconds. Less than a century later, a repeating rifle could shoot off over fifty rounds a minute. And the machine guns? In 1876, the Gatling Gun could fire 200 rounds per minute. No tribal or indigenous military could ever contend with this awesome force.

Once Europe had the motivation and the means, the actual conquest and domination part was the easy proposition. Here was the European Ten Step Guide to Imperialism: 1) ask politely if the people would like to trade, 2) if this fails, park a ship in one of their harbors, launch a few artillery balls, and then repeat step one, 3) if this still fails to win them over, rout the local government and rule from the capital city, 4) if the rebels in the outskirts still continue to resist, send in a land army to put down any rebellions, 5) once the final insurgent gives up, hire the locals to run the economy, making sure they report to the Europeans in charge, 6) invite expatriates from your home country to join you in the capital city where they can assume the swankiest jobs available, 7) make a ton of cash off the labor of the locals, 8) bring over your wife and hire servants to attend to your every need, 9) build summer home in nearby hills, 10) enjoy the fruits of globalization.

In this manner, one by one the world fell to Europe. By 1914, the world had been divided between the United States, France, the Netherlands, Belgium, Portugal, Spain, Austria and Italy. But the trophy for 19th century masters of the universe goes to the founders of the Industrial Revolution, the country that housed the largest city on the planet in 1900, the home of Shakespeare, John Locke and the Beatles...you guessed it...Great Britain. By 1914, "the sun never set on the British Empire," but as you can see, the new kid on the block, the United States of America, had learned a few lessons from their historical mother country and were hanging in there with the big boys.

However, the United States had discovered a far more cost effective way of controlling foreign economies that was low on risks and expense, but heavy on rewards. Throughout Latin America and the South Pacific, the United States rarely had to resort to all out war. Instead they would employ just enough economic incentives and military threats to ensure they could expand their sphere of influence across both Americas, but without the cost of daily administration. In Columbia, the United States "encouraged" the peoples of the isthmus of Panama to break free from Columbian rule. Within months of breaking free, Panama miraculously made a deal with the United States to build a canal across their country, dramatically reducing the transportation costs of shipping across the Atlantic and Pacific. In Hawaii, Dole sugar planters asked for protection from the military, eventually replacing the indigenous queen with democracy, setting the stage for Hawaii to shortly after "voluntarily" join the United States. In Argentina, US Steel built the railroads and US merchants controlled all the trade that touched these rail lines. The United States established the precedent that they would economically favor those in power that allowed American businessmen free reign to expand their industry, and those governments who denied American interests might find themselves facing a well-financed local insurgency. Play ball with American business interests and get rich. Or fight the system and your home-grown government could expect a coup. Not exactly a choice. By 1900, Latin America might have gained their political independence, but their economic independence stood decades away from coming to fruition.

So what happens when one civilization subjugates all others? What occurs when essentially the entire world exists so that the West could make and sell cheap stuff? What does this kind of inequity and hierarchical interaction do to the psyche of the ruled? Of the rulers?

It has become almost expected in recent history to condemn Europeans for their undeniably negative influence on the world. According to these denouncers of all things Western, the world's economies were destroyed, tens of millions died horrific deaths or lived in abject suffering, entire cultures became extinct and racism grew to all-time highs making it impossible for people of different societies to ever interact on an equal footing.

Was this true? What was the Western impact on the globe during and after this age of New Imperialism?

Well, it depends. There was no one experience that all colonizers and colonized shared. Take for instance Malaya (the region we today call Malaysia and Singapore). If you were a local rubber merchant, you prospered; a local farmer, you lost your edible crops; a hunter-gatherer, you found you had to migrate deeper into the forest. If you were a local leader that worked with the Europeans, you were rewarded handsomely; if you objected, you were imprisoned or dealt with more harshly. If you were a Christian missionary, you might convert a few more souls to your cause. If you lived in the cities, you might attend a Western school and buy Western clothes. If you lived in the rural areas you might be able to move your goods even faster to market. And this was just in one British colony. What about all the other situations, all the other nuances of religion, government and local reaction that might have produced an entirely different story? The truth was...there was no singular narrative to reflect European impact on the colonies of Asia, Africa and Latin America.

Yet some themes did develop. Everywhere Europeans went, they improved the infrastructure of the region. They built roads, railroads, dams, hospitals, bridges and schools. They laid plumbing, telegraph and electricity lines. They might have made these choices to improve their own living conditions or ensure the speedy movement of goods, but regardless the motive, when they eventually did leave, they left behind some fairly impressive systems of communication, transportation and public health. They encouraged education, at both the primary and university level, even oftentimes bringing the most elite students back to Europe. These students might then return, educated on the enlightened ideals of Locke, Rousseau and Montesquieu, and demand their own country's independence (though Europe learned the potential risk of this policy, so by the time they took over the African nations, these learning abroad programs had faded out of favor).

They improved the overall health and lifestyle of every society they touched. How can you best gauge the health of the world? Look at the overall population rates. The world started eating better, taking care of their bodies better and living much longer lives. At the time of Christ, we had 300 million people on the planet. 1600 years later, we had only doubled to 600 million people. In the next 300 years, we doubled again to 1.2 billion. But by 1900, once everyone had been touched by Western influence, population numbers exploded like never before. By the year 2000, we were at 6 billion. Europe shared their knowledge of diseases and medicine, as well as improving the overall diets of the indigenous people. They taught the locals how to farm more efficiently, and in cases like Egypt, they even built dams that could double or triple crop outputs. As for quality of life, look what the puritanical Europeans did for some arguably disgusting traditions that still existed in the world in the 19th century. In India, the British banned the practice of *sati* where widows were thrown onto the funeral fires of their husbands. They also banned the practice of marrying girls under the age of eight. They pushed to end slavery across the African continent, a practice that had existed long before the Spanish and Portuguese hijacked the market in the 16th century. Humans ate better, lived healthier and died later. Yes, people still suffered in the world, but they've always suffered. But once the fruits of the Western revolutions spread around the world, these outer nations suffered a heck of a lot less. And yes, many of these effects came not from a European desire to help out their common man, but more self-serving reasons, but when it comes to health, to life and death, doesn't the end sometimes justify the means?

Nevertheless, certain elements of Western contact were harmful, oftentimes appalling. On the battlefield, Western armies slaughtered indigenous armies. European soldiers only recently trained in how to pull a trigger could wipe out a civilization of well-trained warriors yielding only leather shields, bows and arrows. In the Sudan, in the 1898 Battle of Omdurman, a British force of a few thousand wiped out a Sudanese army numbering over 40,000 in a matter of hours. Death toll: Sudanese – 11,000. British – 48. Even outside the battlefield, the brutality often continued unabated. For those who refused to turn their land over to the European settlers or were unable to pay the oppressive taxes assigned, violence became the next logical step. In Tasmania, in an event known as the Black War, settlers were given the order to shoot on sight any aborigines who refused to vacate the land. Essentially, the British settlers lined up, walked across the island and killed everyone they passed. In the Congo, the Belgian oppressors punished local men who didn't meet their harvesting quota by cutting off their ears, kidnapping their families or just killing them as examples until the requisite labor requirement was met. For others, death was a slower process. Pushed off their ancestral lands, the first few generations of locals exposed to European industrialization couldn't adjust, and ended up starving to death, unable to find food in this new world they had inherited.

Economically, the colonized nations started down a path that would make it impossible for them to ever compete with the industrialized nations on an equal playing field. While Europe pushed the envelope of technology and manufacturing efficiency, almost the whole of Latin America, Africa and Southeast Asia was forced into a state of merely delivering the raw materials to Europe. The manufacturing process, and therefore the ability to make a profit, resided solely in the hands of Westerners. They became the haves and the rest of the world became the have-nots. Although these peoples might have entered the global marketplace, they couldn't compete. They could never produce goods at the rate or at the cost of their Western rivals, a crisis many developing nations (in what has recently been called the Third World) still face even today.

Culturally, the rest of the world was made to adjust to the values, traditions and ethics of the West. Imperialists pressured locals to adopt Western notions of proper clothing, appropriate behavior and gender roles. This pressure, coupled with the economic mandates that required peoples to only purchase from their European colonizers, meant regional cultures were oftentimes supplanted, or even replaced. Cultures died. Languages were lost. The world had 20,000+ languages before the Europeans started colonizing. There are only about 6,000 left (and we'll probably lose 3,000 more in the next three decades).

To this day, the rest of the world continues to struggle with how to survive in a world where a steady stream of Western culture fills our every sense, placing a higher value on foreign ideas than on native traditions. In many instances, the rise today of extremist Muslims willing to martyr themselves is not as much a war of religion, as it is one of cultural preservation in a world where the Western way is becoming the only way.

A century later, as transportation and communication networks exponentially advance, seeming to only "flatten" our world even more, we have started to see the cultural exchange going both ways. An American living in Mississippi is as apt to dine at a sushi restaurant as a family in Shanghai might sit down for a McDonald's Value Meal.

Yet, back in 1850, the West's New Imperialism forced countries to evaluate their place in the world and the direction of their civilizations. In the case of two of the oldest civilizations on the planet – the Chinese and the Japanese – the manner in which they reacted to the arrival of the Europeans would forever alter their histories. One nation collapsed. The other prospered. Neither would ever be the same again.

But that is for another chapter.

33

The Last Emperor

China – Qing Dynasty – 1800 > 1919

At the start of the 19th century, the Chinese were in no way
ready for what the next century had in store for them.
Their profits from trade were greater than ever. They were
farming more land than ever. They manufactured a third of the
world's goods. Their people were living longer and their
population had quadrupled in less than 200 years. They weren't
just prospering. They were the kings of the world.

And the encroaching influence of the Western powers
barely registered a hint of concern. Europeans were nothing more
than inconsequential nuisances who from time to time sent
emissaries to spread their Christianity or hawk some useless wares.
But aside from the silver the Europeans brought in from the
American mines, there still wasn't anything of interest Westerners
could produce. The Chinese also restricted these foreigners to
conducting all of their business out of one port – Canton. In 1793,
when the British tried to expand their influence, Emperor
Qianlong didn't mince words in outlining the Middle Kingdom's
perspective:

"The celestial empire abounds in all things and lacks nothing. I set no value on objects strange or ingenious and have no use for your country's products...It behooves you, O King, to respect my sentiments and to display even greater devotion and loyalty in future, so that, by perpetual submission to our Throne, you may secure peace and prosperity for your country...Tremble and Obey!"

Not exactly the words of a man who saw the death of his domain on the horizon. To the Chinese, the fruits of the Industrial Revolution held no value whatsoever. But in the next few decades, Britain proved they weren't willing to take "no" for an answer. The Brits had already established the largest empire in human history, stretching from Australia to Singapore to India to Africa to Canada. One arrogant, misguided little Emperor wasn't going to stop their progress.

And Britain's push to open up China came at exactly the time the local Chinese were starting to get fed up with the ruling family. The Qing Dynasty had become victims of their success. Sure, their population had quadrupled, but there was no new land to feed these new generations. They had outgrown their resources. When the inevitable drought or flood or heat wave hit the fields, famine was always just a season away. For those fleeing the starvation of the countryside for the promises of city life, the reality of urban employment illustrated the futility of their existence. The massive population surge meant wages stayed low. If an employee didn't like what his boss was paying him, there were thousands more desperately waiting outside to accept any meager salary. Living standards dropped, families started killing their babies (girls especially) and many resorted to drugs to escape the misery of life. When the Chinese looked for someone to blame, their pointed fingers usually landed on foreigners.

It was the Manchus, barbarians from Manchuria, who earned the Mandate of Heaven by wrestling away power from the Ming Dynasty in 1644. These Manchus had built on the successes of the Ming, creating the Qing Dynasty that initially expanded the wealth and health of their citizenry. But after a century and a half, their successes could not outweigh their contradictory foreign ideals. Knowing the majority Han Chinese weren't big fans of foreigners, the Manchus secluded themselves in the Forbidden City and reserved all top government positions and benefits for their own people from the north. Their court officials had become corrupt and the regional scholar-bureaucrats cared more about their own personal comfort than maintaining the roads, canals and irrigation systems that made China's economy thrive and kept floods from spoiling crops. The Manchus had also enacted some laws that, though not debilitating, were more than a bit annoying. They banned books, homosexuality and the study of Confucian texts by commoners. They expected all women to act exactly the same – they couldn't talk or laugh in public, couldn't walk and look around at the same time and couldn't wear dresses that rustled in the wind.

But these weren't the foreigners the Chinese should have been worrying about. By 1840, the Qing Dynasty had allowed the population to swell to over 400 million, ruled by a Manchu population that numbered less than six million. But these few million Manchus weren't the ones that would bring down the empire, it would be the few thousand Europeans trading in Canton and living in Macau. These barbarians from the West would be the ones that would set in motion a series of events that for almost a century altered China's place in the world economy.

The Brits were just not willing to tremble and obey the emperor. They weren't willing to accept trading in just one port, cut off from hundreds of millions of would-be consumers. Great Britain wanted more.

The first step Britain took was introducing a product to the Chinese that they just couldn't refuse – opium. To a people increasingly frustrated by their lot in life, opium provided the perfect escape. Opium activates dopamine in the brain, and seconds after being inhaled, it transports the user to another world, free of pain, stress and anxiety. This state of euphoria is in itself addictive, but opium also causes physiological dependence. After a few uses, the body must have it. If not, the user faces the aching limbs, diarrhea, vomiting and insomnia that come with withdrawal. Similar to the other narcotics from the opiate family – heroin and morphine – once a user, always a user.

So with opium, Britain had the ideal good to break into the Chinese market. It was highly addictive, it was easy to transport and it was produced right next door in India. Britain had been looking for a way to exploit Indian labor for decades. Britain was no longer attracted to India's cheap manufacture of clothing (their own Industrial Revolution made Indian fabric almost obsolete), but if Britain could put Indian farmers to the task of growing poppies, they would have themselves a gold mine.

The Brits traded through Chinese middlemen who set up opium dens where those with silver would sit down, take a couple drags from the opium pipe and then lounge around stoned for the rest of the day. After a few decades, few classes were immune to its temptation. By 1840, twelve million Chinese were addicted to this midnight oil. Society was falling apart. Productivity levels dropped and the government was impotent to do anything about it. How could they? 30% of all court officials were likewise addicts. The emperor saw his kingdom crumbling and attempted to cut the trade from within. In 1839, the government passed laws, forbidding the sale and usage of opium. 2000 opium hawkers were imprisoned or executed, and at the port town of Canton, 20,000 chests of opium were destroyed (the Asian version of America's little Tea Party outing).

Emperor Linzexu made one final plea to Queen Victoria, cautioning the Queen that if they didn't stop selling opium, he'd have no choice but to enforce "decapitation or strangulation." He warned:

> *Even though the barbarians may not necessarily intend to do us harm, yet in coveting profit to an extreme, they have no regard for injuring others. Let us ask, where is your conscience? I have heard that the smoking of opium is very strictly forbidden by your country; that is because the harm caused by opium is clearly understood. Since it is not permitted to do harm to your own country, then even less should you let it be passed on to the harm of other countries... if there are still those who bring opium to China then they will plainly have committed a wilful violation and shall at once be executed according to law, with absolutely no clemency or pardon...The barbarian merchants of your country, if they wish to do business for a prolonged period, are required to obey our statues respectfully and to cut off permanently the source of opium.*

The Brits were less than pleased. Opium made up nearly 1/6th of Britain's total GDP, pulling in close to one billion dollars a year in revenue. There was no way the merchants and the government were going to sit back and watch their golden goose perish without a fight. Within a year, British warships pulled up alongside dozens of port towns scattered along the Chinese coast, taking out each, one by one. The Chinese might have had 26 times more men than the Brits, but they were outgunned ten to one, and the Brits had even lined their ships with Indian soldiers to help subdue their Chinese foes. The Opium Wars had begun.

After three painful years of fighting, the Qing emperor saw no hope for victory and surrendered with Queen Victoria's forces right on the doorsteps of the port of Nanking. Many court officials committed suicide rather than see their country cowed by the enemy. For all of history, the Chinese were the cowtowed not the cowtowers. The authorities agreed to the Treaty of Nanking. They ceded Hong Kong permanently (or at least until 1997) to the British and they agreed to open up five ports to trade with Western nations. They could no longer set the tariff rates for imported goods, and most insulting of all, they had to grant extraterritoriality rights to British expatriates roaming their towns. No matter what any Brit did in China, they could not be held liable to Chinese laws. Like ambassadors today who have diplomatic immunity, these extraterritorial privileges meant that Europeans could do anything they wanted, without fear of punishment. If the Han Chinese were disgusted by foreigners before the Opium Wars, their growing hatred of barbarians only intensified in the final half to the 19th century.

Adding injury to insult, the Chinese also had to come up with 21 million ounces of silver to pay for the Opium War. They didn't have this money, so they had to call on their neighbors for loans. And their neighbors were more than willing to lend a hand. But in exchange for the loans, these neighbors wanted collateral, something of Chinese value that would make it worth their while to send over some cash. What these neighbors wanted most was railroad access, so one by one, the Russians, the British and then the Japanese seized control of China's countryside, building railroads connecting inland areas to Pacific ports, with all connected lands becoming the property of the foreign country.

China was falling apart. It was being whittled away by industrialists from Europe and even from East Asia. Their people were starving or stoned. Their infrastructure was outdated and crumbling. Their technological superiority was proven a myth by their embarrassing defeats at the hands of the Europeans and then the Japanese. They were a broken nation.

Imperial officials tried to rectify the situation, but it was too little too late. They sent officials across Europe, looking for strategies to industrialize quickly. They hoped they could hold onto the past by melding Confucian ethics with Western science. Scholar Feng Guifen argued, "What we have to learn from the barbarians is only one thing, solid ships and effective guns" (that's actually two things, Feng). The Manchus tried repairing their broken government by weeding out corrupt officials and creating government banks that would encourage entrepreneurialism.

But the people still starved and the foreigners kept gaining more influence. The peasants started to rise up, demanding not just reforms, but an end to the Qing Dynasty. First, there was the Taiping Rebellion. This war was started in the early 1850s by Hong Xiuquan, a peasant who saw himself as the younger brother of Jesus Christ (yes, you read that right). He felt he was sent by God to free his Chinese brethren from the tyrannical rule of foreign Manchus. This rebellion started with simply a few villages that refused to bow to Manchu authority. But Hong was in the right place at the right time. Many were drawn to his philosophies that promised to kick out the foreigners, redistribute land to the poor, end the private trade that was leading to enormous income disparities and abolish the horridly painful custom of foot binding. Most followers weren't totally buying into his whole Christ-brother declaration, but they were willing to overlook this little bit of insanity for a chance at food and safety.

And it worked. Through guerilla warfare and just pure numbers, by 1860, Hong's forces had 40 million people under their control across south and central China. The Qing forces refused to cede power to Hong, even aligning with French and British forces to push back the movement. But it was too little too late. By the time the rebellion fell in 1864, after a decade of catastrophic civil war, nearly 30 million people had perished due to starvation, disease or force, making it the bloodiest conflict in the history of the world (until of course the 20th century where the two world wars would claim this shameful title). The war left towns abandoned, crops untended and roads reduced to rubble. Peasants liked the idea of robbing from the rich and giving to the poor, and the Communist Party would tap into this desire in the 20th century as it scoured the countryside looking for supporters.

But before the 20th century would arrive, several additional rebellions demonstrated that the Qing Dynasty's hold on the Mandate of Heaven was in its waning days. To the north, the Nien Rebellion took the lives of a couple hundred thousand soldiers and civilians over two decades. To the west, the Dungan Revolt claimed another fifteen million lives. Coupled with the Taiping Rebellion, these costly civil wars disturbed the flow of food and goods through the economy, but also drained the Qing Dynasty's ability to defend itself from external threats.

The greatest external threat came after the Qing's failure to quell the disturbances of a secret society of unemployed men known as the Fists of Righteous Harmony (or "Boxers" as they were known to Westerners impressed by their martial arts skills). These Boxers had one thing in common – their hatred of foreigners. They hated the fact that they brought opium into their country. They hated the fact that Christianity was spoiling their traditional values. They hated the fact that Europeans didn't have to follow the laws of the land. And they hated the fact that their lives were shorter, their bellies were less full and their wages didn't buy what they could, once upon a time. And who was to blame for all of society's ills? Westerners. And which Westerners were most visible in the villages of rural China? Christian missionaries. It was this group of wandering proselytizers that was easiest to denounce, and in the late 1890s, the Boxers started attacking Christian residents, killing missionaries and burning churches. Only a few dozen missionaries ever saw any real danger, but the European powers were taking notice, just waiting for an excuse to deploy their forces and take an even greater chunk of China's economy.

The Empress Dowager, the ruthless, self-absorbed, incompetent widow who took care of the Qing throne while her young children came of age, could have squashed this tension in a heartbeat. The Boxers were nothing compared to the forces unleashed in the Taiping and Dungan rebellions. They would have been no match for Qing forces. But instead of crushing the movement before it gained momentum, she decided to instead give it added support. She threw her official backing behind the Boxers, believing naively that this might be the impetus she needed to get rid of the Europeans.

She couldn't have been more wrong. Once her support was given to the perceived killers of innocent Christian missionaries, the Europeans had the pretext they needed to launch an all-out offensive. In the 19th century, it was near impossible to get the Europeans to agree on anything, but when it came to fresh access to the markets of China, they'd have no problem putting their differences aside. In 1900, an Eight-Nation Alliance made up of Britain, Russia, France, Germany, Austria-Hungary, the United States and Japan (now behaving a lot like the Europeans) joined the ruckus and easily squashed the Boxers. Because the Qing family had supported the Boxers, the peace treaty also went on to include yet another series of paralyzing treaties and humiliating reforms.

After the Boxer Rebellion, Russia saw its chance to move deeper into Manchuria. China was ordered to pay an additional $61 billion as reparations. The Qing Dynasty was allowed to stay in power, but with a catch. They had to adopt Western reforms. The military was reorganized to resemble that of Germany and Japan. The examination system was terminated, replaced with a Western-styled college system. Scholar-bureaucrats were stripped of their powers and Western investors and merchants were encouraged to expand their businesses throughout China.

Any remaining loyalists to the throne had had enough. They were done with the Qing. They hadn't protected the nation from foreigners. They hadn't put food on their tables. They hadn't earned the right to retain the Mandate of Heaven. And in fact, the situation was even getting worse.

The Qing were a lost dynasty, so when Sun Yat Sen returned from exile and organized his own populist movement that sought out the "Three Principles of the People" (get rid of Manchus, form an elected government and guarantee an equal economic status for all), he earned the support of not only tens of millions of peasants, but also the more influential bands of merchants, students and military. In 1911, his forces moved on the capital city and within months the Empress Dowager fled, and the Qing Dynasty knew their time was up.

The Qing emperors had been fighting foes, both internal and external, for almost a century. They were tired, inept and powerless to stop the inevitable change.

But China was a long way from sorting out who would rule after the Qing, for it would first have to survive five decades of civil war, as regional lords fought regional lords, and central governments faced an invasion of epic proportions from their centuries-old island nemesis to the west – Japan.

Life in China would get a lot worse before it would get better, and another 50 million civilians would lose their lives before China got back on track to prosperity. However, they would get back.

But that is for another chapter.

34

An Island on Overdrive

Japan – The Meiji Restoration – 1850 > 1910

Throughout the near-three-century Tokugawa Shogunate, Japan had been fairly successful keeping itself just out of reach of Western influence. Their policy of only dealing with Dutch merchants out of the port of Nagasaki meant that they were able to stay relatively abreast of the comings and goings of the European traders, without having to deal with the economic and social consequences of allowing Westerners access to their world.

But as each decade passed, and as the British, French, Russian and US ships grew more bold in their trading habits, it became harder and harder to ignore their presence. U.S whalers were increasingly seen off shore and once in awhile the odd shipwrecked crew would make its way to the Japanese coast (only to be promptly jailed and expelled as soon as possible). Western envoys kept trying to convince the shogun to reconsider his stance, but time and again, these diplomats were sent off empty-handed. Japan wanted to be left alone.

But the West wouldn't give up. Japan had to be opened. Its strategic location made it the perfect stop for repairs and supplies, and no one could ignore the advantages of being the first country granted the opportunity to tap that market. The United States of America stepped up to the plate first. Once the labyrinth of railroads made the US a transcontinental behemoth, the Far

East was finally within their grasp. The mountains of finished goods streaming continuously out of the factory gates of Illinois, New York and Pennsylvania could now make it to the ports of San Francisco and out to the sea in mere weeks. The factory beasts just needed more "willing" buyers. But in the mid-1800s, Japan wasn't terribly attractive as a market. They remained more or less a feudal society with limited manufacturing capability and few inhabitants with enough money to make trade worthwhile. But they had potential. Even if they might not immediately be the ideal market for America's manufacturing leftovers, Japan could fill in nicely as a strategic port at the gate to the East. Once China was opened, the need for some rest stops to break up the months-long trip became glaringly apparent. Hawaii and the Philippines would unenthusiastically assume that role at the end of the 19th century, but in 1852, the President of the United States (Millard Fillmore) wanted Japan. He called on Commodore Matthew C. Perry to lead a fleet of America's finest ships to encourage Japan to possibly reconsider their stance on international trade.

In 1853, leading a force of four black-hulled ships, Perry arrived at Tokyo Bay and politely asked if he could drop off a letter with the emperor. He was denied. Perry then introduced the Japanese to his 65 cannons, not-so-subtly alluding to the destruction he could hastily rain down on defenseless Edo. He then courteously asked again if he could drop off a letter. This time, the Japanese agreed. Perry delivered the letter which started off "Great and good friend...I am desirous that our two countries should trade with each other, for the benefit both of Japan and the United States" and in case a whaling or fishing vessel should be wrecked "that our unfortunate people should be treated with kindness" and that it would be just lovely if "vessels should be allowed to stop in Japan and supply themselves with coal, provisions, and water." Perry then left Japan, letting the Emperor know he'd be returning in about a year to preferably hear the emperor's favorable reaction. *And...oh by the way...did I already show you the guns on our ships?*

Perry then sailed to Macao, China, picked up a few more ships and returned a year later. During this sojourn, Japan pondered their next move. Resist the Americans and become slaves. There was no way the Japanese could summon a force to rival the American fleet. Japan had purposefully weakened their navy to a few junks able only to make short trips within sight of the islands. But if they acquiesced, gave in and played America's game, not only would the purity of Japanese society be at risk, but who knows which European nation would next come knocking at their bay, parading the latest in military technology, wanting access to Japan's ports. There wasn't really a choice. Japan had seen what had happened to China after the Opium War, and knew the consequences of testing Western weapons. In China, their entire society was left in shambles and no economic decision could be made without consideration of European interests.

These "black ships" symbolically ended the Tokugawa Shogunate. Commodore Perry dropped off his gifts (a miniature train set, a barrel of whiskey, some rifles, a few farm tools and a picture book of American animals), secured the emperor's signature, and headed back triumphant. He would return a hero to the United States, the man who "peacefully" opened up Japan. But in Japan, the devil's ships signaled a wake-up call. Remain feudal and perish. Japan must somehow industrialize. They had to catch up to the West, and they had to do it fast. Europe took almost 400 years to transition from a feudal economy to an industrial economy, surviving revolutions, political and social upheaval, and a horrific initial drop in the standard of living for the common man before the fruits of industrialization finally started kicking in.

But Japan didn't have four centuries. They had four decades.

For industrialization to occur, Japan couldn't just trust the trial and error method employed with inconsistent success in the West. In England, entrepreneurs would invent; they would invest; they would improve transportation, communication and production practices; and then another series of inventions would pop up from the corners of the island, and they'd return to the drawing board and adjust their business models. Japan didn't have time to wait for entrepreneurs to figure out what worked and what didn't. They had no time for setbacks. This revolution wouldn't come from capitalists, the wanna-be industrialists advancing for personal gain. Japan's revolution would come down from above, carefully structured and implemented from a centrally-planned government calling all the shots, ensuring success at any cost.

The first step was reforming the government. The Tokugawa Shogunate had to go. The regional lords (daimyos) initially accepted the treaties with the United States, but because they granted privileged status to the Americans residing in Japan, and because nearly all profits fell back into the hands of the Americans, after fifteen years, the daimyos had endured enough.

The daimyos to the south, who had increasingly gained more independence in the years following America's first contact, combined their forces, and in 1868, fairly easily overthrew the shogunate, restoring the power of the emperor, which at the time rested in the hands of sixteen-year-old Mutsuhito. Mutsuhito would take on the name Meiji – "the Enlightened One" – and as the figurehead to a government of focused and devoted advisors, he would shepherd in an era of massive social, political and economic transformation - the Meiji Restoration.

The Meiji Restoration had two goals – enrich the nation and strengthen the army – and Japan would do whatever it took to achieve these aims. They swallowed their pride and admitted the West's dominance, and unlike their Chinese neighbors to the West, instead of running from this reality, they embraced it, borrowed from it and created a nation able to compete on a level playing field as their pale-skinned, hairy adversaries.

To enrich the nation, Japan had to educate their workforce, improve their ability to create and use technology and transform their method of producing goods. First, they had to figure out the secrets to the West's dominance, so they assembled a contingent of Japan's finest minds and sent them all over the world on a fact-finding mission. The plan was that these 19th century exchange students would enter as guests and then explore every hospital, school, factory, bank, government building, museum and cultural event at their disposal. In 1871, this Iwakura Mission departed Tokyo with dozens of advisors and officials, sixty students and a writer to record every finding. They were then strategically dropped across the globe. If all went as planned, these children would then be raised by Westerners, schooled by Westerners, only to then return to Japan in adulthood where they would one day lead the next generation of industrialization.

But Japan couldn't sit back and wait for these students to come of age. They were running out of time. Across the Yellow Sea, China was falling apart under the weight of foreign domination. Japan would have to swallow their pride and invite back into their most sacred nation the one group they had forever detested – the "hairy barbarians." One by one, the emperor's top advisors pinpointed areas of weakness and then brought in the ideal Western experts to employ their talents. In addition to offering a handsome salary far beyond what the foreigners would have earned in their native countries, the Japanese government also offered these yatoi, or "hired menials," preferential treatment while in-country. They were put up in lavish houses, granted privileged status in business dealings and absolved from having to follow Japanese law. This favored position incensed the traditional Japanese, but they could do nothing about this gross inequity. Japan needed these foreigners. They brought in military experts from Germany, bankers from Switzerland, engineers from England, steel manufacturers from the United States, legal experts from France and artists from Italy. They were costly (oftentimes commanding up to 33% of the annual budget), but they were also temporary. In almost all cases, after three-year terms, they were sent back to their homes. Japan needed their knowledge. Japan didn't need *them*.

Once they had the knowhow, they needed the financing. This was where the government stepped in. The West had such a head start that no individual-created corporation could ever hope to compete with the behemoths from the West. Could a textile manufacturer in Osaka ever expect to make shirts as efficiently and inexpensively as the garment factories streaming out goods from London? Could a steelmaker ever produce at a rate close to what Carnegie's factories spewed out around the clock? Never. Unless these corporations received government assistance. Japan then systematically decided which individuals needed special loans, which corporations needed straight-out government assistance in the form of subsidies and which ones needed to just be government run. By the 1890s, most of the industries in Japan were either directly run or directly supported by the Japanese government. To fund this capital investment and the enormous financial burden of the yatoi, the peasants were taxed mercilessly. Though some moved to the cities and eventually reaped the benefits of industrialization, for the most part, the quality of life for the rice farmers of Japan, the lifeblood of the economy, actually fell during the Meiji Restoration. By 1900, farmers lived shorter, less healthy lives and overall survived a far more dismal existence than did their ancestors centuries earlier. But that was the price the nation had to pay to evolve.

To compete with the Western powers, Japan couldn't continue indefinitely sponsoring Western experts and adapting their inventions. It was a short-term solution to a much larger problem. To continue in this vein meant Japan would always fall one step behind the West, waiting for the technological crumbs to fall off their overseas tables. If they were to sustain long-term growth, their talent must be home-grown, which meant a complete overhaul of the class structure and the education system.

First, the government outlawed feudalism. The day of the daimyo was over. Initially, the emperor's advisors worried the daimyos would resist change, resist the loss of their regional authority and all the associated perks. In what other civilization had a noble class voluntarily given up autonomy? In France? England? The United States? Not a chance. But in Japan, the daimyo realized they would perish if they remained isolated lords instead of formally aligning themselves with the emperor. This choice was made a heck of a lot easier when a few of the most prominent daimyo stepped forward and in a formal ceremony relinquished their authority over their fiefdoms, setting the precedent that the survival of the nation depended on the unchallenged authority of the emperor. The remaining daimyo quickly fell into line. Now, don't be so naïve as to believe these gracious donations were all delivered selflessly. It definitely helped that the emperor decreed the state government would assume all daimyo debts. This unprecedented, bloodless exchange of power meant that by 1871, the wealth and power of the nation all rested in the hands of the imperial court, in the hands of the emperor.

Once the daimyo were removed, the next step was eliminating the samurai. In the two centuries of the Tokugawa Shogunate, the samurai had pretty much become irrelevant leeches, clinging to a heroic history while draining the public's coffers. Their heyday had long since passed, and now they roamed the countryside and the city streets, living off the welfare of the government. They still carried their swords and demanded respect, but their warrior ethos appeared quaint during the Tokugawa Era when violence was essentially eradicated. They'd become soft and worthless, so few were surprised when the Meiji reformers mandated the dissolution of the samurai class. They could no longer carry their swords, they no longer had any more rights than a commoner and they could no longer cut off people's heads if disrespected (many samurai were deeply saddened by the reality that they no longer held universal decapitation rights). Once they lost their funding and their privileges, they had to get jobs. Some joined the military, some joined the industrial workforce and still others returned to school to possibly fill some of the management positions that were surfacing with each new industry. A few tried one last gasp at preserving their honor, but alas, it was too late. The 1877 Satsuma Rebellion (check out Tom Cruise's *The Last*

Samurai for Hollywood's take on this bloody little episode) ended once and for all the samurais as an elite warrior class. The imperial army of conscripts using Western techniques and weapons easily dispatched these relics of the past. The samurai were no more.

With all power in the hands of the emperor and his inner circle, they next set out to influence and mold the minds of the youth. School became compulsory – everyone had to attend. Even before the Meiji Reformation, Japan had some of the highest literacy rates in the world (45% of all men, 15% of all women), but with the reforms, they far surpassed any other Eastern civilization. They studied science and math from books translated from Western texts. But this reliance on all things Western came at a cost. After a few years, the government grew concerned that Japanese values were being supplanted by Western culture. One of the bi-products of encouraging adoption of Western technology was that many Japanese started likewise adopting Western dress, Western food and even the Western trappings of wealth. By the late 1800s, you could walk through the alleys of Tokyo and see Japanese men strolling in full suits, carrying canes and brandishing the latest pocket watch imported from Europe. Women began replacing their kimonos with the elaborately poofy dresses of Victorian England, and families even started eating beef for the first time. Some even partook in ballroom dancing (though even the most ardent Japanese Westophile had to admit this was a pretty ridiculous practice). With each Western adoption, Japan came one step closer to losing its own identity.

In 1878, the emperor saw what was happening to his people and he mandated a return to the Confucian teachings of filial piety and absolute respect for all leaders – especially the emperor. The schools adopted this new edict, and steadily the emperor again became a near-mythical being. Schools adorned their buildings with shrines to the emperor, often showcasing his portrait, scrolls bearing his words or even symbolic tokens of his absolute rule (if lunchboxes existed in Meiji Japan, he probably would have had his face on one of those as well). Each day, Japanese students swore their allegiance to the emperor, believing the highest honor was living and dying in his name. This blind allegiance would prove quite useful in future decades when the government not only needed faithful workers to turn out finished goods, but also impassioned warriors willing to sacrifice at the emperor's request (see World War II).

And year after year, the Meiji reforms proved their worth. The newly adapted agricultural machines and techniques produced a 30% increase in yearly harvests, and the nation's silk production by 1900 made up 1/3 of the world's supply. New industries sprung up as the daimyo started investing their annual government stipends (awarded as a compensation for giving up feudal rights) in potential wealth-generating industries. By the end of the century, Japan made its own railway lines and steam locomotives, produced its own copper and coal for export and shipped textiles across Asia and even back to the West. Yet even as these industries began paying for themselves, the government was still dealing with mounting debt. The cost of industrialization from above exhausted the imperial reserves, and forced the government to look elsewhere for funding.

Enter the zaibatsu. The government chose a select group of families to take over the leading industries. These families - with names such as Nissan, Mitsubishi, Sumitomo and Kawasaki – entered into a scripted alliance with the government where they would provide the initial capital to purchase the company, while the government would ensure subsidies, tax breaks and guaranteed government contracts. Basically, they'd be granted monopolistic control over the major industries of Japan. The government alone no longer had to support industrialization. They shared this responsibility with a few carefully chosen capitalist families. By the start of World War II, fifteen zaibatsu families controlled 80% of the wealth of Japan. Unlike Europe, this was definitely not a revolution led by plucky entrepreneurs from the middling classes. This was a carefully orchestrated creation of wealth and industry from above.

Even with all their advancements, Japan continued to suffer under the unequal treaties instituted by the United States and the other Western states. By 1900, Japan no longer needed the foreign advisors to direct their operations and they certainly didn't need any interference in their commercial trade. The empire first sent the Iwakura Mission to ask for a revision of the treaties. That failed. They then invited the Western countries to conferences in Japan. That failed. They then tried working one on one with nations to hopefully come to some agreement. That too failed. Finally, they thought maybe they could enter some sort of secret agreements with any Western nation who would step up to break this East-West stalemate. But still, the West wouldn't budge.

Time for Plan B. If you can't beat them, join them. If Japan couldn't pull itself out of submission through diplomatic channels, maybe the West would listen a little better if they saw Japan's freshly-created, industrialized military in action. Japan looked west to Korea, a nation that at different times had survived as a vassal state to both China and Japan. Japan didn't want a shared Korea, but it also didn't want an independent Korea. In 1894, when there was some confusion over who would ascend to the throne of Korea, Japan took the opportunity to jump in and claim it. Learning from its own experience with Western imperialists, Japan imposed an unequal treaty on Korea, forcing ports to open and granting extraterritoriality rights to Japanese merchants and diplomats on Korean soil. This displeased China who believed Korea was their puppet, and nobody else's. China then sent in its army, and the Sino-Japanese War was underway. However, weakened by decades of civil war and European oppression, China was no match for the Japanese, losing both at land and at sea, eventually compelled to sign a treaty with Japan that not only ceded territorial influence over Taiwan and Korea, but also imposed a heavy fine on China's already crippled economy.

And for the first time in history, there was a new king of the East. China had been the unquestioned leader of Asia since the first Qin Dynasty, but in just three short decades, they had been replaced. Japan had industrialized. China had refused. Japan sought Western assistance. China resisted the West to the bitter end and it paid the ultimate price. It was only a matter of time before China faded for a few decades into utter chaos.

And for Japan? Their imperialistic desires had only begun to be quenched. Next up – Russia. At the end of the 19th century, Russia too had caught the expansionist bug and wanted to expand deep into Manchuria, a region bordering both the recently acquired Korea and Northern China. Should Russia control this region, they would not only monopolize access to valuable raw materials, but also a direct line to trade with China. This would also place a Western power within striking distance of Japan, a risk the imperial government of Japan could not accept. So in 1904, Japan launched a sneak attack on Russian controlled Port Arthur (if this whole Japanese sneak attack on a naval base doesn't sound familiar, check back in a few chapters when we hit the eve of World War II and you'll see a connection). Tens of thousands of Japanese troops perished (a fact conveniently not mentioned by the Japanese press), but the Russians were caught off guard and eventually forced to retreat. The ensuing Russo-Japanese War, like the conflict with China a decade before, proved the strength of Japan's navy and the resiliency of their conscripted army. Over the next year and a half, close to 200,000 soldiers and civilians died, but the Japanese forces proved an insurmountable foe. Russia surrendered.

Japan had finally arrived. For the first time since the Middle Ages, a non-Western country had defeated a European power. This proved to the Asian community that industrialization and Westernization were not just possibilities, but necessities. In just 35 years, Japan had accomplished what it took the United States and Britain over a century. Japan had become an equal. In 1906, American sociologist Edmund Buckley confirmed that the Japanese had finally become "peers of western peoples." So when the Japanese again requested a revisiting of the unequal treaties, amazingly the British and the Americans acquiesced and removed all of the demeaning components of their previous arrangements.

Japan's remarkable ascent to the brotherhood of industrialized nations wouldn't stop here however. Their next step was a free Asia, an Asia without any European influence whatsoever, a nation beholden to one nation only, an Asia where Japan alone sat at the center of all commerce and foreign relations. It took Japan 35 years to industrialize. In 35 more years they would take their war to the entire West, in what would become the bloodiest war in human history.

But that is for another chapter.

35

Taking Stock of Our Progress

The World at the Turn of the Century – 1880 > 1910

At the dawn of the 20th century, the West was truly the dominant region of the world. The ages of the Muslims, the Indians and the Chinese had passed with each of these once great civilizations forced to bow to the economic whims of European capitalists. All signs pointed to Europe as the preeminent society, able to bend the planet to its will.

Much of this dominance could be attributed to its military firepower. Starting with Napoleon a century earlier, the national budgets of Europe went almost exclusively to the research, the development and the mass production of firearms and the maintenance of massive conscripted armies. Nations spent between 40 and 80% of their entire budgets just on their militaries (compare that to the 5% spent by the US today). Because of this colossal build-up of arms, there wasn't a nation on Earth in 1900 that could come close to rivaling Western force.

But it wasn't just its military that dwarfed the rest of the world's nations. Its industrialized economies spewed out goods at an unprecedented pace. Its banks financed 9/10ths of the global trade. Its steam ships and trains crisscrossed oceans and continents, and its telegraph lines put the world within a few seconds of instant communication.

By any metric, the West was the most technologically advanced society in the history of mankind, but with all of its industrial successes, it still faced monumental challenges from within. Industrialization, global trade networks, bloated bureaucracies and the rising tide of urban population brought to the West all the material successes their nations could imagine, but with them came a laundry list of ailments that would need to be remedied or else risk perennial discord, if not outright revolution.

One by one, the nations of the West adjusted their societies to assuage the fear, pain and frustration that accompanied this newfound prosperity. And the rest of the world took notice of these reforms. This time around, the rest of the world wouldn't ignore the transformations of the West. Their ignorance and overconfidence doomed them a century earlier. They couldn't make the same mistake twice.

In the West, the most alarming threat stemmed from the rapid, intense growth of cities. From 1850 to 1914, Europe's population shot up from 265 million to 468 million, and in America, total population numbers more than quadrupled. And almost all of these people were moving to the cities. Cities offered jobs, housing and a chance at a better life. By 1900, almost 70% of Europe's population lived in cities, and these cities began gobbling up the surrounding towns, forming super-cities connected by mazes of subway and train lines.

But life in these cities was less than enjoyable. The local governments couldn't build tenements or provide basic necessities like sanitation at a pace that could keep up with the swelling populations. Hundreds of thousands of families crammed into poorly ventilated, run-down shacks that lacked the toilets and fresh water necessary to support even a base level of human hygiene. Diseases spread like wildfire and life expectancy levels actually dropped. Going to work meant merely exchanging one nightmare for another. Wages and working conditions were kept at pitifully low levels due to the seemingly endless supply of cheap labor and the average urban laborer worked 16-18 hours a day.

As helpless as their plight appeared, it turned out the urban dwellers' biggest handicap was also their greatest asset – their sheer numbers. If mankind has shown one truth over the millennia, it's that an angry, densely populated, unemployed populace must be appeased. If they unite, they can cause economic disruption, social chaos and they can topple even the most secure regime.

In the 19th and early 20th centuries, workers formed labor unions to lobby for better working conditions, higher salaries and lower hours. Their main threat was always the strike, an across-the-board cessation of labor. If nobody went to work, their bosses would have to concede to their demands. One problem – there was always another starving laborer willing to cross the picket line and accept any job for a pittance. Labor unions realized their opponents weren't merely their employers, but also any recent immigrant not willing to honor the union's tactics. Union members not only yielded picket signs and fiery rhetoric, they also weren't afraid to employ their guns, clubs and their fists to keep would-be workers away from the factories. As their influence swelled, unions forced companies to adjust their policies. But these improvements were inconsistent and oftentimes temporary. For real change to occur, it needed to happen at the national level.

Enter democratic politics. After the 1848 revolutions, the West gradually expanded suffrage so that by the end of the 19th century, almost every nation across Europe granted voting rights to all males. If politicians didn't listen (or at least appear to listen) to the voices of their constituents, their futures in government would have relatively short shelf lives. This was where the labor unions started affecting change. As solid voting blocs willing to throw their support behind a candidate or a political party, the workers of the West exploited this power at the polls. Ineffective or corrupt politicians were increasingly voted out of office. Local governments then chose to spend their revenue on making life more enjoyable for their residents. They built parks, installed electricity, demanded effective police and fire companies and invested significantly in sanitation projects that markedly reduced the spread of waterborne diseases in congested cities (and it markedly reduced the mounds of human excrement on the curbside).

But it was the labor laws that altered human existence. Governments banned child labor and then mandated school attendance. Within a couple generations, a family's future opportunities appeared boundless. Laws established ceilings on the amount of hours an adult could work in a week and enforced wage floors that employers must respect. They funded and trained inspectors to examine factory conditions to ensure the wellbeing of all employees.

The age of social welfare had begun. For generations, governments saw their sovereignty as ordained by the gods, that they could rule by personal whim, that they were beholden to none. Democracy flipped the scales away from the governors to the governed. Power came from the people and it was the people that could retract their support should their leaders ignore their needs. Across the 20th century, Western powers redefined their priorities so that appeasing the masses became of utmost importance. The social contract once only required governments to protect property. The new West required governments to improve everyone's standard of living, so that the years you did walk the earth were free of strife and struggle. By the end of the 20th century, Western laborers worked on average 41 hours per week and in some countries (like Greece, Spain and Italy), you could retire in your mid-50s and receive a full pension. The government would pay you not to work.

And while you weren't working, you increasingly had far more leisure options to fill your days. Up until the 20th century, free time was a luxury for the wealthy. If people socialized at all, it was at church or while working. In 17th century New England, USA, the big highlights of the year were house building parties where neighbors would get together and "raise the roof" on a new home. After a few generations of the Industrial Revolution, city dwellers were so painfully bored by the monotony of their lives that they needed a bit more entertainment than a potluck dinner and a house erection.

The first entertainment choice of the working class was the neighborhood bar. Pubs popped up on every street corner, beer was cheap and a couple pints with some buddies had the amazing ability to deaden the senses and make the futility of life just a tad bit more bearable. Alcoholism hit epidemic levels, destroying families and robbing households of much-needed incomes. Men would pick up their salaries on a Friday and the money would be blown at the bar before they returned home to their starving families. Abuse and then divorce rates escalated, destroying the values and the social norms of the nuclear families. The entitled middle and upper classes watched as the desperate poor regressed into states of squalor, and instead of focusing their attention solely on improving the lot of the masses, they attempted to prevent their consumption of alcohol, not realizing that drunkenness is sometimes more of symptom of misery than a cause. The resulting temperance movements attempted to ban alcohol, at first just on Sunday (the Holy Day), but in some nations (like the United States), it was prohibited on a national level. This prohibition did little to reduce consumption rates, merely driving the production, delivery and purchase underground, creating a black market where rival gangs slaughtered each other over distribution rights.

As upper society tried their hand (and failed) at legislating social behavior, other forms of entertainment developed a mass following. At the turn of the century, spectator sports like boxing, soccer, horse racing and baseball (in the United States) brought together different classes, different races and different faiths under one roof, cheering on their patron sons while jeering the enemy. For those watching punches thrown, shots fired and balls slammed, where you came from was irrelevant. It was "us" against "them" in the sports stadiums of every major metropolitan area. Mix in a little alcohol with some gambling opportunities and sports again proved the perfect recipe for distracting disenchanted denizens of the urban jungle. Like the Romans of old who learned the value of bread and circuses (and maybe some gladiatorial eviscerations thrown in to keep life interesting), the Europeans found there was money to be made and unity to be harvested behind the banner of the local team. As local newspapers exploded and radio connected every household to the day to day feats of a town's native hero, athletes became celebrities and entire generations rallied behind the famed jocks and jockettes of the day. In America, a fairly rotund chap named George Herman "Babe" Ruth grew to be the most recognizable face on the planet, becoming the first athlete to earn more money that his country's head of state. When asked why he deserved to make more money than then president Herbert Hoover, the Babe replied, "I had a better year than" he did.

The celebrity culture wasn't restricted to the rinks, the pitches, the fields and the stadiums of the major cities, the budding film industry produced stars and starlets of the silver screen. Phonographs recorded music on vinyl and then offered them across the country. For the first time, entire nations could all listen to the same music, watch the same films, support the same teams and worship the same personalities. Print news combined with live and recorded entertainment to foster a pop culture that has become a hallmark of Western society. Today, whether you're paying for a carton of milk in Paris, Madrid, New York, London or Berlin, you're bound to pass a magazine rack lined with the latest dirt on your favorite jock, singer, thespian or socialite. A hundred years ago, Western advertisers appreciated the value of pop culture and you can guarantee in another century we'll still be straining our heads to find out the latest on the prepubescent boy band of the week, the female ingénue with a plunging neckline or the naughty athlete who just can't seem to follow the rules of society.

Fortunately for mankind, and womankind, our successes went a little further than grasping the value of a pretty face. The early 20th century saw a radical shift in rights for 51% of the planet. Since the first time man threw seeds in the ground along the major rivers of Eurasia, women have been relegated to the home, restricted to taking care of the kids, keeping the home relatively hygienic and preparing some sort of edible meal from what was left in the cupboard. That was their sphere. And for the next seven thousand years, whether you were living in a hamlet in China or a palace in the Mughal Dynasty or a wooden shack in the American frontier, the rules were the same – men ruled the world and women took care of the home.

But the Industrial Revolution challenged these gender roles. Who made the money, who took care of the kids, who took care of the house – all these responsibilities became a bit murky when families moved to swarming slums, and mom and kids often found they could find more work than could dear ol' dad. In most families, men preserved their patriarchal power, forcing women to continue to fulfill their domestic obligations after earning a paycheck during the daylight hours. This little arrangement was never going to last, and women gradually began demanding more rights – first in the house, but then in the larger society. First, at the turn of the century, the only women truly able to demand more freedoms were the upper and middle class women who were educated, but unemployable. They had the free time, the powerful connections and the brains to exact change. They pushed for temperance laws that would outlaw alcohol, reasonable divorce and inheritance laws that could allow a spouseless-woman to survive, access to contraception that would allow women more control over their bodies, but most importantly, they pressed for the right to vote. These middle and upper class suffragettes petitioned, marched, lobbied, rallied and even died for the right to vote. One radical (or dedicated) proponent of women's rights, a Miss Emily Davison, even jumped in front of King George V's horse during a 1913 derby. The horse trampled and killed her, but her story spread and the tireless five-decade-long struggle for the female vote slowly started to pay off. Finland was the first to grant women the right to vote and when the United States finally ratified the 19th Amendment in 1920, almost every Western nation had embraced true universal suffrage. Many were still wary what women at the ballot box would mean for republican governments, but this crucial step paved the way for epic breakthroughs in gender equality in the workplace, the political sphere and even the bedroom.

Change was coming at a faster rate than ever before thought possible. A man born in 1850 would have more in common with a man born in 1200 than he would with a man born in 1900. The home, the workplace and the public sphere looked nothing like they did before the Industrial Revolution. Civil authorities and local leaders tried to keep up with the times, but the pace of migration and the dissemination of information made their task almost always a losing battle.

For some, the social changes weren't happening fast enough. For some, they demanded an outright toppling of the political and industrial leaders of the West, a situation where the workers of the world would unite and seize the resources of production and government. For others, these social changes meant the urban population was becoming increasingly easier to manipulate. If you could convince an entire city to chant for their beloved athlete, cry for their country's most-cherished performer and die for their social welfare, could you not also convince them to live and die for their nation?

Could you not also convince them to partake in a clash of civilizations, where the winning nation would determine the future of humanity?

Was that possible? Could the attributes that empowered the West to progress so far as a civilization actually be used to blow itself up?

Yep. They could. And they did. Twice.

But that is for another chapter.

36

The War to End All Wars

World War I – 1900 > 1920

At the turn of the 20ᵗʰ century, the West was feeling pretty good about itself. It was on an unprecedented winning streak. In the span of five centuries, except for a few little bumps in the road, it appeared to be perpetually moving forward, with no one able to stop its progress. Nation after nation fell to its advances, so that by 1914, 80% of the world's economy fell under the domain of one of the Western nations and over 60% of the planet was controlled by a Western power. Their industrial production was unparalleled and their military might was unquestioned. With each passing decade, more and more people entered the democratic process, creating governments and worlds in their own image. As food production exploded, living standards improved and the medical industry found more and more ways to keep us from dying, life expectancy rates soared. Free time and entertainment were no longer solely the birthright of a privileged few, as new forms of leisure became accessible to all segments of society. We lived longer, healthier, more enjoyable lives and it appeared nothing could stop the West's continued ascension.

And then Europe blew itself up.

It wasn't enough that the West conquered the rest of the world, they then proceeded to turn their sights on each other, and it was this cannibalistic clash of civilization which forced the West to reevaluate their preconceived notions of superiority. Maybe their way wasn't the best way. Maybe their way actually could lead to the destruction of all humanity.

World War I signaled the end of an era. It was at the time known as "the Great War" or the "war to end all wars," but it would not be either. A greater war would follow within a couple decades, and, if anything, it became the war to start all wars, for the 20th century ended with the infamous claim to being the bloodiest century in human history.

But how did it all begin?

Well, there was no singular cause. Each nation had a different reason for joining; each nation sold its people on a different motivation to embrace the war effort. England was afraid Germany's growing industrial economy would throw a kink in their global empire. Russia wanted a warm water port so they could readily bring supplies to their interior. Bosnia wanted to be free. Austria-Hungary didn't want to let them. France wanted a chunk of land back that they'd lost a few decades earlier. Japan had their eyes on northern China. Italy didn't know whose side it was on, but it liked the idea of making itself bigger. Argentina wanted to sell more beef. And the list goes on and on and on.

Each country grappled with a series of regional, ethnic, national and imperial questions, each threatening to injure their progress if not handled properly, but each promising to advance its status if approached prudently. Though the specifics might have differed, they each fell into one of a few types of tensions that pitted nation versus nation and people versus people. Each tension was the natural manifestation of European policies that directly led to their ability to achieve so much economic and geopolitical success in the previous century. In 1914, these tensions threatened to unravel all that had been achieved.

First, there was the issue of self-determination. Individual peoples wanted to determine their future. In the great land grab that was European imperialism, slews of diverse groups were thrown together in a mish-mash of empires. Regardless of language, religion, culture or historical background, added territories were expected to merely accept their fate and somehow unite under the nationalistic banner of their newfound mother country. Easier said than done. Oftentimes in the great boundary-making schemes of the European powers, they overlooked regional hostilities and desires, putting together groups still healing from centuries of violence, or conversely dividing groups across arbitrarily chosen boundary lines. By 1914, instilled with the ideals of the Enlightenment and inspired by the triumphs of the American and French revolutions, these peoples sought to break free from the empirical hold, setting their own paths toward nationhood. Their imperial lords were less than enthusiastic.

But there was no way a European empire was going to let a minority ethnic group break away. Think of the precedent this would set? Look at the Austrian Empire of 1914. It was made up of Gypsies, Germans, Hungarians, Slovaks, Croats, Italians, Romanians, Czechs, Serbs, Slovenes, Ukrainians, Poles and Arabs. If just one of these groups was granted independence, the rest of the dominos would soon fall, and Austria would be left a skeleton of its former glory. So at the immediate moment these peoples wanted their freedom, their imperial lords had no intention of granting any concessions. But this wasn't just true for Austria. All of Europe had expanded its colonial holdings, and inevitably the conquered wanted to break free from their conquerors.

Which leads to the next issue – imperialism. The European desire to conquer and maintain worldwide territories hit a snag in the early 20th century. All the good land had been passed out. Germany and Italy, the two new kids on the block, wanted their own territories to harvest resources, sell surplus goods and enlist cheap labor. But what was left? In Africa, there was Liberia and Ethiopia. In Asia, there was merely a spattering of hospitable lands still remaining (aside from Japan of course who no one wanted to touch after they so readily dispatched the Russians). Though late to the industrializing party, Germany and Italy still demanded the requisite features of capitalist economies – ready access to foreign markets – which put them directly in conflict with those established powers none-to-thrilled about losing their claims to a rival upstart. And Germany was intimidating. Its investment in research and access to huge deposits of iron ore meant that by 1900 only the United States produced more steel than Germany. Steel meant railroads, steel meant factories, and most worrisome to England, steel meant navies. England had the greatest force on the seas. They were in no mood to deal with any rivals to their throne.

In the first two decades of the 20th century, any threat to one nation's military had to be challenged. England might have had the largest navy, but Germany had the greatest military training. Russia had access to the most soldiers. France had the

Napoleon-spawned superior military tradition. Each of these big four possessed one element of military aptitude that scared the bejeezus out of its neighbors, but each also had a weakness. England's land army was negligible, Germany could be attacked from all sides, Russia was painfully backwards in providing arms and transportation for its troops, and France's military tradition was more impressive in the history books than on the most recent battlefield. To make up for these weaknesses, the European powers started off in an arms race, a quest to see who could build the baddest, most-feared, most destructive military machine imaginable, one so great that no one would ever dare declare war. This belief that advanced weaponry and huge armies could prevent warfare was known as militarism, and it was this homage to armaments that pushed the countries closer to war. Every technological advancement, every increase to the quantity of mobilized soldiers, every military parade made it harder for any real nation to back down. Like the bodybuilder donning a too-snug Under Armour T-shirt who wears a bullseye on his chest the moment he enters a pub, the nations who stockpiled weapons became targets for those other nations wanting to prove their metal.

Unfortunately, this military build-up that was supposedly to prevent war actually created a false sense of superiority that eventually made war seem like a not-so-bad proposition. The standing belief was that because of the extreme cost to produce the weapons and because of these weapons' perceived invincibility, any actual combat would be extremely short-lived. They seemed to ignore the horrific example of the American Civil War that left 600,000 dead in the first of the industrialized wars. They instead merely looked at the Franco-Prussian War of 1870, where France was defeated in a mere weeks. After four decades and a mountain of industrial improvements, wouldn't the next European standoff prove even shorter?

Umm. No. Not exactly. Added to this false sense of military superiority was an added sense of cultural supremacy. In the age of high literacy rates, uniform compulsory education, densely populated cities and the new visual media known as cinema, governments could spew a mountain of propaganda intended to heighten their citizens' love for country. From an early age, children were taught to revere their culture, while condemning that of their neighbors. Germany was home to the masters of sound - Bach, Beethoven and Brahms. England held the masters of the pen - Chaucer, Shakespeare and Locke. France enlightened the West with Rousseau, Montesquieu and Voltaire. Italy brought color to the world with da Vinci, Michelangelo and Raphael. Each nation could claim to be the pillar of the West's development and each likewise believed their government, their economic system and their society surpassed all others. If only they could find a way to decide once and for all who was the best.

They had tried for decades to prove their superiority by expanding their colonial holdings. Their economic and political spheres of influence spread all across the globe. By 1900, there was pretty much nothing left. All of Africa save Liberia and Ethiopia were under European control. All of Asia but Siam (Thailand), Nepal, Bhutan and a few nations in Central Asia answered to the West. Most of the conflicts for sovereignty had been settled in the mid-19th century, but now with Germany and Italy wanting to get in on the colonial action, something had to give. Germany's first target was Morocco (controlled by Spain), and after battles in 1906 and 1911, Germany proved it had only just begun. By 1914, they had moved into East and West Africa, as well as establishing Pacific holdings in New Guinea and Samoa. With no signs of letting up, and with their industrialized economy threatening to eclipse England within a few years, it wouldn't be long before other European colonies felt the weight of the German Empire.

By 1914, the sources of tension were clear. All Europe needed was a fuse to light the fire. That fuse would start in a region that would become known to historians as the powder keg of Europe – the Balkan states. Located just north of Greece and just a bit east of Turkey, the Balkan states were a cornucopia of cultures all vying for independence. For centuries, provinces like Thessaly, Macedonia, Albania, Moldavia, Bulgaria, Serbia and Bosnia all pushed to free themselves from the rule of the Ottoman Empire. At the turn of the century, the Ottoman Empire was on its last legs, unable to control its territories on the periphery, mocked by the West as the "sick man of Europe." By the early 1900s, many of these Balkan states freed themselves from the grasp of the Ottoman Turks. For little Bosnia, freedom from imperial rule was fleeting. In 1908, they were again gobbled up by a voracious empire, but this time it was the adjoining Austro-Hungarian Empire. Austria-Hungary was already a hodgepodge of peoples, barely held together by Franz Joseph who had ruled over this fading empire for over fifty years. Bosnia joined an empire that also tried to unite Germans, Hungarians, Czechs, Slovaks,

Poles, Ukrainians, Slovenes, Serbians, Croats, Romanians and Italians. Many of these peoples had no interest in being ruled by the Austro-Hungarian monarchy, instead preferring to rejoin their brothers in neighboring nations. Remarkably, the Serbians in Bosnia wanted to rejoin this little place called Serbia.

In 1914, Franz Joseph sent his son Franz Ferdinand down to Bosnia to smooth things over with the local Serbians. Franz Ferdinand wanted to reassure these independent-minded Serbians that when his father eventually died and he took the throne, Bosnia would be granted more rights of self-government. Franz Ferdinand was a naïve heir to the throne, believing his appearance alone might calm the Serbian revolutionary movement. But he didn't account for one group – the Black Hand - a terrorist band of young men focused solely on independence for their country, by any means available. When Franz Ferdinand arrived in Bosnia on June 28, 1914, the streets were already lined with assassins carrying knives, guns and even homemade grenades. As the royal prince and his wife made their way down the spectator-lined streets, one member of the Black Hand darted out from the crowd and threw a grenade at the royal car. It merely bounced off the trunk of the Archduke's vehicle, exploding into the rear car following close behind. At this point, Franz Ferdinand's entourage raced away and finished his official duties with regional political figures, before heading back to his car. He wanted to go to the hospital, to hopefully visit the members of his court who had nearly had their heads blown off a few hours earlier. Unfortunately, the chauffer made a wrong turn, probably the most tragic navigational error in the history of driving, for this dead end wound up starting World War I.

Here's where things speed up, so pay close attention. 19-year-old Black Hand terrorist Gavrilo Princip recognized the royal family, took out his gun and shot Franz Ferdinand and his wife Sophie, killing them both. Franz Joseph wanted revenge. No one got to kill his son and get away with it. But who was he to blame? It must have been Serbia that trained these Black Hand terrorists. So Franz Joseph put in place plans to invade Serbia. Serbia called on their big brother Russia to defend them. Austria-Hungary called on Germany's protection. Germany declared war on Russia. Knowing Russia's ally France would soon join in from the West, Germany pre-emptively declared war on France. Germany invaded neutral Belgium, trying to sweep around the north of France and into Paris. Britain came to Belgium's aid and declared war on

Germany. Austria-Hungary then declared war on Russia. Britain's ally Japan then jumped in from across the world and declared war on Germany. And within six weeks of the assassination of Franz Ferdinand, the world was at war.

Many falsely believed the war would be over in a few months. Boys kissed their moms and girlfriends goodbye, hoping to jump into the festivities before it was too late. Teachers, politicians, priests and generals all thought the war would be over by Christmas. No one wanted to be left out of this great adventure.

But then reality set in. This tragedy would not be like any other war in European history. This wouldn't be a series of pitched battles where men could return with stories of glory and victory.

Germany invaded Belgium, hoping to catch France off guard so they could quickly knock out Paris before Russia could mobilize their troops in the East. Russia might have had millions of possible soldiers, but it was still a backwards nation. Germany couldn't imagine a scenario where the antiquated Russian infrastructure could quickly transport their armies to the front line. This brilliant idea to take out France first and then race across the German heartland to take out Russia was known as the Von Shlieffen Plan, and it would fail. After Franz Ferdinand was shot, Russia almost immediately began mobilizing its troops, so when Germany ultimately headed west into France, Russia could actually start invading Germany's eastern border. This messed up the Schlieffen Plan. The German general sent 180,000 troops back across Germany to protect against the Russian invasion. At the same time, the Belgians proved a pesky foe. Germany expected to just march right through the Belgian countryside, but the locals fought back heroically, and the British soon joined in to slow the German invasion even more. Germany eventually did make it into France, pulling to within 60 miles of Paris. They were met by a pretty formidable French force, brought in large part to the front line by the 2000 Parisian taxi cabs who transported troops to the battlefield.

Paris wasn't taken. The German forces were stopped. They then dug deep into the ground, set up trenches in the French countryside and refused to budge. This was where the rest of World War I would take place. Stretching 600 miles from the northern coast of Belgium to the Swiss border, the French and German forces set up a zigzagging network of trenches, and from 1914 to 1918 the conflict degenerated into a muddy, bloody, lethal brawl where millions perished trying to claim a few miles of charred dirt. This stalemate became the Western Front. A similar patchwork of trenches emerged on the Eastern Front as Russian forces squared off against German, Austro-Hungarian and eventual Turkish forces.

For the soldiers dropped into these war zones, the fighting was anything but the romanticized adventure they sought months earlier. There was no place for glory, no place for heroic missions. In the age of Industrialized Warfare, millions of troops could be brought to the front in a few days, armed with the latest weapons, rifles and machine guns that rarely needed to be reloaded. Enthusiastic zeal and bravery meant something on the battlefield before industrialization. But these admirable traits meant nothing when a soldier faced a machine gun shooting close to 600 bullets a minute. The enemy could merely set up the machine gun, point it at waist level, and swivel the gun back and forth, mowing down thousands of troops like a hot knife slicing through butter.

Even though the weapons had changed, the strategies of the officers remained stuck in the Napoleonic Era. Time and time again, officers sitting miles away from the Front, would telegraph in orders. First, they would send a volley of artillery shells hoping to destroy some of the machine guns or bombard the trench-hidden enemy into submission. After a barrage of shells came down around the enemy, the men were then ordered to go "over the top," emerging from their trench to make the deadly trip across no-man's land, weaving between dead and mutilated bodies, mud-filled shell craters and endless miles of barbed wire. Inevitably, they would be forced to return to their trench, leaving another batch of comrades to suffer intolerably on the barren landscape. This cycle of bombardment, attack and retreat became the modus operandi for the first few years of the war, and it would take millions of casualties before officers and scientific advancements moved warfare into the next phase of military conflict.

At each phase of the war, it was not only the bullets and the shells that kept the men perpetually on edge. Trench rats that grew to the size of cats were a constant menace, stealing any remnants of food left unprotected and even sometimes burrowing into the eye sockets of fallen soldiers where they would nest for weeks until eventually the corpse collapsed from within. Lice filled every bodily crevice and clothing seam, only being extracted with doses of melted candle wax on all inflicted areas. Food rations were scarce at best, with many soldiers surviving on less than 1400 calories a day (an average adult male needs about 2500 calories a day). The lack of fresh water and hit and miss hygiene meant that water-borne diseases like dysentery spread across the fronts, leaving men incapacitated, doubled over in constant pain. Latrines filled with human excrement, and when the trenches flooded from the relentless rains, men would walk for weeks in waist-high pools of fecal matter. Feet that could never dry could swell to three times the normal size of a human foot, oftentimes needing to be amputated to prevent the spread of infection.

And those whose bodies didn't succumb to the appalling conditions, often lost their minds. The unremitting shell fire destroyed the minds of the soldiers, leaving them in a seizure-filled daze known as shell shock. Some even resorted to shooting off their own extremities to hopefully earn the golden ticket back to civilization. For those soldiers who had lost all hope, they could merely lift their heads above the sandbagged trench walls, making themselves the perfect targets for enemy snipers concealed amongst the carnage of no man's land.

Over the course of the war, nearly 6,000 men died every single day. Gradually, governments and officers employed a variety of techniques to try and break through the enemy's defenses. Chlorine, phosgene and mustard gas canisters were shot across the battlefield, frequently with unexpected results. In late 1915, a British force launched a gas attack against German forces, only to have the wind change, bringing the fumes back to the friendly side killing or injuring dozens of men. When the gas attacks did work, men fell to the ground stricken with what would be a long, painful death as their eyes burned and their lungs gradually closed, causing death by asphyxiation. Until gas masks were readily deployed, many soldiers found that the best way to fend off the deadly effects of chlorine gas was to urinate in a cloth and then hold it over their mouth and nose with hope that the ammonia would counteract the chlorine. Aside from the inconsistently effective gas attacks, both sides experimented with tanks to carry men across no man's land; tunneling to plant explosive devices under enemy trenches; and even airplanes to be used for reconnaissance and later air raids. In the skies, the Germans also used helium-filled zeppelins (like our modern day blimps) to record enemy troop movements or even drop explosives on city centers.

The leaders soon realized the war would not be won on the battlefield, but back home in the cities and towns where civilian morale would determine the fate of the nation. In a war where civilian labor was crucial to supplying military forces, any lapse in productivity meant soldiers went to the battlefield unable to properly serve their country. Both sides resorted to blockading the seas, destroying all ships intending to feed, clothe or resupply enemy civilians. If they couldn't beat them, they'd starve them. Britain's navy stretched across the North Sea, effectively cutting off Germany from the world. Germany, in turn, went beneath the surface with its unterseeboots (U-boats). These submarines wreaked havoc on trans-Atlantic shipping, sinking over ten million tons of supplies meant for the allies.

World War I also dramatically altered the lives of the millions not enduring the horrors of the front. This was a total war – a war where victory would be secured only if the entire nation contributed to the war effort. In the age of industrialized warfare, the efficiency and capacity of domestic industries can have as much impact on battlefield success as the training and wherewithal of soldiers. From Berlin to London to Chicago, factories spun at full capacity 24 hours a day, churning out food, clothing, medical supplies and armaments faster than ever before. For the nations at war, the men on the front left a huge void back home. And who would step up to fill this void?

This labor vacuum was then filled by women, minorities and farmers leaving their lives in the country for the promise of work in the cities. For women and minorities, this meant an opportunity to prove their ability to contribute to society on par with the white males who previously dominated all levels of industrial life. In America, women were even able to lobby this newfound clout into the passage of suffrage and prohibition laws that granted them the right to vote and outlawed alcohol. Though in the years following the war, life for many reverted back to the stratified roles that defined industrialization, World War I demonstrated the extent to which civil liberties can be expanded for disenfranchised minorities during wartime.

However, for the most part, civil liberties were ignored during WWI. When at war, there is only one goal – victory. The democratic and capitalistic ideals that might have proved the foundations of a civilization during peacetime became nonessential nuisances during war. Governments chose to suspend or even ignore the rights guaranteeing freedom of speech, freedom of press and even habeas corpus (the belief that people can't be arrested without a trial). Contributing to the war effort did not merely mean producing goods, it had to reconsider how they would handle public displays that contradicted the nation's higher goal. Labor union strikes were banned, newspapers carefully chose which information was eventually published, critics who spoke out against the war were jailed and even war letters were censored to ensure morale at across society remained high. Nations who didn't actively repress anti-war sentiment often saw hostilities rise to perilous levels.

During the first few years of the war, the Russian women's cries for bread and peace went unanswered, eventually leading to the 1917 revolutions that ended imperial rule and pulled Russia out of the conflict. By 1917, Germany likewise witnessed growing pacifist sentiment, a condition which similarly contributed to Germany's eventual decision to surrender. Unlike in the age of absolute monarchies where the people's voice could merely be dismissed, the lessons of the French Revolution and the empowerment of the urban masses scared governments. If the civilians back home could not be controlled, the domestic impact could prove more dire than that on the front.

Governments also then played an even larger role in steering their economies. The goal of profit was replaced with the goal of victory. Government-run war industry boards coordinated how natural resources were attained, who would receive the major production contracts, what goods were deemed necessary and even which goods could no longer be purchased. By the end of the war, the British government accounted for nearly 80% of all imports, leaving businesses at the mercy of governmental demands. Also, because both Germany and Britain engaged in unrestricted naval war on all supply ships heading across the Atlantic, countries began rationing foods, hoping to ensure the supply of civilian necessities. Some like the United States even ordered Meatless Mondays or Wheatless Wednesdays to reduce civilian consumption.

For those who played this new economic game, life wasn't all that bad. Huge government contracts meant profits for a few well-positioned entrepreneurs. Yet individual salaries also grew, and with nothing of interest to buy during the war, savings accounts actually strengthened. Countries not directly in the war also benefited as they became suppliers to war-torn Europe. Argentinian beef became famous during World War I (known as "bully beef"), establishing the cattle ranches of Argentina as the dominant suppliers to the world for the rest of the 20th century. For the United States, who sold to both sides of the war during the first year, profits skyrocketed in a number of industries.

Compared to pre-war numbers, US Steel jumped from annual profits of $105 million to $240 million, Utah Copper went from $5 million to $21 million, and the Central Leather Company saw their profits soar over 1100%. War wasn't hell for everyone.

But how would the government pay for this massive consumption of military goods? Governments started getting creative. Some started expanding taxation to include personal salaries. Other countries raised money by selling war bonds. Instead of investing in a company, individuals and firms invested in their country. Most of the return rates were in the 5-6% range. This was a pretty stable investment option during difficult times, a great way for the government to raise money quickly (Germany raised close to 100 billion deutschmarks), and it also had the fortunate side effect of increasing the population's support for the war. When you believe your money is riding on the success of your country, you're going to be far more helpful in ensuring your country wins.

And if all else failed? What if taxes and war bonds proved unable to keep up with the massive cost of maintaining the war (close to $185 billion in 1914 US currency...or about $4.2 trillion in today's currency)? What then? Well, governments then resorted to the easiest, though not so fiscally sound, way of paying bills. Just print more money. Countries started printing and circulating more and more dollars, deutschmarks, lira, drachmas and pounds. This allowed them to find the money to pay their bills, but it also caused the price of all other goods went up as well. This inflation meant that even though workers were making and saving more money, their money wasn't going nearly as far as it used to.

By 1917, for all countries involved (save maybe the United States), the war had gone on long enough. Crippling inflation, mounting casualty lists and insecure governments forced military leaders to seek some miracle offensive that could bring this slaughter to an end. Attempts had already been made to try to break through the deadlock, but each one failed to shift the advantage conclusively to any one side. The alliances were just too evenly matched. The British tried setting up a third front in Turkey that would open up a southern water port to Russia, allowing supplies to flow freely to the Eastern Front. In early 1915, Britain called on its allies from Australia and New Zealand to launch a seaborne invasion of the Turkish coast of the Ottoman Empire. This campaign, known as Gallipoli, was doomed from the start, as Turkish forces had prepared for the onslaught, setting up impenetrable trenches along the coast. The Turks survived the bombardment and the relentless attacks from ANZAC (Australian and New Zealand Army Corps) forces, eventually forcing the Allies to surrender.

On the Western Front, generals still tried to devise plans for one decisive plan that would end the war. Raised on the military victories of Alexander at Gaugemela or Caesar in Gaul or Napoleon at Austerlitz, the military high commands believed they too could break through, if they could just concentrate all of their military might on one critical spot. The Germans struck first when they attacked the small French town of Verdun, strategically a fairly useless little village, but symbolically a critical defensive fortress for centuries. Started in February 1916, Verdun would become the costliest, longest battle in world history. For a mere ten square kilometers of land, both sides staked their entire reputations. The Germans dropped 23 million shells on the French forces, but the French would not budge. General Robert Nivelle, channeling his inner *Lord of the Rings* Gandalf, declared that no matter how much firepower the Germans brought, "They shall not pass!" This unyielding resilience, coupled with Germany's desperate need to breach the French line led to unprecedented casualties. Within a few months, the Battle of Verdun took 700,000 lives, making it the bloodiest battle ever.

Until the Battle of the Somme. Learning little from the futility of Verdun, the French and British forces launched their own offensive, the hopeful battle to end the war. Like in Verdun, the French and British ceaselessly bombarded their enemy's trenches, hoping to somehow destroy both their machine guns' capabilities and their enemy's will to fight. Yet even though the bombings were so deafening that the explosions could be heard nearly 300 miles away in London, the German forces remained resolute. When the French and British soldiers finally went over the top, crossing what they thought would be their final no man's land, they were met by an even more determined German force. The Allies even sent in their cavalry, falsely believing this charge would carry the day. But as the Germans responded with tanks, machine guns and their own artillery, the Somme battlefield became the latest example of how military strategy had failed to account for technological advancements – with appallingly tragic results.

Earlier in the year, Verdun took 700,000 lives. The Somme offensive claimed 1.2 million. And still the war waged on.

In 1917, in an attempt to gain the upper hand and hopefully only have to deal with a one front war, the Germans dug a bit deeper into their bag of tricks. In Russia, during the final weeks of February 1917, mounting food and labor strikes in Petrograd, coupled with the army's refusal to put down the unrest from the starving classes, forced Czar Nicholas II to abdicate his throne, plunging the nation into a period of uncertainty. If only Germany could find a way of nudging this period of uncertainty into one of all-out anarchy, maybe Russia could then be convinced to pull out of the war, leaving Germany free to concentrate all of its troops on the Western Front. Hmm. What to do? What to do? If only there was a man who could be trusted to further weaken Russia's stability. But where could they find a man who had dedicated his life to destroying the economic and political foundations of Russian society? Did a man such as this exist in 1917?

Yes he did, and his name was Vladimir Lenin, and he had made his temporary home in Switzerland. Lenin had been politely asked to leave (aka "exiled") after his brother had been tried and hung for the attempted assassination of the czar, and Lenin proved time and again he was more than willing to accept the torch of revolution. A staunch follower of Marxism, Lenin watched Russia's February Revolution with heightened interest, knowing that if he could only somehow get back into the country, the nation would be ripe for a communist coup.

Little did Lenin know that Germany happened to be in the market for just a disease to help contaminate Russia's feeble power structure. Members of the German high command, specifically state secretary Arthur Zimmerman (remember this name for a few minutes) communicated their desire to transport Lenin to Russia, and in April 1917, Lenin (along with 32 other revolutionaries and two million German-donated rubles to set up the propaganda newspaper *Pravda*) boarded a one-car train that was promptly locked up and sent across the German countryside. When this sealed train finally reached Petrograd, Lenin again took the reins of the communist Bolshevik party, and within six months his 50,000 followers took over the government, installing a communist regime. Running on a campaign of "bread and peace," the Bolshevik Party quickly delivered on their promise to pull Russia out of the war. They agreed in March 1918 to the crippling Treaty of Brest Litovsk that turned over to Germany control of the Ukraine, Lithuania, Estonia, Latvia and Finland. In one broad swoop, Russia lost a quarter of its population, a vast chunk of its western Russian empire and nearly a quarter of its industrial capacity. But the Russian people got what they wanted. Russia was out of the war.

For Germany, it became a race. Could they transport their eastern armies to the Western Front and conquer Paris before the Americans (finally) arrived? A year earlier, on February 3, 1917, US President Woodrow Wilson asked for and received a formal declaration of war against Germany. This announcement was years in the making. From the start of the war, Britain had been waging a massive propaganda campaign to encourage the Americans to enter on the side of the Allies, and once the German high command endorsed a policy of unrestricted submarine warfare on all Ally-bound supply ships, the United States moved closer to officially renouncing relations with Germany. The final straw came when a secret message from Germany's state secretary Arthur Zimmerman (yep, same guy as earlier) was intercepted by British agents. This note promised its intended recipient, Mexico, the territories of Texas, Arizona and New Mexico if they agreed to enter the war on the side of Germany's side. Britain was none too hesitant to share this useful tidbit of information with U.S authorities, and the US was rightfully displeased knowing their neighbors to the south might have ambitions to take back the Southwest. The US declared war on Germany and the mobilization process began. Could the American troops be assembled, trained and then shipped off to the Western Front before the German reinforcements from the east arrived?

Germany got there first. They made one final offensive burst through the Allied lines, making it to within 37 miles of Paris. But this was not enough. By June of 1918, nearly 250,000 US troops entered Allied trenches, and at this point, the German military leaders admitted to the government back home that they could not win the war. Right around the time this admission came to light, Germany was facing a domestic crisis of its own. The four-year blockade of its ports meant food supplies were in high demand and inflationary prices were leaving millions hungry and pushing for concessions. Some even ironically started suggesting communism might be a solution to their current plight (bet the Germans didn't see their little Lenin-sealed-train scheme coming back so soon to kick them in the tuchus). Trying to avoid a messy political revolution, German Kaiser Wilhelm II took a page from his cousin Czar Nicholas II and abdicated his throne. However unlike his cousin who remained in Russia (only to be murdered along with his family), Wilhelm retired to Holland where he lived until 1941. Germany was turned over to the newly-formed Weimar Republic, who, in a bid to stave off a bubbling revolution while simultaneously saving their armed forces from continuing to fight an unwinnable war, surrendered to the Allied forces. So even though the German military was still in France and many falsely still believed it was Germany that was actually on the verge of winning, on November 11, 1918, at 11:11 in the morning, the final gun sounded and all was quiet on the Western Front.

The Great War was over. Total cost in lives – ten million killed on the battlefield. Another twenty million were blinded, maimed or severely injured. These men were Europe's finest, and within four years an entire generation had been wiped out. This would be Europe's lost generation. In the two years after the war another twenty million died of the Spanish Flu when the soldiers from the trenches returned back home and shared their lovely germs with their families and friends. In India alone, more were killed from the Spanish flu than all their battlefield injuries combined.

Every continent had sent men to fight (no, Antarctica didn't send anyone...you're a clever one you are), and every continent saw their economies or their societies impacted in some way. Europe's 19th century imperialism meant that Europe's 20th century conflicts would engross the entire world. World War I marked a turning point in the relative power structure of the planet's civilizations. The European West had imploded and needed time to rebuild. The United States would from there assume the role as the preeminent Western power. The Arab world freed itself from Ottoman control, but their fate would take decades to unfold. Europe's Asia holdings saw a crack in Western hegemony, and many started to dream of and even implement their own journeys toward independence. But before any of the world could move forward, the Allied powers had to first iron out the peace terms for all parties involved. They headed to France, to the Palace of Versailles. The building that was once the symbol of the age of unchallenged monarchies would become the site of the Paris Peace Conference and the creation of the document that would go down in history as the "peace to end all peace."

The Paris Peace Conference began in January of 1919. Delegates from 27 nations arrived, each hoping to have a role in crafting the peace that would lead to a more equal world. Almost more notable than the 27 nations present (countries that ranged from victorious France, Britain and the United States, to Allied supporters like Haiti, Siam, Uruguay and Belgium) were those who weren't. Germany, Austria-Hungary and the Ottoman Empire were denied a seat at the table because they were, of course, the losers. Russia played no role because they had already pulled out a year earlier (though the lands they awarded to Germany would be fair game when it came to dividing up the fruits of victory). At first, the five major players – France, Britain, the United States, Italy and Japan – met to generate the terms of agreement. This large assembly proved unmanageable, so the Japanese were asked to leave (a treatment they would remember in the ensuing decades). Soon after, Italy was likewise excluded from the meetings of the major powers. This left the "Big Three" to essentially create the terms for Germany's surrender.

The leaders of these Big Three – Georges Clemenceau of France, David Lloyd George of Britain and Woodrow Wilson of the United States – not only brought their nation's needs to the table, but also their own personal ideologies for a post-war world. As the nation that bore the brunt of the conflict, both in the total number of casualties and as the main battlefield through the duration of the war, France wanted revenge. They suffered at the hands of the Germans in the 1870 Franco-Prussian War, and after World War I, Clemenceau (the Tiger) and his contingency needed to know a conquered Germany could not again rise to threaten their homeland. David Lloyd George likewise shared in the suffering of the French, however British interests also considered how to punish Germany in a way that would impede the spread of communism across the war-torn European frontier. From across the Atlantic and a late arrival to the war, Woodrow Wilson brought his idealistic personality and his dreams of a world where all nations met repeatedly to discuss and settle all international issues. Wilson was far less willing to punish Germany, more inclined to bring all nations to the table as equal partners.

So at the table was the French Tiger wanting revenge, the American idealist wanting international harmony and the British moderate straddling both sides of the fence. No one was going to get their way, but what resulted was a combination of both extremes, which in essence doomed the treaty from the start. The terms of the treaty dealt first with what to do with Germany. To Wilson's displeasure, Germany was shattered. In the "war guilt clause," Germany was forced to accept sole responsibility for starting the war (which is odd because they remembered something about Austria and a Black Hand back in 1914). Subsequently, Germany then had to pay reparations for the entire war – all weapons, ammunition, clothing, food, soldier salaries...for both sides. Although later many of these reparations (eventually fixed in 1921 at $31.4 billion) would either be forgiven or paid off by foreign loans, the scope of the reparations was overwhelming, especially considering Germany's primary ability to repay the debt was taken away. For fifteen years, they surrendered a region known as the Rhineland to the French, an industrial center producing a large chunk of Germany's economic output. To make matters worse, Germany's African and Asian colonies were divided up between Belgium, Britain, Japan and France. Their European territories were either given to other nations or made independent. Their military capability was also ruined. Their army was limited to a mere 100,000 troops, their navy was ordered to be destroyed off the coast of Scotland and they couldn't build or import military weapons ever again. Germany was left a shell of its former self.

The Austro-Hungarian and Ottoman empires suffered equal treatment. Their holdings were divided amongst the victors or set free. For a few select countries deemed not quite ready to go it alone, the Versailles Treaty established the concept of trusteeships, where Britain and France would guide new nations (Iraq, Palestine and Transjordan to the British and Syria and Lebanon to France) toward the successful creation of their own democracies. Like in the Scramble for Africa, the boundaries drawn stemmed oftentimes more from the needs of the Europeans than from the regional realities of what would soon be called the Middle East. For example, the northern Kurdish population was split amongst multiple countries, one of which was Iraq. Added to Iraq were the warring Shiite and Sunni factions. With the Shiites controlling access to the Red Sea, the Sunnis governing the capital of Baghdad and the Kurds housing huge oil reserves, Britain essentially united three rivals in an attempt to freely extract and transport oil to the world market. To this day, tensions between Kurds, Shiites and Sunnis persist, threatening to unravel any democratic governments fostered under the recent United States' "occupation" of Iraq. In the other trusteeships, similarly questionable boundaries tore apart peoples who had lived together for centuries and forced together groups who had been sworn enemies.

The most obvious case study concerns Britain-controlled Palestine. World War I marked the turning point in the Zionist

Movement, as Jews from across the West started gaining more traction in their attempt to recreate a homeland for God's chosen people – Israel. British post-WWI attempts to peacefully bring together the Palestinian Muslims and displaced Jews failed time and again, and a century later the world has realized that regional peace in this holy land remains unattainable. The Versailles Treaty clearly failed to bring peace to the Middle East.

One bright spot of Versailles should have been the League of Nations. Woodrow Wilson arrived with his Fourteen Points, an ambitious plan to ensure there would never be a World War II. Among these points was the promise of freedom of the seas, the banning of secret alliances and the full support of the notion of self-determination. Any nation or peoples wanting to free themselves from imperial rule should be allowed that opportunity. In his fourteenth point, Wilson envisioned a congress of all nations, a League of Nations, where international disputes would be resolved through diplomacy and compromise and the standard of living for all peoples would be elevated. He envisioned sharing with the world Western education, health practices and notions of meritocracy. The pragmatists Lloyd George and Clemenceau tepidly agreed to this auspicious proposal, and Wilson returned to the United States believing he had architected a system of international governance that would make war, strife and suffering a thing of the past.

But he forgot one thing. The United States was a democracy. Presidents don't make laws. The Congress does. When he presented the League of Nations to the Senate, it was widely debated. Partly out of spite because no Republicans were invited to the Paris Peace Conference, but mostly because the League of Nations could potentially take away war-making powers from Congress, the Senate rejected the proposal. Wilson went from hero to zero. The man who presented the idea to the world couldn't even convince his own people to support it. This rejection essentially doomed the League of Nations from the start. One of the most powerful nations in the world would not be enforcing any of the decisions, essentially making the League of Nations an impotent body unable to back right with might.

And this was just the start of the unraveling of the Versailles Treaty. Within two decades, the economic sanctions spun the world into a Great Depression, the territorial resolutions spawned restlessness and the desire for revenge, and the naïve espousal of self-determination only created dozens of other regional hot spots where violence would become the only way to assure independence. The war to end all wars was resolved by the peace to end all peace.

During the 1920s, a brief economic boom made some believe quite erroneously that the world had been made a better place, but what they would soon discover was this brief respite only masked far deeper problems that eventually pulled the globe into the abyss.

But that is for another chapter.

37

Roaring into Chaos

The Interwar Period – 1920 > 1940

In 1900, Europe awed the world. Their military and economic dominance gave weight to the argument that it was *the* preeminent civilization on the planet. It made sense. If the richest, most technologically advanced, most feared countries all resided west of the Caucasus Mountains, the accepted belief was that their political and economic systems, their values and their culture were likewise superior.

But then they blew themselves up, and in the decades after Versailles, the nations of Europe not only had to rebuild their shattered infrastructures, but also the confidence of their people. The masses had trusted their leaders. Their politicians, their captains of industry and their spiritual guides had all promised that obedience to the state ensured peace and prosperity. World War I fractured that trust, opening all institutions and authority figures to criticism.

Millions recovered from the wounds of war, questioning if capitalist giants pushed war for their own profit, if democratic leaders truly spoke for the people, if the media was merely the puppet of authority figures, if there even was God.

The 1920s and 1930s became an era of experimentation and polarization. Democracy had failed. Was communism or fascism the solution? Capitalism had failed. Should industry then be turned over to the masses or to the government? God hadn't answered prayers. Would science have the answer? Foreign alliances only exacerbated a regional conflict in the Balkans. Was isolationism and protectionism the path to peace?

Factions emerged promoting their agendas, and for every group that was pro-something, another would pop up that was anti-the same thing. These factions might debate ideologies, or they might take their disagreement to the streets. In many cases, these factions created outright movements, leading to philosophical revolutions at the highest level, where dictators could prescribe and enforce universal behavior, philosophy and even ethnicity.

For some, the 1920s meant unprecedented rights. When America passed their 19th Amendment, they became one of the final Western countries to grant voting rights to women. Over the next decade, these same women expanded their political independence into the social sphere. They started wearing more revealing clothing, smoking and drinking with the boys, going out with the girls unescorted and behaving a lot less "ladylike." Women became celebrities on the Silver Screen Nickelodeons (guess how much it cost for a movie ticket?), their voices could be heard by radio across nations, and they started not just entering, but influencing, fields seen before as solely the domain of men. Women like Amelia Earhart completely ignored gender norms, pushing the limits of what society believed possible for a woman, setting and then breaking dozens of aviation records before finally meeting her end somewhere over the Atlantic Ocean. Even in Turkey, a nation only recently escaping the social conservatism of the Ottoman Empire, female novelist Halide Edip became not only a spokeswoman for gender equality, but also a noted political figure campaigning for Turkish independence.

Edip was one of a growing number of "others" who began pushing for rights not honored under white rule. In the United States during World War I, southern blacks fled to northern cities, not only answering the call for replacement labor for the white soldiers, but also fleeing a Jim Crow South that had created painfully debilitating segregation laws that made life even more unbearable than that under slavery. For the colored billions living under European colonial rule, World War I became the tipping point where independence became a possibility. Whether in Vietnam or Nigeria or Indonesia or Malaya, the "tribes" and "natives" started to push for not merely reforms that would give them more political and economic opportunities, but for wholesale independence, free from external control. Many leaders of these campaigns were actually "natives" who had been Western educated (some even going to Europe for their studies), returning with the ideologies of Montesquieu, Locke, Rousseau and Jefferson.

Among these returning liberal-educated sons, India's Mahatma Gandhi stood out as the foremost advocate for home rule. Employing a method of non-violent protest where civil society organizations peacefully gathered to protest inequalities, hoping for either an alteration in policy or a violent government reprisal that could invoke widespread sympathy, Gandhi became the first to show that civil disobedience opens more eyes than do bullets.

But for every step forward towards racial equality, there was always a group pushing to maintain the status quo, and usually this group was made up of threatened white people. Borrowing from the Social Darwinism of the 19th Century that conveniently used science to justify the West's industrial prominence, a generation of eugenicists pushed to ensure racial purity. Some organizations like the American Ku Klux Klan or the German Nazis resorted to public coercion and violence to keep colored people "in their place." These groups hoped to keep undesirables out of everyday life, and unlike today where even those with racist tendencies try to keep their opinions to themselves, in the 1920s, publicly professing the inferiority of the others was socially acceptable. Today some try to discard the racism of the post-WWI era as being merely the extremist views of an isolated group of fringe thinkers. This argument doesn't wash. At the height of their popularity in the 1920s and 1930s, the Ku Klux Klan hit six million members and the Nazi Party surpassed eight million. But these views weren't solely shared by members of these admittedly extremist groups. Eugenicists like politician Winston Churchill, woman's rights advocate Margaret Sanger, novelist H.G. Wells, president Theodore Roosevelt, inventor Alexander Graham Bell and entrepreneur Henry Ford all at one time lobbied for methods of ensuring racial purity. Whether it be by sterilizing undesirable groups like the disabled, the incarcerated or homosexuals, or promoting laws that prevented interracial marriages, these eugenicists actually believed many of society's problems could be solved if we could just find a way to breed out "negative" human traits.

This tension over gender and racial equity was just one of the many paradoxes that tore at the fabric of the societies emerging from the despair of World War I. For every feminist pushing for fair treatment, there was another conservative mother pressuring to keep their nation's daughters chaste and in the kitchen. For every advocate believing Africans and Asians could live in harmony with their European brothers, there was another man working on the most efficient scientific method of ensuring people of different races didn't reproduce. But the list of contradictions didn't stop there. Some believed man should look to science (specifically the breakthroughs in physics and the medical industry) to determine how we should live. Others still believed God had all the answers. Some championed the values of the cities - with their jazz music, neon lights and loose morals. Others still hoped society wouldn't forget their rural roots, remaining pure, innocent and wholesome. Some believed you could legislate human behavior (even outlawing alcohol). Others wanted people to be free to choose their own paths. Some advocated for opening ourselves to the cultures and economies of all peoples. Others believed every nation should turn inward, shutting off trade with other countries and preventing immigration from "inferior" lands. Some thought war could be prevented by making larger, more destructive weapons. Others wanted to halt weapons production altogether, or even sign adorably naïve international agreements that outlawed war (the rarely-mentioned Kellogg-Briand Pact that hypothetically still determines the foreign policy of dozens of its original signatories...including the United States of America).

As the capitalist/democratic ideal lost a bit of its glimmer, other radically new governing ideologies emerged. With the Russian Revolution of 1917, Karl Marx's 19th century theories finally came to fruition (or at least that's the line Vladimir Lenin and the Bolsheviks sold to the Russian people). The promises of communism faded in the 1920s as first Lenin and then Stalin maneuvered to position all power in the hands of an elite few. Karl Marx's vision of a world where the workers of the world would unite, overthrow the capitalist exploiters, and share power and profit equally was abruptly abandoned once Lenin and the Bolsheviks determined power could only be ensured if a few definitional idiosyncrasies could be reinterpreted. By 1930, Stalin had become the unquestioned dictator of Russia, and power was anything but shared. All economic, political and foreign policy decisions originated from the mouth of Stalin and any threats (either perceived or actual) to his authority were either exiled or killed. The inevitable cycle of revolution that had started with the abdication of the tyrant Czar Nicholas II had ended with the reign of the criminally tyrannical Stalin.

But this wasn't how it all started.

Let's go back a few decades. In March of 1917, Czar Nicholas II reluctantly signed his abdication papers in a railroad car outside of Petrograd, ending decades of imperial decay where the Russian royal family proved incapable of meeting the needs of their people. Since the late 19th century, the throne of Russia had come under frequent attacks from a swelling population that continued to survive under medieval conditions. Nicholas, like his ancestors before, failed to adjust to the changing demands of a more mobile, more indignant population. In 1905, Nicholas attempted to appease the populace by consenting to the formation of the Duma, the Russian version of Congress or Parliament. But this representative body existed in name only, with power still residing in the hands of the distant, uninformed royal family and their advisors. By 1916, with the devastation of World War I disproportionately scarring both civilian life and soldiers on the front (many not armed with the latest weapons), the citizens of Petrograd lashed out, first just demanding bread, but eventually calling for the removal of the Czar. When the army refused to defend Nicholas and the Petrograd revolutionaries appeared inconsolable, Nicholas agreed to "voluntarily" step down.

In the ensuing months of the spring of 1917, Russians tasted the utopia they envisioned. The lands of the wealthy were stolen and redistributed. A parliament of the people was created. The Czar and his family were imprisoned. Hundreds of regional councils (soviets) sprung up around the nation, hoping to soon attend to the needs of the population. Russia began its new era of freedom. For a brief moment, Russia was the most equal nation in the world.

But by the summer, any hope of creating a society of equals had faded. Elected leaders jockeyed for power. Groups consolidated authority, creating and expanding political parties. The communist parties of the Mensheviks and the Bolsheviks competed for the right to determine Russia's future. The Mensheviks wanted to work with the middle class, creating a constitutional republic. Lenin's Bolsheviks disagreed. In Lenin's self-serving interpretation of Marx's beliefs, a communist revolution would have to be guided by an elite group of intellectuals holding supreme authority (with Lenin not-so-surprisingly at the top).

Another revolution was needed. Lenin brought back exiled Leon Trotsky from New York City, plans were hatched, and on November 6, 1917, the Bolsheviks successfully, and relatively peacefully, took over the country. In a coordinated effort, they captured critical railroad stations, banks, communication lines and power grids, and then marched into the assembly and merely set up a new government. Few knew what was happening. Even fewer shots were fired.

In the ensuing months, Lenin's Bolsheviks would keep their promise of peace by pulling out of World War I, signing a peace accord that ceded the Ukraine and Belarus to the Germans. Peace was short-lived as a civil war erupted in Russia, pitting the Communist Red Army vs. the White Army made up of former military leaders, prominent members of the middle class and even a sprinkling of British and American troops. This bloody conflict lasted until 1922 when the Red Army emerged victorious. The Union of Soviet Socialist Republics (USSR) was born with Lenin as the unquestioned leader, ruling with an iron fist, killing anyone who threatened his authority (the royal family was knocked off almost immediately – Nicholas, his wife and his children were hacked to shreds, their bodies turned unrecognizable in vats of acid before being deposited across the countryside).

Lenin's authority was unquestioned, but his health failed him. In 1924 he died, but instead of power passing to his protégé Leon Trotsky, the general secretary of the party, Joseph Stalin - a man who had made numerous alliances during the civil war through his control of information and behind the scenes manipulation – elevated himself to party boss. The self-proclaimed "man of steel," engineered not only the discrediting and eventual exile of Trotsky, but also the cunning intimidation of any other challenger who refused to yield to his authority. Once in power, Stalin revealed a pattern of rule that would oppress, but also advance, Russia for the next three decades.

Stalin was a paranoid man (and rightfully so). He had climbed to power through less than official means. Who was to stop a rival from pursuing the same course? Time and again, Stalin authorized purges that would jail, exile and oftentimes kill all would-be adversaries. By 1935, all connected to the Russian Revolution had been taken care of, many even removed from the history books (Stalin prided himself and his ministers of information for their ability to doctor pictures to put Stalin in critical moments in Soviet history, while deleting those actually in attendance). Even Leon Trotsky, the hero of the revolution, was found and assassinated. A member of Stalin's secret police tracked him down in Mexico and stuck an ice pick in his skull

Once Stalin's power was unquestioned, he worked to advance Russia. He knew he needed to catch up to his Western European rivals or the Russian borders would never be safe. He needed the nation to industrialize, and he needed it done in the shortest amount of time possible. This meant turning the entire state into a production machine. Factories were built, ores were mined and all available capital was put back into industrial production. In the countryside, all farms were "collectivized," meaning they were combined into huge industrial farms where previously independent planters became slaves to the field. Any that disagreed were labeled "kulaks" and sent to prison camps in Siberia where they spent their final days mining or searching for food until they eventually froze to death. This collectivization not only turned over agricultural control to the government, but it eventually killed close to 30 million people through starvation, and forced another 20 million into the cities where they became the cogs in Stalin's industrial machine.

Stalin's plan was deadly, but it worked. Russia became the fastest growing economy in the world, and by the mid-1930s, when the rest of the world was suffering through the Great Depression, Russia claimed almost full employment, with their industrial output growing at a rate of over 10% a year. Just when the capitalist countries were falling apart, communist Russia looked like the poster child for progress. For nations around the world emerging from Western colonial control and the destruction of World War I, Stalin's model looked a bit appealing. Sure, his methods might have been a bit intense, but few could argue with the results.

It was this growing attraction to Communism that spawned the second great governmental experiment of the Interwar Period – fascism. In the years following World War I, across Europe, communist parties gained steam. Promising power to the people and a redistribution of property, it wasn't hard to convince a generation in despair of the advantages of Marx's theories. Obviously this made the nations of Europe a bit uneasy. Robbing from the rich and giving to the poor sounds quaint when Robin Hood is the protagonist, but a wholesale redistribution of power and wealth is a bit less romantic. Communism became a viable option amongst all of the factional groups vying for power in the new democracies that materialized in post-war Europe. Oftentimes these communist groups and even the other political parties fought their "democratic" battles not merely with words but with armed forces of thugs. Many citizens grew tired of all this political jockeying for power. They longed for the good ol' days when one man called all the shots. They just wanted peace, order, stability and a return to the glory of an idealized yesteryear.

Enter the fascists. Benito Mussolini was the first to test this system of controlling the hearts, minds and pocketbooks of a country. The genius of fascism is its ability to recognize and take advantage of mankind's weaknesses. Seeing that his Italian compatriots had grown tired of the endless bickering and ineptitude of the democratic process, but also recalling the lure of nationalism in the early stages of the Great War, Mussolini invented fascism. He took the symbol of Roman power – a fascio that had branches bound securely around an axe – to show how if Italians only cared about their individual wants and needs, Italy would surely fail. But united, they could not be defeated. He fashioned a political party that had all the pomp of a military unit. His party members wore black shirts (earning the nickname "the Black Shirts"). He offered medals and awards for party loyalty. He orchestrated massive political rallies complete with patriotic singing, ritualistic chanting and visual spectacles that attracted even his adversaries. For the young men and women looking for role models, something to do and a place where they could channel their aggression and frustration, the Fascism was the answer. Mussolini's party was more than just a vehicle championing an ideology of order, unity and loyalty, it was a paramilitary organization able to stomp any group that stood in their way. Many remained apathetic to the noise of the Fascists, worrying more about their day-to-day life than this new form of politics developing in the cities. And this played right into the hands of Mussolini. His followers adored him. His adversaries feared him. The rest of the nation stayed out of the way. When his Black Shirts marched on Rome in 1922, King Victor Emmanuel appointed Mussolini prime minister, believing he was the only one who could restore stability to the land. This was exactly the opening Mussolini needed. He used his role as prime minister to gradually eliminate democratic restrictions, and by 1925 he was the supreme ruler of Italy – Il Duce.

To the north, the leader of the National Socialist Party in Germany was paying close attention to the theatrics, the manipulations and the evolution of Mussolini. For this man also lived in a nation facing the uncertainty that stemmed from liberal attacks on traditional institutions. For this man also lived in a nation whose collective ego had been damaged by the losses of war. For this man, the Weimar Republic was a bumbling joke and it held a precarious grip on German society, and if he too could create a political party ready to take advantage of a moment of chaos, he too could one day rise to become supreme leader. All this man, this Adolph Hitler, needed was a crisis of unparalleled proportions.

And it was delivered to him on a tarnished silver platter with the coming of the Great Depression.

The Great Depression slammed the United States first, but because by the 1920s most economies were entwined in a web of bank lending and trading partnerships, when one country went down, the entire system crumbled. The causes were many, some preventable, some merely a product of a global economy.

First, banks started making risky loans. Usually it makes sense for banks to loan money to people, organizations (even countries) that can actually pay the money back. Not so during the 1920s. Money was easy, and whether you were a budding middle class consumer taking out some money to buy one of Ford's Model-T's or Germany pleading for the millions needed to pay back the reparations demanded by the Versailles Treaty, banks were far more willing to ignore huge credit risks. What could possibly go wrong if you lent money to people who couldn't pay it back?

Second, banks and individuals took stock speculation to unprecedented levels. Investors were more than willing to throw cash at the new industries – automobiles, radio, chemicals and appliances – but even to companies with no proven track record. From 1924 to 1929, the US stock market rose 275%. People started to believe 30% annual returns on their investments was the norm, not the exception. And because the federal governments of the West (especially in the US) hadn't yet created the regulatory bodies to keep people honest, some people even "started" fake companies, took in investor money and then ran before anyone realized there was never a product to begin with.

Third, the result of risky loans and stock speculation meant banks and average Joes were overleveraged – they owed way more than they could ever hope to pay back. As long as the economies were roaring, as long as radios, cars and refrigerators kept rolling off the assembly lines, and as long as people were acting out of pure irrational optimism, the ride would keep people flying. But financial bubbles always burst. Rational fear inevitably replaces optimism. People eventually want to actually see their money.

This was when the house of fiscal cards came tumbling down.

Investors got worried. Banks got nervous. They wanted their loans repaid and to cash in their stock certificates. In October 1929, a few started selling their stocks, then it was dozens, then hundreds, then everyone started to pull their money out. But this time, there were no buyers for these stocks. Prices on stocks sunk lower. Banks that had invested their depositors' money needed cash. They demanded their borrowers pay back their loans immediately. But they couldn't. So banks stopped lending money. People couldn't invest any more using borrowed money. Corporations couldn't put money into growing their businesses. Governments ran out of money to pay their debts.

And then the people caught wind of what was happening in the financial sector and ran to the banks to withdraw all their money. These "bank runs" happened all over the West, all at the same time, but there was no money to withdraw. The banks had run out of money. Banks closed. Life savings vanished.

With no money being lent, no money in people's pocket books, people stopped buying goods and services. The demand for the luxury goods of the 1920s had already started to slow by the end of the decade – there are only so many refrigerators, vacuum cleaners and cars any one family actually needs. And by 1930, demand died. Companies produced less and fired unneeded employees. Unemployment rates soared to over 25% in America, and over 50% in Western Europe.

There was no money, no jobs, no hope.

Some were hit worse than others. For example, farmers lost everything. With the technological innovations in agricultural production that coincided with the increased demand for foodstuffs during the World War I years, farmers made a killing from 1915-1920. They produced more crops than ever before, bought more farm equipment than ever before and reaped more profits than ever before. But when the war ended and the troops returned, the supply of food soared even higher. What happens when you produce more than your customers need? The price drops. And by 1925, the demand for beef, corn, wheat and rice dropped to levels that made it unprofitable for the mom and pop farmers of the world to continue taking their yields to market.

Whether you were a rice farmer in China or a cattle rancher in Latin America, you couldn't financially make it anymore. Hundreds of millions sold their lands to large corporations and moved to the cities, and what awaited them in the cities?

No jobs. No food. No support system. But having so many millions of economic casualties in one place meant that for the visionary manipulator with a solution and a scapegoat, a movement could be unleashed.

In Germany the conditions were worse than anywhere else in the industrialized world. Following World War I, the economy of Germany roared up and down like no other. The Versailles Treaty demanded Germany pay 132 billion deutschmarks (close to 500 billion US dollars today), but then took away their colonial holdings and their prime industrial region – the Rhineland. There was no way Germany could ever pay the money back. But France and England demanded their restitution. So, Germany came up with the ingenious idea to just print a bunch of money. You want billions of marks? We can give you billions of marks. But with billions of bills circulating through the economy in the early 1920s, their money lost all of its value. At one point, Germany was printing 100 trillion deutschmark banknotes and their currency was exchanging at the rate of 4.2 trillion marks to 1 US dollar. Stories circulated of Germans wallpapering their homes with the money, bringing wheelbarrows full of marks to buy a loaf of bread and even burning money during the winter months for warmth. France and England weren't too pleased with this ploy, and Germans had trouble making ends meet under this bizarre hyperinflation. American bankers stepped in with a solution. They would loan the money to Germany. Germany would use America's loaned money to pay back debts to France and England. France and England would then take this money and buy American goods. As this money cycled through the West, American bankers were essentially financing foreign imports. So when the banking crisis hit America and loans stopped heading east to Germany, the German economy (and soon after the other Western economies) plummeted.

To try to protect their home industries, government leaders then made the mistake of establishing protective tariffs so their citizens would only buy goods and services produced from their homeland. The logic went that if foreign goods cost far more than local goods, people would only buy the stuff produced locally. The American Congress passed the Smoot-Hawley Tariff, taxing over 20,000 imported goods. America's trading partners then responded with reciprocal tariffs on American goods. International trade came to a halt. If corporate sales were hurting in 1930, they were devastated in the ensuing years after these back and forth tariff wars slaughtered sales figures.

Capitalism had failed. Traditional government attempts to fix the system had likewise failed. Leaders had to try something new. Some governments adopted the Keynesian philosophy that encourages the state to prime the pump, willingly going into debt to put people back to work and circulate more money through the economy. Franklin D. Roosevelt in America enforced his New Deal legislation, creating dozens of "alphabet agencies" that built roads, dams, bridges and national parks; establishing regulatory agencies that would prevent the stock market bubbles and irrational banking practices of the Roaring Twenties; and supporting mandatory state investment programs like Social Security and Aid to Families with Dependent Children (aka "welfare") to help the elderly, the disabled, the unemployed and the fatherless. In Scandinavian Europe, the leaders likewise launched a support network of programs to provide for their people by subsidizing secondary and college education, enforcing labor laws favorable to workers and creating state-run health care programs for all citizens.

The West was clearing moving to the left. Some worried too far to the left - too far toward a communist state where powers would be taken from the wealthy and redistributed to the poor. Communist parties gained traction from Greece to Italy to France, and even across the Atlantic to America. In 1932, presidential hopeful Huey Long advocated his "Share Our Wealth" program, where every man could be a king, and where the fat cats of Wall Street would finally be held accountable for their market manipulations (a 1930s version of the Occupy Wall Street movement). His policies scared Americans raised on the values of hard work, meritocracy and the American Dream. Huey Long was assassinated.

In countries like Italy, Japan and Germany, violence of another sort broke out to prevent the evil of communism from spreading. Military and party leaders sparked the people's passions through nationalism and pledges of a return to former glory. By 1932, the right-wing conservative Fascists controlled Italy, the imperialistic military controlled Japan and the Nazis controlled Germany.

The 1920s battles of new vs. old, liberal vs. conservative and modern vs. traditional had now reached global dimensions. Neither side would concede defeat. Neither side would allow the other to spread their ideology. But unlike in the 1920s when these conflicts solved themselves in courts, in assemblies or on the streets, in the 1930s these clashes would take place in the bunkers, in the jungles and on the seas, for the final resolution would require an all-out global war – World War II.

But that is for another chapter.

38

Countdown to Horror

Causes of World War II – 1925 > 1940

The first Great War took on the moniker World War I, but truly the fighting was restricted to the European continent. Yes, some battles popped up in the European colonies in Africa and Asia, guerilla warfare emerged across the Arabian Peninsula and Japan pushed for territorial claims in China. Yes, colonial holdings from across the globe sent their troops to the European theater in support of mother country. And yes, nations from Latin America to Sub-Saharan Africa to the Far East profited by supplying to Europe the critical resources required to sustain an industrialized war. But when you look at the actual fighting, the actual impact on civilians, soldiers, economies, governments and infrastructures, the burden was almost exclusively borne by the Western nations.

World War II was different. It was a true WORLD war.

Sure, in its first few months, it looked a lot like a replay of World War I. Once again, Germany was heading through Belgium on the way to take out France. Once again, France and Britain worked together to put the upstart Germans in their place. Yet quickly, the comparisons stopped and any passive observer could see that this war would end up like no other. Within six years, major offensives would take the Japanese across the Far East, putting them on the doorsteps of Australia, India and the United States. German armies took over governments from Norway to North Africa to Iraq, and then pushed deep into the heart of the Soviet Union. The United States saw their own country attacked (albeit a remote Pacific island state 2000 miles off the coast of California) before sending their troops to three continents to end the Axis menace. Again Latin America stayed pretty much out of the actual fighting (save for Mexico and Brazil who sent in an air force and a 25,000 man army respectively), but again profiting as needed suppliers to the Allies and welcome home to the millions of refugees fleeing their shattered former lives.

World War II was also different because it wasn't too difficult to blame the instigators. Japan and Germany (and to some extent Italy) brought war to the world. Most nations in the 1930s hid behind policies of isolationism and pacifism, refusing to involve themselves in the affairs of other nations. If alliances were what brought the belligerents to conflict in World War I, it would be the fear of alliances that brought the world to its knees in the 1940s. By the end of the 1930s, militarist Japan and fascist Germany and Italy had embarked on a campaign of empire building, all right in front of the faces of the world's powers, yet the onlookers did nothing. Each bold land grab by the aggressors went unchecked, emboldening even further moves. When the nations finally decided to awake from their pacifist slumber, they saw an East Asia and a Europe ruled by Germany and Japan, with all signs pointing to these two nations being far from finished. It would be up to Britain, the United States, the Soviet Union and 23 other allied nations to reverse this course, or within a few years they might all live under the realm of the Nazi Swastika or the Japanese Rising Sun.

During World War II, the accepted motivation as to why the Germans and Japanese plunged recklessly down the course of conquest was that their democratic governments had been hijacked by demented militarist leaders hell-bent on subjugating the inferior peoples of the world. Though evidence definitely exists to support this evil-leader hypothesis, there might be just a bit more to the tale, considering both nations were considered the most advanced, refined civilizations in their respective regions at the turn of the 20th century.

For Germany, Hitler's promises of national pride, full employment and a return to the glory days of Bismarck were welcomed by a population utterly destroyed by the Great Depression. With unemployment rates eclipsing 50% in some regions, Germans flocked to hear the passionate pledges of the uniquely-mustachioed orator. Although the decade after World War I had briefly teased Western Europe with promises of new wealth, new art and new consumer goods, when their economic worlds came crashing down in 1930, many looked for new answers to why a once-mighty people were again brought to their knees. Hitler offered explanations. Hitler offered scapegoats. It was the capitalists of Britain and France who corrupted the economy. It was the traitors of the Weimar Republic who pulled Germany out of a war they were winning and then signed the crippling Versailles Treaty. It was the communists whose lone desire was to pull down the affluence of all those who excelled. And lastly, it was the Jews, who, in Hitler's mind, were co-conspirators with the capitalists, the Weimar Republic and the communists. His growing crowds ignored the details of how the Jews, who numbered less than 1% of the entire German population, could have aligned themselves with groups spanning the political spectrum to such a degree that they could topple German society. All they saw was a reason for their plight.

Hitler didn't merely offer scapegoats; he also outlined how he would pull the nation out of despair. In his penned-in-prison autobiography *Mein Kampf* (*My Struggle*), Hitler spoke of lebensraum, living space for all German people. Hitler dreamed of a world where all Germans, regardless of current national boundary distinctions, would one day be reunited in a greater German empire. Hitler would then secure lebensraum for his people by conquering the Slavs to the east who had more land than they needed, more land than they deserved. The racially inferior Slavs (with the Russians being the largest group) would be crushed, and the breadbasket of Europe would fall into the hands of the "righteous Aryan race." To meet these ends, Hitler would ignore the mandates of Versailles, instead putting Germany on a course of rearmament, where every man and woman wanting employment would be put to work. They would work again, they would be happy again, they would be proud again.

And Hitler delivered. By 1936, Adolf Hitler had achieved near 100% employment. Regardless of attempts made by their leaders, Britain and America couldn't pull out of their depressions. But there was no Great Depression in Germany, not even close. Hitler's government started subsidizing vacations for his citizens –

paying for trips to the Alps, the Mediterranean and nearby lake cottages. He dreamt of a world where everyone would have a car – wagons for his folks (Volkswagens). He built glorious autobahns for the lucrative auto industry, he created Hitler Youth programs that brought together children from all across the nation and he staged elaborate parades where hundreds of thousands trembled at the sight of their beloved Führer.

He gave the people what they wanted – both ideologically and materially – so that by 1939, he had the nation at his fingertips, willing and able to do his bidding (regardless of how demented, sadistic and ill-planned it would become).

In Japan, the nation already had a revered leader – Emperor Hirohito – the only royal figure in the world who could trace his lineage back to the birth of mankind. Like with Hitler, Hirohito had developed a cult of personality where children grew up pledging their lives to this god-like figure. However, unlike Hitler, Hirohito played a minimal role in determining public policy. This was left to the parliament. But by the 1930s, the parliament had essentially handed over power to the militarists, groups of ultra-right wing military leaders who believed capitalism and its evils – profit and individualism – were responsible for the gradual rotting of the Japanese soul. The militarists offered a new Japan, a Japan that once again revered the Emperor above all else, and who by force would secure Japan's future for generations. After a few key assassinations (including Prime Minister Inukai Tsuyoshi who naively sponsored the restrictive London Naval Treaty), no one in parliament dared cross the vision of the militarists.

Similar to how the Germans sought out lebensraum for their people, the Japanese equally wanted living space for their island nation. As a resource-scarce country, Japan depended on trade with East Asia and the United States, but in the 1930s, free trade had come to an end as nations cared more about protecting their domestic economies than with honoring trade agreements with the rest of the world. Japan was vulnerable. Should it be cut off from the global trade network, Japan's industry would be paralyzed and its people would soon starve. The militarists refused to accept this position of dependence. They envisioned a "Greater East Asian Co-Prosperity Sphere," where European powers would be kicked out of East Asia and Japan would replace the West as the sole extractors of resources.

So by the mid-1930s, the course of Japan and Germany's future had been set. Through hyper-nationalism, rapid rearmament and aggressive foreign policies, these two nations emerged from the shadows of the United States and England to claim what they truly believed to be rightfully theirs.

Japan was the first to strike. Since the Sino-Japanese War of the late 19th century, Japan demanded free access to Chinese ports and manufacturing centers. By the early 1900s, they had secured rights to build and manage railroads across Manchuria, connecting Japan to both Chinese industry and Russian transportation networks. But Japan wanted more than just control of the railroads. They wanted Manchuria.

In an amazing bit of catalyst creation, on September 18, 1931, a section of the Japanese railway lines (on Chinese Manchurian soil) was blown up. To the Japanese army, this was clearly the work of Chinese dissidents, so within weeks, over a hundred thousand Japanese invaded Manchuria, under the pretext of protecting Japanese interests from the big, bad Chinese terrorists. Only one problem. It was Japanese soldiers that actually lit the fuse. The explosion was all just a carefully orchestrated con to justify military action. When the facts came out in this Mukden Incident, the League of Nations was appalled and sternly reprimanded (oh no...not a reprimand) the Japanese for their blatant disregard for sacred international relations. Japan was insulted at this lecture, so they left the League of Nations. But they stayed in China.

Hitler paid close attention to this event and the impotence of the League of Nations. If the League basically was basically powerless to stop the Japanese, who else could get away with international murder? The answer came when Italian leader Benito Mussolini sent his army out of Europe in an attempt to restore Italy to the glory days of the Roman Empire. His target – Ethiopia - the last of the African nations not controlled by a European power. Italian troops used machine guns, bombs and poisoned gas, and within a few months they had conquered the Ethiopians. The League of Nations was outraged. They politely asked Mussolini to pull out of Ethiopia or else risk losing access to all oil imports. Mussolini refused and pulled out of the League of Nations. The League did nothing. Again. Mussolini had his mini-Roman Empire, and Hitler saw his opening. It appeared nobody was in the mood to stop naked aggression.

But how would Germany rise to threaten Europe yet again, when it had hypothetically been dismantled by the Versailles Treaty? Adolph Hitler, obsessed with the inequity of the treaty, made it his life mission to exact revenge on the signatories. First, he had to test the waters. What could he get away with before the so-called Allies checked his plans for regional domination? In 1933, he pulled Germany out of the League of Nations. The Allies did nothing. In 1935, he ordered universal conscription for all adult German males, defying Versailles by expanding his army from 100,000 troops to three million. Again, the Allies did nothing. He then started full rearmament, calling on his people's best scientists to create the state-of-the-art weapons that could take the continent by surprise, eventually even creating the largest air force in the world – the Luftwaffe. The Allies still did nothing. Feeling even bolder, Hitler then sent his troops into the Rhineland, the chunk of territory on Germany's western border that had been controlled by France since Versailles. Hitler promised England and France he had "no territorial claims," and that he just wanted to restore Germany's rightful boundaries, but he would never, ever take over any land again. The Allies trusted the humble Hitler and they did nothing.

Hitler then set his sights on his homeland – Austria. He wanted to reunite the once great German peoples – bringing back together again the Austrian and German empires. Hitler contacted Austrian chancellor Kurt Schuschnigg and presented him with an ultimatum he would have to accept – Germany would get to handpick the next chancellor and 2/3 of the Austrian parliament would have to be reserved for members of the Austrian Nazi Party. Hitler brought his troops to the border of Austria just to help Schuschnigg make his decision. Without an option B, he acquiesced, and Austria was essentially annexed by Germany. Hitler justified this annexation, or Anschluss, by marching his 8th Army through the streets of Vienna (which were lined with hundreds of thousands of Nazi "supporters"), and then demanding the nation take a vote to see if the people truly loved their prodigal son. In an amazing vote that I'm sure was 99.75% legitimate, the German annexation of Austria was accepted by 99.75% of the population. For those of you familiar with *The Sound of Music*, that .25% must have included the Von Trapp Family who weren't terribly fond of the Anschluss, and climbed every mountain to get out of Austria instead of living under the Nazi flag.

From there, Hitler made his boldest move to date. To his southeast lay Czechoslovakia, a nation created by Versailles, a nation that housed over three million Germans across its northern border in an area known as the Sudetenland. Hitler claimed these three million helpless Germans were being persecuted by their Czech compatriots (even though in the Sudetenland they outnumbered Czechs ten to one) and, based on the premise of Woodrow Wilson's own theories of self-determination, had the right to join the greater German empire. To his international audience, Hitler again spewed out his promise that he had no greater territorial claims. He just wanted to help out a little brother in need. To solve this problem, the major nations of Europe −Italy, France and England − agreed to join Hitler in Munich, Germany for a conference to decide the fate of Czechoslovakia. A key omission from the invite list was Czechoslovakia itself, who sat on the sidelines, believing erroneously that the French and English would protect Czech sovereignty. They didn't. Hitler was granted the Sudetenland, under the premise that he promised to never, ever take over any territory again. Hitler shook hands on the deal, Prime Minister Neville Chamberlain returned to England boasting that he had secured "peace in our time" and Czechoslovakia was left bewildered to ponder what just happened.

And within five months Hitler took over the rest of Czechoslovakia.

This Munich Conference came to symbolize the ineptness of the West's policy of appeasement towards German aggression. At every step, the French, British and American efforts to merely "appease" Hitler only empowered the Führer to push further. Within three years, he had seized control of the Rhineland, Austria and Czechoslovakia − all without firing a shot.

For Britain and France, the policy of appeasement meant avoiding another Great War, while hopefully buying much-needed time to rearm their countries.

For the Americans, they wanted nothing to do with European infighting. The pervading American sentiment of the time was that involvement in European affairs inevitably led to pointless wars. World War I was supposed to be the war to end all wars, but even after the horrific suffering and the loss of an entire generation of the West's greatest men, within a couple decades, Europe was at it again. In the late 1930s, the United States even attempted to pass a constitutional amendment outlawing war. The United States wanted to retreat back behind its protection of two oceans, hoping to remain pacifist and isolated from world affairs.

Yet as Japan and Germany continued to force their territorial claims, the United States (and especially their president Franklin D. Roosevelt) found it increasingly difficult to maintain a neutral stance. By mid-1937, Japan was not content with merely controlling Manchuria. They wanted full access to the trading centers of China, so in August, they launched their invasion at Shanghai. After months of brutal fighting, Japan finally proved victorious and began heading further inland for the capital city at Nanking. Instead of defending the capital with the most highly trained of the Chinese army, Chiang Kai-Shek ordered the retreat of all troops deep into the heart of China. His thinking was that if the Chinese army could live to fight another day, it could steadily mount a guerilla war campaign against the invading Japanese forces. China could not defeat Japan head to head on the battlefield, but maybe they could win a war of attrition.

Left behind at the capital of Nanking were young, untrained soldiers - an "army" easily defeated by the battle-hardened Japanese forces. What ensued after this quick victory has gone down in history as one of the most barbaric atrocities ever committed during wartime – the Rape of Nanking. Desiring vengeance for their losses at the battle of Shanghai, fueled by notions of racial superiority and left to their own sadistic desires by an indifferent officer corps, the Japanese army unleashed a six week reign of terror that murdered and maimed close to 200,000 citizens. The casualty toll only tells part of the story, as it was the inhuman, grotesque method in which the cruelty was exacted that horrified the international community. Over 50,000 females – from infants to the elderly to even pregnant women - were taken from their homes and raped. Bodies were mutilated and displayed around the city. Soldiers used gathered civilians as target practice, boasting of their tallies as the individual kills surpassed hundreds, then thousands. The degree of depravity will not be here mentioned any further, but as the Western diplomats began circulating the story to their home countries, sentiment grew amongst the leaders that something had to be done.

But the United States could not yet enter. Because the US Congress had passed a series of Neutrality Acts forbidding America from trading with belligerents at war, if the US hoped to extend any aid to the Chinese (and the surviving European governments in future years), they would have to deny that a war even existed. Throughout the final years of the decade, America worked with China's neighboring countries to send in supplies and provide whatever support was possible without openly declaring war with Japan. Through diplomatic channels, the US pleaded with Japan to withdraw its forces from China, and when this failed, they enforced an oil embargo that severely handicapped Japan's ability to wage war, setting the two nations down the inevitable path of confrontation.

Back in Europe, by 1939, the era of appeasement had run its course. The world was shocked when Hitler and Stalin announced their signing of a mutual Non-Aggression Pact, pledging that they would solve all future disputes cordially and they would never attack each other. Having these two sworn enemies sign any agreement was shocking. For two decades they had each pledged the utter destruction of the other. To Hitler, Soviet communism was the ultimate evil. To Stalin, German antagonism posed the greatest threat. So why then would they sign this agreement? Hitler needed to know his eastern front was secure. The Von Schlieffen Plan of 1914 failed because Germany weakened its western line when it had to send millions of men back across Germany to help reinforce the east under assault from Russia. Hitler had no intentions of not invading the Soviet Union. He just didn't want to do it YET. He pretty clearly mapped out his opinion of Stalin in Mein Kampf. See if you can wade through the subtlety of his language:

> *Never forget that the rulers of present-day Russia are common blood-stained criminals; that that they are the scum of humanity which, favored by circumstances, overran a great state in tragic hour, slaughtered and wiped out thousands of her leading intelligentsia in wild blood lust, and now for almost ten years have been carrying on the most cruel and tyrannical regime of all time...*

Not exactly a promise of eternal friendship. Hitler would invade the Soviet Union, topple the inferior Slavic and Jewish people and seize his lebensraum, but not until after France fell to the West. For Stalin, he signed the deal mostly because he needed time. His military corps was void of competent, experienced officers (something Stalin should have thought about before he killed them all in his 1930s paranoid purges), and his troops hadn't exactly proven themselves in conflicts against the oh-so-lethal army of Finland. Plus, part of the pact divided up Poland, with Germany receiving the western half and the Soviet Union regaining the east. This meant that if (when) the Germans did invade, they'd be hindered by what would essentially become a Polish buffer zone.

With his eastern front secure, Hitler blitzkrieg-ed Poland. On the spectrum of military strategy, the German blitzkrieg, or "lightning war," was pretty much the polar extreme of the trench warfare madness of World War I. In World War I, both sides dug themselves in on two sides of a front and then proceeded to blow themselves up for the next four years, all for the right to claim possession of a few precious feet of charred dirt. Blitzkrieg was different. It took the most daring offensives of military history and combined them with the speed and efficiency of mechanized warfare. German armies would coordinate their technologically advanced airforce, artillery and army with the singular purpose of breaking through the front line. But unlike in previous wars where once through the line, generals would painstakingly protect their rear ends, in this revolutionary lightning war, the Germans broke through and then just kept going and going, until they finally reached the invaded nation's capital. At this point, they'd point their tanks at the seat of power and politely encourage the elected officials to kindly turn over the keys to their nation.

This worked pretty darn well. Even with the inevitable hiccups of waging their first military campaign of the blitzkrieg era, Germany still conquered Poland in less than five weeks (and their record the following spring would look even better).

For Britain and France, the invasion of Poland was the final straw. Appeasement proved pointless. There was no appeasing Hitler. Two days after Hitler invaded Poland, on September 3, 1939, Britain and France declared war on Germany. World War II had begun. For the moment, unlike in World War I, it appeared the Soviet Union would stay out of the war, content to control its half of Poland and remain isolated in its communist cocoon.

But then the next six years unfolded. Hitler would capture the rest of continental Europe, plunge his forces deep into the heart of the Soviet Union and cover an empire more vast than anything seen since Genghis Khan. Across the planet, Japan soon made its fateful play for the Pacific, launching a surprise attack across the ocean, awakening the sleeping giant of American industry and turning the two regional conflicts into a global war to decide the fate of humanity.

But that is for another chapter.

39

The Just War

World War II – 1935 > 1947

With Poland carved in half, its carcass left to be devoured by the Germans to the west and the Soviets to the east, the world waited for Hitler's next move. In a span of just over a year, Hitler had added three countries to his trophy case, and he clearly wasn't going to stop there. He craved lebensraum. He created a four million man strong military. He rearmed Germany with the most state of the art weapons known to man. He could not be appeased. But as the world waited for his next attack, Hitler responded with...

Nothing. Poland fell in October 1939, but then the battlefield grew silent. The British and French mobilized their troops preparing for certain invasion. But nothing came. As the winter of 1939-1940 passed without any major German offensive, the international press started labeling this latest conflict the "phony war," or, in a clever little turn of phrase, the "Sitzkrieg." But this only told half the story. True, the German army might have been in a state of self-imposed hibernation, but the German navy was far from dormant. If they were to control Western Europe, they would have to first control the seas and the endless stream of goods flowing eastward from the United States. The Battle of the Atlantic erupted in 1939, and the cat and mouse nautical game of attack, defend, hide, counterattack didn't cease until the final days of the war, but played a critical role in determining who would have the materials necessary to keep their soldiers and cities supplied.

Meanwhile over in Eastern Europe, the Soviet Union proved dissatisfied with merely controlling Poland. They next moved to Finland, an area lost due to the Treaty of Brest-Litovsk that released Russia from World War I. What they thought would take a few weeks ended up taking almost half a year. Masters of their terrain and expert cross country skiers, the Finns (even though at times outnumbered ten to one) bogged the superior Soviet forces down into a painful war against the elements. The Soviets not only had to fight against the Finns, they had to fight the long nights of the Scandinavian winter and survive the bitter cold which at times fell under 40 degrees below freezing. If the cold didn't stop the Soviets, the Finnish army's ingenuity proved quite adept at foiling any Soviet offensive. Anyone who's ever watched the Winter Olympics knows the Scandinavians dominate any event involving shooting and skiing, and when the Soviet army entered Finland with their motorized tanks and explosive artillery, the Finnish Army proved more than up to the task of defending their homeland. Like the diminutive Ewoks who survived the vastly superior Imperial Army (my apologies for the outdated Star Wars reference) with their improvised usage of the elements, the Finns crippled Soviet tanks with a few well-placed logs and homemade sticky bombs, and cleverly blended into the surroundings, knocking off Soviet soldiers one at a time. With an officer corps ripped apart by Stalin's decade-long purge of over 30,000 of the Red Army's finest officers, the Soviet forces repeatedly failed to adapt to the Nordic guerilla warfare that continually outflanked, outpestered and outmaneuvered their much more dominant foe. It wasn't until the spring of 1940 that the Soviets sent in additional troops and the million-strong Soviet Army proved too much for the Finns. In April, Finland finally surrendered, but the respect they had earned from the international community and the vulnerability they had exposed in the Soviet forces would live on far longer than the six long months of what came to be known as the Winter War.

Spring brought in a hollow victory for the Soviets, but for the Nazis and Hitler, spring signaled the beginning of the most successful two-month campaign in Western military history. On April 9, 1940, Germany invaded Denmark and Norway to prevent Britain from securing military bases and ports that could later be used to mount a deadly blockade across the North Sea. Two months later, Denmark and Norway were defeated. The rest of Western Europe followed in kind. Luxembourg fell in three days. The Netherlands took five. Belgium eighteen. And as for France, the nation that at the turn of the 19th century housed the most feared military in all of Europe, for France, surrender came after a mere three weeks. How was this possible? How could the nation surrender that decades earlier had fought to the last man on the fields of the Western Front? What happened?

The answer rested in how France built its defenses during the Interwar Period. One of the greatest military blunders any army can make is preparing for future wars solely using the lessons learned from previous wars. Technology and strategies constantly evolve, and for the combatant who chooses to only refine the methods of the past, defeat is almost always guaranteed. France made this tragic mistake when they decided to invest the bulk of their defense budget on the creation of the Maginot Line – a series of seemingly impenetrable permanent trenches built on the southeastern border separating Germany from France. In theory, the Maginot Line seemed logical. Because so many men died in the waterlogged filth of World War I trench warfare, it seemed logical to instead build concrete, insulated, well-stocked, heavily armed barracks and artillery stations that no German army could penetrate. There were a couple flaws in the plan. First, the trenches stopped at the Ardennes Forest. The French couldn't imagine a scenario where any army could make it through the dense foliage and steep topography of the forest. A poor assumption. Second, the trenches didn't protect the Belgian border. Belgium didn't like the idea of having a series of trenches running across its publicly declared neutral border.

Anyone with a memory of Germany's Schlieffen Plan recognizes that Germans had little problem invading neutral countries to get through France. As for the Ardennes Forest? It wasn't exactly impenetrable. Within a week, the German tank (Panzer) divisions had merely circumvented the Maginot Line, moving relatively freely through France's unprotected eastern border. And what of the Maginot Line and all the French troops who patiently waited for the German onslaught? Those troops? Well, after the German army entered Paris and triumphantly paraded down the Champs Elysees, forcing the French surrender, Nazi forces merely headed east with their tank divisions and covered the ventilation systems with tons and tons of dirt. The Maginot Line became the encased coffins for thousands of French troops, all who remained in the trenches, manning the massive east-facing guns, protecting their nation against a German army that never came (from the right direction anyway).

It wasn't only the French who had suffered humiliation at the hand of Hitler. The British had sent close to 400,000 soldiers to the Belgian frontier to protect what remained of "free" continental Europe, but they too were surprised by the German plunge through the Ardennes Forest, trapping 338,000 British soldiers on the beaches of Dunkirk. The Germans could have sent in their Panzer tank divisions to finish off the Brits, but in what would become the first of many tactical errors, Hitler ordered his tanks to remain back to repair any damages, allowing his prized air force, the Luftwaffe, the glory of finishing off Germany's main rival to hegemony in Europe. This delay allowed the British Navy to launch Operation Dynamo, the rushed evacuation of all the troops remaining on the shores of the English Channel. In the course of a week, nearly all of the troops were brought back to England on any floating device that could be mobilized. In addition to the British naval fleet, an armada of little ships owned by private individuals and corporations rushed to the aid of their desperate comrades. Over 800 fishing, sailing and recreation boats were sent across the channel to aid in any way possible. Although their actual contribution was fairly minimal, the government tried to make the most of a public relations nightmare, labeling this incident the "Miracle of Dunkirk," a triumphant example of how personal sacrifice would be needed to save the nation.

If any Brit still believed this aquatic evacuation would be the last they'd hear from Hitler, they were soon proven quite naïve. Even though most of his commanders who had a lick of common sense argued against trying to invade England, Hitler proceeded regardless, putting into play Operation Sealion (yes…these operation names will steadily get more bizarrely clever). The first phase of the invasion was the destruction of the British Royal Air Force so that the German forces could presumably cross the English Channel unchallenged. The Luftwaffe soon learned the Royal Air Force would be just a bit harder to suppress than the challenges put forth thus far by the inferior air powers of Czechoslovakia, Poland, Norway, Belgium and Denmark. However, many of the pilots from these conquered nations actually fled to Britain and joined up with the RAF, to become, in many cases, the most decorated of all WWII pilots. Adding to the noble resistance of the RAF, the British had perfected the new technology of radar, preventing the Luftwaffe from arriving unnoticed. Through the summer of 1940, the struggle for the skies continued, leading to the combined loss of nearly 3,500 fighter planes (with Germany bearing the brunt of the losses). By the end of the year, the German high command recognized the futility of continuing the campaign and ceased fighter operations. Freshly-elected British Prime Minister Winston Churchill praised the efforts of these pilots and radar operators, declaring that "never in the field of human conflict was so much owed by so many to so few."

Churchill spoke a bit too soon, for the battle for the skies hadn't ended - it had just changed form. Instead of the romanticized dogfights of the Luftwaffe and the RAF, the Germans turned to their bombers to take the war to the heart of civilian life, hoping to destroy the morale of Brits which would in turn hypothetically lead to the British government seeking a swift surrender. The precedent for these civilian bombings was in fact an accident. In the dead of night, German bombers mistook a London neighborhood for a nearby oil field, dropping their payloads on the unsuspecting civilians below. Once the gloves were off and civilians became legitimate targets, Britain sent 81 of its own bombers to Berlin, killing few, but thoroughly ticking off Adolph Hitler. Considering he had recently promised his people they would never be touched by Allied bombings, this attack on Berlin was a bit of a hit to his prestige. Hitler avenged this insult by ordering an all out attack on London. Londoners tried everything in their power to protect themselves from the devastation from above – erecting bomb shelters, blacking out all windows and extinguishing all lights (and even cigarettes), sleeping in subway tunnels, and even shipping off tens of thousands of children to the countryside to live with strangers until the worst of the war had passed (for those of you familiar with *The Lion, the Witch and the Wardrobe*, this little event was what sent the feisty Pevensie family to live with the professor and his Narnia-cluttered closet). After seven months of non-stop bombings and no sign that the British were any closer to surrendering, Hitler stopped this "Blitz" and started looking east for where he would attack next. In these deadly seven months, Luftwaffe bombers destroyed over a million homes and killed nearly 50,000 civilians, but more importantly these months signaled a dramatic shift in the waging of 20th century war. The industrial tools of destruction would no longer be restricted to the battlefields of the open plains. Civilians would suffer the brunt of the devastation, leading to casualty numbers of non-combatants that would eventually dwarf anything man had ever inflicted.

Unable to bring Britain to its knees, Hitler turned to his true target – the Soviet Union. Since the early 1920s, Hitler made no secret of his desire for the vast living space and natural resources of the Soviet Union. He also was disgusted by the Slavic people that inhabited the former Russian nation, as well as the feeble, corrupt communist leadership that kept its people in abject slavery. But wasn't there that pesky little problem of the Non-Aggression Pact signed in 1939 by both Germany and the Soviet Union? Not a problem for Hitler. As the Blitz was losing steam in early 1941, Hitler and his officers began formulating a plan for the invasion of the Soviet Union – Operation Barbarossa (named after Frederick Barbarossa, the German Crusader who was stopped a bit short of reaching Jerusalem when he drowned crossing a river). If the bungle at Dunkirk and the botching of the Blitz were mere errors in judgment, Operation Barbarossa was the most colossal mistake Hitler could have made. Why invade Russia? Why fight a two-front war? Napoleon had taught the world that you might be able to fight your way into Russia, but the winter and the vastness of the territory will make it hard to get out alive. World War I taught Hitler that Germany couldn't expect to survive a war where its troops were divided to fight two weighty foes.

But Hitler ignored history. Call it hubris. Call it blind hatred for other perceived inferior peoples. Call it false hope that Japan would enter the war on the east to hopefully divide Soviet forces. Whatever you want to call it, the choice was stupid. The moment Hitler's troops stepped foot on Soviet soil in June 1941, Germany's chances of a European empire died. Like in his other land assaults, initially the blitzkrieg proved unstoppable. During the summer of 1941, three million troops, stretched over a 2000 mile long front, pushed east deep into the heart of Russia, hoping to destroy Moscow, Leningrad and eventually Stalingrad. In what would become the largest military conflict in human history, with close to eight million Soviet troops pushing against four million German troops, Operation Barbarossa appeared to favor the German army until the most devastating force thus far known to man surfaced in December 1941...

A Russian winter. The whole success of Operation Barbarossa depended on the success of the initial blitzkrieg. Germany took thousands of miles of territory in the first few months of the campaign, but they took too much, too fast. Their supply lines couldn't keep up, their officers couldn't adapt when their fortunes started to change and the devastating winter not only claimed hundreds of lives, but it also sapped the speed of the German mechanized forces. For some reason, man's machines just don't work so well when the temperature hits 40 degrees below freezing. Stopped short of conquering Moscow and with 3.5 million men spread over a near 2000 mile long front, the German high command revisited how next to proceed.

But first Germany and Hitler would have to watch and see how the events were unfolding in the Pacific. In 1938, Germany had hitched its fortune to the Japanese, promising in the Anti-Comintern Pact that if either of the two sides ever went to war with the Soviet Union, they would combine forces to put down the communist threat. But the Japanese military commanders weren't as naïve as Hitler. They had no intention of dividing their forces. By late 1941, Japan had restricted its operations to China and had refused to join in the battle for the Soviet Union. Yet still, the Germans held out hope that the Japanese would soon enter their formidable force into the equation, relieving German troops from the sole responsibility of opposing the seemingly limitless Soviet forces.

Japan disagreed.

In firm control of China, Japan set its sights on the rest of the Far East. If they could only kick out the Europeans, installing themselves as the imperial overlords, Japan could ensure the continued flow of goods into their resource-challenged nation. The rubber and tin of Malaya, the oil and scrap metal of Indonesia and the strategic port cities of the Pacific were all that was needed for Japan to secure and maintain a regional empire. Under the haughty auspices of creating a Greater East Asian Co-Prosperity Sphere (though I'm not sure how much the soon-to-be-conquered peoples "prospered"), Japan sought out to fulfill its goal of an "Asia for Asians."

One roadblock stood in its way – the United States. The United States sustained a powerful military and economic presence in the Philippines, the island nation sitting right at the heart of Japan's desired sphere of influence. Any attempt to wade into foreign politics or exert a military campaign would inescapably run into the meddling hands of the Americans. If only the Japanese could find a way of convincing the United States to stay out of Asian affairs, the East would be ripe for the picking. In the early months of 1941, the highest military officials began planning Operation Z, the attack on the American naval base in Pearl Harbor that would hypothetically buy the Japanese the time they needed to seize the tactical advantage in Asia. In a perfect world, this attack might also wipe out America's naval fleet, pushing back the American navy to the coast of California, a full 5000 miles away from the Japanese islands. Some even believed the attack would so shock the American psyche that the government leaders would plead for an immediate, peaceful resolution. Americans were seen as soft, gluttonous consumers, unwilling to muster the stomach needed for war. Any attack on their homeland (even if it was only a territory few could even pick out on a map, and one that wouldn't become an official state until 1959) would almost certainly paralyze the American population.

The Japanese would pay the price for underestimating American resolve.

But in the closing months of 1941, few would have anticipated such a bold move so close to American soil. In Washington D.C., Japanese diplomats continued to lobby Americans to remove their oil embargo established in July 1941, after Japan's invasion of French Indochina (modern-day Vietnam). Most also assumed any attack would most assuredly be in Asia – the Philippines, or Thailand, or Borneo or even Singapore. But not Hawaii. It was on nobody's radar. Yet, when total contact with the Japanese naval fleet was lost in the last weeks of November, intelligence experts warned an attack was imminent.

After the war, it was these warnings that pointed some conspiracy theorists toward the assumption that President Franklin D. Roosevelt knew of the attacks, but allowed them to take place, knowing they would rally the American people, becoming the catalyst needed to allow legal entry into World War II. As early as November 27th, army and naval officials warned that "an aggressive move by Japan [was] expected" and that "hostile action [was] possible at any moment." Though these warnings might have reached Roosevelt's desk, because Hawaii was never really considered a realistic target, no orders were sent to put the island on the highest alert.

This failure to respond left Pearl Harbor helpless to what would become one of the most daring, successful military operations ever attempted. On the morning of December 7th, 1941, Japan deployed six aircraft carriers, twenty-three submarines and 360 planes. On this Sunday morning, still sleeping off the previous night's frivolity, the American soldiers were completely unprepared for an attack. At 7:48, the first torpedoes hit the port and the first bombs dropped from the skies. With many of the soldiers even ashore and much of the ammunition and weapons stored away in military lockers, when the bullets and bombs started flying, the dazed Americans were barely able to mount any viable resistance.

Within an hour, the American navy had suffered catastrophic damage. Four battleships had been sunk, over 300 airplanes had been damaged or destroyed, and close to 2,500 Americans had lost their lives. When news of this attack reached the American shores, the population was indeed shocked, but scared into surrender? Not a chance. Instead, the worst possible scenario for the Japanese quickly materialized. On December 8th 1941, President Roosevelt condemned the "sudden and deliberate attack," rallying his nation to avenge this "date which will live in infamy," to protect the "very life and safety of our nation." The American people answered this call to action, and within months, millions had enlisted to fight what had become a "just war." Those who didn't put on the uniform, rushed to the manufacturing plants across the nation, creating the American "arsenal of democracy" that would supply the Allies for the duration of the war. In a much-misquoted line attributed to General Yamamoto, the Japanese had awoken "a sleeping giant," and because the United States, when fully mobilized, could produce ten times the industrial output of Japan, this wake-up call signaled the eventual death of the Japanese empire.

But first Germany wanted to get in on the action. Adding to his list of poorly-pondered decisions, three days after the United States declared war on Japan, Hitler foolishly declared war on the United States. Hitler didn't have to fight the US. Sure, he had signed a military alliance with Japan, but by 1941, Hitler wasn't exactly known in the international community for his credibility. So why then did he make the reckless decision to pull the US into the European theater? Was it because he was an illogical madman who actually thought he could defeat the largest economy in the world from across a fairly substantial ocean? Was it because he was sick and tired of the US acting like they were maintaining neutrality, all the while finding creative ways of gifting to London billions of dollars in goods, battleships and even much needed cash? Was it because he thought, after Britain, the US would be the only nation able to stop him on his road to world domination? Was it because he just assumed the US would declare war on

Germany first, and Hitler wanted to be seen as the aggressor not the victim?

Or was it because, by December 1941, Hitler's Operation Barbarossa had ground to a halt on the icy terrain of the Soviet Union, and Hitler believed the only chance Germany had of eventually defeating the Soviets was if the Japanese started attacking from the east. In Hitler's mind, if Germany appeared the trustworthy ally who supported Japan against the United States, then Japan would feel inclined to reciprocate and wage a full-scale war on the Soviet Union.

This assumption was a slight miscalculation. Japan had no intention of touching the Soviet Union. Their grand desire was ensuring the Greater East Asian Co-Prosperity Sphere. Hitler could have the Soviet Union for his own lebensraum, but Japan had a clear focus and understood they could never hope to survive a war against Stalin's forces when Japanese soldiers were already thinly stretched across the islands and peninsulas of Asia.

Nope. Germany would be on its own in the Soviet Union, and with the failure of Operation Barbarossa to secure Moscow, in the spring of 1942, Hitler resorted to Plan B – Operation Case Blue. Although a bit less catchier title than its predecessor, it was equally ambitious. German forces would head south into the heart of the Russian frontier, capturing oil fields and crushing Stalingrad once and for all. But for some reason, the lessons learned from Operation Barbarossa were quickly forgotten. Hitler still believed he could take Russia.

He sent his German forces across the plains of the Soviet Union, bombing Stalingrad into oblivion. But Germany would find it far easier to destroy this city than to control it. When this latest fiasco finally ended, the tide of the war had officially changed. No more would Germany be on the offensive. They would instead spend the rest of the war searching for ways of slowing the Red Army's revenge.

For it was at Stalingrad's Volga River that Hitler would lose close to half a million of his finest soldiers, consequently losing any hope that his Third Reich would rule the world for a thousand years (it was having trouble surviving a decade).

Stalin declared the Soviet Union would make their final stand at Stalingrad. He was willing to transport every last soldier from across the nation, but he would not accept surrender. The choice was victory or death. He ordered, "Not one step backward!" Any hesitant comrade who pulled away from the fighting was promptly shot by their own officers. So when in August 1942, the Luftwaffe bombed Stalingrad into rubble and the German army took over close to 90% of the city, they would find it impossible to take the last 10%. Once the bombs were dropped and the army had entered the city, the battle became days and months of building-to-building clashes where German forces might take control of a factory one day, only to have it recaptured when they moved on to the next neighborhood. Both Stalingrad civilians and the Red Army resorted to guerilla tactics to steadily wear down the German invaders, attacking supply lines, deploying snipers to pick off stragglers, burning their own food supplies to prevent German pillaging and fighting to the death for every last chunk of bombed city rubble. This was anything but a blitzkrieg. Some even scoffed that this subhuman form of urban warfare was more a rattenkrieg, or "rat war."

This was a battle Germany could never win, because for every Soviet soldier that died, three more crossed the Volga River to replace him.

One of the tactical blunders of the German field officers was refusing to advance forces across the Volga River in the early weeks of the battle, which would have severed the city from eastern supplies and men. Stalin was able to bring in 1.5 million new troops from across the fatherland, each crossing the Volga to defend the last remnants of the city. But like the previous year, it was the arrival of winter that again sealed the German's fate. Without winter clothing, tents or sleeping bags, tens of thousands froze to death or lost their feet and hands to frostbite. Tanks and trucks proved useless as the gas turned to a spongy, useless syrup-like mixture. Guns couldn't be loaded, let alone fired, and to top it off, the Luftwaffe stopped being able to fly in replacement supplies, leaving the troops to fend for their lives. Unable to defend themselves, the German 6th Army was completely surrounded and General Friedrich Paulus surrendered what remained of his force. Hitler was disgusted and shocked by such cowardice. He had expected Paulus to kill himself before surrendering, but Paulus chose to save the lives of his near-death soldiers. His noble intentions to save his men proved futile, as only 6,000 of the 108,000 that surrendered actually survived the even more horrifying conditions of the Soviet prisoner-of-war camps.

The Soviet victory at Stalingrad opened the Red Army offensive. Within two months, the Soviets had recaptured all the land the Germans had seized in the previous year, and their sights were firmly set on Hitler and Berlin. They had always had the largest land army on the planet, but by 1943, they were also the best-supplied military force left in Europe. In the first months of Operation Barbarossa, Stalin had dismantled the munitions and armament factories, had his men carry them across the eastern forests and mountains and then had them rebuilt to the far east of the German assault. With their factories up and running and a steady stream of food, weapons and ammunition arriving from their newly-acquired ally (the United States), the Soviet Union was finally able to match their manpower and fervor with much-needed materiel.

Yet Stalin was still less than pleased with the arrangement he had made with his two new allies – the United States and England. In August of 1942, as the first bombs rained down on Stalingrad, Roosevelt and Churchill revealed they would not be able to directly attack Germany from the west. Not yet. Instead they would aim to take out Germany from the south – first by capturing Northern Africa and then heading up the Italian peninsula. That didn't exactly help Stalin. While the Russian Red Army had to fight off 4.5 million German invaders, the British and Americans would be down in North Africa facing the far less formidable Italian army. With no real Option B available, Stalin accepted this attack from the south option, only with the promise of continued supplies and an invasion of France as soon as humanly possible. Every month that the Brits and Americans stayed out of continental Europe meant tens of thousands of Soviet deaths.

The British-American invasion of North Africa actually helped out Stalin's cause far more than he could have hoped. Within a few months, the Italians fell to the Allied forces, compelling Hitler to deplete his eastern army and come to the aid of his Italian partner. These troops, including the famed German Field Marshal Erwin Rommel, were pulled from Operation Barbarossa. They not only held the Axis line, but almost pushed the Allies completely out of Africa. However, unable to defend for too long against the superior Allied forces, the German and Italian armies in Africa surrendered in May of 1943. Once the Allies controlled Tunisia, they invaded Sicily, and by September, Allied forces were landing on the boot of Italy.

By the end of 1943, Germany was a shell of the empire it once held only two years earlier. Bombarded from the East by a Soviet army that eventually conscripted over 29 million men (and eventually killed over 80% of Germany's army), Hitler now had to worry about American and British forces heading up the boot of Italy. At this point, the Big Three – Churchill, Roosevelt and Stalin – met in Teheran, Iran to discuss the final defeat of both Germany and Japan. The Soviet Union agreed to turn its forces against Japan once Germany had surrendered, but only if Britain and the United States invaded France in the spring of 1944. They agreed, and from there, Churchill and Roosevelt ordered what would be the largest amphibious landing in the history of military warfare – Operation Overlord – otherwise known as...D-Day.

By the time Stalin had been informed of the scheduled invasion, Operation Overlord had already been in the planning stage for years, and weeks earlier General Dwight D. Eisenhower (later president of the United States) had been promoted to Supreme Commander of the Allied Forces. One of the major priorities of the invasion of German-occupied France was avoiding the catastrophic losses suffered by other full frontal assaults of the World War I era. Churchill (the architect of the tragic Gallipoli campaign of World War I which failed to take the ground at the expense of 60% of all involved troops) was more than familiar with the dangers of deploying men on beaches heavily defended by entrenched men, and wanted to avoid a repeat of his most infamous failure.

Because the goal was to eventually create a suitable harbor where hundreds of thousands of Allied soldiers could be deployed for the eventual invasion of Germany, initially many advisors recommended Allied powers take a port town to take advantage of the already existing docking infrastructure (specifically the town of Calais). Calais seemed the most logical spot not only because of its port, but because it was the closest landmass to the British island (just 26 miles away from Dover). Unfortunately for the Allies, Hitler could likewise read a map, and subsequently put the bulk of his forces at Calais to prevent the certain attack. The Allies decided to use this expectation to their advantage, actually creating an entire secret plan – Operation Bodyguard – to deceive Hitler into believing the entire Allied army would be hitting Calais in the summer of 1944. False messages were conveyed over the radio, German double-agents now working for the Allies shared false memos, famed US General George Patton was promoted to lead this pseudo-invasion force and even Hollywood set designers were employed to create wooden artillery equipment and inflatable tanks. No actual army ever existed. But that's not what Hitler thought. Even when D-Day, June 6, 1944, finally arrived and thousands of aircraft and naval vessels (to say nothing of the hundreds of thousands of men) descended on the beaches of Normandy, Hitler defiantly prevented his Calais forces from defending Normandy, believing the real invasion was a few hundred miles to the north. Hitler military mistake number 3,741.

Because of the Calais ruse, the comprehensive, meticulous planning of Operation Overlord, the heroic valor of the first troops that landed and the overall scale of the Allied forces, any German resistance proved initially deadly, but ultimately futile. The 400,000 German troops spread across the coast of France were no match for the wave after wave of air bombings, naval bombardments and troop deployments. Within hours, Hitler's Atlantic Wall (the series of trenches, barbed wired fences, pillboxes and hedgehogs protecting the French coast) had been breached, allowing over two million soldiers to enter the European theater at Normandy. Hitler now had to fight forces from all sides, but by no means did the Führer consider surrender. Even with the Soviets closing in from the east and the American and British forces moving in from the west and south, the German leader refused to capitulate. Everyone else saw that the D-Day invasion was the "beginning of the end," but not Hitler. At this point even some of his officers tried to have him assassinated, but when these failed plots (seventeen attempts in total) were uncovered, all involved were quickly tried for treason and executed. And Hitler compelled his forces to carry on.

Within eight months of the landing, Allied forces crossed German borders, and Berlin was within striking distance. In the months since D-Day, as the Allied ground forces liberated nation after nation that had fallen to Nazi rule, from the skies, bombers wiped out German cities with what became almost 24-hour, incessant carpet bombing raids. Fleets of bombers dropped hundreds of thousands of tons of explosives on the cities below, caring little about any one specific target, simply leaving mountains of ruins for the coming Allied forces.

By the end of April 1945, Berlin had been breached. Soviet Red Army forces went door to door, wiping out everything in their path – even looting, torturing and raping civilians. British and American forces then closed in on the city. All that was needed was a sign from Hitler that the war was over. On April 30, 1945, he gave that sign.

Not wanting to endure a humiliating surrender and probable international trial, believing the only honorable military option was to take his own life and not wanting to follow in the footsteps of his ally and mentor Benito Mussolini (who was shot and then had his corpse spat upon, kicked and eventually hung on a meat hook), Hitler decided to commit suicide. At 3:30 in the afternoon, Adolph Hitler gave his wife Eva Braun (who he had just married a couple days earlier) cyanide pills, and after those started to do their job, Hitler stuck his pistol to his head and pulled the trigger. To prevent the mutilation and desecration of his remains, within hours, his trusted officers took his body outside where it was covered with gasoline, burned and then buried. This attempt to conceal Hitler's corpse proved unsuccessful, as months later, Stalin ordered SMERSH (his most trusted intelligence agency) to recover his enemy's final resting place. When the bodies were eventually discovered in a bombed out crater (along with a couple puppy carcasses), they were brought back to Russia, where they remained until the 1970s. Eventually, the Soviet KGB (the equivalent of America's CIA), fearing Neo-Nazis might one day want to use his Soviet burial site as some sort of perverted memorial, dug up the remains, crushed them into a fine powder and then dumped them in the Elbe River.

But in 1945, few were worried about a possible Neo-Nazi memorial in a few decades. They just wanted peace. On May 8, 1945, what remained of a German government surrendered, and the world rejoiced at what would become known as VE Day (Victory in Europe). Hitler's dreams of a thousand-year Third Reich had come to an end (falling just a mere 988 years short of his goal).

The popped champagne bottles and ticker tape parades couldn't last long as there was still one more Axis power to defeat – the Empire of Japan.

The fate of Japan was sealed the moment they invaded Pearl Harbor and unleashed the industrial might of the United States. From that moment on, it was only a matter of time before Japan fell to the superior foe. But the Japanese military brass must not have received the pessimistic memo of their fated demise, for the war waged on for four more years. In the month following Pearl Harbor, the Japanese controlled most of coastal China, the Philippines, Burma, Borneo, Malaya, Indonesia, Singapore, and were on their way to Australia. They appeared unstoppable. With every passing month, the world watched as the patchwork of the Pacific increasingly fell to the Empire of Japan. The final pie piece in what was to be the Greater East Asian Co-Prosperity Sphere was not just an island, but a continent itself – Australia. The final European holding in the Pacific, Australia symbolized the last of the European presence in the East. Once Australia was conquered, Japan could set its sights westward – to India.

But taking Australia would prove a bit more difficult than the previous island nations. Aside from its vast size, distant location and resilient military force (of over a million men who would see action in Asia, Africa and Europe), Australia also had the assistance of the Americans, who finally made a dent in the Japanese juggernaut when they successfully launched a surprise raid on the Japanese mainland on April 18, 1942.

Since the bombing of Pearl Harbor, the American public was looking for some clue that they might actually have a chance in this war. In the early winter months of 1942, the future of the United States was anything but secure. The German forces were wreaking havoc across three continents, and Japan was a matchless, almost alien force, that instilled terror in the hearts of most citizens, especially those on the west coast. For if the United States was to be invaded, it would come from the Pacific. The attack on Pearl Harbor signaled that anything was possible, and the age of America's isolation due to two fairly large bodies of water had come to an end. America looked for something to turn their spirits, and the Doolittle Raid on Japan became just the propaganda coup the nation needed. The Doolittle Raid of April 1942 launched fifteen B-25 bombers off the decks of the aircraft carrier Hornet. Because of the distance of the carrier from Japan and due to the low levels of fuel carried on each plane, the mission was to be a one-way trip (the pilots that survived would ideally make it to the Ally-controlled safe zones of China). Like the bombings of Berlin in the midst of the Blitz, when the bombers dropped their payloads on the outskirts of Tokyo, the arrogance of the aggressor was knocked down a few pegs. The aura of Japanese invincibility had been shattered (though the actual losses – a few buildings destroyed and a couple dozen people killed - due to the Doolittle Raid were strategically irrelevant).

If the Doolittle Raid was merely a symbolic victory, in the next two months, the Battle at Coral Sea and the Battle at Midway would prove the strategic equivalents of Stalingrad and D-Day.

At the Battle at Coral Sea, off the northeast coast of Australia, Japanese and American aircraft carriers faced off in what was the first naval war where neither ship actually saw the other (due to their long-range artillery and launched-off the-deck fighter planes). Although the Japanese might have endured fewer casualties, this battle stopped their months of expansion and forced them to retreat to protecting the lands already conquered. Also, two of the Japanese navy's aircraft carriers would have to be repaired, making them unable to assist in the Battle of Midway.

The Battle of Midway became the beginning of the end in the Pacific. Japan intended to once and for all kick the Americans out of the war, securing their perceived right to control East Asia. Midway Island – a fairly meaningless chunk of dirt midway between the US and Japan – was the sight chosen by the Japanese to launch one final all-out offensive. Unfortunately for the Japanese, the American code breakers had intercepted and translated Japanese plans in advance of the Empire of the Rising Sun, which allowed the American navy to be waiting with all available ships sent to the region. What could have been a disaster for America, sending the remainder of its fleet back to San Diego, turned out to be a devastating blow to Japan's Imperial Navy. Admiral Nagumo ordered his fighter pilots to return to their carriers for refueling and rearming, making them nothing more than sitting ducks to the Navy's fighter planes. In less than a half hour, between 10:00 and 10:25 on June 4, 1942, the Japanese navy was permanently crippled.

Unlike the Battle at Stalingrad (the turning point battle for Europe) where millions perished over months of fighting, Midway meant the loss of only 3,000 seamen, but because four critical aircraft carriers (out of the ten Japan had at the start of the war) sunk to the bottom of the Pacific, Japan's ability to wage an enduring war at sea became almost impossible.

Japan couldn't even properly protect its supply lines. Going to and from the Japanese mainland, Japanese merchant vessels faced relentless raids from the American and Allied forces, who sunk 3,032 vessels – over 10.5 million tons of ships deposited at the bottom of the Pacific (many of which have become lovely dive sites for eager scuba divers).

From Midway Island on, Japan was perpetually on the retreat. The Allies in the Pacific established a two-pronged attack: 1) provide the needed support to local resistance fighters in Japanese-controlled areas, and 2) "island hop" toward Japan, setting the stage for the eventual invasion of the mainland. Island hopping was the strategy of avoiding the major Japanese forces located in the major population centers of East Asia, and instead just focusing on capturing geographically significant chunks of land in the Pacific Ocean. Once occupied, each subsequent island provided the air force runways needed to take the next island. Although outnumbered in almost every case, the Japanese firmly entrenched themselves across each island, guaranteeing high casualty rates and some of the most intensely brutal fighting of the war. After Midway, the Allied forces took dozens of islands such as the Gilbert Islands, the Marshall Islands, the Marianas, Iwo Jima and finally Okinawa. Few of these islands were inhabited by civilians, instead usually coral or volcanic atolls that, to the Allied invaders, looked like nothing more than glorified piles of rocks. After the Battle at Iwo Jima – the famed sight of the iconic flag raising photograph – American B-29 bombers were within striking distance of Japan, and from this point on, Japanese cities suffered through daily and nightly bombing raids whose incendiary bombs left the nation's major cities in ashes.

When Okinawa was finally taken in June 1945 (within weeks of Germany's surrender in Europe) the Allied forces began finalizing plans for an October invasion of Japan – Operation Downfall.

But the invasion was never to be, for on April 24, two weeks after the death of US President Franklin D. Roosevelt, newly sworn-in President Harry S. Truman was briefed on a file that would not only bring World War II to an immediate end, but would change the face of war forever. After almost six years in utter secrecy, the massive research undertaking known as the Manhattan Project had succeeded in creating an atomic bomb.

On August 2, 1939, Einstein wrote a letter to then President Roosevelt, explaining to him that in recent months European physicists had taken the next step in splitting the nucleus of atoms, giving off a ton of energy. Man had actually created an energy source, that, in the words of Einstein, released "vast amounts of power," enabling the construction of "extremely powerful bombs of a new type." And the worst part was, the Germans were far ahead of the Americans in mastering this technology. If the United States didn't jump into the atomic energy game, the Germans could create a super bomb that would allow them to effortlessly conquer the world.

Roosevelt acted on Einstein's recommendation to create a department of atomic energy, thus was born the Manhattan Project. This project combined the knowledge of US, Canadian and British scientists and engineers, all working toward not only developing a bomb, but creating the delivery device that could eventually be used to destroy enemy nations. Although research took place in dozens of universities across the US, the primary facility was created in Los Alamos, New Mexico. Fresh off his supervision of the building of the Pentagon, Colonel Leslie Groves was appointed to run the Los Alamos facility, sequestering 8,000 men and women in a remote laboratory (known as Site Y12), where they couldn't communicate with the outside world. The deadly fruit of their labor emerged on July 16, 1945 when the first of the three bombs was detonated. This Trinity Test proved to the military brass that they had in their control a weapon of unparalleled destructive capability.

There was a bit of concern prior to the scientists igniting this little "gadget." Some thought nothing at all would happen. Others thought once one atom was split, it would lead to a chain reaction that would blow up the entire planet. Both were wrong. Instead a mushroom cloud producing over 20,000 tons of TNT (compared with only seven tons of TNT from the most powerful non-atomic bombs available at the time) threw the world into the nuclear age, in an instant making the United States the most deadly force on the planet.

There were two more bombs left. But should the United States use them?

This question has become the great conundrum of the 20th century. On one side of the argument you have the lesser of two evils stance. The Japanese showed no signs of surrendering. Their warrior tradition, coupled with a mass propaganda campaign depicting Americans as barbarians who only wanted to torture and rape every civilian they captured, led both Japanese soldiers and civilians to believe that suicide was the only honorable way to die. In Okinawa, Japanese soldiers ordered the mass suicide of all civilians, even handing out grenades to help speed the process. Hundreds took their families and jumped off cliffs rather than surrender. The Imperial Navy convinced kamikaze pilots to fly their planes into enemy vessels. Of even greater significance was Emperor Hirohito's call for all citizens to die defending the motherland. There would be no retreat, no surrender.

Based on their experiences in the previous amphibious landings and the mass suicides at Okinawa, the Allies projected that if they were to invade Japan, anywhere from five to ten million Japanese lives would be lost, in addition to the predicted million Allied casualties. This didn't even account for what such a land invasion would do to the psyches of the Allied soldiers, as the enemy would no longer be uniformed soldiers, but three-year-old children, pregnant mothers and elderly men, all fighting to save their emperor and their homes.

If anything, the Americans believed dropping the atomic bombs would actually save lives. Not just the lives of those that would inevitably die in an invasion, but the lives of those that would most certainly die if the US continued their bombing raids. For the previous year, American incendiary bombing raids had already taken the lives of over half a million Japanese civilians in 67 cities, leaving another five million as refugees. Japan was already being bombed off the map.

A few other reasons were introduced by Truman's advisors. First, the United States needed to keep the Soviet Union out of Japan. Stalin had already proven in Germany he had no plans of leaving his conquered territory, and the last thing America wanted to do was to partition the Japanese islands. America needed to end the war before the Soviets entered. Second, on a similar note, America wanted to intimidate the Soviets. Stalin proved he liked the idea of expanding an empire, and this little show of force might make him think twice about pressing further east. Third, the military needed to justify the expense. Two billion dollars (over twenty billion in today's money) was spent on the Manhattan Project. Those in power wanted to see some bang for their buck. And lastly, America was just tired of fighting. They had just defeated Hitler in Germany, and the idea of sending millions over to the Pacific for what would be a catastrophic, monumentally demoralizing offensive just couldn't be justified. Truman had a way of ending the war immediately. He had to use it.

But his critics said otherwise. Why not merely drop the bomb on a nearby island to demonstrate its power? Was it because of racism? Had the military started to believe its own propaganda? Were the Japanese really inferior to the Americans? Weren't atomic bombs far more horrific than conventional bombs? The radiation not only kills the current generation, but sentences future generations to a rash of genetic anomalies. And what about the precedent of using an atomic bomb? Wouldn't this just lead to a global arms race to master the technology (and as the last few decades have played out, this was exactly what happened)?

Taking into consideration all sides, Truman made the fateful decision to drop the two bombs – nicknamed Fat Man and Little Boy (after Colonel Leslie Groves and scientist Robert

Oppenheimer) – on the military ports of Hiroshima and Nagasaki. On August 6th Little Boy was dropped on Hiroshima and on August 9th Fat Man was dropped on Nagasaki. The Americans then pledged to relentlessly drop this death-from-the-sky until the Japanese finally surrendered (which was a bit of a bluff since the US had already exploded the only three bombs it built).

Unable to use their courage, their willingness to sacrifice their lives and their conventional weaponry, Japan had no other choice but to surrender. On August 14th, Emperor Hirohito's voice came over the radio for the first time to the nation, and he announced the surrender of Japan, on the grounds that "the enemy now possesses a new and terrible weapon with the power to destroy many innocent lives and do incalculable damage. Should we continue to fight, not only would it result in an ultimate collapse and obliteration of the Japanese nation, but also it would lead to the total extinction of human civilization."

World War II ended.

The world's reaction was a mixture of jubilation and mass mourning, for what had transpired the previous six years demonstrated the hideously appalling extent man went to direct his new technologies against humanity. When industrialized weapons of death were combined with hyper-nationalism and abject racism, the toll on human lives hit unparalleled levels. Historians like to point to the brutality of Attila the Hun, or Genghis Khan, or Julius Caesar or even the religious crusades of the Middle Ages, but to truly see barbarity, one needs to look no further than World War II.

The sheer numbers alone are staggering. Agreeing to any exact total is nearly impossible as so many regions were impacted and the battlefield deaths only reveal part of the story. Fifteen to twenty million soldiers were killed on the battlefield. Five million soldiers were killed as prisoners of war. This alone made the war one of the deadliest of all time (second only to China's Taiping Rebellion), but it was the impact on civilians that took the carnage to unprecedented levels.

40-60 million civilians died in the course of the war. Some were incinerated in bombing firestorms that drove temperatures past 1500 degrees Celsius and asphyxiated hundreds of thousands of innocent civilians. Some were targeted for scientific experiments where they became nothing more than tortured guinea pigs. Some were shipped to far off camps. Others were merely shot on sight or raped to death. Food supplies were cut off, transportation networks were demolished and homes were turned to rubble. When the final shot was fired, tens of millions of those that survived wandered aimlessly across war torn landscapes, creating a refugee crisis that threatened to extend the suffering for decades.

When it came to treatment of civilians, no country was innocent. The United States, fearing an invasion on the West Coast, expelled 110,000 of its own Japanese-American citizens from the states of Washington, Oregon and California, interning them in camps centered deep in the heart of America. US bombing missions also targeted Japanese and German cities, killing millions of civilians. In Poland, the Soviets systematically pulled out the leaders of the nation – the lawyers, policeman, educators, businessmen – and had hundreds shot and mass buried in an incident now known as the Katyn Massacre. And then, upon entering German lands, these Soviet forces then shot civilians on sight and even tortured and raped tens of thousands of the innocent. Britain sent over 3000 planes over the city of Dresden, a German cultural center with minimal strategic importance, dropping almost 4000 tons of explosives on the homes and public meeting areas below. And those were just the Allies.

The Axis Powers took depravity to a new level. Aside from the Rape of Nanking, the Japanese military set up comfort houses, where local women across Southeast Asia were forced into sex slavery for the duration of the war. In Manchuria, the Japanese set up Unit 731, a biological experimentation center where tens of thousands of Chinese and Korean civilians were purposefully given infectious diseases and then their bodies were opened while still alive to observe the results of the disease.

As for the Germans, their barbarism knew no limits. The sum total of their atrocities has become known as the Holocaust – a period of mass exploitation, expulsion, torture, experimentation and murder. Over twelve million civilians were killed both to further the German war aims, but more specifically to ensure a world free of Nazi-perceived racial impurity. Starting with European notions of Social Darwinism and racial superiority, the century leading up to the Holocaust saw an increasingly prevalent view that reproduction between superior and inferior groups should be prevented at all costs – a philosophy known as eugenics. Although most equate the Holocaust with the senseless slaughter of the Jewish population, over half of the total number killed by the Nazis were other "undesirables," including blacks, Arabs, Gypsies, homosexuals, prisoners, mentally and physically handicapped, Slavs and those political opponents deemed a threat to Nazi superiority.

However, the Holocaust in its public perception deals primarily with the systematic, calculated extermination of the Jews. What started in the 1930s as an attempt to prevent interaction between Jews and non-Jews (restrictive marriage and commerce laws, identification bands, concentration in urban ghettos and even forced sterilization), eventually evolved into the "final solution to the Jewish problem." In the early years of the war, German scientists, officers and businessmen exploited the Jews as slave labor. Eventually they were put into concentration camps where they were starved, beaten, worked to death or even used as human lab subjects in Nazi's bizarre scientific experiments. Under the demented leadership of Josef Mengele, infant twins were sewn together, men were frozen and then revived in boiling water, prisoners were exposed to malaria and poisoned gas, inmates were burned alive with incendiary bombs and countless other defenseless victims were subjected to torture and mutilation to satisfy the whims of German "scientists."

The course of Jewish treatment shifted at the Wannsee Conference on January 20, 1942, when the leaders of the Nazi Party, along with critical military figures from across Europe, met to discuss the mass transportation and eventual execution of all Jews currently residing in German-occupied territories. From across the empire, Jews were crammed into train cars and sent to camps such as Auschwitz, Belzec and Treblinka, where they were stripped, exposed to lethal doses of cyanide and then cremated in gas-fed furnaces. Tens of thousands of Jews were slaughtered daily and within a year nearly the entire Jewish population of Europe had been eradicated. In Warsaw, Poland alone, out of the 500,000 Jews alive at the start of the war, only 200 eventually survived to VE-Day (Victory Day in Europe). Though whisperings of Nazi atrocities had been heard throughout the war, it wasn't until the Allied forces moved into German-occupied territories that the extent of the tragedy was fully revealed.

Across World War II, time after time, humans failed to live up to their humanity. We entered the 20th century believing we were the most civilized, advanced, cultured, enlightened people to ever walk the planet. We had learned more, built more and seen more than any previous generation, but in a few short years we proved that under the guise of war and beholden to a set of extraordinary scientific tools, our insecurities and racist proclivities could still win out over logic and compassion.

World War II had been a total war. Everyone had been touched. Civilians had been for years pounded with propaganda dehumanizing the enemy, while encouraging every man, woman and child to join the war effort. In some nations, wartime production brought the people out of the Great Depression. In others, the factories, neighborhoods and public meeting areas became targets for enemy bombers, making survival, let alone production, nearly impossible. The United States witnessed a mass migration to the cities as minorities, women and rural dwellers filled in for the departed soldiers. Chinese suffered through not only a foreign invasion, but a savage civil war that continued between the communists and the national government. Territories changed hands dozens of times, and across Southeast Asia, the Middle East and North Africa, civilians tried to survive in a world where they were mere pawns in a global game of territorial acquisition.

For soldiers fighting in World War II, there was no singular experience. Whereas trench warfare came to define the first Great War, combat in World War II became almost indefinable. A soldier could fight behind a tank crossing the Tunisian desert. He could live for weeks underwater as his submarine crew struggled to sink merchant vessels attempting to supply enemy combatants. He could storm the beaches of Sicily, the coral atolls of the Pacific or the beaches of Normandy. He could just as likely freeze to death huddled in a hole in Bastogne in temperatures 40 degrees below zero, as he could die marching for miles through 110 degree temperatures on the Bataan Death March or die shot in the head by a sniper perched in the corner of a blown-out factory building in Stalingrad. And his tools of terror were like no other before. Sure, he still had his machine gun, his flamethrower, his knife and his grenade, but now he survived on ships as big as floating islands, fired V2 rockets that soared into the stratosphere and built bombs that required the splitting of atoms. It was in some ways like all the other wars fought before, but at a scale never before seen, using tools of destruction never before envisioned.

The world would need to rebuild from this near-apocalypse. It would need to take stock of what went wrong, punish the aggressors and ensure the world would not merely fall again into chaos within a few short decades. The Paris Peace Conference of World War I proved an abject failure. The world could not survive another botched treaty. For now that man had atomic bombs, the next world conflict would mean the end of humankind.

But that is for another chapter.

40

Farewell to the Age of Empires

Decolonization and Independence Movements – 1920 > 1970

I f ever there was the perfect opportunity for the age of empires to end, it was going to be the years following World War II.

In 1945, all the conditions looked ripe for decolonization, for outright independence, for the dawn of a new era where the peoples of the world were free to choose their own economic, cultural and political paths, free from the soft and hard influence of foreign powers bent on pursuing their own selfish goals.

The European continent sat in utter ruin. Surely, the major Western powers would prioritize getting their own people back to work and feeling safe before they'd ever again concern themselves with some far off, uncivilized colored peoples. Surely, the citizens of Western Europe would rather prevent revolutions in their own backyards before they would allow their politicians to funnel much-needed recovery funds to maintain colonies a continent away. And if Western indifference wasn't enough of a deterrent to re-colonization, surely there was no way the Soviet Union or the United States would allow global power to return to Old Europe.

The two surviving superpowers had no intention of seeing the tremendous cost they bore during the war, both in lives (especially for the USSR) and in economic resources, go for naught. Their uneasy alliance existed almost exclusively to end the new empirical designs of Japan and Germany – that didn't mean they in any way approved of a return to the status quo of the early 20th century. The United Nations put in writing what the victors felt, declaring that empires would no longer be tolerated, that instead the world would strive "to develop self-government, to take due account of the political aspirations of the peoples and to assist them in the progressive development of their free political institutions."

As for the "them" in the previous sentence, the conquered peoples of the world, this appeared their moment in world history to declare and achieve independence. The nations of Africa, the Middle East and East Asia had been teased with independence since World War I, only to see their colonial masters renege on their promises when the probable outcomes appeared to be too expensive or too messy. But just because few nations broke free from their colonial oppressors in the 1920s and 1930s didn't mean that the independence movements had been squashed.

And when the German and Japanese forces unveiled their own armies of imperialism, the global colonial holdings were again pulled into regional clashes. Resources were drained from local economies at a fraction of their value, citizens were drafted to fight in distant theaters and entire colonies were overrun by Axis belligerents. Not only did these invasions remove the European perception of invincibility (Britain surrendered a mere seven days after the Japanese invaded Singapore), but they also fueled nationalistic movements that united local forces to expel this new set of foreign invaders. When World War II ended, victorious colonial forces felt their pivotal role in defeating the Axis powers earned them the right to see the promises of self-determination finally come to fruition.

And at first, it looked like they were getting what they asked for. A ton more countries were actually put on the map. Two decades after Germany and Japan surrendered, four times as many nations existed on the earth than did before the war began. One by one, the nations of the developing world had earned their independence. By the 1960s, on paper, decolonization looked like it was well underway.

But there was no singular story of decolonization. How could there have been when there was no singular story of "colonization"? On one extreme, you had the settler colonies of Australia, New Zealand and the United States where native populations were subjugated, interned or even massacred, essentially wiping out any hint of an indigenous presence. Then there was the political imperialism of India, East Asia and Africa where European authorities dictated their laws from the safety and insulation of their colonial mansions. And then, on the other extreme, there was the more hands-off approach of commercial imperialism where European traders made deals with locals, trading their Western finished goods for some much needed natural resources (but other than that not leaving any noticeable imprint on local culture).

So yes, in 1914, Europe might have economically or politically *influenced* 80% of the planet, but in no way were 1.53 billion individuals following the lead of one tiny little continent northeast of the Atlantic Ocean. In fact, for most of the people living in one of Europe's holdings, from Indonesia to Burma to Zambia to Algeria, once you travelled a few miles from the region's main port city, you'd quickly realize that native life was still ruled by the rhythms of nature and the needs of the family, not the whims of European oppressors.

Yet still, though the degree of domination might have differed, a few patterns of influence popped up regardless of how embedded European authority was in the other nations of the world. And not all Western influences were evil. Everywhere Europeans went, they brought improved communication and transportation networks. They built telegraph lines, paved roads, dug canals, dredged canals and laid down railroad lines. They shared their technology, improving medical care, farming techniques and methods for extracting natural resources. Income levels rose, standards of living increased and overall health and life expectancy rates improved. They brought their education systems to these foreign worlds, and even sent elite students back to Europe to study at the finest institutions. Europeans also set up the institutions that ironically later formed the foundations for the independence movements that eventually became their own undoing.

However, these contributions are almost always ignored as it is far easier to fixate on the numerous, and sometimes horrific, examples of exploitation and oppression. Locals were taxed, enslaved, mutilated and murdered. Europeans sat in their conference tables thousands of miles away, determining arbitrary borders that forced rival tribes to interact and divided clans that had survived together for centuries. Natives were driven off their land, taken away from their families or forced to abandon their farms to cultivate commodities whose value rose and fell based on international demand outside their control. When the demand for cotton or opium or sugar or tea dropped, millions found themselves without the money needed to purchase the necessities of life, and unlike before the implementation of these commodity crop economies, they couldn't exactly eat their opium or cotton harvests to survive during the off years. Europeans further crippled these developing economies by establishing the precedent that their lone value in the global trading networks was the exporting of natural resources to the industrialized nations. They were never given the capacity to turn the cotton into cloth or the diamonds into jewelry. Their economies were trapped in their infancy.

By the mid-20th century, the time appeared ripe for the oppressed to free themselves from their oppressors. Western institutions had proved defective and vulnerable. The Great Depression revealed the weaknesses of capitalism. Conquered peoples were inspired and demanded liberation. And one by one they got their wish. The end of the 20th century paralleled the end of the age of European dominance, and not only created opportunities for some nations to thrive in the world community, but also left behind dangerous power vacuums that were filled with chaos and civil war.

For China, the stakes were the highest. For nearly four thousand years, China stood out as the preeminent civilization in the world, but the Opium War and the incursion of European traders in the mid-19th century triggered a brief blip in China's story where their future no longer rested solely in the hands of their dynastic emperors. Like the periods following previous dynastic failures, the decades following the fall of the Qing Dynasty saw the countryside regress into civil war, but this time foreigners from Europe stood on the sidelines waiting to see if a new empire would earn the Mandate of Heaven or if the regional lords would keep the nation in chaos opening up new avenues for exploitation. It wasn't clear in 1912 what direction China would adopt. Would it partner with European business interests to Westernize the economy? Would it expel all foreigners and isolate itself from the world? Would it revert to the traditional values of Confucianism or adopt the more liberal values pressing in from all sides? Would it look to its scholars for guidance or would the mantle of power be passed to the capitalist entrepreneurs looking to turn China into an industrial giant? And what form of government would it become? A democratic republic? An autocratic dictatorship? Or what about that new form of government being tested by their neighbor to the north - Russia? What about communism?

Initially, the Chinese experimented with democracy. In 1912, they created a Senate, elected a president and then started to write a constitution. But it didn't last. Their first elected president didn't really understand the whole democracy thing. Once in power, he charged his army with destroying all political parties and ceasing any chatter about creating a republic. He ruled as dictator until 1916 when he died and the nation regressed into despair. Power reverted to the regional lords that controlled the countryside. China's future was in doubt. How long would this latest era of crisis last before a new dynasty arose? Or would Western democracy be given another chance?

The Europeans helped the Chinese answer these questions by doing the one thing that has proven able to unite a people locked in regional madness – create a common enemy. And in this case the common enemy would again be the Europeans.

After the end of World War I, the European powers gathered in Versailles to punish the Germans and divvy up the spoils of war. In China, since 1897, the Germans had controlled the eastern Shandong province, after the war, the Chinese only assumed that control of the region would revert back into their hands. They were wrong. The British, the Americans and the French awarded control of Shandong to the Japanese, ignoring the Chinese diplomats at Versailles who pleaded for autonomy.

For the Chinese, the writing was on the wall – the Europeans cared little for Chinese interests. Europeans controlled the game and they would make any rules that would benefit Europeans. Even if that meant allying themselves with the Japanese.

Enough was enough. European imperialism in China had to end. But it wouldn't be warlords or political leaders who confronted the foreign foe. It would be university students. On May 4, 1919, students from the thirteen universities across Beijing gathered at Tiananmen Square (where 70 years later, students would again protest before being sent home by tanks and armed forces). They demanded a reversal of the Shandong agreement and blasted Chinese officials for allowing the spread of the European values of materialism and individualism. These students protested for days and their message spread into the countryside. Their initial goal of a free Shandong never materialized, but they did succeed in uniting China and igniting a sense of nationalism that had gone into hiding for a few generations. The Chinese were proud again to be Chinese, and they began to believe they could expel the barbarians. They also recognized that this revolution would not come from the elite of society. It would have to come from the masses. They would need to unite across the countryside to share the fruits of the economy. This conviction gave birth to the rise of communism.

And once there was the Communist Party, the death of European influence in China was just around the corner. Well, maybe not just around the corner. It still took thirty years, over forty million deaths and a civil war for the soul of China. On one side of this war were the Communist forces of Mao Zedong who spent the 1920s and 1930s recruiting peasants to overthrow their feudal bonds and raise their standard of living. On the other side was the Nationalist Party of Chiang Kai Shek that promised to advance China's interests by going the more Western route of supporting businesses, improving the nation's infrastructure (roads, roads and communication networks) and bringing banking into the 20th century. Both sides wanted an independent China – the Communist Party wanted the Westerners out unconditionally, the Nationalist Party was more willing to work with Westerners to gradually reverse the unjust treaties of the previous century. The Communists fought guerrilla battles from the countryside. The Nationalists built up a strong national military with moneys they earned from imports and from loans secured from European banks. The Nationalists ran the government and the Communists relentlessly pestered their forces across the indefensible Chinese countryside. By the mid-1930s, it appeared the Nationalist Party had the advantage. Mao's forces had retreated to the hills and appeared on their last legs.

Then the Japanese invaded and the tides of China's future turned not on the actions of Mao or Chiang, but on the choices of a warlord from the north – Zhang Xueliang. Zhang's family had controlled Manchuria for decades, but when the Japanese invaded in 1928 and planted a bomb that killed Zhang's father, he flipped into revenge mode and vowed to expel the Japanese. But he had a problem. He couldn't do it alone. He needed help from the Communists *and* the Nationalists. Divided, China had no chance. United, they might be able to defeat Japan, or at least keep them from pushing their forces inland. If he could just find a way to convince the Communists and Nationalists to stop fighting each other and direct their venom against the more dangerous foreign forces. But how could he convince Chiang Kai Shek to sign a truce with his enemy Mao Zedong? How? He kidnapped Chiang, put a gun to his head and encouraged him to stop fighting the Communists.

It worked. The Communists and Nationalists agreed to not kill each other for a few years. They would just kill the Japanese. Mao's Communists used this reprieve to scatter across the nation, securing more and more peasants attracted to the ideology of redistribution of wealth from the rich to the poor, but more drawn to the opportunity to attack Japanese forces. The Nationalists continued to fight the Japanese, tying themselves closer and closer to their Western allies who offered money and weapons to help slow down the Japanese onslaught. This uneasy truce flipped the tide of national support in the Communists' favor, as time and again it appeared the Communists were the better fighters and the Nationalists were merely the soft allies of the West, unable to truly protect China's interests. When the war ended and Japan was no longer the enemy that necessitated a truce, Mao and Chiang resumed their war, but by this time, the Nationalist's credibility had been shot. Mao's party skillfully exposed incidences of Nationalist corruption, highlighted the oppressive taxes of the Nationalist government and circulated stories of Nationalist soldiers dressing in peasant clothing to avoid protecting innocent women and children. If the Chinese people had to choose a horse, they were putting their money on Mao and the Communist Party.

In 1948, Mao used this support to dominate Chiang's forces, eventually forcing him to retreat across the Taiwan Strait with two million of his Nationalist supporters, hoping to fortify their forces so they might one day return to the mainland and restore the Nationalist government to its rightful place.

They never returned. In 1949, Mao proclaimed the birth of a new nation - The People's Republic of China – a nation that would be a republic in name only. Mao was the lone man calling the shots, and his often-misguided efforts lead to millions of deaths.

Both the European and American interests were left supporting a loser. They continued to throw money and weapons at Taiwan (and even still do to this day), but it would be another three decades before mainland China again reopened its doors to

Western influence. But by then, China would have regained its national prestige and would never again deal with the West on foreign terms. China would control its destiny and if the West wanted to play along, they would have to adapt to the whims of the reborn Middle Kingdom.

For China, escaping European influence meant half a century of civil war while embracing a Communist doctrine of peasant revolution. Other countries would likewise feel the pull of capitalism and communism as they wrenched themselves away from colonial shackles, but unlike the violent path taken by China, their neighbor to the west offered another option – civil disobedience.

For India wasn't anything like China. It wasn't merely a nation where a few ports were controlled by Western authorities. India was a colonial holding of Great Britain, utterly subjugated by a foreign nation unwilling to relinquish its dominion. If India was to break free, they couldn't afford a civil war. They had to find a way to unite their four hundred million people to pressure Great Britain to withdraw their forces. They could never match Britain on the battlefield, but maybe they could induce sympathy in the media. Maybe if they followed a man with a revolutionary idea of how to protest nonviolently (instead of a military leader or a political mastermind), maybe they could convince the British public that their independence was a natural right.

For this revolution, they would follow Mahatma Gandhi. A lawyer and a philosopher, Gandhi became the inspiration for a movement that had been decades in the making. Like so many times in history, he was the right man at the right time.

The Great Britain of the 1920s was not the Great Britain of the turn of the century. WWI proved the Brits were not an infallible force. Their century reign of pretty much uninterrupted military successes came to an end. Sure, they might have won World War I, but in 1919, their nation didn't feel too victorious. It was plagued by debt, close to a million of their young men were slaughtered on the battlefields of France and their citizens were left to wonder if they truly were the most civilized people on the planet. Britain could have withdrawn from international affairs and focused on repairing the lives of their countrymen, but instead they attempted to merely pick up where they left off. India was their crown jewel in Asia and they had no intention of granting them independence, no matter what they had promised their South Asian subjects to ensure full support during the war.

In 1919, India was not only further away from independence, it was actually feeling the even deeper sting of colonialism due to the war's carnage. 60,000 Indian men paid the ultimate price of supporting the crown, perishing in the trenches of East Africa and the Western front. To add insult to injury, the Indians were then charged exorbitant taxes to help pull Britain's economy out of turmoil. Like the American colonists 150 years earlier, the Indian colonists had a little trouble swallowing the fact that they not only were responsible for dying in a foreign power's war, but they also then had to illogically pay for this war. But also like the Americans, merely being frustrated wasn't enough to foment a revolution. The people had to be roused out of their passive acceptance of subordination, snapped out of their haze of merely accepting the leftover scraps of their British lords.

For the thirteen colonies of America, there was the "massacre" at Boston.

For India, it was the AmriCzar Massacre.

But unlike the Boston Massacre where only a handful of Bostonians died, many of whom had spent the afternoon badgering the British redcoats, throwing out a series of slurs and pelting them with rocks and snow balls, this Indian tragedy was truly an example of innocents being butchered by seemingly sadistic bullies. On April 13, 1919, in the northern region of AmriCzar, a few thousand men, women and children gathered at a public garden to protest their spiraling downward standard of living. Alarmed by recent riots in neighboring counties, the head of the British forces, Brigadier-General Reginald Dyer, ordered that fifty of his soldiers set up around the periphery of the square and mow down the gathering protesters. They obliged, and within minutes, hundreds of defenseless civilians lay murdered and another thousand were wounded. Word quickly spread of the tragedy and the Indian subjects looked to their hypothetically civilized authorities to right this wrong. Dyer was taken before a military tribunal and forced into an early retirement, but when he returned to Britain he was greeted as a hero.

How could this murderer be celebrated as a hero? Weren't the Brits the ones who championed themselves as enlightened elites, who spent the last few centuries admiring the works of 18th century philosophes who demanded the protesting of unjust political systems and the protection of individual freedoms like assembly and speech? Or maybe in the world of Great Britain, human equality and freedom were rights only granted to Europeans.

Whatever moral authority Britain once held died that spring day. Indians would never be treated as equals as long as they were simply a source of labor and resources that Great Britain could tap into whenever its economy needed a boost.

Enter Gandhi. Gandhi returned to India in 1915 a hero. He had spent the previous two decades in South Africa, after earning his law degree in England. He had become a sort of celebrity in the decade before World War I for standing up to British authorities in South Africa, attempting to end the apartheid system that saw races separated and a caste system propped up where white people had access to the highest paying jobs, while the coloreds were relegated to whatever manual labor they could find. Gandhi himself was thrown off trains for sitting in the white section and refused entry to hotels and restaurants based on his color. It was in South Africa where we first saw the man's methods. He would use the law, he would use the press and he would use the crowds to shine an unflattering light on the inequities of the British realm.

Once he returned to India, he was approached by the Indian National Congress, an organization of wealthy, educated, connected Indians who hypothetically represented Indian interests in colonial government. Yet many of these elite Congressmen had more in common with British authorities than they did with their own people. They had worked since 1885 to gain more privileges for Indians, but they did so within the law, hoping to work towards an amicable understanding with the respected British crown. Their movement never really gained traction, as it was never before a movement of the masses, but more a gathering of the upper class who talked of a better world. They were big on words but small on action. They had assured more power to local governments and expanded the voice of locals, but by the end of World War I, India was still not independent.

Yet when Gandhi arrived, the make-up of the Congress changed. It became less elitist and more welcoming to members of the other castes. It started listening to the grievances from the countryside. With the Amritsar Massacre, it was poised to take the protests to a higher level, and Gandhi would lead this movement.

Gandhi challenged the conventional Indian National Congress platform that supported an end-game where Brits running a British system were replaced with Indians running a British system. He saw how the American Revolution was a revolution in name only and he had no desire to simply replace one aristocratic ruling class with another aristocracy, even if this new one was from South Asia. He espoused the principles of home rule – where Indians would create a unique government system based on India's vibrant past, its complex diversity and its geographic realities. In his book *Hind Swaraj*, Gandhi introduces a new type of freedom, a freedom where the West is rejected, where Indians don't see themselves as beneath the Europeans, but realize it was they who dominated a huge chunk of the planet for most of human history. He also wrote of how the one way to accomplish this true independence was through civil disobedience, by securing rights through suffering. Until Indians were willing to let their bodies, their minds and their pocketbooks suffer, the British would never leave.

So Gandhi started his campaign of nonviolent resistance, a strategy that has since been borrowed countless times by disenfranchised peoples around the globe. He convinced Indians to boycott British goods. He argued they should stop buying British clothes and instead make their own (thus the trademark white outfit Gandhi spun from his own portable spinning machine). He marched across the country, gathering thousands along the way as he protested the British ban on Indian salt, choosing instead to make salt from the sea. He lobbied persecuted employees to go on strike until their companies granted them a fair standard of living. He himself willingly paid the price for independence. He fasted, he was beaten, he was arrested and his life was constantly under threat. But all the while, he moved forward. And all the while, he ensured the full participation of another partner – the media. Without both the British press and Indian press, his movement would have fallen on deaf ears (if even heard at all). Throughout the 1920s and 1930s, one by one, nations were falling to fascist governments that persecuted the helpless. So when stories continued out of India of scores of people beaten by royal officers or of a gaunt, smiling man in rags staggering across the country speaking of the power of free will, England had to take a dose of hypocrisy medicine. Back in England, the powers-that-be started to listen. They realized the falseness of their claim of civilized, moral authority when reports kept rolling in of barbaric treatment of an oppressed people.

Not all approved of Gandhi's tactics. Some wished he would use his influence to foment a communist revolution (a la Mao to the east). Some thought he was an egotistical self-promoter who relished the attention. Others thought he favored Hindus over Muslims. Others thought he was too nice to the Muslims. And back in Britain, parliamentarian Winston Churchill was just annoyed with his entire existence, calling him a "half naked fakir."

Yet in a country of 390 million people, he was never going to get everyone on his side. He didn't need to. But he did move tens of millions. At the start of World War II, Britain had a tenuous hold on India, but it still wouldn't let it be free. When war broke out against Germany, Britain forced India to again support the cause, both with the lives of its young men and its resources needed at the front lines. Gandhi didn't believe India should support British forces, and he chose the heart of the war to launch a more rigorous campaign – the Quit India movement. Tens of thousands marched, protested and boycotted, but Britain had little patience for this resistance when they were trying to manage a war. They threw Gandhi in jail for a few years and focused their efforts on keeping Hitler from taking over the world.

But when World War II ended, Britain realized enough was enough. Again, their economy was in turmoil, but this time their entire country lay in rubble. Britain had no idea how it was going to rebuild itself, let alone how it would finance India's recovery. In 1947, they decided to pull out their troops and their officials. The British forces had no idea what to do about the Muslim vs. Hindu conflicts that were bound to blow up at any moment. Would they turn the country over to a percentage of Muslim officials or a percentage of Hindu officials? Or would they just walk away and let them fight it out for themselves? Instead, the British authorities just invented a new country – Pakistan, and on August 14th and 15th, 1947, Indian and Pakistan became independent nations.

Though the struggle for independence had ended, the civil war began. After the partitioning of South Asia into a Muslim Pakistan and a Hindu India, over twelve million Indians packed up their lives and moved across the country, marking one of the largest migrations in human history. As homes were abandoned and villages were taken over by thousands of belligerent, hungry refugees, there was bound to be conflict. Former allies turned against each other as Muslims fought Hindus for the spoils of independence. Anywhere from 500,000 to a million Indians perished in the beatings, shootings, burnings and famines that resulted from the mass migration. To this day, the legacy of this partition continues to fuel hostilities, as Pakistan and India refuse to accept that the partition and its arbitrary boundaries established by the British parliament should be respected as is.

Gandhi lived long enough to see his country free and then his people implode. A year after the partition he was gunned down by a Hindu extremist who felt Gandhi was too soft on Pakistan. The leader of the independence movement was dead, the two nations were in turmoil and like every other nation that broke free from colonial rule, life would get a heck of a lot worse before it got better.

China and India took two completely different routes to independence, but certain patterns emerged in their stories that would reoccur time and again as scores of countries believe the time was ripe for revolution.

First, across the world, patriotic feelings of nationalism sprouted, as the possibility of rallying against a common foreign enemy stirred many to put their differences aside for the sake of the movement. These nationalistic uprisings were almost always rallied by passionate, inspirational figures who spouted vitriolic attacks at their colonial masters. Second, many of these newly-freed countries experimented with democracy. China dabbled with a republic after the fall of the Qing, India stuck with a republic that has since evolve into the largest democracy in the world, Israel was created by the United Nations as a beacon of republicanism in the midst of a desert of autocratic regimes, and in Vietnam, America actually thought democracy could work, even though a man named Ho Chi Minh was less than thrilled with the notion. Nationalism and the promise of republican governments sparked the independence movements, but almost all decolonized regions soon learned inspiration and governance are two entirely different concepts. Keeping the country would be a lot harder than creating it.

Another pattern that emerged is that almost all decolonized regions immediately devolved into madness, civil war or political infighting. In regions where boundaries had been created haphazardly with no concern for ethnic rivalries (see map of Sub-Saharan Africa), this regression would be bloody and would cripple any chance of fostering stable societies. In nations where ethnicity wasn't the dividing factor, political ideology would rule the day and peoples would decide if they could resolve their differences amicably in a house of parliament (a la India) or have to fight a civil war for the hearts and minds of the nation (Vietnam). For some nations, resolution was impossible and independent nations would have to be created (Korea, Vietnam). For other nations, the conflicts were stopped, not by negotiation, but by force – which leads us to the third pattern.

Autocrats had proven effective at stopping (even if only temporarily) the ethnic hatred that had no clear solution. Often these figures aren't renowned today for their humanitarianism or their pacifist nature, but they did keep the peace in freed nations where rival groups wanted nothing less than total annihilation of their adversaries. Saddam Hussein in Iraq, Sukarno in Indonesia and Marshall Tito in Yugoslavia all stifled ethnic hostility through their ample usage of secret police and not-so-judicious judicial systems. But once these men died (either naturally or by the hands of people not so fond of their rule), tensions sprung again to the surface, meaning persecution and death tolls were soon to follow.

But the one pattern common to all of these decolonized societies was that their little foray into independence, free of outside influence, was always fleeting. Although the French, the British and the Dutch might have pulled back their colonial influence, two remaining superpowers would spend the rest of the 20th century pulling these fledgling nations under their own sphere of influence. For the five decades following World War II, Russia and the United States fashioned a new type of empire, a new way of controlling the economies and the governments of the world. They no longer would colonize. It was just too expensive. And also, the legacy of imperialism rightfully left a bad taste in the mouths of the freshly-freed.

These two new powers set out to carve up the world into a bipolar hegemony, where they each warned, "You're either with us or against us." This new era of imperialism would be known as the Cold War, and if nations thought their societies were shaped by foreign interests before, they hadn't seen nothing yet.

But that is for another chapter.

41

Avoiding Armageddon

The Cold War – 1945 > 1989

Explaining a hot war isn't too tough. One side wants something from another side. The other side would prefer to keep it. Tensions mount. Both sides prepare for conflict. Whether intentional or accidental, a catalyst erupts. One side attacks the other. The other defends itself. Civilians help out. Civilians are killed. One side conquers the other, or one side just gets tired of fighting and gives up. The war ends. A peace deal is set. Life goes on.

That's how a hot war works.

But what about a cold war? How does one of *those* things start?

Within weeks of Germany's surrender, the highest military brass warned that World War III was just around the corner.

Within months, the Soviet Union secured its borders and prepared for yet another invasion from the West. The Americans and Brits tried to slow the Soviets down, pushing their own forces as far east as peace would allow.

Within years, the world was again at war, but this time it wouldn't be a conventional war. It would be something totally different. It would be the Cold War, a near five-decade struggle between the Soviet Union and the United States of America for mastery of the universe.

Their fight was as much for ideological supremacy as it was for geographic influence and self-preservation. From 1946 to 1989, the Soviets and Americans spied, schemed, built up armies, built up weapons, created alliances, prevented alliances, expanded their science, economies and spheres of influence, all with the hopes that when the great civilization day of judgment arrived, their nation would stand alone as the preeminent superpower on the planet (while hopefully preventing a nuclear holocaust that just might vaporize all living creatures).

But the roots of the war didn't actually start in the weeks after Germany's surrender. Like all conflicts, the roots oftentimes find themselves buried deep within a previous conflict. The way one war ends determines when and how the next war will be fought.

In the final stages of war, when victorious powers fail to prepare for the peace, they might as well prepare for another war. The failures at Versailles fueled the tension and rage that spawned World War II. And likewise, the missteps by the Allied powers in the final months of World War II started the world down an even more treacherous path where total annihilation would loom only moments away.

So yes, World War II created the Cold War.

The fragile alliance between America, Britain and the Soviet Union was never meant to last. It was formed to take out Hitler - nothing more, nothing less.

Churchill and Roosevelt never really trusted Stalin. Why would they? His domestic policies killed millions, his secret police and show trials persecuted, prosecuted and then discarded even his closest advisors (fourteen of the original fifteen leaders of the Bolshevik party were murdered or "died" under convenient circumstances) and even Stalin admitted, "I trust no one, not even myself." It didn't help the Allied circle of trust that just a few years earlier, Stalin had actually partnered with Hitler to carve up neutral Poland, before invading Finland, Lithuania, Estonia and Latvia.

So as World War II progressed and the Big Three came together to meet at first Tehran, then Yalta and finally at Potsdam (with Truman replacing the recently deceased Franklin D. Roosevelt), it became more than apparent that America and Britain were two peas from the same idealistic pod, whereas Russia was the obvious odd man out, appeased more out of necessity than out of a shared vision for the future. Tensions arose almost immediately when Britain and America delayed launching a Western offensive, choosing to instead approach Europe from the African front, leaving Russia alone to bear the brunt of the German blitzkrieg.

But dissension over military tactics was the least of their worries; of bigger concern was what to do with Germany, and the world, once the war was over. America and Britain wanted a world where all nations embraced free trade, free markets, free elections, free speech and free choice. Russia wanted to be safe. Sure, Stalin wouldn't be upset if the rest of the world adopted his version of communism, but his number one priority was security. Russia lost a quarter of a million countrymen when Napoleon invaded in 1812, over three million in World War I and over 23 million in World War II. Their nation's borders were seemingly limitless, and the West had frequently shown the propensity for invasion whenever someone got the idea to expand their empire.

But no more. Stalin was done with being vulnerable. He wanted to create a protected ring of satellite nations around Mother Russia, a buffer zone that would if not prevent, at least slow down any attempt to invade Soviet soil.

So in every discussion between the Big Three, it became quite apparent that Stalin had no intention of merely defeating Germany and withdrawing his forces to focus on domestic tranquility. At the Yalta Conference, Stalin was unwavering. He wanted a divided Germany. He wanted Berlin. And he also wanted control of Eastern Europe.

And Churchill and Roosevelt let him have it. They wanted Stalin's consent to a United Nations and his promise to enter the war in the Pacific 90 days after Germany was defeated. The Yalta deal was made, and the fate of the world for the rest of the 20th century had been sealed. In the spring of 1945, General Eisenhower ordered the American troops entering Germany and Eastern Europe to slow down, leaving the Red Army free to occupy Poland, Hungary, Czechoslovakia, Austria and Romania. The Red Army then marched into Berlin, "liberating" the German people from Nazi rule, all the while sanctioning the murder and rape of millions of innocent civilians. Stalin even sanctioned this behavior, believing that people should "understand it if a soldier who has crossed thousands of kilometers through blood and fire and death has fun with a woman or takes some trifle."

As word of Soviet atrocities spread through the Allied High Command and it became glaringly obvious that Stalin would never adhere to his agreement to let all occupied territories hold free elections, Churchill even considered enlisting captured German soldiers and invading Russia once the Nazis had surrendered.

When the Big Three sat down at their final meeting at Potsdam, the groundwork for World War III was being sewn. Power was up for grabs and both the US and the USSR wanted each other to know who would be filling the vacuum. Germany was defeated. Japan was on its final legs. Roosevelt, the calming presence that mediated the tension between Stalin and Churchill, had died. Russia occupied the whole of Eastern Europe, with no intention of leaving. US president Truman knew he had a super-weapon, even subtly letting its existence slip during the talks. The eventual agreements of the Potsdam Conference offered glimpses into a bipolar world, where geopolitical relationships would be divided simplistically using "us against them" terminology.

At Potsdam, the four-way division of Germany and Austria was finalized. Next, the German industrial machines were to be disassembled and sent back to the Soviet Union as restitution. Stalin wanted his "war booty." And finally, all the eastern European countries were to be liberated by the Soviet Union, occupied by the Red Army until they were stable and ready to rule themselves again independently. The Soviets agreed that they would allow Liberated Eastern Europe to have free elections (of course they wouldn't be disappointed if these nations happened to choose communism).

In fact, they wouldn't be disappointed if all recovering nations chose to align themselves with Soviet communism. And in the post-WWII landscape, communism actually looked like a viable option.

When life is going well, communism isn't attractive. People don't just voluntarily exchange a life of prosperity for a life where everyone is equal. Communist equality takes the wealthy down a couple notches to bring up those at the bottom. If there are a ton of people who are prospering (or at least naively believe they have a shot at the good life), they aren't too excited about giving up this promise by sharing their cash with those down below. Humans can be nice, but they're not stupid. Think of it in the terms of academic grading. Who wants to trade in their A- life for a D- existence?

But when life sucks, when your nation is destroyed, when a generation of your young men lie dead or wounded, when your factories have been turned to rubble, when your roads, railroads and ports can't move goods, when your economy is in utter ruin and your people don't know from where the next meal will come, when your life is in misery and your nation is teetering on anarchy, this is when communism is attractive. When your life is an F, a D-doesn't look too bad.

And in 1946, Europe and East Asia were failing. The tyrants of the 1920s and 1930s had taken the world to war. The people wanted power restored to the masses. This was when Marxism had a chance. If ever the workers of the world were going to unite to overthrow the power elite, this was the moment.

It didn't hurt the communist cause that Soviet tanks and soldiers remained stationed all across Eastern Europe. If the allure of communism in times of strife wasn't enough to influence the ballot box, the hundreds of thousands of occupying Soviet troops definitely tipped the scales in the Soviets favor. Stalin had hoped each occupied nation would naturally choose communism, but he quickly learned that even though the conditions were ripe for a series of communist victories, the initial post-war ballot boxes chosen non-communist leaders. Stalin couldn't tolerate this outcome, so he made sure "free elections" would be just a little bit less free. One by one, the nations of Eastern Europe (Poland, Hungary, Czechoslovakia, Romania, Albania and Yugoslavia) started to "choose" communist governments. But with the Soviet Red Army involved in all facets of the election process, Eastern Europe never really had a choice.

England and the United States were less than pleased. In 1946, on a trip to President Harry Truman's hometown in Missouri, Winston Churchill delivered his famous "iron curtain" speech where he warned, "From Stettin in the Baltic to Trieste in the Adriatic an *iron curtain* has descended across the Continent" and that the Communist parties "are seeking everywhere to obtain totalitarian control." To the east of the curtain stood the Soviet Bloc, the network of nations all answering to the mandates of Moscow. To the west was a weakened, vulnerable Europe. Communism had already taken hold of Eastern Europe, and it appeared only a matter of time before the suffering masses to the west likewise followed suit.

America couldn't allow that to happen.

Europe needed money, and a lot of it. The only way America could ensure Soviet influence would never gain a foothold in Western Europe was if prosperity could be quickly restored, making the communist system look like a laughable alternative.

Enter US Secretary of State George Marshall. He proposed to just give Europe money. Not a loan, just a gift. And they would give Europe a lot of it – $12.5 billion from 1948 to 1952. This money was used to: rebuild roads, power plants and factories; to pay for millions of tons of food and clothing; to help restore Europe's ability to rejoin the world as equal players. In one fell swoop, this European Recovery Program (known as the Marshall Plan) not only put Western Europe back on its feet, but more importantly "strengthen[ed] the area still outside Stalin's grasp," firmly locking Western Europe into America's capitalist corner for the remainder of the Cold War.

But economic aid was only part of America's plan to contain the communist menace. In Turkey and Greece, the communist parties grew more powerful, and because of their terrorist campaigns and socialist promises, it appeared only a matter of time before two more puppet nations fell under Stalin's umbrella. Britain tried to fight the movement with covert aid, but the forces of democracy and capitalism needed help on a much grander scale, and on March 12, 1947, President Truman promised to Congress that America would not sit by passively as the Soviet Union supported communist takeovers. He recognized:

> *At the present moment in world history nearly every nation must choose between alternative ways of life. The choice is too often not a free one. One way of life is based upon the will of the majority, and is distinguished by free institutions, representative government, free elections, guarantees of individual liberty, freedom of speech and religion, and freedom from political oppression. The second way of life is based upon the will of a minority forcibly imposed upon the majority. It relies upon terror and oppression, a controlled press and radio, fixed elections, and the suppression of personal freedoms. I believe that it must be the policy of the United States to support free peoples who are resisting attempted subjugation by armed minorities or by outside pressures.*

Truman was "fully aware of the broad implications involved if the United States extended[ed] assistance to Greece" and eventually Turkey. America would essentially become the policemen of the world. Any façade of isolationism would never again be an option. Anytime a nation needed help, America would have to be there. Anytime a leader, whether the head of state or the leader of a revolutionary force, professed the desire to fend off communism, America would have to be there.

The Truman Doctrine ushered in the era of Pax Americana, a world where 500,000 US troops were deployed to keep peace on every corner of the planet. Although by 1950, hundreds of thousands of US troops could be found everywhere from Okinawa to South Korea to the Indian Ocean to the depths of the Arctic Ocean, the bulk of all troops were stationed in West Germany, for it was in Germany where everyone believed World War III was going to start.

By 1948, Germany was still rebuilding from the rubble, and all signs pointed to a standoff between the Soviets and the rest of the allies. Split into four sections by the decrees made at Potsdam, Germany was theoretically to be ruled independently by the French, British, Americans and Soviets. But there was nothing independent about how the western half was rebuilding. The French, British and Americans (the capitalist democracies) made no secret of their partnership in rebuilding their German spheres, leaving the Soviets isolated and able to mold their chunk into yet another satellite communist nation. And all attempts to mask alliances were shattered in 1948, when the three western sections of Germany each adopted one currency, the Deutsche Mark, and agreed to exist as one united economy.

This was too much for Stalin. He couldn't believe Germany was being rebuilt into a regime entirely incompatible with his own desires. In fact, in 1946, he had optimistically assumed that it was only a matter of time before the Americans, French and Brits grew weary of occupation and pulled out of Western Germany altogether, leaving the Soviet Union to reunite all of Germany under the Soviet banner.

The Marshall Plan put a wrinkle in his scheme. The Deutsche Mark adoption went one step further. Unification couldn't be tolerated. If the three sections united under the same currency, it was only a matter of time before they became one nation. Stalin would have to make a stand, and he would do it in Berlin, the capital city of Germany. Like all of Germany, Berlin was also divided into four occupied sections, but Berlin's situation was dangerously unique. The city was located 100 miles inside the Soviet zone, which meant West Berlin was a little democratic, free-market nugget surrounded by communism. Stalin wanted that nugget for himself.

On June 24, 1948, Stalin cut off all trade to the French, British and American sections of Berlin. All roads, all canals, all railroad tracks were severed. Nothing could come in. Nothing could go out. Stalin would cut off the fuel and the food to West Berlin. He thought he could starve his former allies into capitulation. There's no way they would help out the West Berliners. It would only be a matter of time before the French, British and American starving sections came crawling to the Soviets for survival. Stalin would be waiting with open arms.

The US and Britain had a few choices – do nothing and let Stalin win, send in military forces to open up the trade routes or ignore the blockade.

The first two options were unacceptable. The first would only empower Stalin to keep pushing his communist agenda. The second would lead to World War III.

So they chose option three. American and British governments ignored the blockade and instead coordinated an endless stream of supplies to be delivered over the heads of Soviet-occupied East Germany and into the destitute hands of the West Berliners. This Berlin Airlift became the Cold War's first "defense of freedom," lasting close to eleven months, keeping three billion Berliners alive through the winter of 1948. Coordinating the air forces of Canada, Australia, New Zealand, Britain and America, Operation Vittles dropped over two million tons of cargo – everything from blankets to medicine to food to clothing to coal.

And the Soviet Union didn't retaliate. They didn't shoot down the planes or mobilize their troops to stop the dispersal of supplies. And then Stalin gave up, admitting he'd been bested. He re-opened supply lines from Berlin to the West, and on May 12, the airlift ended. Berlin had survived without turning communist, but the battle lines were officially drawn. Two new nations were created. The Soviet section became the ironically named German Democratic Republic (East Germany) and the remaining three sections became the Federal Republic of Germany (West Germany).

America took the alliance that made the airlift possible and expanded it to become NATO, the North Atlantic Treaty Organization. The fifteen founding members of NATO each vowed to come to each other's aid should any ally be attacked. In response, the Soviet Union established its own military alliance - the Warsaw Pact. The European powers had chosen sides. You were either with NATO, or you were with the Warsaw Pact. The Americans and Soviets then started pouring weapons, money and troops into their allies' borders, hoping this massive armament would maintain the status quo for years to come. And it worked. By 1950, the European alliances that had been established in the early days of the Cold War would remain until the downfall of the Soviet Union in 1989. The Soviet Union would have its network of satellite nations across Eastern Europe. And the United States of America had firmly ensconced itself in the future of Western Europe. No more nations would shift alliances after 1950. The expansion of communism had been contained.

But the Cold War was by no means over. It had merely shifted to Latin America, Africa and Asia.

And then to the skies.

One of the signature components of the Cold War was the ceaseless risk of nuclear war. When America dropped its two atomic bombs in 1945, they thought they would have a monopoly on the super weapon for at least a decade. Not exactly. By 1949, the Soviets had perfected their own atomic bomb. Then, in 1952, America regained its military prestige when it successfully tested the considerably more deadly hydrogen bomb (867 times more deadly to be exact). But this time it only took a year before the Soviets caught up and detonated their own hydrogen bomb. American scientific supremacy was under assault. The American hyper-confidence of the post-war years was coming to an end, and on October 4, 1957, technologically superiority seemed like it had shifted once again.

America had symbolically fallen behind the Soviets. It was on this day that the Soviets successfully deposited Sputnik, a basketball-sized satellite with four seven-foot long antenna tales, into space. America was now not only confronted technologically, they were vulnerable. If the Soviets could put satellites into space, could they also hypothetically watch over all American activities, chart its military's every movement and drop bombs out of the sky like a kid dropping water balloons off an apartment balcony?

The US couldn't tolerate any notion of Soviet superiority.

The space race had begun. Whoever controlled the technology that could put satellites into space would also control the technology to deploy nuclear weapons. One man's rocket is another man's missile, and whoever could design a ship that could propel man and machines into space could just as easily deliver nuclear bombs anywhere on the planet.

The US rushed to get the National Aeronautics and Space Administration (NASAS) up and running. They had to get something into space. They had to prove that they were back in the competition. The first few years of America's space program weren't terribly reassuring. Some rockets exploded before even taking off. Others lifted a few feet off the ground and then crumpled back down to earth. And some made it a few miles into the sky, only to spin wildly out of control or burst into flames high above the anxious spectators. Every failure was public. Every failure made America wonder if the Soviets might now actually possess the better society. The Soviets were first with a satellite, the first with a man in space and the first to make it to the moon to take some pictures.

But America would catch up. Vowing in 1961 to put a man on the moon before the end of the decade, President John F. Kennedy put the full weight of the federal government behind the space program. It was a race America could not lose, and on July 20, 1969, Buzz Aldrin and Neil Armstrong landed on the moon, taking "a few small steps" and making a "giant leap for mankind." Since the dawn of the first hunter-gatherers hundreds of thousands of years ago, the moon always sat just beyond our world, bordering the heavens. But in 1969, because of Cold War posturing and the threat of scientific mediocrity, the wealthiest nation on the planet finally bridged the two worlds together, and yet again man had conquered nature.

After the initial landing, the hype surrounding the Soviet and American space programs died down, and funding was steadily withdrawn. But the money kept flowing toward the defense programs in record numbers. At its height in the 1960s, America spent 20% of its GDP on military expenditures, and the Soviets spent over 40%. Much of this went to the production of nuclear weapons as both sides stockpiled arsenals far in excess of what was needed to destroy their foe. At their peak, the Soviets had amassed over 45,000 warheads, the Americans over 32,000. Scientists argued over whether we had enough bombs to blow up the planet five times or fifty times. Tough to say since some bombs are duds, the earth does a pretty good job absorbing radiation and some pesky pieces of life are bound to just not succumb to the blasts. But that wasn't the point of piling up bomb after bomb after bomb.

It was all part of a policy of Mutually Assured Destruction. This MAD scheme promised that whoever fired first would assuredly doom its own nation to nuclear annihilation. You kill me. I kill you. After the Soviet Union and the USA planted their missile silos all across their allies' territories (and even in submarines scouring the depths of the oceans), there wasn't a point on the planet that couldn't be reached by a nuclear bomb within 30 minutes.

Neither side would be stupid enough to use these weapons. Some argue it was the threat of nuclear war that actually kept the peace throughout the Cold War. But "kept the peace" was a bit of an overstatement, considering that just because the two sides couldn't attack each other directly, didn't mean they resisted putting weapons and wars in the hands of developing nations and revolutionaries. No, there was no World War III, but twenty million people did lose their lives because of Cold War aggression, and it was in these proxy wars that tensions would burn hottest.

The world made the mistake of decolonizing at the exact moment the Cold War was heating up. Europe was giving up on its empires. They were too expensive and their people wanted their leaders to focus on domestic issues, not on taking care of some distant peoples on the other side of the world. Western Europe chose to instead use their tax base to fund health care, unemployment benefits, paternity care, college, public housing and pension plans. Though defense spending continued as part of any Western European budget, it no longer dominated discourse, and with the United States bearing the brunt of NATO weapons funding and troop deployment, Europe moved closer toward a welfare state.

And as Europe was focused on rebuilding their economies and protecting their people, the nations of Latin America, Africa and Asia pushed further away from colonial control. The world was soon divided into three types of countries – First World countries that followed America, Second World countries that followed the Soviet Union and Third World countries that were figuring out which way to turn. It was in the Third World that the two superpowers would yield their mighty influence. Every emerging nation would have to choose – trade with America or trade with the Soviet Union. For some the "choice" was never an option. In 1945, America occupied Western Germany, North Korea and Japan. The Soviet Union occupied Poland,

Czechoslovakia, Hungary, Romania, Yugoslavia, Bulgaria and Albania. For these satellite nations, their alliances were already set.

But for every other nation, the revolutionaries would have to choose. Some tried to stay neutral and play the Soviet Union against the United States. Friends with one country one day, the other the next. Some ended up getting caught in civil wars, as regional factions failed to decide unanimously on their ideological course. This was how the proxy wars started.

For America, the two most consequential proxy wars were in Korea and Vietnam. For the Soviet Union, Afghanistan was the quagmire that marked the beginning of the end.

Korea had been divided at the end of World War II. On August 10, 1945 a couple military officers pulled out a National Geographic magazine and decided on the 38th parallel for a division between a Soviet occupied zone and an American zone. The Soviets gained the manufacturing north and the Americans gained control of the capital and agrarian south. The North Koreans had no desire to live in a divided nation, and in 1950, with passive permission from Josef Stalin to proceed, they crossed the 38th parallel, pushing South Korean forces down to the southern tip of the peninsula. The freshly formed United Nations had its first test of legitimacy. How could it claim to be a proprietor of peace if it allowed unprovoked aggression? But the problem was in the makeup of the war-making branch of the United Nations. The Security Council was made up of five permanent members – the USA, Britain, China, France and the Soviet Union – each with veto power. If any one nation vetoed a resolution, the United Nations could not legally take action. So of course, with the Soviets supporting North Korea's offensive, they would inevitably veto any resolution condemning the North Korean invasion. But the Soviet Union made a mistake. They boycotted this meeting of the Security Council, never entered their vote and their absence meant the United Nations could launch their first "peacekeeping" mission.

The United States was way ahead of them. With hundreds of thousands of troops stationed in occupied Japan, the Americans were in Korea within weeks. General Douglas MacArthur, the hero of the WW2 Pacific Theater, swept in behind North Korean troops and eventually pushed them to the Chinese-Korean border. At this point, he pressured President Truman for permission to drop some nuclear bombs on China, who was obviously aiding the North Koreans.

Truman refused. He wasn't going to use nukes again.

China took advantage of America's reticence. Recently crowned Chinese premier Mao Tse Tung ordered 700,000 troops to the border, ultimately commanding them to cross into Korea on October 25, 1950. Over the next three years, the conflict devolved into a murky stalemate. Though both sides agreed to a ceasefire, they could never settle on a peace agreement. To this day, the Korean War has never officially ended and the 38th parallel remains the spot where tensions could one day end the 60-year "break."

Like in Korea, the conflict in Vietnam stemmed from borders created by Westerners and a nationalistic desire to reunite the nation under one government. Following World War II, even under advisement from the United States, France refused to give up their holdings in French Indochina (Laos, Cambodia and Vietnam). The Vietnamese revolutionary Ho Chi Minh was less than pleased, as he had fought to expel the Japanese in the 1940s and felt his proclamation that "all men are created equal" would rally American support for a free Vietnam. He was wrong. America had to have France's support in Europe, and if that meant America had to hypocritically backtrack on their previous anti-imperialistic stance, they would. But Ho Chi Minh's forces were too determined. They'd had enough of strangers in their land. These French soldiers and their American backers were just the latest in a string of foreign oppressors dating back five centuries. During the first few years of the 1950s, Ho's forces slaughtered and embarrassed the French, bringing both sides to Geneva to talk peace treaty.

But in Geneva, the Western powers decided to create two new countries - North Vietnam and South Vietnam – until the region was stable enough to have a united government. General Ho was less than pleased. He believed he had earned the right to rule a united Vietnam.

America's role in this story could have ended at the Geneva Convention of 1954 when the two Vietnams were created, but instead they made the choice to make Vietnam their Asian Berlin. They would not back down and give in to the spread of communism. They saw Ho Chi Minh not merely as a nationalist revolutionary, but as the Southeast Asian transmitter of communism. If America let him take over Vietnam, the dominos would topple one after another – first Laos, then Cambodia, then Thailand, then Malaysia, then the Philippines and then Indonesia.

If they didn't hold the line in Vietnam, within a decade another half a billion souls (and consumers) would be lost to communism.

So America backed the wrong horse. To run South Vietnam, the Americans brought in Ngo Dinh Diem, a Catholic Vietnamese exile, educated in the United States, who was totally unfamiliar with the plight of his Vietnamese brethren. He didn't make any by stealing from the government coffers, giving the prime government posts to his family and friends and persecuting Buddhists. Back in the United States, Americans started questioning their role in this Southeast Asian struggle, as on the nightly news Buddhist monks could be seen dousing themselves with gasoline and lighting themselves on fire to protest the Diem's policies.

Needing to go in a new direction, the CIA supported both the assassination of Diem and the election of a series of equally incompetent leaders. By the mid-1960s, Ho Chi Minh's efforts in South Vietnam accelerated, forcing President Kennedy to increase the number of "advisors" in the region to 12,000. When you think "advisor," you have to think of a soldier, a helicopter pilot, a medic or a military officer. These enlisted American men "advised" the South Vietnamese military on how to defend themselves, sometimes even leading them into battle. As Chinese and Soviet money continued to trickle into North Vietnam and southern Vietnamese communist guerrillas (the Vietcong) expanded their terrorist activities, the US had a choice – escalate or pull out. The ensuing president, Lyndon B. Johnson knew he would have to either "go in with great casualty lists or get out with disgrace." He ended up assuring both.

By 1968, 580,000 Americans were serving in Vietnam, many of whom were forced into combat through a compulsory draft. As the death tolls mounted and the war goals were lost in a haze of rhetoric, an anti-war movement gained momentum. It first started in the quads of colleges across the country, but eventually spread to all classes of society. This was a war Americans no longer wanted to fight, and when they found out their military had expanded the conflict to include bombings of neighboring Laos and Cambodia, the anti-war protests hit an even higher fever pitch. Enough was enough. The government and military brass so no clear path victory. America conceded to "peace with honor," pulling out troops in 1973

With the American forces out of the picture, within two years, the communists took over the southern capital. Vietnam united under communist leadership and across the region...

Nothing happened.

No dominos fell. No other nation succumbed to what once was seen as an inevitability. Vietnam eventually entered into the global market and a generation of Americans was left wondering why they'd ever been sent to Southeast Asia.

The Vietnam War was the most glaring example of American intrusion in regional conflicts, but it was by no means the end of US interference in foreign affairs. The CIA would again prop up dubious figures. Government advisors would again believe the domino theory was a preordained certainty, not merely a cleverly worded geopolitical guess. American military forces would again be challenged by local populations yielding inferior weapons. And America again would be embarrassed on foreign soil. By 1980, a series of questionable involvements in Guatemala, the Congo, Cuba, Angola, Iran, Grenada, Nicaragua and El Salvador each diminished American prestige, gradually fostering an anti-American sentiment that still lingers today.

Vietnam forever damaged America's international stature. The Soviet Union would have its own Vietnam. It would have Afghanistan. After the Soviet Union had secured its western borders by creating the Eastern Bloc, it set its sights on securing a buffer zone to the south by incorporating all the "stans" behind the Soviet shield. By the 1950s, Krygyzstan, Tajikistan, Turkmenistan, Kazakhstan and Uzbekistan all fell to Soviet influence, both for their geographic importance (as grain producers, as links to the Indian Ocean and for their proximity to the oil fields of the Middle East) and for their symbolic currency in the great battle for superpower bragging rights.

One nation held out for decades. Afghanistan. By playing both sides against each other, never formally granting their allegiance to either, Afghanistan benefited from trade with both the Soviet Union and the United States, using these contacts to improve their infrastructure and protect them from outside influences. This all changed in 1979 when the Soviet Union decided to invade and lend support to the local communist revolutionaries. America in turn, through the efforts of Senator Charlie Wilson and CIA operatives, coordinated the transfer of billions of dollars of money and arms (specifically surface to air missiles) to the Mujahideen. The Mujahideen were virulently anti-communist and were willing to protect the autonomy of their nation to the death (they also boasted the membership of one wealthy expatriate from Saudi Arabia who would later play a much different role in America's story...this man was named Osama Bin Laden). The Mujahideen eventually taught the Soviets a lesson others have had to learn the hard way – you might be able to invade Afghanistan, but you're not going to be able to control Afghanistan. After a decade of futile fighting, like with America's foray into Vietnam, close to two million civilians were killed, hundreds of thousands of refugees fled to neighboring countries, tens of thousands of Soviet soldiers died and over $80 billion was needlessly lost in the mountains of Afghanistan. This failed assault not only damaged the Soviet image internationally, but it also caused great tension within the upper echelons of Soviet government as the course of the Soviet's future came under heightening scrutiny.

These destructive, exhaustive proxy wars weren't the only hot spots in the Cold War. Several incidents not only soured Soviet-American relations, but pushed the world into a state of perpetual panic as the question of nuclear war became more one of *when* than *if*.

In 1951, Americans Julius and Ethel Rosenberg were arrested and put on trial for sharing Army military weapons secrets with the Soviets. Their trial and eventual execution set off a wave of paranoia in the United States, as everyone might be a spy. The CIA strengthened their counter-espionage efforts and the government, through the obsessive, paranoid leadership of Senator Joseph McCarthy, went on a "witch hunt" to weed out potential conspirators.

In 1960, the US and the Soviets continually denounced each other's intelligence networks. The Soviets even accused the Americans of flying high-speed spy planes over Soviet soil, recording troop movements and missile construction sites. America fervently denied these actions, but were soon internationally mocked when the Soviets put a captured Gary Powers, a U-2 pilot shot down over Soviet airspace, in front of a television camera. This American embarrassment was soon overshadowed in 1961 when the Soviets erected the Berlin Wall, a series of barbed wire and stone fences created to prevent East Germans from escaping into the capitalist, democratic mecca of West Berlin. America could do nothing, and for the duration of the Cold War, the Berlin Wall would stand as the symbol of the conflict.

Although these incidents each amplified the mistrust and apprehension of the day, it was the Cuban Missile Crisis that brought the world within minutes of World War III. After World War II, Cuba, an island 90 miles off the coast of Florida, had become America's Las Vegas of the Caribbean. The high rollers of America would head down to Havana to party, gamble and mingle with the locals. Cuba had become essentially America's own satellite nation; even President Kennedy later commented how "United States companies owned about 40 percent of the Cuban sugar lands—almost all the cattle ranches—90 percent of the mines and mineral concessions—80 percent of the utilities— practically all the oil industry—and supplied two-thirds of Cuba's imports."

This all changed when Fidel Castro, aided by Latin American revolutionary Che Guevera, lead a small invasion force across the Gulf of Mexico, hid in the hills for months and gradually increased his influence through terrorism, guerrilla activities and very persuasive propaganda. Gaining support against the dictator Fulencio Batista didn't prove too difficult, as he had been for years living the life of a billionaire playboy, crafting crooked deals with American businesses and leaving his people to suffer below the poverty line. In 1958, Castro's army overthrew Batista and within a few years he had nationalized American businesses, ensuring that profits from Cuban resources went into the hands of Cubans.

America couldn't have this. They couldn't have a Marxist demagogue less than 100 miles from the mainland and they couldn't afford to set the precedent that overseas American businesses in Latin America could not be protected. The CIA devised possible coups to overthrow Castro, eventually settling on tacit support for the Bay of Pigs Invasion where Cuban exiles would be trained in Panama, given American ships and planes and then supported officially once they took the island and rallied the locals behind them. The "taking the island" part was a failure. No one rallied behind the counter-revolutionary forces, and America was left trying to convince the world that the B-26 bombers flown by Cubans were somehow stolen from US Air Force bases.

With a bounty on his head, Fidel Castro looked to the East for allies, and the Soviets were more than willing to lend a hand. They first bought all of Cuba's sugar at above market prices and later supplied farm equipment, fuel and nuclear missiles. When American spy planes filmed the construction of missile silos, President Kennedy was faced with a choice.

Allow the missiles or forbid the missiles. Allowing the missiles so close to America's border meant that Washington D.C. could be destroyed within a few minutes and the entire eastern seaboard could not be protected from nuclear attack. Forbidding the missiles meant a global standoff with Premier Kruschev and the Soviet Union, neither known for their willingness to compromise. Kennedy settled on the blockade of Cuba, but cleverly called it a "quarantine." He declared that if the Soviets attempted to break the quarantine, he would be forced to fire on Soviet ships, effectively starting World War III. For thirteen days in October 1961, the world watched, hoping one side would concede. Kruschev blinked first, returning his ships and promising to remove the missiles. In exchange, the Americans promised to never, ever invade Cuba again and even remove some of their missiles from Turkey. The world was saved, but the two sides grasped the severity of the situation, agreeing to put in a direct phone line – the Red Phone – between the two leaders and to tone down the public rhetoric. The world almost blew itself up over an island with sugar plantations. This lethal face-off would never again be repeated.

But by the 1980s, the Cold War didn't appear any closer to coming to a close. To an outsider, it even looked like the hostilities were getting ramped up a bit. The Soviets continued to stockpile nuclear weapons, and President Ronald Reagan vowed he would end the "evil empire." Taking another page from the script of George Lucas, Reagan spoke of a Star Wars-esque Strategic Defense Initiative program (SDI) where the American military could shoot down any missile before it re-entered the atmosphere. Though this project only existed in theory (and to this day has never been successfully pulled off), the Soviet military brass felt their hearts stop for a bit as they foresaw a future where they housed 45,000 missiles that could never be used. This became the beginning of the end.

Reagan believed that if we can't beat you, we'll economically bury you. There was no way the Soviet economy could even consider spending more money on the military. They were tapped out. For decades, the Soviet Union tried to mask the weaknesses of their government-controlled economy. Unlike the United States and other capitalist economies where consumers and the market determine what goods are made and what they should cost, in the Soviet Union, government officials determined what was made, who would make it, how much it would cost and who would buy it. This didn't work so well. Workers had no incentive to work harder. Planners either overestimated or underestimated production quotas. And too much money was spent on defense.

Though the Soviet scientific and military successes might have been the envy of the world, their economy was a joke. Consumers had little choice on what to purchase, and what they could purchase was never produced in enough quantity. Stories surfaced of men attaching dozens of rolls of toilet paper to their bodies, not knowing when the next batch would arrive in the stores. It got so bad that the Soviet Union even turned to America and Canada for help, frequently begging for billions of dollars in grain supplies when their harvests fell short of demand. For too long, the Soviets had focused on military expenditures, and by the 1980s, with the value of all those expenditures seemingly for naught, they had to revisit the Soviet model.

Enter Mikhail Gorbachev. Upon his election, Gorbachev inherited a country on the verge of collapse. Their consumer products were garbage, their environment was becoming an industrial cesspool, their farming had become completely ineffective and their recent string of premiers didn't inspire confidence (one would even frequently drool on himself while speaking publicly). With the improvements in communication and the spread of tourism, the Soviets could no longer keep the curtain closed on the advances of the Western world. The Soviet standard of living fell far below that of Western Europe, and their citizens were no longer appeased by stories of space and military victories. They wanted a higher quality of life. They wanted more freedom.

Gorbachev would deliver. Through his two buzzwords of perestroika (restructuring) and glasnost (openness), Gorbachev promised to reform the system, but what he really did was set the groundwork for a dramatic shift to a capitalist, democratic republic. He invited a more free press, encouraged entrepreneurialism, lobbied for more candidates for all government posts, ended the war in Afghanistan, and most importantly, eased up on control of the Soviet satellite nations. By 1989, the Ukraine, Poland, Hungary, Czechoslovakia, Bulgaria, Romania and even East Germany pushed for more autonomy, and Gorbachev did little to stop these revolutionary movements. When on November 9th Communist Party spokesmen Gunter Shabowski misread a

Soviet mandate and erroneously told a room full of newspaper reporters that the wall would be brought down "immediately, without delay," the floodgates of revolution ripped open.

Thousands gathered at the wall, started knocking out chunks of concrete and then moving back and forth from East to West, daring the East Berlin soldiers to stop them. But the East German forces did nothing. The Soviet military did nothing. And one by one, the Eastern Bloc countries pulled away from Soviet control.

And still, nothing.

By 1991, the Soviet Union was in disarray, and on Christmas Day, the union was dissolved, leaving the fifteen republics to recreate themselves autonomously, and that included Russia.

The Cold War had finally come to an end. For over four decades, the competition between the USSR and the USA had overshadowed all other foreign policy concerns, oftentimes masking regional issues that would explode in the next two decades. Some erroneously believed that with the demise of the Soviet Union and only one superpower remaining, war would come to an end.

Not even close.

The decades of naively looking at the world's problems through the lens of capitalism vs. communism meant that many immoral, flawed and dangerous regimes had endured. Ethnic minorities had been subjugated, and religious intolerance had been concealed. But with the cover of bipolar alliances ripped away, a new generation of political leaders demanded self-rule, a new generation of disenfranchised peoples demanded access to the fruits of the global market, a new generation of ignored nations pushed for their own nuclear warheads and a new generation of religious extremists demanded a return to the adherence of orthodox decrees that would combat the spread of liberal ideals.

The Cold War might have come to a close, but a Pandora's Box of challenges had been opened. How the world would confront these challenges would determine the safety and prosperity of humanity.

But that is for another chapter.

Part II

The Regional Challenges of Today

42

Sub-Saharan Africa

What comes to mind when you think of Africa? Is it the saddening images of malnourished children with distended stomachs? Or maybe soldiers on the back of trucks yielding second-hand machine guns? Do you think of slavery and America's role in kidnapping five million souls, setting the stage for centuries of racial persecution to which we're still recovering from today? If you're over 30, you might think of South Africa's apartheid, and how maybe the US may not be the only country with a less than egalitarian history. Or maybe your perception leans less toward the depressing and cynical. You hear the word Africa, and you think of a safari and the chance to capture one of the big five game animals with your Canon Rebel, while bobbing around in a 4 x 4 through the savannah of the inner continent.

So does that pretty much summarize Africa? A continent where you're as likely to see someone starving to death, shot or terrorized as you are to see a lion, a giraffe or a rhinoceros? Is that Africa?

First of all, like all continents (and all countries for that matter), there is no one singular African experience. Africa is the north, where Islam and Mediterranean cultures dominate. There are the dozens of islands that sit off the mainland – some having more in common with distant Europe or Asia than the African mainland. There are close to a billion people in all of Africa, with 60% living in cities, and the remainder scattered across rain forests, swamplands, mountains, fertile agricultural areas and desolate, arid deserts. Though there might not be one Africa, there are regional similarities that allow the continent to be divided into two regions – North Africa, which has more in common with Dar Al Islam (and the Middle East), and Sub-Saharan Africa, the 47 countries existing below the Sahara Desert – countries like Zambia, Zaire, Tunisia, Congo, Angola and Somalia.

This region shares both a common history and similar course of economic and political development. When outsiders make blanket generalizations of where Africa stands at the moment and what its hopes and realities are for the future, they're talking about Sub-Saharan Africa. And when economists, international aid agencies, political scholars, foreign heads of state and informed media analyze Sub-Saharan Africa, what do they see?

Africa is a mess.

By almost any indicator, Sub-Saharan Africa is the most depressed, suffering, underdeveloped, deadly, hopeless region in the entire world. There are 195 countries recognized by the United Nations. There are 47 countries in Sub-Saharan Africa. When all of these countries are lined up and ranked on any number of criteria, with rare exceptions, it is this region of Africa that fills in slots 148-195. Just take a look at the facts:

- Life Expectancy – The world's average life expectancy at birth is 67.2 years. Japan is at the top with 82.6 years, the U.S. has dropped to 78.3 years and (except for Afghanistan) the bottom 40 spots are all held by Sub-Saharan African nations, with Mozambique coming in with a world-worst 39.2 years.

- Literacy – 84.1% of the planet knows how to read. 40 countries read at a rate above 99%. Sub-Saharan Africa averages a 62% literacy rate. Mali sits at the bottom of the planet at 26.2%.

- Per Capita GDP – One way of measuring a country's wealth is to divide their Gross Domestic Product (how much goods and services are produced in a year) by the number of people in the country – Per Capita GDP. The world's average is $11,200. For Luxembourg (admittedly a tiny little country), it is $88,000 and for the US, it is $46,000. For fourteen African nations, it is below $1000.

- Unemployment – Worldwide, the average number of working-aged adults who want to work but cannot find a job is 14.3%. In Monaco (another itty bitty nation), the number is 0%. The US has hovered around 9% since the 2008 mini-depression. Zimbabwe is at 95% *unemployed*.

- Global Hunger Index – One method of determining the nutritional health of a nation is through the GHI, a formula that adds the percentage of children that die before the age of five, the percentage of children under five that are underweight and the percentage of population that is undernourished. Most industrialized countries have a sum less than one, whereas all of Sub-Saharan Africa is above fifteen, and Chad, Congo and Eritrea are above 30.

Every civilization, region and country has its problems, but none monopolizes the bottom of the heap like Africa (and I'm going to just call it Africa from here on out because the whole "Sub-Saharan Africa" thing is starting to sound a bit long-winded, but you have to promise that you'll remember that this doesn't include North African countries such as Libya, Egypt, Tunisia, Algeria and Morocco).

So, how did this happen? And is there any chance for recovery so that in a hundred years we'll be talking about Africa like we now talk about China or Southeast Asia or Latin America – success stories of development that suffered through periods of uncertainty and despair, only to emerge as regions both able to take care of their own people, but also contribute to the global marketplace?

The "how did this happen" question usually is answered with two possibilities – 1) it's the Europeans' fault or 2) Africa (and Africans) are just different. Both answers are lazy, and both assume the racist argument that one people can dominate another to such an extent that recovery is impossible. Yes, Europeans are to blame for the creation and preservation of many of the economic, social and political institutions and traditions that influence every element of the region's development. But the same could be said for the majority of the rest of the planet, who each at one point or another found itself under the rule of the West. And yes, Africa is different (every region is), but it isn't unfixable. Through different eras, individual nations have proven capable of escaping (although unfortunately sometimes only temporarily) the cycle of poverty and political corruption that perennially keep the region's inhabitants hovering at the level of base survival.

To understand if Africa has a chance of changing its course, we must first look at what created this reality – what are the factors in Africa's control and what are those forced upon them?

Africa wasn't always at the bottom of the society-ranking pyramid. In fact, being that it was the cradle of mankind, the site where humans first emerged, you have to give the region credit for having a head start on the rest of the planet. And before there was the Golden Age of Greece and the Pax Romana, there was the Empire of Ethiopia that challenged Egypt for control of Eastern Africa. By the time Europe was stuck in its Dark Ages, West Africa witnessed the height of the Kingdom of Mali, which controlled trade across the Sahara Desert. In 1324, King Moses of Mali (known as Mansa Musa) embarked on his hajj to Mecca, commissioning a caravan of one hundred camels weighted down by hundreds of pounds of gold and five hundred servants, each yielding a six pound golden walking staff. This little trans-Saharan entourage carried what would be worth over $100 million today, and when they stopped off in Cairo, Mansa Musa was so generous with his gold that he destroyed the market by basically just giving gold nuggets away for free. Around the time Mansa Musa was teasing the Mediterranean world with his medieval bling, in the southern part of Africa, the Shona people were building walled holy structures known as zimbabwes, that still exist to this day (in a country remarkably named Zimbabwe).

So by the time the Portuguese started arriving in Africa in the 1400s, vibrant societies had not only existed, but had played leading roles in trade across the Saharan Desert and across the Red Sea for centuries. By 1500, nearly 2000 different languages existed in Africa, none of which had been written down (which is one of the reasons Europeans readily disregard African history – aside from what was written by Arabic or European traders, there is no written history). Hundreds of tribal societies flourished across the southern half of the continent, a space of land equal to the size of the United States, China and Europe combined, and those at the mouth of critical trade networks or controlling key resources (like iron or gold) had created prosperous, complex kingdoms rivaling those of pre-Renaissance Europe.

Like most of the European explorers of the 15th and 16th centuries, the primary goal of the Portuguese was establishing trade networks linking Europe to the luxury goods and spices of Asia. Financed by Prince Henry the Navigator, and benefiting from their location at the northwestern tip of Africa, Portugal built and maintained forts dotting the western coast of Africa, allowing for the relatively safe passage of goods around Africa and into Asia. Even though the bulk of European interaction with Africa in these early decades was limited to the coastal areas, the lure of gold eventually enticed more inland endeavors, in spite of the threat of malaria and yellow fever that kept the average life expectancy of any European willing to journey inland at a mere one year. Because of the insurmountable threat of disease, until the mid-1800s, the Europeans settled for this pattern of trading weapons, slaves and raw materials at coastal ports (with the occasional foray into the heart of darkness).

This relationship changed in the mid-19th century. At the exact time new medical developments (like the discovery of quinine's anti-malarial benefits) allowed for safer passage inland, Europe was taking its industrialized warfare around the world, carving up the globe into spheres of influence to be governed by the British, French, Belgians, Dutch, Germans, Italians, Spanish and Portuguese. In 1800, the "Scramble for Africa" erupted after a conference in Berlin where the European powers established some ground rules for how to conquer the continent without stepping on each other's toes. This landmark summit marked the beginning of a European-African, dominator-dominated relationship that would last deep into the 20th century. Europe first, and later the United States and Soviet Union, turned the peoples of Africa into mere pawns in their geopolitical conflicts for global supremacy.

First it was the Europeans. By 1900, all of Africa (save for Liberia and Ethiopia) remained under the dominion of the Western powers. Even when the cost of maintaining order outweighed any material benefits, Europe preserved its African hegemony, due in large part to the perceived prestige of vast colonial holdings. The more colonies you had, the better you must be. Ethnically divided and militarily inferior, the African peoples were unable to break free (with rare exception) from European control. It wasn't until two world wars decimated Western society, leaving the European citizenry with little appetite for foreign conquest (and leaving governments with few funds to send abroad), that Africa finally achieved independence. In the 1950s and 1960s, dozens of nations emerged from European domination, only to find themselves subject to the whims of the United States and the Soviet Union, the two latest powers from the north engaged in a contest of "my empire is bigger than yours." Through the Cold War, Africa again found itself the mere regional pawns of a much larger battle where the Americans and Soviets proclaimed, "You are either with us or against us." Newly independent African nations could either choose the path of economic, military and political alliances with the capitalist democracies of the First World or the communist forces of the Second World. With this continued reliance and influence on foreign powers, governments survived without making the difficult, necessary choices that would secure their futures. With the fall of the Soviet Union in the early 1990s and the subsequent end of the Cold War, Africa found itself able to choose its own path for the first time since the early 1800s.

But by this point, the damage was done. African economies were crippled, African governments were corrupt and ineffective and ethnic divisions threatened to turn any disagreement into an excuse for wholesale regional genocide.

European powers can by no means be blamed for all of Africa's problems, but they clearly created the systems, bureaucracies and global precedents that put Africa at a seemingly insurmountable disadvantage. Europeans paralyzed African economies by rendering the continent mere suppliers of natural resources to the rest of the world. Africa is a resource-rich continent, blessed with the ores needed to compete in an industrial market, yet from their first meetings, Europe made their intentions clear – Africans would work to export whatever the European mother country needed, and then these same Africans would import the surplus finished products of Europe. Whether or not they actually desired those goods was irrelevant.

In the late 19th century, much of what lied under Africa's soil (the minerals and commodities needed by the world's manufacturers today) had yet to be discovered, but it was the abundance of land itself that garnered so much attention. Initially, Africa was needed for its ability to grow rubber, palm oil, groundnuts and cocoa. All of these products have a couple things in common – one, they're cash crops, which means they're difficult to eat when the going gets tough, and two, they made African farmers dependent on their European consumers to the north.

Should European tastes or needs change, African economies would suffer. Colonial governments enforced this African dependence on European economic interests, and generations grew up unable to even consider the possibility of entrepreneurialism or how to compete on an equal footing in the budding global trading network.

Not only did European colonial powers undermine Africa's economic development, but they also set the conditions for weak central governments that would be unable to effectively rule their constituencies. Because the European governments in Africa were vastly outnumbered, they used a method of divide and conquer to intensify ethnic tensions and ensure their authority. In each colonial holding, European leaders would choose, sometimes arbitrarily, the ethnic group that would have access to the most prestigious, most powerful and most lucrative professions. These decisions alone intensified ethnic division, but whenever potential indigenous threats emerged, Europeans would lean not so much on their own military superiority to ease the threat, but on alliances with rival clans. That's not to say Europe was hesitant to employ violence. King Leopold's Belgian forces even commissioned local troops to cut off the limbs of any villager suspected of dissension. For those chosen ethnicities put in positions of power, few were ever educated in the Western democratic tradition that became prominent in the 20th century. Whereas leaders of Southeast and South Asian colonies were often schooled in European universities (like Mahatma Gandhi of India, Ho Chi Minh of Vietnam and Lee Quan Yew of Singapore), rarely would an African leader benefit from the social democratic tradition of Europe. When independence movements eventually materialized, almost every African nation was an economically-weakened, socially-fractious, politically-fragile grouping of peoples, speaking dozens (if not hundreds) of different languages, all thrown together in these political entities called countries, with arbitrary boundaries chosen almost always to benefit European needs, rarely taking into account regional realities.

Though Europe clearly played a predominant role in Africa's modern identity, the Africans themselves (primarily the leaders who inherited and then plundered their country's coffers) must be held accountable for the hopeless, wretched Africa that enters the 21st century.

If you were going to point fingers at one group for Africa's squalid state, you need look no further than the generation of kleptocrats who seized power in the decades after World War II, only to leave behind a legacy of personal enrichment and domestic neglect. If a kleptomaniac steals from unassuming peddlers, a kleptocrat steals from entire societies at a seemingly unfathomable scale. Leaders like Mobutu Sese Seko of Zaire and Sani Abacha of Nigeria each embezzled close to $5 billion during their regimes, by directly depositing profits from natural resource exports, stealing from aid money or through systemic graft where the government received kickbacks by overpaying for infrastructure projects (pay a contractor $50 million to make a road when it only costs $5 million...then keep the change), or even by merely taking a hefty percentage from collected taxes. These kleptocrats surrounded themselves with family members and allies, all of whom benefited from a culture of corruption and had a personal stake in maintaining the status quo.

As these corrupt practices became more prevalent, the regional autocrats knew their citizens were itching for revolutions. They took over full control of the media and invested heavily in militaries able to squash any potential uprising. Even when these dictators bowed to international pressure by implementing "democratic reforms," they bastardized the process by fixing elections; intimidating, arresting and murdering political rivals; selectively counting votes; or creating election standards unreachable by the average citizen. As recently as 2008, the elections of Zimbabwe were internationally mocked for their corruption. When Robert Mugabe, president and leader of the Zimbabwean African National Union Party, realized he wasn't going to win the election fairly, his party merely gathered up all the ballot boxes and claimed victory without even counting the votes. It wasn't until months had passed, electoral regulators had been fired, and the wife of one of the candidates had her hands and feet cut off before being burned alive, that Mugabe finally announced the predictable conclusion. In spite of all exit polling data and observations from international bodies, Mugabe won in a landslide. This was 2008.

Every few years, an up and coming politico hopeful might claim to be a servant of the people, a political ideologue immune to the seductive gluttony of African political power, a candidate who promises to right the wrongs of the past, restoring power to the disenfranchised and freeing the nation from arbitrary rule by a legion of heartless aristocrats. Leaders like Seko, Abacha and Mugabe all rose to power as men of the people out to fight the oppressors, but it was only a matter of time – be it weeks, or months or years – before they too succumbed to the system of exploitation, bribery and repression of social and political freedoms. Not unsurprisingly, with every passing election, Africans became more and more apathetic to the promises of democracy.

Because these corrupt regional and central leaders consistently prioritize their own profits and job security over the well being of their people, they frequently make short-sighted economic choices that almost assuredly ensure Africa will languish at the bottom of the world's economies.

First, economic planners continue without fail to choose the short-term profits of natural resource exportation over the more fiscally sound choice of prioritizing and investing in a variety of sectors. Africa basically puts all of its eggs in one basket, and this basket is filled with exhaustible gifts of nature. This resource curse leaves Africa both vulnerable to the importing swings of their buyer nations, but also provides little incentive for long-term investment in manufacturing, industry and education. Why invest in an uncertain future when you can get rich by merely tapping the mineral and fuel reserves hidden beneath the surface? Countries like Singapore, Japan, South Korea (and even Germany and England) lead the world in GDP, but their natural resources pale in comparison to those of Africa. They were forced to look outside their borders for resources and markets for their goods, forced to develop the technology, infrastructure and labor force necessary to survive. If not, they would have remained agricultural nations, stuck in the dark ages of human evolution.

Africa doesn't suffer from the geological disadvantages of a Singapore or a Japan or a South Korea. Yet, they also never created the manufacturing centers able to process these gifts from the earth. Africa remains merely an extraction point in the industrialized production chain, leaving the true profits of production to those nations with the factories, technology, skilled labor and needed infrastructure to reap the benefits of the land.

This precedent for resource extraction, established after the Scramble for Africa and maintained throughout the Cold War, continues today, but this time it's not only the European powers that are using Africa as their own personal mining outlets. Until Africa creates its own manufacturing and distribution hubs, they will remain at the whims of foreign powers. When the economies of the industrialized world flourished in the early 2000s, the price of African commodities likewise skyrocketed, producing national growth rates sometimes eclipsing 10%. But when the factories slowed in 2008, the demand for African commodities likewise plummeted, and the lives of Africans regressed into abject despair.

Because the African nations are so far behind in the global game of industrialization, they can't even come close to producing the goods at the cost or the efficiency of their competitors in Europe, Latin America, and South and East Asia. Subsequently, with every passing year, African resources dwindle while the profits are reaped by countries on foreign continents (not even neighboring nations). Whereas a developing country like Mexico conducts more than 90% of its trade with its two regional neighbors – the United States and Canada, in Africa the trend is almost completely reversed. 80% of their trade totally leaves the continent. It is these distant countries that then process these ores for their own manufacturing and domestic consumption. Angola sends coffee to France, Kenya sends cement to Germany, Zimbabwe sends tobacco to Spain, Zambia sends copper to Japan, Nigeria sends oil to the United States and to China...well, everything goes to China.

In 2008, China surpassed the US as Africa's leading importer of goods – some $60 billion in natural resources ranging from oil to aluminum to chromite to cobalt to steel to zinc to coal to uranium to tantalum (that little black rock used to make your cell phones). And Africa loves trading with China, because their money doesn't come with conditions. China doesn't care how governments treat their citizens or their environments. They just need resources. This disinterest makes it difficult for Western countries to put pressure on Africa to change their behavior. In the early 2000s, when the Sudanese government was murdering its own people, Canada threatened to pull out its funding from the national oil industry. Sudan didn't blink. China was waiting to swoop in and help finance the construction of the pipelines, wells, airports and roads needed to harness and ship the desired oil. China is almost forcing nations to likewise ignore health and environmental standards, or else risk being shut out of key markets.

As the world industrialized, Europe took the lead in designating Africa as a critical resource extraction point, and little has changed in the period since the end of European imperialism, with most Sub-Saharan African countries earning more than 50%

of their GDP through natural resource exports, some seeing that percentage surpass 90%. This resource curse threatens to keep African economies in infancy, unable to create a wide range of employment options that could transform their societies into competitors in the post-industrial age.

Which leads to unemployment. Americans like to fret over their 9% unemployment rate, as if this was the signal of the end times. But if you really want to see true unemployment, take a trip through Africa. With rates that in some regions can surpass 90%, the streets are lined with men merely standing around, unable to find a job. No jobs exist. Even those who are technically "employed" merely exist as subsistence farmers or street hawkers of fast food and plastic knick-knacks.

So if there are close to a billion people living in Africa, shouldn't profit-seeking firms be jumping at the opportunities to hire African laborers? Like in Vietnam, Indonesia, India, or Bangladesh, countries where millions of people move to urban areas seeking any sort of hourly wage, shouldn't Africa offer an appealing labor pool?

Not exactly. Their labor is inefficient and unskilled. The education system is atrocious. In the 1980s, African nations sought to reduce their debt by cutting social services – specifically education funding. So today, teachers are either underpaid or not paid at all. Some teachers just stopped coming to work. Dilapidated school buildings house fifth-hand resources, and most paradoxical of all, students have to pay for these services. African children have to bring coins to school to pay their teacher, or they won't have a teacher. Is it any wonder that only 60% of Africans even achieve a primary school education? Those who eventually do graduate from secondary and post-secondary schools often leave the region for other countries where job opportunities match their skill set. What's left behind in Africa is a labor force that is out-produced by European labor by a ratio of ten to one.

If this dearth of skill wasn't enough to dissuade any would-be entrepreneur, the unreasonable cost of labor becomes the final straw. When all countries are ranked on a "difficulty of hiring index," yet again, Africa stands out as the most problematic. Minimum wages don't match skills, contracts unfairly punish the employer and it is nearly impossible for employers to require workers to put in a 40-hour workweek. Firing an employee isn't any easier. Employers have to pay hefty severance packages, keeping their fired employees on the payroll for weeks and sometimes months, and the paper trail needed to document incompetency borders on ridiculous. These frustrating practices don't even take into account some of the more extreme regional requirements where employers have to pay for an employee family's funeral costs, have to pay for employee family's tuition or have to excuse employees for time lost due to extreme illnesses (AIDS and tuberculosis primarily). The balance of power is tipped so far in the direction of the employees that foreign companies will often bring in their own laborers to actually get the job done cheaply and efficiently. Is it any wonder then that only 3% of all global investment reaches Africa? It's not exactly a profit seekers dream locale.

Africa's dismal economic state isn't unfamiliar to the world community. People, organizations and countries are trying to help, but fortunately this "help" has been as detrimental to African development as the resource curse. There has never before in human history been a region of the world that has received so much financial aid for such an extended period of time as has Africa. And the results call into question if this aid is actually beneficial. There are two types of foreign aid – there are the billions of dollars in remittances sent by African emigrants back to their families in the homeland and then there are the aid dollars, both in loans and in grants, to governments to help improve the social programs for their citizens. Few would argue that the money that directly provides food, water, shelter, health and education to the suffering masses is in any way a negative.

But it is. Today, after four decades of focused assistance from the Western world (about $502 billion), Africa is poorer, its people are hungrier and its democracies are less secure. Although there isn't a direct correlation between aid and suffering, the facts are so telling that the majority of African NGOs have even requested that aid be, if not stopped, at least strongly reconsidered.

But why? When foreign money enters a country, there's more money, which leads to rising inflation, which leads to banks lending less money to control the money supply, which leads to fewer locals being able to create businesses. Next, when foreign money comes into countries, it often comes with stipulations, little rules that the receiving government has to honor. Governments then find themselves listening more to the whims of donor nations than their own people. For example, a country like the United States might demand that wages are increased, that labor is protected and that more stringent environmental laws are followed. Although well-intentioned, these requirements have unexpected negative consequences of making countries less attractive to corporate investment. Why make your Nike shoes in expensive Africa when they can roll off the factory floor in Vietnam for a fraction of the cost? Also, when governments know they have a guaranteed source of income every year from a foreign body, they have less incentive to help out their own people. If there was no outside aid, the parties in power would have to answer to the demands of their people or they would find themselves out of power at the next election.

And the last problem is that relying on outside aid is inconsistent. In 2008, Africa received $20 billion in remittances from African expatriates and $35 billion in foreign aid. After the recession, these numbers plunged. When a household, a company or a country has to tighten their budgets, one of the first cuts they make are charitable donations, and aid to Africa took a huge hit post-2008. The free money stopped coming into the country, and it again became obvious that (like the welfare families of the United States who generation after generation find themselves on the public dole) Africa has plunged into a cycle of poverty from which escape will be impossible unless the charity stops.

If the industrialized world truly wanted to help Africa, they could shut down the tax havens where the kleptocrats store their stolen wealth. $148 billion a year leaves Africa to be protected in one of the scores of countries that encourage overseas deposits. Countries like Bermuda, Switzerland, Singapore, Luxembourg, the Maldives and the Cayman Islands willingly take the money of outsiders, with no questions asked. A billion stolen one day can be deposited in an offshore account the next. Not only does this money not go back to the social programs of individual nations, but the money isn't even circulated through the economy. One might be able to excuse a corrupt autocrat if he at least bought his luxury goods from local stores, but when the money leaves the country, it is lost forever. So if the world truly cared about the course of Africa, they should reconsider their $35 billion in aid, and instead focus on litigation that can prevent the $148 billion fleecing of the African people.

Until these international regulations are implemented, the cycle of political corruption and abuses will continue. Added to these systemic abuses is the rampant violence spreading across the region. Borrowing from the divide and conquer techniques employed by the most ruthless of the European colonizers, political parties and rebel groups today continue to employ intimidation and brutality to secure supporters. Although dozens of civil wars currently run unabated in Cote d'Ivoire, the Democratic Republic of Congo, Somalia, Nigeria, Sierra Leone and Rwanda, it was the conflict in Sudan (most specifically the Darfur region) that monopolized media headlines at the turn of the century.

Since 1955, the northern and southern regions of Sudan had been fighting an on-again, off-again civil war over the South's desire for their own independence. By the 1990s, with Cold War machinations no longer influencing governmental policy, conflict soared again, and international agencies and nations intervened, trying to quell tension. Adding to the north-south conflict, in the rural areas, religious-based rebel groups waged an all-out war (approaching genocide) on neighboring villages, killing some 2.5 million innocents, enslaving generations of youths to fight in local militias and turning six million people into refugees. Finally, in 2011, South Sudan gained their independence, but any political successes pale in comparison to the economic and human cost that leaves both these nations in utter chaos.

The conflict in Sudan brought to the international attention all the issues that consistently plague Africa – political corruption, sadistic militias, human starvation and suffering, international exploitation of regional resources and ethnic tension caused by arbitrary political boundaries. But when South Sudan officially became a country in July 2011, and the atrocities of Darfur ceased to garner front-page attention, the vicious conflicts in Africa by no means subsided. Whether they're fighting for access to better jobs, fighting to overthrow the government in power, fighting to redress an ethnic slight from generations past or fighting for their survival, these conflicts kill tens of thousands of innocent civilians monthly, creating a culture of fear and suffering, while also contributing to a refugee crisis where nine million Africans have lost their homes and currently seek sanctuary in a neighboring land. Oftentimes, this influx of refugees only exacerbates the already tense ethnic balance in the neighboring country, creating yet more conflict, destruction and death.

The frequency of death in Africa runs truly unparalleled in the modern world. While the majority of the world sees people living longer, healthier lives, Africa is going in the opposite direction, with countries like Sierra Leone, Zambia, Swaziland and

Mozambique registering life expectancy rates falling under 40 years.

Though much of these deaths come from lack of access to proper nourishment and the violence of civil conflicts, UN Secretary Kofi Annan declared in 2000 that far more deaths come from AIDS than all the conflicts combined. Although few countries in the world can claim not to be affected by the AIDS epidemic, Africa suffers disproportionately. Of the 33 million people currently infected with the disease, 22 million live in Africa, with close to two million new cases reported annually. These results stem from a combination of naivety, cruelty, social taboos and economic and medical realities. For years, some leaders denied AIDS even existed. Others argued it couldn't be transmitted sexually. Rumors spread that AIDS medicines were actually poisonous (one leading South African health minister even suggested the only treatments were beetroot, garlic, lemons and African potatoes). Condoms carry a stigma both for men and women. Men who wear condoms are seen as less virile. Women hesitate to even request the use of a condom, fearing being labeled promiscuous, or worse, raped or beaten for making such an insulting request.

For those already infected with HIV, the acquisition and distribution of medicines has proven nearly impossible. Medicines are too expensive to purchase and pharmaceutical companies are hesitant to lower prices. In addition, poorly resourced and inadequately staffed health centers and unprotected, decaying infrastructure networks mean that purchased medicine can't even be distributed in a timely manner.

In a bizarre demographic twist, even with the horrific brutality of regional wars, the scarce economic opportunities, the uncertainty of a healthy existence and the constant threat of starvation or death, Africa's population continues to grow – and grow like no other place on the planet. In 1900, Africa had 100 million people. Today its population is over 800 million. It could eclipse two billion by 2050. An average woman will have five to six children in her life. In Niger, the average tops out at 7.5 births per woman. Sub-Saharan African nations can't even support their citizens today. There's no way they will be able to keep these hundreds of millions alive in the future. They are headed toward a population emergency, where no amount of foreign aid can keep this region safe and healthy.

Like the families of medieval Europe who justified large families because the kids could provide needed labor and help support parents in their final years, families continue to believe that their survival depends on multiple births. Coupled with this economic reality, many women - marginalized due to their exclusion from education, employment and property – believe the only way they can contribute to society and ensure their own survival is through reproduction. Governments have been hesitant to provide the funding needed for family planning, contraception, abortions and thoughtful reproductive education. Until governments can turn the corner on this demographic nightmare, African societies will continue to crumble under the weight of an uneducated, unhealthy, resource-starved population.

So is there any hope for this region of Africa?

Here's the problem. Every time it looks like an African nation is turning the corner - getting a handle on election fraud, controlling corruption, providing the needed services to its people, focusing on the short and long term needs of its economy – every time it looks like a nation has reached the tipping point, pulling itself out of the pit of despair, they inevitably fall back.

But still, there are success stories, sometimes undetectable glimmers of hope in a region begging for a bit of optimism. Though Africa is too often painted with the same broad brush, a few nations have made the difficult choices that might help them permanently turn the corner.

Politically, the age of the autocrats is winding down. Since 1989, the number of democracies has risen from 3 to 23. Though this transition has been inconsistent and sometimes ineffective, the adherence to the rule of law has improved in many nations and the freedom of the press and political organizations has progressed. The region is actively trying to prevent a regression to the politics of the past. In the Cote d'Ivoire, to uphold the importance of honoring election results, the international community and the African Union supported the overthrow of Laurent Gbagbo who barricaded himself in his presidential palace and refused to accept the authority of the actual election victor. In the Sudan, the warring northern and southern factions accepted external mediation, agreed to a truce that ended nearly six decades of fighting and formally created the new nation of South Sudan. The International Criminal Court has taken action to track down illegally laundered funds and hold kleptocrats accountable for their autocratic rule and their fleecing of their nations. Taking a page out of the 2011 Arab Spring handbook, a new generation of Africans, the "Cheetah Generation," are using social media to exact reforms and hold government agencies accountable.

African health standards have seen gradual improvements. In Rwanda, the government established a National Office of Population that recommended and implemented widespread reforms and national public information campaigns that resulted in an improvement of contraceptive use from 4% to over 26% in two decades. Countries like Liberia have doubled their health facilities and improved immunization rates to over 90%. Using insecticide-treated bed nets and anti-malarial drugs has radically reduced the number of malarial cases in Ghana, Kenya and Tanzania.

Economically, save for the global recession started in 2008, African economies have steadily improved since 1995 – averaging annual GDP growth rates surpassing 5%. In places like the Nile Valley, farmers are seeing their crop yields explode through technological innovation and implementation of modern farming and irrigation strategies.

Though still lagging behind other regions, trade and investment in Africa has doubled in the first decade of the 21st century. Due to regional and international efforts (led most noticeably by Bono, the lead singer of U2) to help the struggling economies of Africa, numerous Western and industrialized nations have embraced the Heavily Indebted Poor Country Initiative, offering to just ignore the debt commitments of African economies. Indebted countries simply don't have to pay back what they owe.

Africa is on the mend.

The key from here is that these changes must become permanent, enumerated in law books, ingrained in the culture and repeated through formalized structures, so that when flawed men inevitably rise to power or neighboring strife unavoidably spills across the border, the nations' future remain assured. For until those changes are permanent, the African nations surviving below the Sahara will continue to sink back into the pits of despair that have disastrously become the norm and not the exception.

But Africa isn't the only developing region on the cusp of chaos, trying to emerge from the dark shadow of European imperial rule. Across the Atlantic Ocean lies Latin America, a continent and a people slowly emerging from centuries of exploitation, and similarly dealing with ethnic, political and social realities that threaten to derail their development.

But that is for another chapter.

43

Latin America

Until the turn of the century, Latin America and Sub-Saharan Africa had forged fairly similar paths through world history. Once upon a time (well...500 years ago), thousands of indigenous tribes survived on subsistence farming, scattered across these two massive continents, divided by vast, unsurpassable environmental boundaries, the beneficiaries of bountiful ecosystems that were theirs for the taking. Regional empires had developed – the Mayas, Aztecs and Incas in Latin America and the empires of Mali, Songhai and Zulu in Africa – but these were the exception and not the norm, and millions existed outside the grip of these dominant kingdoms.

Within a century of European exploration, both Latin America and Africa suffered at the hands of European imperialism, first losing their land, then seeing their peoples enslaved and then suffering through centuries of fragmented states created seemingly randomly by colonial masters. Both regions were puppets in geopolitical games orchestrated across oceans, first by the

Europeans and then through the Cold War decades by the US and the Soviet Union who vied for absolute obedience of all newly-independent nations.   And both regions fell behind in the industrialization race to wealth, seeing their nations used as simply supply and demand hubs for global goods, but never as manufacturing centers where real fortunes could be made.

In recent decades, there appeared few signs Latin America would emerge from colonial rule any better off than did the Africans.   In 1969, America's National Security Adviser Henry Kissinger dismissed the Chilean foreign minister, admitting that "(Latin America) is not important.   History has never been produced in the South...what happens in the South is of no importance."

Latin America was viewed as merely the unspoken domain of the United States – a hemisphere under the implicit control of their big brother to the north. As long as Latin America did as the US demanded, they would be left alone, but if ever they steered a course that didn't match the US's vision of a Western future, they could count on America's military entering their borders to help clear up any confusion.   Subservient to the West, crippled by economic stagnation, governed by a revolving door of military dictators (caudillos) who prioritized expanding and conserving their own supremacy over the dislocation and misery of their own people, Latin America was a lost continent.

But in the 1990s, Latin America started to separate itself from its northern brothers, charting a new path for itself, that although inconsistent and far from solidified, could stand out as the model for all developing nations.

Before looking at how Latin America altered its future, first you need to know what actually Latin America is. You have to go back to the mid-19th century to find the term's origin, back to France's Napoleon III. In the 1860s, Bonaparte's nephew wanted to recreate a French empire so he had his cartographers and public relations reps start speaking of this region as united by a shared history.   If he could convince all the Portuguese and Spanish-speaking peoples that they somehow were linked to France (a la the Latin language), he could possibly justify why he was invading Mexico (which would allow him to then hypothetically unite the rest of the continent).   Yet considering in 1860, French was only spoken in Haiti, French Guiana and a couple of tiny islands in the Caribbean (and the Spanish and Portuguese speakers weren't exactly clamoring for French occupation), Napoleon's vision never caught on and the French foray into Latin America ended when his puppet emperor to the Mexican throne was shot in the face by a firing squad in 1867.

The French Empire in the Americas died in 1867, but the name still sticks, and today Latin America has become the general term for Mexico, Brazil, Argentina, Haiti, Cuba, Chile and all of the other countries that make up the 43 nations of Central America, the Caribbean and South America.

The first component of Latin American that immediately stands out is its expanding economy. In the mid-1980s, the governments of Latin American began to one by one embrace the advantages of free trade, abandoning their protective policies of the early part of the 20th century. During the Great Depression, many developing nations (and even many developed nations) believed the best way to support their local businesses was to prevent foreign competition. This became known as import substituting industrialization, where prohibitive tariffs punished imports, encouraging citizens to only buy locally. This worked initially, but if a company is to thrive it must continue to grow its market. This was the lesson that the West has been teaching the world for the past century, and it's why today McDonalds has 33,000 outlets worldwide, CocaCola can be bought in over 200 countries and General Motors sells more cars in Brazil, Russia, China, Mexico and Uzbekistan combined than they do in the United States. If you want to expand, you have to sell to your neighbors, even if that means you have to consider sending your stuff to neighbors that live 15,000 miles away. And when you agree to sell stuff to these neighbors, you don't punish them with painful import taxes (tariffs).

This decision to remove tariffs led to the adoption of dozens of bilateral and regional trade agreements. NAFTA, the North American Free Trade Agreement linking Canada, the United States and Mexico, started the ball rolling in 1994, and since then Latin American nations have partnered with nations in the region, with Europe, with Africa, and most recently, and most profitably, with China. Aside from the multination pacts like the EFTA with Europe, the DRCAFTA between the US, Central America and the Dominican Republic, and Mercosur which links the largest South American nations, close to a hundred other pacts have been ratified in the last decade. This has led to billions of dollars of goods passing through Latin American ports.

However, the trade agreements with the outside world come with risks. Latin America almost exclusively sells commodities. Whether its wheat and corn from Argentina, oil from Venezuela, copper from Chile, sugar and beef from Brazil or natural gas and timber from Bolivia, the bulk of the economies of Latin America make money from resources whose value fluctuates widely in the world market and whose long term profits aren't guaranteed. These resources are then taken by the industrialized economies of Europe, East Asia and the United States, turned into manufactured goods, and then sold back to South America. Latin America is in many cases still the beginning and the end of the supply and demand chain. For their economies to thrive long-term, they must expand their human and technological capital. That's where there's money to be made. For example, in Bolivia, China mines lithium, transports it back to China, turns it into batteries and then sells these batteries to the world. Should Bolivia ever nurture their own skilled, educated labor pool, they could keep the battery production in country, not only increasing profits in the short-term, but creating a workforce that could later be utilized in other industries as well.

But at the moment, nations find it difficult to not jump on the commodities bandwagon. There's just too much easy money to be made. China has surpassed the United States as the top trading partner of numerous Latin American countries, especially since Chinese trade deals come with no strings attached (which holds particular appeal to dictators with questionable agendas like Hugo Chavez of Venezuela). China really doesn't care what you do in your country, just as long as you keep buying and selling goods. Subsequently, in the first decade of the 21st century, Chinese imports from Latin America exploded from $5 billion to $90.3 billion annually, and exports expanded at a similar rate ($4.5 billion to $88 billion). But these profits come at a cost. For decades, America was seen as an oppressive, condescending patriarch who constantly demanded their trading partners enforce labor laws, intellectual property regulations, counter-narcotics policies and political corruption deterrents. China couldn't care less. This indifference could mean that much of the American-pressured progress made toward fostering a protected, liberal, fair market could be reversed. Or it could will become internally motivated to ensure their economies progress while striving to protect the environment and their labor force.

In forging its own path of progress, Brazil has proven the role model for Latin America. It too trades with China, it too has abandoned import-substituting industrialization and it too has confirmed dozens of free trade agreements. It however has the sixth largest economy in the world (recently passing Britain on Christmas 2011) and should pass France for fifth place within the next five years. It's made all the right decisions and it has primed itself to not only be an economic leader for years to come, but has also emerged as the unofficial spokesman for Latin America in geopolitical discussions.

Much of Brazil's recent success can be attributed to the leadership of Luiz Inácio Lula da Silva, the man Barack Obama recently called the "most popular politician on earth." He left office in 2010 with an approval rating above 70% (for comparison, George Bush left at 22%, and Obama hovers in the low 40s), a remarkable feat for any exiting politician, but especially for one who governed in Latin America, a region known more for its military coups and fanatical dictators than for its stable democracies. But Lula was the exception. He entered office in 2003 on a platform of *zero fome* – or "no hunger" – promising to tackle the income inequality of Brazil so every man, woman and child could be assured two meals a day. To achieve this lofty goal, he directed billions of dollars toward education and free public school lunches, while also ensuring access to water for subsistence farmers in even the most remote provinces.

Once he had taken care of his people, he then set out to take care of his country, and then his continent. He challenged the 20th century norm where Latin American countries danced to the tune of the gringos to the north, announcing at the beginning of his term that he would no longer merely react to the needs of the US. Lula realized Brazil could no longer flourish if they relied exclusively on a trading relationship with the US. He had to look for other trade allies, beyond even Europe, to the emerging economies of Russia, India, China and South Africa. This was a risky move, but in the post-Cold War era where "you're either with us or against us" partnerships seemed juvenile and outdated, it was a move that paid off. Brazil now exports over $200 billion a year (of which only $19 billion goes to the US), including not just the ores and crops that so many other Latin American nations produce, but also the high-skilled manufactured goods like cars, planes, computers and petrochemicals. They've diversified their economy, and now they can compete with the big boys.

And they've also made the region stronger. They've acted as both trading partners and intermediaries, linking many of the Latin American economies in partnerships that exist outside Western influence. Unlike in recent decades where outsiders attempted to impose their ideologies on local governments, Brazil has played the role of mediator, bringing all sides to the table to discuss, consensus-build and then move forward. But in no way does this mean Brazil is soft. With the thirteenth largest military in the world, and with a nuclear program that has developed both enrichment facilities and missile systems, Brazil always has the mettle to back up the mediation. Taking a page from America's foreign policy, Brazil can foster piece by yielding either the promise of a trading partner or the threat of the military. Because of its role in mitigating regional disputes, because of its status as an economic powerhouse and because of its geopolitical links to the most important nations of the world, Brazil has become a voice in international organizations, often speaking as the lone representative of Latin America. At the G20 economic summits, at the World Trade Organization conferences and even at the United Nations, Brazil has positioned itself as the voice that must be heard. They might even be the lone nation able to convince the United Nations that the current structure of the UN Security Council (with France, China, England, the US and Russia as the only permanent members) is merely an archaic representation of "hereditary claims," not an accurate or fair illustration of who will truly dominate the 21st century.

Even with a Brazil as an emerging, respected regional role model, continuing crises threaten the stability and health of the region. The foremost problems facing Latin America are the rampant violence, the mounting narcotics industry and the staggering poverty. Latin America is home to 21 of the 23 nations with the highest homicide rates in the world (thanks South Africa and Russia for breaking up the monopoly.) If you live in Latin America your chances of getting kidnapped, mugged, robbed or killed are as much as ten times the global average.

Take Brazil for example. If Brazil is the crown jewel of Latin America, you'd expect it to be relatively immune from the vices that are tearing apart the region. Not exactly. Corruption runs rampant across Brazil, from the local cops who extort bribes from street vendors, to the local politicians who make millions off Olympics and World Cup construction projects, to even former president Lula who is under investigation for buying election votes.

The current Brazilian administration has signaled its intent to crack down on federal and local corruption, both through the media and through tougher legislation. Lula's romanticized reign has been tarnished even further the last couple years, not only because of the mounting accusations of corruption, but because the economy has stalled since 2012. The middle class now wonders if Brazil's greatest growth years might be behind them. As the economy stagnates, acts of violence continue to escalate (Brazil is embarrassingly home to 15 of the 50 most violent cities in the world). And at the exact moment economic and social stats have turned dire, Brazilians look all around and see tens of billions of dollars of state funds being thrown into preparations for the 2014 World Cup and 2016 Olympics. Brazilians have been promised that these projects would lead to lasting infrastructure improvements (but just ask Greece how Olympic investments "helped" the long-term progress of their economy). In the summer of 2013, tens of thousands of disenchanted protestors took their frustration to the streets, and the less-than-charismatic government officials proved ill-prepared to respond to the calls for political and economic reform. If this discontent is not handled effectively, Brazil's global games might become the showcase for their recent reversal of fortune and how a nation that was one minute the darling of Latin America, can the next minute appear simply another struggling state.

Another issue Latin American political leaders hope does not become a global focus when the international sports media rolls into town is the regional narcotics industry that increasingly feeds the addictions of their American neighbors to the north. From the time of the Aztecs and the Incas, marijuana and coca leaves were enjoyed by the indigenous populations (though the chewed coca plant produced a high only 1% of that of contemporary nose candy). Usage rates remained relatively restricted to the indigenous clans of Latin America until the United States encouraged Mexican immigration during World War II. These migrant farmers brought their marijuana, and it quickly caught on. By the 1960s, the drug was no longer the rural drug of farmers and migrant laborers, but the drug of choice of an educated and elite younger population. Then in the 1980s, marijuana was displaced by cocaine, the new drug of the rich, and by 2010, the United States of America ruled the world in yet another category – highest usage of illegal drugs. The World Health Organization reported in 2010, that approximately 43% of

Americans have smoked pot and about 17% have snorted cocaine – far and away the highest rates reported in the world. One of the bi-products of being the richest country in the world is you can always buy happiness in a pill, a powder or a leaf if consumerism just isn't giving you the high from the good ol' days.

But this US demand has fueled a huge rise in crime not only deep in the heart of South America, but also in the towns just south of the US-Mexican border. In the first decade of the 21st century, it appeared every attempt by the government to reduce the kidnappings, mutilations and murders only seemed to make matters worse. In Mexico, the regional leaders and police departments had for decades turned a blind eye to the drug business, if they cartels promised to not hurt civilians. This passive acceptance allowed a few major cartels to establish regional fiefdoms, where they controlled not only the cannabis production and distribution, but also the budding methamphetamine trade.

But in 2006, when President Felipe Calderon announced he would be upping the anti-drug campaign to permanently wipe out drug-related violence, the tenuous status quo devolved into utter anarchy. Leaders of the top cartels were arrested, but instead of these incarcerations decreasing the violence, the policy had an inverse effect. Heirs to the cartel thrones stepped up and engaged in hundreds of turf wars, killing and maiming innocent bystanders, leaving a trail of decapitated corpses, blood-filled streets and mass graves, turning Mexico into this generation's "killing fields." The cartels acted in utter indifference to the vigilant actions of Mexican police officials and even the military, forcing even the mayor of Tijuana to discourage Southern California tourists from making trips south of the border.

This pattern of cartels persisting even in the face of fresh governmental pressure can be seen in the drug producing countries of Bolivia, Columbia and Peru, but also in many of the Caribbean islands that have become layovers for drug shipments heading to the United States. In Columbia, a nation that has received billions of dollars in US aid to counter the narcotics industry, coca plants continue to be grown miles away from the eyes of government officials. The drug trade now plays a key role in politics, funding the activities of the revolutionary organization FARC (Fuerzas Armadas Revolucionarias de Columbia – Revolutionary Armed Forces of Columbia). FARC now controls more than 40% of the countryside, becoming little more than a drug cartel with political ambitions, and the civil war that resulted from the power struggle has thus far taken over 600,000 lives.

The situation in Columbia does show signs of getting better, as US and regional authorities crack down on the manufacture and distribution of illicit drugs, and FARC officials have actually agreed to sit down and talk peace options. But these nations are also recognizing the balloon effect of the war on drugs. Squeeze out the production and crime in one area, it'll only blow up in another. As the Columbian drug industry starts to decrease, it has popped up in neighboring Venezuela and Brazil. Solve one problem. Create another. There will be no quick solution to this problem, as long as there is millions to be made up north.

Regardless of where the blame resides – whether in the US with all its druggies or in Latin America with its drug lords and thugs – the problem is clearly out of control. The drug trade grosses close to $50 billion a year, and in 2011, Mexico saw its drug-related homicide numbers hit its highest mark in history with a reported 16,466 deaths (16,400 more than were registered just six years earlier). The Americas are losing the war on drugs, and if the demand and the supply aren't both reduced significantly in the coming years, this will turn out to be the deadliest war in Latin American history.

Not surprisingly, with the upswing in violence, the lack of employment opportunities and the limited access to education, millions still head north each year for the promise of the United States and the American Dream. Yet, with the post 9/11 border tightening and the recent conservative push to build walls and strengthen border security, the trek to los Estados Unidos is stopping far further south of the border. This migration has seen population density rates skyrocket not just in Mexico's largest cities (like Mexico City with its 21 million inhabitants), but also in the rural areas and manufacturing towns that sprung up after NAFTA. Now towns across Mexico, and growingly across Latin America, have to deal with migratory patterns that are bringing together the displaced with the already suffering indigenous populations. This melting of ethnicities creates not only cultural clashes, but also changes the political atmosphere as governments must now attend to the needs of an increasingly diverse electorate.

And it is this poverty and lack of opportunities that will remain Latin America's biggest concerns moving forward. Ironically, since 2009, Latin America has been one of the few regions in the world to actually demonstrate an improvement in income equality. Some of that progress can be attributed to the fact that poverty rates were so low for the last half of the 20th century that they had nowhere else to go but up. In 2000, Bolivia, Columbia, Paraguay, Peru and Argentina each maintained poverty rates above 40%, and even Brazil saw 40 million of its citizens living on less than $2 a day. However, over the last few years, millions have risen above the poverty line, and the discrepancy between the haves and the have-nots has shrunk. Governments are spending more money educating their people, providing health care and pension benefits and enforcing tax collection from the wealthiest of its citizens. Plus, most significantly, as Latin American countries continue to expand their manufacturing industries to meet the demand of the world economies recovering from the 2008 recession, there are simply more jobs available. In the coming years, Latin America should see even more jobs come to the region as pharmaceutical companies, automobile manufacturers, investment banks and medical tourism providers expand to fill market demand.

A totally different way of confronting the cycle of poverty in Latin America was offered by Hugo Chavez, with his communist experiment in Venezuela. Hugo Chavez rode into the presidency in 1999, quickly took over all the nation's private oil companies and turned petroleum exports into his key to economic recovery. He would make money from oil exports and then pass it out to his people. And for a few years, this strategy worked. Poverty rates decreased, education and health levels improved and Chavez was seen as the savior of the poor. He pulled the billions in oil profits from the richest rich, and used it to fund the medical industry and schools across the country. He cut the poverty rate in half and provided elderly retirement benefits to over two million Venezuelans.

But then, his megalomania and poor economic planning got the best of him and his country started falling apart. The government ignored non-oil producing industries, allowing many to fall bankrupt or produce substandard products (in 2012, Conviasa, the nation's lone public airline, was banned from European airspace because its planes were seen as too dangerous to fly). As Chavez wanted all the credit for the economy's recovery, his federal agencies controlled pricing and production quotas for all goods and services, which unavoidably led to market shelves stocking far too much bathroom cleanser, and far too few bottles of milk. In fall of 2012, when Chavez won his re-election bid by only 11% of the votes, his shallow victory was seen by many outsiders as proof that his popularity was fading. Considering he had done everything possible to fix the election – limiting opposition TV time to six minutes a day, threatening voters to cast their ballots for his party, imprisoning opposition leaders – he should have been able to manufacture a far larger margin. His victory quickly proved a back-page story, as days later, Chavez admitted his cancer had returned, and within a few months he was dead. Venezuela now faces the choice of how to replacer a dictator who claimed to rule under the guise of a democracy. To what extent will the nation continue to adopt Chavez's unique take on communism? Will future leaders seize this rare opportunity to diversify their economy to ensure all parties can best benefit from their resource gift? And was Venezuela's communist experiment simply a random outlier, or might other nations likewise tryout the outdated system?

Latin America is in flux. In recent years, there have been glimmers of hope, but there have also been indisputable pictures of cruelty and barbarism. There have been nations who have produced stable governments with diverse economies and an increasingly-educated workforce, yet there are still nations that pillage the natural resources for short-term gains or appease the political desires of a corrupt autocracy. There are millions who look outside their home country for a chance at safety and prosperity, and there are millions who have realized that these hopes rest no longer in the United States, but in Latin America where the economic opportunities are increasing.

Latin America is on the cusp of moving beyond developing, to becoming developed, possibly following in the footsteps of the one region – East Asia - that appears to have figured out how to participate as equals in the global economic game, while also bringing its people up from squalor.

But that is for another chapter.

44

Japan

Japan poses a conundrum. On one hand it's the success story of the developing world. Little more than an economic puppet to the Western world at the turn of the century, Japan jumped on the industrialization fast track, eventually kicking Europe out of Asia in the 1940s, and then recovering from the ruin of World War II, rebuilding itself into the second largest economy in the world.

On the other hand, it's a cautionary tale to all industrialized countries that economic superiority is only temporary in this world of globalization, and risky or short-sighted banking and corporate policies will eventually burst any bubble.

It boasts the oldest life expectancy in the world. It also suffers from an aging population that threatens to wipe out all retirement benefits.

It clings to an ethnic purity that features a nation of close to 99% citizens of pure Japanese heritage. But its restricted immigration policies handicap its ability to yield a labor force able to keep up with global demand.

It's usually the first country to embrace technological innovation, and its workers have become the model of productive efficiency. It also suffers from a culture of depression and intolerance where suicide rates dwarf the rest of the world, and millions hole themselves in their homes, fully amputated from society.

So which Japan do we accept? The one that stands as the model of what humans and economies can achieve, or the one that presents a foreboding glimpse into what can result when a flourishing economy is the sole goal?

In August of 1945, Japan was a civilization on the verge of extinction. A generation of Japan's finest men gave their lives to the Imperial Army. Relentless, indiscriminate American firebombings left close to a hundred Japanese cities in ashes. Nagasaki and Hiroshima were left to crawl out of their atomic holocaust. The Emperor's feeble voice was heard for the first time on the radio, formally surrendering to American forces. Factories lay impotent. Transportation and communication networks were useless. Millions needed to be mourned, homes needed to be rebuilt and mouths had to be fed.

Economic recovery was improbable. Regression to a pre-industrial state appeared the more likely scenario.

But then Japan did the unthinkable. Not only did they mend their war wounds, they surpassed all worldly expectations. First protected by the American occupying forces, then subsidized and shielded from foreign competition by the Japanese government, industry boomed. By 1960, the atrocities of the Second World War were pushed deep into the Japanese psyche, and a full-fledged recovery was underway. By 1980, the economic miracle that was Japan had come to fruition. By 1990, Japan reached deep into the pockets of the western world. It felt like everyone was listening to Sony Walkmans, playing Nintendo Game Boys, driving Honda Preludes and sampling sushi and California Rolls. Even America itself was falling to Japanese businesses. The pinnacle of Japan's ominous influence hit when a group of Japanese businessmen (a few of whom had made their money through less than legal means) had the gall to buy America's prized golf course – Pebble Beach. The Cold War was ending, America was looking to raise taxes to recover from their late 1980s financial crisis and Japan sat on the threshold of unmatched economic superiority. Their GDP had catapulted them to #2 in the world, and dozens of think tanks wondered if America should turn a bit more Japanese.

And then their bubble burst.

On December 29, 1989 the Nikkei 225 (Japan's version of the Dow Jones Industrial Average stock index) hit 38,957. It would never come close to that number again. Over the next decade, bit by bit, little by little, the stock market fell and never recovered. Unlike the Great Depression, where stocks crashed almost overnight, the Japanese stock market collapse was more of a slow bleeding than a severed appendage. It hit a low of 7,054 in 2009, and even today, over two decades after it almost hit 40,000, the Japanese stock market barely even flirts with the 10,000-point level.

And the housing market took an equally bad hit, dropping over 70% in value from its bubbled highs of the late 1980s when loans were cheap, interest rates hovered near zero and even the most risky consumer could borrow money. In the most coveted business districts of Tokyo, rents on office spaces could eclipse $200,000 a square foot (a SQUARE FOOT!). A small bed is 35 square feet, so in the fantasy world of Japanese real estate, a chunk of land the size of a bed would go for $7 million. And people somehow thought it would keep going up. These people got burned the hard way. Some of these more posh districts in the major cities saw their value drop by up to 99%.

Japan had been exposed. The decades of fooling with Adam Smith's invisible hand had come back to bite them hard. The government's over-eagerness to intervene and protect home industries, the corporate leaders' willingness to preserve detrimental business models and investors' inability to grasp the inevitable gravitational pull on inflated assets – all of these behaviors played a role in yanking Japan back to reality. And in the years since 1990, in the "lost decades" that have ensued, Japanese policymakers (and those industrial nations who fear a similar slump) have had to revisit what about the Japanese model to determine what practices could one moment create a miracle, and the next, spawn a nightmare.

Japan developed some bad habits over the years. The nation relied on a type of corporate welfare, where companies took care of employees for life. Once in the door, a young 20-something could see his next fifty years lined with a steadily increasing salary, guaranteed health benefits and reduced-priced corporate housing. When you were hired, you didn't join a firm, you joined a family. You arrived to a workplace strewn with banners, plaques and slogans broadcasting the virtues of your protective kin. Your company protected you, and you offered your undying allegiance to your company. Your salary moved up incrementally with each year of service, regardless of your continued usefulness. By the 1980s, close to 90% of the Japanese population saw themselves as middle class. Savings rates climbed to the highest in the world (nearly 25% of annual income). The young deferred to the old, and the old deferred to the managers. Everyone was taken care of...at least until the unlimited growth reached its limit.

Throughout the Cold War, Japan had been protected – protected from the realities of a truly open marketplace. As the lone bastion of democracy in East Asia, America provided them unfettered support, gobbling up any good the Japanese could shoot out of their plants. Starting with the Korean War, American-Japanese relations flipped. Japan was no longer the fledgling economy where America could dump all of its surplus products. Instead, America became the mass importer of Japanese goods – buying their cars, electronics, computers and machine tools. None of these exports were natural resources. All required the education, skills and efficiency of the Japanese workforce. The worker was the key to exports, and exports were a key to the economic miracle.

But as China emerged from its self-imposed industrial exile, Russia pulled itself from outdated communist control and the Southeast Asian Tigers (Singapore, Hong Kong, Taiwan and South Korea) proved themselves equally able to produce high-end manufactured goods, the Japan's near-monopolistic control of the region started to fade.

Corporate Japan was slow to adjust. Unneeded workers were kept on staff. Product lines that didn't have a market were still made. Banks still gave out loans like the economy would never shrink and governments bailed out companies that started to struggle. The end of the miracle was apparent in the early 1980s, but economic advisors and corporate leaders refused to adapt.

The lost decades of the 1990s and 2000s made this failure to adapt no longer an option, and today the government faces a host of demographic and economic realities that threaten to destroy the long-term viability of the Japanese model. The foremost problem for Japan is their people. They're just too healthy, and they live too long. Longevity is good if you're talking about your grandparents, it's bad when you're running a country. The average life expectancy of a Japanese citizen born today is 82.9 years, the highest rate in the world. For their southern island region Okinawa, the figures were ridiculous. Okinawa has more centenarians than most countries have 60-year-olds. The Japanese have better diets, better access to health care and better communal ties – the formula for longevity.

But longevity comes with a price - especially when families are simultaneously having less and less children. Japan's birth rate averages 1.09 children per woman – the lowest rate in the entire world (if you don't include Monaco with its whopping 35,000 citizens). Families just don't want to have kids. Whether it's because daycare options are obsolete, workdays are the longest in the world (25% work over 60 hours a week) or couples just prefer to spend their time and money on themselves, Japan isn't reproducing fast enough to replace all those millions of retirees heading into their sunset years. Japan's workforce is also diminishing because of their staunch resistance to immigration. Japan has a history of closing its doors to immigrants, and even today they are 98.5% Japanese and 1.5% "other." No other country even comes close to this homogeneity. England is 82% British. Germany is 88% German. China has 92% Han Chinese. The United States? Well, they're a hodgepodge of everything from Mexican to Puerto Rican to Vietnamese to Laotian to Irish to Turkish to Arab to Persian. If the US is the great melting pot of the world, Japan is its frozen ice cube.

Unlike the rest of the nations of the world suffering from the strains of overpopulation, Japan became the first industrialized power forced to manage underpopulation. In 2011, for the first time, they're population actually decreased from 128 million to 127 million, and if their birth rates continue at this meek rate, by 2050, they'll have lost 25% of their population. Less people equals less workers. Less workers equals less goods being produced and less taxes being paid. Less taxes equals less revenue available to pay for all the social welfare and infrastructure programs that keep the nation healthy and the country running smoothly. The government has a few choices - convince people to head to the bedroom and make babies, convince their population that immigration is essential for survival or create more machines to do the work of humans.

The first one would be a tough sell (although countries like Singapore do produce some fairly clever commercials to reverse the birth curse), but the second two are already underway. Japan has begun encouraging regional foreigners to emigrate, establishing labor contracts with neighboring countries. Japan hopes to pull in over 10,000 employees a year from Vietnam (promising wages of $1500 a month) to fill openings in the fishing and agricultural industries and the Philippines is currently training members of its workforce to satisfy the nursing and caregiver demands of Japan's aging population. As more and more workers begin to work and live amongst the ethnically Japanese, their society will inevitably have to manage the nativist-immigrant tensions facing all industrialized countries. And if the workers don't come to Japan, Japan will take their businesses to the workers. Whereas Japan is running out of laborers, nearby India has more than they know what to do with. Over 800 Japanese firms now operate in India, taking advantage of the 720 million Indians under the age of 30 who provide not just an endless stream of workers, but also a huge demand for anything the factories can spew.

Outsourcing might increase corporate profits, but it doesn't increase Japan's revenue base from payroll taxes. Immigration will only solve part of the labor challenge, and its potential cultural threats might hamper its long-term viability. Because of Japan's resistance to accept foreigners, it will have to continue to expand the reach of mechanization if it hopes to continue to compete with the other industrial giants through the 21st century. For the last few decades, what Japan lacked in human hands, it made up for with machines. Unlike anywhere else in the world, the retail sales workforce has been replaced with vending machines. Why hire a salesman when you can plug in a machine? By 2010, Japan had one vending machine for every 23 people (Britain comes in a distant second with one per 55 people). They have machines for drinks and snacks like the rest of the world, but they also have some for underwear, beer, cigarettes, live crab, music, ice, eggs, umbrellas, flowers, shoes and vegetables. Today vending machines have even become wi-fi hotspots, providing Internet access to up to 50 feet from the coin and bill operated stores in a box (and with coffee sold at the adjacent machine, Japan has essentially created Vending Internet Cafes).

The most remarkable (albeit a bit disturbing) goods in a machine are the capsule hotels that started popping up in Tokyo and other major Japanese cities in the late 1980s. These six foot long, five foot wide boxes have TVs, coat hooks, clean linens and a pillow made of rice husks, all for the low price of $640 a month. They all stack on top of each other, so basically you're climbing into stacked coffins for the chance at a covered night's sleep. Initially created for the drunken Tokyo businessmen who missed the last train out of town, today they've become a cheaper alternative for those trying to survive in the city in an uncertain job market with limited affordable housing options. Since the 2008 global recession, city officials have even tried to expand the number of "capsules," as more and more residents have resorted to creating tent cities and cardboard box homes. For a city that boasts the fourth most skyscrapers in the world, Tokyo awkwardly needs to focus a bit more on the shelter crisis going on at the street level.

These capsules, tents and cardboard boxes all illuminate the greater economic problems that cause Japan's leaders their fair share of sleepless nights. In 2010, Japan's debt to GDP ratio was the worst in the world. Their GDP was $5 trillion. Their debt was $10 trillion. In 2011, the United States passed the 100% debt to GDP ratio. Japan hovers about 200%. But Japan's debt is a bit different than America's. America's debt is held in large part by foreign banks and foreign countries. 46% of US debt is held by people, companies and countries living outside the US (with China accounting for 8% of the debt). In Japan, the story is totally different. Japan borrows from itself. 95% of Japan's debt is to its own people, to its own banks. With household and corporate savings eclipsing $19 trillion, the Japanese government can always call on its own citizens when it needs to borrow more money. They might not receive enough revenue through taxes, but they more than make up for it by merely borrowing from within, and as long as the banks and the citizens don't ask for all of their money back (and are content with just receiving the interest payments), this little loaning scheme will continue to keep Japan afloat. But if ever the investors get nervous and start calling in all their debts, Japan would be unable to pay back all its lenders. It would run out of money. But the odds are in favor of the Japanese government continuing this nationalized ponzi scheme (an investment form of trickery where new investors pay off the interest of earlier investors...do a Google search for imprisoned guru Bernie Madoff for more details), as the banks and the people can't envision pulling out their money to invest it elsewhere. It's Japan or nothing.

Corporations have been restructuring themselves to compete globally without risking the long-term viability of their firms. They're hesitant to offer "employee for life" guarantees. They're more willing to hire part-time workers or outsource. They're now more willing to hire women (though the Japanese glass ceiling will be far harder to crack than America's). They're more willing to fire aging or inefficient employees, terminate product lines that don't make any more money and stop investing in dangerous real estate or new technology ventures that might come back to haunt their bottom line for years to come. The government has likewise turned away from their role as an enabling, co-dependent father figure, willing to bail out struggling companies or twist the markets in favor of Japanese goods. Since the 1960s, Japan manipulated trade agreements or mass purchased steel, rubber and ores from neighboring countries to give home industries an absolute advantage over their competitors. Not anymore. Japanese officials are more inclined to let the invisible hand of the market toss out bungling businesses so only the competent survive.

The nation has had difficulty looking to the government for stability. They've gone through seven prime ministers in seven years, and in December 2012, Shinzo Abe took his second crack at the top seat in the government (he had resigned in 2007 due to poor health and the suicide of one of his ministers). Abe came in with a plan to reverse the deflation of recent years. He would encourage banks to lend more money (a difficult task considering interest rates are already at 0%), call on businesses to raise salaries and invest more public money into businesses and infrastructure projects. This brand of "Abeonomics" hasn't yet taken off. Banks are hesitant to offer negative interest rates (actually paying people to borrow their money), and few CEOs will risk raising wages with no guarantee that the prices of goods and services will likewise go up.

The one area where Prime Minister Abe has gained national support is his hard line stance on both North Korea and China. At a time when China is looking to flex its regional muscles, and newly appointed North Korean leader Kim Jong Un repeatedly ups the tension level in the Far East by pursuing a nuclear program and threatening to point his conventional weapons at key Asian targets, Japan is looking for a leader who likewise presents an aura of strength. Abe increased the military budget of Japan for the first time in decades and reemphasized its strategic military partnership with the United States.

Abe also won't back down on territorial disputes, specifically the islands of Senkaku (known as Diaoyu to the Chinese). Both nations claim sovereignty over the uninhabited islands and the rights to any natural resources (aka oil and natural gas) found nearby. The islands lay in the no man's land of territorial claims, right about 200 miles between each nation. Each country also maintains historical claims to the islands. The Chinese argue that in 1892 their Empress Cixi claimed the islands for one of her medicine men to grow herbs. The Japanese say their claims go back even further, as fisherman and ornithologists scoured the islands for bird poop. These flimsy territorial declarations not only illuminate current conflicts souring relations between China and Japan, but also bring to the surface tensions that still remain following the barbarism of World War II. As both nations compete for the resources and markets of East Asia, they will continue to bump into each other to ensure their own economic survival.

As Japan moves into its next phase of economic development, it risks leaving a generation materially less well-off than its parents and, in many cases, emotionally battered. Japanese workers are finding it harder and harder to acquire the trappings of wealth that once seemed a birthright. In 2012, their savings rates for the first time turned negative (a tragic plunge from the 25% savings rates highs of the 1970s), as more were willing to go into debt than forego a life of material comfort. They work longer hours, but with less job security. They navigate agonizingly through the ultra-competitive and endless stream of entrance exams, after-school tutoring and yearly assessments, where only the strongest emerge with a top-end education, and many are left behind in education's wake.

An uncertain future has wreaked havoc on the nation's psyche. In the recently produced World Map of Happiness, Japan scored 90 out of 178 countries. It's difficult to ascertain depression rates, as Japan's culture scorns the analysis and treatment of mental health issues, but in the last decade, two troubling patterns have developed that speak to deeper schisms in the nation's psyche and threaten to reach crisis proportions if steps aren't taken quickly to curb their predominance.

First is the issue of hikikomori. Translated it might mean "going inward," but in reality it is when a person fully withdraws from society, choosing instead to close themselves up in an apartment, a bedroom, a kitchen or even a bathroom, refusing to ever leave. Like with depression, exact figures are difficult to tabulate, but some estimate as many as one million Japanese have chosen hikikomori. To some, this is an issue of parental indulgence. Parents, usually middle or upper class, allow their adult children to stay indoors, feeding them, providing them shelter, bringing them their needed worldly goods, basically enabling their hermit existence. To others, it goes beyond lax parenting, and says more about a society that puts too much pressure on young adults, a society that prescribes one accepted lifestyle, forcing many to choose self-imposed isolation to peer rejection. Once these recluses have checked out, some return to the land of the living after a few months, but some remain locked indoors for decades, and with the Internet promising to deliver all necessities to their doorsteps, this behavior will continue to expand as economic conditions worsen and more seek an escape from the stresses of daily living.

For some Japanese, the retreat to seclusion is not enough. They instead choose to take their own lives. Over the last decade, Japanese suicide rates have remained the highest in the world, averaging over 30,000 deaths a year, and with each year the numbers only increase. Like with the "hikkis" who are often running from despair, suicides most often result from an economic loss (most notably a job) or from a personal tragedy like a break-up, an incident of bullying or a scandal. In 2007, cabinet minister Toshikatsu Matsuoka hung himself after being accused of stealing from the government, illegally claiming over $200,000 in electricity, gas and water bills for his government office building (even though the building's utility costs were free). At the time of his death, some political officials actually believed he took the honorable way out, and this reaction reveals how the Japanese cultural values of self-sacrifice and saving face might actually encourage suicide. From the Tokugawa Era through to World War II, valiant heroes took their own lives, rather than suffer a public embarrassment.

Yet today, instead of the ritual seppuku belly ripping of samurai or the aeronautical sacrifices of the kamikaze pilots, men and women take their own lives most frequently by merely jumping in front of a train or overdosing on pills in an apartment. And unlike the ritual deaths of the past, these deaths actually end up bringing more pain and economic suffering to their families. Although some suicide victims establish life insurance policies that will pay off all their debts once they've died, most end up costing their parents even more money. To discourage railway suicides that inevitably impact the morning commute, the government has established a "delay fee" of over a million dollars, charged to the families of the deceased. For those who take their lives in an apartment, the landlords or the property owners must charge the family for clean-up fees, lost rent and sometimes complete renovation of the complex, as few want to be linked to death in any form.

The government has recognized that suicide, and to some extent hikikomori, are growing problems for their nation, but have offered few solutions. Japan is a society that disdains the public admission of emotional flaws, so early identification of potential mental health risks is almost impossible. This resistance to open dialogue is also met with limited resources. Few suicide hotlines even exist in Japan (only 24,000 suicide calls are taken a year in Japan versus 2.4 million counseled annually in England), and medical insurance agencies often refuse to pay for mental health treatment. Of late, the government has funded fact-finding investigations as to the causes and potential treatments for these destructive behaviors, but little progress has been made, leaving Japan highly vulnerable to rising rates of depression, withdrawal and even suicide.

But all is not lost. The tragedy of the 2011 March earthquake and tsunami exposed a few of the flaws in Japan's political and economic systems, but it also revealed the cultural strength and resiliency that bodes well for the chances of this nation assessing where it stands and taking the painful, yet needed, steps towards recovery. On March 11, 2011, a 9.0 earthquake lasting nearly six minutes struck off the northeast coast of Japan, triggering a series of deadly aftershocks and an even deadlier tsunami. Within an hour of the first quake, a wave of water measuring over 120 feet overran the coastal areas, demolishing entire cities, depositing a trail of over 23 million pounds of debris across the countryside. Close to 20,000 lives were lost, over 40,000 buildings were destroyed, hundreds of thousands of Japanese citizens were displaced, and damages surpassed $300 billion.

As would be expected for such an unparalleled disaster (see Hurricane Katrina 2005), the government was slow to adapt. Relief efforts were poorly coordinated, the scope of the damage was not accurately gauged and disseminated to the public, and basic necessities like fuel, food and medicine took weeks to make it to the hardest hit regions. However, within weeks, the government gained control of the situation, mobilizing its Self-Defense Forces and accepting aid from foreign countries. In the months since, the government has reduced taxes for the region, increased efforts to relocate the displaced and funded the cleaning up and reconstruction of the damaged regions. But some wonder if the damaged regions should even be rebuilt. Sitting on rim of the Pacific Ring of Fire, Japan has always been vulnerable to devastating seismic activity, and many feel to rebuild exposed coastal regions would prove futile.

The nuclear disaster at the Fukushima nuclear power plant triggered powerful memories of the tragedy of the World War II bombings, convincing a bulk of the citizenry to push for an end to Japan's reliance on nuclear power. Prior to the nuclear meltdown, between 30-50% of all Japan's power needs were satisfied by nuclear power, but since the disaster, government officials have scrapped plans to build fourteen additional plants, and have had to now pursue alternative sources for energy.

A year later, a deeper level of discontent and malaise has settled into the nation's consciousness. The spirit of volunteerism and self-sacrifice that immediately accompanied the disaster has been replaced with an uneasiness over Japan's future. The media's self-restraint and unwillingness to sensationalize personal tragedy has been replaced with a more critical media inclined to shed a somber light on the flaws in society. Japan is nervous. A bright future is far from guaranteed. Japan watches as rivals China and America warn about how they both hope to avoid becoming the "next Japan" as if their current state is one of despair and hopelessness.

But Japan is anything but a failed state. Its people still live longer, healthier, more prosperous lives than about 99% of the planet, and their economy and culture show no signs of passively fading off into the annals of failed civilizations. Japan has recovered from annihilation time and time again, and if history chooses to repeat itself, these last two lost decades will merely be a bump in the road of what had become a true global success story.

But that is for another chapter.

45

China

China's back. Again. In the summer of 2010, China's economic output officially passed that of Japan, ending the island nation's 42-year reign as the second largest economy in the world, and symbolically closing the book on the darkest two century chapter in China's history. For those familiar with China's epic story, a couple hundred-year slump was nothing new for the civilization rooted in the Mandate of Heaven where rulers rise and fall, foreign powers briefly oppress, and civil wars, famine and destitution cripple the country. But in the end, China always recovers.

In 2010, after two centuries of embarrassment at the hands of Japanese and European invaders; after the maniacal, narcissistic misdirected and debilitating rules of first Empress Cixi and then decades later Mao Tse Tung; and after a string of civil wars, purges and lethally foolish reforms, China entered the 1980s uncertain if it would ever recover. When the protests at Tiananmen Square in 1989 presented to the world a people willing to stand in front of an oppressive system (aka "tank") to demand their just human rights, many believed that, like the Soviet republics, the age of communist rule in China would soon come to an end.

The forecasters were not even close. From those protests, China didn't dissolve into chaos, but instead went on a two-decade economic, military and political evolution that pulled the nation from a backwards "century of humiliation" and advanced it to become a superpower threatening to dislodge the United States of America from its pedestal.

Look at the stats. China's 2011 GDP surpassed $7.3 trillion (only the United States produced more). China exports $1.9 trillion in goods every year (tops in the world). Over the last twenty years, China's economy has grown at a double-digit percentage rate for all but four of those years (and in five of those 20 years, they surpassed 20% growth). China now holds the three largest banks in the world (replacing Bank of America and Citibank). China graduates over a million scientists and engineers from college every year (the United States barely hits 250,000 graduates, and its two leading majors are business and psychology). China has supplanted Japan and the Baby Tigers (South Korea, Hong Kong, Taiwan and Singapore) as the regional economic and military power. China has 240 nuclear bombs (fourth most on the planet) and maintains an active military of close to 2.5 million soldiers (nearly twice that of second place America).

The 2008 Beijing Olympics were a symbolic coming-out party for China. From its Opening Ceremonies to its mildly disturbing ability to control the weather, China showed the world that it had arrived and was not merely a nation able to produce the billions of toys, porcelain plates and knick-knacks that line our shelves and fill our closets. Staged more to impress the world than to showcase the athletes, the $44 billion Olympian production will probably never be duplicated again.

2008 marked another changing of the guard as the global recession first destroyed the American economy, bursting the over-inflated housing bubble and revealing the financial machinations of Wall Street "pure" capitalists, and then threatened to bring down the rest of the world's markets. As nation after nation succumbed to harsh austerity measures and saw unemployment rates skyrocket while production rates plummeted, China emerged from the crisis relatively unscathed - some could argue even stronger than before. When in 2009 Secretary of State Hillary Clinton arrived in China to advise the government ministers on how best to weather the economic storm, she was met by officials who struggled to see what benefit they could gain from American instruction. Maybe, it is the Americans who should revisit their economic model. Maybe it is America's stalled democratic system and corrupt financial industry that should heed the Chinese precedent.

The student had become the teacher. The West's century-long paternalistic treatment of China no longer matched the reality of the economic and geopolitical climate. China had become a major player on the world stage, leaving many historians and economists to ponder if the age of Pax Americana was coming to an end and the era of Chinese hegemony was upon us.

However, before sounding the death knell of the American republic and the birth of China's unparalleled supremacy, China must first resolve a series of threats if they hope to continue on their seemingly unstoppable upward trajectory. For as much as pundits might want to believe China can only keep rising at a double-digit rate, history has shown us through the Tulip bubble of 1637, the railroad bubble of the 1840s, the stock market bubble of the 1920s, the Internet bubble of the 1990s and the housing bubble of the 2000s that what goes up, must come down. The gravitational realities of the invisible hand are inescapable. So the question isn't if, but when. When will the Chinese boom become a Chinese bust?

The warning signs are many, but their costs might not be felt for decades, but they will be felt. First, China must deal with the threat of inflation. Double-digit growth often leads to double-digit inflation. As incomes increase and as more goods are produced, more money is circulated. China is in the midst of its own housing bubble; average home values tripled from 2005 to 2010. This type of too much, too fast growth was seen in Japan in the 1980s and America at the turn of the millennium, and both situations didn't end well.

China must also deal with its rising income inequality. Americans and the West fret over the inequity of the 1%, fearing that one class controls all the wealth. China's already headed down that same path. Though it might have the #2 ranked economy in the world, when it comes to per capital GDP, China falls to 25th place. This inequality prevents China from developing a middle class able to consume the goods necessary to sustain China's economic miracle. Although millions of skilled and unskilled laborers migrate to urban areas every year, purchasing the goods that keep an economy humming, China still disproportionately relies on exports to fuel their economy. This means that if the other countries stop buying, say during a worldwide economic recession, China invariably suffers. China's domestic consumption (the amount of goods and services its own people buy) accounted for only 34.9% of its GDP in 2010 (compared to 71.2% in the United States). China is a nation of savers, not a nation of buyers. This is great when it comes to investment, not so great when it comes to fueling an economy. If China can't find a way to grow their economy internally, they will perennially be vulnerable to the whims of other nations' buying practices.

As China's economy has grown, as cities have swelled, as billions of dollars in state and private investment in infrastructure projects has trickled down to the furthest corners of the nation, corruption has inevitably crept into every day transactions and jeopardizes the legitimacy of regional governments. Whenever a society goes through rapid economic expansion, there is money to be made by middlemen, those willing to grant favors to the highest bidder. 77% of China believes their local government officials are corrupt. With all the billions of dollars flowing to build roads, dams, bridges, communication lines, high-speed railways and state-sponsored businesses, local officials inevitably skim off the top to ensure the moneys flow to their province.

The most alarming (yet somewhat comical) example of the prevalence of corruption and the depth to which it pervades Chinese society came out in 2012 with the suspicious death of British businessman Neil Heywood. On November 15, 2011, Heywood was found dead in his hotel room, and initial reports claimed it was from alcohol poisoning, which was odd because many of Heywood's friends claimed he never drank alcohol. When the toxicology reports surfaced, noting traces of potassium cyanide, it became obvious that Heywood was poisoned. Who would have the means and the motivation to poison a British businessman? This was where the story started to look more like the plot of a quickly forgotten episode of CSI Shanghai than an actual turn of events.

Heywood was a friend of Gu Kailai, the wife of Bo Xilai. Bo was a prominent politician in the Chinese politburo whose career trajectory looked limitless. He had proven himself a popular figure, making a name for himself as the Communist Party chief of Chongqing, vowing to stamp out corruption while making Chongqing a haven for foreign investment and technological advancement. The problem was, Bo himself was quite corrupt, and it turns out that Heywood helped Bo and his wife Gu embezzle millions of dollars into offshore accounts. When Heywood threatened to expose Bo for his hypocrisy, Gu had him killed. As the media lens focused more on Bo Xilai's political and professional dealings, they discovered he had a history of kidnapping, torture, threats and graft that dated back decades. Because of Bo's position and the bizarre, sometimes shocking details surrounding the scandal, many in both China and abroad wondered if the story of the rise and fall of Bo Xilai was more the norm than the exception. For if corruption is as embedded in Chinese society as polls might suggest, China will have to embrace an era of progressive legislation and enforcement comparable to the American progressive legislation of the early 20th century.

But it won't be tales of homicides or income inequality or even distressing levels of domestic consumption that will obstruct Chinese prosperity. It'll be demographic trends that threaten to disrupt China's greatest asset – its seemingly inexhaustible supply of young, educated labor. China is the most populated country on the planet. At 1.33 billion, China's population surpasses the combined population totals of the third through seventh largest countries in the world – the United States, Indonesia, Brazil, Pakistan and Nigeria (India had to be ignored because they're at 1.2 billion and it messes up my argument). At around 20% of the world's population, you wouldn't think China would have an impending labor shortage, but they do. Let's call it the 160-160-160 problem.

As of 2010, China had 160 million people that were 60 years old or older, 160 million families with only one child and 160 million migrants who had moved to the cities. These numbers scare economists because of the direction they are headed and the subsequent implications of this demographic shift. China's cohort of elderly people will continue to swell as health care and economic conditions improve. In just 50 years, China has increased its life expectancy from less than 40 to 74.5 for females and 70.7 for males. In the West, this feat took close to two centuries. Because China has expanded life expectancy at such a remarkable rate, their society has not had the time to properly prepare a health care, pension and infrastructure systems able to meet the inevitable needs of this greying population. By 2030, China could have more senior citizens than any country in the world, but not the money or the services to care for them.

Compounding the problem of decreased mortality rates is a frightening decrease in fertility rates. In 1979, recognizing how the population pressure was hurting their nation's progress, China instituted a One-Child Policy, where families would be penalized a "social child raising fee" for having more than one child. Intended initially to apply to only one generation, three decades later, provinces continue to enforce the policy, and to this day, nearly 400 million births have been prevented. Some families are exempt from the policy due to exceptions related to gender, next of kin or rural status. Others merely have paid the fine (up to $70,000 based on a couple's income level). Even though exceptions exist, the One-Child Policy has dramatically impacted the ability of China to replace its population. Industrializing societies already witness a decrease in fertility as living standards improve, but China has compounded the problem with their forced compliance. Over the next decade the number of 20- to 24-year-olds will decrease from 125 million to 68 million, and with each future generation, the numbers will continue to drop. Though China might have 1.33 billion people now, by 2030, it will probably cap out at 1.5 billion, and then steadily decline.

A decline from 1.5 billion seems like it would benefit the society, but not when over half your population is made up of unproductive old people who mostly spend their money on health services, not exactly the type consumption that fuels an economy. Not when your population is physically unable to work. Not when your population drains money from the government's treasury instead of filling it through payroll taxes. As each succeeding generation decreases in number, all of the age-related purchases will likewise decrease. Less babies mean less strollers, stuffed animals, diapers and baby formula. Less teenagers mean less schools, gadgets, cinema attendance and video games. Less young adults mean less weddings, cars, houses and furniture.

Less people also mean less girls. China is clearly still a patriarchal society, preferring male children to female children, and with the advent of ultrasound machines (China owns the most of these little contraptions in the world), Chinese couples increasingly use this sex determination technology to choose their one child's gender. This form of in utero infanticide means that for every 130 boys born in China, only 100 girls are born. This gender inequity has already led to some creative methods of dealing with a dearth of female options. Children are forced to marry first cousins. Brothers share a wife. Some 30 million single men will die never being married. What will happen as this discrepancy only increases? Will crime increase? Will homosexuality rates increase? Will sex trafficking and the purchase of foreign brides increase?

What will happen to a society outnumbered by the old and by males? Over the next few decades, China will find out.

If China's domestic issues weren't worrisome enough, their increasingly formidable impact on international affairs continues to frustrate and challenge regional and global powers. China appears to abide by the policy of "anything goes as long as there's money to be made." Whereas the United States and other Western liberal, free-market democracies often put human rights stipulations on their trading partners, China has no qualms about working with the less-altruistic regimes around the world. It's kind of hard for America to force the governments of Iran, North Korea and Sudan into altering their oppressive policies that brutalize their citizens, when always in the background is China willing to sweep in and accept all available resource exports. China needs the gifts of nature (especially oil), and if they have to make deals with the devil, they won't shed a tear or feel guilty when the international community condemns their seemingly-callous business practices. G8 countries such as Canada, France, Germany, the United Kingdom and the United States hope that China will see their seat at the table as an opportunity to become a global leader, willing to leverage their economic power to make the world a better place for humanity. China right now cares more making a buck (or a yuan).

China also is expectedly defensive when it comes to dealing with regional powers. Only recently did China emerge from the patriarchal, sometimes condescending, influence of foreign powers, and they have no intention of returning to a state of subservience. Their military strength stands behind only Russia and the United States. With a 21st century navy, a land army that dwarfs any other country's and a couple hundred nuclear warheads at their disposal, China is a formidable force that must be handled delicately. Because of China's economic and military influence, over the last three decades their relations with their neighbors has skewed in their favor. Towards Russia, China no longer takes orders from their supposed communist fathers, but instead Russia is one of China's most trusted trading partners. Their 2,640 mile border has even been demilitarized. Towards India, China has developed a mutually beneficial relationship that has seen trade explode from a mere $332 million in 1992 to $60 billion in 2012. Though these "Chindia" trade agreements prevent tensions from reaching the point of once return seen in their 1962 border war, China continues to recognize India's threat as both countries race to establish permanent relationships with nations to not only import essential resources, but to nail down markets for their expanding industries.

The nation that harbors the greatest hostility toward China is Taiwan. Ever since Chiang Kai Shek retreated to the island, securing an alliance with the United States and refusing to recognize Mao's communist control of the mainland, tensions between the two nations have always flirted with disaster. Not wanting to accept the reality of a Communist China, for decades America only recognized Taiwan as the true Republic of China. Taiwan sent a representative to the United Nations to fill China's seat. To many, this was a farce, as 98% of China's population was under communist control. In the 1970s, America changed their strategy, recognizing two countries – mainland China and Taiwan. To this day, America treats Taiwan as an independent country. But China still believes Taiwan is merely a province that should be returned to communist control. Neither side appears willing to surrender their claim to sovereignty as Taiwan continues to purchase the latest in military technology from the United States, and China consistently makes overtures toward returning Taiwan (or Formosa as it was called once upon a time) to their dominion. But for now, they've agreed to exist relatively peacefully, tied by a shared cultural background and connected by mutually beneficial economic interests.

North Korea is a whole different story. Decades ago, both North Korea and China were impoverished, backwards, pre-industrial nations who shared a vision of a communist future. In the words of Mao, they were "as close as lips and teeth." But the lips and teeth aren't so close anymore. With the appointment of Kim Jong Un to the head of North Korea after the death of his father, tensions between North Korea and the rest of the world hit feverish levels. China has tried to be supportive of North Korea, neutralizing UN sanctions and voting down interventionist plans. This isn't so much because Chinese officials agree with the unbalanced swaggering of North Korean leaders or the nation's continued pursuit of nuclear weapons, it's because the alternative is even less attractive. Should North Korean leadership fall, violence would ensue and two things would probably happen – millions would cross the North Korean border into China, and Korea would probably become united behind the support of the United States. China has no desire to manage a refugee crisis, and they're even less inclined to see American troops near their border. The status quo is just fine for now. If only Kim Jong Un would shut up.

As foreign countries debate China's interactions with regional neighbors, they're also a bit taken aback by its domestic policies. Environmentally, China isn't exactly helping out the planet. In 2007, they surpassed the United States as the greatest emitter of greenhouse gases and carbon dioxide. 23% of the world's carbon dioxide comes from China. China likes to argue that their carbon dioxide emissions per person are far less than that of the United States (4.03 tons per person vs. 21.75 tons per person), but this ratio is irrelevant as Mother Earth isn't exactly handing out global warming rebates to those countries minimizing their per capita environmental destruction. China is hesitant to ratify any international agreements that might restrict their manufacturing output, especially when the United States isn't exactly the global leader in putting their money where their mouth is (the US was one of four countries – Afghanistan, Andorra and Sudan – out of 195 to NOT sign the Kyoto Protocol that aimed to reduce man's impact on global warming). As China's economy continues to expand, and as they increasingly rely on coal and oil to fuel their boom, the atmosphere will continue to bear the brunt of their development.

But China definitely knows there's a problem. Pollution continually chokes the skies, with air quality readings often approaching toxic levels. Sixteen out of the twenty most polluted cities in the world are in China, and 1.2 million Chinese citizens die yearly from pollution-related diseases (most notably cancer). Because everyone now has access to cell phones and these phones can download air quality apps, the government can no longer mask the true level of contamination. In January 2013, Air Quality Index readings hit 755 (anything above 100 is considered dangerous) in Beijing, and its citizens protested the government's seemingly oblivious reaction to the crisis. They know the government could change the air quality if they actually cared. They did it prior to the 2008 Beijing Olympics. But alas, the coal factories still burn, the citizens still smoke and the cars keep clogging up the streets (with the numbers expected to quadruple by 2030).

As tens of millions migrate from the countryside every year, and as factories continue to prioritize profits over environmental health, the air quality will continue to deteriorate.

International observers also feel their hands are tied when it comes to China's human rights abuses. Freedom of speech is not a Chinese inalienable right. Those who speak their mind can be jailed, tortured or even killed. The press is anything but free.

Rigorous Internet censorship has led to what some call "The Great Firewall of China." Emails are filtered, websites are blocked, blogs are analyzed and Internet connections crawl. After the revolutionary events of the Arab Spring, the ministers of information blocked all emails containing the words "today," "tomorrow" or even "jasmine" (in reference to the Jasmine Revolution in Tunisia). This hypersensitive attempt to prevent negative discourse ended up having a greater impact disrupting the purchase of tea than it did forestalling any rebellious behavior. In addition to preventing its people from gaining a comprehensive view of international affairs, China also tends to block Internet communication that might depict domestic affairs in a negative light. In June of 2011, after a traffic accident in Mongolia incited regional protests, China immediately blocked all searches for "Mongolia" and cut off all communication from the region. This censorship, coupled with a dozens of seemingly random arrests, quickly quieted the insurrection. What China doesn't know can't hurt it.

So why don't the people protest? In 1989, people were willing to sacrifice their lives in Tiananmen Square for the sake of personal freedoms and liberal government. If the youths of the 1980s were willing to confront the oppressive central government twenty years ago, why not today?

First of all, China does still protest. In 1993, there were 8,700 "mass incidents" of protest involving more than 100 people. In 2010, there were 127,000. In 2013, just a few weeks after the appointment of new president Xi Jinping, Chinese journalists in the province of Guangzhou went on strike condemning the government's censorship of their articles. The Chinese definitely still protest. They just protest differently. Back in 1989, it was college students and city dwellers that demanded change. Today, the protests occur mostly in the rural provinces, and the issues aren't just freedom of press, freedom of speech and free elections, the issues relate more to regional decisions that negatively affect households. Maybe a regional official accepted bribes. Maybe a group of factory workers were laid off and wanted more compensation. Maybe a neighborhood wanted reparations for homes torn down to make way for a new railway. Maybe they didn't like a new land tax on their farm plot. But these protests aren't about Communist Party policies. They're about regional director choices.

The Communist Party is, for the most part, beloved by the Chinese people. Why? Is it because the Communist Party censors the media, suppresses public assembly and prohibits any damaging comments made toward the central government? Or are the people actually happy? For the most part, the Chinese are content. They've seen their wages increase, their nation's prestige rise and their health and security improve. Their lives are better. They also know what can happen to countries emerging from the Maoist-Stalinist post-WWII models. Of the 34 communist countries that once existed, only four still remain – China, Vietnam, North Korea and Cuba. The other 30 who have abandoned one-party communist rule have seen their nations digress into civil war, economic depression or societal anarchy, oftentimes emerging with an even more oppressive authoritarian leader. China has carefully avoided the daunting obstacles of entering the global marketplace, and has instead become the poster child for how a government can better guide an economy than can the invisible hand of capitalism. When China weathered the 2008 recession with their economy still intact, the Chinese people once and for all recognized they were part of something pretty impressive. The Communist Party has made minor concessions to opening up the political process – securing secret balloting, encouraging multiple candidates for regional posts, allowing the media more freedoms and voluntarily transferring power to a new generation of leaders at the 18th National Party Congress of the Communist Party in the fall of 2012. But the Communist Party is here to stay.

Martin Jacques, author of *When China Rules the World* offers another explanation for why the Chinese aren't revolting against Communist rule and demanding a multiparty democracy that protects individual freedoms. Jacques argues that China's relationship with their government is like that of a son to their father – to be respected, to be feared, to be trusted. Unlike the West's notion of a social contract where the people have been taught to demand more from their government and where over the centuries the church, the aristocracy and regional powers have all attempted to wrestle power away from the state, Jacques argues that in China, the population trusts that the government alone has absolute power. And they're totally OK with that. Their empire stretches back 3000 years, and the central government has time and again proven capable of making China the preeminent civilization on the planet.

But for how long will the people be content to let this government rule? Just as history shows us how the Chinese willingly deferred power to the state for thousands of years, it has also shown us that when the government proves unable to handle economic strife and threats from abroad, the people have no problem ousting their leaders. So what happens when the other shoe drops? What happens if Europe and the United States enter yet another depression and stop consuming all the wares of Chinese factories? What happens when the government starts spending trillions of dollars on public welfare programs to support the elderly? What happens when China's huge labor advantage starts to dissipate as less and less couples have children? What happens when China's economy can no longer grow at the double-digit levels of the past, and the income disparity becomes a bit less tolerable to the masses?

What happens when people aren't so healthy, wealthy and optimistic? Will they start caring a little more for their personal freedoms? Will they start to distrust their leaders just a bit more?

And what happens when 1.3 billion citizens get angry? Can the Chinese miracle continue indefinitely?

We'll just have to see.

But that is for another chapter.

46

India

Like China, India is on no singular track. It has become two Indias. One is the India of growth, wealth and prosperity, where GDP rates continue to rise at 8% a year, where 200 million members of the middle class vie to buy the latest gadget, where health care stands out atop the world and where universities provide an education second to none. The other India is a nation of abject poverty, where 250 million survive on less than a dollar a day, where clean water is sparse, where schools are primitive, where hospitals are medieval and where plumbing is a luxury.

One need not travel far to see these two Indias. Though clearly the rural-urban divide exaggerates the differences, the mere taxi journey from airport to hotel can feel like a trip across a millennia, as much as a ride through a city. One block, you might see towering high-rises, urban nouveau riche singles donning the latest frock from Manish Arora, neon cinemas trumpeting the latest Bollywood feature or Lamborghini Gallardos daring the city's police. The next block, you could just as easily pass a man defecating on the side of the road, a sacred cow stopping traffic, limbless beggars pleading for a coin or decaying shacks doubling as markets for weeks-old produce.

But can a nation of 1.21 billion people, a nation where 30 different languages are spoken by at least a million people, a nation that can be home to the Dalai Lama and also 165 million Muslims (to say nothing of the 700+ million Hindus) - can this nation be divided merely in two? Can a nation home to the Himalayan Mountains, the Thar Desert, marshy swamplands, tropical rainforests and over 3800 miles of coastline - can this nation be split in two?

In fact, there are hundreds of Indias, and it is this diversity that separates India from the world. China might have the most people on the planet, but 92% of China's citizens consider themselves the same race – the Han – and they all bow to the same political party – the communists. The United States might hold legitimate claims as the most diverse nation, and critics might even like to say that the United States has the largest income disparity in the world. But India's diversity dwarfs that of America, with over a billion people either divided by race, religion or caste, and as for income disparity, it's hard to challenge a nation that boasts 48 billionaires, but also 650 million living in poverty.

It is India's diversity that poses so many of the different challenges it faces; yet, this unique demographic reality may be the key that allows India to progress into the future.

But the road ahead will not be easy.

In recent decades, India appeared right on the cusp of securing its place among the world's elite. Since 1990, India's GDP has grown at an average rate of 8% per year, becoming the 9th largest economy in the world. But unlike China, India isn't making a name for itself by supporting hundreds of millions of factory laborers willing to assemble, glue, connect, wire, tie and paint the trinkets that make their way onto Walmart shelves. In the pharmaceutical industry, India doesn't anymore just make cheap generic drugs to sell on the wholesale market (merely copying and mass producing the work of others), it's becoming a major player in research and development, and with tens of thousands of engineers and scientists graduating every year from Indian universities, the potential for India to become a hub for prescription drugs appears quite promising. They've also jumped into international car manufacturing, with Tata Motors rolling out the cheapest car in the world – the $2800 Nano. Sure, its engine under the back seat might make passengers a bit nervous, its wheels are about the size found on a three-year-old's tricycle and its maximum speed of 65 miles per hour won't attract the thrill-seeking crowd, but with its ridiculously low price, India hopes to corner the market for car buyers just needing wheels that will get them from point A to point B.

Though the pharmaceutical industry has potential and the tiny Tata might steal some business from the Koreans and Japanese, it's in the IT sector that India has truly made a name for itself. In 2005, New York Times author Thomas Friedman came out with the book *The World is Flat*, introducing the world to Bangalore, India's version of Silicon Valley, where software is designed and phone centers are manned. Soon after, Bangalore became the symbol for American jobs heading overseas. Companies had learned that if you want a job done quickly and cheaply, you call India. If you're Bank of America and need someone to answer calls from homeowners looking to refinance their mortgage, call India. If you're an entrepreneur starting up a company and need someone to design your website, call India. If you're running an accounting firm and need someone to handle all the tax paperwork during a hectic season, call India. You can save up to 90% on labor costs, and because India is on the other side of the world, you can contract a project when you're walking out the door at 6:00 in the evening, and when you arrive the next morning, the project will be sitting in your email box. This wealth of talented, cheap labor has transformed how companies source their labor, but also how individuals task out their day-to-day responsibilities.

If you don't believe me, try it. Say you want someone to turn your notes into a Powerpoint presentation – just go to a website called odesk.com, type up a job description, pay $1 through Paypal, and within a couple hours, you'll have a finished product better than anything you could have spat out. And that's just at the household level. Companies are outsourcing to India everything from creating Ipad apps to providing voices for videos to manufacturing Twitter "followers" or Facebook "likes" to enhance your popularity. If it can be done online or on a phone, it can be done cheaper (and oftentimes better) in India. Don't believe me still? Next time you call a 1-800 number, ask where the phone operator is from. They have to tell you. And there's a 97.4% chance it's a city somewhere in India.

With all this new money to be made in India's emerging economies, the middle class has exploded to over 200 million, many of these are young twenty-somethings with budding expendable incomes they can blow on consumer goods. And the number one consumer good they want to get their hands on is the cell phone. India has the fastest growing telecom market in the world, boasting the cheapest rates on the planet. As telecom companies expand, so has their reception range, meaning even the villager living in the most desolate mountain pass can now connect to the world. Today, over 76% of the country owns a cellphone, meaning 920 million cell phones could be ringing at any one time (almost three times the number of those found in the US). If they're not texting or chatting, they're "scrapping" (Facebooking) on Orkut.

For those willing to emerge from the digital world, India's cuisine, its fashion industry and its cinema offer limitless options for even the most discriminate palette. Their movie industry alone (known to the world as Bollywood and familiar to most audiences for its smiling couples who always seem to find a way to dance around trees) surpasses Hollywood in total viewership, with some three billion annual moviegoers paying to see any one of the hundreds of films produced each year.

India has taken their mounting economic influence and applied it to their geopolitical reach. It is now seen as a major global player, creating free trade agreements across the region, potentially one day linking ports from the Philippines to Afghanistan (a la Canada, Mexico and the US's NAFTA). As they steadily finalize trading partnerships with the countries of West Africa, the Middle East and South Asia, Indian interests oftentimes come head to head with Chinese corporations and Chinese government officials hoping to likewise expand their influence in these emerging markets. But today, India is no longer a minor player, passively bowing to either their Chinese neighbor to the east or to the nations of the West. India's human capital and technological ascendancy has set it up as a nation with first world economic potential.

Now that India has molded an economy that can compete with the big boys, it has likewise compiled a military that is not only respected, but feared. India has become the number one arms importer in the world, and they are currently one of only nine countries with a nuclear bomb. Though they prefer not to use these weapons and have shown time and again their willingness to compromise instead of mobilize, the sheer volume of their arsenal makes them a force to be reckoned. India no longer wants to be seen patronizingly as a developing country emerging from European domination, but instead desires to show the world they are an economic and a military leader in their own right. They even resolutely refused aid from other countries during their recent natural disasters (2004 tsunami, 2005 earthquake and the 2006 flooding), wanting to demonstrate that they are a creditor to the world, not a borrower.

India looked like it was on a roll. Their economy was expanding, their culture was flourishing, their military was proliferating and their people were prospering. They were the vowel in the BRIC countries, joining Brazil, Russia and China as the nations that were threatening to supplant Western dominance, potentially ushering in a new model of government efficiency and economic management.

But then the 2008 recession hit, and all the successes that the media had been championing started to fade and the realities of a nation in peril again emerged. Like every other nation emerging from an industrial revolution, India's gilded veneer of economic success merely masked institutional, governmental, demographic and societal flaws that (though diminished) never vanished from India's unpleasant reality. In the first few months after America's descent into its own Great Recession, India hinted that it might survive relatively unscathed. But this pipedream quickly faded, replaced with stark truths that have no easy solution.

Foremost on the minds of politicians and economists is what to do with the poor? What do you do with 300 million people living below the poverty line? 300 million who can't get to school, can't get to the doctor and can't put food on their table? Do you help them or let them fend for themselves? If you help them today, you impede your economy today. But if you let them starve, you destroy your future (to say nothing of your karma). So over the last decade, politicians have more often than not chosen to help them. It's been the right moral choice, but it's also been the prudent choice. In a nation of dozens of political parties (two of which are communist) where incumbents rarely win and the masses are always waiting for a hero to come in and save the day, any would-be politician would be stupid to not promise to fleece the rich and protect the poor. If you want the vote from the countryside, you better have a plan that can inspire the poor from the countryside. For when you live in the largest democracy in the world, every vote counts, and often the hungriest voters are the easiest to sway.

So, India officials experiment. They add new programs, take over private businesses and pass out billions of dollars. Some of these programs work, some of the businesses excel and some of the money reaches the hands of those in need. There are success stories. In the state of Bihar, government reps realized only a third of all girls actually went to school past the 8th grade, and their literacy rates hovered around 50%. The solution? Give the girls bikes - over 800,000 bikes and counting since 2006. And it's working. Dropout rates plummeted, literacy rates soared and Bihar had a success story. Other regions clamored to follow the lead, and steadily millions across the nation are overcoming the hardest hurdle of their education – getting to school.

A far more ambitious plan is the Mahatma Gandhi National Rural Employment Guarantee Act, a program that guarantees 100 days of work for anyone willing to apply. You sign up, you have a job. Like the Civilian Conservation Corps used by Roosevelt during the Great Depression, men and women build roads, dig canals, construct bridges, repair dams and plant trees - any odd job that might help their community. Started in 2006, over 47 million households benefit from the plan, at a cost of some $9 billion to the federal government.

Cost is just one reason this program, and hundreds of others, have come under heightened scrutiny in recent years. Some wonder how sustainable it is to earmark close to $10 billion a year on a program that feels like it was created more for good PR than for actually improving a community. Because the laborers are almost all unskilled, many of the projects are completed pretty shabbily, meaning the government has to hire other engineers to go back in and fix their initial mistakes.

But the biggest issue with all these federal and local programs is corruption. The allocated money rarely reaches the hands of those in need. Instead, officials line their own pockets, and the wealthy and middle class claim benefits they don't even deserve. You don't have to turn too many pages in the newspaper to uncover yet another case of a politician taking a kickback or an entrepreneur stealing from the impoverished. Programs that start off with the grandest of good intentions inevitably fall when the immorality of man steps in. For example, some farmers are given electricity for free, and diesel and petroleum are delivered at discounted rates. Gas that would cost $1 a gallon on the open market costs a farmer only twelve cents. This seemed like a good idea, but the problem was, the poorest farmers don't use electricity. They don't own tractors that use gas. They dig irrigation ditches with their hands. So the people who need the financial help don't get it, and ironically, the corporate farms with their electrical sprinklers and army of tractors see their profits soar. And every year, the power industry loses another $8 billion in revenue, all for a scheme that was doomed from the start.

If it wasn't for the fact that the corruption takes food from the mouths that most need it, the corruption could seem almost comical. In one instance in 2012, Chief Minister Mayawati of the state of Uttar Pradesh wanted to pay tribute to the untouchables (the lowest caste in India) by building a series of national parks in their honor. But Mayawti must have misunderstood the meaning of the words "honor" and "tribute," instead filching millions of dollars from the program. She had trees planted, uprooted and then planted again. She charged millions of dollars for palm trees that her workers merely threw in a ditch and let rot. She billed $15 million for elephant statues, yet the sculptors only got $1.5 million for their efforts (only her purse knows where the missing $13.5 million went).

Not all the corruption occurs on such a grand scale. Sometimes it could just mean lying about your identity and falsely collecting meals from one of the food banks. Nearly half of all food aid money ends up in the hands of the upper class. The government has tried to curb this habit of fleecing the poor by assigning everyone a special identity card that designates their level of poverty. This card, or even in some states a fingerprint scan, then becomes your ticket to collecting government-funded rations.

But even though officials know their allocated moneys have a good chance of not reaching the intended hands, they keep crafting programs that might temporarily please the poor, but almost always hinder entrepreneurs. In 2012, the Indian parliament approved a series of retroactive taxes that hoped to punish businesses for transactions dating back to 1962. India hopes this scheme will recoup over $7 billion in taxes on any merger that transpired over the last four decades. So if back in

1997, a British cell phone company bought an Indian battery company, the government could sue them based on a new tax code created in 2012. The US Constitution outlaws this type of ex post facto law, but the Indian representatives feel it's a totally fair method of recovering lost revenue. But the international community is a bit scared. If India is allowed to tax mergers from the past, what other profits from years ago can be taxed? This doesn't exactly give foreigners a great deal of confidence in starting a company or making deals in India.

Entrepreneurs' hands are also tied when it comes to hiring cheap labor. When most countries go through an industrial revolution, they can count on cheap, plentiful labor to keep costs low and profits high, allowing for companies to grow and expand. India has created a system that punishes entrepreneurs. New business owners can't afford to hire cheap labor, because the government is already guaranteeing jobs above market value to anyone who wants to work. How can a guy start a company making T-shirts when nobody wants to work for him because they make more money digging ditches for the government? India's huge supply of labor is its biggest advantage, but India's trying to push its economy through an industrial revolution while protecting its people. But that's not how countries industrialize. Sure, when companies are getting rich, poor people suffer, but that's what every England, Germany, United States, Canada, Japan and Russia had to go through. If India continues to interfere with the invisible hand of capitalism, all they're assuring is many more decades of stalled growth and pre-industrial living conditions.

Not only is the government obstructing growth in the private sector, it's not exactly doing a great job in their own public sphere. The most visible organizations operated by the Indian government are Indian Railways and Indian Air – both of which are dangerous, inept and constantly teetering on bankruptcy. Air India ran out of money years ago, but the government deemed the firm too big to fail and constantly bailed it out, even giving it another $3.4 billion in 2011. Pilots still go on strike, fuel prices still spiral out of control and airplanes still sit grounded on runways.

Indian Railways is an even bigger mess. The trains are overcrowded, poorly maintained and questionably hygienic. Six billion passengers travel the rail annually, with tens of thousands dying from one of the hundreds of accidents. Almost 15,000 die a year just crossing the railroad tracks (since footbridges are rarely installed). One of the crowning symbols of Indian Railways ineptitude is the dozens of bonfires that light up on the tracks whenever a train pulls out of a station. You see, as a cost-cutting measure, Indian toilets come without plumbing; there's merely a hole in the floor. So, for all those that do their business while the train is stopped in station, a lovely little mound of fecal joy starts to build on the tracks. Once the trains depart, the designated crapmen (chosen from the 1.4 million railway employees) have the fun job of walking amongst the tracks, lighting all the mounds with their torches. Lovely. The trains could be fixed, the footbridges could be installed and the toilets could be piped if only the rail line would raise ticket prices, but of course, in the land where no politician wants to be disliked by the masses, no one would ever willingly attach their name to a bill that would punish any struggling commuter. So the trains will continue to crash and the poo will continue to burn.

For awhile, prognosticators believed India's changing demographics might prove to be the key to the "economic miracle" that jumpstarted Southeast Asia in the 1980s and 1990s. In those countries, families stopped having children and started living longer. When this happened, governments and families spent less money on clothes, housing and education, and started putting their money into research, infrastructure and savings accounts. When governments didn't have to worry about building schools and paying teachers, they could fix roads and finance engineers. With its improved sanitation, drinking water and health care, India's mortality rates started to drop in the 1990s, and fewer and fewer families had three-plus kids (due in part because Indian women started entering the workforce and didn't want to have as many kids). These smaller families could then put all of their resources into educating these fewer children, and when they reached adulthood, this next generation would have higher skills, better health, and because less of them would be graduating, they would receive higher salaries. This worked for awhile, but it was inconsistent. Some regions saw a drop in birth rates and an increase in life expectancy, but many of the rural regions continued to see birth rates hover in the 5-7 children range for many farming families. This unequal demographic shift meant that the whole country didn't move forward, just a few of the urban regions.

And now, this demographic shift towards fewer children scares Indian planners for the same reason China and Japan are a bit nervous about their future prospects. By 2050, 316 million Indians will be 60 years or older, and because old people and their diseases (like diabetes, cancer, heart disease and dementia) are expensive, this will be a huge drain on government resources. Who will be paying taxes to support these elderly drains on the economy? Will it be the 650 million people living below the poverty line? This creates a pretty huge burden for the middle class – all they'll have to do is come up with enough taxable income to support a billion people in need. That'll be interesting to see unfold.

Initially, this demographic shift appeared to benefit the plight of women. India has long been a patriarchal society. India was once the nation that forced its wives to jump into funeral fires if their husbands passed away. Females were always seen as a burden; families would have to come up with crippling dowries just to get another family to take their daughters off their hands. India's recent economic growth hinted at a potential end to this treatment. But alas, in the world of the two Indias, gains have been inconsistent. Sure, millions of women graduate with a college education, move into high paying service professions, and even choose their spouses based on romantic interest and other personal preferences. But there's still the other India - the India where families still practice fetacide, aborting their females at a rate that bares only 933 girls for every 1000 boys born. For the girls that survive, dowries still exist, and in recent years the tragedy of dowry deaths is becoming more common. One girl every hour dies due to some dispute about the value of the dowry. Some girls commit suicide under the strain of the families fighting; others are killed by the husband's family once the money has changed hands. Many families even look at dowries as an easy way to get rich quick – pledge to have your son marry the unattractive daughter of a wealthy family, then find a way to have the daughter reach a premature end.

Even women who have escaped the plight of the deadly dowries can still find themselves victims of violence and persecution. India is now the second leading purchaser of guns in the world (of course the US is #1), many of which are bought by women fearing for their safety. The number of reported sex crimes increases every year, and women who engage in any sort of public displays of affection can be targeted by the more conservative members of society. One group known as the Shiv Shena even go as far as to destroy flowers, cards and attack any woman who appears too modern.

These archaic gender behaviors gained international attention in December 2012 when a young urban couple was kidnapped and assaulted after hopping on a bus. After the male student was knocked unconscious, the 23-year-old female student was gang raped by five men, one of whom sodomized her with a lead pipe before ripping open her intestines. These gruesome details first circulated through social media channels, stirring thousands to march in protest to the horrific incident. The young woman died thirteen days after the incident, and the resulting firestorm of demonstrations only escalated. Marchers not only demanded stricter penalties for rape (some even clamoring for the death penalty), but also a complete overhaul of an apathetic judicial system. Across India, police readily dismiss any claims of female abuse and the courts can indefinitely delay cases involving sexual predators. Local politicians only exacerbated the situation by ordering the police to open fire on the protestors, attacking them with water cannons and tear gas. Federal politicians then added fuel to the fire by going as far as to blame the woman by saying she deserved it by being out too late, and that she could have avoided the whole messy affair had she just apologized to her assailants and called them "brother."

Three months later, the rape incident clearly was not going to be forgotten. The driver of the bus allegedly killed himself while in prison (though his family claimed he was raped and killed), a Swiss tourist was gang-raped by seven men after cycling through the forest and a three-year-old girl died after being raped in a public bathroom. Though sexual violence against women has been an appalling reality for women for generations in India, the fact that these three incidents were perpetrated against first a young, educated member of the middle class, then against a foreign tourist and finally against a toddler, could mean that politicians might now pass tougher rape laws (even impacting marital relations), and Indian society might have to start grappling with how males and females are treated from their earliest ages. However, all signs point to these cases of violence only increasing in the coming years as affluent, educated young adults live side-by-side with those lacking any hope for a brighter future.

One moment India can appear one of the more advanced civilizations; the next it looks like a medieval slum existing at the lowest level of human interaction. While India struggles to create a more equitable society where not only a select few benefit from the trappings of wealth, the nation also must contend with an increasing number of regional threats.

Foremost among these threats is their neighbor to the north – Pakistan. Since 1947, when Britain removed itself from South Asia, creating the independent nations of Pakistan and India, both governments have fought to control the northwestern Kashmir region. Kashmir is the Yosemite National Park of the Asia – crystal clear lakes, flowered forests and majestic Himalayan peaks. In 1947, the region was majority Muslim with a Hindu leader. Because the British mandated popular sovereignty (each state could choose which nation they joined), both Pakistan and India felt they had the best shot for retaining Kashmir. Eventually, the Hindu leader chose to join India, and ever since, the Muslim majority has fought to reverse this decision both diplomatically and militarily.

Sometimes these struggles are merely played out through rhetoric in the local media or in public demonstrations, but since the late 1990s, local freedom fighters have begun targeting Hindu officials and communities, and some even claim the Kashmir region became a training ground for Al Qaeda, the militant terrorist group responsible for the September 11th attacks on the United States. India has considered using military force to squash the insurgency and punish the Pakistanis for sending moral and material support to the Kashmir insurgents, but war has always been averted. One of the benefits of both sides holding nuclear bombs is that both sides are hesitant to pull the trigger and use their full military capability, knowing any war could end in nuclear annihilation. So what ends up happening is a lot of back and forth name-calling and posturing, but both sides are wary of crossing the military line. In 2002, weeks after a group of Pakistani-supported terrorists bombed the Indian Parliament, both nations mobilized their troops to the disputed border area – 500,000 Indian troops moved to within miles of 300,000 Pakistani troops. But after the men had been lined up and the artillery had been set up within striking distance, both sides agreed to stand down. The risks were just not worth intervention.

Since that conflict, militant groups have survived in Kashmir, going dormant for months or years, but then striking out when it appears the momentum has swung out of their favor. In early 2013, when the Indian government carried out the execution of a man tied to the 2003 planned attack on India's parliament, the Kashmiri people took to the street decrying the Indian government for their allegedly fraudulent judicial system. One of the militant organizations, the Hizbul Mujahedeen, then attacked an Indian camp, killing five soldiers. The Indian government responded with restrictive curfews, keeping the Kashmiri people off the streets for their own safety. Just when it appeared tensions had cooled, it became quite obvious that the conflict over control of Kashmir has been anything but settled.

Though India has proven willing and able to intervene with force, they have tried to increasingly employ "soft power" – a geopolitical strategy where India will continue to invest heavily in the latest in weaponry and military training, but will never actually use their force unless attacked. They want to look big and intimidating, but they don't want to have to actually use their forces. Ever since the embarrassing 1962 border conflict war with China, India has been rightfully gun shy, almost always blinking first when faced with regional threats. They don't see their path to regional prominence needing a pre-emptive military ideology, instead relying on trade agreements that will link all the regions. The nation founded by the pacifist Gandhi continues to seek to resolve its conflicts without bloodshed. And it seems to be working. Even with precarious Pakistan, trade seems to be the key to peace. In recent years, borders have been opened and daily Indian truckloads of almonds, oranges and sandals are offloaded in Pakistan, and their cargo trailers are replaced with shipments of onions, chiles and potatoes. No money changes hands – just one trailer is replaced with another trailer. This isn't exactly free trade, but it's a start. For two nations struggling to recover from the economic downturn following the 2008 recession, this 21st century version of bartering is a step in the right direction.

Unfortunately, creating trade partnerships and stockpiling weapons won't deter all of India's regional threats. India must also deal with an upswing in terrorist activity and insurgent movements, many of which are led by a Muslim population believing it has been marginalized by a Hindu-dominated government. Though Muslims represent 13% of India's population, they fill less than 3% of all security, bureaucratic and upper echelon civil jobs. Muslims have become almost a fifth caste – one that is the least educated, the least supported and the least employed. This perception of inequality, as well as India's growing acceptance of Western notions of beauty, behavior and entertainment, has inspired a younger generation of militants to demand change through overt action. The 2008 Mumbai hotel attacks that led to the deaths of

164 people could become more commonplace if the federal government doesn't create a more effective method of combating home-grown and foreign-sponsored terrorism. Following these 2008 attacks, the federal government failed to immediately react, due in large part to the autonomy it grants every state. Without a coordinated effort to combat terrorism across the entire nation, the states will be ill-prepared to mount a comprehensive campaign to monitor and diffuse radical forces.

But as much as India has so much to fear, it also has so much to hope for, because its potential is limitless. It's located in the center of Asia, the perfect conduit for all trade going from Asia to Africa and Europe. It has top-notch universities that annually graduate tens of thousands of scientists and engineers. It has a huge middle class that will only continue to grow (and continue to buy). It has the largest democracy in the world with 714 million citizens casting votes every election. It has an economy that might be slowing, but it's still growing faster than most of industrialized nations and could, in a few decades, become the world's fourth largest economy.

India has a ton of potential, but what its people do with this potential has yet to be seen. Will it find a way to move forward, delicately balancing the needs of the masses with the needs of the entrepreneurs? Or will it remain "two Indias" – one of affluence, one of abject poverty. Over 1.2 billion people are waiting to find out.

But that is for another chapter.

47

The Middle East

Ahh...the Middle East. What glories come to mind? A magical land of lush forests, babbling brooks and mystical valleys. A blissful land home to giggling cherubs and jovial seniors. A technologically savvy land that spawns the latest innovations and inspires generation after generation of entrepreneurs to design and mass produce the gadgets that fill our pockets and line our shelves. A tolerant land where homosexuals walk hand in hand through city squares, the young frolic and gyrate to the freshest hip hop tunes and women don the latest Parisian fashions on their way to their 87th floor offices overlooking a bustling metropolis below.

Ahh yes, the Middle East – the once cradle of civilization and the present beacon of hope, liberty and peace that all nations hold as the pinnacle of humanity.

But wait. Does that vision not exactly jibe with your notions of the Middle East? Does it possibly contradict the headlines you've read, the actors you've seen and the politicians you've followed?

So I guess your Middle East is instead a land of oil, of deserts, of gluttonous sultans living in golden palaces, of turbaned shepherds pulling camels, of ticked-off bearded men calling for the death of all Americans, of women hidden behind black hoods, of terrorists calling for the destruction of Israel, of rogue nations vying for membership in the Axis of Evil, of millions of homogenous Muslims all marching to the same Quranic beat, hating the West for all of its splendor, jealous of the West for just being so darn much better at everything?

Be honest, is this your Middle East? A sad, depressed, backward land of angry Muslims who happen to live on top of the greatest surplus of petrol gold on the planet?

And you're actually right...about as right as you'd be if you said America is the land of scantily clad bikini'd hotties jiggling around on cars as they try to sell you a can of Coors Light. As right as you'd also be if you said America is the land of religious fanatics who blow up abortion clinics, and all Americans believe that Jonah hung out for three days in a whale and that humans only first appeared back in 4004 BC when Adam and Eve developed an apple craving.

If you travel throughout the Middle East, you'll see the stereotype, but there's also a heck of a lot going on that you've never witnessed, and a heck of a lot going on that even our most learned foreign policy analysts missed. For decades, there was an accepted Middle East narrative that passed for truth.

But then there was the Arab Spring and everyone had to reassess the Middle East. How in less than six months did the nations of Tunisia, Egypt and Libya throw off the shackles of autocracy when it was just assumed that the bulk of the Middle East just passively accepted their leaders as they trudged through their days waiting the afterlife? Wasn't the only way to overthrow a dictator and form a democracy was to have a foreign invader enter their borders and altruistically guide them to the promised land? And what about the threat of Muslim extremists? If the all-powerful autocrats were overthrown, wouldn't all the millions of terrorists come out of hiding, take over the military and then blow up the world (after first of course flattening Israel)?

How was this Arab Spring possible? And why didn't anyone see it coming?

The Arab Spring, or to some the "Arab Awakening," actually started in the winter of 2010. On December 17, 2010, in the Tunisian town of Sidi Bouzid, a fruit and vegetable vendor named Mohamed Bouazizi set himself on fire to protest his years of being abused by authorities and his frustration over not being able to provide for his family. As chief breadwinner of his family, this 26-year-old man had, since his childhood, worked the streets, earning barely over $140 a month. On December 16, local authorities approached Bouazizi and ordered him to produce a valid vendor permit. He had no permit. And after he refused to pay a bribe, he was mocked, beaten and his scales and vegetables were confiscated. Utterly defeated and humiliated, he bought some gas, went to the governor's office and set himself on fire. He died a couple weeks later in a hospital. 5,000 marched at his funeral procession, and soon these thousands became tens of thousands, and soon this death of a street vendor became the inspiration for a generation to fight back and challenge the authority that had left their lives in despair.

Bouazizi's story of hopelessness, persecution and retribution spoke to the masses, and to the youth especially, for they too had suffered long enough under exploitive, brutal, seemingly omnipotent regimes who appeared more inclined to fleece their people than provide opportunities for all. Enough was enough. They were as mad as hell and they weren't going to take it anymore.

Within five months, protests broke out across the Arab world. From Syria to Bahrain, Morocco to Saudi Arabia, Tunisia to Jordan, a generation of desperate, frustrated Arabs took to the streets, believing the time had finally come to reform the flawed, antiquated economic and political systems. They pointed to the monarchs and autocrats who preserved their power through militaries willing to crush any anti-government sentiment. They spoke of corrupt government officials who lived off kickbacks, of police taking bribes to ignore growing crime, hospitals taking bribes before administering medical care, even schools taking bribes before admitting children. They chastised their heads of states for siphoning off oil revenue instead of distributing it back into the economy. With oil prices surpassing $100 a barrel, the region pulls in over $1 trillion a year in revenue, but this money rarely makes it past the hands of the royal families and their network of loyal cronies. They complained of the limited opportunities for the younger generation. 65% of the Arab world is under 30 years old, but even the educated find they can't find work in a society where governments care little about improving infrastructure or supporting entrepreneurs and job growth. Why get an education when there are no jobs available once you graduate?

Like the protesters of the West who rallied around the Occupy Wall Street movement, the Arab underclass opposed income inequality, both within their nation and between nations in the Arab region. The United Arab Emirates per capita GDP hovers around $59,000 a year. Neighboring Yemen averages an appalling $1,800. But per capita GDP numbers are misleading. Saudi Arabia might average a health $23,000, but almost all the wealth rests in the hands of the Al-Saud royal family, a few thousand multimillionaires (and billionaires - King Abdullah bin Abdulaziz is worth $18 billion) who control everyday life, keeping twenty million Arabs (of the nations 27 million) in poverty. The Al-Saud family is worth $1.9 trillion, almost all the money made through oil revenue. Had this money been returned to the people, Saudi Arabia would be one of the world's most prosperous nations, but royals have instead used the money to line their stables with prized ponies, find new ways for their interior decorators to use gold and occasionally buy huge chunks of stock in US companies like Twitter, Apple and Disney. But the Al-Saud family is not alone in using their nation's resource wealth to craft lives of utter gluttony. Most of the money comes from the government's control of oil. Unlike in the United States where oil revenue is split between companies like Shell, Exxon Mobil and Chevron, in the Arab world, the royal families are the oil companies. President Sheikh Khalifa bin Zayed of the United Arab Emirates is worth $15 billion. Sheikh Hamad bin Khalifa al Thani of Qatar is worth $2.4 billion. Sultan Qaboos bin Said of Oman is worth only $700 million. But not all money comes from oil exploitation. King Muhammad VI of Morocco holds a fortune in excess of $2.5 billion from his monopoly of the nation's phosphate mines. And much of these fortunes aren't spent on buying the wares manufactured in their home countries or investing in national industries. Instead, Arab royals are famous for their outrageous European shopping sprees or for stashing their money in Western stock markets or offshore bank accounts.

For decades, this opulence and corruption was relatively hidden from the public's eyes. The government-controlled media prevented negative reports of their behavior, and the military was used to persecute, pressure, arrest, interrogate and incarcerate any individual, assembly or political party who dared question their actions. On a person-to-person basis, Arabs still talked about the daily corruption that made life intolerable, but mass scale public discussion of ruling family abuses rarely existed. It couldn't. It was immediately squashed. This media muzzle became a bit more difficult as the Internet, cell phones and satellite TVs brought to light not only the exploitation and injustices of their own worlds, but also the promises and possibilities available in the outside world. Arabs were suddenly just a Google search or a Wikipedia click away from having their frustrations validated, and the cult of personality surrounding their leaders was gradually demystified.

Tunisians could read that President Ben Ali stole billions from the nation's treasury, depositing it in Swiss bank accounts. Egyptians read that their President Hosni Mubarak had amassed a wealth of over $70 billion, making him the richest man in the world, and that along the way he had stashed billions in gold bars in England, millions in private jets, villas and hotels scattered across Europe and the United States and set up secret prisons to hold anyone not willing to play by the rules of his family's game. Libya read that their very own Mumar Gaddafi was a certifiable nutter. Everyone knew his fashion sense was a bit bizarre – he could look one day like a military officer doubling as an African safari guide and the next day look like a pop music transvestite who had raided the wardrobes of Elton John, Michael Jackson and Liberace. But the Internet revealed a whole other world of eccentricity and oddity. Gaddafi used his state fortune to fund his plastic surgery, create secret sex caves for a slew of young women, travelled with an all-female, gun-toting Amazonian Guard and wrote love songs and kept photo albums in honor of US Secretary of State Condoleeza Rice. The more they found out, the more Arabs discovered about their leaders, the more they couldn't believe they had to follow these morally bankrupt, slightly disturbed gluttons.

In November 2012, the website Wikileaks revealed not only the actions of the Arab regimes, but also the United States' role in propping up crooked governments and empowering the suppression of opposition groups. For years, bloggers had called out their leaders for their nepotistic, narcissistic behavior. But Wikileaks took the discussion global, becoming the great whistleblower of Arab autocratic malfeasance, and because US and European interests were named as co-conspirators, outside nations could not intervene in any future uprisings without validating claims that the West actually supports autocratic regimes as long as they protect Western economic interests.

The Arab Awakening then began. Protesters took to the streets. Their signs and chants condemned the rise in food prices, the dearth of jobs, the corruption and kickbacks demanded at every stage of society and the government's seeming disregard for their complaints. From here, the marches, rallies and protests went the way of Gandhi's and MLK's own movements of civil disobedience. Tens of thousands gathered. The police and the government overreacted, injuring, then arresting, then creating martyrs. With each government reaction, the movement spread. This was where the Internet came in handy, turning the movement into a social media revolution. Tunisians took to their Twitter, their Facebook and their YouTube accounts to report the events of the day and spawn support. The government tried to control this spread of information by shutting down websites, but this censorship only further symbolized the government's repressive measures, and because of the nature of the Internet, bloggers merely opened other sites, ensuring their now maligned messages would have an even greater audience.

The government was fighting a losing battle. Every reaction only further incited the movement, while calling into question their own authority. And then the military turned. They refused to fire on their own people, realizing they could either ride the wave of change or be crushed by it. Seeing the writing on the wall, on January 14, 2011, Tunisian president dissolved his government, hopped on a plane and eventually landed in exile in Saudi Arabia.

The first domino had fallen. The Arab world reacted in awe. What just happened? People protested, the government fought back, people protested some more, the leader fled. All within a few weeks? Was it really that easy to end decades of persecution?

One by one, across the Arab world, protests broke out, first in Algeria, then Lebanon, then Jordan, then Oman, then Saudi Arabia, and then, on January 25th, they broke out in the most populated, oldest country in the Middle East – Egypt. If Tunisia was a mere blip on the international radar, the events in Egypt kept the entire world on edge. If Egypt fell, the whole Middle East might turn. And after Eight Days of Revolution, President Mubharrak's regime likewise fell. The combination of protests, marches and heavy-handed military reaction turned the people against Mubharrak and then eventually turned the world against Mubharrak. Long time ally, the United States, at first merely asked for an "orderly transition," believing Mubharrak might be able to either hand over power to his second in command or make some symbolic concessions that would send the people back to their homes. But Mubharrak, the United States and the watching world were wrong. The people wanted nothing of their old president, and this time they felt empowered by the actions of their Tunisian brothers. Hundreds of thousands gathered in Tahrir Square, ignoring the unintelligible, rambling pleas of the man some called "the Pharaoh," instead refusing to stand down until the government had been overthrown.

So on February 11th, the "Friday of Departure," Mubharrak resigned. The government was turned over to the military. The second Arab nation had fallen. This was no longer an isolated incident in a little-known country called Tunisia. This was an Arab Revolution.

Then came the next wave of protests - Yemen, Iraq, Bahrain, Libya, Kuwait and Morocco. All faced major protests, yet not all went the path of Tunisia and Egypt. The leaders of Jordan, Oman, Bahrain, Kuwait and Morocco avoided a total revolution by agreeing to alter the structure of their government, the legitimacy of their elections, the relative freedom of speech and the rampant nepotism. Countries like Syria and Yemen regressed into states of civil war as both the governments and the revolutionaries refused to back down. Libya likewise descended into civil war, but as the atrocities mounted and international observers believed Gaddafi was willing to exact genocide to maintain power, the United Nations Security Council approved the deployment of peacekeeping troops and military support to protect the civilians and topple Gaddafi's regime. Led by the British and the French, the UN forces destroyed the Libyan government's ability to wage war. Fighting continued into the fall of 2011, and on October 20, 2011, Gaddafi was pulled out of a sewer, quivering and hiding from his pursuers. He was stripped, beaten and then shot to death.

A year later, the final assessment of the Arab Awakening had yet to be written – three autocrats were overthrown, two nations plunged into a civil war that could last for years, one (Iraq) was emerging from a decade of sectarian chaos instigated by an American invasion and the remaining ten Arab states appeared to have survived the upheaval by only slightly altering their modus operandi.

Still today, the political future of the Middle East is totally up in the air. Even after the region comes to terms with the true impacts of the Arab Spring on individual rights, economic opportunities and good governance, they will still have to contend with a host of larger problems that were issues long before a vegetable vendor set himself on fire in Northern Africa. Afghanistan and Iraq will see US troops depart, and the resulting sectarian violence could spread into surrounding regions. Militant Islamic extremist organizations continue to grow and threaten to choke not only the process of democratizing, but also offend regional allies. Iran might finally reveal the nuclear bomb they've been teasing the world with for over a decade. And of course, there's Israel and the unsolvable duel between Muslims and Jews for control of their Kingdom of Heaven.

For the Middle Eastern nations – Tunisia, Egypt, Libya, Iraq - testing the unsure waters of their post-autocratic era, Turkey stands as sole model of a country able to move toward liberal, democratic, capitalist systems while not selling out their adherence to Islam. Turkey has proven able to run free elections, debate legislative reforms in a civilized manner, expand the scope of personal freedoms and radically improve economic opportunities for all (especially the swelling middle class). Under the stewardship of a staunchly Sunni Muslim Prime Minister Tayyip Erdogan, the Turks have created a secular government without abandoning their Muslim roots. The ruling party, the Justice and Development Party (AKP), runs on a platform of remaining pious to Allah, but just working harder. Like the Puritan work ethic that founded America, the Turkish ethos has become one of adhering to the pillars of Islam, but not at the expense of busting your butt to advance your education and to improve your economic options. The AKP constantly looks for opportunities to expand the standard of living of its people, not merely because it's the right thing to do, but because it's politically expedient. In a country where you're always just an election away from losing your job, savvy leaders understand the #1 rule of politics – "it's the economy stupid." For all the talk of how to reconcile the seemingly contradictory ideologies of conservative religious adherence and progressive economic and political development, Turkey has found that when the people have jobs, have a future, have hope, they're more willing to ignore the pull of militant Islamism.

And it's working. Turkey's GDP has grown at a near double digit clip for almost a decade, both women and men look to futures in the marketplace and over 60% of its population now belong to the middle class (compared to less than 40% for Egypt). Internationally, Turkey has also avoided extremist agendas by following the middle road – working with the West, while also aligning itself with Arab nations – careful not to alienate either side since one group holds the keys to their economic fate, the other the keys to their souls. They've been able to accomplish this by also pulling in the reigns on their military, preventing them from playing a daily role in the suppression of individual rights and also thwarting them from direct intervention in neighboring disputes. The AKP's has held firm to its regional policy of "zero problems with neighbors" by setting up trade agreements with Iran, Syria and Iraq, providing mediation to nations at odds and supporting the Arab League and other Middle Eastern multilateral organizations. For decades, Middle Eastern nations bowed to external European forces to help mitigate their disputes. Now, Turkey has become the big brother they might all just need.

But even Turkey is not without its warts. In June 2013, Turkish protesters took to the streets, claiming Erdogan had taken recent election results as a mandate that he could expand his dictatorial power, imposing his will and his vision on the entire country. Though tens of thousands of disenchanted Turks lined city parks demanding the resignation of their prime minister, the police soon aggressively took control, injuring over 7000 protesters, killing five individuals in the process. Erdogan might still be seen regionally as the role model for how to steward a Muslim nation, but his own people now increasingly see him as a power-hungry bully willing to enact Gestapo-esque tactics to keep his people in line (even taking over the news media during the protests, having CNN Turk run penguin documentaries instead of actual coverage of the dissent). Turkey has proven that even the most admired system of government comes with challenges.

Whether or not the budding Middle Eastern administrations will be able to likewise pursue a moderate, economically dynamic path is yet to be determined. Iraq might have a head start in the fun game of democracy building, albeit they also have a few more hurdles to surpass seeing that their nation is also pulling itself out of a decade long war that destroyed their infrastructure and took the lives of over 150,000 soldiers and civilians. Now I don't want to get into the background of the war. I'm not going to talk about how in the post 9/11 war on terror era, President George Bush, his team of experts and the intelligence community were positive Iraq was developing weapons of mass destruction that would assuredly fall into the hands of terrorists who would then yet again attack American soil. I'm not going to talk about how the media and the Congress took this information and supported the pre-emptive invasion of Iraq in 2003. I definitely don't want to then get into the embarrassing fact that after months of searching for these weapons of mass destruction, the powers that be had to admit there were no weapons (and hadn't been since 1991), and worse yet, Iraq had no connection to the terrorists responsible for the 9/11 bombings. I don't want to then have to explain that once US officials realized they'd screwed up, they cleverly changed the narrative to justify US involvement as one of regime change, where American forces would remove a universally despised despot - Saddam Hussein - to pave the way for a democratic revolution. If I bring up that lofty little goal, I would then have to talk about how the US might have had a good plan of how to win the war, but they had devised a crappy plan on how to win the peace, leaving cities and countrysides across Iraq vulnerable to insurgents who plunged the nation into years of deadly, indiscriminate violence that crippled the economy and left Iraqis in a far more vulnerable state than they had been under Saddam Hussein.

But I don't want to get into any of that.

So let's just start in January 2012. President Barack Obama pulled US troops out the previous December and now the coalition government began working to ensure a bright, happy, prosperous future for its people. One small problem. Its people hate each other. You see, Iraq has three groups – the Shiites, the Sunnis and the Kurds. The Sunnis are the minority (about 15% of the population), but they have run the country for the last four centuries. They've relegated the majority Shiites (60%) to the lowest level jobs, which leads to just a tad bit of bitterness. Then there are the Kurds (20%), also a minority (a much less religious group than the Shiites and Sunnis), but their people control the rich oil fields of the north and pretty much just want to be left alone, and since 1991, with American support, they've lived autonomously in a place they like to call Kurdistan, fairly removed from Iraqi politics. For the last three decades, the three groups didn't kill each other because Saddam Hussein (a Sunni) killed anyone who threatened to break his "peace." His logic was a bit sadistic, but it worked. After Saddam fell (first captured, then tried, then hung), the Americans kept the fragile peace by spreading their military around the regional hotspots and even helped the Iraqis draw up a constitution that would involve (placate) each of the three major groups.

But none of the three groups are buying it. They each believe that the other groups won't honor their responsibilities in the government, and they each will continually vie to increase their power. So, Sunni officials boycott parliament because they believe the Shiite prime minister is trying to secure a dictatorship, the Sunni vice-president uses government funds to hire hitmen to hunt down Shiite officials, the Kurds keep pushing to remain independent and militants from neighboring countries continue to stream in hoping to impede Iraq's transition to democracy. All the while, neighbor Iran watches with anticipation for a time when their Shiite brothers will emerge victorious, possibly forging an impenetrable bond between the two once-enemies.

So it could get a lot worse before it gets better. If you were a gambling man, dropping a wager on civil war in Iraq would probably be a fairly secure bet. The nation has no recent history of working out its problems civilly and because each of the three demographics fears genocide should the opposition gain control, sectarian conflict and violence are almost assured. However, there have been some recent glimmers of hope. To ensure the survival of his flimsy coalition, Prime Minister Maliki has spent the last couple years reinterpreting his executive powers. He sometimes chooses to not enforce approved legislation, he has put his most loyal military officers in positions of authority and he has at times used the military as his own personal security force, arresting those who object to his policies. But his approval ratings continue to improve. How is that possible? Aren't the Iraqi people disgusted that their nation appears to returning to an autocracy? Don't they care?

To be honest, the form of government is really the least of Iraq's concerns. The two biggest issues – stability and economic opportunities – appear to be coming together under Maliki's watch. Last year, Iraq surpassed Iran as the #2 supplier of oil to the world, producing over three million barrels of oil today (and this number could continue to grow to nine million barrels per day by 2020). This $100 billion in revenue has trickled down to the hands of the Iraqi people, and they see their daily lives steadily improving. Iraq has also seen a relative reprieve from the incessant violence. Iran is dealing with its own internal issues, and the regional militants who spent the last decade causing chaos in Iraq, have exported their terror to the civil war in Syria.

In 2013, Syria became the powder keg of the Middle East. What started in March 2011 as a few protests opposing the military's treatment of boys caught spraying anti-government graffiti, has devolved into an all-out civil war that has killed over 30,000 soldiers and civilians and imprisoned another 40,000. President Bashar al-Assad, leader of the minority Ba'ath Party, has ruled Syria with an iron fist, trying to hold together a country that is more a network of independent fiefdoms than a unified nation. The minority Shiites have controlled Syria for decades, establishing an awkward alliance with the Kurds and the Christians. The Sunni majority (accounting for 74% of the population, but relegated to agricultural and menial labor) have used the Arab Spring and support from the United States, Turkey, Saudi Arabia and Qatar to mount an insurgency across the countryside, taking over numerous towns and inflicting far more damage on Syrian forces than was to be expected. Many of the Sunni insurgents learned urban warfare techniques during the Iraqi War, making it difficult for the Syrian armed forces to gain an upper hand. In early 2013, the Russian military advised Syria to simply drop bombs on any city that might house insurgents (a tactic the Russians employed during the Chechen War), even if Assad might lose some international public relations points.

Assad and his Shiite ruling party refused to give up any ground. They couldn't. Their survival depended on controlling the government. If the Sunnis ever took over power, they would want revenge for the decades of oppression, inevitably enacting a policy of ethnic cleansing that would rival the Rwanda massacres of the 1990s. This ominous possibility has led to a relative stalemate, where neither side is willing to surrender, but neither side yet holds the advantage to break through to victory. Potentially the balance could be shifted if foreign nations (the US specifically) threw more support behind one side, but at this point, no one really knows if a clear victory would actually be a beneficial result in the long term. Maybe a stalemate is what is best for the region (and the survival of the vulnerable ethnic groups).

The Syrian civil war also threatens to blow up into a full-scale regional war. In May 2013, tensions went up a few notches when evidence emerged that Syria had used chemical weapons (sarin gas) on insurgents in March, that a border town in Turkey was shattered by two car bombs and that Israel had deployed missile strikes on Syrian territory to knock out an alleged arms trade between Iran and Shiite Hezbollah insurgents. Syria has become a proxy war for Iran and Israel, with the Iranians sending guns, ammunition and missiles to Hezbollah, endangering Israeli borders. As more and more information files in and regional belligerents start flexing their muscles, we can only hope that cooler heads prevail before the Middle East devolves into an all-out war.

Over in Egypt, the possibility for a smooth transition is equally murky. The Egyptians might have overthrown their minority dictator, but they in no means secured stability. In June 2012, the military-run interim government reluctantly swore in its first post-Mubarak executive – President Muhammad Morsi. Morsi led the Freedom and Justice Party, the political wing of the Muslim Brotherhood, the once-banned political party that was the perennial thorn in the side of Mubarak throughout his tenure. University of Southern California-schooled Morsi returned to Egypt and spent his adulthood challenging Mubarak's corrupt government and rigged elections, landing himself in jail time and time again.

Now that Morsi is the one heading the state, Egyptians and regional leaders wonder what direction will be forged and if a change in ideology can even lead to lasting, far-reaching progress. Because of Morsi's connection to the Muslim Brotherhood, some wonder how far to the religious right will the government turn. Will it bow to the Salafists who demand strict adherence of ninth century Sharia law, demanding the separation of the sexes in all public and professional spheres and adoption of conservative economic and education practices? Or will it try to follow the path of the Turkish Justice and Development Party, retaining and valuing Muslim faith while pursuing a democratization agenda that also emphasizes free market capitalism? And regardless of what Morsi, the Freedom and Justice Party and their coalition government desire, who will actually enforce their mandates?

How many of the 500,000 Egyptian soldiers actually support this new government? How many of the hundreds of thousands of bureaucrats who benefited from Mubarak's web of corruption will want to adopt a more legitimate method of interacting in all public and economic transactions? If you're an Egyptian general used to pocketing millions on weapons sales, are you excited about this new era of transparency? If you're a post office employee or a marriage license secretary used to getting a kickback just for mailing a letter or processing a document, how excited are you to know that your salary will be your only source of income? And how excited are the people for the bickering, infighting, politicking and deadlocking that inevitably follow pure democracy? What's worse? Not getting your way when you never had a say in government or knowing you now have a say, but your opinion isn't supported by the majority? It could get a lot messier in Egypt before it gets better.

Tunisia and Libya have a slight advantage over Egypt – they never had any government that even slightly resembled a democracy, so they are essentially starting with a clean slate. When Egyptians think of democracy, they automatically remember the years of rigged elections and phony legislative initiatives. Mubarak was able to get anything he wanted passed through his parliament, sometimes combining a whole laundry list of unrelated resolutions – from military expenditures, to education reform, to personal investments, to corporate regulation – all into one yes or no vote. Tunisians and Libyans never knew democracy and have no preconceived notions of the institution, so they're sucking in all they can from the successful governments (especially Turkey's) of the region, hoping they'll start off on the right foot. But like Egypt, the footprints of their despots will last far longer than the men who marked their territory. Mubarak might be jailed, Ben Ali might be living in exile and Hussein and Qadafi might be dead, but the powerful elites, intimidating secret polices and corrupt state structures will be far harder to overthrow than were the men who sat at the top of the crooked pyramids.

In the fall of 2012, Tunisia and Libya illuminated another problem with emerging democracies – they are ill-equipped to prevent mass demonstrations and terrorist incursions. In Tunisia, a mob scaled the American embassy walls, killed four employees and then raided the nearby American school. In Libya, US Ambassador Christopher Stevens was assassinated in October at the hands of terrorists attempting to commemorate the anniversary of the 9/11 attacks. Emerging democracies in the Middle East will remain unstable for possibly years to come, and it is this instability that has made them attractive targets for Islamic extremists looking to make a mark.

For the remaining Middle East nations that didn't fall, their administrations will need to decide how much they want to do (or even need to do) to evolve to address this "Awakening." Syria and Yemen have refused to acquiesce to the demands of the people, violently repressing the protesters and making only superficial shows at reforming their rule. The remaining Middle East regimes in Jordans, Saudi Arabia and Oman took a cue from the 19th century European states who avoided the anarchy and turmoil of the French Revolution by modifying their method of conducting elections and business, and by granting a few liberties to the people. This form of "authoritarian upgrading" might mean that the ruling party might invite the creation of a few more political parties (though any that become too successful will have to be "dealt with"), they might expand voting rights to women, they might fire a few top officials who seem a bit too close to the ruling family or they might even rescind rulings that appear just a bit too medieval (like the Saudi Arabian law that lashed a woman ten times for driving a car). But really, these absolute monarchies of the Middle East have little intentions of exacting any real reforms. Most just hope they can endure the storm, trusting that this little event known as the Arab Spring was nothing more than a blip in their self-conceived, enlightened dictatorships.

And unfortunately, for the four nations on the verge of a democratic transition, the truth is...these revolutions, this Arab Awakening, this once in a century opportunity expand freedom, they might lead to...no real change at all. It might merely be the transfer of power from one elite group to another. They might even follow the cycle of revolutions that saw a Napoleon Bonaparte replace a King Louis XIV, a Josef Stalin replace a Czar Nicholas II and a Mao Tse Tung replace the Qing Dynasty. Revolutions that often start with the noblest intentions of overthrowing aristocracy often succumb to the even more iron fists of megalomaniacal dictators. So if history has any lessons for us, there might be a whole lot more chaos, a whole lot more civil war and a whole lot more one-man rule before the Middle East makes any more than a perfunctory shift toward democracy.

And who's to say that enlightened dictatorship isn't the best form of government for this region? Instead of being a homogenous region of like-minded thinkers, the Middle East harbors the full spectrum of cultural and social perspectives, many of which cannot be readily resolved. How can a region come to terms with the issue of homosexuality when conservatives call for flogging, imprisonment and the death penalty for any man thought guilty of sodomy? Some towns even separate vegetables in markets based on their anatomical likeness. How about gender equity? In a society where some believe only those able to penetrate others are seen as powerful, in a society where women can be jailed or gang raped for walking with an unrelated man, in a society where 42% of all females are illiterate, how can these women gain the equality they see online in the likenesses of Oprah, Hillary or Condoleeza? Maybe only a respected dictator can gradually push through legislation that expands rights to the disenfranchised, while still appeasing the demands of the Islamists. Maybe in a society where extremist agendas have percolated for centuries, democracy is a formula for failure.

Democracy might even lead to a revival of Islamism. In the late 1990s and early 2000s, organizations like Al Qaeda, Hamas and Hezbollah appeared to be the only outlet for protest against Western-backed, autocratic regimes. But with the events of 9/11 and the continued attacks on innocent civilians, the mainstream Muslim community started to distance itself from the jihadists who were willing to violently end Western influence under the auspice of uniting all Muslims under one caliphate from Jakarta to Istanbul. The goals of these jihadists became too narrow and their values contradicted the teachings of the Quran. People cared more about smooth roads, functioning electricity and available jobs than they did about punishing the infidel. With the Arab Spring, the common enemy was no longer the West, but their nation's own head of state and his inability to develop the economy. With this focus on day-to-day economic issues, the jihadist agenda felt outdated and out of touch with the majority's needs.

This gradual increase in anti-jihad sympathies could reverse if the nations adopting democracy plunge into chaos or foreign nations continue to influence and support autocratic regimes. In Iraq, the decade of civil war became a breeding ground for jihadist militants wanting to test their battle readiness on American soldiers and anti-Islamist sympathizers. Al Qaeda and its adherents are only waiting for other regions, like Yemen or Syria, to jump into the conflict and continue their convoluted mission to advance their narrow anti-Western agenda.

For American officials, they must also strongly reconsider their role in supporting Middle Eastern governments. As the events of Iraq unfolded, many critics argued – why Iraq? If the goal was to overthrow a corrupt despot, any number of candidates in the region fit the description, many of which would pose a lot less risk than going after the twelfth largest military in the world. Why not Yemen? Or Bahrain? Or Syria? Or the granddaddy-of-them-all...Saudi Arabia?

The reason is America has had a less than consistent position on regimes in the region (and not just in the Middle East, but around the world). Since the Cold War era, the United States developed the following hierarchy for supporting foreign governments: Priority #1 - Democratic leader favorable to US policy. Priority #2 - Autocrat (monarch, military leader, president for life) favorable to US policy. Priority #3 - Other. The US didn't like the "other" option and basically propped up regimes that might not have been favorites of their population, but also only supported regime change when they didn't agree with the regime.

In the case of Saudi Arabia, as long as they continued to grant the US access to their 267 billion barrels of oil reserves and promised to remain America's biggest purchaser of military equipment, they could continue to handicap their economy, persecute their people and maintain one of the more unequal societies on the planet. One could argue that this isn't a passive stance of "we'll leave you alone to take care of your own business," but more one of "we'll make it possible for you to stay in power for all eternity."

Between 2006-2009, Saudi Arabia purchased over $39 billion in US military equipment, and in 2010 they pledged to buy $60 billion more in aircraft, naval vessels and intelligence equipment that would not only protect them from foreign threats, but would also enable them to prevent any uprising from taking hold.

When the Arab Spring hit in 2011, Saudi Arabia was better prepared than any other nation to squelch the protest – they put tens of thousands of troops on the ground, took over the media airwaves reminding everyone about their religious duty to listen to their elders and monitored and shut down any websites or Internet communication that posed a threat to the status quo. It worked. The Saud family's control remains absolute.

America has to be careful though, because in today's world of Wikileaks and anti-US sentiment, it wouldn't take much to revitalize Al Qaeda in the region. When Arab Spring Part II inevitably breaks out, if it seems like it's American foreign policy that is bankrolling the political and military elite, demonstrations and protests might start again calling for "Death to America."

Until then, the greatest foreign threat to the Middle East comes not from a Western boogeyman, but from Iran, who appears on the cusp of unveiling its own nuclear bomb. For close to a decade, Iranian president Mahmoud Ahmadinejad has frustrated national leaders with his unrelenting quest to join the nuclear-armed community of nations. To this point, America and its anti-nuclear proliferation allies have relied on empty threats in the vein of "If you don't stop trying to make nuclear weapons, we're going to sternly ask you again to stop trying to make nuclear weapons." But the US's hands were relatively tied, as there was no way they were going to back their verbal threats with any military might – three wars in Iraq, Afghanistan and Iran wouldn't do well for America's economy and it might even look a heck of a lot like World War III. Even with America's slew of boycotts, their cyber attacks on Iranian computer systems and their assassinations of critical engineers and scientists, Ahmadinejad remained undeterred.

He's going to have his bomb, and there's nothing anyone can do to stop him, for he knows, once a country has the bomb, its relationship with the world changes. He never again has to worry about invasion from a regional or distant foe. He can come to the table of geopolitical and economic discussions as a relative equal, not as a patronized inferior. He could even blow Israel off the map (a threat the Israelis might just take out preemptively).

But more than likely, when Iran gets the bomb (and it's only a matter of when at this point), probably not much will change. Israel will still have the most powerful military in the Middle East. They'll still have the most nukes in the Middle East. This isn't going to start any arms races in the Middle East. Libya, Algeria, Iraq, Syria and Egypt all considered going after the bomb, but realized the cost and the expertise was beyond them. Iran is probably not going to give the bomb to terrorists since those pesky ideologues can't be trusted not to use the bomb against their supplier. Sure, they'll continue to support Syria, Hezbollah, the Taliban and Al Qaeda with a "what are you going to do about it?" philosophy, but aside from being a bit more assertive, Iran isn't stupid.

Or at least the world better hope they're not.

But by the end of 2013, the psychosis of Ahmadinejad might be irrelevant. His term was up in August, and the presidential elections saw the victory of Dr. Hassan Rouhani, a seemingly stable politician less likely to make the absurd, combative, bombastic statements of his predecessor. Within days of winning the presidency, Rouhani promised a "new era...of moderation and justice, not extremism." One can only hope.

But the election revealed again to the outside world that Iranian democracy is nothing like the American version championed across the 20th century. The true power brokers in Iran are the Supreme Leader Ayatollah Ruhollah Khomeini, the Guardian Council (his advisors) and the Revolutionary Guard Corps (his secret police that act outside the law and control every facet of politics and economics). If the Supreme Leader wants something to happen, it will happen. He is the puppet master behind the scenes and regardless of what changes Rouhani envisions, all policies will still need to be vetted by Khomeini and his Guardian Council. Losing the favor of the Supreme Leader guarantees political ostracism. Ahmadinejad learned this reality first hand, after he angered the clerics and the Guardian Council, by claiming he was related to a religious prophet and destroying the economy by garnering international sanctions. Ahmadinejad is not a popular man to the outside world, but he didn't exactly win a lot of fans within Iran either.

Which leaves us with the final conflict in the Middle East – the fight over the Holy Land. Israel. This is the one we most commonly hear about and the one that will almost assuredly never get resolved. Who gets the Holy Land? Do the Jews get the land promised to them by God? Or do the Muslims get the land secured to them by Allah? Should the Palestinians regain control of the region they were forced out of following World War II? Or should the Israelis maintain control over the region they spent two thousands years trying to regain after being exiled by the Romans? Both sides have claims. Both sides have been persecuted. Neither side plans on giving in anytime soon.

However, the tide might be turning. In recent years, Israel has lost sympathy from the world community. Following the Nazi atrocities of World War II, international agencies and nations (especially the United States) were willing to turn a blind eye to the aggressive policies of the newly formed Israel. The lone capitalist, Judeo-Christian democrachy in the region, Israel was justifiably wary of its vulnerable position. Jews had spent 2000 years wandering from country to country. They were a people without a nation. They had suffered through countless atrocities and persecution for centuries, culminating in the worst episode of cruelty in man's history. And in the decades after World War II, the Arab world had no interest in seeing these displaced people return to their homeland. Until Israel could secure its borders, it would be exposed and susceptible to foreign invasion.

But Israel is no longer the underdog. They have one of the, if not *the*, most state of the art militaries in the world, their Mossad intelligence agency is second to none and they have a couple hundred nuclear bombs that they've never been held accountable for. To top it all off, they've mounted two wars to expand their territory, creating a humanitarian and refugee crisis that continues to plague both the Palestinians kicked out of their homes and the neighboring countries of Jordan, Syria and Lebanon that have reluctantly accepted these emigrants.

For many in the Middle East, the Israeli treatment of Palestinian Arabs is the symbolic rallying point for Arabs against the oppressive, hypocritical policies of the West. How can a nation built on the foundation of democracy marginalize nearly half its population?

Most Israelis support a two-state option – a Palestine for Arabs and an Israel for Jews – though most Jews believe the Palestinians won't be able to keep their side of the bargain and will certainly resort to continued violence. But even though the majority of the population supports a two-state solution, the chances of it ever passing through Israeli parliament are miniscule. They have a coalition government where the two biggest political parties together only control 40% of the available seats, which means it would be almost impossible to get any contentious resolution through the legislative branch. Plus, many Palestinians don't even want a two-state option. In Israel, there are currently 1.5 million Palestinians living amongst five million Jews. Many of these and these Palestinian Arabs aren't exactly jumping at the chance to have a united Palestine. Sure, they'd be with their ideological brethren, but most would rather live where the jobs are – Israel. These Palestinians would rather be employed and living amongst the enemy, than poor living with their religious brothers.

What then will happen to the Middle East? It might erupt into a true revolution where nation after nation embraces the hiccups of democracy. It might devolve into civil war and sectarian violence as warring factions struggle for their perceived survival. Or, it might just proceed as it has for centuries, with autocratic monarchs ensuring the spoils for their families and the society's elites, hoping that the masses passively accept the status quo.

Anything might happen.

But that is for another chapter.

48

Russia

History might not repeat itself, but some regions seem to have a habit of regressing into roles that have dominated for centuries. No matter the state of the world, the evolution of industries or the disposition of their people, some places on earth just have difficulty escaping their past.

So here they go again. Russia entered the 21st century the same way they entered the 17th, 18th, 19th and 20th centuries. They have a lone autocrat calling all the shots from Moscow. They have an elite oligarchy controlling all of the major resources. Their government polices the media, silences opposition and breeds apathy. They fear the allure of Europe might pull their people to the West, so they close off their borders and ensure a widening sphere of influence keeps their vast nation buffered from the influence of outsiders. They have more farmland than anywhere else on the planet, but their people still starve. They seem to have one foot in the world of the advanced countries, but one still stuck in the quagmire of the developing world.

Russia is a paradox of extremes, and it is no closer to resolving these disparities than it was under the reign of Peter the Great or Catherine the Great or even Josef Stalin. In fact, it looks like they're heading backwards.

After the fall of the Soviet Union in 1989, Russians briefly experimented with democracy and capitalism.

They failed.

Russia opened up its polls to free elections and opened up public industries and lands to the highest bidder. It released its hold on the Soviet satellite nations, allowing each to pursue its own destiny. Russia turned inward, hoping the wonders of the free markets and the invisible hand would sweep in and compensate for decades of mismanagement and outdated business practices.

Opportunistic moguls who had friends in the right places swept in and gobbled up the factories, mines and farms from the government, buying them for kopecks on the ruble. These moguls became billionaires. The former Soviet republics degenerated into chaos, totally unprepared for self-rule. By 1998, Russia was a mere shadow of its former self. Its people were mired in a recession that left banks closed and 60% of their population below the poverty line. Boris Yeltsin had won another election, but everyone knew the democratic process was a sham, and that corruption and ballot tampering ruled the system. The nation that was once a superpower had failed at communism, and it now seemed like it would likewise fail at their bastardized form of capitalism and democracy.

Then Vladimir Putin took over. But more importantly, then oil prices started going up. China and India needed energy and Russia had the oil, the natural gas, the coal and the timber to fill their insatiable hunger. Within a decade, Russia was clearly recovering. Its people were no longer suffering, but were actually flourishing. Unemployment dropped to 15% and many proclaimed Putin their savior. He had rescued their economy and restored their pride.

Putin then turned his forces on neighboring Georgia, invading the nation who teased Europe into believing it was going to enter NATO. Russia could not lose one of its holdings to the West. They might not be the Soviet Union anymore, but they were not exactly feeble and willing to release their neighbors from their sphere of influence. The international community was frustrated with Russia's land grab, but they did nothing. The

Russia of the early 21st century was starting to look a heck of a lot like the one that ruled over Eurasia for the whole of the 20th.

Russia had crawled back from its self-inflicted purgatory, and the world watched to see if this was Russia's permanent reality or merely a blip on their road to joining the world of liberal democracies and free market capitalists.

But Russia doesn't have to follow the path of the rest of the world because it is by far the most resource-rich country on the planet. It has what the world needs. It has $7 trillion in oil reserves, $19 trillion in natural gas reserves, $23 trillion in coal reserves and $28 trillion in timber reserves. Russia's getting rich. By 2013, they'd already stocked up a savings account worth $527 billion. They were no longer a debtor nation. Their economy was spinning.

This reliance on resources brought prosperity to the Russian people, but it also masks a ton of problems that threaten to bring down the current government should the price of energy plummet. In 2013, oil prices hovered around the $93 a barrel range. Just fifteen years ago, it sat at around $12 a barrel. What happens if the commodities markets collapse? What hidden problems will be exposed?

First, the Russian government under Vladimir Putin has created an unsettling, symbiotic relationship between big business and the state. Seeing how the privatization of Russian industries destroyed the economy in the 1990s, Putin pushed for what he calls "national champions," companies willing to pursue not only profits, but also do the bidding of the government whenever called upon. Here's how the system works. The Russian regime approaches a business to see how open they would be to a partnership with the government. If they decline, the Russian court system steps in. They inevitably find some minute offense or CEO indiscretion, and use this information to "legally" liberate the company from its private owners. The authorities then turn over title to an entrepreneur willing to play ball and bow to government interests. In one very public example of this type of hostile takeover, energy company Yukos was charged with tax evasion. Oddly enough their tax bill came to 111% of their actual profits, an odd figure considering other energy companies paid less than 20% of their total revenue. The courts didn't care about the lack of logic. They forced Yukos into bankruptcy and their assets were auctioned off to the highest bidder loyal to Putin. In this manner,

Putin has built up a cadre of companies intensely loyal to his cause, not willing to cross him should they ever disagree.

This inconsistent, shameless interpretation of the law has scared off would-be investors from around the world. Who would want to start up a company in Russia when the government could shut it down at any moment? Would Dell Computers? Coca Cola? IKEA? Who would risk it? And because Russia has made foreign investment so unappealing, countries have also made it near impossible for Russian companies to expand overseas. The logic being – if you don't support us, we won't support you. This unspoken blackout of Russian industries has put a ceiling on the growth of Russia's manufacturing sector. Likewise, the resource curse has handicapped the development of other industries. There's no Russian software or pharmaceutical or automobile giant that even comes close to rivaling those goods created in Europe, East Asia or the United States. Can you even name a consumer good exported by Russia (aside from vodka and caviar)?

Putin has also attempted to seal off any criticism of his policies – a task far more difficult in the age of the Internet. Russians have shown a willingness to protest in recent years. Tens of thousands marched on the capital city after Putin's 2011 phony election, and some have even begun staging flash mobs to denounce his policies. In 2012, the shock rock, punk band Pussy Riot, a group known for their colorful costumes and political messages, staged a musical protest at a Christian church. The Russian government wasn't huge fans of the girl band's antics. Trying to escape prosecution, a few of the bandmates fled the country, but two others were arrested and then sentenced to imprisonment. This trial gained international recognition and illustrated how there was an undercurrent of discontent hidden beneath the economic prosperity of recent years. The disenchanted protesters have yet to unify, but should Russian authorities continue to come down hard on civil disobedience, or should Russia's economic fortune shift, a possible political challenge could be ripe for action.

Yet even though local industries are paralyzed and freedom of speech really isn't that free, the majority still herald the reign of Putin. They remember all too well the despair of the late 1990s. They also know that income inequality is monumental in Russia, but unlike in other countries where the rich stay rich and the poor stay poor, in Russia, wealth can come and go at a moment's notice. In the last fifteen years, 90% of Russians claim to have seen their salaries drop below the poverty line. You can be middle class one moment, destitute the next. One of the reasons for this oddity is that Russian companies don't fire people when the economy drops. In the United States, if a company needs to cut back, they simply lay off thousands of their employees. In Russia, everyone stays on, but they all take a pay cut. In this manner, during a recession, millions more see their standard of living drop than they would in a standard capitalist structure (though they won't see their depth of despair go as deep as those who find themselves fired with no hope for employment).

Russian inequality also stems from geographic realities. Russia's resources are unequally distributed. Ten regions (out of 83) produce 75% of the country's wealth. Live in those regions, you're doing well. Live outside them, you're going to struggle to make ends meet. Workers also suffer because industries are often placed far away from other resources. Under Stalin and his party officials, clusters of manufacturing plants were placed far away from Russia's western borders to ensure if Europe ever invaded, their industries would be safe. But there's a problem with this logic. These industries can be stuck out in the middle of a forest, instead of next to an airport or a port or a canal. Not only does it cost the firm a ton of money to get their product to market, for all their employees living in the boonies, purchasing luxury items, or even necessities, is near impossible. Of course, the easiest solution to this problem is to move to the cities out west. But this immigration has only exacerbated the problem, as more and more regions out east struggle to maintain any level of economic stability.

Urban migration is one of many demographic nightmares facing Russia. Its people are sick, depressed and old. Russia's alcoholism, murder and suicide rates are distressingly high. Their people contract tuberculosis, hepatitis and AIDS at rates that rival Sub-Saharan Africa. Their prenatal care is horrible, so millions are born with abnormalities. The Russian military recently claimed that 23% of their conscripts had physical disorders and 21% had mental disorders. The average life expectancy rate is 61 years for men and 73 years for women (a larger gender discrepancy rating than anything you'll find in Europe or North America). Even with these short life spans, the plunge in birth rates and minimal immigration means that Russia is getting smaller. In 2013, it had 143 million people. By 2050, that number could drop to 128 million. This reduced adult population will have trouble replacing the workforce, but will also struggle to replenish the needed military quotas, and for a nation that has seemingly imperialistic aspirations, this could cause a problem.

Since 2008, Russia has made every inclination that it wants to again be a major player in global issues. Because of its permanent seat on the United Nations Security Council and its veto power, it will continue to play a critical role in world affairs. But this isn't enough for Russia. Every clue suggests Russia would love to have its former satellite nations back under its domain. When the nations of the Caucasus Mountains (Georgia, Armenia and Azerbaijan) pushed for democratic reforms and inclusion in the European Union, Russia stepped in and ensured that wouldn't occur. They openly passed out Russian passports to residents of these countries, and then conveniently claimed they might need to invade the nations to ensure their "citizens" were protected.

This refusal to allow democratic reforms has put Russia at odds with the United States. Although it has been hesitant to match force with rhetoric, the United States has condemned Russia's meddling in regional affairs, especially when it prevents democracy from sprouting. Likewise, Russia has been less than enthusiastic about supporting the countries of the Middle East and Northern Africa caught up in the Arab Spring. More a fan of business as usual, Russia is a bit nervous about meddling in the affairs of other countries (unless of course, Russia is the one determining the course of the affairs). And to Russia, the Arab Spring is more a harbinger of anarchy than one of stability. Whether it's in Syria or Libya or Egypt, Russia would much prefer a dictator able to keep violent factions in line, than a fledgling democracy unable to satisfy the needs of the multiple extremist ideologues. Russia also sees these Arab revolutions as opening up possible breeding grounds for radical terrorists who might one day return to Russian territories to exact their extremist agendas. The tragic massacre of 400 school children in the province of Chechnya still disturbs local and federal officials, and the idea of a new generation of terrorists on their soil causes grave concern.

For these reasons – the desire to prevent chaos and the creation of terrorist training grounds – Russia has been unable to support attempts by the United States and European nations to intervene in Middle Eastern conflicts. In Libya, when civilians were at risk of being wiped out by Muammar Gaddafi's forces, Russia chose to abstain from the UN vote, allowing England and France to create a coalition that provided air support to the rebel forces. But then the forces pulled out, leaving Libyans to contest who would have the right to fill the power void. It is this abandonment of responsibility that truly frustrates Russian foreign policy makers. In Iraq, and soon in Afghanistan, America has shown the willingness to engage militarily, but unwilling to see peace through to fruition. Once US troops pulled out of Iraq, the nation slid back into sectarian conflicts, and the same will probably hold true for Afghanistan when UN forces are pulled out in 2014. Russia does not want the same for Syria. If the Sunni rebels take over power, their fear is that they will want to exact revenge on the Shiite and Christian minorities, turning first Syria and then the rest of the Middle East into one huge religious war. Russia would prefer the status quo.

But America has a problem with the status quo, as this means dictators are allowed to oppress their people and democracy is stifled. In the first few years of Barack Obama's presidency, US-Russian relations actually improved. Vice President Joe Biden coined this improvement of relations a "reset" – a chance to start all over again as allies. Initially this reset worked. The US and Russia signed a nuclear weapons treaty, the Russians agreed to have American aircraft fly over their soil and the World Trade Organization even admitted Russia (with some needed convincing from US diplomats). But all of this goodwill has come to an end with the America's dealings with Russia over Syria and the Middle East. America would like Russia to just get in line and follow the American lead. Russia would prefer working with their partners Iran, Syria and even Israel to broker some kind of peace in the region, while allowing nations to independently determine their fates.

This puts the two nations at conflict – a situation they have grown quite accustomed to over the past hundred years.

Where Russia goes from here is anyone's guess. Will they reform their political system before the government loses all sense of legitimacy? Will they expand their industries so that they are not so reliant on a few natural resources? Will they find a way to separate the business from the government so that the entrepreneurial spirit can truly be tapped? Will they find a way to feed their people and keep them healthy so that their nation doesn't lose their ability to compete with the still expanding nations of the world?

Or will they do nothing and simply hope that their resource gift never becomes a resource curse?

We'll just have to wait and find out.

But that is for another chapter.

49

Europe

The Europe that entered the 21st century found itself in a much different position than the one that had entered the 20th. The continent was no longer home to the preeminent power players on the planet; decades earlier, it had surrendered its geopolitical stewardship to the United States. It no longer had the most feared military, the most prolific economy or the most cloned culture. Again, those titles went to the US.

But to signal Europe's demise would be a bit premature. Though it might not be number one anymore, it hasn't exactly fallen off the charts. When it comes to military spending, Europe still holds spots four, five and nine (United Kingdom, France and Germany respectively). When it comes to GDP, Europe still pops up fourth, fifth, seventh and eighth (Germany, France, United Kingdom and Italy). As for culture, the whole world might no longer clamor for everything European, but the world still has a hard time not following the goals of Europe's footballers, the cuisine of Europe's top chefs and the tunes turned out by Europe's musicians. And when the world travels, where do they end up? Overwhelmingly, Europe – ranking first, fourth, fifth, sixth, seventh and eighth (France, Spain, Italy, Turkey, United Kingdom and Germany). And when organizations like Forbes or the Economist rank the best places in the world to live (based on criteria like material well-being, gender equality, life expectancy and government performance), Europe overwhelmingly earns almost all the top spots.

Not too shabby considering Europe is home to only about 10% of the world's population and 6.9% of the world's land.

But like the rest of the world, Europe's status is precarious, its future prosperity anything but guaranteed. It suffers from many of the same demographic dangers facing developed regions on other continents. Its economic progress has been inconsistent, its regional stability is shaky and its governments have not exactly instilled total confidence that they'll be able to have the answers when their societies inevitably deteriorate.

One of the most noticeable changes in Europe over the last few decades has been the formation of the European Union. The EU is a system of political and economic partnerships that have steadily expanded since the early 1950s. The EU emerged as a possible solution to the centuries of violence, competition and nationalistic movements that continually made it impossible for European nations to consistently prosper in peace. Since the time of Napoleon, it seemed like political, economic and military leaders all saw European development as a zero sum game – one nation's success was another nation's failure. This rivalry inevitably led to conflict, and after the decimation of World War II, the continent's leaders knew something had to change.

What if instead of fighting for resources and prestige, they linked up and benefited from the advantages of scale? What if instead of trying to prevent their neighbors from trading, they actually worked with their neighbors to open up markets and natural resources for all to share? What if instead of seeing each other as enemies bent on ruin, they saw each other as allies seeking a shared success?

Europe knew they could never form a republic a la the United States of America, but why not form a federation of mutually beneficial partnerships? The first partnership started with just six nations who wanted to link together their coal and steel production to compete with the massive production levels of the Soviets and the Americans. But since that first economic alliance of six, the number of member states has expanded to 27 (with six candidate countries currently vying for inclusion), and these members have since adopted a common currency (the Euro), a governing body (the European Parliament), a continental bank (the European Central Bank) and a judicial body (the Court of Justice).

And to this point, it's worked, possibly becoming the most effective international organization in the history of the planet. It has taken away borders, allowing Europeans to trade and travel from member state to member state without showing their passport or paying tariffs. It has improved the entire continent's standard of living. It has led to the sharing of ideas and individuals like never before. But most importantly, it has kept the peace. There was a time not too long ago when it seemed like every generation saw another European war, and as the technologies industrialized, each successive war was proving more deadly. The first half of the 20th century was the most violent in human history. But the second half witnessed relative stability in the region, and we've all seen how Europe's peace has meant the world's peace.

Yet, the European Union is not without its struggles. The biggest issue facing the EU is its long-term economic sustainability. The 2008 recession wiped out the world's economies, while also drawing attention to the fundamental flaws in each nation's economic systems. In Europe, the member countries saw how quickly one country's corrupt or inept economic practices could threaten to bring down the entire system. It wasn't just one failing economy that was endangering the group, it was five – the PIIGS (Portugal, Ireland, Italy, Greece and Spain). Each nation had allowed flawed, short-sighted practices to engulf their nation in massive debt to the point that they needed bailouts from the more prosperous nations, or risk falling into depressions that could last for decades.

In each of these failing nations, the same theme kept popping up – their governments were spending more money than they were bringing in. Italy is the classic example of a failed economic system. The government spends money recklessly and has few checks and balances to make sure the funds are not wrongly distributed. Disability benefits go to workers who aren't injured, swollen pensions support multiple generations living under the same roof and government subsidies go to firms that don't need them (taxi drivers get paid for not even driving passengers).

Foreign companies are hesitant to relocate their offices to Italy as the government has made it almost impossible to fire incompetent workers and the bungling, bloated state bureaucracies mean a company could spent months jumping through all the paperwork hoops required just to get your business up and running.

To make matters worse, the Italian government can barely collect enough taxes to keep the economy running. Tax codes are rarely applied consistently (and it's a running joke that if you actually pay the taxes you owe, you're some sort of a gullible sucker). Workers rarely claim to the government what they actually earn (most luxury car owners fill out tax forms stating they make less than $30,000 a year).

One of the huge problems with democracy is that a politician's primary motivation is to get elected, and what better way to appeal to the average voter than to promise to cut their taxes and increase their benefits. Politicians also need money to run campaigns, so big donors are "taken care of" once their backed horse comes into office. Corruption has almost become an expected bi-product of democracy, as plum government jobs are passed out to cronies and the most profitable government contracts fall into the laps of the most generous campaign benefactors. But there's only so much you can promise before you destroy the government's ability to function.

And it's not just Italy. Greece tosses away billions in entitlement programs to their citizens, paying out huge pension retirements to workers once they hit 55 years old, allotting over 440 million euros to daughters of deceased government workers and funding hundreds of random committees whose missions are questionable at best (one such committee manages Lake Kopais which dried up in the 1930s). Portugal loses millions in revenue by supporting 31 days of paid holiday leave a year. Cyprus has created a pension system that pays its elected officials double their earnings in retirement. And the governments of Ireland and Spain lost billions of dollars in real estate investments that went belly-up after the 2008 recession.

And here's the problem with all of this lost money. Money has to come from somewhere. Someone has to pay for all these programs when tax revenue consistently comes up short. So what do countries like Spain, Portugal, Ireland, Greece, Italy and Cyprus do when they run out of money? They take out loans - huge loans - from countries more than willing to make some cash charging interest. Trillions of dollars flowed from the banks of Germany, Belgium, England and France down to the struggling economies of the EU. This situation was always precarious.

What would happen when the debtor nations couldn't pay back the creditor nations? Europe found out after the 2008 recession. One by one, the struggling nations of the EU asked for debt relief, saying essentially, "Sorry, we just can't pay you back...would you mind just forgetting about the money you lent us?" The creditor nations had a choice – let the countries go bankrupt (and they'd get none of their money back) or bail them out (give them more money with hopes that their economies will get moving again). They chose the second option, and in 2010, the EU set up the European Financial Stability Facility, an organization charged with passing out money to those EU countries in crisis. From 2010 to 2013, these bailouts surpassed $500 billion, but there's no guarantees another round of bailouts won't be on the horizon.

But this money didn't come without a few conditions. The EU wasn't going to just throw good money after bad. They needed promises from the bailed out countries that they'd change their behaviors, that they'd adopt austerity measures – practices that would spend less money on entitlements and take in more revenue from taxes. These cuts would be the bitter pill Europeans would have to take if they wanted to rescue their economies from imminent collapse. Across Europe, governments froze salaries, reduced the number of paid holidays, extended the retirement age, cut off aid to education and arts programs, wiped out hundreds of thousands of unnecessary government jobs, decreased spending on defense, cut energy subsidies for families in winter, increased corporate and household tax rates, installed road tax machines and attached new taxes to junk food, alcohol and cigarettes.

Impacted Europeans have been less than pleased. Unemployment levels skyrocketed. Household income levels plummeted. Consumer spending died. And the people started fuming. Streets filled with protests, violence and vitriolic graffiti. In Portugal, an organization published the tax numbers of their elected officials so people started cheekily charging purchases to their politicians. In Greece, 300,000 protesters gathered outside the parliament building to warn the legislators that they best not take away their entitlements. In London, college students attacked the car of Prince Charles in opposition of the 80% cuts to university spending. Still today, the masses are suffering and there are no signs yet that austerity is working. Some nations (like Cyprus) considered voting to just ignore the conditions of the bailout, calling the EU's bluff. Will the EU really let nation's go bankrupt? Healthy nations (like Germany who has a balanced budget) are being held hostage by the indebted nations, but the precedent has been set that the haves will continue to help out the have-nots. When will enough be enough?

Some nations are even considering leaving the EU. Candidates for office now run on platforms promising to leave the EU, blaming the federation for their economic failings. If a debtor nation leaves the EU, its government can ignore the austerity conditions and return to business as usual (though it might be hard to find another country willing to lend them money after it proved to be a less than trustworthy borrower). If a debtor nation leaves the EU, it can then reestablish its old currency, letting its value float downward with the markets. Because the Euro stays strong because of the economic strength of northern members, the southern European nations can't take advantage of their nation's struggling economies. Usually, when a nation's economy is in the tank, the value of their currency drops, making it attractive for tourists and investors to blow their foreign currency abroad. But today, foreigners would rather go to Turkey or Morocco then get fleeced on the beaches of Portugal, Spain or Greece. More importantly, devaluing the currency would also allow local businesses to export more goods, as foreigners would get more bang for their buck if they bought from the depressed economies.

But the odds are, most countries won't leave. At least not yet. They'll continue to experiment with austerity measures, eliminating the entitlement programs that on one hand cripple the economy, but on the other hand make European cities some of the most attractive places to live in the world. European governments have so fully taken on an active role in the social welfare of their citizens that even the most liberal US Democrat would be nervous.

Take Sweden for example. Sweden offers universal health care, unemployment insurance, retirement benefits, child allowance payments for each kid, "free" college tuition and sixteen months of paid paternity/maternity leave (dads are forced to take a month off or they lose the whole benefit). These benefits come at a cost. Workers can expect to pay 48% of their salary to taxes, and purchased goods come with a 25% tax. Life might be healthy, but life is expensive. And it also isn't perfect. In recent years, Sweden has seen a rise in suicide rates, out-of-wedlock pregnancies and drug addiction – stats that don't exactly point to welfare being a cure-all for all of man's ills.

Because of their inviting social programs and promises of employment (coupled with their proximity to the developing nations of Africa and Eurasia), Europe has witnessed a huge increase in immigration in recent years. And they need it. Like the rest of the developing world, Europe is getting old. Nineteen of the twenty oldest countries in the world are in Europe. By 2050, the average age of a European will rise to 52.3 years old (in Uganda it's currently 15.1 years). So who will pay for all the welfare programs? Who will be paying for the pensions of the millions living in retirement, expecting handouts from the government? The answer comes from the south and the east. From the Middle East, North Africa and Eastern Europe, millions enter the EU every year, moving freely between the countries, looking for the best chance at a livelihood. These migrants definitely add to the tax base of the countries, but unfortunately, many that are now arriving are also old or likewise reproduce at a relatively low rate. Europe needs babies now, or their demographic deficit will cause havoc in a few decades. France has tried another option – state-sponsored fertility encouragement programs. The government wants big families, and passed liberal maternity leave laws, while also offering income incentives and mandating companies provide part-time work for moms.

Many countries favor increasing population from within, as the ideology of hatred towards foreigners has gradually captured a following. Like the xenophobic eugenicists of the early 20th century who scapegoated immigrants for all their world's ills (culminating with Hitler's sadistic attempts to ensure racial purity), today a new generation of nativists have emerged, many taking prominent roles in government. The 2008 recession and resulting high rates of unemployment have empowered political parties to take a more right-wing stance, denouncing the presence of foreigners. Once in office, they pass laws that ban headscarves or clothing not appropriate for work, or even the construction of mosques (laws not-so-subtly targeting Muslims).

Ironically, these policies have done little to dissuade immigration, but have actually united Muslims who before were separated by class, nation of origin and religious practice. Fearing for their safety or avoiding persecution, Muslims have begun insulating themselves from the mainstream culture. This isolation has only perpetuated the frustration with "others" as nations have begun deporting those that don't fully assimilate. France alone saw its deportation rates climb above 35,000 in 2012, supported strongly by Interior Minister Claude Gueant who declared, "we reject...those that live by their own laws." And there are growing signs that the mainstream public is starting to share these xenophobic tendencies.

In 2011, the fertilizer bombing of Oslo and the massacre of 21 children at a summer camp on Utoya Island exposed the depth of hatred building in northern Europe. A survey conducted by the European Social Survey found that 68% of those surveyed believed immigrants cause crime and 38% believed immigrants make a country worse. Nativist-foreigner relations didn't exactly soften in May 2013, after a couple Muslim extremists ran over a former British soldier and then proceeded to hack him to pieces with a machete. On camera, these two demented men claimed the murder was in response to all the NATO killings in Afghanistan. Regardless the reason, mutilations in full daylight don't exactly bring out the best in man's nature.

And if conditions continue to spiral downward with the new string of austerity measures, the culture of scapegoating and ethnic discrimination will only intensify. Europe doesn't have to look too far back into its past to remember a time where persecution of minorities went beyond just words. Their leaders will need to make sure it never happens again. To this point, right wing extremists spewing anti-immigration vitriol have had limited actual impact once in power, but economic uncertainty could turn their radical views more mainstream.

At the exact time Europe looks inward to handle issues of immigration, it is also playing an increasingly important role in international policy. American authority and prestige have diminished in recent years, leaving an opening for another power center to play the role of mediator and thought leader. Europe not only has the firepower to impose its will, it also better employs soft power (diplomacy and trade agreements) to link regions in conflict. Unlike the United States that has waffled on issues of human rights and environmental protection, Europe tends to not just talk the talk, but they also walk the walk. Europe gives 50% of all the world's foreign aid to nations in need. And European countries didn't just sign Geneva agreements on military behavior or the Kyoto Protocol on environmental emissions and then proceed business as usual. They actually enforced changes. Europe sets the tone that international agreements should have weight, and that no lone nation can be above the rest. Likewise, their track record of social welfare has become more the model for developing nations than has the American version where citizens are perceived to be left to fend for themselves.

European nations also subscribe to the philosophy that free trade is the best antidote for hostilities. Look no further than the European Union. It has become the hallmark for how open borders lead to open relationships. Sure, the EU isn't without strife, but arguing in a conference room or in the press can't compare to the arguments that used to end up in the trenches and the battlefields. The European Union has extended free trade agreements to countries across the globe, from Singapore to South Africa, from Peru to Palestine, from Chile to Mexico. If the EU had its way, the world would turn into a GU, a Global Union where all the world's peoples moved and traded freely as members of one world, not independent, insulated entities protecting their own markets at all costs.

But all this talk of foreign aid, free trade and international organizations doesn't mean Europe isn't willing to unleash their firepower should push come to shove. They make up 21% of the world's military spending (China accounts for only 5%), they have 100,000 troops currently stationed in offensives around the world and they (France and the UK) also have nuclear weapons, the ultimate show of force. In recent years, Europe has also shown the willingness to not simply follow the lead of the United States. In the decades following World War II, it was rare for a European nation to sway from American foreign policy.

But with the end of the Cold War, European nations increasingly voted against American aggression, most notably in the 2003 war against Iraq where only Poland and the UK actually sent troops to join the "Coalition of the Willing." Aside from not simply rubber-stamping US foreign policy, European powers have recently taken command of military expeditions, most notably in Libya where they supported local rebel forces in their ouster of warlord dictator Muammar Gaddafi.

Whether they employ soft power or hard power, Europe will be called on to mediate disputes in their region. They'll need to determine what role they'll play in the Syrian civil war, the conflicts between Palestine and Israel and the new democracies that emerged from Arab Spring. They also must face the constant threat of terrorism that has, in recent years, seen European homelands targeted far more frequently than those on American soil. How they answer these threats will determine to what extent the world continues to look at Europe as the moral compass for international affairs. The recession of 2008 exposed both Europe's own economic failings and the sub-culture of ethnic hatred that threatens to destroy the moral fabric of the continent.

The world is waiting to see how Europe responds.

But that is for another chapter.

50

The United States of America

And now we come to the end. And what better place to wrap up than with the United States of America? In recent years, it's become en vogue to claim that the Golden Age of America is behind us, that the once revered and feared American Empire no longer holds sway in the world, that some up and coming nation might remove America from its global sway. Or worse yet, that America is self-destructing from within, that its gluttonous values, its rigged economic systems and its hopeless political landscape will soon trash whatever is left of a once mighty people.

I'm just not buying it.

I just don't see what the doomsayers see. Yes, if you're comparing the US to a utopia, it inevitably comes up short. But when you compare it to other actual countries (not mere theoretical ideals), it's doing OK. Let's just see how America stacks up.

It has the largest economy in the world - $15 trillion and counting – and the largest military in the world. Its troops are on 700+ bases in 156 different countries. It houses the most sought after universities in the world. Its Hollywood movies dominate. Its musicians sell millions of albums. Its franchises (Subway, McDonald's, 7-11, Burger King and Pizza Hut to name a few) sell goods everywhere. Its Coca-Cola is only NOT sold in Cuba and North Korea. It exports to the world the most cars, the most airplanes, the most computers, the most weapons, the most medical equipment, the most pharmaceutical drugs and the most food. It's on track to be the #1 exporter of oil by 2017. It has the most immigrants in the world. It would attract the most tourists in the world, if not for that darn Eiffel Tower. It gives out the most patents and copyrights. It has the most Fortune 500 companies. It has the most billionaires.

It looks like America is doing just fine.

But that doesn't mean the US doesn't have problems. Oh, it has a host of issues, roadblocks and conflicts that threaten to cause its people frustration and anxiety for years to come, but none of these is going to realistically bring down its civilization. America has always proven to be resilient, and its economic and political systems have always found a way of making life work.

Yet for another generation, America's greatest strength is its greatest weakness. America is a pluralistic society, welcoming all people and all ideas. Subsequently, its society has always lived in a paradox.

It might have the richest people, but it also has a huge income disparity. It might have incredibly fit people, but its obesity rates are scary. It might offer the best musical and cinematic offerings, but it also spews out a ton of garbage. It's the most religiously diverse nation on the planet, but it also has had a habit of persecuting those who believe in non-traditional faiths. Its people might claim its form of democracy is the best in the world and that it should be embraced by all other nations, but its people also believe its government is inept, ineffective and corrupt.

But the existence of the extremes doesn't mean the United States will ever cease being a free society. Over time its leaders have learned how to sever the bad while preserving the good.

Today is no different. The question has always been, who gets to define what is "good."

Americans have the right to be anything they want to be.

One of the things it seems they want to be is fat. Obesity is defined as someone who has a Body Mass Index (BMI) over 30. It basically determines how much fat your body stores. For a woman who's 5'4", this would mean she weighs over 175 pounds. For a man who is 6' tall, he would weigh over 220. And America has the most of these obese people on the planet – 35.7% as of 2013 (and this doesn't even include those that are overweight – some 71% of Americans are overweight). Most worrisome is that the trend is only getting worse. Close to 20% of America's children are obese. Americans take in an average of 3,770 calories a day, while the average person only needs about 2000 calories a day. America is fat and it's getting fatter.

Obesity impacts not just our health, but our economy. Being overweight is directly related to increased rates of heart disease, stroke, respiratory problems, sleep apnea, cancer and diabetes (rates of Type 2 diabetes have been doubling annually for the last decade). 300,000 people die before their time because of their weight. If you're sick in America, it's probably because you're fat. And being overweight is costly. Americans (both private individuals and the government) pay over $150 billion a year treating the effects of obesity. The desire to consume food is not only killing us physically, it's killing us economically.

Recognizing this issue, Americans have stepped up to tackle this problem. The health industry is booming. There are over 29,000 health clubs in the US. Natural and organic food stores have seen sales surpass 85% growth the past five years running, with no signs of it slowing down. At the school level, the US Department of Agriculture just launched their "The School Day Just Got Healthier" program. Since most kids eat the bulk of their calories at school, if America wants to see a change, it needs to hit kids while their young. School cafeterias across the country have adopted the new federal requirements, adding more vegetables, low fat milk and nutritious grains, while taking away foods high in sodium and fat. The days of eating powdered donuts, French fries and chocolate milk for lunch are a thing of the past. Kids now are eating fruit salad, broiled chicken and brown rice.

But fighting the battle at schools will not be enough. To truly change the American diet, the country would need to revisit how it buys food and how it prepares food. A few years back, Time Magazine took a series of pictures for a photo essay on "What the World Eats." They arranged families around dinner tables lined with all the food they had purchased for the week. Families from Mongolia to Chad to Japan to Italy to Kuwait to Mexico participated. And what did we find out? Americans eat a ton of packaged food. They like their food symmetrical, easy to stack and easy to store. Fresh fruits, vegetables and raw meat are a rarity. Their food comes in cans, boxes and bags and can be prepared in a few minutes by zapping it in the microwave. On average, Americans spend only 75 minutes a day eating (one of the lowest levels in the world) and this directly correlates to their weight. Countries that spend a long time preparing meals and take time to enjoy them, often consume less calories and therefore pack on fewer pounds. If Americans ever truly wanted to lose weight, they'd get out of the drive-thru lanes, sell their microwave ovens and stop by the market a few times a week (not filling two carts full every Saturday morning).

Some cities and states have tried to legislate people into eating better. New York City Mayor Michael Bloomberg tried to ban large cups of soda (it was shot down in court). Some states require fast food restaurants to post the nutrition levels of their items. Some states are pondering fat taxes that will punish those who eat sweet or salty foods. But if Americans learned anything from their past, it's that they better be wary of legislating personal behavior. Back in the 1920s, the Prohibitionists outlawed alcohol and which resulted in the dawn of the gangster age where mob bosses like Al Capone and Lucky Luciano filled the streets with blood as they tried to corner the market on black market booze. Americans might not want to see how far their citizens are willing to go to ensure they get their Krispy Kreme fix, their helping of chicken nuggets or their Big Gulp.

Speaking of getting their fixes, America is starting to change its stance on what to do about its drug culture. Increasingly Americans are taking drugs (and I'm not talking about the prescription kind, though 49% of Americans take some sort of a pill every month), and many wonder if it's worth it anymore to fight it. Since Richard Nixon first launched the War on Drugs in 1971, the US has spent well over a trillion dollars, and they have little to show for their efforts. America leads the world with people in jail for drug-related crimes – over 500,000 incarcerated and counting - yet it also still leads the world in illegal drug use (22 million Americans a year). In recent years, many states have taken a page from Prohibition repeal, and have actually reversed their policies on prohibiting marijuana use. The thinking being, that people are going to do it anyway, so states might as well save the money on law enforcement costs and make some money on the related tax revenue (which combined could save the country over $75 billion a year). First, states made it legal to inhale/ingest marijuana for medicinal purposes. Then, they decriminalized it, so if you got caught, you'd get nothing more than a traffic ticket-sized warning. And today, after pot ballot measures passed in November 2012, states like Colorado and Washington are trying to determine how best to roll out (pun intended) this new good to grocery chains. In the not-to-distant future, you might find a bag of weed tucked in between a bottle of Tylenol and a box of Bandaids. The verdict is still out on what this will do to drug usage, as the past few years have shown that the reduced penalties for marijuana usage has led to increased usage of all illicit drugs.

One of the impetuses for resolving the complications caused by both obesity and drug usage is that the effects have disproportionately damaged minority groups. Obesity rates of African-Americans and Hispanic Americans far exceed those of White Americans (49.5% and 40.4% respectively, compared to 34.3%). Likewise, incarceration rates clearly show the disparity amongst ethnicities. One in every nine black men is in jail. One in every 36 Hispanic men is in jail. And one in every 106 white men is in jail.

These disproportionate effects on minorities have to be confronted as the faces of America are changing. Back when America was founded and the first census was taken in 1790, the United States was home to about four million people, with 3.2 million being white (80%), and the rest black. A century later, the United States reached 62 million people, and the breakdown went 87% white, 12% black and 0.1% Asian. And by 1960, the population hit 179 million, divided up into 89% white, 10% black, 1% Hispanic and .2% Asian.

Flash forward fifty years. Look at America today. In 2012, America's population was 308 million. 72% were white, 17% were Hispanic, 13% were black and 5% were Asian (this doesn't add up to 100% because some people are of mixed heritage). At this rate, it is predicted that whites will become a minority in 2043. So what does this mean for America? First, America has always drawn the line between being a melting pot and a mixing bowl. Do our different ethnicities truly merge together to form one society, or do we fragment and form independent cultures, some in conflict with others? At the turn of the 20th century, immigrants were forced to assimilate. They changed their names, changed their languages and often left behind their culture from the Old World. As the ethnic percentages have changed, the question has become – what America are different ethnicities supposed to assimilate to?

And do they even have to assimilate at all anymore? In Los Angeles alone there is Chinatown, Koreatown, Little Tokyo, Leimert Park (African-Americans), Boyle Heights (Mexican-Americans) and Persian Square (home to the most Iranians outside Iran). Whether America chooses to see this diversity as an asset or a hindrance remains to be seen, but as some states become more diverse than others (40% of Californians are non-white, whereas nineteen states have fewer than 20% non-white citizens), America has the potential to become two Americas, one living on the coasts that is multi-colored and one living in the center which is monochromatic.

Ethnicity isn't the only part of America's demographics that are changing. The American household looks vastly different than it did just fifty years ago. At the tail end of the 1950s, the average American household started when a 22-year-old man married a 20-year-old woman. One year later, they had the first of their three children, and the father would then make enough money to support the household without even having a college degree (only about 7% had a university diploma).

Fifty years later, we have a different America. The average man doesn't get married until he's 28, and the average woman waits until she's 26. Married couples on average have only two children, but many couples are choosing to not even have kids at all (called DINKs – Double Income No Kids). 42% of all Generation X-ers born after the 1970s haven't had kids and they might not ever.

And then there's divorce. Divorce rates hovered in the low 20% range until the 1970s, when it skyrocketed to over 50% where it remains today. Many couples have decided to not even get married at all, choosing to instead live together in sin.

So what happened? How did America go from being a land where Dad worked while Mom cooked, cleaned and made sure little Suzy and Bobby grew up, to a land where Dad and Mom might not even be married, and if they did marry, there was a coin flip chance they'd end up one day divorced?

A few things happened. First, the birth control pill was invented. Once women started being able to control their own contraception, they increasingly wanted to have fewer and fewer kids, and they also wanted to stay in their careers later and later (which meant when they did want to have kids, they were too old and it wasn't so easy anymore to reproduce). Second, in 1973, the Supreme Court came down with their *Roe vs. Wade* ruling that made it illegal to outlaw abortions. Like with contraception, women could now better control unwanted pregnancies and better determine their future. Third, no fault divorce laws were passed. Before the 1970s, to divorce your spouse, you had to prove one of the big three – addiction, abuse or adultery. But by 1977, nine states had adopted no fault divorce laws, where you could just claim in the "Reason for Divorce" box – "Irreconcilable Differences." Women started getting out of doomed marriages, willing to give the whole single mom thing a shot.

And fourth, girls started playing sports. This one sounds a bit odd, but in 1972 Congress passed an amendment to the Civil Rights Act of 1964, and in the most important section for girls – Title IX – schools were mandated to provide equal opportunities for boys' and girls' after school activities. If you have a boy's swim program, you better have a place for girls. If you have a boy's volleyball team, you better have a girl's volleyball team. If you have a football team, you better let the girls try out, or you better create an opportunity for them to play something during that season (field hockey or lacrosse usually did the trick). Female participation in high school sports jumped more than anyone could have anticipated. In 1972, 294,000 girls played high school sports. Today that number has jumped up to 3.2 million. So what does playing sports have to do with households? Well, more girls playing sports means more girls learning leadership, determination and teamwork, which means more girls get scholarships, which means more girls attend college, which means more girls can be successful in the workplace, which means more girls develop identities outside simply making babies.

The combination of revolutions in family planning, a redefinition of divorce and expanded participation in extracurricular activities has increased the amount of women in the workforce, decreased the amount of women getting married young and having children young and increased the prevalence of divorce. Those realities, plus more welfare benefits for single mothers and a change in societal values where men no longer feel responsible for the care of their children, have created the greatest number of single mothers in America's history. Today, 9.9 million mothers raise their children as the head of household, many of whom do so without the help of a father. 27% of all these single mothers live in poverty, making up the largest single group in America. Because many of the children growing up in poor households themselves go on to become poor, America has created a cycle of poverty where your parents' marital status has become the single biggest factor determining your economic fate in adulthood. On average, children of poor parents are less healthy, less motivated, less safe and less exposed to role models in different income classes. As the rates of single parenthood and poverty continue to rise, federal and state governments will need to determine to what extent they provide safety nets to single parents below the poverty line with children, or to a greater extent, to any family below the poverty line.

But still, for the majority of women, the major issues in their lives are not dealing with divorce or raising children without help from a man. Two of the bigger issues are the lingering traditions of objectifying women and the enduring inequality in the workplace where women still earn less than men and have more difficulty rising to management positions. The objectification of women is nothing new in American, or really in any society. But today, as children spend over six hours a day in front of a screen, bombarded with media in the form of Internet, music, television or cinema, third party producers of images have far more control over our gender perceptions than ever before. Once upon a time, your view of the world was determined by your family, your town, your newspaper.

Today, those groups continue to play a factor in your perception of reality, but for many, media plays an even larger role. These makers of myth present idealized female forms that no mere mortal could ever replicate. To say nothing of the power of airbrushing, makeup, enhanced undergarments and a skilled plastic surgeon, models are still chosen from body types that make up less than 2% of the adult population. There's no way you can look like a model walking down the runway on Victoria's Secret Fashion Show, and there's no way you're looking like the model on the cover of Vogue, Cosmo, Elle or InStyle.

But that doesn't stop women from trying. Plastic surgery rates have not just doubled or tripled, in some cases they've gone up over 1000%. Women now lift their stomachs, their butts, their legs, their arms, their cheeks and their foreheads. They add silicone to their breasts and suck cellulite out of their tummies. And for those without the money to blow on the surgery of the month, many fall victim to eating disorders. In the course of their lives, one in six women will suffer from bulimia or anorexia in their lives, and many more will develop fitness obsessions, all in the vain of creating a body that will be wanted by society.

And even though these stats don't come as a surprise anymore, the media industries seem little-inclined to do anything about it. During the 2013 Super Bowl, carmaker Audi depicted a high school boy stealing his father's car and then running up to a strange woman and kissing her without her consent (aka...assault), and infamous sexist ad maker GoDaddy presented a dorky science dude awkwardly locking lips with a female judged less for her intelligence than for her appearance. At the Oscar Awards, women are still paraded up and down the Red Carpet as fans cheer their latest outfits, and talk show hosts ask truly cognitively-revealing questions like "Who did you do your hair?" and "Who are you wearing?"

And the music video industry has yet to turn the corner on their presentation of women, as artists such as Rihanna, Nicki Minaj, Lady Gaga and Katy Perry still sell more albums due to their ability to gyrate their groins, hike up their mini-skirts or shoot whipped cream out of their brassieres (Katy Perry can be blamed for the last one). All the while, a whole new generation of male Country, Rap and Rock stars continue to brag about their conquests of pretty little ladies. And with YouTube now running videos 24 hours a day, your videos won't be seen by just a few hundred thousand fans. They could be seen by hundreds of millions (and in 2013, the misogynistic, catchy, slightly disturbing video for "Gangam Style" eclipsed the one billion hit mark).

Outside the world of media, women still suffer. In the workplace, women have found that their gender was oftentimes an impediment to success. Just fifty years ago, job ads in newspapers came in two different sections – one for men and one for women. Female job openings were almost always clerical, with the occasional opening for a nurse or a teacher. Women could type, file, answer phones and look pretty for when a customer entered the office. The Civil Rights Act of 1964 outlawed such practices, making it illegal to advertise or hire for a job position based on race, religion, national origin or gender. But anyone who thought this law would actually change common practice didn't exactly understand how social change worked in American society. Blacks were officially freed from slavery in 1865. Yet, the vast majority of them remained destitute farmers in the South for another century. *Brown vs. Board of Education* made it illegal to segregate in schools. Yet, it took another decade before blacks and whites actually went to school together. So although this 1964 law mandated equal employment, actual practice took a lot longer to catch up to the idealized goal.

Five decades later, the US is still coming up a bit short in what it promised. In 1964, for the same job, a woman on average made 59.1% of a man's salary. In 2013, a woman still only makes 77.1% of a man's salary (and that number has more or less flat-lined for the last decade). When it comes to types of jobs available to women and men, stereotypes still exist. Women make up 11% of all engineers, 16% of all scientists, 31% of all lawyers and 34% of all doctors. These numbers show a dramatic improvement over the past few decades, but huge barriers exist to this day. In 2012, the National Academy of Science conducted an experiment where they two identical resumes to faculty members asking to be the graduate student's mentor. The only difference in these two resumes was one came from John and one came from Jennifer. John ended up being viewed as the better, brighter, more accomplished candidate, and he was even offered a salary substantially higher than Jennifer's. And these are the people that teach the future.

But gender bias isn't restricted to grizzly old college professors. One hundred high school students were presented with the following situation:

> *A man and his son are driving home from dinner one night and they get into a horrible car accident. They are both unconscious and rushed to the hospital. At the hospital they are put into two separate rooms. The doctor walks into the boy's room and states, "I can't operate on this patient. He is my son." How is this possible?*

Of the one hundred students queried, 52 stated it was because the doctor was his homosexual other father, 31 stated it was because the doctor was his mother and seventeen gave up because riddles scare them. As much as these responses show how far the younger generation has come in accepting homosexual parents, it's fairly interesting how America's comfort with gender preference has leap-frogged its comfort with gender equity.

Gender equity goes beyond what fields of jobs are available. It also influences what level job is within reach. The term "glass ceiling" was created to illustrate how women might be able to enter certain fields, but there is an invisible ceiling that prevents them from being seen as management material. In 1990, 38% of management jobs went to women. Two decades later, that number has only grown to 39%. In 2013, of the 500 largest companies in America, eighteen were run by women (that was six better than the year before, so if you're judging the number based on percent growth, women are doing phenomenally well). The number for entrepreneurs looks a bit more hopeful as 44% of all small businesses are owned by women. Female entrepreneurs employ eighteen million workers and generate over $2 trillion in revenue.

Women are steadily approaching equity in the workplace, but society will need to find a way of jumpstarting women's wages, while also ensuring fair access to upper management positions. Unfortunately, by the time this battle enters the adult business sphere, gender inequities are already firmly in place. To truly change cultural expectations, Americans have to revisit the education system. But unfortunately, US schools are already burdened with solving all 4,631 of the nation's other problems.

It's no secret US schools are failing. Pick a stat and you'll be depressed. US students rank 14th in the world in reading, 17th in science and 25th in math. 17% of students will use drugs during the day. 77% of high school students will be bullied. The freshman graduation rate is only 78.2% (though this is the highest rate in over forty years). Over 370,000 teenage girls will give birth this year.

They're not learning as much as they should, they're doing drugs and having unprotected sex more than they should and they're just not being nice to each other. But few signs point to it getting any better. Schools were charged with improving achievement of ALL students, so with both George Bush's *No Child Left Behind* program and Barack Obama's *Race to the Top*, teachers began prioritizing test scores over learning. Gone are the days of dodgeball, class musicals and Thanksgiving paper bag turkeys. At the youngest grades, in the most struggling schools, students constantly complete drill and kill assessment sheets that mimic the high stakes tests they'll take each year. A school's funding and future depends on the test scores, so teachers oftentimes forsake the inspirational activities for the ones that might correlate with success on an objective achievement test. To this point, it's not clear if *Race to the Top* is working, as reported data can be interpreted from different angles. Students are scoring better on tests, but is that because the students are learning more, or is it because the tests are becoming easier or is it because teachers are teaching the test? Critics of *No Child Left Behind* claim that it created a generation of test takers who lack the creativity and ingenuity to become leaders in their adulthood. Improved high school graduation rates point more to the failing economy and the fact that few high school students would consider dropping out after 2008 as there was a pretty good chance no jobs would be available for them.

Once high school students graduate high school, there's no guarantee college will be an option for them. For the upper echelon of students, for those who packed in 10+ APs, played three sports, sung lead in their school's rendition of *Wicked*, founded a service club that provided microfinancing to unemployed women in Cambodia and invented an incubator for newborns in India, for these elite few, college used to be a no-brainer, but now the costs are so prohibitive that even our best and brightest have to reconsider if college is an option. In 1940, only 5% of the workforce had a college degree. Today, 40% of Americans have a college degree. The largest determining factor of your financial success as an adult is your degree of education. If you don't have a college degree, you're going to struggle. Yes, there are exceptions, but they're rare (and you're not allowed to bring up Bill Gates, Mark Zuckerberg or Tiger Woods...if you can invent code or drive a golf ball 350 yards, you can drop out of college too).

The #1 reason why college is beyond so many Americans is cost. Let's take two schools UC Berkeley and Harvard – one a public school, one private, both with decent reputations. In 1960, the average salary was $4,700. It cost $2260 to go to Harvard and $680 to go to Berkeley (and these costs included everything – tuition, room, board, vinyl records). Flash forward to 2013. The average salary has risen to $51,413. Harvard today costs $64,954 per year. Berkeley costs $32,884. Those numbers look freakishly high (multiply them times four to get really nervous), but let's compare percentages. In 1960, you'd have to spend 48% of your dad's income to go to Harvard and 14% of his income to go to Berkeley. Today, you'd spend 127% of his annual income to go to Harvard and 64% of his income to go to Berkeley. It costs a ton more any way you look at it.

But it's not just how much it costs today. For those who decide to take out student loans, you could be stuck with a $100K bill that you will be trying to pay off for the next twenty years (which could be a bit of a problem if you graduate college during a recession and there are no jobs available for you). Because of the huge cost of education, the best and brightest aren't always the ones attending college, but more the ones who can afford it. Sometimes these roster spots even go overseas. In fact, many public universities have started actively recruiting overseas, hoping these foreign students will pay the full tuition that will hopefully compensate for the lack of money state universities now receive from the government. America has created a situation where the children of the rich are the only ones who have the opportunity stay rich, and for the poor, the chance at the American Dream is increasingly becoming an inaccessible myth. If the cost of colleges doesn't come down, or if the federal government or private interests don't find some better way of funding or delivering a college education, millions of Americans will see their opportunities extinguished through no fault of their own.

This is the world that greets the Millennials (the name given to the generation that followed Generation X, which was the generation that followed the Baby Boomers). These are the ones who first graduated from college in the post-2000 mini-recession, didn't have enough money yet to benefit from the housing bubble of the 2000s or have since graduated from college in the post-2008 Great Recession world. They're praised for being uber-tech savvy and scorned for being ultra-materialistic. But they have no money, and their odds of getting more money seem lower than any generation over the past century. They've graduated to a world of corporate layoffs, global outsourcing and strict bank lending practices that prevent them from getting credit cards and home and car loans.

When the 2008 recession hit, their unemployment rates hit 17%. Worse yet, their underemployment rates eclipsed 50% (underemployment is when you take a job way under your skill set). These graduates are managers at the local GAP, barristas at Starbucks, clerks at Hilton Hotels or waiters at your local Olive Garden. Oh, they might have jobs, but they're not exactly living the dream. Enterprise Rent-A-Car boasts that it's the largest employer of college graduates in America. That's a lovely stat. I'm sure a chance at coordinating a fleet of Ford Fusions and Chevy Aveos was just what kept these college grads focused as they pulled all-nighters doing finals week. And because they walk away from college with a ton of debt (72% have over $25,000 in student loan debt, 6% have over $75,000), they're forced to stick with these jobs just to make sure they stay ahead of their minimum monthly payments.

And if college grads are taking all of these service jobs, what are all the non-college grads doing?

That's the real problem. It's one thing to be underemployed, it a whole other thing to be living off a minimum wage salary with no benefits. The federal minimum wage is $7.25 an hour, which equates to about $1200 a month, which comes out at just over $14,600 a year. The poverty line for a family of four is $23,050 a year, so if just Mom is working at a minimum wage job, you're below the poverty line. 16% of Americans live below the poverty line. But it's not just the poorest of the poor that are suffering, middle class wages have essentially froze the last two decades, meaning you make the same amount you did back in the 1990s, but with inflation, everything costs a heck of a lot more. It's tougher and tougher making ends meet, and as manufacturing jobs head overseas (the one industry that employed the bulk of high school graduates in the 20th century), more and more people struggle to keep up with the cost of living.

But that doesn't mean there isn't wealth in America. Oh, there's wealth. It's just in the hands of a smaller and smaller pool of the super rich. America is living through the greatest income disparity since the 1920s – the decade known as the Roaring Twenties, the era before the Great Depression. How rich are the super rich? Let's just take the two richest guys in America – Bill Gates and Warren Buffet. As of 2013, they were worth $72,700,000,000 and 59,700,000,000 respectively. Let's see how many regular people equal these two guys and they're combined wealth of $132,400,000,000. I could just say these guys have more money than 135 countries earn in a year, but that's too hard to wrap your head around. Let's just see how many people living at the poverty line add up to their salaries. How many? 5,227,765. Two dudes equal over five million people. Let's look at it another way. $100,000 a year sounds like a healthy salary. How long would it take for someone making $100K a year to earn as much as these two guys currently hold in stocks and salary? Oh...just about 1.3 million years. These two guys make over $4000 a second. They made as much as I make in a year in the time it took you to read this last paragraph.

And that's just two guys. The top 1%, the richest three million people, control 40% of our national wealth. Through a combination of upper class friendly tax laws, increased corporate profits due to layoffs and industry innovations and a growing number of entrepreneurs who got rich off the dot.com and technology booms, the rich keep getting richer and richer. They pay themselves well.

In the fall of 2011, it looked like the 99% might have had enough of the income disparity. Inspired by the Arab Spring movement and organized by a Canadian anti-consumerist news organization called Adbusters, a group of 2,000 marchers descended on Wall Street in October, eventually occupying Zuccotti Park. These protestors claimed they were against corporate greed and income inequality. The Occupy Movement soon caught on around the world, with protests popping up in 82 countries, some of which are continuing to this day. And all of these demonstrators were united by one event, the catalyst that opened the world's eyes to the level of corruption and corporate greed at the highest levels of the business world and the government, the catalyst that continues to this day to threaten to bring down the economic systems of developed and developing countries – the 2008 Great Recession.

For most tuning in to life in 2008, the Great Recession came out of nowhere. Life had been going well for the previous few years. Housing prices were up and the stock market was booming. It appeared the American financial industry had figured out new ways of making money for themselves, for investors and for American corporations.

The truth was they had created nothing new. What they had created was yet another pyramid scheme where those who jumped in during the early years made a ton of money, but those who threw their money into the game after the riches were already made, these late-to-the-party investors, they lost everything.

When the crisis came, it blew up in just a few months. First came the news that Lehman Brothers, the fourth largest investment bank in the United States, had declared bankruptcy. Then came news that other banks might be folding. Then the stock market dropped even deeper. The Dow Jones Industrial Average dropped from a high of 14,000 to a low of 6,594 on March 5, 2009. The government tried to stop the bleeding by brokering mergers between banks and by bailing out the larger banks, giving them $700 billion. The government then tried to avert the next catastrophe by bailing out the auto industry with $43 billion in loans to help pay pensions and medical benefits to their employees, and to jumpstart their businesses.

But regardless of what steps the government made, they were all just Band-Aids. The economy was dying. Companies laid off millions. Unemployment rates surpassed 10%, the highest rate since the Great Depression. Banks stopped loaning money. They were worried borrowers might never pay them back. Seventeen million homeowners lost their properties when they could no longer pay their mortgages. Americans were out of work, homeless and hopeless. Taking a page out of President Roosevelt's New Deal, President Obama tried to prime the pump and get the economy spinning again by infusing over $780 billion for infrastructure improvements across America. Americans would be put to work building bridges, paving roads and constructing dams, and local governments would be helped out as the federal government granted them money to keep paying for medical insurance, education and energy.

And steadily the economy started recovering. It took years, but banks started lending money again and companies started hiring again. The stock market surpassed its previous high and people started moving back into homes.

But in the back of everyone's mind lies the lingering thought, "When will it happen again?"

To answer that question we need to see how it happened the first time.

Nobody wants to hear this, but it happened because of greed, the American desire for short-term fixes. Americans of all classes, of all segments of society, wanted more, but they didn't want to pay their dues to get it.

But let's not worry about greed for now, let's focus on two tangibles – the housing bubble and derivatives. An investment "bubble" is when the cost of a good (its perceived value) far outweighs its actual value, but people keep buying it anyway, making the bubble expand even further, until inevitably, it pops, and the value of the good plunges far below even its actual worth.

In the 2000s, the bubble revolved around real estate. In the 1990s, President Clinton pressured home lenders to loosen their requirements for loan eligibility, making it possible for every family, regardless of race, class, credit history or income, to buy a home. George Bush took this pressure one step further by arguing,

"You don't have to have a lousy home. The low-income home buyer can have just as nice a house as anybody else."

Lenders had what they wanted. The government basically gave them permission to give loans to people who they knew wouldn't be able to pay them back. And the average American household jumped at the opportunity. They took out loans for properties way beyond their budget, buying McMansions on their middle class salaries. They refinanced their homes, taking the money to pay for education, health care, recreational vehicles and all the electronic gadgets available at your local Best Buy. But what happened to these loans? Didn't the banks lose money when borrowers couldn't/didn't pay back their loans?

Ahh...that's where it gets interesting, dare I say *brilliant*.

In the 1990s, investment banks had created this little investment tool called a derivative. Usually, investors buy stocks in companies or they invest in commodities like gold, soybeans or oranges. If the value of the company or the commodity goes up, shareholders make money. Fairly straightforward. But the investment bankers wanted a new way of making money, a new way of making even more money. They created the derivative. A derivative is an investment not in a product, but in the expected movement of the product. For example, you could bet money (pardon me, "invest" money) on a stock actually dropping in value. You could wager that it might hit a certain price. Or, you could even bet on the weather if you wanted. But the key factor that makes these derivatives so fascinating, yet disturbing, is that they aren't regulated. All stocks and bonds are regulated by the Securities and Exchange Commission. Roosevelt created this body to ensure the wild speculation and corruptive practices of the Roaring Twenties never held the nation hostage again.

Congress forgot about this little nugget of history, and passed laws preventing anyone from regulating derivatives, and by the end of the 1990s, over $50 trillion was traded on the derivatives market, without any government regulations whatsoever.

And once the markets had derivatives, the financial industry had a place to put all these bad loans. They'd repackage them with other loans and then sell them to big-time investors under a clever name that masked their actual value. Let's walk you through the loan process. Let's say you buy a house in Portland, Oregon and take out a loan from Pacific Northwest Mortgage. This bank then immediately turns around and sells your loan to

Bank of the United States. You receive a note in the mail saying your loan has been transferred to a new bank. You really don't care who gets your money, so you throw the notice away, remember to write "Bank of the United States" on your mortgage checks each month and then get back to your life. Your loan, however, gets bundled up with tens of thousands of other loans – some made to reliable borrowers (prime loans) and others made to huge credit risks (subprime loans). And then Bank of the United States renames this little package of loans. They might call it the "Emerging Development and Reorganization Mutual Fund." Then investment brokers get on the phone and start calling all their big-time investors - retirement funds for entire states, huge corporations with cash to spend or even small countries. They market these new bundles as being the best thing you can do with your money.

For awhile, this little scheme worked. Banks kept giving out loans, investors kept gobbling them up and everyone was getting rich. Until something happened.

People couldn't pay their monthly mortgage. They started realizing maybe they can't afford a $3000 a month mortgage when they only make $3500 a month. So they stopped paying. They defaulted. Banks had to foreclose on their properties and repossess them. And what happened to the little bundles of loans that were being sold around the world? They started losing value quickly? 5% one day. Then 20%. Then 50%. They plummeted.

But the investment bankers had already planned for this inevitability. They had bought insurance on all these investments, so when they tanked, they would make money on them tanking. And who was the company that was insuring all these loans? Insurance companies like AIG – American International Group. But what happens if all the subprime home loan bundles start dying? Well, AIG would then go bankrupt. The investment bankers had planned for this as well. They had bought derivatives that their insurance companies would go bankrupt.

So, they'd make money in the good times, and they'd make money in the bad times.

But what would happen if the entire market fell apart all at once. What if all of a company's investments fell at the same time? What if there wasn't enough insurance or derivative income to keep the investment companies afloat?

What happens then? Well, this is when the banking industry claimed, and rightfully so, that they were "Too Big to Fail." If all the banks failed, then the entire economy would fall apart. Nobody would be able to borrow money – not state and local governments, not corporations, not individuals. Nothing would be made. Nothing would be bought. It would be economic Armageddon.

This was when the government stepped in and started bailing out the banks, bailing out the auto industry and bailing out state governments. And we solved all of the problems that got us into this mess, didn't we?

Well, not exactly. Investment banks can still buy and sell unregulated derivatives. Local banks can still make risky loans (though they're scared to do so...and in fact rarely give loans if at all). The banks that were too big to fail before the recession, only got *bigger*. Bank of America merged with Countrywide and Merrill Lynch; Wells Fargo merged with Wachovia; and JP Morgan took over Bear Stearns. The investment industry is even too bigger to fail. And the SEC has few powers to actually stop the bankers from turning to the dark side again, should the opportunity present itself.

So why didn't the federal government do more to prevent some of the pitfalls that put America in this predicament in the first place?

Why not? For the same reasons this current Congress has seen its approval ratings drop to 13%. It seems like in today's political landscape, no one is willing to compromise, that every conversation, every issue becomes a zero-sum death match, where one side can't appear to lose so they have to ensure that the other side doesn't appear to win. So, every couple months, pundits at CNN, FOX and MSNBC count down to the fiscal cliff or the debt ceiling or the latest on the government's credit rating, manufacturing crisis after crisis after crisis, warning us that if such and such date comes and passes without an agreement, the world will end and we'll all be eating canned brussel sprouts in our 1950s bomb shelters. The crisis days unsurprisingly come and go, we're all still alive and Congress loses whatever remaining credibility it had left.

Today's politics has come down to the Republicans versus the Democrats. It appears their #1 priority is always winning the next election. And the best way to win? Make the other guy look bad. Label any of his proposals fascist or communist or socialist or anti-American and you're guaranteed to see bills die on the Senate or House floor. Even when committees bargain and compromise behind closed doors, even when a bill has enough votes to pass with a majority, the minority party in the Senate can always pull out the filibuster card. The filibuster is a lovely little invention of the 19th century, where Senators can delay votes on hot button issues by simply talking, talking about whatever they want – Mom's favorite cookbook, a few chapters from *Fifty Shades of Grey* or their opinions on which American Idol winner is the dreamiest. As long as they are willing and able to stand at the podium, they can talk, and they don't have to sit down until they have to pee, they need something to eat or the rest of the Senate takes a vote of cloture (67%) to shut them up. And because no party has enough votes to pass a call for cloture, the filibuster, or at least the threat of a filibuster, more or less prevents any substantive legislation from ever passing through Congress, let alone getting to the desk of the President of the United States.

So the country forever sits in a state of gridlock. And this stalemate doesn't just relate to economic issues, it hits on every topic that might arise. After the 2012 school shooting in Newton, Connecticut, the American public rightfully believed this was the time for us to revisit our gun control laws. In the span of 22 months, a Congresswoman had been shot in the head while giving a speech at a shopping mall, twelve moviegoers were shot dead at opening night of the new Batman film and now 27 teachers and children died in the classrooms of Sandy Hook Elementary School. If ever there was a time to revisit the conversation, the weeks and months after Sandy Hook was that time.

Not that we would ever really contemplate getting rid of guns (that's not even an option considering there are more guns in America than people), just that we might debate the need for your average citizen to own a machine gun. But what happened when the gun legislation hit the floors of Capitol Hill? The vitriolic extremists from both sides of the political spectrum went into overdrive, threatening and name-calling their opponents to such an extent that compromise was doomed from the start. Three months later, Obama stood in front of his White House podium with the relatives of the fallen children, scolding Congress for their inaction, "Shame on us if we've forgotten." No bill had yet passed through Congress, and Obama had no idea if or when he would look at a piece of legislation that might actually impact gun violence in America.

Why has it become so tough to get laws passed in America? Was this what the Founding Fathers envisioned over two hundred years ago when they delivered their version of democracy to the thirteen colonies to be ratified? What's gone wrong? Is our legislative system bloated, paralyzed or just dysfunctional?

Yes, yes and yes.

Over the past two centuries, the federal government has grown into the beast no one could have predicted. Prior to the Great Depression, the only times most Americans ever thought of the US government was when they had to mail a letter or when they saw a soldier in uniform walking down the street. But then the Great Depression hit, and households alone proved ill-equipped to alleviate the suffering. Enter the federal government. And since the 1930s, the federal government's responsibilities have spiraled out of control. They regulate everything from the cost of corn, to trade relations with Zimbabwe, to the legality of gay marriage, to the maintenance of Niagara Falls, to the production of medicine, to the repair of bridges, to the disability insurance of returning soldiers, to terrorist threats from splinter cells, to the possible victor in college basketball's March Madness tournament. Back in 1930, Roosevelt had six assistants. Today, Obama has over one hundred. The sheer volume of stuff the president, Congress and Supreme Court have to sift through is mind-boggling, and because every view is permitted in America, everyone feels their issue of the moment is the most critical concern to face the United States in the history of the union.

Coupled with the crushing scale of the government's responsibilities is the perpetual harassment and analysis of the choices made by the White House and Capitol Hill. The fourth branch of America – the media – is now on a 24-hour news cycle, where airtime must always be filled with images and analysis that will keep the attention-deprived viewers from turning the channel or clicking to another news site. Adding to the traditional news networks (ABC, CBS, NBC, Fox and CNN), a new generation of professional and amateur bloggers and watchdogs record every bit of political intrigue, sometimes even inventing news topics to increase viewership. But here's the problem with democracy. It's actually kind of boring. 19th century German politician Otto von Bismarck once admitted that "there are two things in life you never want to see being made – laws and sausages." In his era, and in the decades after, the media left the politicians relatively alone to make back-room deals or to pontificate in closed assemblies for the benefit of their colleagues. But laws were passed. But now, because of the limitless news programs and the millions of civilians with a cellphone, politicians are paranoid that a comment made or a stance taken could one day prevent them from being electable when the next cycle of balloting rolls along. So they guard their words, they fear compromise and they basically follow the party line, believing it's better to have allies of incompetence than speak their mind and be left adrift without party support.

And of course there's the influence of lobbyists. The urban Washington DC legend goes that the term "lobbyist" was created back in the mid-19th century, when you would have to wait in the lobby of the Willard Hotel for President U.S. Grant to stop by if you ever wanted to see your law get past the oval office. Since that time, lobbyists have become the key fixture in Washington politics. But they do provide a service. With the tens of thousands of pieces of legislation or initiatives that can be proposed in any one term, there is no way legislators can be expected to know all the different angles on all the different issues that cross their desks. Enter the lobbyists. Ideally, they would inform legislators of the pros and cons of a decision, and leave the decision-making to the Congress and the President. But over the decades, lobbyists and campaign fundraisers have developed a symbiotic relationship where financial assistance can be tied to political perspectives. And while close to 90,000 individuals lobby (though only 11,000 are registered "lobbyists"), not all lobbyists were created equal. Lobbying is a $3.5 billion a year industry, and those corporations, unions and organizations with the deepest pockets oftentimes have the largest influence on the direction of the country. Not exactly what James Madison intended when he drafted the Constitution.

The reality of obstinate political parties, invasive media and persuasive lobbyists isn't going to change anytime soon. And now that America is no longer in the midst of a Cold War, they don't even have a common enemy anymore to fear or hate. At least for the five decades after World War II, politicians could come together on one thing – their fear and hatred of communism. But now, even America's foreign policy divides its polities.

Discussing the scope of American foreign policy is almost impossible, because America's foreign policy involves essentially every country. Just look back at the last eight chapters and you'll see that the course of every country in the world is reliant to some extent on America. Look no further than the 2008 Recession to see how a financial crisis in the United States, and the subsequent drop in demand for consumer goods, decimated most nations' economic health. One of the bi-products of America's "policeman of the world" post-WWII mentality and the fact that Americans are the number one consumers of energy and consumer goods in the world ($11 trillion in 2012 – five times more than #2 Japan), is that the United States is, like it or not, embedded in every corner of the planet. There was an expression in the mid-18th century that when France sneezed, the whole of Europe caught a cold. Well, in the 21st century, when the United States sneezes, the whole world gets pneumonia.

So, instead of going one by one down the list of countries to scrutinize America's degree of influence, let's instead look at a few foreign policy themes that Obama and future presidents will have to handle.

When Obama took office in 2008, he pledged to pull United States troops out of two countries – Iraq and Afghanistan. He's already made true on his promise in Iraq, and America's role in Afghanistan looks to be coming to a close in 2014. These two wars drained over $1 trillion from America's economy, cost over 4,000 American lives and injured another 100,000 troops. But American withdrawal came not from any overwhelming evidence that the conflicts in the region had been resolved. In Iraq, Saddam Hussein might be dead, but sectarian strife between the Shiites, Sunnis and Kurds could still erupt into an all-out civil war at any moment. In Afghanistan, the Taliban has been shelled into submission, and, along with the remnants of the Al Qaeda terror network, have skulked back into society. But when NATO troops leave in 2014, there are no guarantees they won't simply come out of hiding and re-establish their sovereignty over war-torn Afghanistan.

So the questions for the United States are, first, will they follow through on their commitment to withdraw? But more importantly, if and when the worst-case scenarios come to fruition, to what extent will American leaders resist the urge to toss US military forces back into unwinnable situations? If ten years of war didn't bring peace, is there really anything more America can expect with Iraq III or Afghanistan II? Staying neutral will be especially difficult in Afghanistan, as neighboring Pakistan, home to Islamic militants *and* a nuclear arsenal, could prove to be a foe that could present an even more imminent threat to American soil.

Pakistan usually gets overlooked in any discussion on nuclear threats to the United States. Usually, all eyes focus on Iran and North Korea's attempts to enrich uranium and develop operational nuclear arms programs. Though for years, both Iran and North Korea claimed they were pursuing nuclear energy for purely domestic energy needs, the last few years have revealed that these hollow statements were nothing more than insulting ruses. Both programs appear to be within just a few years of finally realizing the fruit of their nuclear ambitions, as sanctions and threats have proved impotent. At least in Iran, there appears to be a glimmer of hope that a change in leadership in 2013 might put more stable minds in power. Mahmoud Ahmadinejad's influence over the government is in its waning days, as both the clerics and the educated classes have grown tired of listening to his unstable public ramblings and suffering through the economic despair caused by international sanctions. But the question remains, if Iran continues to develop their nuclear program (even under a new regime), what will be the breaking point for Israel? Iran has denied Israel's legitimacy, threatening to blow it off the map. Will Israel, the other nuclear power in the region, take matters into their own hands and take out Iran's nuclear plants militarily? And if so, will America sit back and passively watch their #1 ally in the Middle East take war to one of the pillars of the Axis of Evil, or will it commit both money and military might to the cause? This would be bad. Very bad.

North Korea's another story. Unlike in Iran where its leader is on his final legs, in North Korea, the fresh-faced boy-child Kim Jong Un jumped into power at the end of 2012 and has made it his mission to prove to the military leadership and his adoring followers that he is a supreme leader to be feared. After a failed first rocket launch, North Korea has since successfully sent a rocket into space, demonstrating their desire to not just develop nuclear bombs, but to also manufacture delivery systems to instill fear in every nation bordering the Pacific Ocean. In March of 2013 it appeared that every day some other declaration of death came out of Kim's mouth. First, he ordered an end to the six-decades-long Korean War ceasefire. Then he released a video showing North Korea attacking Washington D.C. and imprisoning the 140,000 US expats living in Seoul (all to the uplifting background track – "We Are the World"). He then threatened Japan and the

US that he had his conventional artillery (the largest stockpile in the world) pointed at Tokyo and Hawaii. This wasn't the first time a North Korean leader had let his mouth get ahead of him, but the world doesn't yet know what to make of this boy and his toys. In a perfect world, his bombastic proclamations will calm down once he's proven his point that he's the unquestioned heir to the North Korean throne. But we don't always live in a perfect world.

While America is worrying about what to do with rogue nations intent on America's destruction, it will also need to ensure it continues to develop strategic and economic partnerships with those not bent on their annihilation. In the decade after 9/11, foreign policy experts focused their attention on those nations that could aid in foiling terrorist plots on US soil. Preventing another attack trumped all other policy decisions, so nations outside North Africa, the Middle East and Eurasia were moved to the back burner. During this decade, the nations of East Asia, Sub-Saharan Africa and Latin America pushed their own agendas without consideration for US interests. China ended up sweeping in and developing near monopolies on resources in the developing economies of Latin America and Africa, and nations like Brazil, South Korea, Singapore, India and South Africa established regional partnerships excluding the interests of the United States. America's Cold War spheres of influence no longer apply, and the US will need to establish how future relationships can be mutually beneficial, instead of believing other nations will simply accept the often-lopsided dealings of the latter half of the 20th century.

And then there's Israel - America's foreign policy elephant in the room. Since the 1970s, no other country has retained the US's unwavering support like Israel. The US commits $3.1 billion of aid every year to Israel, the US provides Israel with state of the art military weaponry and training and the US has always been Israel's staunchest advocate in the United Nations (even when they invaded adjoining countries or killed civilians on freight ships). But America will need to decide if their partnership is unconditional. Obama journeyed to Israel in spring of 2013 and advocated for an independent Palestinian state. Lovely words, but words also stated by former presidents Bush II, Clinton and Bush I. At what point will America throw their support behind the Palestinians and push more aggressively for an independent nation? Ever?

The true point where America will need to reconsider their indissoluble alliance with Israel is when it comes to life with a nuclear Iran. Israel can't tolerate a nuclear Iran. Israel would be unwise to invade Iran unilaterally (the rest of the Muslim Middle East would descend into a horrific holy war), but if the US gets involved, America has a problem. Almost all of Iraq's oil goes through the Strait of Hormuz, surrounded by the Iranian military. If America is pulled into a war in Iran, they could see the oil supply to the world shut down, leading to another global recession. But more important than any profits lost through an oil embargo, the United States would lose all credibility in the region, and all the nations emerging from the Arab Spring would be hard-pressed to involve America in their development. The world doesn't want another Judeo-Christian vs. Muslim war. It destroyed the region in the 12th century. It could lead to World War III in the 21st century.

But enough with all the doomsday prognostications.

Right now, America is doing just fine. It has some warts, some roadbumps and some challenges it will need to overcome. But what nation doesn't?

If you've learned anything in your readings, it's that the world has always struggled. But it has been out of our deepest, darkest hours that we as a species have cultivated our most creative solutions. Our world's story is one of strife and peace, one of deterioration and progress, one of recognizing problems and finding innovative ways of moving forward. We are healthier, more peaceful and more connected than ever before in human history. It is this connectedness that some might argue could lead to our demise. Or maybe it leads to our even more prosperous evolution. For we have proven time and again that when we combine our resources, our minds and our objectives, we can construct worlds far superior than those our ancestors endured.

We're still moving forward.

And our story still has a few more chapters left to be written.

Index

CPSIA information can be obtained
at www.ICGtesting.com
Printed in the USA
LVOW10s0052240518

578342LV00001B/8/P